When should I travel to get the best airfare?
Where do I go for answers to my travel questions?
What's the best and easiest way to plan and book my trip?

frommers.travelocity.com

Frommer's, the travel guide leader, has teamed up with **Travelocity.com**, the leader in online travel, to bring you an in-depth, easy-to-use resource designed to help you plan and book your trip online.

At **frommers.travelocity.com**, you'll find free online updates about your destination from the experts at Frommer's plus the outstanding travel planning and purchasing features of Travelocity.com. Travelocity.com provides reservations capabilities for 95 percent of all airline seats sold, more than 47,000 hotels, and over 50 car rental companies. In addition, Travelocity.com offers more than 2,000 exciting vacation and cruise packages. Travelocity.com puts you in complete control of your travel planning with these and other great features:

Expert travel guidance from Frommer's - over 150 writers reporting from around the world!

Best Fare Finder - an interactive calendar tells you when to travel to get the best airfare

Fare Watcher - we'll track airfare changes to your favorite destinations

Dream Maps - a mapping feature that suggests travel opportunities based on your budget

Shop Safe Guarantee - 24 hours a day / 7 days a week live customer service, and more!

Whether traveling on a tight budget, looking for a quick weekend getaway, or planning the trip of a lifetime, Frommer's guides and Travelocity.com will make your travel dreams a reality. You've bought the book, now book the trip!

A New Star-Rating System & Other Exciting News from Frommer's!

In our continuing effort to publish the savviest, most up-to-date, and most appealing travel guides available, we've added some great new features.

Frommer's guides now include a new **star-rating system.** Every hotel, restaurant, and attraction is rated from 0 to 3 stars to help you set priorities and organize your time.

We've also added **seven brand-new features** that point you to the great deals, in-the-know advice, and unique experiences that separate travelers from tourists. Throughout the guide look for:

Finds   Special finds—those places only insiders know about

Fun Fact   Fun facts—details that make travelers more informed and their trips more fun

Kids   Best bets for kids—advice for the whole family

Moments   Special moments—those experiences that memories are made of

Overrated Places or experiences not worth your time or money

Tips   Insider tips—some great ways to save time and money

Value   Great values—where to get the best deals

We've also added a **"What's New"** section in every guide—a timely crash course in what's hot and what's not in every destination we cover.

Other Great Guides for Your Trip:

Frommer's Washington State

Frommer's Oregon

Frommer's Vancouver & Victoria

Frommer's®

Seattle & Portland

2002

by Karl Samson

with Jane Aukshunas

Here's what the critics say about Frommer's:

"Amazingly easy to use. Very portable, very complete."
—Booklist

"The only mainstream guide to list specific prices. The Walter Cronkite of guidebooks—with all that implies."
—Travel & Leisure

"Complete, concise, and filled with useful information."
—New York Daily News

"Detailed, accurate and easy-to-read information for all price ranges."
—Glamour Magazine

Hungry Minds™

Best-Selling Books • Digital Downloads • e-Books • Answer Networks
e-Newsletters • Branded Web Sites • e-Learning

New York, NY • Cleveland, OH • Indianapolis, IN

About the Author

Karl Samson and **Jane Aukshunas,** a husband-and-wife travel-writing team, make their home in the Northwest, where they've never been able to decide which city they like best, Seattle or Portland. Together, they also cover the rest of Washington and Oregon for Frommer's. In addition, Karl is the author of *Frommer's Arizona.*

Published by:

Hungry Minds, Inc.

909 Third Avenue
New York, NY 10022

ISBN 0-7645-6534-6
ISSN 1045-9308

Edited by Dog-Eared Pages, Inc.
Production Editor: Heather Gregory
Cartographer: Nicholas Trotter
Photo Editor: Richard Fox
Production by Hungry Minds Indianapolis Production Services

Special Sales

For general information on Hungry Minds' products and services, please contact our Customer Care department; within the U.S. at 800-762-2974, outside the U.S. at 317-572-3993, or fax 317-572-4002. For sales inquiries and reseller information, including discounts, bulk sales, customized editions, and premium sales, please contact our Customer Care department at 800-434-3422.

Manufactured in the United States of America

5   4   3   2   1

Contents

List of Maps ix

What's New in Seattle & Portland 1

1 The Best of Seattle   4

1 Frommer's Favorite Seattle
   Experiences 6
   *Site Seeing: The Best Seattle
   Websites* 7

2 Best Hotel Bets 8
3 Best Dining Bets 10

2 Planning Your Trip to Seattle   12

1 Visitor Information 12
2 Money 12
3 When to Go 13
   Seattle Calendar of Events 14

4 Health & Insurance 16
5 Tips for Travelers with
   Special Needs 17
6 Getting There 21

3 Getting to Know Seattle   25

1 Orientation 25
   The Neighborhoods in Brief 28
2 Getting Around 32

Driving a Bargain in Seattle 34
Fast Facts: Seattle 36

4 Where to Stay in Seattle   38

1 Downtown & First Hill 39
2 The Waterfront 47
3 Pioneer Square & the
   International District 48
4 Belltown & Pike Place Market ...48
5 Queen Anne & Seattle Center ...50
6 Lake Union 54

7 Capitol Hill & East Seattle 55
   Family-Friendly Hotels 56
8 North Seattle (The University
   District) 57
9 Near Sea-Tac Airport 58
10 The Eastside 58

5 Where to Dine in Seattle   61

1 Restaurants by Cuisine 62
2 Downtown & First Hill 65
   Family-Friendly Restaurants 69
3 The Waterfront 70
4 Pioneer Square & the
   International District 70

5 Belltown & Pike Place Market ...72
6 Queen Anne & Seattle Center ...78
7 Lake Union 82
8 Capitol Hill & East Seattle 84
9 North Seattle (Including
   Fremont, Wallingford &
   the University District) 85

10 West Seattle 86
11 The Eastside (Including Bellevue & Kirkland) 87
12 Coffee, Tea, Bakeries & Pastry Shops 88
13 Quick Bites 90

6 Exploring Seattle 91

Suggested Itineraries 91
1 On the Waterfront 94
2 Pike Place Market to Pioneer Square 95
Good Times in Bad Taste 96
3 Seattle Center & Lake Union Attractions 98
Space Needle Alternatives 100
4 The Neighborhoods 101
On the Trail of Dale Chihuly . . .103
5 Parks & Public Gardens 106
Fish Gotta Swim 107
6 Especially for Kids 109
7 Organized Tours 110
8 Outdoor Pursuits 114
9 Spectator Sports 118
10 Day Spas 120

7 Strolling Around Seattle 121

Walking Tour 1: The Pioneer Square Area 121
Walking Tour 2: Fun, Funky Fremont 125

8 Seattle Shopping 129

1 The Shopping Scene 129
2 Shopping A to Z 130

9 Seattle After Dark 141

1 The Performing Arts 141
2 The Club & Music Scene 145
3 The Bar Scene 148
Ballard, A Pioneer Square Alternative 149
4 The Gay & Lesbian Scene 150
5 More Entertainment 151
6 Only in Seattle 152

10 Side Trips from Seattle 153

1 The San Juan Islands 153
2 Mount Rainier 166
3 Ferry Excursions from Seattle . . .169
4 East of the City: A Waterfall & Wineries Loop 172

11 The Best of Portland 176

1 Frommer's Favorite Portland Experiences 177
Site Seeing: The Best Portland Websites 178
2 Best Hotel Bets 179
3 Best Dining Bets 181

12 Planning Your Trip to Portland   183

1 Visitor Information 183
2 Money 183
3 When to Go 183
Portland Calendar of Events ...184
4 Tips for Travelers with Special Needs 187
5 Getting There 188

13 Getting to Know Portland   190

1 Orientation 190
Did You Know? 193
The Neighborhoods in Brief ...194
2 Getting Around 196
Fast Facts: Portland 199

14 Where to Stay in Portland   202

1 Downtown 203
2 Nob Hill & Northwest Portland 210
Family-Friendly Hotels 211
3 Jantzen Beach (North Portland) & Vancouver, Washington 211
4 The Rose Quarter & Irvington ...212
5 The Airport Area & Troutdale ...214
6 The Southwest Suburbs (Lake Oswego & Beaverton) 215

15 Where to Dine in Portland   216

1 Restaurants by Cuisine 216
2 Downtown (Including the Skidmore Historic District & Chinatown) 222
3 Northwest Portland (Including the Pearl District & Nob Hill) ...227
4 Southwest Portland 234
5 Northeast Portland (Including Irvington) 234
Family-Friendly Restaurants ...235
6 Hawthorne, Belmont & Inner Southeast Portland 236
7 Westmoreland & Sellwood ...239
8 Coffee, Tea, Bakeries & Pastry Shops 240
9 Quick Bites & Cheap Eats 242

16 Exploring Portland   243

Suggested Itineraries 243
1 Downtown Portland's Cultural District 244
2 Skidmore Historic District & the Willamette River Waterfront 245
3 Washington Park & Portland's West Hills 249
Great Photo Ops 250
4 Other In-Town Attractions 252
5 Portland's Other Public Gardens 253
The World's Smallest Park 254
6 Outlying Historical Attractions 254
7 Especially for Kids 257
8 Organized Tours 258
9 Outdoor Pursuits 260
10 Spectator Sports 264
11 Day Spas 265

17 Strolling Around Portland   266

Walking Tour 1:
Old Town & Downtown 266

Walking Tour 2:
Fountains & Public Art 269

18 Portland Shopping   273

1 The Shopping Scene 273

2 Shopping A to Z 273

The City of Books 276

19 Portland After Dark   281

1 The Performing Arts 281

2 The Club & Music Scene 284

3 The Bar Scene 286

*Portland's Brewing Up a
Microstorm* 289

4 The Gay & Lesbian Scene 291

5 At the Movies 291

20 Side Trips from Portland   292

1 The Columbia Gorge &
Mount Hood Loop 292

2 The Northern Oregon Coast ...297

3 A Winery Tour 300

4 Mount St. Helens National
Volcanic Monument 302

Appendix A: Seattle & Portland in Depth   305

1 Seattle Past & Present 305

  Dateline 305

2 Portland Past & Present 309

Dateline 309

*Of Shanghaied Sailors
& Floating Brothels* 311

Appendix B: For International Visitors   314

1 Preparing for Your Trip 314

2 Getting to the United States ...318

3 Getting Around the
United States 319

*Fast Facts: For the
International Traveler* 320

Index   325

General Index 325

Seattle and Environs
Accommodations Index 335

Portland and Environs
Accommodations Index 336

Seattle and Environs
Restaurant Index 336

Portland and Environs
Restaurant Index 337

List of Maps

Greater Seattle Orientation 29

Accommodations: Downtown, First Hill, the Waterfront, Pioneer Square & Belltown 40

Accommodations—North: Seattle Center, Lake Union, Capitol Hill & the "U" District 52

Dining: Downtown, the Waterfront, Pioneer Square, the International District & Belltown 66

Dining: Queen Anne/Seattle Center, Lake Union, Capitol Hill & North Seattle 80

Seattle Attractions 93

Seattle Center 99

Walking Tour 1: Pioneer Square 123

Walking Tour 2: Fremont 127

Seattle Excursions 155

The San Juan Islands 157

Mount Rainier National Park 167

Greater Portland 191

Portland Accommodations 204

Portland Dining 220

Portland Attractions 246

Walking Tour 1: Old Town & Downtown 267

Walking Tour 2: Fountains & Public Art 271

Portland Excursions 293

The Columbia Gorge & Mount Hood Loop 295

The Northern Oregon Coast 299

Mount St. Helens National Volcanic Monument 303

An Invitation to the Reader

In researching this book, we discovered many wonderful places—hotels, restaurants, shops, and more. We're sure you'll find others. Please tell us about them, so we can share the information with your fellow travelers in upcoming editions. If you were disappointed with a recommendation, we'd love to know that, too. Please write to:

Frommer's Seattle & Portland 2002
Hungry Minds, Inc. • 909 Third Avenue • New York, NY 10022

An Additional Note

Please be advised that travel information is subject to change at any time—and this is especially true of prices. We therefore suggest that you write or call ahead for confirmation when making your travel plans. The authors, editors, and publisher cannot be held responsible for the experiences of readers while traveling. Your safety is important to us, however, so we encourage you to stay alert and be aware of your surroundings. Keep a close eye on cameras, purses, and wallets, all favorite targets of thieves and pickpockets.

New! Frommer's Star Ratings & Icons

Every hotel, restaurant, and attraction listing in this guide has been ranked for quality, value, service, amenities, and special features using a star-rating scale. In country, state, and regional guides, we also rate towns and regions to help you narrow down your choices and budget your time accordingly. Hotels and restaurants in the Very Expensive and Expensive categories are rated on a scale of one (highly recommended) to three stars (exceptional). Those in the Moderate and Inexpensive categories rate from zero (recommended) to two stars (very highly recommended). Attractions, towns, and regions are rated according to the following scale: zero stars (recommended), one star (highly recommended), two stars (very highly recommended), and three stars (must-see).

In addition to the rating system, we also use seven icons to highlight insider information, useful tips, special bargains, hidden gems, memorable experiences, kid-friendly venues, places to avoid, and other useful information:

| Finds | Fun Fact | Kids | Moments | Overrated | Tips | Value |

The following abbreviations are used for credit cards:

AE	American Express	DISC	Discover	V	Visa
DC	Diners Club	MC	MasterCard		

FROMMERS.COM

Now that you have the best guidebook for a great trip to the Pacific Northwest, visit our website at **www.frommers.com** for travel information on nearly 2,000 destinations. With features updated regularly, we give you instant access to the most current trip-planning information available. At Frommers.com, you'll also find the best prices on airfares, accommodations, and car rentals—and you can even book travel online through our travel booking partners. At Frommers.com, you'll also find the following:

- Daily Newsletter highlighting the best travel deals
- Hot Spot of the Month/Vacation Sweepstakes & Travel Photo Contest
- More than 200 Travel Message Boards
- Outspoken Newsletters and Feature Articles on travel bargains, vacation ideas, tips & resources, and more!

What's New in Seattle & Portland

The only thing constant in the world of travel is change, and Seattle and Portland are no exceptions. Highlighted below are some of the most significant new developments in these two cities this past year.

SEATTLE

ORIENTATION Prepare for sticker shock when riding the **Washington State Ferries** (© **800/84-FERRY** or 888/808-7977 within Washington state, or 206/464-6400; www.wsdot. wa.gov/ferries/). Due to reduced funding, which was brought on by a voter tax-reduction initiative, ferry fares have been climbing. As of this writing, it will now cost you $10 each way for a car and driver to ride the Bainbridge Island or Bremerton ferry during the summer months. Luckily, walk-on and passenger fares haven't jumped quite as much, and these ferry passengers still get a free ride back to Seattle from either Bainbridge Island or Bremerton.

ACCOMMODATIONS The **Elliott Grand Hyatt Seattle,** 721 Pine St. (© **800/233-1234** or 206/ 262-0700; www.elliotthotel.com), which opened in the summer of 2001, immediately became Seattle's most prestigious business hotel. With its emphasis on luxury and high-tech amenities, and with room rates to prove, this is one of Seattle's first truly world-class hotels. See the full review in chapter 4.

Equally luxurious and with even more high-tech features, the **Willows Lodge,** 14580 NE 145th St.,

Woodinville (© **877/424-3930** or 425/424-3900; www.willowslodge. com), boasts much more of a Northwest feel than the Elliott. Located in the wine country 30 minutes north of downtown Seattle, this lodge is surrounded by beautiful gardens. It shares a parking lot with the acclaimed Herbfarm restaurant (see below) and even has two guest rooms decorated in Herbfarm country French style. However, most of the guest rooms at the Willows Lodge feature bold contemporary styling that incorporates lots of wood and stone. See the full review in chapter 10.

DINING The single biggest piece of news on the Seattle restaurant scene this year has been the opening, after years of planning, of the new Herbfarm restaurant. **The Herbfarm,** 14590 NE 145th St., Woodinville (© **206/784-2222;** www.theherb farm.com) is the Northwest's most expensive and most celebrated restaurant, the ultimate expression of the Northwest's bounty, with an emphasis on fresh, herb-driven preparations, all of which are matched with regional wines. In keeping with its country-inn heritage, the Herbfarm is located out on the edge of Seattle's suburban sprawl. See chapter 10.

For those Seattle visitors with less money to spend on their vacation meals, we've added some of our new favorite restaurants around town. For the freshest sushi in Seattle, head to **Shiro's Sushi,** 2401 Second Ave. © 206/443-9844). The flavors of West Africa are the specialty at

Belltown's **Afrikando,** 2904 First Ave. (© **206/374-9714**). At the tiny **Koraku,** 419 Sixth Ave. © **206/624-1389**), in the International District, you'll find classic Japanese home-cooking. Seattle is crazy about French food and has an abundance of French restaurants in all prices ranges. **Le Pichet,** 1933 First Ave. © **206/256-1499**), is one of the least expensive and most authentic of the city's French restaurants and is conveniently located in the Pike Place Market area. For reasonably priced fresh seafood in a waterfront setting away from the crowds of tourists on the downtown waterfront, head north 10 minutes to **Chinook's at Salmon Bay,** 1900 W. Nickerson St. © **206/283-4665**), which overlooks a commercial marina that is the winter home to the Alaska fishing fleet. Over on the Eastside, you'll find great ethnic cuisines from around the world at **Beach Café,** 1270 Carillon Point, Kirkland. © **425/889-0303**), which has a great waterfront setting at the Carillon Point development in Kirkland. See chapter 5 for full reviews of these and other Seattle favorites.

SIGHTSEEING   To add further authenticity to its African savanna exhibit and to provide visitors (especially children) with insight into what life is like for Africa's human inhabitants, he **Woodland Park Zoo,** 5500 Phinney Ave. N. (© **206/684-4800;** www.zoo.org), has added an African Village. It doesn't feel like a Hollywood stage set, but is instead a well-researched rendition of a contemporary African village with a surprisingly authentic feel.

If you have a keen interest in contemporary art and are planning to be over on the Eastside (the high-tech communities on the east side of Lake Washington) in the Bellevue or Kirkland areas, you may want to stop in at the new **Bellevue Art Museum,** 510 Bellevue Way NE, Bellevue (© **425/**519-0770;   www.bellevueart.org). This museum has already begun booking some major touring exhibitions, but also emphasizes art education and regional artists.

See chapter 6 for complete coverage of Seattle's sightseeing attractions.

PORTLAND
ORIENTATION   The **Portland Oregon Visitors Association (POVA),** 1000 SW Broadway, Suite 2300, Portland, OR 97205 (© **877/678-5263** or 503/275-9750; www.travelportland.com), moved its visitor center into a new and very conveniently located facility right on (actually under), Pioneer Courthouse Square, downtown Portland's central plaza. This plaza is the site of various events throughout the year and is within a few blocks of most of Portland's top downtown hotels.

Also here at the new visitor center, you'll find **Ticket Central** (© **503/275-8358**), which sells both full-price advance-purchase tickets to a wide range of Portland area concerts and events, but also sells half-price day-of-show tickets.

On the public transportation front, Portland continues to break new ground. Summer 2001 saw the opening of the **Portland Streetcar** (© **503/238-RIDE;** www.portlandstreetcar.org), which now connects downtown Portland with the Pearl District and the Nob Hill neighborhood, Portland's two trendiest neighborhoods. This streetcar line is the first new streetcar in the United States in 50 years. By the time you read this the new **Airport Max** (© **503/238-7433;** www.tri-met.org) should be up and running, making Portland the only city on the West Coast with a light-rail system that serves an airport terminal.

To make Portland even easier to get around by public transit, Tri-Met also expanded downtown's **Fareless Square** (an area in which all buses, trolleys, and streetcars are free) to include the Rose Quarter neighborhood on the east side of the Willamette River. The Rose Quarter is the site of the Rose Garden arena, the Oregon Convention Center, and the Lloyd Center Mall.

See chapter 13 for complete details on learning your way around Portland.

DINING   With the closing of Atwater's, which was located high atop a downtown skyscraper, Portland lost its best restaurant with a view. However, for view-seeking visitors to Portland, there is a great alternative that we've added to this edition of the book. The **Chart House,** 5700 SW Terwilliger Blvd. (© **503/246-6963**), offers not only great views across Portland to Mount Hood and Mount St. Helens but also the best clam chowder in Portland (and plenty of good seafood and steaks as well). Another restaurant worth searching out is the **Veritable Quandary,** 1220 SW First Ave. (© **503/227-7342**), which, though it has been around for many years, recently went through a renovation and an upgrading of its menu.

See chapter 15 for full reviews of these and other favorite Portland restaurants.

SIGHTSEEING   After many years of moving from one temporary space to another, Portland's **American Advertising Museum,** 211 NW Fifth Ave. (© **503/226-0000;** www.ad museum.org), finally settled into a permanent space this year. The new museum facility, located between Chinatown and the trendy Pearl District, is small but packs a lot of fun exhibits into its small space.

If you'll be visiting Portland with your kids, be sure to check out the new home of Portland's children's museum. **CM2—Children's Museum 2nd Generation,** 4015 SW Canyon Rd. (© **503/223-6500;** www.portland cm2.org), as the museum is now known, is conveniently located across the parking lot from the Oregon Zoom, which makes for a great double whammy of a kids' outing. Both the zoo and the children's museum are located in Washington Park, a sprawling green space in the forested hills to the west of downtown Portland.

See chapter 16 for full coverage of Portland's sightseeing attractions.

1

The Best of Seattle

Imagine yourself seated at a table on the Seattle waterfront, a double tall latte and an almond croissant close at hand. The snowy peaks of the Olympic Mountains are shimmering on the far side of Puget Sound, and the ferryboats are coming and going across Elliott Bay. It's a summer day, and the sun is shining. (Hey, as long as we're dreaming, why not dream big?) It just doesn't get much better than this, unless of course you swap the latte for a microbrew and catch a 9:30 summer sunset. No wonder people love this town so much.

OK, so the waterfront is as touristy as San Francisco's Fisherman's Wharf, but what a view! Seattle is a city of views, and the must-see vista is, of course, the panorama from the top of the Space Needle. With the 21st century in full swing, this image of the future looks decidedly mid-century modern, but still, it's hard to resist an expensive elevator ride in any city. And you can even take a monorail straight out of *The Jetsons* to get there (and pass through the Experience Music Project en route).

EMP, as the Experience Music Project has come to be known, is Seattle's latest architectural oddity. Its swooping, multicolored, metal-skinned bulk rises from the foot of the Space Needle, proof that real 21st-century architecture looks nothing like the vision of the future people dreamed of when the Space Needle was built for the 1962 Seattle World's Fair. EMP is the brainchild of Microsoft cofounder Paul Allen, who built this rock 'n' roll cathedral to house his vast collection of Northwest rock memorabilia.

Paul Allen's money is also hard at work changing the architectural face of the south end of downtown Seattle, where, on March 26, 2000, the Kingdome stadium came down, imploded to make way for a new football stadium home for Allen's Seattle Seahawks. Allen has also developed much of the land around the old Kingdome site into office space, renovating the old Union Station building and adding the unusual glass-walled "waterfall building," which appears to have a waterfall cascading down its windows when it rains.

Paul Allen projects aside, Seattle has become one of the nation's most talked-about and popular cities, and life here has been changing dramatically in recent years. An influx of urban residents has brought a new vibrancy to the downtown area, and as the city has grown wealthier and more sophisticated, it has built itself chic urban condominiums, a new symphony hall, a gorgeous new baseball stadium (Safeco Field), new hotels, and countless upscale restaurants and shops. By the end of 2002, the new football stadium should be up and running. Still in the works are a light-rail system and a new aquarium—though these latter two projects are still a couple of years away.

It's clear that Seattle has not grown complacent. Sure, it's become a very congested city, with traffic problems rivaling those of L.A. And yes, the weather really is lousy for most of the year. But Seattle manages to overcome these minor inconveniences—in large part by spilling out into the streets and parks whenever the sun shines. To visit Seattle in the summer is to witness an exodus; follow the lead of the locals and head for the great outdoors. Should you be brave enough to visit in the rainy season, don't despair: There are compensations for such misfortune, including a roof on Pike Place Market and an espresso bar on every block.

WATER, WATER EVERYWHERE . . . & FORESTS & MOUNTAINS, TOO

Though the times may be a-changing for Seattle, one thing has stayed the same—the beautiful and wild landscape that surrounds the city. The sparkling waters of Elliott Bay, Lake Union, and Lake Washington wrap around this city of shimmering skyscrapers, and forests of evergreens crowd the city limits. Everywhere you look, another breathtaking vista unfolds. With endless boating opportunities and beaches and mountains within a few hours' drive, Seattle is ideally situated for the outdoor pursuits that are so important to the fabric of life in the Northwest.

Few other cities in the United States are as immersed in the outdoor aesthetic as Seattle. The Cascade Range lies less than 50 miles to the east of downtown Seattle, and across Puget Sound stand the Olympic Mountains. In the spring, summer, and fall, the forests and mountains attract hikers, mountain bikers, anglers, and campers, and in winter the ski areas of Snoqualmie Pass and Stephens Pass attract downhill and cross-country skiers.

Though impressive mountains line both the city's eastern and western horizons, a glance to the southeast on a sunny day will reveal the city's most treasured sight—Mount Rainier, a 14,410-foot-tall dormant volcano that looms large, so unexpected that it demands your attention. When "The Mountain is out," as they say here in Seattle, Seattleites head for the hills.

However, as important as The Mountain is to Seattle, it is water that truly defines the city's character. To the west lies Elliott Bay, an arm of Puget Sound; to the east is Lake Washington; and right in the middle of the city is Lake Union. With so much water all around, Seattle has become a city of boaters, who take to the water in everything from regally appointed yachts to slender sea kayaks. The opening day of boating season has become one of Seattle's most popular annual festivals.

A CITY DRIVEN BY CAFFEINE

Despite Seattle's affinity for its nearby natural environment, this city is best known as the coffee capital of America. To understand Seattle's coffee addiction, it is necessary to study the city's geography and climate. Seattle lies at almost 50° north latitude, which means that winter days are short. The sun comes up around 7:30am, goes down as early as 4:30pm, and is frequently hidden behind leaden skies. A strong stimulant is almost a necessity to get people out of bed through the gray days of winter. Seattleites love to argue over which espresso bar or cafe in town serves the best coffee (and the answer isn't always Starbucks, despite its massive expansion across the country).

Seattle's popularity and rapid growth, however, have not been entirely smooth. The streets and highways have been unable to handle the increased traffic load, and commuting has become almost as nightmarish as it is in California, from whence so many of the city's recent transplants fled (ironically, partly due to the traffic congestion). With roads growing ever more crowded and the cost of living continuing to rise, Seattle may not be the Emerald City it once was, but it remains a city in a singularly spectacular setting and a superb summertime vacation destination.

1 Frommer's Favorite Seattle Experiences

- **Taking in the Sunset from the Waterfront.** On a clear summer day, the setting sun silhouettes the Olympic Mountains on the far side of Puget Sound and makes the view from the Seattle waterfront truly memorable. Try the rooftop park at the Bell Street Pier, Myrtle Edwards Park at the north end of the waterfront, or the lounge at the Edgewater Hotel.

- **Riding a Ferry Across Puget Sound.** Sure you can spend $16 to $30 for a narrated tour of the Seattle waterfront, but for a fraction of that, you can take a ferry to Bremerton or Bainbridge Island and see not just Elliott Bay but plenty more of Puget Sound. Keep an eye out for porpoises, orcas, and bald eagles.

- **Eating Your Way through Pike Place Market.** Breakfast at Le Panier, espresso at the original Starbucks, lunch at Café Campagne, a martini at the Pink Door, dinner at Chez Shea, Celtic music at Kells, and a nightcap at Il Bistro—that's how you could spend a day at Pike Place. Between stops on this rigorous itinerary, you can people-watch, listen to street musicians, and shop for everything from fresh salmon to tropical fruits to magic tricks to art glass to live parrots.

- **Relaxing over a Latte.** If the rain and gray skies start to get to you, there is no better prescription (short of a ticket to the tropics) than a frothy latte in a cozy cafe. Grab a magazine and just hang out until the rain stops (maybe sometime in July).

- **Wandering Around Fremont.** This quirky neighborhood considers itself the center of the universe, but it's really a little bit left of center. Retro clothing and vintage furniture stores, cafes, a couple of brewpubs, a great flea market, and the city's best public art make this the most eccentric neighborhood in Seattle.

- **Attending a Show at the Fifth Avenue Theatre.** This historic theater was designed to resemble the imperial throne room in Beijing's Forbidden City. Can you say ornate? Nothing else in Seattle compares, including the show onstage.

- **Going to the Spring Flower and Garden Show.** Each spring, gardening madness descends on the Washington State Convention and Trade Center in the form of one of the largest flower-and-garden shows in the country. There are more than 5 acres of garden displays and hundreds of vendors.

- **Catching Concerts at Bumbershoot.** It isn't often that you can agonize about picking one great music performance over another, but that's just what you have to do at the annual Labor Day music and arts extravaganza known as Bumbershoot. Whether your tastes run to Grieg or grunge, salsa or swing, you'll have plenty of choices.

- **Riding the Monorail.** Though the ride is short, covering a distance that could easily be walked in half an hour, the monorail provides a different perspective on the city. The retrofuturist transport, built for the Seattle World's Fair in 1962, ends at the foot of the Space Needle and even passes right through the Experience Music Project.

- **Spending an Afternoon at Volunteer Park.** Whether or not the day is sunny, this park on Capitol Hill is a great spot to spend an

ℹ️ Site Seeing: The Best Seattle Websites

If you're surfing the Web in search of information on Seattle, the following sites are great places to start.

- **http://seattle.citysearch.com**: CitySearch includes listings and reviews for dining, nightlife, shopping, and more by neighborhood and date (with a handy interactive calendar). In addition to places and events, you can also check the weather or get driving directions.

- **www.seeseattle.org**: Here at the official Seattle–King County Convention and Visitors Bureau website, you can take a virtual tour of the Emerald City, then click on the "What's Happenin'" icon for a calendar of events and attractions (from museums, to theaters, to shopping, to sports) around town. The Seattle FAQ addresses issues such as "What is with you Seattle folks and your coffee?" and "Where is the grave site of Bruce Lee?"

- **www.seattletimes.com**: A solid virtual version of Seattle's print stalwart, the *Seattle Times,* offers many of the paper's stories online. There's also an entertainment section with information on movies, theater, and concerts around town.

- **www.seattleweekly.com**: *Seattle Weekly* is Seattle's main arts-and-entertainment weekly and provides detailed information on what's happening in film, music, theater, and the arts. The weekly also features an extensive dining guide and database of restaurant reviews.

- **www.seatac.org/seatac**: At the Seattle-Tacoma International Airport's website, you'll find maps of individual terminals to help you find your way around. Parking and transportation news also comes in handy. Here you can also keep tabs on any construction projects underway at the airport. A large list of links will point you to everything from freeway traffic updates to local lodging.

- **www.wsdot.wa.gov/ferries**: This is the official website for Washington State Ferries, which are an essential part of any visit to Seattle. This site offers route destinations, schedule and fare information, a calendar of events, and an online ferry reservation service for ferries to Sidney, British Columbia (near Victoria), as well as a section of things to do at various stops along the ferry routes.

afternoon. You can relax in the grass, study Chinese snuff bottles in the Seattle Asian Art Museum, marvel at the orchids in the park's conservatory, or simply enjoy the great view of the city from the top of the park's water tower.

- **Enjoying a Day at the Zoo.** The cages are almost completely gone from this big zoo, replaced by spacious animal habitats that give the residents the feeling of being back at home in the wild. Zebras gallop, brown bears romp, river otters cavort, elephants stomp, and orangutans swing. The levels of activity here make it clear that the animals are happy with their surroundings.

- **Strolling Through the Arboretum in Spring.** Winters in Seattle may not be long but they do lack color. So, when spring hits, the sudden bursts of brightness it brings are reverently appreciated. There's no better place in the city to enjoy the spring floral displays than the Washington Park Arboretum.

• **Walking, Jogging, Biking, or Skating a Seattle Path.** There are several paved trails around Seattle that are ideal for pursuing any of these sports. The trail around Green Lake is the all-time favorite, but the Burke-Gilman/Sammamish River Trail, the trail along the western shore of Lake Washington, the trail along Alki Beach, and the trail through Myrtle Edwards Park at the north end of the Seattle waterfront are equally good choices.

• **Sea Kayaking on Lake Union.** Lake Union is a very urban body of water, but it has a great view of the Seattle skyline, and you can paddle right up to several waterfront restaurants. For more natural surroundings, paddle to the marshes at the north end of the Washington Park Arboretum.

• **Exploring a Waterfront Park.** Seattle abounds in waterfront parks where you can gaze out at distant shores, wiggle your toes in the sand, or walk through a remnant patch of old-growth forest. Some of our favorites include Discovery Park, Seward Park, Lincoln Park, and Golden Gardens Park.

2 Best Hotel Bets

See chapter 4, "Where to Stay in Seattle," for complete reviews of all these accommodations.

• **Best Historic Hotel:** Built in 1924, the **Four Seasons Olympic Hotel,** 411 University St. (© **800/223-8772** or 206/621-1700; www.fourseasons.com/seattle), is styled after Italian Renaissance palaces and is by far the most impressive of Seattle's handful of historic hotels. The grand lobby is unrivaled.

• **Best for Business Travelers:** If your company has sent you to Seattle to close a big deal, insist on the best. Stay at the new **Elliott Grand Hyatt Seattle,** 721 Pine St. (© **800/233-1234** or 206/262-0700; www.elliotthotel.com), and you can avail yourself of all kinds of high-tech amenities, not least of which is complimentary high-speed Internet access. If you're here on Microsoft business, head for the **Woodmark Hotel on Lake Washington,** 1200 Carillon Point, Kirkland (© **800/822-3700** or 425/822-3700). Rooms have two phones,

computer hookups, and most have water views.

• **Best for a Romantic Getaway:** Though Seattle has quite a few hotels that do well for a romantic weekend, the **Inn at the Market,** 86 Pine St. (© **800/446-4484** or 206/443-3600; www.innatthemarket.com), with its Elliott Bay views, European atmosphere, and proximity to many excellent (and very romantic) restaurants, is sure to set the stage for lasting memories.

• **Best Trendy Hotel:** The **W Seattle,** 1112 Fourth Ave. (© **877/W-HOTELS** or 206/264-6000; www.whotels.com), one of a chain of ultrahip hotels that have become popular with the dot-com generation, has brought to Seattle a high-end hipness that also emphasizes service. Dressing entirely in black is de rigueur.

• **Best for Families:** Located just across the street from Lake Union, the **Silver Cloud Inns Seattle–Lake Union,** 1150 Fairview Ave. N. (© **800/330-5812** or 206/447-9500; www.silvercloud.com), is far enough from downtown to be affordable and yet in a great location overlooking the lake and not far from Seattle Center. There are indoor and outdoor pools, and several restaurants right across the street.

- **Best Moderately Priced Hotel:** The **Best Western University Tower Hotel,** 4507 Brooklyn Ave. NE (© **800/WESTERN** or 206/634-2000; www.universitytower hotel.com), is surprisingly reasonably priced for what you get, which is one of the most stylish contemporary hotels in Seattle. Ask for a room on an upper floor, and you'll also get good views.
- **Best Budget Hotel:** Located a 5-minute drive from Seattle Center, the **Howard Johnson Express Inn,** 2500 Aurora Ave. N. (© **877/284-1900** or 206/284-1900; www.hojo.com), may not be the newest budget hotel in town, but it certainly has the best views. Set high on the northern slopes of Queen Anne Hill, the motel has a great view of Lake Union.
- **Best B&B:** Set in the Capitol Hill neighborhood, the **Gaslight Inn,** 1727 15th Ave. (© **206/325-3654;** www.gaslight-inn.com), is a lovingly restored and maintained Craftsman bungalow filled with original Stickley furniture. Lots of public spaces, very tasteful decor, and a swimming pool in the backyard all add up to unexpected luxury for a Seattle B&B.
- **Best Service:** The **Alexis Hotel,** 1007 First Ave. (© **800/426-7033** or 206/624-4844; www.alexishotel.com), a downtown boutique hotel, is small enough to offer that personal touch.
- **Best Location:** Located on a pier right on the Seattle waterfront, **The Edgewater,** Pier 67, 2411 Alaskan Way (© **800/624-0670** or 206/728-7000; www.noble househotels.com), is only 5 blocks from Pike Place Market and the Seattle Aquarium and 3 blocks from the restaurants of Belltown. The Waterfront Streetcar, which goes to Pioneer Square and the International District, stops right in front of the hotel; and ferries to Victoria, British Columbia, leave from the adjacent pier.
- **Best Health Club:** So, you're on the road again, but you don't want to give up your circuit training. Don't worry; bring your Lycra and book a room at the **Bellevue Club Hotel,** 11200 SE Sixth St., Bellevue (© **800/579-1110** or 425/454-4424; www.bellevueclub.com), where you'll have access to a huge private health club complete with indoor Olympic-sized pool.
- **Best Hotel Pool:** Most city-center hotels stick their swimming pool (if they have one at all) down in the basement or on some hidden-away terrace, but at the **Sheraton Seattle Hotel and Towers,** 1400 Sixth Ave. (© **800/325-3535** or 206/621-9000; www.sheraton.com/seattle), you can do laps up on the top floor with the lights of the city twinkling all around you.
- **Best Views:** If you're not back in your room by sunset at **The Edgewater,** Pier 67, 2411 Alaskan Way (© **800/624-0670** or 206/728-7000; www.noblehousehotels.com), you won't turn into a pumpkin, but you will miss the smashing sunsets over the Olympic Mountains on the far side of Puget Sound.
- **Best Room Decor:** If you plan to spend a lot of time in your room, then a room at the **Bellevue Club Hotel** in Bellevue, 11200 SE Sixth St. (© **800/579-1110** or 425/454-4424; www.bellevue club.com), is the place to be. The

rooms here are plush enough to please the most demanding of hedonists.

- **Best for Pets:** If you'll be traveling to Seattle with your pooch and don't mind shelling out big bucks for a top-end hotel, then the **Alexis Hotel,** 1007 First Ave. (© **800/426-7033;** www.alexishotel.com), is the place for you. For an additional $25, they offer a special "Pet Amenities" package that includes dog treats, distilled water and water bowl, morning and afternoon walks, and a copy of the book *Seattle Dog Lovers Companion.*

3 Best Dining Bets

See chapter 5, "Where to Dine in Seattle," for complete reviews of all the restaurants mentioned below.

- **Best Spot for a Romantic Dinner:** At **Chez Shea,** Corner Market Building, 94 Pike St., Suite 34 (© **206/467-9990**), in a quiet corner of Pike Place Market, candlelit tables, subdued lighting, views of ferries crossing the bay, and superb meals add up to the perfect combination for a romantic dinner.

- **Best Waterfront Dining: Palisade,** Elliott Bay Marina, 2601 W. Marina Place (© **206/285-1000**), has a 180° view that takes in Elliott Bay, downtown Seattle, and West Seattle. Never mind that it also has great food and some of the most memorable decor of any Seattle restaurant, with a saltwater tide pool pond in the middle of the dining room and beautiful koa wood details everywhere.

- **Best View:** There's no question here. **SkyCity at the Needle,** Seattle Center, 400 Broad St. (© **800/937-9582** or 206/905-2100), has the best views in Seattle—360° worth of them. Sure it's expensive, but there's no place in town with views to rival these.

- **Best Outdoor Dining with a View:** Located up at the north end of the waterfront, a bit removed from most of the tourist hubbub, **Anthony's Pier 66 & Bell Street Diner,** 2201 Alaskan Way (© **206/448-6688**), combines quality food with a great dockside deck and plenty of variety in pricing.

- **Best Wine List: Canlis,** 2576 Aurora Ave. N. (© **206/283-3313**), has been around for almost 50 years, so the folks here have had plenty of time to develop an extensive and well-thought-out wine list.

- **Best Value:** While Wild Ginger usually gets all the accolades for its Pan-Asian cuisine, Belltown's little **Noodle Ranch,** 2228 Second Ave. (© **206/728-0463**), is every bit as good, despite a more limited menu.

- **Best for Kids:** Located on the south shore of Lake Union, **Cucina!Cucina!,** Chandler's Cove, 901 Fairview Ave. N. (© **206/447-2782**), is Seattle's most popular family restaurant because of all the things they do here to make dining out fun for kids. Adults like it, too.

- **Best Service: Canlis,** 2576 Aurora Ave. N. (© **206/283-3313**), is a Seattle tradition, the perfect place to close a big deal or celebrate a very special occasion. When you want to be pampered, the professional staff at Canlis will do just that.

- **Best French:** Tucked into a quiet courtyard in a secluded corner of Pike Place Market, **Campagne,** Inn at the Market, 86 Pine St. (© **206/728-2800**), is a casually elegant little restaurant that makes the most of fresh market produce, meats, and fish. You can even enjoy views of Elliott Bay with your country French meal.

- **Best Italian:** With so many Italian restaurants in Seattle these days, it's tough deciding which is the best. If you've got the bucks, though, **Il Terrazzo Carmine,** 411 First Ave. S. (© **206/467-7797**), in Pioneer Square, is as likely a candidate as any for a big night on the town.

- **Best Northwest Cuisine:** Chef Thierry Rautureau at **Rover's,** 2808 E. Madison St. (© **206/325-7442**), combines his love of Northwest ingredients with his classic French training to produce his own distinctive take on Northwest cuisine.

- **Best Seafood:** Chef Tom Douglas seems to be able to do no wrong, and at **Etta's Seafood,** 2020 Western Ave. (© **206/443-6000**), he focuses his culinary talents on more than just his famed crab cakes.

- **Best Steaks:** The **Metropolitan Grill,** 820 Second Ave. (© **206/624-3287**), in downtown Seattle, serves corn-fed, aged beef grilled over mesquite charcoal. Steaks just don't get any better than this.

- **Best Burger:** Peppered bacon, cheddar cheese, and grilled onions on a thick, juicy burger all inside a chewy Italian roll—this is the combination that makes the **Belltown Pub and Cafe** burger the best in town, 2322 First Ave. (© **206/728-4311**).

- **Best Desserts:** At **The Famous Pacific Dessert Company,** 127 Mercer St. (© **206/284-8100**), you can indulge in out-of-this-world desserts throughout the day. The location is perfect for enjoying a posttheater piece of cake.

- **Best Late-Night Dining: Palace Kitchen,** 2030 Fifth Ave. (© **206/448-2001**), is an urbane palace of food, where chef Tom Douglas serves tasty specialties from the grill and rotisserie until 1am. The bar here is also a happening place.

- **Best Espresso: Torrefazione,** 320 Occidental Ave. S. (© **206/624-5847**), 622 Olive Way (© **206/624-1429**), and a couple of other locations, serves its brew in hand-painted Italian crockery, and offers delectable pastries to accompany your espresso.

2

Planning Your Trip to Seattle

Seattle has in recent years become one of the West Coast's most popular vacation destinations and as its popularity has grown, so too has the need for previsit planning. Try to make your hotel and car reservations as far in advance as possible—not only will you save money, but you won't have to struggle to find accommodations after you arrive. Summer is the peak tourist season in Seattle, and from June through September downtown hotels are often fully booked for days or even weeks at a time. Consequently, reservations—for hotel rooms, rental cars, or a table at a restaurant—are imperative. If you plan to visit during the city's annual Seafair summer festival in late July and early August, when every hotel in town can be booked, reservations are especially important.

Oh, yeah, and about that rain. Seattle's rainy weather may be infamous, but Seattleites have ways of dealing with the dreary days. They either put on their rain gear and head outdoors just as if the sun were shining or retreat to the city's hundreds of excellent restaurants and cafes, its dozens of theaters and performance halls, its outstanding museums, its many movie theaters, and its excellent bookstores. They rarely let the weather stand in the way of having a good time, and neither should you.

Although summer is the best time to visit, Seattle offers year-round diversions and entertainment, and because it is still a seasonal destination, hotel rooms here are a real bargain during the rainy months between October and April.

1 Visitor Information

If you still have questions about Seattle after reading this book, contact the **Seattle–King County Convention and Visitors Bureau,** 520 Pike St., Suite 1300, Seattle, WA 98101 (© **206/461-5840;** www.seeseattle.org), which operates a Visitor Information Center inside the Washington State Convention and Trade Center, 800 Convention Place, Galleria Level.

For information on other parts of Washington, contact the **Washington State Tourism Office,** P.O. Box 42500, Olympia, WA 98504-2500 (© **800/544-1800** or 360/725-5051; www.experiencewashington.com).

2 Money

ATMs are linked to a national network that most likely includes your bank at home. **Cirrus** (© **800/424-7787;** www.mastercard.com) and **PLUS** (© **800/843-7587;** www.visa.com) are the two most popular networks; check the back of your ATM card to see which network your bank belongs to. Use the 800 numbers to locate ATMs in your destination. Other ATM networks found in the Seattle area are Accel, The Exchange, and Interlink. Expect to pay $1.50 or $2 each time you withdraw money from an ATM, in addition to what your home bank charges.

ATMs have made **traveler's checks** all but obsolete. But if you still prefer

Travel Tip

Photocopy your driver's license, and credit cards (with the number to call in case a credit card is stolen). If your wallet or purse gets stolen, you'll be glad you did.

the security of traveler's checks to carrying cash (and you don't mind showing identification every time you want to cash one), you can get them at almost any bank, paying a service charge that usually ranges from 1% to 7%. You can also get **American Express** traveler's checks online at www.americanexpress.com or over the phone by calling ✆ **800/221-7282;** by using this number, Amex gold and platinum cardholders are exempt from the 1% fee. AAA members can obtain checks without a fee at most AAA offices. If you opt for traveler's checks, be sure to keep a record of the serial numbers, separate from the checks, of course, so you can claim a refund in an emergency.

Credit cards are invaluable when traveling. They are a safe way to carry money, they provide a convenient record of all your expenses, and they're accepted practically everywhere.

At most banks, you can get a cash advance with your credit card at the ATM if you know your PIN number,

but this should only be used as an emergency measure, since interest begins mounting immediately on cash advances—you'll pay dearly for the privilege.

Almost every credit-card company has an emergency 800 number that you can call if your wallet or purse is stolen. They may be able to wire you a cash advance off your credit card immediately; and in many places, they can deliver an emergency credit card in a day or two. Visa's U.S. emergency number is ✆ **800/227-6811.** American Express cardholders and traveler's check holders should call ✆ **800/221-7282** for all money emergencies. MasterCard holders should call ✆ **800/307-7309.** Odds are that if your wallet is gone, the police won't be able to recover it for you. But it's still worth calling them (your credit-card company or insurer may require a police report). Cancel your credit cards before you do anything else, however.

3 When to Go

THE WEATHER

Let's face it, Seattle's weather has a bad reputation. As they say out here, "The rain in Spain stays mainly in Seattle." I wish I could tell you that it isn't so, but I can't. It rains in Seattle—and rains and rains and rains. However, when December 31 rolls around each year, a funny thing happens: They total up the year's precipitation, and Seattle almost always comes out behind such cities as Washington, D.C., Boston, New York, and Atlanta. So, it isn't the *amount* of rain here that's the problem—it's the number of

rainy or cloudy days, which far outnumber those of any of those rainy eastern cities.

Most of Seattle's rain falls between October and April, so if you visit during the summer, you might not see a drop the entire time. But just in case, you should bring a rain jacket or at least an umbrella whenever you come. Also, no matter what time of year you plan to visit Seattle, be sure to bring at least a sweater or light jacket. Summer nights can be quite cool, and daytime temperatures rarely climb above the low 80s. Winters are not as cold as in the East, but snow does fall in Seattle.

Because of the pronounced seasonality of the weather here, people spend as much time outdoors during the summer as they can, and accordingly, summer is when the city stages all its big festivals. Because it stays light until 10pm in the middle of summer, it's difficult to get Seattleites indoors to theater or music performances. But when the weather turns wet, Seattleites head for the theaters and performance halls in droves.

To make things perfectly clear, here's an annual weather chart:

Seattle's Average Temperature & Days of Rain

	Jan	Feb	Mar	Apr	May	June	July	Aug	Sept	Oct	Nov	Dec
Temp. (°F)	46	50	53	58	65	69	75	74	69	60	52	47
Temp. (°C)	8	10	11	15	18	21	24	23	21	16	11	8
Rain (days)	19	16	17	14	10	9	5	7	9	14	18	20

SEATTLE CALENDAR OF EVENTS

Seattleites will hold a festival at the drop of a rain hat, and summers here seem to revolve around the city's myriad festivals. To find out what special events will be taking place while you're in town, check the "Ticket" arts-and-entertainment section of the Friday *Seattle Times* or pick up a copy of *Seattle Weekly.* Remember, festivals here take place rain or shine. If you want to know more specific dates than those listed here, take a look at the calendar of events on the **Seattle–King County Convention and Visitors Bureau website** (www.see seattle.org), which is updated as dates become available.

January

Seattle International Boat Show (© **206/623-2034**), Stadium Exhibition Center. At one of the biggest national shows, more than 1,500 boats of every style and size are displayed. Mid-January.

February

Chinese New Year, International District. Each year's date depends on the lunar calendar (it may fall in January some years). The year 2002 (4700 in the Chinese designation) is the Year of the Horse, and the Chinese New Year falls on February 12. Call © **206/382-1197** for information.

Northwest Flower & Garden Show (© **800/229-6311** or 206/789-5333; www.gardenshow. com), Washington State Convention and Trade Center. Massive show for avid gardeners. Early to mid-February.

April

Cherry Blossom and Japanese Cultural Festival (© **206/684-7200**), Seattle Center. Traditional Japanese spring festival. Mid- to late April.

May

Opening Day of Boating Season, Lake Union and Lake Washington. A parade of boats and much fanfare as Seattle boaters bring out everything from kayaks to yachts. For information call © **206/325-1000.** First Saturday in May.

Seattle International Film Festival, at theaters around town. At this highly regarded film festival, new foreign and independent films are screened for several weeks. To find out what films will be showing and when, consult the website at www.seattlefilm.com, or call © **206/464-5830.** Mid-May to mid-June.

Northwest Folklife Festival (© **206/684-7300;** www.nw folklife.org). This is the largest folk festival in the country, with dozens of national and regional folk musicians performing on numerous stages. In addition, there are crafts vendors from all over the Northwest, lots of good food, and dancing too. The festival takes place at the Seattle Center, and admission is by donation. Memorial Day weekend.

Pike Place Market Festival (© 206/587-0351), Pike Place Market. A celebration of the market, with lots of free entertainment. Memorial Day weekend.

Seattle International Children's Festival (© 206/684-7338 or 206/684-7346; www.seattleinternational.org), Seattle Center. Hungarian gypsy musicians, a Chinese martial arts ballet, Yoruba drummers from Nigeria—these are just some of the acts that you might see at this festival that celebrates world cultures through the performing arts. Mid- to late May.

June

Fremont Fair (© 206/726-2623; www.fremontfair.com), Fremont neighborhood. A celebration of the summer solstice with a wacky parade, food, arts and crafts, and entertainment in one of Seattle's favorite neighborhoods. Third weekend in June.

Out to Lunch (© 206/623-0340). Free lunchtime music concerts in plazas and parks throughout downtown. Mid-June through early September.

July

Fourth of Jul-Ivar's fireworks (© 206/587-6500; www.ivars.net), Myrtle Edwards Park, north end of Seattle waterfront. Fireworks over Elliott Bay. July 4.

AT&T Family Fourth at Lake Union (© 206/281-8111), Lake Union. Seattle's other main Fourth of July fireworks display. July 4.

Wooden Boat Festival (© 206/382-BOAT; www.cvb.org), Lake Union. Wooden boats, both old and new, from all over the Northwest. Races, demonstrations, food, and entertainment. July 4th weekend.

Chinatown/International District Summer Festival (© 206/382-1197), International District. Features the music, dancing, arts, and food of Seattle's Asian district. Second weekend in July.

Bite of Seattle, Seattle Center (© 206/232-2982; www.biteofseattle.com). Sample offerings from dozens of Seattle's restaurants, as well as a wine-tasting exhibit. Third weekend in July.

Seafair (© 206/728-0123; www.seafair.com). This is the biggest Seattle event of the year, with daily festivities—parades, hydroplane boat races, an air show with the navy's Blue Angels, a Torchlight Parade, ethnic festivals, sporting events, and open house on naval ships. Events take place all over Seattle. Early July to early August.

Bellevue Art Museum Fair (© 425/454-3322), Bellevue Square shopping mall, Bellevue. This is the largest arts and crafts fair in the Northwest. Late July.

August

Chief Seattle Days (© 360/598-3311), at Suquamish tribal headquarters. Celebration of Northwest Native American culture across Puget Sound from Seattle. Third weekend in August.

September

Bumbershoot, the Seattle Arts Festival (© 206/281-8111; www.bumbershoot.org). Seattle's second most popular festival derives its peculiar name from a British term for an umbrella—an obvious reference to the rainy weather. Lots of rock music and other events pack Seattle's youthful set into Seattle Center and other venues. You'll find plenty of art and crafts on display too. Labor Day weekend.

Seattle Fringe Theatre Festival (© 206/342-9172; www.seattle fringe.org), various venues. Avant-garde, experimental, and otherwise uncategorizable plays and theater performances from a wide variety of companies. Late September.

October

Salmon Days Festival (© 425/ 392-0661). This festival in Issaquah, 15 miles east of Seattle, celebrates the annual return of salmon that spawn within the city limits. First full weekend in October.

November

Elliott's Oyster New Year (© 206/ 623-4340), Elliott's Oyster House, Seattle. Summer months are not the best for oysters, but as the cooler weather returns, so does the bounty of oysters. To celebrate this occasion, oyster lovers slurp down more than two dozen different types here at Elliott's on Pier 56. Beginning of November.

Seattle Marathon (© 206/729-3660), around the city. What with all the hills, you have to be crazy to want to run a marathon in Seattle, but plenty of people show up in running shoes every year. First Sunday after Thanksgiving.

December

Seattle Christmas Ships (© 206/ 623-1445), various locations. Boats decked out with imaginative Christmas lights parade past various waterfront locations. **Argosy Cruises** (© 800/642-7816 or 206/ 623-1445; www.argosycruises.com) offers tours; see chapter 6, "Exploring Seattle," for more details. Throughout December.

AT&T New Year's at the Needle, Seattle Center. The Space Needle ushers in the new year by bursting into light when midnight strikes. Call © 206/443-2100 for information. December 31.

4 Health & Insurance

WHAT TO DO IF YOU GET SICK AWAY FROM HOME

If you suffer from a chronic illness, consult your doctor before your departure. For conditions like epilepsy, diabetes, or heart problems, wear a **Medic Alert Identification Tag** (© 888/633-4298; www. medicalert.org), which will immediately alert doctors to your condition and give them access to your records through Medic Alert's 24-hour hot line.

Pack prescription medications in your carry-on luggage. Carry written prescriptions in generic, not brand-name form, and dispense all prescription medications from their original labeled vials. If you wear contact lenses, pack an extra pair in case you lose one.

If you get sick, you may want to ask the concierge at your hotel to recommend a local doctor—even his or her own—or call the doctor referral line listed on p. 36 of "Fast Facts: Seattle." If you can't find a doctor who can help you right away, try the emergency room at the local hospital (also listed in the "Fast Facts" in chapter 3, "Getting to Know Seattle"). Many emergency rooms have walk-in-clinics for emergency cases that are not life threatening. You may not get immediate attention, but you won't pay the high price of an emergency room visit. In an emergency, phone © 911.

TRAVEL INSURANCE

Most travelers' needs are met by their existing insurance policies (your homeowners' insurance should cover lost or stolen luggage, for example), but if you have any concerns, contact your insurance company before you leave home and ask them to detail what they'll cover. Some credit- and charge-card companies may insure you against travel accidents if you buy plane, train, or bus tickets with their cards. If you do decide you need additional specific travel coverage, most travel agents can sell you any number of insurance packages tailored to fit your specific needs. But check your existing policies first, and don't buy more than you need.

Among the companies offering specialized travel insurance policies are **Access America** (© **800/284-8300;** www.accessamerica.com), **Travel Guard** (© **877/216-4885;** www.travel-guard.com), and **Travelex Insurance Services** (© **888/457-4602;** www.travelex-insurance.com).

Trip-cancellation insurance may be a good idea if you've paid a large portion of your vacation expenses up front, say, by purchasing a package tour. (But don't buy it from your tour operator—talk about putting all of your eggs in one basket! Buy it from an outside vendor instead.) Coverage should cost approximately 6% to 8% of the total value of your vacation, so a $3,000 trip could be insured for around $210.

Your homeowner's or renter's insurance should cover stolen luggage. The airlines are responsible for losses up to $2,500 on domestic flights if they lose your luggage; if you plan to carry anything more valuable than that, keep it in your carry-on bag.

5 Tips for Travelers with Special Needs

FOR TRAVELERS WITH DISABILITIES

The greatest difficulty of a visit to Seattle for anyone who is restricted to a wheelchair is dealing with the city's many steep hills, which rival those of San Francisco. One solution for dealing with downtown hills is to use the elevator at the Pike Place Market for getting between the waterfront and First Avenue. Also, by staying at The Edgewater hotel, right on the waterfront, you'll have easy access to all of the city's waterfront attractions and can use the Waterfront Streetcar for getting between the Pike Place Market and Pioneer Square area. Also keep in mind that the downtown bus tunnel, which connects the International District to Westlake Center shopping mall and is wheelchair accessible, can make traveling across downtown somewhat less strenuous.

When making airline reservations, always mention your disability. Airline policies differ regarding wheelchairs and Seeing Eye dogs.

Most hotels now offer wheelchair-accessible accommodations, and some of the larger and more expensive hotels also offer TDD telephones and other amenities for the hearing and sight impaired.

Many of the major car-rental companies now offer hand-controlled cars for drivers with disabilities. Avis can provide such a vehicle at any of its airport locations in the United States with 72-hour advance notice; Hertz requires between 24 and 48 hours of advance reservation at most of its locations. **Wheelchair Getaways** (© 800/642-2042; www.wheelchair-getaways.com) rents specialized vans with wheelchair lifts and other features for travelers with disabilities in about 40 cities across the United States.

Travelin' Talk Network, P.O. Box 1796, Wheat Ridge, CO 80034 (© **303/232-2979;** www.travelintalk.net), operates a website for travelers with disabilities, and each month e-mails a newsletter to members ($19.95 for a lifetime membership) with information about discounts, accessible hotels, trip companions, and other traveling tips. Those without Internet access can also subscribe and receive two newsletters by mail every other month. Another online newsletter and database, **www.access-able.com**, is operated by the same company. You'll also find relay and voice numbers for hotels, airlines, and car-rental companies on Access-Able's user-friendly site, as well as links to accessible accommodations, attractions, transportation, tours, local medical resources and equipment repairers, and much more.

Moss Rehab ResourceNet (www. mossresourcenet.org) is a great source for information, tips, and resources relating to accessible travel. You'll find links here to a number of travel agents who specialize in planning trips for disabled travelers.

Travelers with disabilities might also want to consider joining a tour that caters specifically to them. **Accessible Journeys (** © **800/TINGLES** or 610/521-0339; www.accessible journeys.com), for slow walkers and wheelchair travelers, offers excursions to the Northwest. **Wilderness Inquiry (** © **800/728-0719** or 612/ 676-9400; www.wildernessinquiry. org) offers a kayaking trip to the San Juan Islands for persons of all abilities.

Amtrak's (© **800/USA-RAIL;** www.amtrak.com) services for disabled passengers include wheelchair assistance and special seats with 24 hours' notice. Passengers with disabilities are also entitled to a discount of 15% off the lowest available rail fare at the time of booking. Documentation from a doctor or an ID card proving your disability is required. Amtrak also provides wheelchair-accessible sleeping accommodations on long-distance trains, and service animals are permitted and travel free of charge. Amtrak publishes a handbook called "Access Amtrak," which tells you all you need to know about traveling on Amtrak when you have a disability; call © **877/268-7252** to order it and allow 7 to 10 days for delivery. Amtrak's TDD number is © **800/ 523-6590.**

On **Greyhound** (© **800/229-9424;** www.greyhound.com) buses, a companion can accompany a person with a disability at no charge (you must inform Greyhound in advance; they'll ask for proof of disability and will want to confirm that the companion is truly necessary and capable of helping the disabled passenger). Call © **800/752-4841** at least 24 hours in advance to discuss other special needs. Greyhound's TDD number is © **800/ 345-3109.**

If you plan to visit Mount Rainier or Olympic National Park, you can avail yourself of the **Golden Access Passport.** This lifetime pass is issued free to any U.S. citizen or permanent resident who has been medically certified as disabled or blind (you will need to show proof of disability). The pass permits free entry into national parks and monuments and can be obtained through the visitor's center at either Mount Rainer or Olympic National Park.

You can join the **Society for Accessible Travel and Hospitality (SATH;** © 212/447-7284; www.sath.org) to gain access to their vast network of connections in the travel industry. They provide information sheets on destinations and referrals to tour operators that specialize in traveling with disabilities. Their quarterly magazine, *Open World,* is full of good information and resources.

FOR GAY & LESBIAN TRAVELERS

Seattle is one of the most gay-friendly cities in the country, with a large gay and lesbian community that's centered around the Capitol Hill neighborhood. In Capitol Hill you'll find numerous bars, nightclubs, stores, and bed-and-breakfast inns catering to the gay community. Broadway Avenue, Capitol Hill's main drag, is also the site of the annual Gay Pride March, held each year in late June.

The *Seattle Gay News* (© 206/324-4297; www.sgn.org) is the community's newspaper, available at bookstores and gay bars and nightclubs.

Beyond the Closet, 518 E. Pike St. (© 206/322-4609), and **Bailey Coy Books,** 414 Broadway Ave. E. (© 206/323-8842), are the gay community's two main bookstores and are good sources of information on what's going on within the community.

The **Lesbian Resource Center,** 2214 S. Jackson St. (© 206/322-3965), is a community resource center providing housing and job information, therapy, and business referrals.

The **Gaslight Inn** and **Bacon Mansion** are two gay-friendly bed-and-breakfasts in the Capitol Hill area; see chapter 4, "Where to Stay in Seattle," for full reviews. For information on gay and lesbian bars and nightclubs, see "The Gay & Lesbian Scene" in chapter 9, "Seattle After Dark."

If you want help planning your trip, the **International Gay & Lesbian Travel Association (IGLTA;** © 800/448-8550 or 954/776-2626; www.iglta.org) can link you up with the appropriate gay-friendly service organization or tour specialist. With around 1,200 members, it offers quarterly newsletters, marketing mailings, and a membership directory that's updated quarterly. Members are kept informed of gay and gay-friendly hoteliers, tour operators, and airline and cruise-line representatives. **GayWired Travel Services (www.gaywired.com)** is another great trip-planning resource; click on "Travel Services."

Out and About (© 800/929-2268 or 415/486-2591; www.outandabout.com) offers a monthly newsletter packed with good information on the global gay and lesbian scene. Its website features links to gay and lesbian tour operators and other gay-themed travel links, plus extensive online travel information to subscribers only. *Out and About*'s guidebooks are available at most major bookstores and through www.adlbooks.com.

FOR SENIORS

Don't be shy about asking for discounts, but always carry some kind of identification, such as a driver's license, that shows your date of birth, especially if you've kept your youthful glow. In Seattle, most attractions, some theaters and concert halls, tour companies, and the Washington State Ferries all offer senior-citizen discounts. These can add up to substantial savings, but you have to remember to ask.

Discounts abound for seniors, beginning with the 10%-off-your-airfare deal that most airlines offer to anyone age 62 or older. In addition, a number of airlines have clubs you can join and coupon books you can buy that may or may not increase your savings beyond that base 10% discount, depending on how often you travel, where you're going, and how long you're going to stay. Always ask an airline whether it has a club for seniors or sells coupon books, either of which often qualifies "mature" travelers for discounted tickets.

Both **Amtrak** (© 800/USA-RAIL; www.amtrak.com) and **Greyhound** (© 800/752-4841; www.greyhound.com) offer discounts to persons over 62.

Many hotels offer senior discounts. **Choice Hotels** (Clarion Hotels, Quality Inns, Comfort Inns, and Sleep Inns), for example, give 20% off their published rates to anyone over 60 depending on availability, provided you book your room through their nationwide toll-free reservations numbers (not directly with the hotels or through a travel agent).

If you plan on visiting either Mount Rainier National Park or Olympic National Park while in the Seattle area, you can save on park admissions by getting a **Golden Age Passport,** which is available for $10 to U.S. citizens and permanent residents age 62 and older. This federal government pass allows lifetime entrance privileges. You can apply in person for this passport at a national park, national forest, or other location where it's honored, as long as you can show reasonable proof of age.

If you aren't a member of the **American Association of Retired Persons** (**AARP**), 601 E St. NW, Washington, DC 20049 (© **800/424-3410;** www.aarp.org), do yourself a favor and join. This association provides discounts for many lodgings, car rentals, airfares, and attractions throughout Seattle, although you can sometimes get a similar discount simply by showing your ID.

Grand Circle Travel is another of the literally hundreds of travel agencies specializing in vacations for seniors (347 Congress St., Suite 3A, Boston, MA 02210 (© **800/221-2610** or 617/350-7500; www.gct.com). *But beware:* Many of them are of the tour-bus variety, with free trips thrown in for those who organize groups of 20 or more. Seniors seeking more independent travel should probably consult a regular travel agent. **SAGA International Holidays,** 222 Berkeley St., Boston, MA 02116 (© **800/343-0273;** www.saga holidays.com), offers inclusive tours and cruises for those 50 and older. SAGA also sponsors the more substantial "Road Scholar Tours," which are fun-loving but with an educational

bent, and is an agent for Smithsonian Institution tours.

If you'd like to do a bit of studying on vacation in the company of like-minded older travelers, consider looking into **Elderhostel,** 11 Avenue de Lafayette, Boston, MA 02110-1746 (© **877/426-8056;** www.elder hostel.org).

The Mature Traveler, a monthly newsletter on senior citizen travel, is a valuable resource. It is available by subscription ($32 a year) from GEM Publishing Group by calling © **800/460-6676.** GEM also publishes *The Book of Deals,* a collection of more than 1,000 senior discounts on airlines, lodging, tours, and attractions around the country; it comes free with the newsletter subscription, but is available by itself for $9.95.

Specialty books on the market for seniors include *Unbelievably Good Deals and Great Adventures That You Absolutely Can't Get Unless You're Over 50* (Contemporary Books). Also check out your newsstand for the quarterly magazine *Travel 50 & Beyond,* or subscribe online at www.travel50andbeyond.com for $9.95.

FOR FAMILIES

Many of the city's hotels allow kids to stay free in their parents' room—be sure to ask. Some budget hotels also allow children to eat for free in the hotel's dining room. Also, note that most downtown hotels cater almost exclusively to business travelers and don't offer the sort of amenities that will appeal to families—a swimming pool, game room, or inexpensive restaurant. For information on hotels that are good for families, see the "Family-Friendly Hotels" box in chapter 4.

At mealtimes, many of the larger restaurants, especially along the waterfront, offer children's menus. You'll also find plenty of variety and low prices at the many food vendors' stalls at the Pike Place Market. There's also a food court in Westlake Center shopping mall. For information on restaurants that cater to families, see the "Family-Friendly Restaurants" box in chapter 5, "Where to Dine in Seattle."

For information on family attractions in Seattle, see the "Especially for Kids" section of chapter 6.

Note: If you plan on traveling to Canada, be sure to bring your children's birth certificates.

An excellent resource for family travel, including information about hotel deals for families, is **Family Travel Times,** a bimonthly newsletter published by FTT Marketing. To subscribe or get information, contact *Family Travel Times* (© **888/ 822-4388** or 212/477-5524; www. familytraveltimes.com). For $39 per year, you get six issues of the newsletter and discounts on other publications and back issues.

Family Travel Forum (© **888/ 383-6786;** www.familytravelforum. com) is another helpful source of information and travel discounts for families planning trips. You can receive a newsletter in the mail and/or access information online to read tips on traveling with children, staff-written travel articles, and members' firsthand accounts of experiences in various destinations. Each issue of the newsletter focuses on a specific theme, from traveling with teens to intergenerational travel. A comprehensive annual membership is $48, or you can subscribe simply to the online service for $28 annually or $3.95 monthly.

6 Getting There

BY PLANE
THE MAJOR AIRLINES
The **Seattle-Tacoma International Airport** (© **800/544-1965** or 206/ 431-4444; www.seatac.org/seatac) is served by about 30 airlines. The major carriers include: **Air Canada** (© 800/ 247-2262; www.aircanada.ca), **Alaska Airlines** (© 800/426-0333; www. alaskaair.com), **America West** (© 800/235-9292; www.americawest. com), **American** (© 800/433-7300; www.im.aa.com), **Continental** (© 800/525-0280; www.continental. com), **Delta** (© 800/221-1212; www. delta.com), **Frontier** (© 800/432-1359; www.frontierairlines.com), **Horizon Air** (© 800/547-9308; www.horizonair.com), **Northwest/ KLM** (© 800/225-2525; www.nwa. com), **Shuttle by United** (© 800/ 748-8853; www.united.com), **Southwest** (© 800/435-9792; www. southwest.com), **TWA** (© 800/221-2000; www.twa.com), **United** (© 800/241-6522; www.united.com), and **US Airways** (© 800/428-4322; www.usairways.com).

For information on flights to the United States from other countries, see "Getting to the United States" in Appendix B, "For International Visitors."

Seaplane service between Seattle and the San Juan Islands and Victoria, British Columbia, is offered by **Kenmore Air** (© **800/543-9595** or 425/ 486-1257; www.kenmoreair.com), which has its Seattle terminals at the south end of Lake Union and at the north end of Lake Washington.

There is also helicopter service to Seattle's Boeing Field from Victoria and Vancouver, British Columbia, on **Helijet Airways** (© **800/665-4354;** www.helijet.com). The flights take about 35 minutes from Victoria and about 90 minutes from Vancouver (depending on the connection, as you must connect in Victoria for the flight to Seattle). Ballpark round-trip airfares are about C$369 (Canadian dollars) between Victoria and Seattle and about C$687 between Vancouver and Seattle.

FLY FOR LESS: TIPS FOR GETTING THE BEST AIR-FARES

If you happen to be flying from another city on the West Coast or somewhere else in the West, check first with Frontier Airlines, Shuttle by United, Alaska Airlines, Horizon Airlines, or Southwest. These airlines often have the best fares between western cities.

Check your newspaper for advertised **sales** or call the airlines directly and ask if any promotional rates or special fares are available. You'll almost never see a sale during the peak summer vacation months of July and August, or during the Thanksgiving or Christmas seasons; but in periods of low-volume travel, you should pay no more than $400 for a cross-country flight.

Note, however, that the lowest-priced fares are often nonrefundable, require advance purchase of 1 to 3 weeks and a certain length of stay, and carry penalties for changing dates of travel. So, when you're quoted a fare, make sure you know exactly what the restrictions are before you commit. If you already hold a ticket when a sale breaks, it may even pay to exchange your ticket, which usually incurs a $50 to $75 charge.

If your schedule is flexible, ask if you can secure a cheaper fare by staying an extra day, staying over Saturday night, or flying midweek. (Many airlines won't volunteer this information, so be aggressive and ask the reservations agent lots of questions.)

Consolidators, also known as bucket shops, are a good place to find low fares. Consolidators buy seats in bulk from the airlines and then sell them back to the public at prices below even the airlines' discounted rates. Their small boxed ads usually run in the Sunday travel section of newspapers at the bottom of the page. Before you pay, however, ask for a confirmation number from the consolidator and then call the airline itself to confirm your seat. Be prepared to book your ticket with a different consolidator—there are many to choose from—if the airline can't confirm your reservation. Also be aware that bucket shop tickets are usually nonrefundable or rigged with stiff cancellation penalties, often as high as 50% to 75% of the ticket price. And when an airline runs a special deal, you won't always do better with a consolidator.

Council Travel (℡ 800/226-8624; www.counciltravel.com) and **STA Travel** (℡ 800/781-4040; www.sta-travel.com) cater especially to young travelers, but their bargain basement prices are available to people of all ages. **Travel Bargains** (℡ 800/AIR-FARE;** www.1800airfare.com) was formerly owned by TWA but now offers the deepest discounts on many other airlines, with last-minute purchases available. For discount and last-minute bookings, contact **McCord Consumer Direct** (Air for Less) (℡ 800/FLY-FACTS or 800/FLY-ASAP; www.better1.com), which can often get you tickets at significantly less than full fare. Other reliable consolidators include **1/800-FLY-CHEAP** (www.flycheap.com); **Cheap Tickets** (℡ 800/377-1000; www.cheaptickets.com); and **TFI Tours International** (℡ 800/745-8000 or 212/736-1140), which serves as a clearinghouse for unused seats. There are also "rebators," such as **Travel Avenue** (℡ 800/333-3335 or 312/876-1116; www.travelavenue.com), which rebate part of their commissions to you.

It's also easy to search the **Internet** for cheap fares—though it's still best to compare your findings with the research of a dedicated travel agent, if you're lucky enough to have one, especially when you're booking more than just a flight. Among the better-respected virtual travel agents are **Travelocity** (**www.travelocity.com**),

Expedia (www.expedia.com), **Yahoo! Travel** (http://travel.yahoo.com), and **Orbitz** (www.orbitz.com). **Smarter Living** (www.smarter living.com) is a great source for discount Internet deals. And don't forget to check the airlines' own websites for special Internet bargains.

BY CAR

Seattle is 1,190 miles from Los Angeles, 175 miles from Portland, 835 miles from Salt Lake City, 810 miles from San Francisco, 285 miles from Spokane, and 110 miles from Vancouver.

I-5 is the main north-south artery through Seattle, running south to Portland and north to the Canadian border. I-405 is Seattle's east-side bypass and accesses the cities of Bellevue, Redmond, and Kirkland on the east side of Lake Washington. I-90, which ends at I-5, connects Seattle to Spokane in the eastern part of Washington. Wash. 520 connects I-405 with Seattle just north of downtown and also ends at I-5. Wash. 99, the Alaskan Way Viaduct, is another major north-south highway through downtown Seattle; it passes through the waterfront section of the city.

One of the most important benefits of belonging to the **American Automobile Association** (© 800/222-4357; www.aaa.com) is that it supplies members with emergency road service and towing services if you have car trouble during your trip. You also get maps and detailed Trip-Tiks that give precise directions to a destination, including up-to-date information about areas of construction. In Seattle,

AAA is located at 330 Sixth Ave. N. (© 206/448-5353).

See "Getting Around" in chapter 3 for details on driving, parking, and car rentals in Seattle.

BY FERRY

Seattle is served by **Washington State Ferries** (© 800/84-FERRY or 888/808-7977 within Washington state, or 206/464-6400; www.wsdot.wa.gov/ferries), the most extensive ferry system in the United States. Car ferries travel between downtown Seattle and both Bainbridge Island and Bremerton (on the Kitsap Peninsula) from Pier 52, Colman dock. A passenger-only ferry sails for Bremerton from this dock as well. A passenger-only ferry to Vashon Island uses the adjacent Pier 50. Car ferries also sail between Fauntleroy (in west Seattle) and both Vashon Island and the Kitsap Peninsula at Southworth; between Tahlequah at the south end of Vashon Island and Pt. Defiance in Tacoma; between Edmonds and Kingston (on the Kitsap Peninsula); between Mukilteo and Whidbey Island; between Whidbey Island at Keystone and Port Townsend; and between Anacortes and the San Juan Islands and Sidney, British Columbia (on Vancouver Island near Victoria). See "Getting Around," in chapter 3, for fare information.

If you are traveling between Victoria, British Columbia, and Seattle, there are several options available from **Victoria Clipper,** Pier 69, 2701 Alaskan Way (© 800/888-2535 from outside Seattle and Victoria, 206/448-5000, or 250/382-8100 in

---

Impressions

. . . on a famous ferry going into famous Seattle, dusk on a November night, the sky, the water, the mountains are all the same color: lead in a closet. Suicide weather. The only thing wrong with this picture is that you feel so happy.

—*Esquire* magazine

Victoria; www.victoriaclipper.com). Throughout the year, a ferry taking either 2 or 3 hours makes the trip ($79–$125 round-trip for adults). The lower fare is for advance-purchase tickets. Some scheduled trips also stop in the San Juan Islands.

BY TRAIN

There is **Amtrak** (© **800/872-7245;** www.amtrak.com) service from Vancouver, B.C., to Seattle and from Portland and as far south as Eugene, Oregon, on the *Cascades* (a high-speed, European-style Talgo train). The train takes about 4 hours from Vancouver to Seattle and 3½ to 4 hours from Portland to Seattle. One-way fares from Vancouver to Seattle are usually between $23 and $34, and fares between Portland and Seattle are usually between $23 and $36. Booking earlier will get you a less expensive ticket. There is also Amtrak service to Seattle from San Diego, Los Angeles, and San Francisco, and Portland on the *Coast Starlight,* and from Spokane and points east on the *Empire Builder.* Amtrak also operates a bus between Vancouver and Seattle.

Like the airlines, Amtrak offers several discounted fares; although they're not all based on advance purchase, you have more discount options by reserving early. The discount fares can be used only on certain days and hours of the day; be sure to find out exactly what restrictions apply. Tickets for children ages 2 to 15 cost half the price of a regular coach fare when the children are accompanied by a fare-paying adult. Amtrak's website features a bargain fares service, Rail SALE, which allows you to purchase tickets for one-way designated coach seats at great discounts. This program is only available on **www.amtrak.com** when you charge your tickets by credit card.

Also inquire about money-saving packages that include hotel accommodations, car rentals, tours, and so on with your train fare. Call © **800/ 321-8684** for details.

BY BUS

The **Greyhound bus station,** Eighth Avenue and Stewart Street (© **800/ 231-2222** or 206/628-5526), is located a few blocks northeast of downtown Seattle. **Greyhound** bus service provides connections to almost any city in the continental United States. Several budget chain motels are located only a few blocks from the bus station. It's a bit farther to the Hosteling International–Seattle hostel, yet walkable if you don't have much luggage. Otherwise you can grab a free ride on a Metro bus.

3

Getting to Know Seattle

Because it is surrounded on three sides by water, built on six hills, and divided into numerous neighborhoods, Seattle can be a very confusing city. While most of its top attractions are located downtown, there are places of interest in other areas, too, including eclectic neighborhoods and attractive parks. The city's charms aren't all right in your face. This chapter, which includes information on the city's layout, its neighborhoods, and the basics of how to get around, should help you get out and explore so you can get to know the real Seattle.

1 Orientation

ARRIVING

BY PLANE

Seattle-Tacoma International Airport (© 800/544-1965 or 206/431-4444; www.seatac.org/seatac), most commonly referred to simply as Sea-Tac, is located about 14 miles south of Seattle.

Inside the arrivals terminal, you'll find a **Visitor Information Desk** (© 206/433-5218) in the baggage-claim area across from carousel no. 8. It's open daily from 9am to 6pm. However, this desk cannot make hotel reservations for you.

Also at the airport, you'll find a Thomas Cook currency exchange desk (© 206/248-0401) and branches of all the major car-rental companies (for further details see "Getting Around," later in this chapter).

GETTING INTO THE CITY BY CAR There are two main exits from the airport: From the loading/unloading area, take the first exit if you're staying near the airport. Take the second exit (Wash. 518) if you're headed to downtown Seattle. Driving east on Wash. 518 will connect you to I-5, where you'll then follow the signs for Seattle. Generally, allow 30 minutes for the drive between the airport and downtown—45 minutes to an hour during rush hour.

During rush hour, it's sometimes quicker to take Wash. 518 west to Wash. 509 north to Wash. 99 to Wash. 519 (which becomes the Alaskan Way Viaduct along the Seattle waterfront).

GETTING INTO THE CITY BY TAXI, SHUTTLE, OR BUS A **taxi** into downtown Seattle will cost you about $32. There are usually plenty of taxis around, but if not, call **Yellow Cab/Graytop** (© 206/622-6500) or **Farwest Taxi** (© 206/622-1717). The flag-drop charge is $1.80; after that, it's $1.80 per mile.

Gray Line Airport Express (© 800/426-7505 or 206/626-6088; www.graylineofseattle.com) provides service between the airport and downtown Seattle daily from about 5am to 11pm and is your best bet for getting to downtown. These shuttle vans pick up from two booths outside the baggage claim area—one outside Door 24 and one outside Door 8. Shuttles operate every

20 minutes and stop at the following hotels: Madison Renaissance, Crowne Plaza, Four Seasons Olympic, Seattle Hilton, Sheraton Seattle, Westin, and Warwick. Fares are $8.50 one-way and $14 round-trip. Connector service to the above hotels is also provided from numerous other downtown hotels, as well as from the Amtrak station, the Washington State Ferries ferry terminal (Pier 52), and the Greyhound station. Connector service is free from some downtown hotels, but from other locations, it costs $2.50 one-way or $5 round-trip; call for details.

Shuttle Express (© **800/487-7433** in Washington, or 425/981-7000; www.shuttleexpress.com) provides 24-hour service between Sea-Tac and the Seattle, North Seattle, and Bellevue areas. The rate to downtown Seattle is about $21 plus $3 for an additional person. You need to make a reservation to get to the airport, but to leave the airport, simply call when you arrive. Push 48 on one of the Traveler's Information Center courtesy phones outside the baggage-claim area. If you arrive at a time when the Gray Line shuttle is not operating or are heading to one of the Eastside communities such as Bellevue or Kirkland, this is going to be your best bet for getting into town.

Metro Transit (© **800/542-7876** in Washington, or 206/553-3000; http://transit.metrokc.gov) operates two buses between the airport and downtown. These buses leave from near Door 6 (close to baggage carousel 1) of the baggage claim area. It's a good idea to call for the current schedule when you arrive in town. Bus 194 operates (to Third Avenue and Union Street or the bus tunnel, depending on the time of day) every 30 minutes weekdays from 4:55am to 8:33pm, weekends from about 6:20am to 7:20pm. Bus 174 operates (to Second Avenue and Union Street) every 30 minutes from 4:47am to 2:43am (from 5:45am on Saturday and from 6:49am on Sunday). Bus trips take 30 to 40 minutes depending on conditions. The fare is $1.25 during off-peak hours and $2 during peak hours.

BY TRAIN OR BUS

Amtrak (© **206/382-4125**) trains stop at King Street Station, which is located at Third Avenue South and Jackson Street, within a few blocks of the historic Pioneer Square neighborhood and adjacent to the south entrance of the downtown bus tunnel. Any bus running north through the tunnel will take you to within a few blocks of most downtown hotels. The Waterfront Streetcar also stops within a block of King Street Station and can take you to the Hotel Edgewater.

The **Greyhound bus station,** Eighth Avenue and Stewart Street (© **800/231-2222** or 206/628-5526), is located a few blocks northeast of downtown Seattle not far from Lake Union and Seattle Center. Several budget chain motels are located only a few blocks from the bus station. It's a bit farther to the Hostelling International–Seattle hostel, yet walkable if you don't have much luggage. Otherwise, you can grab a free ride on a Metro bus.

BY CAR

See section 6, "Getting There," at the end of chapter 2, and section 2, "Getting Around," later in this chapter.

VISITOR INFORMATION

Visitor information on Seattle and the surrounding area is available by contacting the **Seattle–King County Convention & Visitors Bureau Visitor Information Center,** Washington State Convention & Trade Center,

800 Convention Place, Galleria Level, at the corner of Eighth Avenue and Pike Street (© **206/461-5840;** www.seeseattle.org). To find it, walk up Union Street until it goes into a tunnel under the Convention Center. You'll see the information center on your left. Alternatively, you can enter the building from Pike Street.

CITY LAYOUT

Although downtown Seattle is fairly compact and can easily be navigated on foot, finding your way by car can be frustrating. The Seattle area has been experiencing phenomenal growth for more than a decade, and this has created traffic-congestion problems. Here are some guidelines to help you find your way around.

MAIN ARTERIES & STREETS   There are three interstate highways serving Seattle. Seattle's main artery is I-5, which runs through the middle of the city. Take the James Street exit west if you're heading for the Pioneer Square area, take the Seneca Street exit for Pike Place Market, or the Olive Way exit for Capitol Hill. I-405 is the city's north-south bypass and travels up the east shore of Lake Washington through Bellevue and Kirkland (Seattle's high-tech corridor). I-90 comes in from the east, crossing one of the city's two floating bridges, and ends at the south end of downtown.

Downtown is roughly defined as extending from the stadium district just south of the Pioneer Square neighborhood on the south, to Denny Way on the north, and from Elliott Bay on the west to I-5 on the east. Within this area, most avenues are numbered, whereas streets have names. Exceptions to this rule are the first two roads parallel to the waterfront (Alaskan Way and Western Avenue) and avenues east of Ninth Avenue.

Many downtown streets and avenues are one-way. Spring, Pike, and Marion streets are all one-way eastbound, while Seneca, Pine, and Madison streets are all one-way westbound. Second and Fifth avenues are both one-way southbound, while Fourth and Sixth avenues are one-way northbound. First Avenue and Third Avenue are both two-way streets.

To get from downtown to Capitol Hill, take Pike Street or Olive Way. Madison Street, Yesler Way, or South Jackson Street will get you over to Lake Washington on the east side of Seattle. If you are heading north across town, Westlake Avenue will take you to the Fremont neighborhood, and Eastlake Avenue will take you to the University District. These two roads diverge at the south end of Lake Union. To get to the arboretum from downtown, take Madison Street.

FINDING AN ADDRESS   After you become familiar with the streets and neighborhoods of Seattle, there is really only one important thing to remember: Pay attention to the compass point of an address. Most downtown streets have no directional designation attached to them, but when you cross I-5 going east, most streets and avenues are designated "East." South of Yesler Way, which runs through Pioneer Square, streets are designated "South." West of Queen Anne Avenue, streets are designated "West." The University District is designated "NE" (Northeast), and the Ballard neighborhood, "NW" (Northwest). So if you're looking for an address on First Avenue South, head south of Yesler Way.

Another helpful hint is that odd-numbered addresses are likely to be on the west and south sides of streets, whereas even-numbered addresses will be on the east and north. Also, in the downtown area, address numbers increase by 100 with each block as you move away from Yesler Way going north or south and as you go east from the waterfront.

Remembering Seattle's Streets

There is an irreverent little mnemonic device locals use for remembering the names of Seattle's downtown streets, and since most visitors spend much of their time downtown, this little phrase could be useful to you as well. It goes like this: "Jesus Christ made Seattle under protest." This stands for all the downtown east-west streets between Yesler Way and Olive Way/Stewart Street—Jefferson, James, Cherry, Columbia, Marion, Madison, Spring, Seneca, University, Union, Pike, Pine.

STREET MAPS   If the streets of Seattle seem totally unfathomable to you, rest assured that even longtime residents sometimes have a hard time finding their way around. Don't be afraid to ask directions. You can obtain a free map of the city from one of the two Seattle–King County Convention & Visitors Bureau Visitor Information Centers (see above).

You can buy a decent map of Seattle in most convenience stores and gas stations around the area, or for a greater selection, stop in at **Metsker Maps,** 702 First Ave. (② **206/623-8747;** www.metskers.com).

If you're a member of AAA, you can get free maps of Seattle and Washington state, either at an AAA office near you or at the Seattle office, 330 Sixth Ave. N. (② **206/448-5353**).

THE NEIGHBORHOODS IN BRIEF

DOWNTOWN This is Seattle's main business district and can roughly be defined as the area from Pioneer Square in the south, to around Pike Place Market in the north, and from First Avenue to Eighth Avenue. It's characterized by steep streets, high-rise office buildings, luxury hotels, and a high density of retail shops. This is also where you'll find the Seattle Art Museum and Benaroya Hall, which is home to the Seattle Symphony. Because hotels in this area are convenient to both Pioneer Square and Pike Place Market, this is a good neighborhood in which to stay. Unfortunately, the hotels here are the most expensive in the city.

FIRST HILL Known as Pill Hill by Seattleites, this hilly neighborhood, just east of downtown across I-5, is home to several hospitals as well as the Frye Art Museum and a couple of good hotels.

THE WATERFRONT The Seattle waterfront, which stretches along Alaskan Way from roughly Washington Street in the south to Broad Street and Myrtle Edwards Park in the north, is the most touristy neighborhood in Seattle. However, in recent years, Seattleites have been reclaiming the waterfront as a new residential area, and the north end of Alaskan Way is now lined with water-view condos. In addition to the many tacky gift shops, greasy fish-and-chips windows, and tour-boat docks, the waterfront also has the city's only waterfront hotel (The Edgewater), the Seattle Aquarium, and a few excellent seafood restaurants.

PIONEER SQUARE The Pioneer Square Historic District, known for its restored 1890s buildings, is centered around the corner of First Avenue and Yesler Way. The tree-lined streets and cobblestone plazas make this one of the prettiest downtown neighborhoods. Pioneer Square (which refers to the neighborhood, not a specific square) is

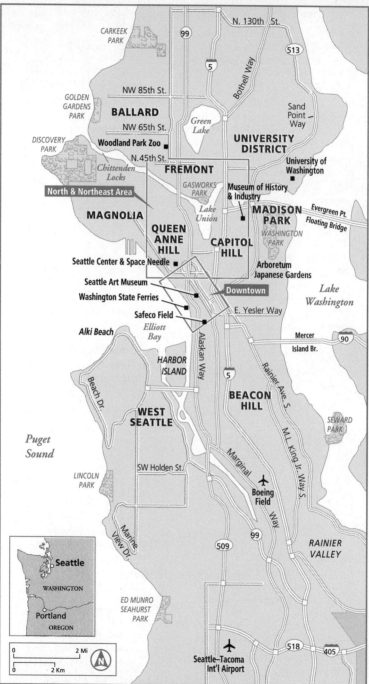

CARKEEK PARK

N. 130th St.

99

513

5

Bothell Way

GOLDEN GARDENS PARK

NW 85th St.

Green Lake

Sand Point Way

BALLARD

NW 65th St.

UNIVERSITY DISTRICT

DISCOVERY PARK

Woodland Park Zoo ■

N.45th St.

University of Washington ■

Chittenden Locks

FREMONT

North & Northeast Area

GASWORKS PARK

Museum of History & Industry ■

MAGNOLIA

Lake Union

MADISON PARK

Evergreen Pt. Floating Bridge

QUEEN ANNE HILL

CAPITOL HILL

WASHINGTON PARK

Seattle Center & Space Needle ■

Arboretum Japanese Gardens

Lake Washington

Seattle Art Museum ■

Downtown

Washington State Ferries ■

E. Yesler Way

Safeco Field ■

Alki Beach

Elliott Bay

Mercer Island Br.

90

Alaskan Way

HARBOR ISLAND

5

BEACON HILL

Rainier Ave. S.

SEWARD PARK

Beach Dr.

Puget Sound

WEST SEATTLE

M.L. King Jr. Way S.

LINCOLN PARK

SW Holden St.

Marginal

✈ Boeing Field

Marine View Dr.

509

99

RAINIER VALLEY

Seattle

WASHINGTON

Portland

OREGON

ED MUNRO SEAHURST PARK

518

405

0   2 Mi

0   2 Km

✈ Seattle–Tacoma Int'l Airport

full of antiques shops, art galleries, restaurants, bars, and nightclubs. Because of the number of bars in this neighborhood, late nights are not a good time to wander here. Also, the number of street people in this area can be off-putting to many visitors.

THE INTERNATIONAL DISTRICT The most distinctive of Seattle's neighborhoods, the International District (known to locals as the I.D.) is home to a large Asian population. Here you'll find the Wing Luke Asian Museum, Hing Hay Park (with an ornate pagoda), Uwajimaya (an Asian supermarket), and many other small shops and restaurants. The International District begins around Fifth Avenue South and South Jackson Street. While this neighborhood is interesting for a stroll, there really isn't a lot to do here.

BELLTOWN Located in the blocks north of **Pike Place Market** between Western and Fourth avenues, this area once held mostly warehouses, but over the past decade has become gentrified. Today Belltown is ground zero for upscale Seattle restaurants and is also home to numerous nightclubs. Keeping all the restaurants in business are the residents of the neighborhood's many new high-rise condominiums. The area is popular with a young, hip crowd.

QUEEN ANNE HILL Queen Anne is located just northwest of **Seattle Center** and offers great views of the city. This affluent neighborhood, one of the most prestigious in Seattle proper, is where you'll find some of Seattle's oldest homes. Today the neighborhood is divided into the Upper Queen Anne and Lower Queen Anne neighborhoods. Upper Queen Anne has a very peaceful

neighborhood feel and abounds in inexpensive restaurants. Lower Queen Anne, adjacent to the theaters and Opera House at Seattle Center, is something of a theater district and has a more urban vibe.

CAPITOL HILL To the northeast of downtown, centered along Broadway near Volunteer Park, Capitol Hill is Seattle's main gay community and is also a popular shopping district. Broadway sidewalks are always crowded, and it is nearly impossible to find a parking place in the neighborhood. While there are lots of inexpensive restaurants in the area, few are really worth recommending. This is also the city's main hangout for runaways and street kids, many of whom have become involved in the city's infamous heroin scene. There are many old homes and mansions on Capitol Hill, and this is where you'll find many of the city's bed-and-breakfast inns.

MADISON PARK One of Seattle's more affluent neighborhoods, Madison Park fronts the western shore of Lake Washington, northeast of downtown. Its centerpiece is the University of Washington Arboretum, including the Japanese Gardens. There are several excellent restaurants here, at the end of East Madison Street.

UNIVERSITY DISTRICT As the name implies, this neighborhood in the northeast section of the city surrounds the University of Washington. The U District, as it's known to locals, provides all the amenities of a college neighborhood: cheap ethnic restaurants, bars, pubs, espresso bars, and music stores. There are several good hotels in the neighborhood that offer substantial savings over comparable downtown Seattle hotels.

WALLINGFORD This neighborhood is another of Seattle's up-and-comers. Located just west of the University District and adjacent to Lake Union, it's filled with small, inexpensive-but-good restaurants. There are also interesting little shops and an old school that has been renovated and is now filled with boutiques and restaurants.

FREMONT Located north of the Lake Washington Ship Canal between Wallingford and Ballard, Fremont is home to Seattle's best-loved piece of public art—*Waiting for the Interurban*—as well as the famous Fremont Troll sculpture. This is Seattle's wackiest neighborhood and is filled with eclectic shops and ethnic restaurants. During the summer, there's a Sunday flea market and outdoor movies on Saturday nights. If you have time to visit only one neighborhood outside of downtown, make it Fremont.

MAGNOLIA This affluent residential neighborhood lies to the west of Queen Anne Hill. Although the neighborhood has a few cafes, restaurants, and bars, these are frequented primarily by area residents. Magnolia is, however, home to Palisade, one of Seattle's best waterfront restaurants. The west side of Magnolia borders the sprawling Discovery Park, Seattle's largest green space.

BALLARD In northwest Seattle, bordering the Lake Washington Ship Canal and Puget Sound, you'll find Ballard, a former Scandinavian community now known for its busy nightlife but with remnants of its past still visible. Ballard is one of Seattle's up-and-coming neighborhoods and is undergoing a pronounced change in character. There are now art galleries and a few interesting boutiques and shops along the tree-shaded streets of the neighborhood's old commercial center. It's definitely worth a stroll here to see what's happening.

THE EASTSIDE Home to Bill Gates, Microsoft, countless high-tech spinoff companies, and seemingly endless suburbs, the Eastside lies across Lake Washington from Seattle proper and is comprised of the fast-growing cities of **Kirkland, Bellevue, Redmond, Bothell,** and a few other smaller communities. As the presence of Bill Gates's media-hyped mansion attests, there are some pretty wealthy neighborhoods here; but wealth doesn't necessarily equal respect, and the Eastside is still much derided by Seattle citizens, who perceive the Eastside as an uncultured bedroom community.

WEST SEATTLE West Seattle, across the wasteland of the port facility from downtown Seattle, is not just the site of the ferry terminal for ferries to Vashon Island and the Kitsap Peninsula. It's also the site of Seattle's favorite beach (Alki), which is as close to a Southern California beach experience as you can get in the Northwest. This is also the site of the waterfront restaurant with the best view of Seattle: Salty's on Alki.

BAINBRIDGE ISLAND Seattle's most exurban bedroom community. Though it is only a 35-minute ferry ride, Bainbridge feels worlds away from the inner city asphalt to the east. Green, green, green is the best way to characterize this rural residential island. Downtown Bainbridge Island (formerly known as Winslow), the island's main commercial area, has the feel of an upscale San Francisco Bay Area community. When you hear about Seattle's quality of life, this is what most people are talking about.

2 Getting Around

BY PUBLIC TRANSPORTATION

BY BUS   The best thing about Seattle's **Metro** bus system (© **800/542-7876** in Washington, or 206/553-3000; http://transit.metrokc.gov) is that as long as you stay within the downtown area, you can ride for free between 6am and 7pm. The Ride Free Area is between Alaskan Way (the waterfront) in the west, Sixth Avenue and I-5 in the east, Battery Street in the north, and S. Jackson Street in the south. Within this area are Pioneer Square, the waterfront attractions, Pike Place Market, the Seattle Art Museum, and almost all of the city's major hotels. Three blocks from S. Jackson Street is Safeco Field (where the Mariners play), and 6 blocks from Battery Street is Seattle Center. Keeping this in mind, you can see a lot of Seattle without having to spend a dime on transportation.

The Ride Free Area also encompasses the Metro Tunnel, which allows buses to drive underneath downtown Seattle, thus avoiding traffic congestion. The tunnel extends from the International District in the south to the Convention Center in the north, with three stops in between. Commissioned artworks decorate each of the stations, making a trip through the tunnel more than just a way of getting from point A to point B. It's open Monday through Friday from 5am to 7pm and Saturday from 10am to 6pm (closed Sundays and holidays). When the Bus Tunnel is closed, buses operate on surface streets. Because the tunnel is within the Ride Free Area, there is no charge for riding through it, unless you are traveling to or from outside of the Ride Free Area.

If you travel outside the Ride Free Area, fares range from $1.25 to $2, depending on the distance and time of day. (The higher fares are incurred during commuter hours.) Keep in mind when traveling out of the Ride Free Area that you pay when you get off the bus. When traveling into the Ride Free Area, you pay when you get on the bus. Exact change is required; dollar bills are accepted.

BY WATERFRONT STREETCAR   In addition to the bus system, **Metro** (© **800/542-7876** in Washington, or 206/553-3000; http://transit.metrokc.gov) also operates old-fashioned streetcars that follow a route along the waterfront from Pier 70 to Pioneer Square and then east to the corner of Fifth Avenue S. and S. Jackson Street, which is on the edge of the International District. These streetcars are more tourist attraction than commuter transportation and actually are much more useful to visitors than are most of the city's buses. Tourist sites along the streetcar route include Pioneer Square, the Seattle Aquarium, IMAX-Dome Film Experience, and Pike Place Market. In summer, streetcars operate Monday through Friday from 6:46am to 11:28pm, departing every 20 to 30 minutes; on Saturday, Sunday, and holidays from 8:46am to 11:58pm (shorter hours in other months). One-way fare is $1 in off-peak hours and $1.25 in peak hours (75¢ for youth ages 5–17); exact change is required. If you plan to transfer to a Metro bus, you can get a transfer good for 90 minutes. Streetcars are wheelchair accessible.

Value Discount Passes

On Saturday, Sunday, and holidays, you can purchase an All Day Pass for $2; it's available on any Metro bus or the Waterfront Streetcar, and it's good for anywhere outside the Ride Free Area.

BY MONORAIL If you are planning a visit to Seattle Center, there is no better way to get there from downtown than on the **Seattle Monorail** (*©* **206/ 905-2600;** www.seattlemonorail.com), which leaves from Westlake Center shopping mall (Fifth Ave. and Pine St.). The elevated trains cover the 1.2 miles in 2 minutes and pass right through the middle of the Experience Music Project as they arrive and depart from Seattle Center. The monorail operates Monday through Friday from 7:30am to 11pm, Saturday and Sunday from 9am to 11pm. Departures are every 10 minutes. The one-way fare is $1.25 for adults and 50¢ for seniors and children ages 5 to 11.

BY WATER TAXI During the past few summers a water taxi has operated between the downtown Seattle waterfront (Pier 54) and Seacrest Park in West Seattle, providing access to West Seattle's popular Alki Beach and adjacent paved path. For a schedule of service, check with Metro (*©* **206/553-3000;** www. metrokc.gov/kcdot/tp). The one-way fare is $2 (free for children under age 5). Also free with a valid bus transfer or all-day pass.

BY FERRY **Washington State Ferries** (*©* **800/84-FERRY** or 888/808-7977 within Washington state, or 206/464-6400; www.wsdot.wa.gov/ferries/) is the most extensive ferry system in the United States, and while these ferries won't help you get around Seattle itself, they do offer scenic options for getting out of town (and cheap cruises, too). From downtown Seattle, car ferries sail to Bremerton (60-min. crossing) and Bainbridge Island (35-min. crossing), and passenger-only ferries sail for Bremerton (30-min. crossing) and Vashon Island (25-min. crossing). From West Seattle, car ferries go to Vashon Island (15-min. crossing) and Southworth (35-min. crossing), which is on the Kitsap Peninsula. One-way fares between Seattle and Bainbridge Island or Bremerton, or between Edmonds and Kingston via car ferry are $8 ($10 from mid-May to mid-Oct) for a car and driver, $4.50 for adult car passengers or walk-ons, $2.20 for seniors, and $3.20 for children ages 5 to 18. Car passengers and walk-ons only pay fares on westbound car ferries. One-way fares between Fauntleroy (West Seattle) and Vashon Island or between Southworth and Vashon Island are $10.25 ($13 from mid-May to mid-Oct) for a car and driver, $2.90 for car passengers or walk-ons, $1.40 for seniors, and $2.10 for children ages 5 to 18.

BY CAR

Before you venture into downtown Seattle in a car, keep in mind that traffic congestion is bad, parking is limited (and expensive), and streets are almost all one-way. You'll avoid a lot of frustration and aggravation by leaving your car outside the downtown area.

Depending on what your plans are for your visit, you might not need a car at all. If you plan to spend your time in downtown Seattle, a car is a liability. The city center is well serviced by public transportation, with free public buses in the downtown area, the monorail from downtown to Seattle Center, and the Water-front Streetcar connecting Pike Place Market and Pioneer Square by way of the waterfront. You can even take the ferries over to Bainbridge Island or Bremerton for an excursion out of the city. Most Seattle neighborhoods of interest to visi-tors are also well served by public buses. However, if your plans include any excursions out of the city, say to Mount Rainier or the Olympic Peninsula, you'll definitely need a car.

CAR RENTALS Car-rental rates vary as widely and as wildly as airfares, so it pays to do some comparison-shopping. In Seattle, daily rates for a compact car might run anywhere from around $25 to $60, with weekly rates running

(Value Driving a Bargain in Seattle

For the best deal on a rental car, make your reservation at least a week in advance. It also pays to call several times over a period of a few weeks just to check prices. You're likely to be quoted different rates every time you call, since rates fluctuate based on demand and availability. Remember the old Wall Street adage: Buy low!

Always ask about special weekend rates, promotional rates, or discounts you might be eligible for (AAA, AARP, corporate, Entertainment Book). Also make sure you clarify whether there is a charge for mileage. And don't forget to mention that you're a frequent flyer: You might be able to get miles for your car rental.

If you have your own car insurance, you may have collision coverage. If you do not hold your own policy, your credit card may provide collision coverage, allowing you to decline the collision-damage waiver, which can add a bundle to the cost of a rental. (Gold and platinum cards usually offer this perk, but check with your card issuer before relying on it. Note that while many cards provide collision coverage, they do not provide liability coverage.)

If, when you're picking up your car, the person at the rental desk tries to get you to rent a larger car than you reserved, don't do it. This is usually a ploy to get you to pay for an upgrade that you are about to receive free of charge because the size car you reserved is no longer available.

If there's any way you can arrange to pick up your car somewhere other than the airport, you can save the 10% airport concession fee.

It's always smart to decline the gasoline plans offered by rental agencies and simply plan on returning your rental car with a full tank of gas. The prices the rental companies charge you to fill your tank when you don't do it yourself are usually a rip-off.

between $150 and $350. Rates are, of course, highest in the summer and lowest in the winter, but you'll almost always get lower rates the farther ahead you reserve. Be sure to budget for the 18.5% car-rental tax (and, if you rent at the airport, an additional 10% airport concession fee, for a whopping total of 28.5%!).

All the major car-rental agencies have offices in Seattle and at or near Seattle-Tacoma International Airport. Companies with a desk and cars inside the terminal include **Alamo** (© 800/327-9633 or 206/433-0182; www.goalamo. com), **Avis** (© 800/831-2847 or 206/448-1700; www.avis.com), **Budget** (© 800/527-0700 or 206/682-2277; www.budgetrentacar.com), **Hertz** (© 800/654-3131 or 206/248-1300; www.hertz.com), and **National** (© 800/227-7368 or 206/433-5500; www.nationalcar.com). Companies with desks inside the terminal but cars parked off the airport premises include **Dollar** (© 800/800-4000 or 206/433-6768; www.dollar.com), **Enterprise** (© 800/736-8222 or 206/382-1051; www.enterprise.com), and **Thrifty** (© 800/367-2277 or 206/625-1133; www.thrifty.com).

PARKING   On-street parking in downtown Seattle is expensive, extremely limited, and, worst of all, rarely available near your destination. Most downtown parking lots (either above or below ground) charge from $12 to $20 per day, though many lots offer early-bird specials that allow you to park all day for around $8 if you park before a certain time in the morning (usually around 9am). With a purchase of $20 or more, many downtown merchants offer City-Park tokens that can be used for $1 off parking fees in many downtown lots (mostly in the main shopping district around Sixth and Pine). Look for the CityPark signs.

You'll also save money by parking near the Space Needle, where parking lots charge $4 to $6 per day. The parking lot at Fifth Avenue North and North Republican Street, on the east side of Seattle Center, charges only $4 for all-day parking if you show up with three or more people in your car. The Pike Place Market parking garage, accessed from Western Avenue under the sky bridge, offers free parking if you park for less than an hour (just enough time to run in and grab a quick bite). If you don't mind a bit of a walk, try the parking lot off Jackson Street between Eighth and Ninth avenues in the International District. This lot charges only $5 to park all day on weekdays. Also in the International District, the Lower Queen Anne neighborhood, and a few streets south of Seattle Center, you'll find free 2-hour on-street parking.

DRIVING RULES   A right turn at a red light is permitted after coming to a full stop. A left turn at a red light is permissible from a one-way street onto another one-way street.

If you park your car on a sloping street, be sure to turn your wheels to the curb—you may be ticketed if you don't. When parking on the street, be sure to check the time limit on your parking meter. Some allow only as little as 15 minutes of parking, while others are good for up to 4 hours. Also be sure to check whether or not you can park in a parking space during rush hour.

Stoplights in the Pioneer Square area are particularly hard to see, so be alert at all intersections.

BY TAXI

If you decide not to use the public-transit system, call **Yellow Cab/Graytop** (© **206/622-6500**) or **Farwest Taxi** (© **206/622-1717**). Taxis can be difficult to hail on the street in Seattle, so it's best to call or wait at the taxi stands at major hotels. The flag-drop charge is $1.80; after that, it's $1.80 per mile. A maximum of four passengers can share a cab; the third and fourth passengers will each incur an extra charge of 50¢.

ON FOOT

Seattle is a surprisingly compact city. You can easily walk from Pioneer Square to Pike Place Market and take in most of downtown. Remember, though, that the city is also very hilly. When you head in from the waterfront, you will be climbing a very steep hill. If you get tired while strolling downtown, remember that between 6am and 7pm, you can always catch a bus for free as long as you plan to stay within the Ride Free Area. Cross the street only at corners and only with the lights in your favor. Jaywalking, especially in the downtown area, is a ticketable offense.

FAST FACTS: Seattle

AAA The **American Automobile Association** ((© 800/222-4357; www.aaa. com) has a local Seattle office at 330 Sixth Ave. N. ((© 206/448-5353).

Airport See "Getting There" in chapter 2, and "Arriving," in section 1 of this chapter.

American Express In Seattle, the Amex office is in the Plaza 600 building at 600 Stewart St. ((© 206/441-8622). The office is open Monday through Friday from 8:30am to 5:30pm. For card member services, phone (© 800/ 528-4800. Call (© 800/AXP-TRIP or go to **www.americanexpress.com** for other locations or general information.

Area Code The area code in Seattle is **206**; it's **425** for the Eastside (including Kirkland and Bellevue), and **253** for south King County (near the airport).

Car Rentals See section 2, "Getting Around," earlier in this chapter.

Climate See section 3, "When to Go," in chapter 2.

Dentist Contact the **Dentist Referral Service,** the Medical Dental Building, 509 Olive Way, Suite 1052 ((© 206/448-CARE).

Doctor To find a physician, check at your hotel for a referral, or call the **Medical Dental Building,** 509 Olive Way, Suite 1052 ((© 206/448-CARE). See also "Hospitals" below.

Emergencies For police, fire, or medical emergencies, phone (© 911.

Hospitals Hospitals convenient to downtown include **Harborview Medical Center,** 325 Ninth Ave. ((© 206/731-3000), and **Virginia Mason Hospital and Clinic,** 925 Seneca St. ((© 206/583-6433 for emergencies, or 206/ 624-1144 for information).

Information See "Visitor Information" in section 1 of this chapter.

Internet Access First, ask at your hotel to see if it provides Internet access. If not, **Kinko's,** 1335 Second Ave. ((© 206/292-9255) and other locations, is an alternative.

Liquor Laws The legal minimum drinking age in Washington state is 21. Aside from on-premise sales of cocktails in bars and restaurants, hard liquor can only be purchased in liquor stores. Beer and wine are available in convenience stores and grocery stores. Brewpubs tend to sell only beer and wine, but some also have licenses to sell hard liquor.

Newspapers & Magazines The *Seattle Post-Intelligencer* and *Seattle Times* are Seattle's two daily newspapers. *Seattle Weekly* is the city's free arts-and-entertainment weekly.

Pharmacies Conveniently located downtown pharmacies include **Rite Aid,** 802 Third Ave. ((© 206/623-8827), and **Pacific Drugs,** 822 First Ave. ((© 206/ 624-1454). However, these two stores have fairly limited hours. For 24-hour service, try **Bartell Drug Store,** 600 First Ave. N. ((© 206/284-1353), which is located upstairs from Larry's Market.

Photographic Needs **Cameras West,** 1908 Fourth Ave. ((© 206/622-0066), is the largest-volume camera and video dealer in the Northwest. Best of all, it's right downtown and also offers 1-hour film processing. It's open

Monday through Saturday from 9:30am to 6pm, and on Sunday from noon to 5pm.

Police For police emergencies, phone © **911.**

Restrooms There are public restrooms in Pike Place Market, Westlake Center, Pacific Place, Seattle Center, and the Washington State Convention & Trade Center. You'll also find restrooms in most hotel lobbies and coffee bars in downtown Seattle.

Safety Although Seattle is a relatively safe city, it has its share of crime. The most questionable neighborhood you're likely to visit is the Pioneer Square area, which is home to more than a dozen bars and nightclubs. By day, this area is quite safe (though it has a large contingent of street people), but late at night, when the bars are closing, keep your wits about you. Also take extra precautions with your wallet or purse when you're in the crush of people at Pike Place Market. Whenever possible, try to park your car in a garage, instead of on the street, at night.

Smoking Although many of the restaurants listed in this book are smoke-free establishments, there are also many Seattle restaurants that do allow smoking. At most high-end restaurants, the smoking area is usually in the bar/lounge, and although many restaurants have separate bar menus, most will serve you off the regular menu even if you are eating in the bar. There are very few smoke-free bars in Seattle.

Taxes In Seattle you'll pay an 8.8% sales tax, and in restaurants, you'll also pay an additional 0.5% food-and-beverage tax on top of the sales tax. The hotel-room tax in the Seattle metro area ranges from 11.6% to 15.8%. On rental cars, you'll pay not only an 18.5% car-rental tax, but also, if you rent at the airport, an additional 10% airport concession fee, for a whopping total of 28.5%! You eliminate 10% of this by renting your car somewhere other than the airport.

Taxis See section 2, "Getting Around," earlier in this chapter.

Time Seattle is on Pacific time (PT) and daylight saving time, depending on the time of year, making it 3 hours behind the East Coast.

Transit Info For 24-hour information on Seattle's Metro bus system, call © **800/542-7876** in Washington, or 206/553-3000. For information on the Washington State Ferries, call © **800/84-FERRY** or 888/808-7977 in Washington, or 206/464-6400.

Weather Currently, Seattle has no phone number for weather information. Check the *Seattle Times* or *Seattle Post-Intelligencer* newspapers for forecasts. If you want to know how to pack before you arrive, go to **www.cnn.com/weather** or **www.weather.com**.

4

Where to Stay in Seattle

Seattle is close on the heels of San Francisco as a West Coast summer-in-the-city destination, so its hotels stay pretty much booked solid for July and August, even with the recent proliferation of high-end hotels downtown. If you aren't on an expense account, you may be faced with sticker shock when you see what these places are charging. But if you're willing to head out a bit from downtown, you'll find prices a little easier to swallow.

As the city has grown more affluent and urban in recent years, the hotel scene has also become more sophisticated. San Francisco's hip aesthetics are slowly spilling over into Seattle, and there are now postmodern chic hotels around town, as well as historic hotels and characterless convention hotels. This all adds up to plenty of options for the traveler planning a trip to Seattle.

Seattle's largest concentrations of hotels are located downtown and near the airport, with a few good hotels in the University District and also over in the suburbs of Bellevue and Kirkland (on the east side of Lake Washington). If you don't mind high prices, downtown hotels are the most convenient, but if your budget won't allow for a first-class business hotel, try to stay near the Space Needle, in the Lower Queen Anne neighborhood, or in the University District where prices are more reasonable.

Be sure to make reservations as far in advance as possible, especially if you plan a visit during Seafair or another major festival. See the "Seattle Calendar of Events" on p. 14 for the dates of major festivals.

In the following listings, price categories are based on rates for a double room (most hotels charge the same for a single or double room) in high season. Keep in mind that the rates listed do not include taxes, which add up to 15.8% in Seattle.

For comparison purposes, we list what hotels call "rack rates" or walk-in rates—but you should never have to pay these highly inflated prices. Various discounts are often available that will reduce these rates, so always ask if there are any specials or discounted rates available (and check the hotel's website for Internet specials). At inexpensive chain motels, there are almost always discounted rates for AAA members and senior citizens.

Room rates are almost always considerably lower from October through April (the rainy season), and downtown hotels often offer substantially reduced prices on weekends throughout the year (while budget hotels often charge more on weekends).

A few hotels include breakfast in their rates; others offer complimentary breakfast only on certain deluxe floors. Most Seattle hotels offer nonsmoking rooms, while most bed-and-breakfast inns are exclusively nonsmoking establishments. Most hotels, but few inns, also offer wheelchair-accessible rooms.

HELPING HANDS

If you're having a hard time finding a room in your price range, consider using the services of **Pacific Northwest Journeys** (© **800/935-9730** or 206/ 935-9730; www.pnwjourneys.com). This company specializes in itinerary planning, but also offers a reservation service. The charge is $45 per reservation; however, you can usually make that up in savings on just a 2-night stay. If you're going to be in town for longer than that, you'll definitely save money. Last-minute reservations are often possible, too. A phone and e-mail consultation service is also available for people who have already done a lot of planning but who want a little more assistance with setting out their itinerary.

Every year from November through March, more than two dozen Seattle hotels offer deep-cut discounts on their rooms through the **Seattle Hotel Hotline**'s (© **800/535-7071** or 206/461-5882) Seattle Super Saver Package. Room rates under this plan are generally 50% of what they would be in the summer months. Any time of year, you can call this hot line for help with making hotel reservations.

Seattle is a city of diverse neighborhoods, and in many of those neighborhoods, there are fine B&Bs. Often less expensive than downtown hotels, these B&Bs provide an opportunity to see what life in Seattle is like for the locals. We've listed some of our favorites in the pages that follow, but to find out about other good B&Bs in Seattle, contact the **Seattle Bed & Breakfast Association** (© **800/348-5630** or 206/547-1020; www.seattlebandbs.com). Alternatively, you can contact **A Pacific Reservation Service** (© **800/684-2932** or 206/ 439-7677; www.seattlebedandbreakfast.com), which represents dozens of accommodations, mostly bed-and-breakfast homes, in the Seattle area. A wide range of rates is available. The **Northwest Bed and Breakfast Reservation Service** (© **877/243-7782** or 503/243-7616; www.nwbedandbreakfast.com), is another option.

1 Downtown & First Hill

Downtown Seattle is the heart of the city's business community and is home to numerous business hotels. Although these properties are among the most conveniently located Seattle hotels, they are also the most expensive choices and are designed primarily for business travelers on expense accounts, not vacationers. However, many of these hotels do offer discounted weekend rates and winter rates. While there are plenty of good restaurants in this area, they tend to fall into two categories—cheap lunch spots and expensive dinner places.

VERY EXPENSIVE

Alexis Hotel ★★   Listed in the National Register of Historic Places, this century-old building is a sparkling gem in an enviable location halfway between Pike Place Market and Pioneer Square and only 3 blocks from the waterfront, the Seattle Art Museum, and Benaroya Hall. Throughout the hotel there's a pleasant mix of old and new, contemporary and antique; this combination, together with an extensive art collection and the cheerful and personalized service, give the Alexis a very special atmosphere. Classic styling with a European flavor prevails in the guest rooms, each of which is unique. Almost half of the rooms here are suites, including very comfortable fireplace suites with whirlpool baths. However, the spa suites are the real winners, offering lots of special amenities, plus whirlpool tubs in exceedingly luxurious bathrooms. The hotel's highly

Accommodations: Downtown, First Hill, the Waterfront, Pioneer Square & Belltown

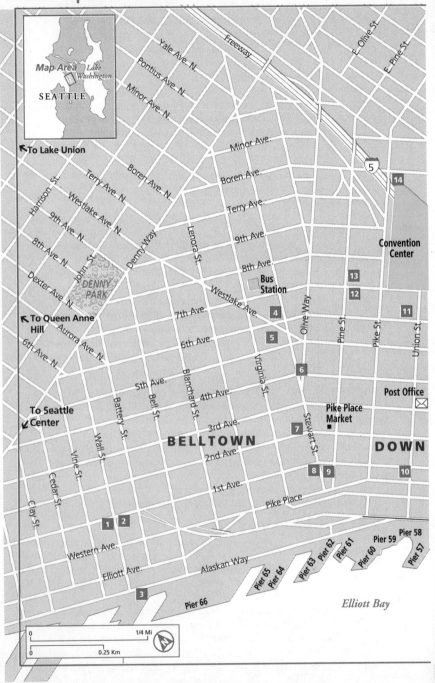

Map Area
Lake Washington
SEATTLE

To Lake Union

To Queen Anne Hill

To Seattle Center

Yale Ave. N.
Pontius Ave. N.
Minor Ave. N.
Freeway
E. Olive St.
E. Pine St.

Boren Ave. N.
Minor Ave.
Boren Ave.
Terry Ave.
9th Ave.
8th Ave.

Terry Ave. N.
Westlake Ave. N.
Harrison St.
9th Ave. N.
8th Ave. N.
Dexter Ave. N.
Aurora Ave. N.
6th Ave. N.

John St.
Denny Way
Lenora St.
Westlake Ave.

DENNY PARK

Convention Center

Bus Station

Olive Way
Pine St.
Pike St.
Union St.

Post Office

Pike Place Market

DOWN

7th Ave.
6th Ave.
5th Ave.
Blanchard St.
4th Ave.
3rd Ave.
2nd Ave.
1st Ave.

Battery St.
Bell St.
Wall St.
Vine St.
Cedar St.
Clay St.

Virginia St.
Stewart St.

BELLTOWN

Pike Place

Western Ave.
Elliott Ave.
Alaskan Way

Pier 66
Pier 65
Pier 64
Pier 63
Pier 62
Pier 61
Pier 60
Pier 59
Pier 58
Pier 57

Elliott Bay

0   1/4 Mi
0   0.25 Km

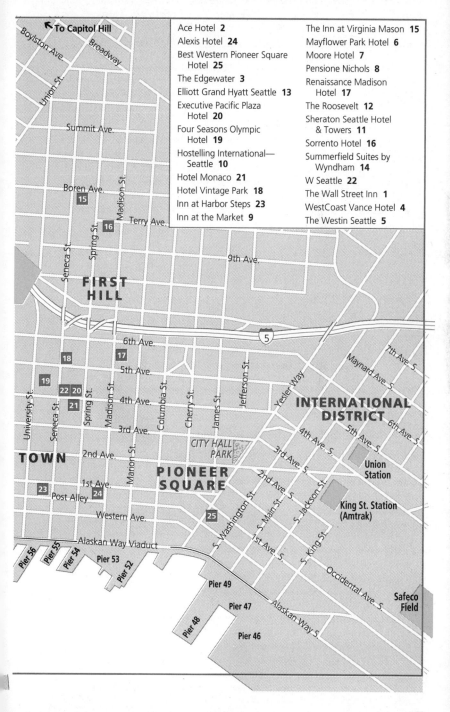

To Capitol Hill

Boylston Ave.
Broadway
Union St.
Summit Ave.
Boren Ave.
Madison St.
Spring St.
Seneca St.
Terry Ave.
9th Ave.
FIRST HILL
6th Ave.
5
5th Ave.
18
17
Maynard Ave. S.
7th Ave. S.
19
22 20
21
University St.
Seneca St.
Spring St.
Madison St.
4th Ave.
3rd Ave.
Columbia St.
Cherry St.
James St.
Jefferson St.
Yesler Way
INTERNATIONAL DISTRICT
5th Ave. S.
6th Ave. S.
4th Ave. S.
2nd Ave.
Marion St.
CITY HALL PARK
3rd Ave. S.
TOWN
1st Ave.
23
Post Alley
24
PIONEER SQUARE
2nd Ave. S.
S. Washington St.
S. Main St.
S. Jackson St.
Union Station
King St. Station (Amtrak)
25
Western Ave.
Alaskan Way Viaduct
Pier 56
Pier 55
Pier 54
Pier 53
Pier 52
1st Ave. S.
King St.
Occidental Ave. S.
Safeco Field
Pier 49
Pier 47
Pier 48
Alaskan Way S.
Pier 46

Ace Hotel **2**
Alexis Hotel **24**
Best Western Pioneer Square Hotel **25**
The Edgewater **3**
Elliott Grand Hyatt Seattle **13**
Executive Pacific Plaza Hotel **20**
Four Seasons Olympic Hotel **19**
Hostelling International— Seattle **10**
Hotel Monaco **21**
Hotel Vintage Park **18**
Inn at Harbor Steps **23**
Inn at the Market **9**

The Inn at Virginia Mason **15**
Mayflower Park Hotel **6**
Moore Hotel **7**
Pensione Nichols **8**
Renaissance Madison Hotel **17**
The Roosevelt **12**
Sheraton Seattle Hotel & Towers **11**
Sorrento Hotel **16**
Summerfield Suites by Wyndham **14**
W Seattle **22**
The Wall Street Inn **1**
WestCoast Vance Hotel **4**
The Westin Seattle **5**

recommended restaurant, **The Painted Table,** serves creative Northwest cuisine (see the full review in chapter 5, "Where to Dine in Seattle"). There are also complimentary evening wine tastings.

1007 First Ave. (at Madison St.), Seattle, WA 98104. ✆ 800/426-7033 or 206/624-4844. Fax 206/621-9009. www.alexishotel.com. 109 units. $295 double; $525–$825 suite. AE, DC, DISC, MC, V. Valet parking $23. Pets accepted with $25 fee per stay. **Amenities:** Restaurant (Northwest), lounge; exercise room and access to nearby health club; Aveda day spa; steam room; concierge; tour desk; 24-hour room service; massage; babysitting; laundry/dry cleaning; concierge-level rooms. *In room:* A/C, TV, fax, dataport, minibar, hair dryer, iron.

Elliott Grand Hyatt Seattle ✫✫✫
Luxury and technology merge at this, Seattle's newest downtown luxury hotel, which opened in summer 2000 and immediately raised the bar for all of Seattle's business hotels. A spacious lobby full of regionally inspired glass art and a Willem de Kooning sculpture outside the hotel's front door set the tone the moment you arrive. Business travelers, take note: You will not find a more up-to-the-minute, business-savvy hotel in this city. Likewise, if you are accustomed to always staying in the very finest hotels, book your room here.

However, unless you spring for something pricier than the basic "deluxe guest room," you're going to be a bit cramped. The least expensive rooms at this hotel are definitely designed for solo business travelers. These rooms, and all the other rooms and suites in the hotel, come with three phone lines (one a cordless phone), complimentary high-speed Internet access, two dataports, and an in-room safe large enough for your laptop. Although the health club is well outfitted and stylishly designed, there is no swimming pool, which means families might want to opt for the Four Seasons instead. The large, multilevel dining room provides a number of different ambiences for different meals.

721 Pine St., Seattle, WA 98101. ✆ 800/233-1234 or 206/262-0700. Fax 206/625-1221. www.elliotthotel. com. 425 units. $370–420 double; $445–$3,000 suite. AE, DC, DISC, MC, V. Valet parking $28. **Amenities:** Restaurant (New American), lounge; health club with Jacuzzi, sauna, and steam room; concierge; business center; 24-hour room service; massage; laundry/dry cleaning. *In room:* A/C, TV, dataport and high-speed Internet access, fridge, coffeemaker, hair dryer, iron, safe.

Four Seasons Olympic Hotel ✫✫✫
If nothing but classically elegant surroundings will do, then head straight for the Four Seasons Olympic Hotel, an Italian Renaissance palace. Without a doubt, this hotel has the grandest lobby in Seattle. Gilt-and-crystal chandeliers hang from the arched ceiling, and ornate moldings grace the glowing hand-burnished oak walls and pillars. Although many of the guest rooms tend to be rather small (with either two twin beds or one king), all have been recently renovated and are now very elegant. If you crave extra space, opt for one of the suites, of which there are more than 200 (however, be aware that the executive suites aren't much bigger than the hotel's deluxe rooms). For plush surroundings, excellent service, and great amenities, this hotel can't be beat. (Although the Four Seasons doesn't have a full-fledged children's program, it does offer amenities such as kids' menus, kids' robes, baby supplies, and the like.)

In keeping with the overall character of the hotel, **The Georgian** is the most elegant restaurant in Seattle (with prices to match); its menu combines creative Northwest and continental cuisines (see chapter 5, "Where to Dine in Seattle," for a full review).

411 University St., Seattle, WA 98101. ✆ 800/223-8772, 800/821-8106 (in Washington state), 800/268-6282 (in Canada), or 206/621-1700. Fax 206/682-9633. www.fourseasons.com/seattle. 450 units. $315–$385 double; $365–$1,850 suite. AE, DC, MC, V. Valet parking $26. Pets accepted. **Amenities:**

3 restaurants (Continental/Northwest, seafood), 2 lounges; health club with indoor pool, exercise machines, Jacuzzi, and saunas; spa; concierge; downtown courtesy shuttle; business center; shopping arcade; 24-hour room service; massage; babysitting; laundry/dry cleaning. *In room:* A/C, TV, dataport, minibar, coffeemaker, hair dryer, iron.

Hotel Monaco ★★

Housed in a building that was once a telephone company switching center, the Monaco is one of downtown Seattle's hippest business hotels, attracting a young and affluent clientele. If you've got a keen sense of cutting-edge style, you'll likely appreciate the eclectic over-the-top retrocontemporary design here. The lobby features reproductions of ancient Greek murals, while guest rooms are done in wild color schemes, with bold striped wallpaper. All rooms and suites have stereos with CD players. For a view of Mount Rainier, ask for rooms 1019, 1119, or 1219. Missing your pet? Call the front desk, and a staff member will send up a pet goldfish for the night. Sazerac, the hotel's restaurant, is as boldly designed as the rest of the hotel and serves New American cuisine. At the adjacent bar, be sure to order the restaurant's namesake cocktail. There are also complimentary evening wine receptions.

1101 Fourth Ave., Seattle, WA 98101. ℂ 800/945-2240 or 206/621-1770. Fax 206/624-0060. www.monaco-seattle.com. 189 units. $275–$295 double; $355–$960 suite. AE, DC, DISC, MC, V. Valet parking $24. Pets accepted. **Amenities:** Restaurant (Southern/New American), lounge; exercise room and access to nearby health club; concierge; business center; 24-hour room service; massage; babysitting; dry cleaning. *In room:* A/C, TV, fax, dataport, minibar, coffeemaker, hair dryer, iron.

Hotel Vintage Park ★★

Small, classically elegant, and exceedingly romantic, the Vintage Park is a must for both lovers and oenophiles. These rooms are perfect for romantic getaways, and every guest room is named for a Washington winery. Each evening in the library-like lobby, there's a complimentary wine tasting featuring Washington vintages (plus late-night port as well). Throughout the hotel, you'll likely also spot numerous references to grapes and wine—even the minibars are stocked with Washington wines. Rooms vary quite a bit here, but when you see the plush draperies framing the beds and the neo-Victorian furnishings in the deluxe rooms, you'll likely want to spend your days luxuriating in the plush surroundings with the one you love. Deluxe rooms have the best views (including some views of Mount Rainier). The bathrooms are small but have attractive granite counters. Standard rooms, though smaller and less luxuriously appointed, are still very comfortable, and surprisingly, their bathrooms are larger than those in the deluxe rooms.

1100 Fifth Ave., Seattle, WA 98101. ℂ 800/624-4433 or 206/624-8000. Fax 206/623-0568. www.hotel vintagepark.com. 126 units. $255–$300 double; $525 suite. AE, DC, DISC, MC, V. Valet parking $24. Pets accepted. **Amenities:** Restaurant (Italian), lounge; access to nearby health club; concierge; 24-hour room service; massage; laundry/dry cleaning. *In room:* A/C, TV, fax, dataport, minibar, hair dryer, iron.

Renaissance Madison Hotel ★★

Despite its large size, the Madison is quieter and less hectic than most convention hotels, and its rooftop restaurant and swimming pool with a view make it is a good choice for leisure travelers as well as the corporate crowd. The biggest drawback is that the hotel is a bit of a walk from the waterfront (and it's all uphill coming back). Most rooms are larger than average and many have views of either Puget Sound or the Cascade Range. For the best views, ask for a room on the west side of the hotel. In the bathroom, you'll find plenty of counter space. Prego, the hotel's Italian restaurant, is up on the 28th floor and has eye-catching views of Seattle. The rooftop indoor pool with a view is by far the best reason to stay here.

515 Madison St., Seattle, WA 98104. ℂ **800/278-4159** or 206/583-0300. Fax 206/624-8125. www. renaissancehotels.com. 553 units. $250–$280 double; $750–$2,000 suite. AE, DC, DISC, MC, V. Valet parking $21; self-parking $20. **Amenities:** 2 restaurants (Italian, Continental), 2 lounges; indoor rooftop pool; exercise room; Jacuzzi; concierge; business center; 24-hour room service; massage; babysitting; dry cleaning; concierge-level rooms. *In room:* A/C, TV, dataport, minibar, hair dryer, iron.

Sorrento Hotel ✦   With its wrought-iron gates, palm trees in the entrance courtyard, and plush seating in the octagonal lobby, the Sorrento, which first opened its doors in 1909, has a classic elegance and old-world atmosphere. Unfortunately, the guest rooms are not nearly as nice as the lobby would suggest, and considering the rates, they're rather overpriced. No two rooms are alike, and most are set up for business travelers. Although more than half the units are suites, even these can be quite cramped. The hotel does boast commanding views of downtown Seattle from its setting high on First Hill, and yet downtown Seattle is only a few steep blocks away (and there's complimentary downtown limousine service). If you do stay here, be sure to ask for a room on the west side of the hotel; you'll have a view of the city and Puget Sound. The hotel's dining room is a dark, clubby place, and in the lounge, which has live jazz piano, you can get light meals, afternoon tea, and cocktails. In the summer, cafe tables are set up in the hotel's courtyard.

900 Madison St., Seattle, WA 99104-1297. ℂ **800/426-1265** or 206/622-6400. Fax 206/343-6155. www.hotelsorrento.com. 76 units. $235–$250 double; $280–$1,700 suite. AE, DC, DISC, MC, V. Valet parking $21. Pets accepted with $50 deposit. **Amenities:** Restaurant (Northwest/Mediterranean), lounge; exercise room; concierge; business center; salon; room service; massage; laundry/dry cleaning. *In room:* A/C, TV, dataport, minibar, coffeemaker, hair dryer, iron.

W Seattle ✦✦   The W hotel chain has won plenty of national attention and devoted fans for its oh-so-hip accommodations, and here in the land of dot.coms and espresso, the W is a natural. The lobby has the look and feel of a stage set, with dramatic lighting and sleek furniture. Here at the W Seattle, not only are the rooms beautifully designed and filled with lots of plush amenities, but they also tend to be larger than those at other W hotels. If you can spring for an additional $50 per night, the -09 or -02 "Cool Corner" rooms are worth requesting. Guest rooms are full of great perks such as Aveda bath products, goose-down comforters, and CD players (there's a CD library available from which you can borrow some disks).

1112 Fourth Ave., Seattle, WA 98101. ℂ **877/W-HOTELS** or 206/264-6000. Fax 206/264-6100. www. whotels.com. 419 units. $229–$390 double; from $500 suite. AE, DC, DISC, MC, V. Valet parking $22. Pets accepted. **Amenities:** Restaurant (New American), lounge; exercise room and access to nearby health club; concierge; business center; 24-hour room service; laundry/dry cleaning. *In room:* A/C, TV, dataport, minibar, coffeemaker, hair dryer, iron, safe.

EXPENSIVE

Inn at Harbor Steps ✦✦   Located on the lower floors of a modern apartment building across the street from the Seattle Art Museum, this inn offers an excellent location that's convenient to all of downtown Seattle's major attractions. The guest rooms, which overlook a courtyard garden, are so spacious that they feel like apartments. Styling leans decidedly toward the Martha Stewart aesthetic. There are gas fireplaces in every room, and the largest rooms have whirlpool tubs. The only real drawback here is the lack of views. In the same building as the hotel, you'll find the Wolfgang Puck Cafe, which features contemporary food and decor, plus water views. There is also complimentary afternoon wine and tea.

1221 First Ave., Seattle, WA 98101. (C) **888/728-8910** or 206/748-0973. Fax 206/748-0533. www.foursisters. com. 30 units. $175–$230 double. Rates include full breakfast. AE, DC, MC, V. Parking $15. **Amenities:** Restaurant (New American), lounge; 2 indoor pools; health club with Jacuzzi, sauna, basketball court; concierge; room service; babysitting; coin-op laundry; dry cleaning. *In room:* A/C, TV, fax, dataport, fridge, coffeemaker, hair dryer, iron.

Mayflower Park Hotel ★★

If your favorite recreational activities include shopping or sipping martinis, the Mayflower Park is for you. Built in 1927, this historic hotel is connected to the upscale Westlake Center shopping plaza and is within a block of both Nordstrom and The Bon Marché. Most rooms here are furnished with an eclectic blend of contemporary Italian and traditional European pieces. Some rooms still have small and old-fashioned bathrooms, but there are plans to renovate all the bathrooms by early 2002. The smallest guest rooms here are very cramped, but these standard rooms are also scheduled to be renovated by early 2002. If you crave space, ask for one of the larger corner rooms or a suite. Martini drinkers will want to spend time at the hotel's **Oliver's Lounge,** which serves the best martinis in Seattle and has free hors d'oeuvres in the evening. The hotel's **Andaluca** restaurant is a plush, contemporary restaurant serving a highly creative cuisine (see chapter 5, "Where to Dine in Seattle," for a full review).

405 Olive Way, Seattle, WA 98101. (C) **800/426-5100,** 206/382-6990, or 206/623-8700. Fax 206/382-6997. www.mayflowerpark.com. 171 units. $150–$210 double; $165–$365 suite. AE, DC, DISC, MC, V. Valet parking $21. **Amenities:** Restaurant (Mediterranean/Northwest), lounge; small state-of-the-art exercise room; concierge; 24-hour room service; laundry/dry cleaning. *In room:* A/C, TV, dataport, coffeemaker, hair dryer, iron.

Sheraton Seattle Hotel and Towers ★★★

At 35 stories, this is one of the two largest hotels in Seattle. Because it's so large, it does a brisk convention business, and you'll almost always find the building buzzing with activity. But don't let the crowds put you off. There's a reason so many people want to stay here—the hotel does things right and captures much of the essence of Seattle in its many features. There's a collection of art glass in the lobby and a 35th-floor exercise room and swimming pool with great views of the city. **Fuller's,** the hotel's highly recommended main restaurant serves excellent Northwest cuisine (see chapter 5, "Where to Dine in Seattle," for a complete review), and, of course, there's an espresso stand in the lobby. The rooms don't have much character, but they do offer plenty of space and some decent views from the higher floors. For even more space, book one of the king rooms, which are designed for business travelers.

1400 Sixth Ave., Seattle, WA 98101. (C) **800/325-3535** or 206/621-9000. Fax 206/621-8441. www.sheraton. com/seattle. 840 units. $140–$405 double; $220–$750 suite. AE, DC, DISC, MC, V. Valet parking $24; self-parking $22. **Amenities:** 4 restaurants (Northwest, American, oyster bar, pizza), 2 lounges; indoor pool; exercise room; Jacuzzi; sauna; concierge; business center; 24-hour room service; massage; babysitting; dry cleaning; concierge-level rooms. *In room:* A/C, TV, dataport, minibar, coffeemaker, hair dryer, iron, safe.

The Westin Seattle ★★★

The 47-story Westin caters primarily to conventions and tour groups and consequently can be crowded and impersonal, especially during the busy summer months. This said, it's still one of the better downtown choices. Not only do the hotel's cylindrical twin towers provide interesting vistas from most of the higher floors, but there are also two excellent restaurants and a pool (only a few downtown hotels have them). Primarily because of their unusual curved walls of glass and the fact that the beds face out to the views, guest rooms here are some of the nicest in town. The views are some of the best in the city, so you'll really get to savor the fact that you're in the land of the Space Needle, Puget Sound, and the Olympic Mountains. Of course, some rooms have much better views than others (ask for a western view), and the higher up you get, the better the vistas.

1900 Fifth Ave., Seattle, WA 98101. (C) 800/WESTIN-1 or 206/728-1000. Fax 206/728-2259. www.westin. com. 891 units. $149–$345 double; $495–$2,500 suite. AE, DC, DISC, MC, V. Valet parking $24; self-parking $22. Small pets accepted ($25 per night). **Amenities:** 3 restaurants (Euro-Asian, Japanese, American), lounge; large indoor pool; 2 exercise rooms; Jacuzzi; concierge; business center; 24-hour room service; laundry/ dry cleaning. *In room:* A/C, TV, dataport, minibar, coffeemaker, hair dryer, iron.

MODERATE

Executive Pacific Plaza Hotel (★) (*Value*)   There aren't too many reasonably priced choices left in downtown Seattle, but this hotel, built in 1928, offers recently renovated, moderately priced rooms and a prime location. You're halfway between Pike Place Market and Pioneer Square, and just about the same distance from the waterfront. However, despite the tasteful new decor, the rooms are still small (verging on tiny) and sometimes quite cramped. Also, be aware that there's no air-conditioning here, and west-facing rooms can get warm in the summer. Bathrooms, although very small, were completely upgraded during the recent renovation. Currently, the room rates here are only slightly higher than at motels near the Space Needle, which makes this place a great deal. However, you can bet that it won't be long before the rates take a jump to reflect the new modern furnishings.

400 Spring St., Seattle, WA 98104. (C) 800/426-1165 or 206/623-3900. Fax 206/623-2059. www.pacificplaza hotel.com. 160 units. May–Sept $114–$145 double; Oct–Apr $96–$135 double. Rates include continental breakfast. AE, DC, DISC, MC, V. Parking $14. **Amenities:** Restaurant (American); access to nearby health club; concierge; business center; dry cleaning. *In room:* TV, dataport, coffeemaker, hair dryer, iron.

The Inn at Virginia Mason (★)   You may think we've sent you to a hospital rather than a hotel when you first arrive on Pill Hill—but don't have a heart attack. This is definitely a hotel, though it is adjacent to the Virginia Mason Hospital. Regardless of the fact that most guests are here because of the hospital, the hotel is a good choice for vacationers, too, with its economical rates, quiet location, and proximity to downtown. There's a roof sun deck for soaking up rays, and just off the lobby, there's a shady little courtyard. Because this is an old building, room sizes vary, but most have large closets, modern bathrooms, and wingback chairs. Deluxe rooms and suites can be quite large, and some have whirlpool baths and fireplaces. The hotel also keeps good company: The Sorrento Hotel, a great place to stop in for a drink, is only a block away.

1006 Spring St., Seattle, WA 98104. (C) 800/283-6453 or 206/583-6453. Fax 206/223-7545. 79 units. $120– $175 double; $165–$245 suite. DC, DISC, MC, V. Parking $7–$8. **Amenities:** Restaurant (American); access to nearby health club; room service; laundry/dry cleaning. *In room:* TV.

The Roosevelt, A WestCoast Hotel (★)   With a small lobby decorated to resemble a library in an old mansion (complete with bookshelves around the fireplace and a grand piano off to one side), the Roosevelt is a 1929-vintage hotel with plenty of class. Be forewarned, though, that rooms here tend to be quite small, and rates can be high for what you get, unless you're visiting in the rainy season or can get some sort of discounted deal. The smallest rooms, known here as studios, have one double bed and a tiny bathroom with a shower only (no tub) and are very cramped. For more space, you'll have to opt for a queen or king room. Most units have small bathrooms with little counter space. The largest rooms verge on being suites and have double whirlpool tubs. The hotel's restaurant, which is more than 80 years old, specializes in grilling meat and fish over applewood. In the bar, a wild array of "objets d'junk" hangs from the ceiling.

1531 Seventh Ave., Seattle, WA 98101. © 800/426-0670 or 206/621-1200. Fax 206/233-0335. www.west coasthotels.com/roosevelt. 151 units. $140–$220 double. AE, DC, DISC, MC, V. Valet parking $18. **Amenities:** Restaurant (American), lounge; exercise room; concierge; room service; laundry/dry cleaning. *In room:* A/C, TV, dataport, coffeemaker, hair dryer, iron.

Summerfield Suites by Wyndham ⭐ (Value) Located just a block uphill
from the Washington State Convention and Trade Center, this hotel caters primarily to business travelers who need a bit of extra room for getting work done while in town. However, the hotel is about equidistant between the waterfront and the hip Capitol Hill shopping and nightlife district, which makes it a good choice if you're just here for fun. Suites are definitely the better choice, though even they're not as big as you would expect. The suites do, however, have two TVs, two phones, and king-size beds. Many rooms have good views that take in the Space Needle, but be aware that a lot of the rooms also get traffic noise from both the freeway and Pike Street. Local restaurants will deliver meals to your room.

1011 Pike St., Seattle, WA 98101. © 800/833-4353 or 206/682-8282. Fax 206/682-5315. www.wyndham. com. 193 units. $129 double; $189–$360 suite. Rates include continental breakfast. AE, DC, DISC, MC, V. Valet parking $18. **Amenities:** Small outdoor pool; exercise room and access to nearby health club; Jacuzzi; concierge; downtown courtesy shuttle; coin-op laundry; dry cleaning. *In room:* A/C, TV, dataport, coffeemaker, hair dryer, iron.

INEXPENSIVE

Hostelling International—Seattle This conveniently located hostel,
housed in the former Longshoreman's Hall, which was built in 1915, is popular with young European and Japanese travelers. The hostel is located between Pike Place Market and Pioneer Square, only 2 blocks away from the waterfront, which makes it very convenient for exploring downtown Seattle. A kitchen and luggage-storage facility make this a solid budget alternative. From some of the hostel's rooms, there are views of Puget Sound. To find the hostel, walk down Post Alley, which runs through and under Pike Place Market, to the corner of Union Street

84 Union St., Seattle, WA 98101. © 888/622-5443 or 206/622-5443. Fax 206/682-2179. www.hiseattle.org. 199 beds. $19–$21 per person for members in dorms; $50 double in private room; $76 for up to 4 people in family room. AE, MC, V. Parking in area garages $12–$16. **Amenities:** Coin-op laundry. *In room:* No phone.

2 The Waterfront

The waterfront is Seattle's most touristy neighborhood, yet it also has the city's finest views and is home to several worthwhile attractions and activities. Although there's only one hotel here, it should be the top choice of anyone wanting to spend a Seattle vacation in the thick of things.

EXPENSIVE

The Edgewater ⭐⭐ (Value) Located on a pier at the north end of the water-
front, the Edgewater is Seattle's only waterfront hotel and is designed to resemble a deluxe mountain or fishing lodge. In fact, it's difficult to believe that the crowded streets of downtown Seattle are only steps away. The views out the windows are among the best in the city, and sunsets are memorable. On a clear day you can see the Olympic Mountains rising across Puget Sound. Pull up a seat between the lobby's river-stone fireplace and the wall of glass that looks out on

busy Elliott Bay, and you'll see why this is one of our favorite Seattle hotels. The hotel's restaurant and lounge also both serve up those same views. The mountain-lodge theme continues in the rooms, which feature rustic lodgepole pine furniture and fireplaces. While the least expensive rooms here overlook the parking lot (and city), opt for a water-view room if you can afford it. The rooms with balconies, though they're a bit smaller than other rooms, are our top choice. Beatles fans can even stay in the same suite the Fab Four had when they visited (and fished out the window) back in 1964.

Pier 67, 2411 Alaskan Way, Seattle, WA 98121. ✆ **800/624-0670** or 206/728-7000. Fax 206/441-4119. www.edgewaterhotel.com. 236 units. May–Oct $189–$309 double, $449–$1,250 suite; Nov–Apr $149–$269 double, $399–$850 suite. AE, DC, DISC, MC, V. Valet parking $16. **Amenities:** Restaurant (Pacific Rim/international), lounge; exercise room and access to nearby health club; courtesy bikes; concierge; business center; room service; laundry service; dry cleaning. *In room:* A/C, TV, dataport, coffeemaker, hair dryer, iron.

3 Pioneer Square & the International District

The historic Pioneer Square area is Seattle's main nightlife district and can be a pretty rowdy place on a Saturday night. However, by day, the area's many art galleries and antiques stores attract a very different clientele. While Pioneer Square can be a very interesting area to explore in the daylight, you'll have to be prepared to encounter a lot of street people. Warnings aside, this is one of the prettiest corners of Seattle and the only downtown neighborhood with historic flavor. The International District lies only a few blocks away from Pioneer Square—again, a good place to explore by day but less appealing at night. There is only one recommendable hotel in the area.

EXPENSIVE

Best Western Pioneer Square Hotel ✵   Located right in the heart of the Pioneer Square historic district, this hotel is only recommended for urban dwellers accustomed to dealing with street people and noise. Pioneer Square is Seattle's nightlife district and gets especially raucous on weekend nights. If you're in town to party (or to attend a baseball game), there's no more convenient location in the city. However, take care on the streets around here late at night. Guest rooms are, for the most part, fairly small (some are positively cramped) and furnished in a classic style.

77 Yesler Way, Seattle, WA 98104. ✆ **800/800-5514** or 206/340-1234. Fax 206/467-0707. www.pioneer square.com. 75 units. July–Sept $149 double, $239 suite; Oct–June $129–$139 double, $219–$229 suite. Rates include continental breakfast. AE, DC, DISC, MC, V. Parking $14. **Amenities:** Concierge; business center; room service; dry cleaning. *In room:* A/C, TV, dataport, hair dryer.

4 Belltown & Pike Place Market

Belltown has for several years now been Seattle's fastest growing urban neighborhood, sprouting dozens of restaurants and several good hotels. If your Seattle travel plans include lots of eating out at hip restaurants, then Belltown is the place to stay. Belltown begins at the edge of the Pike Place Market neighborhood, which is home to still more great restaurants and a couple of lodging options. Pike Place Market is one of Seattle's top attractions and is a fascinating place to explore. If you aren't going to stay on the waterfront, this area makes an excellent alternative.

EXPENSIVE

Inn at the Market ✵✵   For romance, convenience, and the chance to immerse yourself in the Seattle aesthetic, it's hard to beat this small, European-style hotel located right in Pike Place Market. A rooftop deck overlooking the harbor provides a tranquil spot to soak up the sun on summer afternoons and further adds to this hotel's distinctive sense of place. Don't look for a grand entrance or large sign here; there's only a small plaque on the wall to indicate that the building in fact houses a tasteful and understated luxury hotel (and two excellent French restaurants).

To make the most of a stay here, make sure to get one of the water-view rooms, 18 of which have wide bay windows that overlook Puget Sound and can be opened to let in refreshing sea breezes. However, even if you don't get a water-view room, you'll still find spacious accommodations and large bathrooms. The decor is tastefully elegant and gives the feel of an upscale European beach resort. If you need more room than a standard hotel room offers, consider the bi-level town house suites.

Campagne, the hotel's formal main dining room, serves excellent southern French fare, while **Café Campagne** offers country-style French food amid casual surroundings (see chapter 5 for full reviews of both restaurants).

86 Pine St., Seattle, WA 98101. ℂ 800/446-4484 or 206/443-3600. www.innatthemarket.com. 70 units. $180–$310 double; $285–$380 suite. AE, DISC, MC, V. Parking $17. **Amenities:** 3 restaurants (southern French, country French, juice cart); access to nearby health club; courtesy downtown shuttle; concierge; room service; dry cleaning. *In room:* A/C, TV, dataport, minibar, coffeemaker, hair dryer, iron, safe.

MODERATE

Pensione Nichols   It's never easy finding an economical downtown-area lodging with character, but that's exactly what you'll discover at this European-style B&B, located in the heart of Pike Place Market. It's a popular choice with younger travelers and families. The budget-priced units with shared bathroom are all on the third floor of the building, and though most of the eclectically furnished rooms don't have windows, they do have skylights. However, most guests spend their time in the comfortable dining and lounging area, which has huge windows overlooking Elliott Bay. If you want to splurge, the two suites are quite large and have private bathrooms and windows with water views. Be prepared to climb a lot of stairs.

1923 First Ave., Seattle, WA 98101. ℂ 800/440-7125 or 206/441-7125. www.seattle-bed-breakfast.com. 12 units, 10 with shared bathroom. $110 double with shared bathroom; $195 suite with private bathroom. 2-night minimum on summer weekends. Rates include breakfast. AE, DC, DISC, MC, V. Parking $10. Pets accepted. *In room:* No phone.

The Wall Street Inn ⓖ ⓥalue Located in the heart of Belltown, upstairs from El Gaucho (Seattle's most stylish steak house), this B&B was once a sailors' union boardinghouse. Today, the rooms are bright and modern, and a few still have kitchenettes. There's a comfortable living room with leather couches and a fireplace, and a small deck with a barbecue. In addition to the morning breakfast, there are always cookies, coffee, and tea set out in the afternoon. Although Belltown is Seattle's most self-consciously hip neighborhood, this is a traditionally styled, comfortable, and conveniently located base from which to explore the city. Best of all, there are loads of great restaurants within a few blocks.

2507 First Ave., Seattle, WA 98121. ℂ 800/624-1117 or 206/448-0125. Fax 206/448-2406. www.wallstreet inn.com. 20 units. $100–$179 double. Rates include deluxe continental breakfast. AE, DC, DISC, MC, V. Valet parking $10. **Amenities:** Access to nearby health club; bike rentals; concierge; business center; massage; coin-op laundry. *In room:* TV, dataport, fridge, coffeemaker, hair dryer, iron.

WestCoast Vance Hotel ⓖ ⓥalue Built in the 1920s by lumber baron Joseph Vance, this hotel has a very elegant little lobby with wood paneling, marble floors, Oriental carpets, and ornate plasterwork moldings. Accommodations vary in size and style, and some are quite small (bathrooms are uniformly small and have showers only); corner rooms compensate with lots of windows and decent views. Furniture is in keeping with the style of the lobby and for the most part is fairly upscale. If you're here on business or don't care about exercise facilities (there's neither a pool nor an exercise room), this hotel offers good value and a convenient location for a downtown business hotel. With the convention center only a couple of blocks away, this hotel also does puts up a lot of convention-goers.

620 Stewart St., Seattle, WA 98101. ✆ 800/325-4000 or 206/441-4200. Fax 206/441-8612. www.westcoast hotels.com/vance. 165 units. Apr–Sept $110–$170 double; Oct–Mar $80–$140 double. AE, DC, DISC, MC, V. Parking $15. **Amenities:** Restaurant (nuevo Latino), lounge; access to nearby health club; concierge; room service; dry cleaning. *In room:* A/C, TV, dataport, coffeemaker, hair dryer, iron.

INEXPENSIVE

Ace Hotel   Belltown is Seattle's trendiest neighborhood and the Ace, in the heart of Belltown, is the city's hippest economy hotel, sort of a B&B (without the breakfast) for young scene-makers. White-on-white and stainless steel are the hallmarks of the minimalist decor. Brick walls and wood floors have been painted white—even the TVs are white. Wall decorations are minimal, except in those rooms with 1970s photo murals of the great outdoors. Platform beds and blankets salvaged from foreign hotels add to the chic feel of these rooms, as do the tiny stainless steel sinks and shelves in the rooms with shared bathrooms. Basically, aside from the eight large rooms with private bathrooms, this place is a step above a hostel; it's aimed at the 20- and 30-something crowd out to make the scene in Seattle. Be aware, however, that the walls here are paper-thin and the people staying here tend to stay up late. Don't plan on going to sleep early.

2423 First Ave., Seattle, WA 98121. ✆ 206/448-4721. Fax 206/374-0745. www.theacehotel.com. 23 units, 15 with shared bathroom. $65–$85 double with shared bathroom; $130–$175 double with private bathroom. AE, DC, DISC, MC, V. Parking $12. Pets accepted. *In room:* TV, dataport, coffeemaker.

Moore Hotel   OK, this place is nothing fancy, and the rooms aren't in the best shape. However, you just won't find too many acceptable downtown-area hotels in this price range, so it's fine for young travelers and other low-maintenance types who don't demand perfection from cheap accommodations. The lobby, with its marble, tiles, and decorative moldings, is in much better shape than the rooms, but if you've ever traveled through Europe on a tight budget, you'll know what to expect from this place. You certainly can't beat the Belltown location. Trendy restaurants and nightclubs line First and Second avenues starting about a block from the hotel, and Pike Place Market is only 2 blocks away. There's a hip restaurant/lounge on the premises, as well as an adjacent theater that stages rock concerts. Ask for a room with a view of the Sound.

1926 Second Ave., Seattle, WA 98101. ✆ 800/421-5508 or 206/448-4851. Fax 206/728-5668. www.moore hotel.com. 140 units, 45 with shared bathroom. $39 double with shared bathroom; $59–$85 double with private bathroom. MC, V. Parking $12. **Amenities:** Restaurant (American), lounge. *In room:* TV.

5 Queen Anne & Seattle Center

The Queen Anne neighborhood is divided into both an Upper Queen Anne and a Lower Queen Anne. The upper neighborhood is an upscale residential area with an attractive shopping district. However, most of the hotels listed here are in the lower neighborhood, which conveniently flanks Seattle Center. There are also lots of inexpensive restaurants in the area, which makes this neighborhood a good choice if you're on a budget.

MODERATE

Comfort Suites Downtown/Seattle Center 👍 (Kids)   Although it's none too
easy to find this place (call and get specific directions for the approach you'll be taking), the bargain rates and spacious new rooms make this chain hotel worth searching out. Since the Comfort Suites is located only 3 blocks from the Seattle Center, you could feasibly leave your car parked at the hotel for most of your stay and walk or use public transit to get around. Be sure to ask for a room away from the busy highway that runs past the hotel. If you've brought the family, the suites are a good deal, and the proximity to Seattle Center will help moms and dads keep the kids entertained.

601 Roy St., Seattle, WA 98109. ℂ **800/517-4000** or 206/282-2600. Fax 206/282-1112. www.comfortsuites. com. 158 units. $99–$129 double; $129–$149 suite. Rates include continental breakfast. AE, DISC, MC, V. Free parking. **Amenities:** Exercise room; downtown courtesy shuttle; coin-op laundry. *In room:* A/C, TV, dataport, fridge, coffeemaker, hair dryer, iron, free local calls.

Inn at Queen Anne   Located in the Lower Queen Anne neighborhood close
to Seattle Center and numerous restaurants and espresso bars, this inn is housed in a converted older apartment building. Though the rooms here aren't as nice as those at the nearby MarQueen, they're comfortable enough, albeit sometimes a bit cramped and not entirely modern. The convenient location and economical rates are the big pluses here. There's also a pleasant garden surrounding the hotel.

505 First Ave. N., Seattle, WA 98109. ℂ **800/952-5043** or 206/282-7357. Fax 206/217-9719. www. innatqueenanne.com. 68 units. May–Sept $99–$109 double, $119–$159 suite; Oct–Apr $89 double, $109–$139 suite. Rates include continental breakfast. AE, DC, DISC, MC, V. Parking $10. **Amenities:** Coin-op laundry; dry cleaning. *In room:* TV, kitchen or kitchenette, fridge.

MarQueen Hotel 👍 (Kids) (Finds)   Located in the up-and-coming neighborhood
of Lower Queen Anne, this recently renovated historic hotel is in a 1918 brick building. Seattle Center, with its many performance venues and museums, is only 3 blocks away, and from there you can take the monorail into downtown. Although the hotel is geared toward business travelers (with lots of high-tech amenities), it's a good choice for vacationers as well. Guest rooms are spacious, though a bit oddly laid out due to the hotel's previous incarnation as an apartment building. Many rooms have separate little seating areas and full kitchens, which makes this a good choice for families (especially considering the proximity to Seattle Center's kid-oriented attractions). Lots of dark wood trim and hardwood floors give rooms here a genuinely old-fashioned feel. There's an excellent espresso bar in the hotel building and numerous good restaurants nearby.

600 Queen Anne Ave. N., Seattle, WA 98109. ℂ **888/445-3076** or 206/282-7407. Fax 206/283-1499. www. marqueen.com. 53 units. $125–$185 double; $195–$325 suite. AE, DC, DISC, MC, V. Valet parking $12. **Amenities:** Restaurant (espresso bar); access to nearby health club; day spa; concierge; room service; massage; laundry service; dry cleaning. *In room:* A/C, TV, dataport, kitchen, minibar, fridge, coffeemaker, hair dryer, iron.

INEXPENSIVE

Days Inn Town Center   Conveniently located near the Seattle Center and
within walking distance (or a free bus ride) of the rest of downtown Seattle, this three-story chain hotel offers large, clean accommodations. There's a combination restaurant and bar on the premises if you don't feel like going out.

2205 Seventh Ave., Seattle, WA 98121. ℂ **800/DAYS-INN** or 206/448-3434. Fax 206/441-6976. 91 units. $79–$139 double. AE, DC, DISC, MC, V. Free parking. **Amenities:** Restaurant (American), lounge. *In room:* A/C, TV.

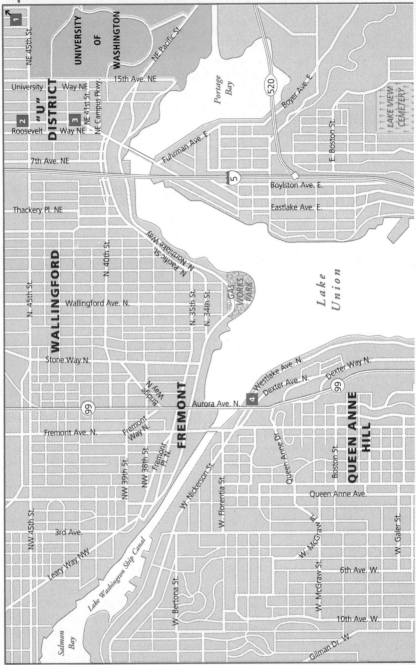

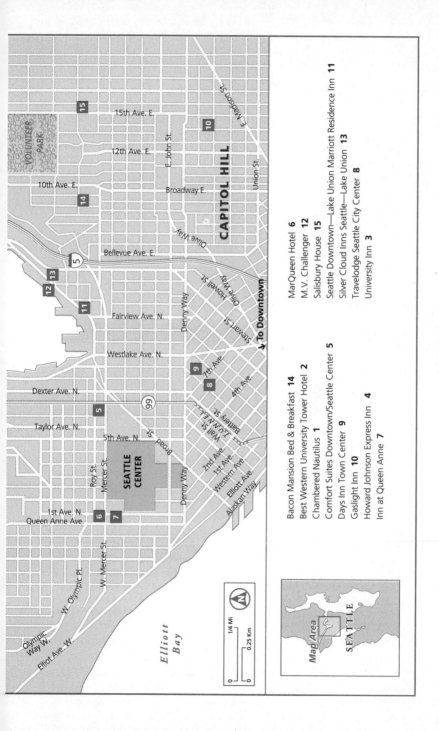

Bacon Mansion Bed & Breakfast **14**
Best Western University Tower Hotel **2**
Chambered Nautilus **1**
Comfort Suites Downtown/Seattle Center **5**
Days Inn Town Center **9**
Gaslight Inn **10**
Howard Johnson Express Inn **4**
Inn at Queen Anne **7**

MarQueen Hotel **6**
M.V. Challenger **12**
Salisbury House **15**
Seattle Downtown—Lake Union Marriott Residence Inn **11**
Silver Cloud Inns Seattle—Lake Union **13**
Travelodge Seattle City Center **8**
University Inn **3**

Howard Johnson Express Inn ⭐ *(Value)*   Located on the eastern slopes of Queen Anne Hill, overlooking Lake Union and the distant Cascade Range, this older motel is just a short drive (or bus ride) from Seattle Center and is just across the Aurora Bridge from Fremont, which has lots of inexpensive restaurants. The best guest rooms, which can usually be had for around $80 to $85 in the summer, have balconies overlooking Lake Union. Right next door to the motel you'll find Canlis, one of Seattle's top restaurants—even if you can't afford to eat here, you can still have a drink at the bar and soak up the atmosphere.

2500 Aurora Ave. N., Seattle, WA 98109. ☎ **877/284-1900** or 206/284-1900. Fax 206/283-5298. www. hojo.com. 94 units. $72–$90 double. Rates include continental breakfast. AE, DC, DISC, MC, V. **Amenities:** Seasonal outdoor pool. *In room:* A/C, TV, coffeemaker.

Travelodge—Seattle City Center   This conveniently located downtown motel can be a bit overpriced for what you get, but the location, midway between the Westlake Center shopping mall and Seattle Center, makes it a fairly convenient choice if you don't mind doing a bit of walking (alternatively, from here you can ride the bus for free within downtown Seattle). The rooms are up to motel standards (and include free local calls—a nice perk), and some even have balconies and views of the Space Needle.

2213 Eighth Ave., Seattle, WA 98121. ☎ **800/578-7878** or 206/624-6300. Fax 206/233-0185. www. travelodge.com. 73 units. $76–$189 double. Rates include continental breakfast. AE, DC, DISC, MC, V. Free parking. **Amenities:** Tour desk. *In room:* A/C, TV, coffeemaker, safe.

6 Lake Union

Lake Union, located less than a mile from downtown and lined with houseboats, marinas, and waterfront restaurants, has a quintessentially Seattle character. Floatplanes use the lake as a runway, and there are several places around the lake where you can rent a kayak, canoe, or rowboat. If you are happiest when you're close to the water, but want to avoid the crowds of the Seattle waterfront, this area is an excellent alternative.

EXPENSIVE

Silver Cloud Inns Seattle–Lake Union ⭐⭐ *(Kids)* *(Value)*   Located across the street from Lake Union, this moderately priced hotel offers good views (some of which take in the Space Needle). The rooms are big and filled with lots of amenities, which makes them convenient for long stays and family vacations. The two swimming pools (one indoors and one out) should also appeal to kids. Although the hotel doesn't have a restaurant of its own, there are plenty of waterfront restaurants within walking distance. Floatplane tours also leave from right across the street. This is a good value for such a great location.

1150 Fairview Ave. N., Seattle, WA 98109. ☎ **800/330-5812** or 206/447-9500. Fax 206/812-4900. www. silvercloud.com. 184 units. June–Sept $160–$240 double; Oct–May $140–$215 double. Rates include continental breakfast. AE, DC, DISC, MC, V. Free parking. **Amenities:** 1 indoor pool and 1 outdoor pool; exercise room and access to nearby health club; 2 Jacuzzis; courtesy local shuttle; business center; laundry service; dry cleaning. *In room:* A/C, TV, dataport, kitchenette, fridge, coffeemaker, hair dryer, iron, free local calls.

MODERATE

The MV Challenger *(Finds)*   If you love ships and the sea and want a taste of Seattle's water-oriented lifestyle, consider stowing away onboard the MV *Challenger*, a restored and fully operational 1944 tugboat. If, however, you need lots of space, this place is definitely not for you. Guest rooms are as tiny as you would expect berths to be on any small boat. However, for nautical types, a stay here is a memorable experience—and you just can't beat the marina location and waterside views. The location, at the south end of Lake Union, puts you a bit of a hike (or a short bus ride) from downtown, but there are lots of waterfront restaurants within walking distance. This is a great place for a weekend getaway or romantic vacation. There are also two berths on a second, much more modern boat.

Yale Street Landing, 1001 Fairview Ave. N., Suite 1600, Seattle, WA 98109-4416. © 800/288-7521 or 206/340-1201. Fax 206/332-0303. www.tugboatchallenger.com. 10 units, 3 with shared bathroom. $85–$185 double. Rates include full breakfast. AE, DC, DISC, MC, V. Free parking.

Seattle Downtown–Lake Union Marriott Residence Inn ★★ A bit removed from downtown Seattle but across the street from Lake Union, this Marriott Residence Inn is within a couple of blocks of several waterfront restaurants, making a stay here a quintessential Seattle experience. A seven-story atrium floods the hotel's plant-filled lobby court with light, while the sound of a waterfall soothes traffic-weary nerves. All accommodations here are suites, so you get quite a bit more space for your money than you do at downtown hotels. You'll also have use of a full kitchen, complete with dishes, so you can prepare your own meals if you like, though breakfasts are provided. The suites here, though generally quite spacious, don't have much character, though they do have phones and televisions in the bedrooms and living rooms, and there are large desks as well. The hotel has no restaurant of its own, but there are several restaurants right across the street, and one of these provides the hotel's room service. Amenities include complimentary cookies and coffee, Wednesday-night guest receptions, and a grocery-shopping service.

800 Fairview Ave. N., Seattle, WA 98109. © 800/331-3131 or 206/624-6000. Fax 206/223-8160. www.residenceinn.com/sealu/. 234 units. $115–$210 1-bedroom suite, $169–$350 2-bedroom suite. Rates include expanded continental breakfast. AE, DC, DISC, MC, V. Parking $12. Pets accepted with $10 fee per day. **Amenities:** Indoor lap pool and children's pool; exercise room; Jacuzzi; sauna/steam room; concierge; downtown courtesy shuttle; room service; laundry/dry cleaning. *In room:* A/C, TV, dataport, kitchen, coffeemaker, hair dryer, iron.

7 Capitol Hill & East Seattle

Capitol Hill, located a mile or so uphill and to the east of downtown Seattle, is a neighborhood with a split personality. It's a hangout for the 20-something crowd, and it has a vibrant gay scene; it's also home to numerous large restored homes, many of which have been converted into bed-and-breakfast inns. If you prefer B&Bs to corporate hotels, this is the best neighborhood in which to base yourself. Although Capitol Hill is a bit of a walk from downtown, the neighborhood has good public bus connections to downtown.

MODERATE

The Bacon Mansion Bed & Breakfast ★ As the name implies, this is a big place (a 9,000-sq.-ft. Tudor built in 1909, to be precise) and has all the accouterments of a mansion—a crystal chandelier, a grand piano, a huge dining-room table, and a library. Located on a shady stretch of Broadway 2 blocks beyond Capitol Hill's busy commercial area, the inn combines a quiet residential feel with proximity to a hip shopping and dining scene. Decor includes a mix of antiques and period reproductions, with an abundance of floral prints. Although you may catch a glimpse of the Space Needle from the Capitol Suite, other rooms lack views. Two of the rooms are located in the old carriage house.

959 Broadway E., Seattle, WA 98102. © 800/240-1864 or 206/329-1864. Fax 206/860-9025. www.baconmansion.com. 11 units, 2 with shared bathroom. $84–$99 double with shared bathroom; $104–$174 double

ⓚ Kids Family-Friendly Hotels

MarQueen Hotel *(see p. 51)* Located within a few blocks of Seattle Center and its many attractions, this converted apartment building provides a convenient location for families, and spacious suites with kitchenettes.

Seattle Marriott Sea-Tac Airport *(see p. 58)* With a huge jungly atrium containing a swimming pool and whirlpool spas, kids can play Tarzan and never leave the hotel. There is also a small game room that will keep the young ones occupied if need be.

Silver Cloud Inns Seattle–Lake Union *(see p. 54)* Located right across the street from Lake Union and with a good family restaurant (Cucina!Cucina!) a short walk away, this modern hotel is a good choice for families. There are also two swimming pools and big rooms.

with private bathroom. Rates include expanded continental breakfast. AE, DISC, MC, V. **Amenities:** Massage. *In room:* TV, dataport, hair dryer.

The Gaslight Inn ⓕ Anyone enamored of Craftsman bungalows and the arts-and-crafts movement of the early 20th century should enjoy a stay in this 1906 home. Throughout the inn, there are numerous pieces of Stickley furniture, and everywhere you turn, oak trim frames doors and windows. The common rooms are spacious and attractively decorated with a combination of Western and Northwestern flair, and throughout the inn's two houses, there are lots of art-glass pieces. A library filled with interesting books and magazines makes a comfortable spot for a bit of free time, or, if it's cold out, take a seat by the fireplace. In summer, guests can swim in the backyard pool or lounge on the deck. Guest rooms continue the design themes of the common areas with lots of oak furnishings and heavy, peeled-log beds in some rooms. An annex next door has a studio and six suites with kitchens, dining areas, and separate bedrooms and living rooms. One of these suites, done in a contemporary style with an art-glass chandelier, has a fireplace and an outstanding view of the city. The innkeepers here can provide a wealth of information about the surrounding Capitol Hill neighborhood, which is the center of Seattle's gay scene.

1727 15th Ave., Seattle, WA 98122. ⓒ 206/325-3654. Fax 206/328-4803. www.gaslight-inn.com. 16 units, 2 with shared bathroom. $88–$148 double; $128 studio; $148–$198 suite. Rates include continental breakfast. AE, MC, V. Off-street parking for suites. **Amenities:** Small outdoor pool; access to nearby health club; concierge; laundry service. *In room:* TV, dataport, hair dryer, iron.

Salisbury House Located on tree-lined 16th Avenue East, this grand old house has a wide wraparound porch from which you can enjoy one of Seattle's prettiest streetscapes. Inside there's plenty to admire as well. Two living rooms (one with a wood-burning fireplace) and a second-floor sun porch provide plenty of spots for relaxing and meeting other guests. On sunny summer days, breakfast may even be served in the small formal garden in the backyard. Guest rooms all have queen-size beds with down comforters, and one has a fireplace and a whirlpool tub. One of the other rooms has an old claw-foot tub in the bathroom. Breakfasts here are deliciously filling and might include fresh fruit, juice, quiche, fresh-baked muffins or bread, and oatmeal pancakes.

750 16th Ave. E., Seattle, WA 98112. ℭ **206/328-8682.** Fax 206/720-1019. www.salisburyhouse.com. 5 units. $105–$165 double. Rates include full breakfast. AE, MC, V. *In room:* Dataport, hair dryer, iron.

8 North Seattle (The University District)

Located 10 to 15 minutes north of downtown Seattle, the University District (more commonly known as the "U" District) will appeal primarily to younger travelers. However, the neighborhood offers less expensive accommodations than downtown, yet is still fairly convenient to Seattle's major attractions. Also nearby are the Burke Museum, Henry Art Gallery, the Museum of History and Industry, the Woodland Park Zoo, and, of course, the University of Washington. As you would expect in a university neighborhood, there are lots of cheap restaurants, making this an all-round good choice for anyone on a budget.

MODERATE

Best Western University Tower Hotel *★★ Value*   Despite the location away from downtown, this is one of Seattle's handful of hip hotels, and the modern art deco decor will surround you in retro style. Best of all, it's considerably cheaper than comparable downtown hotels, and if you need to be near the university, this is definitely the top choice in the neighborhood. You'll even get views of downtown Seattle, distant mountains, and various lakes and waterways. Every room here is a large corner units, which means plenty of space to spread out and plenty of views from the higher floors. Boldly styled furnishings will appeal to anyone with an appreciation for contemporary furniture design. Bathrooms are small, though.

4507 Brooklyn Ave. NE, Seattle, WA 98105. ℭ **800/WESTERN** or 206/634-2000. Fax 206/547-6029. www. universitytowerhotel.com. 155 units. May–Sept $99–$179 double; Oct–Apr $89–$139 double. Rates include continental breakfast. AE, DC, DISC, MC, V. Free parking. **Amenities:** Restaurant (espresso bar); exercise room. *In room:* TV, fax, dataport, coffeemaker, hair dryer, iron.

Chambered Nautilus Bed and Breakfast Inn *★*   Located on an apartment-lined street in the University District, this inn sits high above the street atop an ivy-covered embankment. The Georgian Colonial inn is out of view of the street, and the shady forest surrounding the inn gives it a very secluded feel (you'll hardly realize you're in the middle of the city). The antique-filled inn, which dates from 1915, has a homey feel, and innkeepers Joyce Schulte and Steve Poole make sure guests are comfortable and well fed. Four of the rooms have porches, and some have mountain views (third-floor rooms have the best views). Be advised that this inn is not recommended for anyone who has trouble climbing stairs. Four suites, designed for long-term stays, are located in an adjacent house.

5005 22nd Ave. NE, Seattle, WA 98105. ℭ **800/545-8459** or 206/522-2536. Fax 206/528-0898. www. chamberednautilus.com. 10 units. $99–$129 double; $134–$144 suite. Rates include full breakfast. AE, MC, V. *In room:* TV, dataport, hair dryer, iron.

University Inn *★*   Located within easy walking distance of the university, this renovated 1960s vintage hotel offers surprisingly attractive rooms, many of which have views of Lake Union. Although the standard rooms have only showers (no tubs) in their bathrooms, they make up for this shortcoming with small balconies. The deluxe rooms are more spacious, and those on the west side of the hotel offer glimpses of Lake Union (the best views are in winter). For even more room and the best views, opt for one of the junior suites, which have large windows, microwaves, small refrigerators, and coffeemakers (ask for room 331, which has a view of Mount Rainier).

4140 Roosevelt Way NE, Seattle, WA 98105. © **800/733-3855** or 206/632-5055. Fax 206/547-4937. www.universityinnseattle.com. 102 units. $95–$139 double. Rates include continental breakfast. AE, DC, DISC, MC, V. Free parking. Pets accepted ($10 fee per day). **Amenities:** Restaurant (international); small outdoor pool; exercise room and access to nearby health club; Jacuzzi; massage; coin-op laundry; dry cleaning. *In room:* A/C, TV, dataport, safe, free local calls.

9 Near Sea-Tac Airport

The airport is 20 to 30 minutes south of downtown Seattle, and other than convenience, there's nothing to recommend this area as a place to stay.

EXPENSIVE

Seattle Marriott Sea-Tac Airport 🌟🌟 *Kids*   With a steamy atrium garden in which you'll find plenty of tropical plants, a swimming pool, and two whirlpool tubs, this resortlike hotel is an excellent choice if you're visiting during the rainy season. There are even waterfalls and totem poles for that Northwest outdoorsy feeling; and best of all, it's always sunny and warm in here (which is more than you can say for the real Northwest outdoors). In the lobby, a huge stone fireplace conjures up images of a remote mountain lodge and helps you forget that this is really an airport hotel. With its stone pillars, rough-hewn beams, and deer-antler chandeliers, the hotel's restaurant perpetuates the lodge feel. Guest rooms don't have the same lodge feel as the public areas, but they're comfortable enough. To get the most out of your stay here, try to get one of the rooms with a view of Mount Rainier.

3201 S. 176th St., Seattle, WA 98188. © **800/228-9290** or 206/241-2000. Fax 206/248-0789. www.marriott.com. 459 units. $129–$189 double ($79–$134 on weekends); $225–$650 suite. AE, DC, DISC, MC, V. Parking $12. Pets accepted. **Amenities:** Restaurant (American), lounge; indoor atrium pool; exercise room; Jacuzzi; sauna; small game room; concierge; car-rental desk; airport shuttle; business center; room service; massage; laundry/dry cleaning; concierge-level rooms. *In room:* A/C, TV, dataport, coffeemaker, hair dryer, iron.

MODERATE

WestCoast Sea-Tac Hotel 🌟   Located almost directly across from the airport's main entrance, this modern hotel provides comfortable accommodations designed for business travelers. Guest rooms are generally quite large (if you need space, this is the place). In superior king rooms, you also get evening turndown service, coffee and the morning newspaper, plush terry-cloth robes, and an honor bar. The hotel backs to a small lake, but only a few rooms have lake views.

18220 International Blvd., Seattle, WA 98188. © **800/426-0670** or 206/246-5535. Fax 206/246-9733. www.westcoasthotels.com/seatac. 146 units. $99–$135 double. AE, DC, DISC, MC, V. Free parking. Pets accepted. **Amenities:** Restaurant (American), lounge; outdoor pool; exercise room; Jacuzzi; sauna; courtesy airport shuttle; room service; laundry/dry cleaning. *In room:* A/C, TV, dataport, coffeemaker, hair dryer, iron.

INEXPENSIVE

Among the better and more convenient inexpensive chain motel choices are **Motel 6** (Sea-Tac Airport South), 18900 47th Ave. S. (© **206/241-1648**), charging $56 to $61 double; **Super 8 Motel**, 3100 S. 192nd St. (© **206/433-8188**), charging $86 to $93 for a double; and **Travelodge Seattle Airport,** 2900 S. 192nd St. (© **206/241-9292**), charging $66 to $90 for a double.

10 The Eastside

The Eastside (a reference to this area's location on the east side of Lake Washington) is comprised of the cities of Bellevue, Kirkland, Issaquah, and Redmond. This is Seattle's main high-tech suburb. Should you be out this way on business, you may find an Eastside hotel more convenient than one in downtown Seattle. Surprisingly, two of the most luxurious hotels in the entire Seattle area are here on this side of Lake Washington. If it isn't rush hour, you can usually get from the Eastside to downtown in about 20 minutes via the famous floating I-90 and Wash. 520 bridges.

VERY EXPENSIVE

Bellevue Club Hotel ✿✿✿   In its gardens, architecture, and interior design, this hotel epitomizes contemporary Northwest style. Beautifully landscaped gardens surround the entrance, and there are works of contemporary art throughout the public areas. The "club" in this hotel's name refers to a state-of-the-art health club that has everything from an indoor running track and a 50-meter Olympic-sized pool to indoor squash and outdoor tennis courts (there's also a full-service spa), but even if you aren't into aerobic workouts, this hotel has much to offer. You won't find more elegant rooms anywhere in the Seattle area. Accommodations are extremely plush, with the high-ceiling garden rooms among our favorites. These have a floor-to-ceiling wall of glass, massive draperies, and a private patio facing onto a beautiful garden. Luxurious European fabrics are everywhere, giving rooms a romantic feel. Bathrooms are resplendent in granite and glass, and most have whirlpool tubs. The same elegant contemporary design seen in the lobby is found in the hotel's Polaris Restaurant.

11200 SE Sixth St., Bellevue, WA 98004. ✆ **800/579-1110** or 425/454-4424. Fax 425/688-3101. www. bellevueclub.com. 67 units. $250–$310 double ($125–$230 weekends); $550–$1,450 suite ($325–$895 weekends). AE, DC, MC, V. Parking $5. **Amenities:** 2 restaurants (Northwest), lounge, espresso bar; indoor pool; terrific, expansive health club with Jacuzzi, saunas, steam rooms, tennis courts, racquetball courts, squash courts, aerobics studios; concierge; business center; 24-hour room service; massage; babysitting; laundry/dry cleaning. *In room:* A/C, TV, dataport, minibar, coffeemaker, hair dryer, iron, safe.

EXPENSIVE

Best Western Bellevue Inn ✿   The Bellevue Inn is one of the few hotels in the Seattle area that captures the feel of the Northwest in its design and landscaping. The sprawling two-story hotel is roofed with cedar-shake shingles, and the grounds are lushly planted with rhododendrons, ferns, azaleas, and fir trees. Guest rooms here are quite sophisticated and upscale, with elegant country French furnishings and decor. Bathrooms include plenty of counter space.

11211 Main St., Bellevue, WA 98004. ✆ **800/421-8193** or 425/455-5240. Fax 206/455-0654. www.best western.com/bellevueinnbellevuewa. 181 units. May–Sept $159–$179 double; Oct–Apr $129–$149 double. AE, DC, DISC, MC, V. Free parking. **Amenities:** Restaurant (American), lounge; pool; exercise room; car-rental desk; laundry/dry cleaning. *In room:* A/C, TV, dataport, fridge, coffeemaker, hair dryer, iron.

The Woodmark Hotel on Lake Washington ✿✿   Despite all the lakes and bays in the area, Seattle has a surprising dearth of waterfront hotels. Although Kirkland's Woodmark Hotel is 20 minutes from downtown Seattle (on a good day), it is the metro area's premier waterfront lodging. Surrounded by a luxury residential community, the Woodmark has the feel of a beach resort and looks out over the very same waters that Bill Gates views from his nearby Xanadu. While there are plenty of lake-view rooms here, you'll pay a premium for them. Creek-view rooms, which are the least expensive, offer a pleasant view of an attractively landscaped little stream. Floor-to-ceiling windows that open are a nice feature on sunny summer days, and high-speed Internet access was being added to the rooms in fall 2001. The hotel's dining room is pricey; for cocktails and afternoon tea, there's the cozy Library Bar, which often has live piano music in the evenings. In addition, complimentary late-night snacks and drinks are available.

1200 Carillon Point, Kirkland, WA 98033. ℭ **800/822-3700** or 425/822-3700. Fax 425/822-3699. www.the woodmark.com. 100 units. $205–$260 double; $320–$1,800 suite. AE, DISC, MC, V. Valet parking $12; self-parking $10. **Amenities:** Restaurant (New American), lounge; exercise room; full-service spa; concierge; room service; massage; babysitting; laundry service; dry cleaning. *In room:* A/C, TV, dataport, minibar, coffeemaker, hair dryer, iron, safe.

INEXPENSIVE

Extended StayAmerica–Bellevue ✯   Located just off I-405 near downtown Bellevue, this modern off-ramp motel caters primarily to long-term guests. To this end, the rooms are all large, have kitchenettes, and offer free local calls. If you're only staying for a few days, you'll have to pay around $100, but if you stay for a week, rates drop to around $65 per day. This is about the most expensive of the Seattle area's Extended StayAmerica hotels, so if you don't mind staying in a different less upscale suburb, you can find even lower rates.

11400 Main St., Bellevue, WA 98009. ℭ **800/EXT-STAY** or 425/453-8186. Fax 425/453-8178. www.extended stay.com. 148 units. $89–$99 double ($440–$470 weekly). AE, DISC, MC, V. Free parking. **Amenities:** Coin-op laundry. *In room:* A/C, TV, dataport, coffeemaker, kitchenette, fridge.

Where to Dine in Seattle

With its abundant fresh seafood, Northwest berries, rain-fed mushrooms, and other market-fresh produce, Seattle has become something of a culinary capital. Although the dot-com crash may soon be winnowing out the restaurants that can't weather hard economic times, the Seattle restaurant scene still has plenty of vitality. However, don't be surprised if by the time you arrive some of the hot new restaurants of last year have gone out of business, the victims of too much competition and leaner times. The local chefs who used stints at long-established restaurants as launching pads for their own ventures are now finding it a little difficult to keep their tables filled. The Belltown neighborhood, just north of Pike Place Market along First, Second, and Third avenues, was for many years ground zero for trendy and expensive restaurants, and this is the neighborhood expected to be hit hardest by downfall of the "New Economy." This said, we're sure there will still be plenty of good restaurants around despite the lack of dot-com cash.

The abundant cash of the boom times saw the opening of loads of high-style (and high-priced) restaurants in Belltown. Small fortunes were spent on interior decor so that beautiful people could have beautiful surroundings in which to see and be seen. All this translated into high food prices, with entrees averaging around $20 at the upper-end Belltown restaurants. The offerings in most of these restaurants is not exactly comfort food and not exactly Northwest cuisine,

but rather something in between—call it American Regional, sort of a California cuisine redux. However, one constant is the emphasis on fresh Northwest ingredients, and Belltown's proximity to Pike Place Market makes this easy.

The financially challenged need not despair. Despite the many high-priced restaurants, you can still get a cheap meal in hip Belltown. Not all of the neighborhood posers are flush with cash, and there are plenty of budget eateries lined up side by side with the pricier places. These lesser stars in the Belltown firmament serve everything from African to Vietnamese fare, and while the atmosphere may not be as swanky, they all have a dash of style. With slower economic times, these places have been doing booming business.

One Seattle dining trend that has not changed is the city's near obsession with seafood. You may be aware that wild salmon in the Northwest are rapidly disappearing from the region's rivers, but this doesn't bar nearly every menu in the city from featuring salmon. Much of it is now hatchery fish, or fish imported from Canada or Alaska. Along with the salmon, there are dozens of varieties of regional oysters available. Dungeness crabs, another Northwest specialty, may not be as large as king crabs, but they're quite a bit heftier than the blue crabs of the eastern United States. You may also run across such unfamiliar shellfish as razor clams and geoducks (pronounced "gooey dux"). The former is shaped like a straight razor and can be chewy if not prepared properly, and the latter is a bivalve of prodigious proportions (as heavy as 12 lb.) that now is so highly prized in Asia that it rarely ever shows up on Seattle menus.

With so much water all around, you would be remiss if you didn't eat at one or more waterfront restaurants while in Seattle, and you'll certainly have plenty of choices. You'll find restaurants on the shores of virtually every body of water in the area. Views take in not only water, but also everything from marinas to Mount Rainier, the Space Needle to the Olympic Mountains. We have listed waterfront restaurants in appropriate neighborhood categories below.

1 Restaurants by Cuisine

AFRICAN
Afrikando ★ (Belltown & Pike Place Market, $$, p. 73)

AMERICAN
Belltown Pub and Cafe ★ (Belltown & Pike Place Market, $, p. 78)

Icon Grill ★ (Belltown & Pike Place Market, $$, p. 75)

Maggie Bluffs Marina Grill ★ (Queen Anne & Seattle Center, $, p. 82)

Merchants Cafe (Pioneer Square & the International District, $, p. 72)

Red Mill Burgers (North Seattle, $, p. 86)

Virginia Inn ★ (Belltown & Pike Place Market, $, p. 78)

AMERICAN REGIONAL
Bluwater Bistro ★ (Lake Union, $$, p. 82)

The 5 Spot ★ (Queen Anne & Seattle Center, $, p. 82)

Matt's in the Market ★★ (Belltown & Pike Place Market, $$, p. 76)

Palace Kitchen ★★ (Belltown & Pike Place Market, $$, p. 77)

BAKERIES & PASTRY SHOPS
Boulangerie ★ (North Seattle, $, p. 90)

Dilettante Chocolates ★★ (Capitol Hill & East Seattle, $, p. 90)

The Famous Pacific Dessert Company ★★ (The Seattle Center & Queen Anne Areas, $, p. 89)

Grand Central Baking Company ★ (Pioneer Square & the International District, $, p. 89)

Le Panier (Belltown & Pike Place Market, $, p. 89)

Macrina ★★ (Belltown & Pike Place Market, $, p. 89)

Three Girls Bakery (Belltown & Pike Place Market, $, p. 89)

BARBECUE
Pecos Pit BBQ (Pioneer Square & the International District, $, p. 72)

CAFES, COFFEE BARS & TEA SHOPS
Bauhaus Coffee & Books (Capitol Hill & East Seattle, p. 89)

Café Allegro (North Seattle, $, p. 89)

Caffe Ladro Espresso Bar & Bakery (The Seattle Center & Queen Anne Areas, $, p. 88)

The Crumpet Shop ★ (Belltown & Pike Place Market, $, p. 88)

LUX coffeebar (Belltown & Pike Place Market, $, p. 88)

Queen Anne Caffe Appassionato ★★ (The Seattle Center & Queen Anne Areas, $, p. 88)

Still Life in Fremont Coffeehouse ★ (North Seattle, $, p. 89)

Teahouse Kuan Yin (North Seattle, $, p. 89)

Torrefazione★★ (Pioneer Square
& the International District,
$, p. 88)

Uptown Espresso (The Seattle
Center & Queen Anne Areas,
$, p. 89)

Zeitgeist Art/Coffee★ (Pioneer
Square & the International
District, $, p. 88)

CHINESE

Hing Loon★ (Pioneer Square &
the International District, $,
p. 71)

CONTINENTAL

The Georgian★★ (Downtown,
$$$$, p. 65)

FRENCH

Cafe Campagne★★ (Belltown &
Pike Place Market, $$, p. 74)

Campagne★★ (Belltown & Pike
Place Market, $$$, p. 73)

Le Pichet★ (Belltown & Pike
Place Market, $$, p. 76)

Virginia Inn★ (Belltown & Pike
Place Market, $, p. 78)

HIMALAYAN

Himalayan Sherpa Restaurant★
(North Seattle, $, p. 86)

INTERNATIONAL

Beach Cafe★★ (The Eastside,
$$, p. 87)

Marco's Supperclub★ (Belltown
& Pike Place Market, $$,
p. 76)

Matt's in the Market★★
(Belltown & Pike Place Market,
$$, p. 76)

Shea's Lounge★★ (Belltown &
Pike Place Market, $$, p. 77)

ITALIAN

Assaggio★★ (Belltown & Pike
Place Market, $$, p. 74)

Cucina!Cucina!★ (Lake Union, $,
p. 83)

Il Bistro★ (Belltown & Pike Place
Market, $$$, p. 73)

Il Terrazzo Carmine★★ (Pioneer
Square & the International
District, $$$, p. 71)

The Pink Door★ (Belltown &
Pike Place Market, $$, p. 77)

Salumi★ (Pioneer Square & the
International District, $, p. 72)

Serafina★★ (Lake Union, $$,
p. 83)

Trattoria Mitchelli★ (Pioneer
Square & the International
District, $$, p. 71)

JAPANESE

Koraku (Pioneer Square & the
International District, $, p. 71)

Shiro's★★ (Belltown & Pike Place
Market, $$, p. 77)

LATE-NIGHT

Bluwater Bistro★ (Lake Union,
$$, p. 82)

El Gaucho★★ (Belltown & Pike
Place Market, $$$$, p. 72)

The 5 Spot★ (Queen Anne &
Seattle Center, $, p. 82)

Flying Fish★★ (Belltown & Pike
Place Market, $$, p. 75)

Hing Loon★ (Pioneer Square &
the International District, $,
p. 71)

Palace Kitchen★★ (Belltown &
Pike Place Market, $$, p. 77)

The Pink Door★ (Belltown &
Pike Place Market, $$, p. 77)

Shea's Lounge★★ (Belltown &
Pike Place Market, $$, p. 77)

Trattoria Mitchelli★ (Pioneer
Square & the International
District, $$, p. 71)

LATIN AMERICAN

Fandango★★ (Belltown & Pike
Place Market, $$, p. 75)

MEDITERRANEAN

Andaluca★★ (Downtown, $$,
p. 68)

Palace Kitchen★★ (Belltown &
Pike Place Market, $$, p. 77)

Palomino★★ (Downtown, $$,
p. 69)

NORTHWEST

Andaluca ₳₳ (Downtown, $$,
p. 68)

Canlis ₳₳₳ (Queen Anne &
Seattle Center, $$$, p. 79)

Chez Shea ₳₳₳ (Belltown &
Pike Place Market, $$$, p. 73)

Dahlia Lounge ₳₳ (Belltown &
Pike Place Market, $$, p. 74)

Flying Fish ₳₳ (Belltown & Pike
Place Market, $$, p. 75)

Fuller's ₳₳ (Downtown, $$$,
p. 65)

The Georgian ₳₳ (Downtown,
$$$$, p. 65)

The Herbfarm (The Eastside,
$$$$, p. 87)

Kaspar's Restaurant & Wine Bar
₳₳ (Queen Anne & Seattle
Center, $$$, p. 79)

The Painted Table ₳₳
(Downtown, $$$, p. 68)

Palisade ₳₳₳ (Queen Anne &
Seattle Center, $$$, p. 79)

Palomino ₳₳ (Downtown, $$,
p. 69)

Rover's ₳₳₳ (Capitol Hill & East
Seattle, $$$$, p. 84)

Shea's Lounge ₳₳ (Belltown &
Pike Place Market, $$, p. 77)

SkyCity at the Needle ₳₳ (Queen
Anne & Seattle Center, $$$$,
p. 78)

Yarrow Bay Grill ₳₳ (The
Eastside, $$$, p. 87)

PAN-ASIAN

Dahlia Lounge ₳₳ (Belltown &
Pike Place Market, $$, p. 74)

Noodle Ranch ₳ (Belltown &
Pike Place Market, $, p. 78)

Wild Ginger Asian Restaurant and
Satay Bar ₳₳ (Downtown, $$,
p. 69)

PIZZA

Pizzeria Pagliacci ₳ (Queen Anne
& Seattle Center, $, p. 82)

QUICK BITES

Briazz Cafe (Downtown, $,
p. 90)

DeLaurenti ₳₳ (Belltown & Pike
Place Market, $$, p. 90)

Piroshky, Piroshky (Belltown &
Pike Place Market, $, p. 90)

Three Girls Bakery (Belltown &
Pike Place Market, $, p. 90)

Westlake Center shopping
mall food court (Downtown,
$, p. 90)

World Class Chili ₳ (Belltown &
Pike Place Market, $, p. 90)

SEAFOOD

Anthony's Pier 66 & Bell Street
Diner ₳₳ (The Waterfront, $$,
p. 70)

The Brooklyn Seafood, Steak, and
Oyster House ₳₳ (Downtown,
$$$, p. 65)

Chinook's at Salmon Bay ₳
(North Seattle, $$, p. 85)

Elliott's ₳₳ (The Waterfront, $$,
p. 70)

Etta's Seafood ₳₳ (Belltown &
Pike Place Market, $$, p. 75)

Flying Fish ₳₳ (Belltown & Pike
Place Market, $$, p. 75)

Ivar's Salmon House ₳₳ (Lake
Union, $$, p. 83)

Kaspar's Restaurant & Wine Bar
₳₳ (Queen Anne & Seattle
Center, $$$, p. 79)

McCormick and Schmick's ₳₳
(Downtown, $$, p. 69)

McCormick and Schmick's
Harborside ₳ (Lake Union,
$$, p. 83)

Ponti Seafood Grill ₳₳ (North
Seattle, $$$, p. 85)

Ray's Boathouse and Cafe ₳₳
(North Seattle, $$, p. 86)

Salty's on Alki Beach ₳ (West
Seattle, $$$, p. 86)

Third Floor Fish Cafe ₳₳ (The
Eastside, $$$, p. 87)

STEAK

El Gaucho ₳₳ (Belltown & Pike
Place Market, $$$$, p. 72)

Metropolitan Grill ₳₳ (Down-
town, $$$, p. 68)

THAI

Siam on Broadway (Capitol Hill & East Seattle, $, p. 84)

Siam on Lake Union ⟨★ (Lake Union, $, p. 84)

VEGETARIAN/NATURAL FOODS

Cafe Flora ⟨★ (Capitol Hill & East Seattle, $, p. 84)

Gravity Bar ⟨★ (Capitol Hill & East Seattle, $, p. 85)

2 Downtown & First Hill

VERY EXPENSIVE

The Georgian ⟨★★ NORTHWEST/CONTINENTAL   Nowhere in Seattle will you find a more rarefied atmosphere than at The Georgian, where you'll feel as though you're dining in an elegant palace. The soaring ceiling is decorated with intricate moldings, and the huge windows are framed by luxurious curtains. The meals are serious haute cuisine—the sort of formal dinners that are uncommon in casual Seattle—and the attentive service will likely have you convinced that your table is the only one being served. So, if you happen to be celebrating a very special occasion and have an appreciation for such dishes as veal chops and sweetbreads or roast pheasant breast with truffled yams and seared duck liver, you'd be hard-pressed to find a more memorable dining experience in Seattle. As you would expect, the wine list is well suited to both the food and the restaurant's ambience.

In the Four Seasons Olympic Hotel, 411 University St. ☎ 206/621-1700. Reservations recommended. Main courses $29–$37.50. AE, DC, DISC, MC, V. Mon 11:30am–2:30pm, Tues–Thurs 11:30am–2:30pm and 5:30–10pm, Fri–Sat 11:30am–2:30pm and 5:30–10:30pm, Sat 6:30am–noon and 5:30–10:30pm, Sun 11:30am–2:30pm (tea served Mon–Fri 2:30–3:30pm, Sat–Sun 1:30–2:30pm).

EXPENSIVE

The Brooklyn Seafood, Steak, and Oyster House ⟨★★ SEAFOOD   Designed to look as if it's been here since the great Seattle fire, the Brooklyn is, in fact, housed in one of the city's oldest buildings. The specialty here is definitely oysters, with about 10 different types piled up at the oyster bar on any given night. If oysters on the half shell don't appeal to you, there are plenty of other tempting appetizers, ranging from cilantro-battered calamari to Dungeness crab cakes and smoked-duck spring rolls. For a classic Northwest dish, try the alder-planked king salmon (roasted on a slab of alder wood). In addition, there are simply prepared aged steaks, and such dishes as seafood pasta in parchment or grilled black tiger prawns in a morel mushroom and brandy cream sauce.

1212 Second Ave. ☎ 206/224-7000. www.thebrooklyn.com. Reservations recommended. Main courses $10–$15 at lunch, $16–$35 at dinner. AE, DC, DISC, MC, V. Mon–Fri 11am–3pm; Mon–Thurs 5–10pm, Fri 5–10:30pm, Sat 4:30–10:30pm, Sun 4–10pm.

Fuller's ⟨★★ NORTHWEST   Fuller's, named for the founder of the Seattle Art Museum, is dedicated to both the culinary and the visual arts of the Northwest. Each dish is as beautifully presented as it is superbly prepared, and surrounding you in this very elegant dining room are works of art by some of the Northwest's best artists. Fuller's menu changes seasonally, but Northwest flavors with Asian and Mediterranean accents predominate. A recent spring menu included such appetizers as ahi tuna carpaccio with a coconut emulsion and buttermilk fried quail with a fava-bean purée and a balsamic reduction. Among the main dishes were porcini-dusted striped bas with red-wine risotto and salmon

Dining: Downtown, the Waterfront, Pioneer Square, the International District & Belltown

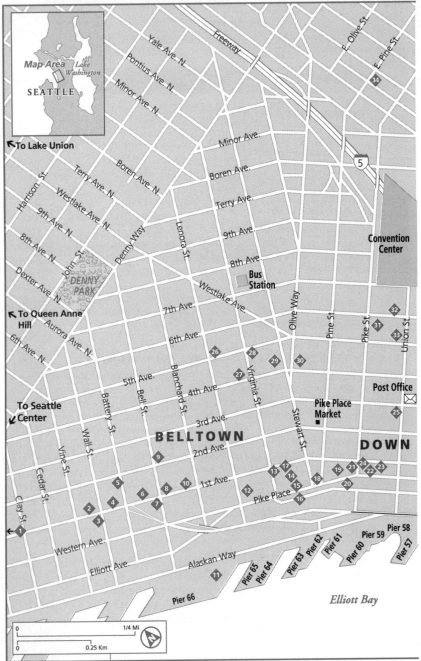

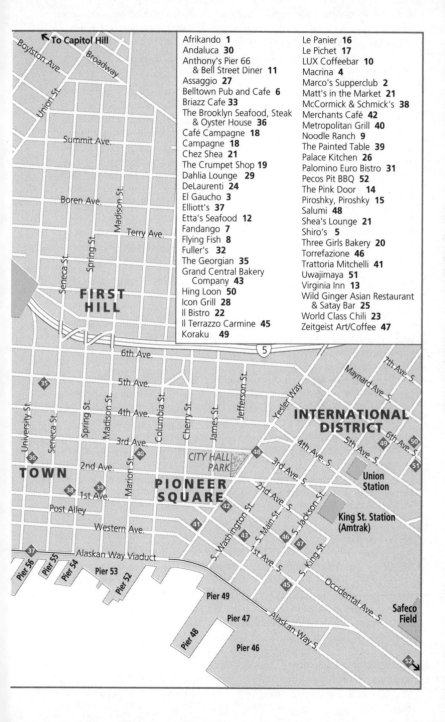

Afrikando **1**
Andaluca **30**
Anthony's Pier 66 & Bell Street Diner **11**
Assaggio **27**
Belltown Pub and Cafe **6**
Briazz Cafe **33**
The Brooklyn Seafood, Steak & Oyster House **36**
Café Campagne **18**
Campagne **18**
Chez Shea **21**
The Crumpet Shop **19**
Dahlia Lounge **29**
DeLaurenti **24**
El Gaucho **3**
Elliott's **37**
Etta's Seafood **12**
Fandango **7**
Flying Fish **8**
Fuller's **32**
The Georgian **35**
Grand Central Bakery Company **43**
Hing Loon **50**
Icon Grill **28**
Il Bistro **22**
Il Terrazzo Carmine **45**
Koraku **49**

Le Panier **16**
Le Pichet **17**
LUX Coffeebar **10**
Macrina **4**
Marco's Supperclub **2**
Matt's in the Market **21**
McCormick & Schmick's **38**
Merchants Café **42**
Metropolitan Grill **40**
Noodle Ranch **9**
The Painted Table **39**
Palace Kitchen **26**
Palomino Euro Bistro **31**
Pecos Pit BBQ **52**
The Pink Door **14**
Piroshky, Piroshky **15**
Salumi **48**
Shea's Lounge **21**
Shiro's **5**
Three Girls Bakery **20**
Torrefazione **46**
Trattoria Mitchelli **41**
Uwajimaya **51**
Virginia Inn **13**
Wild Ginger Asian Restaurant & Satay Bar **25**
World Class Chili **23**
Zeitgeist Art/Coffee **47**

with vanilla bean paste and ginger velouté. For a fuller Fuller's experience, there are four-, six-, and eight-course tasting menus. The wine list reflects the seasonal changes on the menu. Don't miss the displays of glass art in the hotel lobby.

In the Sheraton Seattle Hotel and Towers, 1400 Sixth Ave. ℂ 206/447-5544. Reservations recommended. Main courses $24–$34; tasting menus $55–$95. AE, DISC, MC, V. Tues–Sat 5:30–10pm.

Metropolitan Grill 🏵🏵 STEAK   Fronted by massive granite columns that make it look more like a bank than a restaurant, the Metropolitan Grill is a very traditional steakhouse that attracts a well-heeled clientele, primarily men in suits (often out to impress business associates and clients). When you walk in the front door, you're immediately confronted by a case full of meat, from filet mignon to triple-cut lamb chops (with the occasional giant lobster tail tossed in). Perfectly cooked 28-day-aged steaks are the primary attraction, and a baked potato and a pile of thick-cut onion rings complete the ultimate carnivorous dinner. Financial matters are a frequent topic of discussion here, and the bar even has a "Guess the Dow" contest. I hope you sold high, since it'll take some capital gains to finance a dinner for two here.

820 Second Ave. ℂ 206/624-3287. Reservations recommended. Main courses $10–$20 at lunch, $18–$42 at dinner. AE, DC, DISC, MC, V. Mon–Fri 11am–3pm and 4:30–11pm; Sat 4–11pm, Sun 4:30–10pm.

The Painted Table 🏵🏵 NORTHWEST   At The Painted Table, an upscale-yet-casual restaurant at the luxurious Alexis Hotel, every dish is beautifully arranged. However, it isn't just what's on the dish that's a work of art, it's the dish itself. Every table is set with hand-painted plates created by West Coast ceramic artists. Should you take a fancy to your plate, you can take it home with you for about the price of dinner (or maybe dinner for two) on top of what you'll spend for your actual meal here.

The menu changes frequently, but always features the best of Pike Place Market ingredients combined in creative ways. A recent spring menu included coriander-crusted ahi with shaved fennel, apples, and citrus marinade; a terrine of foie gras with mango marmalade and strawberry-Port syrup; and a two-clam linguini made with Manila and razor clams. For dessert, we wouldn't miss the "s'more," chocolate ganache topped with vanilla-bean meringue and homemade graham crackers.

In the Alexis Hotel, 92 Madison St. ℂ **206/624-3646**. www.paintedtableseattle.com. Reservations recommended. Main courses $12–$17.50 at lunch, $19–$30 at dinner; multicourse tasting menu $60 ($80 with wine). AE, DC, DISC, MC, V. Mon–Fri 6:30am–10am and 11:30am–2pm, Sat–Sun 7:30am–noon; daily 5:30–10pm.

MODERATE

Andaluca 🏵🏵 NORTHWEST/MEDITERRANEAN   Located in the Mayflower Park Hotel, this sumptuous restaurant mixes the traditional and the contemporary like no other place in town. To step through its doors is to enter a world of vibrant artistry, in both decor and cuisine. Specialties include such dishes as traditional Spanish *zarazuela* (shellfish stew) and *cabrales* (crusted beef tenderloin with Spanish blue cheese and grilled pears). The menu is divided into small and large plates, so you'll find something to satisfy your appetite regardless of its size. Don't miss the Dungeness crab tower, made with avocado, palm hearts, and gazpacho salsa—it's a work of art. Keep in mind that you can assemble a meal of small plates here and get away with a smaller bill.

In the Mayflower Park Hotel, 407 Olive Way. ℂ 206/382-6999. www.andaluca.com. Reservations recommended. Main courses $18.50–$30.50, small plates $3–$9.25. AE, DC, DISC, MC, V. Mon–Thurs 6:30–11am,

---

Kids Family-Friendly Restaurants

Maggie Bluffs Marina Grill *(see p. 82)*   Located at a marina overlooking Elliott Bay and downtown Seattle, this economical place has food the kids will enjoy and provides crayons to keep them occupied while they wait. Before or after a meal, you can take a free boat ride across the marina to an observation deck atop the breakwater.

Ivar's Salmon House *(see p. 83)*   This restaurant is built to resemble a Northwest Coast Native American longhouse and is filled with artifacts that kids will find fascinating. If they get restless, they can go out to the floating patio and watch the boats passing by.

Cucina!Cucina! *(see p. 83)*   Every day's a party at this lively Italian restaurant on Lake Union, and kids always get special treatment (pictures to color, puzzles to do, pizza dough to shape and then let the kitchen cook). Birthdays are even better!

11:30am–2:30pm, and 5–10pm; Fri–Sat 6:30–11am, 11:30am–2:30pm, and 5–11pm; Sun 7am–noon and 5–9pm.

McCormick and Schmick's ☆☆ SEAFOOD   Force your way past the crowds of business suits at the bar and you'll find yourself in a classic fish house—complete with cafe curtains, polished brass, leaded glass, and wood paneling. Daily fresh sheets commonly list more than 30 seafood entrees and feature well-prepared seafood dishes such as grilled steelhead with artichokes and spinach, Dungeness crab and shrimp cakes with red-pepper aioli, and cedar-plank-roasted salmon with berry *beurre rouge*. There are also usually a half dozen or more different varieties of oysters available. In late afternoons and late evenings, bar appetizers are only $1.95. If the restaurant is crowded and you can't get a table, consider sitting at the counter and watching the cooks perform amazing feats with fire.

1103 First Ave. ☎ 206/623-5500. Reservations recommended. Main courses $7–$26. AE, DC, DISC, MC, V. Mon–Fri 11:30am–11pm, Sat 4:30–10pm, Sun 4:30–9pm (bar menu served later).

Palomino ☆☆ NORTHWEST/MEDITERRANEAN   Located on the upper level of the City Centre shopping center, only a block away from Nordstrom and Pacific Place, this large and casual restaurant, though part of a chain, has a decidedly Seattle feel due to its many art-glass chandeliers. Anything from the applewood-fired oven is a good bet, and the pizzas are particularly tasty, as are the juicy spit-roasted chickens. For dessert, you'd be remiss if you didn't order the tiramisu. The convenient location and somewhat moderate prices make this a good choice if you want to save your vacation money for shopping at Nordstrom.

1420 Fifth Ave. (in City Centre). ☎ 206/623-1300. www.palominoseattle.com. Reservations recommended. Main courses $9–$17 at lunch, $15–$28.50 at dinner. AE, DC, DISC, MC, V. Mon–Thurs 11:15am–2:30pm and 5–9:30pm, Fri 11:15am–2:30pm and 5–10pm, Sat noon–3pm and 5–10:30pm, Sun noon–3pm and 5–9:30pm.

Wild Ginger Asian Restaurant and Satay Bar ☆☆ PAN-ASIAN   This Pan-Asian restaurant has long been a Seattle favorite and is now located across the street from Benaroya Hall. Pull up a comfortable stool around the large satay grill and watch the cooks grill little skewers of anything from chicken to scallops to pork to prawns to lamb. Each skewer is served with a small cube of sticky rice and pickled cucumber. Order three or four satay sticks and you have a meal. If you prefer to sit at a table and have a more traditional dinner, Wild Ginger can accommodate you. Try the Panang beef curry (rib-eye steak in pungent curry sauce of cardamom, coconut milk, Thai basil, and peanuts). The lunch menu contains many of the dinner entrees, but at lower prices.

1401 Third Ave. © **206/623-4450.** Reservations recommended. Satay $2.75–$5.50; main courses $8.75–$22.50. AE, DC, DISC, MC, V. Mon–Thurs 11:30am–3pm and 5–11pm, Fri 11:30am–3pm and 5–midnight, Sat 11:30am–3pm and 4:30pm–midnight, Sun 4:30–11pm. Satay Bar until 1am nightly.

3 The Waterfront

MODERATE

Anthony's Pier 66 & Bell Street Diner *&&* SEAFOOD   The Anthony's chain has several outposts around the Seattle area, but this complex is the most convenient and versatile. Not only is there an upscale and stylish seafood restaurant with good waterfront views, but Anthony's also includes a moderately priced casual restaurant and a walk-up counter as well. The bold contemporary styling and abundance of art glass set this place apart from most of the waterfront restaurants. The upscale crowd heads upstairs for the likes of Asian-inspired seafood dishes, and the more cost-conscious stay downstairs at the Bell Street Diner where meals are much easier on the wallet (though far less creative). For the higher prices, you get better views, as long as you don't get stuck at the counter that overlooks the exhibition kitchen. In summer, the decks are the place to be.

2201 Alaskan Way. © **206/448-6688.** www.anthonys.com. Reservations recommended. Pier 66 main courses $15–$35; Bell Street Diner main courses $7.50–$30. AE, MC, V. Pier 66 Sun–Thurs 4:30–10:30pm, Fri–Sat 5–11:30pm; Bell Street Diner Sun–Thurs 11:30am–10:30pm, Fri–Sat 11:30am–11:30pm.

Elliott's *&&* SEAFOOD   While most of its neighbors are content to coast along on tourist business, Elliott's actually aims to keep locals happy by serving some of the best seafood in Seattle. Although the restaurant is right on the waterfront, the view really isn't that great. However, if you're looking for superbly prepared fresh seafood, Elliott's is an excellent bet. The oyster bar can have as many as 20 varieties of oysters available, so this is definitely the place to get to know your Northwest oysters. Salmon and Dungeness crabs are always on the menu and are usually prepared any of several different ways. However, with so many oysters in your midst, you might just want to start with oysters on the half shell and then move on to the pan-fried oysters. For lunch, the mesquite-grilled ahi tuna tacos with wasabi lime sauce and mango salsa are terrific.

Pier 56, Alaskan Way. © **206/623-4340.** Reservations recommended. Main courses $9–$17 at lunch, $16–$36 at dinner. AE, DC, DISC, MC, V. Sun–Thurs 11am–10pm, Fri–Sat 11am–11pm. Closes 30 min. to 1 hr. later in summer.

4 Pioneer Square & the International District

In addition to the two International District restaurants listed below, you'll also find a large all-Asian food court at **Uwajimaya,** 600 Fifth Ave. S. (© **206/624-6248**), a huge Asian supermarket. The food court has stalls serving the food of different Asian countries. It all smells great, and everything is good and cheap, which makes this a great place for a quick meal. The bus tunnel entrance is right across the street, which makes Uwajimaya easy to reach even from the north end of downtown.

EXPENSIVE

Il Terrazzo Carmine *☆☆* ITALIAN   One of the finest Italian restaurants in Seattle, Il Terrazzo Carmine is tucked into the back of an office building in the Pioneer Square area and overlooks a hidden waterfall terrace. Despite the odd location amid the saloons and bars of Seattle's main nightlife district, this is a big-time power lunch and business dinner spot, attracting lots of diners in business suits. The power brokers and others in the know come for the rarefied atmosphere, professional service, and reliably fine Italian fare. A couple of unusual pastas worth trying include the venison-stuffed ravioli with mushroom sauce and fettuccine with chicken livers, sun-dried tomatoes, and mushrooms. If you're in the mood for a steak, consider the *filetto al barolo and pancetta,* a prime-cut tenderloin roasted with wine and pancetta sauce.

411 First Ave. S. ℂ **206/467-7797.** Reservations recommended. Pastas $11.50–$16; main courses $10.50–$17 at lunch, $19.75–$34 at dinner. AE, DC, DISC, MC, V. Mon–Fri 11:30am–2:30pm and 5:30–10pm, Sat 5–10pm.

MODERATE

Trattoria Mitchelli *☆* ITALIAN/LATE-NIGHT   Located in the heart of Pioneer Square, Trattoria Mitchelli serves good, basic Italian food in a cozy spot with a friendly old-world atmosphere. An old wooden-topped lunch counter in a room with classic hexagonal tile floors is a popular after-work and late-night gathering spot, and conversation is lively. You can't go wrong here with the fettuccine con pollo, pizza from the wood-fired oven, or the pasta of the week served with your choice of sauce. For a rich dessert, dig into a caramello, a creamy caramel with toasted walnuts and whipped cream. If you're a night owl, keep Mitchelli's in mind—full meals are served until 4am, catering to the starving hordes who pour out of the area's many bars after last call.

84 Yesler Way. ℂ **206/623-3883.** Reservations accepted only for parties of 6 or more people. Main courses $9–$16. AE, MC, V. Mon 7am–11pm, Tues–Fri 7am–4am, Sat 8am–4am, Sun 8am–11pm.

INEXPENSIVE

Hing Loon *☆* CHINESE/LATE-NIGHT   Bright fluorescent lighting, big Formica-top tables, devoid of atmosphere—this is the sort of place you'd pass by without a thought if you were aimlessly searching for a restaurant in the International District. With so many choices in a few square blocks, it's easy to be distracted by fancy decor. But forget the rest and take a seat in Hing Loon. Seafood is the house specialty, and none is done better than the oysters with ginger and green onion served on a sizzling platter. The restaurant makes all its own noodles, so you can't go wrong ordering chow mein or chow fun—but be prepared for a large helping. Pork dishes tend to be fatty.

628 S. Weller St. ℂ **206/682-2828.** Main courses $4.50–$9.50. DC, MC, V. Sun–Thurs 10am–midnight, Fri–Sat 10am–2am.

Koraku *Finds* JAPANESE   Eating lunch at this little International District hole in the wall is like ducking into a back-street cafe in Japan. Only slightly larger than a walk-in closet, Koraku feels as though it hasn't changed in half a century or more, which seems to be just fine with the regular patrons, most of whom will be speaking Japanese. The menu is limited to a handful of daily specials, of which the fried mackerel lunch is our favorite.

419 Sixth Ave. © **206/624-1389.** Main courses $4.50–$6.50. No credit cards. Mon–Tues and Thurs–Fri 11am–5pm.

Merchants Cafe AMERICAN   Merchants Cafe is Seattle's oldest restaurant and looks every bit of its 100-plus years. A well-scuffed tile floor surrounds the bar, which came around the Horn in the 1800s, and an old safe and gold scales are left over from the days when Seattle was the first, or last, taste of civilization for Yukon prospectors. At one time the restaurant's basement was a card room, and the upper floors were a brothel. In fact, this may be the original Skid Row saloon (Yesler Way was the original Skid Road down which logs were skidded to a sawmill). Straightforward sandwiches, salads, and soups are the mainstays of the menu.

109 Yesler Way. © **206/624-1515.** Main courses and sandwiches $5.50–$8. AE, MC, V. Mon–Thurs 11am–9pm, Fri–Sat 11am–2am, Sun 11am–4am.

Pecos Pit BBQ *(Finds)* BARBECUE   This barbecue joint, located in an industrial area south of Pioneer Square, looks like an old gas station with picnic tables out front, and the first thing you'll notice is the line of about 30 people standing in front of the walk-up window. The second thing you'll notice is that the bag they give you comes with five napkins and a spoon. Yep, this joint is both popular and a great place to ruin a good shirt, but those sandwiches sure are tasty. Unless you're a confirmed fire-eater, don't go beyond "mild" unless you want to feel your lips burning long after you've finished eating. Pecos Pit BBQ may be out of the way, but it's well worth the drive.

2260 First Ave. S. © **206/623-0629.** Sandwiches $5.50. No credit cards. Mon–Fri 11am–3pm.

Salumi *(R)* *(Finds)* ITALIAN   For many folks, salami is a guilty pleasure. We all know it's got way too much fat, but it tastes too good to resist. Now, raise the bar on salami, and you have the artisan-cured meats of this closet-size eatery near Pioneer Square. The owner makes all his own salami (as well as traditional Italian-cured beef tongue). Order up a meat plate with a side of cheese and some roasted red bell peppers, pour yourself a glass of wine from the big bottle on the table, and you have a perfect lunchtime repast in the classic Italian style. Did I mention the great breads and tapenades? Wow! If you're down in the Pioneer Square area at lunch, don't miss this place.

309 Third Ave. S. © **206/621-8772.** Reservations not accepted. Main courses $4.50–$9.50. AE, DC, DISC, MC, V. Tues–Fri 11am–4pm.

5 Belltown & Pike Place Market
VERY EXPENSIVE

El Gaucho *(R R)* LATE-NIGHT/STEAK   Conjuring up the ghosts of dinner clubs of the 1930s and 1940s, this high-end Belltown steak house seems like a Fred Astaire film set. The pure theatrics make this place a must if you're in the mood to spend big bucks on a thick, juicy steak. Although you might get a better steak at one of the other high-end steakhouses in town, you just can't duplicate the experience of dining at El Gaucho. Stage-set decor aside, the real stars of the show here are the 28-day dry-aged Angus beef steaks, which are among the best in town, but expect to drop a bundle on the perfect steak. All the classics are here, too, including Caesar salad tossed tableside, and chateaubriand carved before your eyes. Not a steak eater? How about venison chops, an ostrich filet, or Australian lobster tail? There's also a classy bar off to one side, a separate cigar lounge, and for after-dinner dancing, the affiliated Pampas Room nightclub.

2505 First Ave. ℭ **206/728-1337**. www.elgaucho.com. Reservations recommended. Main courses $16–$90. AE, DC, MC, V. Mon–Sat 5pm–1am, Sun 5–11pm.

EXPENSIVE

Campagne ✰✰ COUNTRY FRENCH   With large windows that look out over the top of Pike Place Market to Elliott Bay, Campagne is an unpretentious, yet elegant, French restaurant. With such a prime location, it shouldn't be surprising that Campagne relies heavily on the wide variety of fresh ingredients that the market provides. The menu leans toward country French, with such dishes as pâté de campagne or lamb loin and lamb sausage with a potato *galette* (potato cake). There are always several interesting salads as well.

Budget tip: One of Seattle's great culinary deals can be had here at Campagne between 5:30 and 6:30pm daily, when three-course dinners are available for only $30.

Inn at the Market, 86 Pine St. ℭ **206/728-2800**. www.campagnerestaurant.com. Reservations recommended. Main courses $22–$35; 3-course prix fixe dinner $30. Bar menu midnight. AE, DC, MC, V. Daily 5–10pm.

Chez Shea ✰✰✰ NORTHWEST   Quiet, dark, and intimate, Chez Shea is one of the finest restaurants in Seattle, and with only a dozen candlelit tables and views across Puget Sound to the Olympic Mountains, this is an ideal setting for romance. The menu changes with the season, and ingredients come primarily from the market below. On a recent summer evening, dinner started with savory basil panna cotta and then moved on to potato-leek bisque. There are usually five choices of entree; among these were a pan-roasted salmon filet with a sesame glaze and rhubarb-ginger compote and a shiitake mushroom and spinach lasagna. Though dessert is a la carte, you'll find it impossible to let it pass you by. While there are equally fine restaurants in the city, none has quite the romantic atmosphere as Chez Shea.

Pike Place Market, Corner Market Building, 94 Pike St., Suite 34. ℭ **206/467-9990**. www.chezshea.com. Reservations highly recommended. Prix fixe 4-course dinner $43. AE, MC, V. Tues–Sun 5:30–10:30pm.

Il Bistro ✰ ITALIAN   What with the fishmongers and crowds of tourists, Pike Place Market might not seem like the place for a romantic candlelit dinner. However, romantic dinners are what Il Bistro is all about. This restaurant takes Italian cooking very seriously and in so doing also puts the Northwest's bountiful ingredients to good use. The menu includes such mouthwatering starters as calamari sautéed with fresh basil, garlic, vinegar, and tomatoes. Hundreds of loyal fans insist that Il Bistro's rack of lamb with wine sauce is the best in Seattle, and we'd have to agree. However, the pasta here can also be a genuine revelation when served with garlic, brandy, or vodka cream sauce. You'll find this basement trattoria down the cobblestone alley beside the Market information kiosk.

93-A Pike St. and First Ave. (inside Pike Place Market). ℭ **206/682-3049**. Reservations recommended. Pastas $13–$18; main courses $20–$40. AE, DC, MC, V. Sun–Thurs 5:30–10pm, Fri–Sat 5:30–11pm; late-night menu until 1am; bar nightly until 2am.

MODERATE

Afrikando ✰ *(finds)* AFRICAN   Trendy Belltown seems an unlikely place for a casual restaurant specializing in the unfamiliar flavors of West Africa, but that's exactly what you'll find here at the Seattle Center end of the neighborhood. We love the hearty African home cooking here. The bold and spicy flavors of hot climates merge with the influences of France in West Africa, so you can expect some unusual flavor combinations. Start your meal with the spicy and delicious halibut soup, which has a thick tomato base and maybe split a plate of the *akra* fritters, which are made with black-eyed peas. Although the *thiebu djen,* a Senegalese fish dish is hard to resist, we always go for the *mafe,* a dish of baked chicken topped with a homemade habanero sauce and accompanied by root vegetables smothered in peanut sauce. Be sure to try the strong Senegalese tea.

2904 First Ave. ☎ 206/374-9714. Reservations recommended for 4 or more. Main courses $9–$18. MC, V. Mon–Fri 11am–2:30pm; Mon–Sat 5–10pm, Sun 4–9pm.

Assaggio ☆☆ ITALIAN   Assaggio has long been one of Seattle's favorite Italian restaurants. The large, casual restaurant has an old-world feel, with a high ceiling, arches, and Roman-style murals on the walls. However, what really recommends this place is the excellent food. For a starter, you might try the grilled radicchio wrapped in pancetta ham and topped with a balsamic vinaigrette. Pastas come from all over Italy, but it's hard to beat the *pappardelle boscaiola* with pancetta ham and wild mushrooms in a wine cream sauce. There are also such standbys as lamb shanks with herbs and veal saltimbocca.

2010 Fourth Ave. ☎ **206/441-1399.** www.assaggioseattle.com. Reservations recommended. Main courses $10–$17 at lunch, $13–$25 at dinner. AE, DC, DISC, MC, V. Mon–Fri 11:30am–2:30pm; Mon–Sat 5–10pm.

Cafe Campagne ☆☆ *Finds* FRENCH   This cozy little cafe is an offshoot of the Inn at the Market's popular Campagne, a much more formal French restaurant, and though it's in the heart of the Pike Place Market neighborhood, it's a world away from the market madness. We like to duck in here for lunch and escape the shuffling crowds. What a relief—so civilized, so very French. The dark and cozy place has a hidden feel to it, and most people leave feeling like they've discovered some secret hideaway. The menu changes with the seasons but Monday through Saturday there is always a daily rotisserie special such as stuffed quail or leg of lamb marinated with garlic and anchovy. These are definitely the meals to have here. The cafe also doubles as a wine bar and has a good selection of reasonably priced wines by the glass or by the bottle.

Great Brunch Choices

For brunch, there are some great options around the city. Try **Cafe Flora, Ivar's Salmon House, Palisade, Ponti Seafood Grill, Salty's on Alki,** or **SkyCity at the Needle.** All these places have complete reviews in the appropriate neighborhood sections of this chapter.

1600 Post Alley. ☎ 206/728-2233. Reservations accepted for dinner only. Main courses $11–$18. AE, DC, MC, V. Mon–Thurs 8–11am, 11:45am–3pm, and 5–10pm; Fri–Sat 8–11am, 11:45am–3pm and 5:30–11pm; Sun 8am–3pm and 5–10pm.

Dahlia Lounge ☆☆ PAN-ASIAN/NORTHWEST   The neon chef holding a flapping fish may suggest that the Dahlia is little more than a roadside diner, but a glimpse at the stylish interior will likely have you thinking otherwise. One look at the menu, one bite of any dish, will convince you that this is one of Seattle's finest restaurants. Mouthwatering and succulent Dungeness crab cakes, a bow to Chef Tom Douglas's Maryland roots, are the house specialty and should not be missed. The menu, influenced by the far side of the Pacific Rim, changes regularly, with the lunch menu featuring many of the same offerings at slightly lower prices. For dessert, it takes a Herculean effort to resist the crème caramel, and it's way too easy to fill up on the restaurant's breads, which are baked in the adjacent Dahlia Bakery.

2001 Fourth Ave. ℂ 206/682-4142. www.tomdouglas.com. Reservations highly recommended. Main courses $18–$26. AE, DC, DISC, MC, V. Mon–Fri 11:30am–2:30pm; Mon–Thurs 5:30–10pm, Fri–Sat 5:30– 11pm, Sun 5–10pm.

Etta's Seafood ✸✸ SEAFOOD   Seattle chef Tom Douglas's strictly seafood (well, almost) restaurant, Etta's, is located smack in the middle of the Pike Place Market area, and of course, serves Douglas's signature crab cakes (crunchy on the outside, creamy on the inside), which are not to be missed (and if they're not on the menu, just ask). Don't ignore your side dishes, either; they can be exquisite and are usually enough to share among the table. In addition to the great seafood dishes, there are always a few other fine options, including several that date from Douglas's Café Sport days in the early 1980s. Stylish contemporary decor sets the mood and assures that this place is as popular with locals as it is with tourists.

2020 Western Ave. ℂ 206/443-6000. www.tomdouglas.com. Reservations recommended. Main courses $10–$28. AE, DC, DISC, MC, V. Mon–Thurs 11:30am–10pm, Fri 11:30am–11pm, Sat 9am–11pm, Sun 9am–10pm.

Fandango ✸✸ LATIN AMERICAN   Fandango is the latest culinary offering from local celebrity chef Christine Keff, who also operates the ever-popular Flying Fish restaurant diagonally across the street from this establishment. The focus here is on the sunny flavors of Latin America, and Fandango's menu is filled with combinations you aren't likely to have ever encountered this far north before. This just might be the only place in the city where you can a get a *huitlacoche* quesadilla (made with a corn fungus that's considered a delicacy in Mexico). Whether you order the Brazilian seafood stew, suckling pig, or sea scallops with almonds, oranges, and capers, you'll enjoy some real taste treats. If you're lucky, you just might find grilled bananas on the dessert menu, and be sure to try a *mojito* cocktail.

2313 First Ave. ℂ 206/441-1188. Reservations recommended. Main courses $15–$20. DC, MC, V. Daily 5pm–midnight (until 2am in the bar).

Flying Fish ✸✸ LATE-NIGHT/NORTHWEST/SEAFOOD   Chef Christine Keff has been on the Seattle restaurant scene for many years now, and with Flying Fish, she hit on something the city really wanted. Not only are there the bold combinations of vibrant flavors demanded by the city's well-traveled palates, but the hip Belltown restaurant serves dinner past midnight every night, keeping late-night partiers from going hungry. Every dish here is a work of art, and with small plates, large plates, and platters for sharing, diners are encouraged to sample a wide variety of the kitchen's creations. To keep the locals coming back, the menu changes almost daily, but keep an eye out for the smoked rock shrimp spring rolls, which are positively sculptural. The festive desserts are often so decorated that they're a miniparty on the plate. There's also a huge wine list.

2234 First Ave. ℂ 206/728-8595. www.flyingfishseattle.com. Reservations recommended. Main courses $15–$23. DC, MC, V. Daily 5pm–1am.

Icon Grill ✸ AMERICAN   With every inch of wall space covered with framed artwork, colorful art glass hanging from chandeliers, and overflowing giant vases, this place goes way overboard with its decor, but that's the exactly what makes it so fun. Basically, it's an over-the-top rendition of a Victorian setting gone 21st century. The food is mix of basic comfort food (including a molasses-glazed meat loaf that locals swear by) and moderately more inventive dishes such as a grilled pear salad, lemon-rosemary game hen, and rhubarb-and-rosemary-glazed lamb shank. Unfortunately, the food can be unpredictable, so don't come here just for a culinary experience, but rather for a Seattle experience.

1933 Fifth Ave. ✆ **206/441-6330.** Reservations recommended. Main courses $10.50–$33. AE, MC, V. Mon–Fri 11:30am–2pm; Sun–Mon 5:30–9pm, Tues–Thurs 5:30–10pm, Fri–Sat 5:30–11pm.

Le Pichet ☆ FRENCH   Seattle seems to have a thing for French restaurants. They're all over the place in this city, with a surprising number clustered around Pike Place Market, and Le Pichet is one of our favorites. The name is French for "pitcher," and is a reference to the traditional ceramic pitchers that are used for serving inexpensive French wines. This should give you an idea that this is a very casual spot, the sort of place where you can drop by any time of day, grab a stool at the bar, and have a light meal. Almost everything served here is made fresh on the premises, and with lots of small plates and appetizers, it's fun and easy to piece together a light meal of shareable dishes. We like the salad made with goat cheese wrapped in ham and served on curly endive and dandelion greens, the warm salt cod purée with garlic and olive, and the country-style pâté, which here is served with honey and walnuts.

1933 First Ave. ✆ **206/256-1499.** Reservations recommended. Main courses $15–$16. MC, V. Sun–Mon and Thurs 8am–midnight, Fri–Sat 8am–2am.

Marco's Supperclub ☆ *Finds* INTERNATIONAL   This Belltown restaurant has a casual ambience that belies the high-quality meals turned out by its kitchen. The menu draws on cuisines from around the world, so even jaded gourmets may find something new here. Don't miss the unusual fried sage leaves appetizer, which comes with a variety of dipping sauces or the mussels in a spicy chipotle-pepper broth. Among the entrees, the Jamaican jerk chicken with sautéed greens and sweet potato purée is a standout. On the seasonal menu, you might encounter the likes of Tuscan bread salad, pan-seared halibut with Lebanese walnut-pepper sauce, or mushroom tamales. If you enjoy creative cookery at reasonable prices, check this place out.

2510 First Ave. ✆ **206/441-7801.** Reservations highly recommended. Main courses $14–$20. AE, MC, V. Sun–Thurs 5:30–11pm, Fri–Sat 5:30pm–midnight.

Matt's in the Market ☆☆ *Finds* AMERICAN REGIONAL/INTERNA-TIONAL   Quite possibly the smallest gourmet restaurant in Seattle, Matt's is a tiny cubbyhole of a place in the Corner Market Building, which is directly across the street from the market information booth at First and Pike. There are only a handful of tables and a few stools at the counter here, and although the kitchen takes up almost half the restaurant, the cooks still have little more than the space of a walk-in closet in which to work their culinary magic. The menu changes regularly, with an emphasis on fresh ingredients from the market stalls only steps away, and there's a good selection of reasonably priced wines. The menu pulls in whatever influences and styles happen to appeal to the chef at that moment, perhaps Moroccan, perhaps Southern. This is a real Pike Place Market experience.

94 Pike St. ✆ **206/467-7909.** Reservations not accepted. Main courses $8–$9 at lunch, $15–$18 at dinner. MC, V. Tues–Sat 11:30am–2:30pm and 5:30–9:30pm.

Palace Kitchen ★★ AMERICAN REGIONAL/LATE-NIGHT/MEDITER-RANEAN   This is the most casual of chef Tom Douglas's three Seattle establishments, with a bar that attracts nearly as many customers as the restaurant. The atmosphere is urban chic, with cement pillars, simple wood booths, and a few tables in the front window, which overlooks the monorail tracks. The menu is short and features a nightly selection of unusual cheeses and different preparations from the apple-wood grill. To begin a meal, we enjoy the Spanish white anchovies, but wood-grilled chicken wings with cilantro sour cream are also a big hit. Entrees are usually simple and delicious and often draw on Southern influences, as in the pan-seared halibut with grits and orange-rosemary sauce. For dessert, the coconut cream pie is an absolute must, but there's also always a daily cheese selection.

2030 Fifth Ave. ℂ 206/448-2001. www.tomdouglas.com. Reservations not accepted. Main courses $11–$25. AE, DC, DISC, MC, V. Mon–Fri 11:30am–2:30pm; daily 5pm–1am.

The Pink Door ★ ITALIAN/LATE-NIGHT   Pike Place Market's better restaurants tend to be well hidden, and if we didn't tell you about this one, you'd probably never find it. There's no sign out front—only the pink door for which the restaurant is named (look for it between Stewart and Virginia streets). On the other side of the door, stairs lead to a cellarlike space, which is almost always empty on summer days, when folks forsake it to dine on the deck with a view of Elliott Bay. What makes this place so popular is as much the fun atmosphere as the Italian food. There's a tarot card reader in residence, and sometimes there's a magician. Most nights in the bar there's some sort of Felliniesque cabaret performer. Be sure to start your meal with the fragrant roasted garlic and ricotta-Gorgonzola spread or the house-made tapenade. From there, you might move on to an Italian classic such as lasagna or something made with fresh seafood from Pike Place Market.

1919 Post Alley. ℂ 206/443-3241. Reservations recommended. Main courses $14–$20. AE, MC, V. Tues–Sat 11:30am–2am, Sun 4–11pm.

Shea's Lounge ★★ NORTHWEST/INTERNATIONAL/LATE-NIGHT   Convenient, casual, economical, romantic. What's not to like about this hidden jewel in Pike Place Market? This is the lounge for the ever-popular Chez Shea, and it's one of the most sophisticated little spaces in Seattle. Romantic lighting and a view of the bay make this a popular spot with couples, and whether you just want a cocktail and an appetizer or a full meal, you can get it here. The menu features gourmet pizzas, combination appetizer plates, a few soups and salads, and several nightly specials such as seared rare ahi tuna with chilled Asian noodles tossed in Thai red-curry peanut sauce. You can even order dishes from the main restaurant's menu. The desserts are divinely decadent. This is a great spot for a light or late-night meal.

Pike Place Market, Corner Market Building, 94 Pike St., Ste. 34. ℂ 206/467-9990. Reservations not accepted. Main courses $13–$26. AE, MC, V. Tues–Thurs and Sun 4:30pm–midnight, Fri–Sat 4:30pm–2am.

Shiro's ★★ JAPANESE   If ogling all the fresh fish at Pike Place Market puts you in the mood for some sushi, there is no question of where to head. Shiro's serves the best sushi in the city. It's fresh, flavorful, and perfectly prepared. Eat at the sushi bar here and you'll be rubbing shoulders with locals and visiting Japanese businessmen, all of whom know that sushi maestro Shiro Kashiba has a way with raw fish. Be sure to order at least one of Shiro's special rolls, and, if you're feeling adventurous, this is definitely the place to try sea urchin roe (you won't find it any fresher anywhere). For sushi dessert, try the smoked eel drizzled with a sweet sauce.

2401 Second Ave. (206/443-9844. Reservations recommended. Sushi $2–$12; main courses $17.50–$20.50. MC, V. Daily 5:30–9:45pm.

INEXPENSIVE

Belltown Pub and Cafe (*Kids* AMERICAN   Located in Belltown in what was once a sleeping bag factory, this lively pub serves a surprisingly varied menu. Although you'll find everything from spaghetti and meatballs to smoked salmon mousse here, the bacon and cheddar burger is hard to pass up. It's definitely one of the best burgers in Seattle—thick, juicy, well flavored, and set on a large, chewy roll. Accompany your burger with a pint from one of the many microbrew taps. More sophisticated palates may prefer the likes of chicken marsala or smoked-salmon ravioli with some wine chosen from a fairly decent wine list. There are tables on the sidewalk in summer, and huge wooden booths for when the weather is inclement. This place is family friendly, which is a rarity in trendy Belltown.

2322 First Ave. (206/728-4311. www.belltownpub.com. Reservations accepted. Main courses $8.25–$20. AE, MC, V. Sun–Thurs 11:30am–midnight, Fri–Sat 11:30am–1am.

Noodle Ranch (*Finds* PAN-ASIAN   This Belltown hole-in-the-wall serves Pan-Asian cuisine for the hip-yet-financially-challenged crowd. It's a lively, boisterous scene, and the food is packed with intense, and often unfamiliar, flavors. Don't miss the fish grilled in grape leaves with its nice presentation and knockout dipping sauce. In fact, all of the dipping sauces here are delicious. The Mekong grill—rice noodles with a rice wine vinegar and herb dressing topped with grilled pork, chicken, catfish, or tofu—is another dish not to be missed. You'll also find the likes of Laotian cucumber salad and Japanese-style eggplant. In fact, there are lots of vegetarian options. Although the place is frequently packed, you can usually get a seat.

2228 Second Ave. (206/728-0463. Main courses $7–$11.25. AE, MC, V. Mon–Thurs 11am–10pm, Fri 11am–11pm, Sat noon–11pm.

Virginia Inn (* AMERICAN/FRENCH   In business since 1903, this restaurant/bar near Pike Place Market is a cozy spot for lunch or a cheap dinner. Big windows let lots of light into the small room, but if the sun is shining, most people try to get a seat on the sidewalk patio. This has long been a favorite hangout of Belltown residents and is as popular for its microbrews as it is for its food. The crab cakes are a perennial favorite here.

1937 First Ave. (206/728-1937. Reservations accepted only for parties of 5 or more. Main courses $7.50–$10.50. AE, MC, V. Daily 11:30am–10pm.

6 Queen Anne & Seattle Center

VERY EXPENSIVE

SkyCity at the Needle (** NORTHWEST   Both the restaurant and the prices are sky-high at this revolving restaurant, located just below the observation deck at the top of Seattle's famous Space Needle. But because you don't have to pay extra for the elevator ride if you dine here, the high prices start to seem a little bit more in line with those at other Seattle splurge restaurants. OK, so maybe you'd get better food somewhere else, and maybe you can dine with a view at other Seattle restaurants, but you won't get such a spectacular panorama anywhere but here. The menu works hard at offering some distinctly Northwestern flavor combinations but still has plenty of familiar fare for those diners who aren't into culinary adventures. Steak and seafood make up the bulk of the menu, with a couple of vegetarian options as well. We recommend coming here for lunch. The prices are considerably more reasonable and the views, encompassing city skyline, Mount Rainier, and the Olympic Mountains, are unsurpassed.

Space Needle, 400 Broad St. ✆ **800/937-9582** or 206/905-2100. www.spaceneedle.com. Reservations highly recommended. Main courses $15–$30 at lunch, $26–$42 at dinner. Weekend brunch $34.50 adults, $21.50 children 5–12. AE, DC, DISC, MC, V. Mon–Fri 10am–2:45pm and 4:30–10:15pm, Sat–Sun 8am–2:45pm and 4:30–10:15pm.

EXPENSIVE

Canlis 𝄐𝄐𝄐 NORTHWEST   A Seattle institution, Canlis has been in business since 1950. A major remodeling a few years back gave the restaurant a stylish new look that mixes contemporary decor with Asian antiques, and Canlis continues to make improvements aimed at luring in Seattle's new movers and shakers. The Northwest cuisine, with Asian and continental influences, keeps both traditionalists and more adventurous diners content. Steaks from the copper grill are perennial favorites here, as are the spicy Canlis prawns. You'll definitely want to dress up for a meal here. This is the perfect place to close a big deal or celebrate a very special occasion. To finish, why not go all the way and have the Grand Marnier soufflé? Canlis also has one of the best wine lists in Seattle.

2576 Aurora Ave. N. ✆ **206/283-3313.** www.canlis.com. Reservations highly recommended. Main courses $22–$50; chef's tasting menu $95 with wines. AE, DC, DISC, MC, V. Mon–Sat 5:30–midnight. Valet parking $5.

Kaspar's Restaurant & Wine Bar 𝄐𝄐 NORTHWEST/SEAFOOD Located in the Lower Queen Anne neighborhood, Kaspar's has long been a favorite with Seattleites, offering many dining options for various hungers and pocketbooks. Throughout the year, chef Kaspar Donier puts on interesting special dinners, and for the connoisseur and oenophile there are wine-tasting dinners. For light meals, drinks, and desserts, head for the wine bar. The menu here places an emphasis on seafood (don't miss the scallops) and draws on worldwide influences, such as Asian antipasto, braised lamb shank, or chicken with a hoisin-honey glaze. Kaspar's is also justly famous for its desserts.

19 W. Harrison St. ✆ **206/298-0123.** www.kaspars.com. Reservations recommended. Main courses $14–$24; prix fixe dinners $35–$65. AE, MC, V. Tues–Thurs 4:30–10pm, Fri–Sat 4:30–11pm.

Palisade 𝄐𝄐𝄐 NORTHWEST   With a panorama that sweeps from downtown to West Seattle and across the sound to the Olympic Mountains, Palisade has one of the best views of any Seattle waterfront restaurant. It also happens to have fine food and inventive interior design (incorporating a saltwater pond, complete with fish, sea anemones, and starfish, in the middle of the dining room). The extensive menu features dishes prepared on a searing grill, in a wood-fired oven, in a wood-fired rotisserie, and in an applewood broiler—it all adds up to is many choices of flavorful seafoods and meats. There's also an excellent and very popular Sunday brunch here. Palisade is not easy to find, but it's more than worth the trouble to search it out. Call for directions.

Elliott Bay Marina, 2601 W. Marina Place. ✆ **206/285-1000.** Reservations recommended. Main courses $17–$48. AE, DC, DISC, MC, V. Mon–Fri 11:30am–2pm and 5–10pm, Sat noon–2pm and 4:30–10pm, Sun 10am–2pm and 4:30–9pm.

Dining: Queen Anne/Seattle Center, Lake Union, Capitol Hill & North Seattle

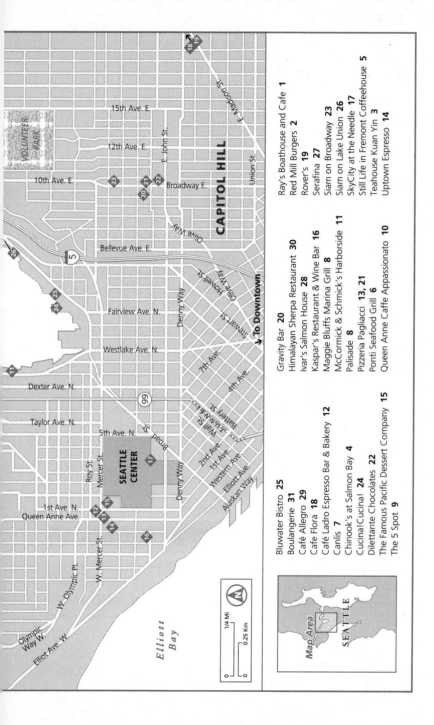

VOLUNTEER PARK

15th Ave. E.

12th Ave. E.

10th Ave. E.

E. John St.

Broadway E.

Union St.

E. Madison St.

CAPITOL HILL

Olive Way

Bellevue Ave. E.

Olive Way

Howell St.

Stewart St.

Olive Way

To Downtown

Fairview Ave. N.

Denny Way

Westlake Ave. N.

7th Ave.

4th Ave.

Dexter Ave. N.

99

Battery St.

2nd Ave.

1st Ave.

Taylor Ave. N.

5th Ave. N.

Broad St.

Wall St.

Western Ave.

Elliott Ave.

Roy St.

Mercer St.

SEATTLE CENTER

Denny Way

Alaskan Way

1st Ave. N.
Queen Anne Ave.

W. Mercer St.

W. Olympic Pl.

Olympic Way W.

Elliot Ave. W.

Elliott Bay

Map Area

SEATTLE

N

1/4 Mi
0.25 Km

Bluwater Bistro **25**
Boulangerie **31**
Café Allegro **29**
Cafe Flora **18**
Café Ladro Espresso Bar & Bakery **12**
Canlis **7**
Chinook's at Salmon Bay **4**
Cucina!Cucina! **24**
Dilettante Chocolates **22**
The Famous Pacific Dessert Company **15**
The 5 Spot **9**

Gravity Bar **20**
Himalayan Sherpa Restaurant **30**
Ivar's Salmon House **28**
Kaspar's Restaurant & Wine Bar **16**
Maggie Bluffs Marina Grill **8**
McCormick & Schmick's Harborside **11**
Palisade **8**
Pizzeria Pagliacci **13, 21**
Ponti Seafood Grill **6**
Queen Anne Caffe Appassionato **10**

Ray's Boathouse and Cafe **1**
Red Mill Burgers **2**
Rover's **19**
Serafina **27**
Siam on Broadway **23**
Siam on Lake Union **26**
SkyCity at the Needle **17**
Still Life in Fremont Coffeehouse **5**
Teahouse Kuan Yin **3**
Uptown Espresso **14**

81

INEXPENSIVE

The 5 Spot *(R)* AMERICAN REGIONAL/LATE-NIGHT   The 5 Spot is one of Seattle's favorite diners. Every 3 months or so, the restaurant changes its menu to reflect a different regional U.S. cuisine. Maybe you'll find Brooklyn comfort food or Cuban-influenced Miami-style meals featured on the menu, but you can bet whatever's featured will be filling and fun. The atmosphere here is pure kitsch—whenever the theme is "Florida," the restaurant is adorned with palm trees and flamingos and looks like the high school gym done up for prom night. This bustling diner is popular with all types, who appreciate the fact that you won't go broke eating here. To find The 5 Spot, look for the neon coffee pouring into the giant coffee cup sign at the top of Queen Anne hill.

1502 Queen Anne Ave. N. ⓒ 206/285-SPOT. www.chowfoods.com. Reservations accepted only for parties of 6–10. Main courses $6.75–$10.25 at lunch, $8.75–$17.75 at dinner. MC, V. Daily 8:30am–midnight.

Maggie Bluffs Marina Grill *(R) (Kids)* AMERICAN   It isn't easy finding affordable waterfront dining in any city, and Seattle is no exception. However, if you're willing to drive a few miles from downtown Seattle, you can save quite a few bucks at this casual marina restaurant located at the foot of Magnolia Bluff (northwest of downtown Seattle). The menu is fairly simple, with burgers and fish and chips, but also includes a few more creative dishes. The restaurant overlooks a marina and, while the view is partially obstructed by a breakwater, you can still see Elliott Bay, West Seattle, downtown, and even the Space Needle. There are crayons to keep the kids entertained, and after a meal, you can walk out Pier G and take a free shuttle boat to an observation deck atop the breakwater. The patio dining area is immensely popular on sunny summer days.

Elliott Bay Marina, 2601 W. Marina Place. ⓒ 206/283-8322. Reservations not accepted. Main courses $7–$11.50. AE, DISC, MC, V. Mon–Fri 11:30am–9pm, Fri 11:30am–10pm, Sat–Sun 9am–11:30pm.

Pizzeria Pagliacci *(R)* PIZZA   Pagliacci's pizza has repeatedly been voted the best in Seattle, and they now have three popular locations. Although you can order a traditional cheese pizza, there are much more interesting pies on the menu, such as pesto pizza or the sun-dried tomato primo. It's strictly counter service, but there are plenty of seats at each of the bright restaurants. For those in a hurry or who just want a snack, there's pizza by the slice. There's another Pagliacci at 426 Broadway E. (ⓒ **206/324-0730**).

550 Queen Anne Ave. N. ⓒ **206/285-1232**. www.pagliacci.com. Reservations not accepted. Pizza $11.50–$20. AE, MC, V. Sun–Thurs 11am–11pm, Fri–Sat 11am–1am.

7 Lake Union

MODERATE

Bluwater Bistro *(R)* AMERICAN REGIONAL/LATE-NIGHT   Although this restaurant is located on the shore of Lake Union, its views are limited, which is probably why the Bluwater Bistro is more popular with locals than with tourists. However, you can watch seaplanes taking off and landing right in front of the restaurant. Best of all, the prices here are considerably lower than at most tourist-targeted waterfront restaurants around town. Good choices include the New York steak topped with blue cheese and, at lunch, the fish tacos. You'll find this little bistro on the next pier north of Cucina!Cucina! This is also a popular watering hole for marina types who arrive by boat.

1001 Fairview Ave. N. (on Lake Union). ⓒ **206/447-0769**. www.bluwaterbistro.com. Reservations accepted only for parties of 6 or more. Main courses $6.75–$12.75 at lunch, $14.75–$21 at dinner. AE, MC, V. Daily 11:30am–2am.

Ivar's Salmon House 🏮🏮 *Kids* SEAFOOD   With a view of the Space Needle on the far side of Lake Union, flotillas of sea kayaks silently slipping by, sailboats racing across the lake, and powerboaters tying up at the dock out back,
this restaurant on the north side of Lake Union is quintessential Seattle. Add to
the scene an award-winning building designed to resemble a Northwest Coast
Indian longhouse, and you have what just might be the very best place in town
for a waterfront meal. OK, so maybe, just maybe, you can find better food at a
few other waterfront places, but none has the unequivocally Seattle atmosphere
you'll find at Ivar's Salmon House. This place is a magnet for weekend boaters
who abandon their own galley fare in favor of Ivar's clam chowder and famous
alder-smoked salmon. Lots of artifacts, including long dugout canoes and historic photographic portraits of Native American chiefs, make Ivar's a hit with
both kids and adults. Bear in mind that this restaurant's popularity means that
service can be slow; just relax and keep enjoying the views.

401 NE Northlake Way. 🅒 **206/632-0767.** www.ivars.net. Reservations recommended. Main courses
$8–$15 at lunch, $13–$27 at dinner. AE, MC, V. Mon–Thurs 11am–10pm, Fri–Sat 11am–11pm, Sun 10am–
2pm and 3:30–10pm.

McCormick and Schmick's Harborside 🏮 SEAFOOD   With its waterfront
setting and views of the marinas on the west side of Lake Union, this restaurant
has the best location of any of Seattle's McCormick and Schmick's restaurants.
The menu, which changes daily, includes seemingly endless choices of appetizers, sandwiches, salads, and creative entrees. Just be sure to order something with
seafood, such as seared rare ahi with a nori (seaweed) wrap and wasabi;
Parmesan-crusted petrale sole; or blackened catfish with tequila and rock shrimp
sauce. Sure, there are meat dishes on the menu, but why bother (unless you only
came here for the excellent view)? Bar specials for $1.95 are available in the late
afternoon and late evening, and there are always plenty of varieties of oysters on
the half shell.

1200 Westlake Ave. N. 🅒 **206/270-9052.** www.mandsharborside.com. Reservations recommended. Main
courses $6–$25. AE, DC, DISC, MC, V. Mon–Fri 11:30am–11pm, Sat–Sun 11:30am–3pm (summer only) and
4–11pm.

Serafina 🏮🏮 RUSTIC ITALIAN   Off the beaten tourist track, Serafina is
one of our favorite Seattle dining spots. It has a nice touch of sophistication but
overall, it's a relaxed, neighborhood sort of place. The rustic, romantic atmosphere underscores the earthy, country-style dishes served here. The antipasti Serafina is always a good choice for a starter and changes daily. It's also hard to resist
ordering at least one of the bruschetta appetizers, which come with any of three
different toppings. Among the pasta offerings you might find a rabbit ragout
served over papperdelle pasta or veal meatballs in a green olive-tomato sauce
served over Italian *strangozzi* pasta. If you've brought a big appetite, try the
mixed grill. There's live music (mostly jazz and Latin) several nights each week.

2043 Eastlake Ave. E. 🅒 **206/323-0807.** www.serafinaseattle.com. Reservations recommended. Pastas
$8–$16; entrees $14–$22. MC, V. Mon–Fri 11:30am–2pm; Sun–Thurs 5:30–10pm, Fri–Sat 5:30–11pm.

INEXPENSIVE

Cucina!Cucina! 🏮 *Kids* ITALIAN   Although it's part of a local restaurant
chain, Cucina!Cucina! is a good bet not only for its waterfront view and reliable
pizzas and pasta, but for its lively party atmosphere. Located at the south end of
Lake Union, this restaurant is also a favorite of Seattle families because of all
the special attention kids are given here. But just because families are welcome

doesn't mean this place isn't fun for grown-ups, too. In summer, the deck is the place to be.

Chandler's Cove, 901 Fairview Ave. N. ℭ 206/447-2782. www.cucinacucina.com. Call ahead to place name on wait list. Main courses $9–$19. AE, DC, DISC, MC, V. Sun–Thurs 11:30am–10pm, Fri–Sat 11:30am–11pm (open 1 hr. later in summer).

Siam on Lake Union ⊛ THAI   Although this large, casual restaurant, one of the best Thai restaurants in Seattle, isn't located right on the lake, it's close enough to be convenient if you're staying at one of the hotels in Lake Union. The *tom yum* soups, made with either shrimp or chicken, are among the richest and creamiest we've ever had—also some of the spiciest. If you prefer your food less fiery, let your server know. Just remember that they mean it when they say very hot. The pad Thai (spicy fried noodles) is excellent, and the *nua phad bai graplau* (spicy meat and vegetables) is properly fragrant with chiles and basil leaves. A second, smaller restaurant, Siam on Broadway, is located at 616 Broadway E. (ℭ **206/324-0892**).

1880 Fairview Ave. E ℭ 206/323-8101. Reservations recommended on weekends. Main courses $7.25–$12. AE, DC, MC, V. Mon–Thurs 11:30am–10pm, Fri 11:30am–11pm, Sat 5–11pm, Sun 5–10pm.

8 Capitol Hill & East Seattle

Also worth trying in this area are **Siam on Broadway,** 616 Broadway E. (ℭ **206/324-0892**), which is affiliated with Siam on Lake Union (see the listing just above), and **Pizzeria Pagliacci,** 426 Broadway E. (ℭ **206/324-0730**), which is affiliated with the Pizzeria Pagliacci in the Lower Queen Anne neighborhood (see the review on p. 82).

VERY EXPENSIVE

Rover's ⊛⊛⊛ NORTHWEST   Tucked away in a quaint clapboard house behind a chic little shopping center in the Madison Valley neighborhood east of downtown, this is one of Seattle's most acclaimed restaurants. Thierry Rautureau, Rover's much-celebrated and award-winning chef, received classical French training before falling in love with the Northwest and all the wonderful ingredients it has to offer an imaginative chef. Voilà! Northwest cuisine with a French accent.

The delicacies on the frequently changing menu are enough to send the most jaded of gastronomes into fits of indecision. Luckily, you can simply opt for one of the fixed-price dinners and leave the decision making to a professional—the chef. Culinary creations include such offerings as smoked salmon and cucumber salad, spice-infused pinot noir sorbet, and venison with caramelized turnips and Armagnac sauce. Vegetarians, take note: You won't often find a vegetarian feast that can compare with the ones served here.

2808 E. Madison St. ℭ 206/325-7442. www.rovers-seattle.com. Reservations required. 5-course menu degustation $70 (vegetarian) and $80; chef's 8-course grand menu $115. AE, DC, MC, V. Tues–Sat 5:30–about 9:30pm.

INEXPENSIVE

Cafe Flora ⊛ VEGETARIAN   Big, bright, and airy, this Madison Valley cafe will dispel any ideas you might have about vegetarian food being boring. This is meatless gourmet cooking and draws on influences from around the world—a vegetarian's dream come true. One of the house specialties is a portobello Wellington made with mushroom-pecan pâté and sautéed leeks in a puff pastry. While the menu changes weekly, unusual pizzas (such as roasted fig, Walla Walla onion masala chutney, toasted hazelnuts, and goat cheese) are always on the menu. On weekends, a casual brunch features interesting breakfast fare.

2901 E. Madison St. © **206/325-9100.** www.cafeflora.com. Reservations accepted only for parties of 8 or more. Main courses $9.25–$16. MC, V. Tues–Fri 11:30am–10pm, Sat 9am–2pm and 5–10pm, Sun 9am–2pm and 5–9pm.

Gravity Bar ✦ VEGETARIAN/NATURAL FOODS   If you're young and hip and concerned about the food that you put into your body, this is the place for a quick, cheap meal on Capitol Hill. The juice list includes all manner of unusual combinations, with catchy names like Dragon Slayer, Martian Martini, or 7-year Spinach. The postmodern, neoindustrial decor is the antithesis of the wholesome juices and meals served here.

415 Broadway E. © **206/325-7186.** Meals $4.50–$7.50; juices $2.50–$5.25. MC, V. Sun–Thurs 10am–10pm, Fri–Sat 10am–11pm.

9 North Seattle (Including Fremont, Wallingford & the University District)

EXPENSIVE

Ponti Seafood Grill ✦✦ SEAFOOD   Situated at the south end of the Fremont Bridge overlooking the Lake Washington Ship Canal (not officially in north Seattle), Ponti is one of Seattle's most elegant and sophisticated restaurants. The menu here, which changes weekly, has an international flavor that roams the globe from Thailand to Italy, though it also offers some solidly Northwestern creations. Perennial favorites among the appetizers include Dungeness crab spring rolls with a chile-lime dipping sauce, and the Cajun barbecued prawns. The weekly listing of fresh seafoods might include the likes of grilled rare ahi with a coconut-rice cake or a simple penne pasta with grilled prawns. The lunch menu includes some of the same dishes served at dinner (though at sometimes half the price), which makes this restaurant a good bet for a gourmet midday meal on a tight budget. Before or after you dine here, take a walk around Fremont to check out the funky shops and eclectic public art.

3014 Third Ave. N. © **206/284-3000.** Reservations recommended. Main courses $8–$14 at lunch, $16–$29 at dinner. AE, DC, DISC, MC, V. Mon–Fri 11:30am–2:30pm, Sun 10am–2:30pm (brunch); Sun–Thurs 5–10pm, Fri–Sat 5–11pm.

MODERATE

Chinook's at Salmon Bay ✦ SEAFOOD   Seattle's Fishermen's Terminal, the winter home of the large Alaska fishing fleet, is located just across the Lake Washington Ship Canal from the Ballard neighborhood. Overlooking all the moored commercial fishing boats, you'll find one of Seattle's favorite seafood restaurants, a big, casual, boisterous place with walls of windows looking out onto the marina. With a long menu featuring seafood fresh off the boats, this place tries to have a little something for everyone. However, our recommendation is to go for the alder-plank-roasted salmon with maybe some oyster stew to start things off.

The only real problem with this place is that it isn't very easy to reach. Take Elliott Avenue north from the downtown waterfront, continue north on 15th Avenue West, take the last exit before crossing the Ballard Bridge, and follow the signs to Fishermen's Terminal. Before or after a meal, stroll around the marina and have a look at all the fishing boats.

1900 W. Nickerson St. © **206/283-4665.** Reservations not accepted. Main courses $7–$20. AE, DISC, MC, V. Mon–Thurs 11am–10pm, Fri 11am–11pm, Sat 7:30am–11pm, Sun 7:30am–10pm.

Ray's Boathouse and Cafe ✸✸ SEAFOOD   When Seattleites want to impress visiting friends and relatives, this restaurant often ranks right up there with the Space Needle, the ferries, and Pike Place Market. The view across Puget Sound to the Olympic Mountains is superb. You can also watch the boat traffic coming and going from the Lake Washington Ship Canal, and bald eagles can often be seen fishing just offshore. Then there's Ray's dual personality—upstairs there's a lively (and loud) cafe and lounge, while downstairs there's a much more formal and sedate scene. The upstairs menu is more creative and less expensive than the one downstairs but even upstairs, you can order from the downstairs menu. The crab cakes are delicious and are packed full of crab, and the smoked scallops are tender and delicately flavored. The black cod glazed with sake kasu is a typically Northwestern preparation well worth trying. Whatever your mood, Ray's has got you covered. No reservations are taken for dinner upstairs, and waiting times of up to an hour are not unusual (which is why the bar gets so lively).

6049 Seaview Ave. NW. ✆ **206/789-3770.** www.rays.com. Reservations recommended (not accepted for dinner in cafe). Main courses $16–$45 (Boathouse), $8.50–$17 (Cafe). AE, DC, DISC, MC, V. Boathouse Mon–Thurs 5–10pm, Fri 5–10:30pm, Sat 4:30–10:30pm, Sun 4:30–10pm. Cafe Sun–Thurs 11:30am–10pm, Fri–Sat 11:30am–10:30pm.

INEXPENSIVE

Himalayan Sherpa Restaurant ✸ *Finds* HIMALAYAN   If you've ever been to Nepal, you may not remember the food with the fondest of memories. But should you be struck with pangs of nostalgia for that trek you once did, you might be interested to know that you can relive your fonder Himalayan culinary memories in Seattle's University District. The food here is both surprisingly authentic and far superior to most of the Nepali food served in budget restaurants in Nepal. For the full experience, opt for the Nepalese fixed menu or the Himalayan Sherpa combo. With a minimum of four people and an hour's notice, the restaurant can also prepare a traditional Tibetan hot-pot (*gyakok*) dinner for you.

4214 University Way NE. ✆ **206/633-2100.** www.himalayansherpa.com. Reservations recommended. Main courses $6.50–$15. AE, MC, V. Daily 10am–10pm.

Red Mill Burgers AMERICAN   Located just a little north of the Woodland Park Zoo, this retro burger joint is tiny and always hoppin' because everyone knows they do one of the best burgers in Seattle. Try the verde burger, made with Anaheim peppers for just the right amount of fire. Don't miss the onion rings. Burgers here are definitely multinapkin affairs.

312 N. 67th St. ✆ **206/783-6362.** Burgers $3–$5. No credit cards. Tues–Sat 11am–9pm, Sun noon–8pm.

10 West Seattle

EXPENSIVE

Salty's on Alki Beach ✸ SEAFOOD   Although the prices here are almost as out of line as those at the Space Needle, and the service is unpredictable, this restaurant has *the* waterfront view in Seattle, and the food is usually pretty good. Because the restaurant is set on the northeast side of the Alki Peninsula, it faces downtown Seattle on the far side of Elliott Bay. Come at sunset for dinner and watch the setting sun sparkle off skyscraper windows as the lights of the city twinkle on. On sunny summer days, lunch on one of the two decks is a sublimely Seattle experience. Don't be discouraged by the ugly industrial/port area you drive through to get here; Salty's marks the start of Alki Beach, the closest Seattle comes to a Southern California beach scene. Just watch for the giant rusted salmon sculptures swimming amid rebar kelp beds and the remains of an old bridge (hey, Seattle even recycles when it comes to art).

1936 Harbor Ave. SW. ℂ 206/937-1600. www.saltys.com. Reservations recommended. Main courses $20–$40. AE, DC, DISC, MC, V. Daily 11am–11:30pm.

11 The Eastside (Including Bellevue & Kirkland)

By far the most celebrated restaurant on the Eastside is the **Herbfarm,** a much-lauded restaurant serving herb-driven Northwest cuisine. The restaurant's nine-course dinners are legendary in the Northwest. For information on this restaurant, which in 2001 moved into a new building in Woodinville, see the review on p. 174, in chapter 10, "Side Trips from Seattle."

EXPENSIVE

Third Floor Fish Cafe ★★ SEAFOOD   Take the elevator up to the third floor of this downtown Kirkland restaurant for fabulous views of Lake Washington and seafood cooked with an expert touch. The atmosphere is very clubby and the clientele tends to be well off and well dressed. It's the superb seafood that pulls them in; you might start with Dungeness crab spring rolls or house-cured salmon tartare. As at so many other restaurants around town, seared ahi tuna is currently very popular, here served with a peppercorn crust and whatever seasonal sides strike the fancy of the chef. Seared scallops have also become quite popular in Seattle; here they might be served with a potato gratin, carrot purée, and crispy onions. There's also an extensive, well-chosen wine list, and five- and seven-course tasting menus are available nightly.

205 Lake St. S., Kirkland. ℂ 425/822-3553. www.fishcafe.com. Reservations recommended. Main courses $19–$32. AE, DC, DISC, MC, V. Daily 5pm–closing. Lounge 4pm–closing.

Yarrow Bay Grill ★★ NORTHWEST   The combination of Northwest cuisine and a view across Lake Washington to Seattle has made this restaurant, in the upscale Carillon Point retail, office, and condo development, a favorite of Eastside diners. The setting is decidedly nouveau riche and about as close as you get to a Southern California setting in the Northwest. The menu is not so long that you can't make a decision, yet long enough to provide some serious options. The Thai-style crab cake appetizers with a sweet mustard sauce are favorites of ours, as is the peanut-chile dusted calamari. Entrees are equally divided between seafoods and meats, with at least one vegetarian dish on the menu daily. Keep in mind that the menu changes daily. Nearly every table has a view, and there is a great deck for good weather. By the way, rumor has it that this restaurant is a favorite of Bill Gates.

1270 Carillon Point, Kirkland. ℂ 425/889-9052. www.ybgrill.com. Reservations recommended. Main courses $17–$39. AE, DC, DISC, MC, V. Mon–Fri 11:30am–2:30pm, Sun 10am–2:30pm (brunch); daily 5:30–10pm.

MODERATE

Beach Café ★★ INTERNATIONAL   Affiliated with the Yarrow Bay Grill, which is located just upstairs, this casual waterfront cafe is the Eastside's best bet for an economical and creative meal with a view. In summer, the patio dining area just can't be beat. The menu circles the globe bringing a very satisfying mélange of flavors to Bellevue diners. The weekly specials further add to the international flavor. On a recent visit, the Caribbean was the theme of the week and the Haitian *griots* (pork marinated in orange juice, habanero chiles, chives, and onions) was spicy and full of unusual flavor.

1270 Carillon Point, Kirkland. ⓒ 425/889-0303. www.ybbeachcafe.com. Reservations recommended. Main courses $13–$24. AE, DC, DISC, MC, V. Mon–Thurs 11am–10:30pm, Fri–Sat 11am–11pm, Sun 11am–10pm.

12 Coffee, Tea, Bakeries & Pastry Shops

CAFES, COFFEE BARS & TEA SHOPS

Unless you've been on Mars for the past decade, you're likely aware that Seattle has become the espresso capital of America. Seattleites are positively rabid about coffee, which isn't just a hot drink or a caffeine fix anymore, but rather a way of life. You'll never be more than about a block from your next cup. There are espresso carts on the sidewalks, drive-through espresso windows, espresso bars, gas station espresso counters, espresso milk shakes, espresso chocolates, even eggnog lattes at Christmas.

Starbucks, the ruling king of coffee, is seemingly everywhere you turn in Seattle. They sell some 36 types and blends of coffee beans. **SBC,** also known as Seattle's Best Coffee, doesn't have as many shops as Starbucks, but it does have a very devoted clientele. Close on the heels of Starbucks and SBC is the **Tully's** chain, which seems to have opened an espresso bar on every corner that doesn't already have a Starbucks or an SBC. However, serious espresso junkies swear by **Torrefazione** and **Caffe Appassionato.** If you see one of either of these chains, check it out and see what you think.

Coffee bars and cafes are as popular as bars and pubs as places to hang out and visit with friends. Among our favorite Seattle cafes are the following (organized by neighborhood):

PIONEER SQUARE & THE INTERNATIONAL DISTRICT

The Pioneer Square location of **Torrefazione** ✵✵, 320 Occidental Ave. S. (ⓒ **206/624-5847**), with its hand-painted Italian crockery, has a very old-world feel. The foam on the lattes here is absolutely perfect. Great pastries, too. Other Torrefaziones can be found at 622 Olive Way (ⓒ **206/624-1429**), 1310 Fourth Ave. (ⓒ **206/583-8970**), and in Fremont at 701 N. 34th St. (ⓒ **206/ 545-2721**).

Zeitgeist Art/Coffee ✵, 171 S. Jackson St. (ⓒ **206/583-0497**), with its big windows and local artwork, is popular with the Pioneer Square art crowd. Luckily, there's a dictionary on hand so you can look up the word *zeitgeist.*

BELLTOWN & PIKE PLACE MARKET

The Crumpet Shop ✵, 1503 First Ave. (ⓒ **206/682-1598**), in Pike Place Market, specializes in its British namesake pastries but also does scones. It's almost a requirement that you accompany your crumpet or scone with a pot of tea.

LUX coffeebar, 2226 First Ave. (ⓒ **206/443-0962**), in stylish Belltown, is a retrohip hangout popular with design school students. Indulge in lowbrow, low-key luxury while sipping a latte and perusing the latest design magazines.

THE SEATTLE CENTER & QUEEN ANNE AREAS

Queen Anne Caffe Appassionato ✵✵, 1417 Queen Anne Ave. N. (ⓒ **206/ 270-8760**), an attractive little espresso bar right at the top of Queen Anne Hill (and just a short drive from the Space Needle), serves what many Seattleites contend is the best espresso in Seattle. We just might agree.

Caffe Ladro Espresso Bar & Bakery ✵✵, 2205 Queen Anne Ave. N. (ⓒ **206/282-5313**), in the heart of the pleasant Queen Anne area, has the feel of a cozy neighborhood coffeehouse. There's another Caffe Ladro in the Mar-Queen Hotel building in Lower Queen Anne at 600 Queen Anne Ave. N. (© **206/282-1549**).

Uptown Espresso, 525 Queen Anne Ave. N. (© **206/285-3757**), with its crystal chandelier, gilt-framed classical painting, and opera music on the stereo, has a very theatrical, European feel. Good baked goodies and Internet access, too. There's another Uptown in Belltown at 2504 Fourth Ave.

CAPITOL HILL & EAST SEATTLE
Bauhaus Coffee & Books ✧, 301 E. Pine St. (© **206/625-1600**), on the downtown edge of Capitol Hill, is a great place to hang out and soak up the neighborhood atmosphere. There are always lots of interesting 30-something types hanging out reading or carrying on heated discussions.

NORTH SEATTLE
Café Allegro, 4214 University Way NE (© **206/633-3030**), located down an alley around the corner from University Way in the U District, is Seattle's oldest cafe and a favored hangout of University of Washington students. Keep looking; you'll find it.

Still Life in Fremont Coffeehouse ✧, 709 N. 35th St. (© **206/547-9850**), in the eclectic Fremont neighborhood, harks back to hippie hangouts of old. It's big and always crowded, offering good vegetarian meals and great weekend breakfasts, too.

Teahouse Kuan Yin, 1911 N. 45th St. (© **206/632-2055**), in the Wallingford neighborhood, is one of Seattle's favorite coffee alternatives. This Asian-inspired tea shop not only serves an amazing variety of teas, but also sells all manner of tea paraphernalia.

BAKERIES & PASTRY SHOPS
PIONEER SQUARE & THE INTERNATIONAL DISTRICT
Grand Central Baking Company ✧, 214 First Ave. S. (© **206/622-3644**), in Pioneer Square's Grand Central Arcade, is responsible for awakening Seattle to the pleasures of rustic European-style breads. This bakery not only turns out great bread, but also does good pastries and sandwiches.

BELLTOWN & PIKE PLACE MARKET
Le Panier, 1902 Pike Place (© **206/441-3669**), located in the heart of Pike Place Market, is a great place to get a croissant and a latte and watch the market action.

Macrina ✧✧, 2408 First Ave. (© **206/448-4032**), a neighborhood bakery/cafe in Belltown, serves some of the best baked goodies in the city and is a cozy place for a quick, cheap breakfast or lunch. In the morning, the smell of baking bread wafts down First Avenue and draws in many a passerby.

With a wall of glass cases full of baked goods and a window facing onto one of the busiest spots in Pike Place Market, **Three Girls Bakery,** 1514 Pike Place, Stall no. 1 (© **206/622-1045**), is a favorite place to grab a few pastries or other goodies to go. There is, however, a counter in back where you can sit down.

THE SEATTLE CENTER & QUEEN ANNE AREAS
Located near the northwest corner of Seattle Center, **The Famous Pacific Dessert Company** ✧✧, 127 Mercer St. (© **206/284-8100**), is an out-of-the-way pastry shop that serves some of the most delicious desserts you'll find in Seattle. A great posttheater spot.

CAPITOL HILL & EAST SEATTLE

Basically, **Dilettante Chocolates** ✸✸, 416 Broadway E. (© **206/329-6463**), is a chocolate restaurant that happens to be Seattle's leading proponent of cocoa as the next drink to take the country by storm. If you don't order something with chocolate here, you're missing the point.

NORTH SEATTLE

Let's say you've spent the morning or afternoon at the zoo and you're suddenly struck with a craving for a fresh apple tart or an almond croissant. What's a person to do? Make tracks to **Boulangerie** ✸, 2200 N. 45th St. (© **206/ 634-2211**), a Wallingford neighborhood French pastry shop, that's what.

13 Quick Bites

If you're just looking for something quick and cheap and don't want to resort to McDonald's or Burger King, consider grabbing a wrap. It can be just about anything in a tortilla and has become the food of choice in Seattle these days. Keep your eyes out for a **World Wraps** (of which there are many all around the city).

For variety of types of foods available, it's hard to beat the food court on the top floor of **Westlake Center** shopping mall, 400 Pine St. If you're downtown at lunch and just want a gourmet sandwich and pasta salad that you can grab out of a case, stop by **Briazz Cafe,** 1400 Fifth Ave. (© **206/343-3099**).

MARKET MUNCHING

There are few Seattle activities more fun than munching your way through Pike Place Market. There are dozens of fast-food vendors in the market, and it is nearly impossible to resist the interesting finger foods and quick bites. Here are some of our favorite places:

If you're planning a picnic, **DeLaurenti** ✸✸, at 1435 First Ave. near the Market's brass pig (© **206/622-0141**), is the perfect spot to get your pâté, bread, and wine.

Piroshky, Piroshky, 1908 Pike Place (© **206/441-6068**), lays it all out right there in its name. The sweet or savory Russian filled rolls are the perfect finger food.

Three Girls Bakery, 1514 Pike Place, stall no. 1 (© **206/622-1045**), has not only the bread-and-pastry window on the sidewalk, but a lunch counter as well.

World Class Chili ✸, inside the Market's south arcade at 1411 First Ave. (© **206/623-3678**), really lives up to its name. If you're a chili connoisseur, don't pass it by.

To give direction to a tour of Pike Place Market, why not spend the morning or afternoon shopping for interesting picnic items, then head up to the north end of the waterfront to Myrtle Edwards Park? Or, since a picnic of foods from Pike Place Market should be as special as the food shopping experience, consider heading a bit farther afield, perhaps to Discovery Point, Seattle's waterfront urban wilderness (take Western Avenue north along Elliott Bay to Magnolia and follow the signs). Another good place for a picnic is in Volunteer Park, high atop Capitol Hill. Alternatively, you could have your picnic aboard a ferry headed to Bainbridge Island (a 30-min. trip) or to Bremerton (a 1-hr. trip).

6

Exploring Seattle

I hope you've got a good pair of walking shoes and a lot of stamina (a double latte helps), because Seattle is a walking town. The city's two biggest attractions—the waterfront and Pike Place Market—are the sort of places where you'll spend hours on your feet poking into nooks and crannies. When your feet are beat, you can relax on a tour boat and enjoy the views of the city from out on the waters of the Puget Sound, or you can take a 2-minute rest on the monorail, which links downtown Seattle with Seattle Center, which is home to both the Space Needle and the Experience Music Project. If your energy level sags, don't worry, there's always another espresso bar on the next block.

By the way, that monorail ride will now take you right through the middle of Paul Allen's Experience Music Project, the Frank Gehry–designed rock music museum. Paul Allen, who made his millions as one of the cofounders of Microsoft, is also busily changing the face of the south end of downtown. Here he has renovated Union Station and developed the area

adjacent to where the city's new football stadium is being built. (By the way, Allen also owns the Seattle Seahawks football team that will play in the new stadium.) That stadium is scheduled to be ready for the 2002 football season, but the Seattle Mariners have already settled into their impressive $500 million Safeco Field, which debuted in 1999 as one of the few stadiums in the country with a retractable roof.

However, despite Seattle's many downtown diversions, the city's natural surroundings are still its primary attraction. You can easily cover all of Seattle's museums and major sights in 2 or 3 days, and with the help of the itineraries below, you should have a good idea of what not to miss. These itineraries will provide a good overview of the history, natural resources, and cultural diversity that have made Seattle the city it is today.

Once you've seen what's to see indoors, you can begin exploring the city's outdoor life. A car is not entirely necessary, but it's helpful, and if you want to head farther afield—say to Mount Rainier, the San Juans, or the Olympic Peninsula—it's a must.

SUGGESTED ITINERARIES

If You Have 1 Day

Start your day at **Pike Place Market,** Seattle's sprawling historic market complex. In the market, you can buy fresh salmon and Dungeness crabs packed to go, peruse the offerings of produce and flower vendors, buy art and crafts directly

from the makers, and explore the dark depths of the market for unusual shops.

After you've had your fill of the market, head down the Pike Hill Climb to the Seattle waterfront. Directly across the street from the foot of the Hill Climb is Pier 59, site of the **Seattle Aquarium,** where you can learn about the sea life of the region and, next door at the IMAXDome, catch an IMAX film about Mount St. Helens.

If you walk south from the aquarium to Pier 55, you can set sail on a 1-hour **harbor tour cruise.** A variety of other boat excursions are also available along the waterfront. You'll pass numerous overpriced seafood restaurants (most with good views and some with good food), as well as quite a few fish-and-chips counters.

When you pass the Washington State Ferries Colman Dock terminal, head away from the waterfront and into the historic **Pioneer Square** area. If you have an appreciation for bad humor and history, the **Seattle Underground Tour** (see "Good Times in Bad Taste" on p. 96) will provide a little fun and give you a good idea of Seattle's early history.

After exploring Pioneer Square aboveground, head up James Street to the bus tunnel entrance and catch a free bus north to the Westlake Center station. In Westlake Center, an upscale shopping center, you can catch the monorail to Seattle Center, where, if you're a rock music fan, you can explore the **Experience Music Project** and ride the elevator to the top of the **Space Needle,** a great place to finish a long day's exploration.

If You Have 2 Days

If you have 2 days, you can be more leisurely than the rather hectic 1-day itinerary above. On your first day, spend a bit more time in Pike Place Market before heading down to the waterfront. After exploring the aquarium, consider doing the **Tillicum Village Tour,** which includes a boat excursion to Blake Island State Park, where you'll be fed a salmon dinner and entertained with traditional Northwest Coast Native American masked dances.

Start your second day in Pioneer Square and take the Seattle Underground Tour. Then wander over to the nearby **International District (Chinatown)** and have lunch (Hing Loon is one of our favorite spots; see chapter 5, "Where to Dine in Seattle"). After lunch, take the free bus through the bus tunnel to the **Seattle Art Museum.** After exploring the museum, continue north to Westlake Center and take the monorail to Seattle Center, where you can check out the **Experience Music Project** or head to the top of the **Space Needle.**

If You Have 3 Days

Start off by following the 2-day strategy outlined above. On your third day, do something very Seattle. Rent a sea kayak on Lake Union, go in-line skating in Green Lake Park, or rent a bike and ride the Burke-Gilman Trail. Wander around the funky **Fremont** neighborhood and maybe go to the **Woodland Park Zoo** or the **Burke Museum,** depending on your interests.

If You Have 4 Days or More

On your fourth and fifth days, plan to take a trip or two outside the city to nearby Mount Rainier, Snoqualmie Falls, Bainbridge Island, the San Juan Islands, or Mount St. Helens. All these trips can be turned into overnighters or longer (see chapter 10, "Side Trips from Seattle," for details on the first four destinations; see chapter 20, "Side Trips from Portland," for an excursion to Mount St. Helens).

Seattle Attractions

To Airport →

Broadway

7th Ave. S.

Maynard Ave. S.

5th Ave. S.

4th Ave. S.

6th Ave. S.

Washington St.

S. Main St.

Safeco Field

INTERNATIONAL DISTRICT

Union Station

King St. Station (Amtrak)

Occidental Ave. S.

Yesler Way

S. Jackson St.

King St.

3rd Ave. S.

2nd Ave. S.

1st Ave. S.

Alaskan Way

Jefferson St.

CITY HALL PARK

PIONEER SQUARE

Pier 47

Pier 46

James St.

Cherry St.

Columbia St.

FIRST HILL

Marion St.

Terry Ave.

9th Ave.

8th Ave.

7th Ave.

6th Ave.

5th Ave.

4th Ave.

3rd Ave.

2nd Ave.

1st Ave.

Western Ave.

Pier 49

Pier 48

Madison St.

Spring St.

Seneca St.

University St.

Union St.

Pike St.

Pine St.

DOWNTOWN

Post Office

Alaskan Way Viaduct

Pier 52

Pier 53

Pier 54

Pier 55

Pier 56

Pier 57

Pier 58

Pier 59

Pier 60

Pier 61

Pier 62

Pier 63

Elliott Bay

CONVENTION CENTER

Olive Way

Terry Ave. N.

9th Ave. N.

8th Ave. N.

Westlake Ave. N.

Bus Station

← To Seattle Center & Space Needle

Stewart St.

Virginia St.

BELLTOWN

4th Ave. N.

1st Ave.

Pier 64

Pier 65

Pier 66

Alaskan Way

1/5 Mi

0.2 Km

Argosy Cruises **9**
Bank of America Tower **15**
Frye Art Museum **16**
IMAXDome Theater **10**
Klondike Gold Rush
  National Historical Park **3**
Occidental Park **4**
Odyssey—The Maritime
  Discovery Center **14**
Pike Place Market **13**
Safeco Field **2**
The Seattle Aquarium **11**
Seattle Art Museum **12**
Smith Tower **6**
Tillicum Village Tours **9**
Underground Tour **5**
Washington State Ferries **7**
Wing Luke Asian Museum **1**
Ye Olde Curiosity Shop **8**

Map Area

SEATTLE

1 On the Waterfront

The Seattle waterfront, which lies along Alaskan Way between Yesler Way in the south and Bay Street and Myrtle Edwards Park in the north, is the city's most popular attraction. Yes, it's very touristy, with tacky gift shops, saltwater taffy, T-shirts galore, and lots of overpriced restaurants, but it's also home to the Seattle Aquarium, the IMAXDome Theater, Odyssey—The Maritime Discovery Center, and Ye Olde Curiosity Shop (king of the tacky gift shops). Ferries to Bainbridge Island and Bremerton, as well as several different boat tours, also operate from the waterfront. This is also the best place to hire a horse-drawn carriage for a spin around downtown.

You'll find the Washington State Ferries terminal at **Pier 52,** which is at the south end of the waterfront near Pioneer Square. (A ferry ride makes for a cheap cruise.) At **Pier 55,** you'll find excursion boats offering harbor cruises and trips to Tillicum Village on Blake Island. At **Pier 56,** cruise boats leave for trips through the Chittenden (Ballard) Locks to Lake Union. See section 7, "Organized Tours," later in this chapter, for details. Here you'll also find the Bay Pavilion, which has a vintage carousel and a video arcade to keep the kids busy.

At **Pier 59,** you'll find the Seattle Aquarium (see below for details), the IMAXDome Theater (see below), and a small waterfront park. Continuing up the waterfront, you'll find **Pier 66,** the Bell Street Pier, which has a rooftop park. This is also the site of Odyssey—The Maritime Discovery Center (see below), which is dedicated to the history of shipping and fishing in Puget Sound, and Anthony's, the hippest restaurant on the waterfront (see chapter 5 for a full review). At **Pier 67,** you'll find the Edgewater hotel, a great place to take in the sunset over a drink or dinner (see chapter 4, "Where to Stay in Seattle," for details).

Next door, at **Pier 69,** you'll come to the dock for the ferries that ply the waters between Seattle and Victoria, British Columbia, and at **Pier 70,** you'll find the *Spirit of Puget Sound* cruise ship (see p. 112 for details). Just north of this pier is grassy Myrtle Edwards Park, a nice finale to a very pleasant waterfront. This park has a popular bicycling and skating trail, and is the northern terminus for the Waterfront Streetcar, which can take you back to your starting point.

⟨Value Saving Money on Sightseeing

If you're a see-it-all, do-it-all kind of person, you'll definitely want to buy a **CityPass** (📞 707/256-0490; www.citypass.com), which gets you into the Space Needle, Pacific Science Center, Seattle Aquarium, Woodland Park Zoo, and Museum of Flight at a savings of 50% if you visit all six attractions. The pass also includes a harbor cruise with Argosy Cruises. The passes, good for 9 days from date of first use, cost $33.50 for adults, $29 for seniors, and $21.50 for children. Purchase your CityPass at any of the participating attractions.

You might also want to drop by the **Seattle–King County Convention and Visitors Bureau Visitor Center,** Washington State Convention & Trade Center, 800 Convention Place, Galleria Level, at the corner of Eighth Avenue and Pike Street (📞 206/461-5840; www.seeseattle.org). Here you can grab a copy of the "Seattle's Favorite Attractions" booklet, which includes coupons good for discounts at numerous area attractions.

IMAXDome Theater ⊛ The IMAXDome is a movie theater with a 180° screen that fills your peripheral vision and puts you right in the middle of the action. This huge wraparound theater is adjacent to the Seattle Aquarium, and for many years now has featured a film about the eruption of Mount St. Helens. Various other special features are screened throughout the year, and in 2002, *Island of the Sharks* and *Dolphins* will both be showing here.

Pier 59, 1483 Alaskan Way. ℂ 206/622-1868. www.seattleimaxdome.com. Admission $7 adults, $6.50 seniors, $6 youth, free under 5 (IMAXDome–Aquarium combination tickets available). Screenings daily beginning at 10am. Closed Christmas. Bus: 15 or 18; then walk through Pike Place Market to the waterfront. Waterfront Streetcar: To Pike Place Market stop.

Odyssey—The Maritime Discovery Center Sort of an interactive promotion for modern fishing and shipping, this facility at the north end of the Seattle waterfront is aimed primarily at kids and has more than 40 hands-on exhibits highlighting Seattle's modern working waterfront and its links to the sea. Exhibits include a kid-size fishing boat, a virtual kayak trip through the Puget Sound, and a live radar center that allows you to track the movement of vessels in Elliott Bay. In another exhibit, you get to use a simulated crane to practice loading a scale model of a cargo ship.

Pier 66 (Bell Street Pier), 2205 Alaskan Way. ℂ 206/374-4000. www.ody.org. Admission $6.75 adults, $4.50 seniors and students, free for children under 5. Tues–Sat 10am–5pm, Sun noon–5pm. Bus: 15 or 18; then walk through Pike Place Market to the waterfront. Waterfront Trolley: Bell Street Station.

The Seattle Aquarium ⊛⊛ Although not nearly as large and impressive as either the Monterey Bay Aquarium or the Oregon Coast Aquarium, the Seattle Aquarium is still quite enjoyable and presents well-designed exhibits dealing with the water worlds of the Puget Sound region. The star attractions here are the playful river otters and the sea otters, as well as the giant octopus. There's also an underwater viewing dome, from which you get a fish's-eye view of life beneath the waves, and each September, you can watch salmon return up a fish ladder to spawn. Of course there are also plenty of small tanks that allow you to familiarize yourself with the many fish of the Northwest. There's also a beautiful large coral-reef tank, as well as many smaller tanks that exhibit fish from distant waters.

Pier 59, 1483 Alaskan Way. ℂ 206/386-4300. www.seattleaquarium.org. Admission $9 adults, $8 seniors, $6.25 ages 6–18, $4.25 ages 3–5 (joint Aquarium–IMAXDome tickets also available). Labor Day–Memorial Day daily 10am–5pm; Memorial Day–Labor Day daily 9:30am–7pm. Bus: 15 or 18; then walk through Pike Place Market to the waterfront. Waterfront Streetcar: To Pike Place Market stop.

2 Pike Place Market to Pioneer Square

Pike Place Market and the Pioneer Square historic district lie at opposite ends of First Avenue; midway between the two is the Seattle Art Museum.

The **Pioneer Square** area, with its historic buildings, interesting shops, museum, and **Seattle Underground Tour** (see the box titled "Good Times in Bad Taste," below), is well worth exploring. We've outlined a **walking tour** of the area in chapter 7, "Strolling Around Seattle."

Pike Place Market ⊛⊛⊛ Pike Place Market, originally a farmers' market, was founded in 1907 when housewives complained that middlemen were raising the price of produce. The market allowed shoppers to buy directly from producers, and thus save on grocery bills. By the 1960s, however, the market was no longer the popular spot it had been. World War II had deprived it of nearly half its farmers when Japanese Americans were moved to internment camps. The

Good Times in Bad Taste

If you love bad jokes and are fascinated by the bizarre (or maybe this describes your children), you won't want to miss the Underground Tour and a visit to Ye Olde Curiosity Shop. Together, these two outings should reassure you that, espresso, traffic jams, and Microsoft aside, Seattle really does have a sense of humor.

If you have an appreciation for off-color humor and are curious about the seamier side of Seattle history, **The Underground Tour,** 608 First Ave. (© 206/682-4646; www.undergroundtour.com), will likely entertain and enlighten you. The tours lead down below street level in the Pioneer Square area, where you can still find the vestiges of Seattle businesses built before the great fire of 1889. Learn the lowdown dirt on early Seattle, a town where plumbing was problematic and a person could drown in a pothole. (Tours are held daily. The cost is $9 for adults, $7 for seniors and students ages 13–17 or with college ID, $5 for children ages 6–12; children under 6 are discouraged.)

Ye Olde Curiosity Shop, 1001 Alaskan Way, Pier 54 (© 206/ 682-5844), is a cross between a souvenir store and Ripley's Believe It or Not! The collection of oddities was started in 1899 by Joe Standley, who developed a more-than-passing interest in strange curios. It's weird! It's tacky! It's always packed! See Siamese-twin calves, a natural mummy, the Lord's Prayer on a grain of rice, a narwhal tusk, shrunken heads, a 67-pound snail, fleas in dresses—all the stuff that fascinated you as a kid.

postwar flight to the suburbs almost spelled the end of the market, and the site was being eyed for a major redevelopment project. However, a grassroots movement to save the 9-acre market culminated in its being declared a National Historic District.

Today it is once again bustling, but the 100 or so farmers and fishmongers who set up shop on the premises are only a small part of the attraction. More than 200 local craftspeople and artists can be found here, selling their creations. There are also excellent restaurants, and hundreds of shops fill the market area. Street performers serenade milling crowds. At the information booth almost directly below the large Pike Place Market sign, you can pick up a free map and guide to the market. Watch for Rachel, the giant piggy bank, and the flying fish at the Pike Place Fish stall.

Victor Steinbrueck Park, which is at the north end of the market at the intersection of Pike Place, Virginia Street, and Western Avenue, is a popular lounging area for both the homeless and people just looking for a grassy place in which to sit in the sun. In the park, you'll find two 50-foot-tall totem poles.

For a glimpse behind the scenes at the market and to learn all about its history, you can take a 1-hour guided **Market Heritage Tour** (© 206/682-7453, ext. 653, for information and reservations). Tours are offered Wednesday through Saturday at 11am and 2pm and Sunday at noon and 2pm. Tours depart from the market's Heritage Center, 1531 Western Ave. (take the Skybridge to the Market Garage and then take the elevator to the Western Avenue level). The

Heritage Center is an open-air building filled with historical exhibits. Tours cost $7 for adults and $5 for seniors and children under age 18).

One-hour tours are also offered by the **Pike Place Market Merchants Association** (© **206/587-0351;** www.seattlespublicmarket.com). The tours, which are offered by reservation and cost $7 for adults and $5 for seniors and children under 12, include a healthy dose of fun and facts plus a bit of fiction. You'll even get to meet some market merchants and learn their stories.

See the section titled "Market Munching" at the very end of chapter 5 for a rundown of some of our favorite market food vendors.

Between Pike and Pine sts. at First Ave. © **206/682-PIKE.** www.pikeplacemarket.org. Mon–Sat 10am–6pm, Sun 11am–5pm. Closed New Year's Day, Easter, Thanksgiving, Christmas. Bus: 15 or 18. Waterfront Streetcar: To Pike Place Market stop.

Klondike Gold Rush National Historical Park

It isn't in the Klondike (that's in Canada) and it isn't really a park (it's a single room in an old store), but this is a fascinating little museum. "At 3 o'clock this morning the steamship *Portland,* from St. Michaels for Seattle, passed up [Puget] Sound with more than a ton of gold on board and 68 passengers." When the *Seattle Post-Intelligencer* published that sentence on July 17, 1897, it started a stampede. Would-be miners heading for the Klondike goldfields in the 1890s made Seattle their outfitting center and helped turn it into a prosperous city. When they struck it rich up north, they headed back to Seattle, the first U.S. outpost of civilization, and unloaded their gold, making Seattle doubly rich. It seems only fitting that this museum should be here. Another unit of the park is in Skagway, Alaska.

117 S. Main St. © **206/553-7220.** www.nps.gov/klse. Free admission. Daily 9am–5pm. Closed Thanksgiving, Christmas, and New Year's Day. Bus: 15, 16, 18, 21, or 22. Waterfront Streetcar: To Occidental Park stop.

Seattle Art Museum 🎭🎭

Two blocks from Pike Place Market, Jonathon Borofsky's *Hammering Man,* an animated three-story steel sculpture, hammers away in front of the Seattle Art Museum. Inside you'll find one of the nation's premier collections of Northwest Coast Indian art and artifacts and an equally large collection of African art. Exhibits cover European and American art ranging from ancient Mediterranean works to pieces from the medieval, Renaissance, and Baroque periods. A large 18th-century collection and a smaller 19th-century exhibition lead up to a large 20th-century collection that includes a room devoted to Northwest contemporary art. (There's also a smattering of Asian art at this museum, but the city's major collection of Asian art is at the Seattle Asian Art Museum in Volunteer Park; see below for details.) Free guided tours of the different collections are offered.

Throughout the year there are special exhibits, as well as film and music series. Between June 20 and September 15, 2002, the *Corot to Picasso* special exhibit will feature European masterworks, including art by Monet, Degas, Cézanne, Kandinsky, Seurat, Rodin, and, of course, Picasso and Corot. At the same time, there will be an exhibit of Degas bronzes. Beginning October 17, 2002, there will be an exhibit of works by Diego Rivera, Frida Kahlo, and other 20th-century Mexican artists.

100 University St. © **206/625-8900.** www.seattleartmuseum.org. Admission $7 adults, $5 seniors and students, free 12 and under. Free first Thurs of each month (free for seniors on first Fri of each month). Admission ticket also valid at Seattle Asian Art Museum if used within 1 week. Tues–Sun 10am–5pm (Thurs until 9pm). Also open on Martin Luther King Day, Presidents' Day, Memorial Day, and Labor Day. Closed Thanksgiving, Christmas, and New Year's Day (open holiday Mondays). Bus: 10, 15, 18 or any bus using the bus tunnel.

3 Seattle Center & Lake Union Attractions

Built in 1962 for the World's Fair, Seattle Center is today not only the site of Seattle's famous Space Needle—it's a cultural and entertainment park that doubles as the city's favorite festival grounds as well. Within Seattle Center's boundaries, you'll find the Experience Music Project (EMP), the Pacific Science Center, the Seattle Children's Museum, the Seattle Children's Theatre, Key Arena (home of the NBA's Seattle Supersonics), the Seattle Center Opera House, a children's amusement park, a fountain that is a favorite summertime hangout, the Intiman Theatre, and the Bagley Wright Theatre. See p. 109, "Especially for Kids," for further details on Seattle Center attractions that young travelers will enjoy.

The Center for Wooden Boats ✷   This unusual little museum, located adjacent to the Northwest Seaport/Maritime Heritage Center, is basically a collection of wooden boats of all kinds. Most of the boats are tied up to the docks surrounding the museum's floating boathouse, but some are stored in dry dock (on the dock itself). Dedicated to the preservation of historic wooden boats, the center is unique in that many exhibits can be rented and taken out on the waters of Lake Union. There are both rowboats and sailboats. Rates range from $12.50 to $37.50 per hour (call for hours of availability). Individual sailing instruction is also available.

1010 Valley St. (Waterway 4, south end of Lake Union). ✆ 206/382-2628. www.cwb.org. Free admission. May–Labor Day daily 11am–6pm; Labor Day–May Wed–Mon 11am–5pm. Bus: 17.

Experience Music Project ✷✷   The brainchild of Microsoft cofounder Paul Allen and designed by architect Frank Gehry, who is known for pushing the envelope of architectural design, this rock 'n' roll museum is a massive multicolored blob at the foot of the Space Needle. Originally planned as a memorial to Seattle native Jimi Hendrix, the museum grew to encompass not only Hendrix, but all of the Northwest's rock scene (from "Louie Louie" to grunge) and the general history of American popular music.

One museum exhibit focuses on the history of guitars and includes some of the earliest electric guitars, which date from the early 1930s. The museum even has a sort of rock 'n' roll thrill ride, which has been featuring funk music since the museum's opening. The "ride" consists of a platform of seats that are bounced around giving you the sensation of being on a roller coaster. However, the most popular exhibits here (after the Jimi Hendrix room) are the interactive rooms. In one you can play a guitar, drums, keyboards, or even DJ turntables. In another, you can experience what it's like to be onstage performing in front of adoring fans.

In the museum's main hall, known as the Sky Church, there are regularly scheduled concerts. To help you get the most out of your visit (and at almost $20 for a ticket, you certainly expect plenty), every visitor is issued a Museum Exhibit Guide (MEG), a hand-held electronic player filled with recorded audio clips explaining the various exhibits. Expect long lines in the summer and leave plenty of time to see this unusual museum.

325 Fifth Ave. N. ✆ 877/EMPLIVE or 206/EMPLIVE. www.emplive.com. Admission $19.95 adults, $15.95 seniors, $14.95 children ages 7–12, free for children 6 and under. Daily 9am–11pm. Bus: 1, 2, 3, 4, 13, 15, 16, 18, 24, or 33. Monorail: From Westlake Center at Pine St. and Fourth Ave.

Northwest Seaport/Maritime Heritage Center   Although this marine heritage center at the south end of Lake Union is currently little more than a

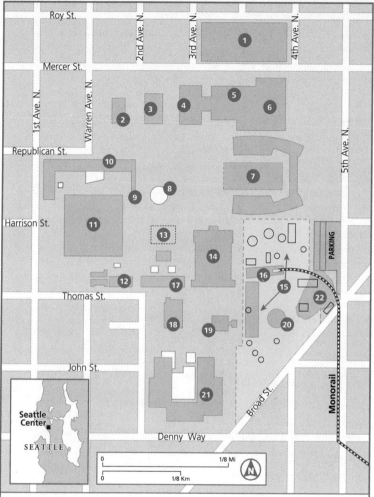

Amusement Park Areas **15**
Bagley Wright Theatre **2**
Center House & Children's Museum **14**
Exhibition Hall **4**
Experience Music Project **22**
Flag Pavilion **17**
Flag Plaza **13**
International Fountain **8**
Intiman Playhouse **3**
The Key Arena **11**
Memorial Stadium **7**

Mercer Arena **6**
Mercer Street Parking Garage **1**
Monorail Terminal **16**
Mural Amphitheatre **19**
Northwest Crafts Center **9**
Northwest Rooms **10**
Opera House **5**
Pacific Science Center **21**
Seattle Center Pavilions **12**
Seattle Children's Theatre **18**
Space Needle **20**

C Space Needle Alternatives

If you don't want to deal with the crowds at the Space Needle but still want an elevated downtown view, you have some alternatives. One is the big, black **Bank of America Tower** (*C* 206/386-5151) at the corner of Fifth Avenue and Columbia Street. At 943 feet, this is the tallest building in Seattle (twice as tall as the Space Needle), more stories (76, to be exact) than any other building west of the Mississippi. Up on the 73rd floor, you'll find an observation deck with views that dwarf those from the Space Needle. Admission is only $5 for adults and $3 for seniors and children. It's open Monday through Friday from 8:30am to 4:30pm.

Not far from the Bank of America Tower, you'll find the **Smith Tower,** 506 Second Ave. (*C* 206/622-4004). Opened in 1914, this was Seattle's first skyscraper and, for 50 years, was the tallest building west of Chicago. Although Smith Tower has only 42 stories, it still offers excellent views from its 35th-floor observation deck, which surrounds the ornate Chinese Room, a banquet hall with an ornate carved ceiling. An lavish lobby and original manual elevators all make this a fun and historic place to take in the Seattle skyline. The observation deck is open May 15 to October 31, daily from 10am to 4pm; admission is $5 for adults, $3 for seniors, students, and children ages 6 to 12.

If you've ever seen a photo of the Space Needle framed by the high-rises of downtown Seattle, it was probably taken from **Kerry Viewpoint** on Queen Anne Hill. If you want to take your own drop-dead photo of the Seattle skyline from this elevated perspective, head north from Seattle Center on Queen Anne Avenue North and turn left on West Highland Drive. When you reach the park, you'll immediately recognize the view.

Another great panorama is from the water tower in **Volunteer Park** on Capitol Hill at East Prospect Street and 14th Avenue East. See p. 106.

shipyard for the restoration of three historic ships, it has grand plans for the future. If you're a fan of tall ships and the age of sail, you can pay a visit to the 1897 schooner *Wawona,* which is currently under restoration. Also being restored are a 1904 lightship, an 1889 tugboat, and a 1933 salmon troller. Throughout the year, there are folk music concerts ($10) on the deck of this boat (call for details), and on the second Friday of each month, there's a free Chantey Sing from 8 to 10pm. Nearby, at Chandler's Cove (901 Fairview N.), you'll also find the gift shop and the few small exhibits of the **Puget Sound Maritime Historical Society** (*C* 206/624-3028).

1002 Valley St. *C* 206/447-9800. www.nwseaport.org. Free admission/suggested donation. Tues–Sun noon–5pm. Bus: 17.

Pacific Science Center *C* *C* *Kids* Although its exhibits are aimed primarily at children, the Pacific Science Center is fun for all ages. The main goal of this sprawling complex at Seattle Center is to teach kids about science and to instill a desire to study it. To that end, there are life-sized robotic dinosaurs, a butterfly house and insect village (with giant robotic insects), a Tech Zone where kids can play virtual-reality soccer or play tic-tac-toe with a robot, and dozens of other fun hands-on exhibits addressing the biological sciences, physics, and chemistry. The August Bubble Festival is always a big hit, as is April's Gross Out Week. There's a planetarium for learning about the skies (plus laser shows for the fun of it), and an IMAX theater. There are always special exhibits, so be sure to check the schedule when you're in town.

200 Second Ave. N., Seattle Center. ☎ 206/443-2880. www.pacsci.org. Admission $8 adults, $5.50 ages 3–13 and seniors, free for children under 2. IMAX $6.75–$7.50 adults, $5.75–$6.50 ages 3–13 and seniors, free for children under 2. Laser show $5–$7.50. Various discounted combination tickets available. Mid-June to Labor Day daily 10am–6pm; Labor Day to mid-June Mon–Fri 10am–5pm, Sat–Sun and holidays 10am–6pm. Closed Thanksgiving and Christmas. Bus: 1, 2, 3, 4, 13, 15, 16, 18, 24, or 33. Monorail: To Seattle Center.

The Space Needle ★★   From a distance it resembles a flying saucer on top of a tripod, and when it was built for the 1962 World's Fair, the 605-foot-tall Space Needle was meant to suggest future architectural trends. Today the Space Needle is the quintessential symbol of Seattle, and at 520 feet above ground level, the observation deck provides superb views of the city and its surroundings. There are displays identifying more than 60 sites and activities in the Seattle area, and high-powered telescopes let you zoom in on distant sights. You'll also find a pricey restaurant atop the tower (see the review of SkyCity on p. 78). If you don't mind standing in line and paying quite a bit for an elevator ride, make this your first stop in Seattle so you can orient yourself. There are, however, cheaper alternatives if you just want a view of the city (see the box titled "Space Needle Alternatives," above).

Seattle Center, Fourth Ave. N at Broad St. ☎ 800/937-9582 or 206/905-2100. www.spaceneedle.com. Admission $11 adults, $9 seniors, $5 ages 5–12, free under 5. No charge if dining in either restaurant. Summer daily 8am–midnight; other months Sun–Thurs 9am–11pm, Fri–Sat 9am–midnight. Valet parking $10 for 4 hr. Bus: 1, 2, 3, 4, 13, 15, 16, 18, 24, or 33. Monorail: From Westlake Center at Pine St. and Fourth Ave.

4 The Neighborhoods

See chapter 7 for walking tours of Pioneer Square and Fremont.

THE INTERNATIONAL DISTRICT

While Seattle today boasts of its strategic location on the Pacific Rim, its ties to Asia are nothing new. This is evident in the International District, Seattle's main Asian neighborhood, which is centered between Fifth Avenue South and 12th Avenue South (between South Washington Street and South Lane Street). Called the International District rather than Chinatown because so many Asian nationalities have made this area home, this neighborhood has been the center of the city's Asian communities for more than 100 years. You can learn about the district's history at the Wing Luke Museum (see below), where you can also pick up a walking-tour map of the area.

There are many restaurants, import stores, and food markets, and the huge **Uwajimaya** is all of these rolled up in one (see the listing on p. 138 of chapter 8, "Seattle Shopping," for details).

At the corner of Maynard Avenue South and South King Street, you'll find **Hing Hay Park,** the site of an ornate and colorful pavilion given to the city by Taipei, Taiwan.

Wing Luke Asian Museum   Despite much persecution over the years, Asians, primarily Chinese and Japanese, have played an integral role in developing the

Northwest, and today the connection of this region with the far side of the Pacific has opened up both economic and cultural doors. The exhibits at this small museum, located in the heart of Seattle's International District (Chinatown) and named for the first Asian American to hold public office in the Northwest, explore the roles various Asian cultures have played in the settlement and development of the Northwest. Many of the museum's special exhibits are meant to help explain Asian customs to non-Asians. If you're walking around Chinatown, this museum will give you a better appreciation of the neighborhood, but the exhibits tend to have a narrow range of appeal.

407 Seventh Ave. S. ℂ 206/623-5124. www.wingluke.org. Admission $4 adults, $3 students and seniors, $2 ages 5–12, free for children under 5. Free on first Thurs of every month. Tues–Fri 11am–4:30pm, Sat–Sun noon–4pm. Closed New Year's Day, Easter, July 4, Labor Day, Thanksgiving, Christmas eve, and Christmas day. Bus: 7, 14, 36, or any southbound bus using the bus tunnel (get off at the International District station).

FIRST HILL (PILL HILL) & CAPITOL HILL

Seattle is justly proud of its parks, and **Volunteer Park,** on Capitol Hill (drive north on Broadway and watch for signs), is one of the most popular. Here you'll find not only acres of lawns, groves of trees, and huge old rhododendrons, but also an old water tower that provides one of the best panoramas in the city. A winding staircase leads to the top of the water tower, from which you get 360° views. On the observatory level there is also an interesting exhibit about the Olmsted Brothers and the system of parks they designed for Seattle. To find the water tower, park near the Seattle Asian Art Museum if you can, and walk back out of the parking lot to where the road splits. The view from directly in front of the museum isn't bad either.

Frye Art Museum ℱ   Located on First Hill not far from downtown Seattle, this museum is primarily an exhibit space for the extensive personal art collection of Charles and Emma Frye, Seattle pioneers who began collecting art in the 1890s. The collection focuses on late-19th-century and early-20th-century representational art by European and American painters, and there are works by Andrew Wyeth, Thomas Hart Benton, Edward Hopper, Albert Bierstadt, and Pablo Picasso, as well as a large collection of engravings by Winslow Homer. In addition to galleries filled with works from the permanent collection, there are temporary exhibitions throughout the year.

704 Terry Ave. (at Cherry St.). ℂ 206/622-9250. www.fryeart.org. Free admission. Tues–Sat 10am–5pm (Thurs until 9pm), Sun noon–5pm. Closed July 4, Thanksgiving, Christmas, and New Year's Day. Bus: 3, 4, or 12.

Seattle Asian Art Museum ℱ   Housed in a renovated Art Deco building, the Asian art collection has an emphasis on Chinese and Japanese art but also includes pieces from Korea, Southeast Asia, South Asia, and the Himalayas. Collections of Chinese terra-cotta funerary art, snuff bottles, and Japanese netsukes (belt decorations) are among the museum's most notable. One room is devoted to Japanese ceramics, while three rooms are devoted to Chinese ceramics. The central hall is devoted to the stone religious sculptures of South Asia (primarily India). There are frequent lectures and concerts.

1400 E. Prospect St., Volunteer Park (14th Ave. E. and E. Prospect St.). ℂ 206/654-3100. www.seattleart museum.org. Admission $3 adults, free 12 and under. Free to all on first Thurs and first Sat of each month (free for seniors on first Fri of each month). Admission ticket plus $4 will get you into the Seattle Art Museum if used within 1 week. Tues–Sun 10am–5pm (Thurs until 9pm). Closed Thanksgiving, Christmas, and New Year's Day (open holiday Mondays). Bus: 7, 9, or 10.

On the Trail of Dale Chihuly

For many years now, Northwest glass artist Dale Chihuly, one of the founders of the Pilchuck School for art glass north of Seattle, has been garnering nationwide media attention for his fanciful, color-saturated contemporary art glass. From tabletop vessels to massive window installations, his creations in glass have a depth and richness of color treasured by collectors across the country. His sensuous forms include vases within bowls reminiscent of Technicolor birds' eggs in giant nests. His ikebana series, based on the traditional Japanese flower-arranging technique, are riotous conglomerations of color that twist and turn like so many cut flowers waving in the wind.

There's no one place in Seattle to see a collection of his work (although a glass museum is in the works in Tacoma), but there are numerous public displays around the city. Up on the third floor of the **Washington State Convention and Trade Center,** Pike Street and Eighth Avenue, there is a case with some beautifully lighted pieces. In the lobby of the **Sheraton Seattle Hotel,** 1400 Sixth Ave., there are works by Chihuly and other Northwest glass artists from the Pilchuck School. (If you want to dine surrounded by art glass, including work by Chihuly, make a reservation at the Sheraton's ever-popular Fuller's restaurant.) The **City Centre shopping arcade,** 1420 Fifth Ave., has displays by numerous glass artists, including Chihuly. Don't miss the large wall installation beside this upscale shopping arcade's lounge (out the back door of FAO Schwartz). You'll also find two Chihuly chandeliers in **Benaroya Hall,** Third Avenue between Union and University streets, which is the home of the Seattle Symphony.

Want to take home an original Chihuly as a souvenir of your visit to Seattle? Drop by the **Foster/White Gallery,** 123 S. Jackson St. (② 206/622-2833), in Pioneer Square, or in Kirkland at 126 Central Way (② 425/822-2305). However, you'll usually find more affordable Chihuly pieces at **Portfolio Glass,** 1425 Fourth Ave. (② 206/748-9166).

If you happen to be in **Tacoma,** 32 miles south of Seattle, you can see more of his work at the **Tacoma Art Museum,** 1123 Pacific Ave. (② 253/272-4258), which is open Tuesday through Saturday from 10am to 5pm (Thurs until 8pm) and Sunday from noon to 5pm. Just up the street from here, at Tacoma's restored Union Station (now the federal courthouse), there is a fascinating large installation in a massive arched window.

Volunteer Park Conservatory ✯   This stately old Victorian conservatory, built in 1912, houses a large collection of tropical and desert plants, including palm trees, orchids, and cacti. There are seasonal floral displays also.

1400 E. Galer St. ② 206/684-4743. Free admission. May 1–Sept 15 daily 10am–7pm; Sept 16–Apr 30 daily 10am–4pm. Bus: 7, 9, or 10.

NORTH SEATTLE (INCLUDING THE U DISTRICT, FREMONT & MONTLAKE)

The **Fremont District,** which begins at the north end of the Fremont Bridge near the intersection of Fremont Avenue North and North 36th Street, is Seattle's funkiest and most unusual neighborhood. Even livelier, though not nearly as eclectic or artistic, the **University District** (known locally as the U District) has loads of cheap restaurants and all the types of shops you would associate with a college-age clientele. However, the main attractions for visitors are the two excellent museums on the university campus and the nearby Museum of History and Industry, which is just across the Montlake Bridge from the U District.

Burke Museum ⚡ Located in the northwest corner of the University of Washington campus, the Burke Museum features exhibits on the natural and cultural heritage of the Pacific Rim. Permanent exhibits include *Life & Times,* which covers 500 million years of Washington history (and prehistory) with lots of fossils, including a complete mastodon, on display. The second permanent exhibit, *Pacific Voices,* focuses on the many cultures of the Pacific Rim and their connections to Washington state. There is also a smaller temporary exhibit gallery. In front of the museum stand three modern totem poles that were carved in the style of the 1870s and 1880s. From February 7 to September 7, 2002, the museum has scheduled a special exhibit on Northwest earthquakes.

17th Ave. NE and NE 45th St. ⓒ 206/543-5590. www.burkemuseum.org. Admission $5.50 adults, $4 seniors, $2.50 students, free for children under 6. Daily 10am–5pm (Thurs until 8pm). Closed July 4, Thanksgiving, Christmas, and New Year's Day. Bus: 7, 43, 70, 71, 72, or 73.

Henry Art Gallery The focus here is on contemporary art with retrospectives of individual artists, as well as exhibits focusing on specific themes or media. Photography and video are both well represented, and for the most part, the exhibits are the most avant-garde in the Seattle area. Located on the west side of the University of Washington campus, this museum benefits from large well-lit gallery spaces that are illuminated by pyramidal and cubic skylights that can be seen near the main museum entrance. There's also a cafe here and a small sculpture courtyard. Parking is often available at the Central Parking Garage at NE 41st Street and 15th Avenue NE.

University of Washington, 15th Ave. NE and NE 41st St. ⓒ 206/543-2280. www.henryart.org. Admission $6 adults, $4.50 seniors, free for students and children under 14. Pay what you wish Thurs 5–8pm. Tues–Sun 11am–5pm (Thurs until 8pm). Closed July 4, Thanksgiving, Christmas, and New Year's Day. Bus: 7, 43, 70, 71, 72, and 73.

Museum of History and Industry (MOHAI) ⚡ If the Seattle Underground Tour's vivid description of life before the 1889 fire has you curious about what the city's more respectable citizens were doing back in those days, you can find out here, where re-created storefronts provide glimpses into their lives. Located at the north end of Washington Park Arboretum, this museum explores Seattle's history, with frequently changing exhibits on more obscure aspects of the city's past. While many of the displays will be of interest only to Seattle residents, anyone wishing to gain a better understanding of the history of the city and the Northwest may also enjoy the exhibits here. There's a Boeing mail plane from the 1920s, plus an exhibit on the 1889 fire that leveled the city. This museum also hosts touring exhibitions that address Northwest history. Although not actually in north Seattle, this museum is just across the Montlake Bridge from the University District.

McCurdy Park, 2700 24th Ave. E. (C) **206/324-1126**. www.seattlehistory.org. Admission $5.50 adults, $3 seniors and ages 6–12, $1 for ages 2–5, free under 2. Daily 10am–5pm. Closed Thanksgiving, Christmas, and New Year's Day. From I-5, take Wash. 520 east (exit 168B) to the Montlake exit and go straight through the stoplight to 24th Ave. E and turn left. Bus: 25 or 43.

Woodland Park Zoo 🌟🌟 *Kids*   Located in north Seattle, this sprawling zoo has outstanding exhibits focusing on Alaska, tropical Asia, the African savanna, and the tropical rain forest. The brown bear enclosure, one of the zoo's best exhibits, is a very realistic reproduction of an Alaskan stream and hillside. In the savanna, zebras gambol and antelopes and giraffes graze contentedly near a reproduction of an African village that opened in 2001. An elephant forest provides plenty of space for the zoo's pachyderms. The gorilla and orangutan habitats are also very well done, and there's a large walk-through butterfly house ($1 additional fee) during the summer months. Don't miss the giant Komodo lizards from Indonesia. A farm animal area and petting zoo are big hits with the little ones.

5500 Phinney Ave. N. (C) **206/684-4800**. www.zoo.org. Admission $9 adults, $8.25 seniors and college students, $6.50 disabled and children ages 6–17, $4.25 ages 3–5, free for children 2 and under. Mar 15–Apr 30 daily 9:30am–5pm; May 1–Sept 14 daily 9:30am–6pm; Sept 15–Oct 14 daily 9:30am–5pm; Oct 15–Mar 14 daily 9:30am–4pm. Parking $3.50. Bus: 5.

SOUTH SEATTLE

Museum of Flight *Kids*   Located right next door to busy Boeing Field, 15 minutes south of downtown Seattle, this museum will have aviation buffs walking on air. Within the six-story glass-and-steel repository are displayed some of history's most famous planes.

To start things off, there's a replica of the Wright brothers' first glider, and from there the collection of planes brings you to the present state of flight. Suspended in the Great Hall are more than 20 planes, including a 1935 DC-3, the first Air Force F-5 supersonic fighter, and the Gossamer Condor, a human-powered airplane, plus there are some 34 other planes on display. You'll also see one of the famous Blackbird spy planes, which were once the world's fastest jets (and you can even sit in the cockpit of one of these babies). A rare World War II Corsair fighter rescued from Lake Washington and restored to its original glory is also on display. Visitors also get to board the original Air Force One presidential plane, used by Eisenhower, and can sit in the cockpit of an F/A-18 Hornet fighter. An exhibit on the U.S. space program features an Apollo command module. Of course, you'll also see plenty of Boeing planes, including a reproduction of Boeing's first plane, which was built in 1916. The museum also incorporates part of Boeing's old wooden factory building from its early years.

While any air-and-space museum lets you look at mothballed planes, not many have their own air-traffic control tower and let you watch aircraft taking off and landing at an active airfield. During the summer months, biplane rides are also usually offered from in front of the museum.

See p. 114 for information on a tour of the Boeing plant.

9404 E. Marginal Way S. (C) **206/764-5720**. www.museumofflight.org. Admission $9.50 adults, $8.50 seniors, $5 ages 5–17, free for children under 5. Free first Thurs 5–9pm. Daily 10am–5pm (until 9pm Thurs). Closed Thanksgiving and Christmas. Take exit 158 off I-5. Bus: 174.

THE EASTSIDE

Bellevue Art Museum 🌟   This new institution in the city of Bellevue, which is located on the east side of Lake Washington and about a 20- to 30-minute drive from downtown Seattle, is rather unusual as art museums go. Although

Insider Tip

University of Washington campus parking is expensive on weekdays and Saturday mornings, so try to visit the Burke Museum or Henry Art Gallery on a Saturday afternoon or a Sunday, when parking is free.

there are several large galleries that host shows and installations by regional and national artists, the museum is really all about allowing the public to interact with artists. To this end, the museum stages the Northwest's largest and most highly regarded art fair each summer in late July. During the rest of the year, there are artists in residence and frequent artist demonstrations. The museum also has several classrooms in which art classes are held throughout the year. Although this museum usually isn't worth making a special trip to Bellevue, you might want to stop by if you happen to be on the Eastside and are an art aficionado.

510 Bellevue Way NE, Bellevue. © 425/519-0770. www.bellevueart.org. Admission $6 adults, $4 seniors and students, children under 6 free. Free for everyone third Thurs of each month. Wed–Fri noon–8pm, Tues and Sat 10am–5pm, Sun noon–5pm. Closed Thanksgiving and Christmas, New Year's Day, Easter, and July 4th. From Seattle, take Wash. 520 east over the Evergreen Point Bridge to I-405 south, then take Exit 13A onto NE 4th St., continue west, and then turn right onto Bellevue Way NE. Alternatively, take I-90 east over Lake Washington to the Bellevue Way Exit, and drive north on Bellevue Way for approximately 2 miles.

5 Parks & Public Gardens

PARKS

Seattle's many parks are what make this such a livable city. In the downtown area, **Myrtle Edwards Park** ⚘, 3130 Alaska Way W. (© **206/684-4075**), at the north end of the waterfront, is an ideal spot for a sunset stroll with views of Puget Sound and the Olympic Mountains. The park includes a 1¼-mile paved pathway.

Freeway Park, at Sixth Avenue and Seneca Street, is one of Seattle's most unusual parks. Built right on top of busy Interstate 5, this green space is more a series of urban plazas, with lots of terraces, waterfalls, and cement planters creating walls of greenery. You'd never know there's a roaring freeway beneath your feet. Unfortunately, although this park is convenient, it often has a deserted and slightly threatening feel due to the isolated nature of the park's many nooks and crannies.

For serious communing with nature, however, nothing will do but **Discovery Park** ⚘⚘, 3801 West Government Way (© 206/386-4236). Occupying a high bluff and sandy point jutting into Puget Sound, this is Seattle's largest and wildest park. You can easily spend a day wandering the trails and beaches here. The park's visitor center is open daily from 8:30am to 5pm. Discovery Park is a 15-minute drive from downtown; to reach the park, follow the waterfront north from downtown Seattle toward the Magnolia neighborhood and watch for signs to the park. When you reach the park, follow signed trails down to the beach and out to the lighthouse at the point. Although the lighthouse is not open to the public, the views from the beach make this a good destination for an hour's walk. The beach and park's bluff-top meadows both make good picnic spots.

Up on Capitol Hill, at East Prospect Street and 14th Avenue East, you'll find **Volunteer Park** ⚘⚘, 1247 15th Ave. East (© **206/684-4075**), which is surrounded by the elegant mansions of Capitol Hill. It's a popular spot for sunning

Fish Gotta Swim

While salmon in the Puget Sound region have dwindled to danger-ously low numbers in recent years, it is still possible in various places to witness the annual return of salmon.

In the autumn, on the waterfront, you can see returning salmon at the **Seattle Aquarium,** which has its own fish ladder. However, the very best place to see salmon is at **Hiram M. Chittenden Locks,** 3015 NW 54th St. (© 206/783-7059), which are located a 10-minute drive north of downtown Seattle (drive north from the waterfront on Elliott Avenue, which becomes 15th Avenue West; after crossing the Ballard Bridge, turn left on Market Street and follow this road for about 1 mile). Between June and September (July and August are the peak months), you can view salmon through underwater observation win-dows as they leap up the locks' fish ladder. These locks, which are used primarily by small boats, connect Lake Union and Lake Washington with the waters of Puget Sound, and depending on the tides and lake levels, there is a difference of 6 to 26 feet on either side of the locks. The locks and surrounding park are open daily from 7am to 9pm, and the visitor's center is open daily from 10am to 6pm (closed Thanksgiv-ing, Christmas, and New Year's Day). Take bus 17.

East of Seattle, in downtown **Issaquah,** salmon can be seen year-round at the Issaquah Salmon Hatchery, 125 Sunset Way (© **425/ 391-9094**). However, it is in October that adult salmon can be seen returning to the hatchery. Each year in October, the city of Issaquah holds a Salmon Days Festival to celebrate the return of the natives.

and playing Frisbee, and it's home to the Seattle Asian Art Museum (see p. 102), an amphitheater, a water tower with a superb view of the city, and a conserva-tory filled with tropical and desert plants (see p. 103). With so much variety, you can easily spend a morning or afternoon exploring this park.

On the east side of Seattle, along the shore of Lake Washington, you'll find not only swimming beaches but also **Seward Park** ✸, 5898 Lake Washington Blvd. (© **206/684-4075**). While this large park's waterfront areas are its biggest attraction, it also has a dense forest with trails winding through it. Keep an eye out for the bald eagles that nest here. This park is south of the I-90 floating bridge off Lake Washington Boulevard South. From downtown Seattle, follow Madison Street northeast to a right onto Lake Washington Boulevard.

In north Seattle, you'll find several parks worth visiting. These include the unique **Gasworks Park** ✸, 2101 N. Northlake Way, at Meridian Avenue North (© **206/684-4075**), at the north end of Lake Union. This park has, in the mid-dle of its green lawns, the rusting hulk of an old industrial plant. Kite Hill is the city's favorite kite-flying spot. North of here, on Green Lake Way North near the Woodland Park Zoo, you'll find **Green Lake Park** ✸✸, 7201 E. Green Lake Dr. N. (© **206/684-4075**), which is a center for exercise buffs who jog, bike, and skate around the park on a 2.8-mile paved path. It's also possible to swim in the lake (there are changing rooms and a beach with summer lifeguards), and there are plenty of grassy areas. For information on renting in-line skates or a bike for riding the path here, see pp. 115 and 117.

North of the Ballard neighborhood, you'll find **Golden Gardens** 🌸🌸, 8499 Seaview Ave. NW (✆ **206/684-4075**), which, with its excellent views of the Olympic Mountains and its somewhat wild feeling, is our favorite Seattle waterfront park. Not only are there great views, but there are also some small wetlands and a short trail. However, Golden Gardens is best known as one of Seattle's best beaches, and although the water here is too cold for swimming, the sandy beach is a pleasant spot for a sunset stroll. People often gather here on summer evenings to build fires on the beach. To reach this park, drive north from the waterfront on Elliott Avenue, which becomes 15th Avenue West; after crossing the Ballard Bridge, turn left on Market Street and follow this road for about 2 miles (it will change names to become NW 54th Street and then Seaview Avenue NW).

PUBLIC GARDENS
See also the listing for Volunteer Park Conservatory on p. 103.

Bellevue Botanical Gardens 🌸   Any avid gardener should be sure to make a trip across one of Seattle's two floating bridges to the city of Bellevue and the Bellevue Botanical Garden. Although this 36-acre garden opened only in 1992, it has matured very quickly and has become one of the Northwest's most talked-about perennial gardens. The summertime displays of flowers, in expansive mixed borders, are absolutely gorgeous. There is also a Japanese garden, a shade border, and a water-wise garden (designed to conserve water).

Wilburton Hill Park, 12001 Main St., Bellevue. ✆ **425/452-2750**. www.bellevuebotanical.org. Free admission. Daily 7:30am–dusk; visitor center daily 9am–4pm. Take the NE Fourth St. exit off I-405.

Carl S. English, Jr. Ornamental Gardens   Located beside the Hiram M. Chittenden Locks in the Ballard neighborhood of north Seattle (a 10-min. drive north of downtown), this park is home to one of Seattle's prettiest little botanical gardens. Although relatively small, the gardens contain more than 500 species of plants.

Hiram M. Chittenden Locks, 3015 NW 54th St. ✆ **206/783-7059**. Free admission. Daily 7am–9pm.

Japanese Garden   Situated on 3½ acres of land, the Japanese Garden is a perfect little world unto itself, with babbling brooks, a lake rimmed with Japanese irises and filled with colorful koi (Japanese carp), and a cherry orchard (for spring color). A special Tea Garden encloses a Tea House, where, between April and October, on the third Saturday of each month at 1:30pm, you can attend a traditional tea ceremony. Unfortunately, noise from a nearby road can be distracting at times.

Washington Park Arboretum, Lake Washington Blvd. E. (north of E. Madison St.). ✆ **206/684-4725**. Admission $2.50 adults; $1.50 seniors, persons with disabilities, and ages 6–18, free for children under 6. Mar daily 10am–6pm, Apr–May daily 10am–7pm; June–Aug daily 10am–8pm; Sept–Oct daily 10am–6pm; Nov daily 10am–4pm. Closed Dec–Feb. Bus: 11.

Washington Park Arboretum 🌸   Acres of trees and shrubs stretch from the far side of Capitol Hill all the way to the Montlake Cut, a canal connecting Lake Washington to Lake Union. Within the 230-acre arboretum, there are 5,000 varieties of plants and quiet trails that are pleasant throughout the year but which are most beautiful in spring, when the azaleas, cherry trees, rhododendrons, and dogwoods are all in flower. The north end of the arboretum, a marshland that is home to ducks and herons, is popular with kayakers, canoeists (see

p. 117 in "Outdoor Pursuits," below, for places to rent a canoe or kayak), and bird-watchers. A boardwalk with views across Lake Washington meanders along the water in this area (though noise from the adjacent freeway detracts considerably from the experience). Free tours are offered Saturday and Sunday at 1pm.

2300 Arboretum Dr. E. © 206/543-8800. Free admission. Daily 7am to dusk; Graham Visitors Center daily 10am–4pm. Enter on Lake Washington Blvd. off E. Madison St.; or take Wash. 520 off I-5 north of downtown, take the Montlake Blvd. exit, and go straight through the first intersection. Bus: 11, 43, or 48.

6 Especially for Kids

In addition to the listings below, kids will also enjoy many of the attractions described earlier in this chapter, including the **Pacific Science Center** (see p. 100), the **Seattle Aquarium** (see p. 95), the **IMAXDome Theater** (see p. 95), **Odyssey** (see p. 95), and the **Woodland Park Zoo** (see p. 105).

Even the surliest teenagers will think you're pretty cool for taking them to the **Experience Music Project** (see p. 98).

Adolescent and preadolescent boys seem to unfailingly love **Ye Olde Curiosity Shop** and the **Seattle Underground Tour** (see the "Good Times in Bad Taste" box on p. 96). Younger boys also seem to love the **Museum of Flight** (see p. 105).

When the kids need to burn off some energy, see section 5, "Parks & Public Gardens," above, for descriptions of Seattle's best recreational areas; section 8, "Outdoor Pursuits," later in this chapter, will give you the lowdown on for beaches, biking, in-line skating, and more. You can also take the kids to a sporting event; Seattle supports professional football, basketball, and baseball teams. See section 9, "Spectator Sports," later in this chapter.

You might also be able to catch a performance at the **Seattle Children's Theatre** (© 206/441-3322; www.sct.org), or the **Northwest Puppet Center,** 9123 15th Ave. NE (© 206/523-2579; www.nwpuppet.org).

Children's Museum *Kids* Seattle's Children's Museum is located in the basement of the Center House at Seattle Center. The museum includes plenty of hands-on cultural exhibits, a child-size neighborhood, a Discovery Bay for toddlers, a mountain wilderness area, a global village, and other special exhibits to keep the little ones busy learning and playing for hours.

Center House, in Seattle Center. © 206/441-1768. www.thechildrensmuseum.org. Admission $5.50 per person. Daily 10am–5pm. Closed Thanksgiving, Christmas, and New Year's Day. Bus: 1, 2, 3, 4, 13, 15, 16, 18, 24, or 33. Monorail: from Westlake Center at the corner of Pine St. and Fourth Ave.

Seattle Center *Kids* If you want to keep the kids entertained all day long, head to Seattle Center. This 74-acre cultural center and amusement park was built for the Seattle World's Fair in 1962 and stands on the northern edge of downtown at the end of the monorail line. The most visible building at the center is the **Space Needle** (see p. 101), which provides an outstanding panorama of the city from its observation deck. However, of much more interest to children is the **Fun Forest** (© 206/728-1586), with its roller coaster, log flume, merry-go-round, Ferris wheel, arcade games, and minigolf. Seattle Center is also the site of the **Children's Museum** (see above) and **Seattle Children's Theatre** (© 206/441-3322; www.sct.org). This is Seattle's main festival site, and in the summer months hardly a weekend goes by without some special event or another filling its grounds. On hot summer days, the **International Fountain** is a great place for kids to keep cool (bring a change of clothes).

305 Harrison St. ✆ **206/684-7200**. www.seattlecenter.com. Free admission; pay per ride or game (various multiride tickets available). Fun Forest: June–Labor Day Mon–Thurs noon–11pm or midnight; spring and fall Fri 7–11pm, Sat noon–11pm, Sun noon–8pm. Bus: 1, 2, 3, 4, 13, 15, 16, 18, 24, or 33. Monorail: from Westlake Center at the corner of Pine St. and Fourth Ave.

7 Organized Tours

For information on the **Seattle Underground tour,** see box titled "Good Times in Bad Taste" on p. 96.

WALKING TOURS

In addition to the walking tours mentioned here, there are two different Pike Place Market tours offered by market organizations. See the Pike Place Market listing on p. 95 for details.

If you'd like to explore downtown Seattle with a knowledgeable guide, join one of the informative walking tours offered by **See Seattle Walking Tours** (✆ **425/226-7641;** www.see-seattle.com). The tours visit Pike Place Market, the waterfront, the Pioneer Square district, and the International District. Tours are split into two parts ($15 per person for part one, $10 per person for part two).

You can also learn lots of Seattle history and wander through hidden corners of the city on 2-hour tours run by **Duse McLean** (tel] **425/885-3173**). These tours start with a ride through the Bus Tunnel to the International District and then make their way back north to Pike Place Market, taking in historic buildings, public art, and scenic vistas. Tours are $15 per person and are offered year-round by reservation.

If you'd like an insider's glimpse of life in Seattle's International District, hook up with **Chinatown Discovery Tours** (✆ **425/885-3085;** www.seattlechamber. com/chinatowntour). On these walking tours, which last from 1½ to 3 hours, you'll learn the history of this colorful and historic neighborhood. "A Touch of Chinatown" is a brief introduction to the neighborhood. The "Chinatown by Day" tour includes a six-course lunch. "Nibble Your Way Through Chinatown" provides a sampling of flavors from around the International District. The "Chinatown by Night" tour includes an eight-course banquet. Rates (for four or more on a tour) range from $12.95 to $38.95 per person (slightly higher for fewer than four people).

BUS TOURS

If you'd like an overview of Seattle's main tourist attractions, or if you're pressed for time during your visit, you can pack in a lot of sights on a tour with **Gray Line of Seattle** (✆ **800/426-7532** or 206/626-5208; www.graylineofseattle. com). Half-day tours are $27 for adults, $13.50 for children; full-day tours are $39 for adults, $19.50 for children. Many other tours, including tours to Mount Rainier National Park and to the Boeing plant in Everett, are also available.

From mid-May through mid-October, Gray Line also offers a **Trolley Tour** on a bus made up to look like an old trolley. The tour is really a day pass that allows you to use the trolley, which follows a set route that passes nearly all the major tourist attractions in downtown Seattle. The trolley stops several places along the waterfront and at Seattle Center, Pike Place Market, the Seattle Art Museum, and Pioneer Square. Tickets are $16 for adults and $8 for children. Because buses in downtown are free and because both the Waterfront Streetcar and the monorail to Seattle Center cost no more than $1.25, the trolley is not a very good deal; but if you don't want to worry about finding the right bus stop,

---

Seattle by Duck

Paul Revere would have had a hard time figuring out what to tell his fellow colonists if the British had arrived by Duck. A Duck, if you didn't know, is a World War II vintage amphibious vehicle that can arrive by land or sea, and these odd-looking things are now being used to provide tours of Seattle both on land and water. Duck tours take in the standard Seattle sights but then plunge right into Lake Union for a tour of the Portage Bay waterfront, with its many houseboats and great views. Ninety-minute tours leave from near the Space Needle and cost $20 for adults and $10 for kids. Contact **Seattle Duck Tours** ⚓ (② **800/817-1116** or 206/441-DUCK). Tours leave from a parking lot across from the Space Needle. Because these tours encourage Seattle visitors to get a little daffy while they're in town, they are very popular; reservations are recommended.

---

it's worth considering. There's also a $36 family pass that allows two adults and up to four children use the trolley for 2 days.

To glimpse a bit more of Seattle on a guided van tour, try the "Explore Seattle Tour" offered by **Customized Tours and Charter Service** (② **800/770-8769** or 206/878-3965), which charges $35 per person. This tour stops at Pike Place Market, Ballard Locks and Fish Ladder, and the Klondike Gold Rush Historical Park. This company also offers a tour to the Boeing plant ($40) and a Snoqualmie Falls and wineries tour ($40 per person, four person minimum).

BOAT TOURS

In addition to the boat tours and cruises mentioned below, you can do your own low-budget cruise simply by hopping on one of the ferries operated by **Washington State Ferries** (② **800/84-FERRY** or 888/808-7977 within Washington state, or 206/464-6400; www.wsdot.wa.gov/ferries/). Try the Bainbridge Island or Bremerton ferries out of Seattle for a 1½- to 2½-hour round-trip. There are both car ferries and foot ferries on the Bremerton run; the passenger-only ferries leave from the dock to the south of the car ferry terminal in Seattle. For more information on these ferries, see "Getting Around," in chapter 3, "Getting to Know Seattle."

If you don't have enough time in your vacation scheduled to fit in an overnight trip to the San Juan Islands, it's still possible to get a feel for these picturesque islands by riding the San Juan Islands ferry from Anacortes to Friday Harbor. These ferries depart from Anacortes, which is located 75 miles north of Seattle. If you get off in Friday Harbor, you can spend a few hours exploring this town before returning to Anacortes. It's also possible to take the first ferry of the day from Anacortes, ride all the way to Sidney, British Columbia, and then catch the next ferry back to Anacortes. However, if doing this trip in one day, you won't have any time to spend in Victoria. Alternatively, if you have more money to spend (and even less time), there are boat tours of the San Juan Islands that depart from the Seattle waterfront. For information on ferries and boat excursions to the San Juan Islands, see chapter 10.

For a boat excursion that also includes a salmon dinner and Northwest Coast Indian masked dances, consider coughing up the cash for the **Tillicum Village Tour** ⚓⚓, Pier 55 (② **800/426-1205** or 206/933-8600; www.tillicumvillage.com). Located at Blake Island State Park across Puget Sound from Seattle and only accessible by tour boat or private boat, Tillicum Village was built in conjunction with the 1962 Seattle World's Fair. The "village" is actually just a large restaurant and performance hall fashioned after a traditional Northwest Coast longhouse, but with totem poles standing vigil out front, the forest encircling the longhouse, and the waters of Puget Sound stretching out into the distance, Tillicum Village is a beautiful spot. After the dinner and dances, you can strike out on forest trails to explore the island (you can return on a later boat if you want to spend a couple of extra hours hiking). There are even beaches on which to relax. Tours cost $65 for adults, $59 for seniors, $25 for children ages 5 to 12, and are free for children under age 5. Tours are offered daily from May through early October; other months on weekends only. If you can opt for only one tour while in Seattle, this should be it—it's unique, truly Northwestern, the salmon dinner is pretty good, and the traditional masked dances are fascinating (although more for the craftsmanship of the masks than for the dancing itself).

Seattle is a city surrounded by water, and if you'd like to see it from various aquatic perspectives, you can head out with **Argosy Cruises** ✯ (C **800/ 642-7816** or 206/623-1445; www.argosycruises.com). Offerings include a 1-hour harbor cruise (departs from Pier 55; $16 adults, $14 seniors, and $10 children ages 4–12), a 2½-cruise through the Hiram Chittenden Locks to Lake Union (departs from Pier 56; $30 adults, $28 seniors, $16 children ages 4–12), and two cruises around Lake Washington (a 2-hr. cruise departs from the AGC Marina at the south end of Lake Union and a 1½-hr. cruise departs from downtown Kirkland on the east side of the lake; $26 adults, $24 seniors, $14 children ages 4–12). The latter two cruises will take you past the fabled Xanadu built by Bill Gates on the shore of Lake Washington. However, of all these option, we'd recommend the cruise through the locks; although this is the most expensive outing, you get not only good views but also the chance to navigate the locks.

Want a meal with your cruise? Try one of Argosy Cruises' lunch or dinner cruises (lunch cruises: $42–$46 for adults, $26–$29 for children ages 4–12, $38–$42 for seniors; dinner cruises: $78–$83 for adults, $52–$56 for children ages 4–12, $74–$79 for seniors). These cruises are aboard a ship that conjures up the style of the *Titanic,* albeit on a much smaller and less luxurious scale. Meals are prepared on board the ship by one of our favorite waterfront restaurants, so these cruises get our vote for best dinners afloat. Reservations are recommended for all cruises.

Less expensive dinner cruises are offered on board the very modern *Spirit of Puget Sound,* Pier 70 (C **206/674-3500;** www.spiritofpugetsound.com). This big sleek yacht does lunch, dinner, and moonlight party cruises. Adult fares range from $28 to $35.50 for lunch cruises and from $44 to $65 for dinner cruises.

Looking for a quieter way to see Seattle from the water? From May 1 to October 15, **Emerald City Charters,** Pier 54 (C **800/831-3274** or 206/624-3931; www.sailingseattle.com), offers 1½- and 2½-hour sailboat cruises. The longer excursions are at sunset. Cruises are $23 to $38 for adults, $20 to $35 for seniors, and $18 to $30 for children under age 12.

(Value Money-Saving Tip

The **Ticket/Ticket** booth under the big clock at Pike Place Market sometimes has boat tour tickets available at discounted prices. If your schedule is flexible, be sure to check here first.

Seattle Noir

If your tastes run to the macabre, you might be interested in the **Private Eye on Seattle** ✵ tours (© 206/365-3739; www.privateeyetours.com) offered by Windsor Olson. These somewhat bizarre van tours are led by a retired private investigator who shares stories of the interesting and unusual cases he handled over his 40 years as a private eye in the Emerald City. Tours are $20 per person. To balance things out, Olson also offers a tour of some of Seattle's most distinctive churches ($25 per person).

For information on ferries and boat excursions to the San Juan Islands, see chapter 10.

VICTORIA EXCURSIONS

Among Seattle's most popular boat tours are day-long excursions to Victoria, British Columbia. These trips are offered by **Victoria Clipper** ✵✵, Pier 69, 2701 Alaskan Way (© 800/888-2535, 206/448-5000, or 250/382-8100 in Victoria; www.victoriaclipper.com), and operate several times a day during the summer (once or twice a day in other months). The high-speed catamaran passenger ferry takes 2 to 3 hours to reach Victoria. If you leave on the earliest ferry, you can spend the better part of the day exploring Victoria and be back in Seattle for a late dinner. Round-trip fares range from $59 (7-day advance purchase) to $125 for adults, $59 (7-day advance purchase) to $115 for seniors, and $49.50 to $62.50 for children ages 1 to 11 (between mid-Oct and mid-May, one child travels free with each adult paying for a 7-day advance purchase round-trip fare). Some scheduled trips also stop in the San Juan Islands during the summer. Various tour packages are also available, including an add-on tour to Butchart Gardens. Overnight trips can also be arranged.

For more information on Victoria, pick up a copy of *Frommer's Vancouver & Victoria.*

SCENIC FLIGHTS & HOT-AIR BALLOON RIDES

Seattle is one of the few cities in the United States where floatplanes are a regular sight in the skies and on the lakes. If you'd like to see what it's like to take off and land from the water, you've got a couple of options. **Seattle Seaplanes** ✵, 1325 Fairview Ave. E. (© 800/637-5553 or 206/329-9638), which takes off from the southeast corner of Lake Union, offers 20-minute scenic flights over the city for $57.50.

If you'd rather pretend you're back in the days of *The English Patient,* you can go up in a vintage biplane with **Olde Thyme Aviation** ✵ (© 206/730-1412; www.oldethymeaviation.com), which operates from the Museum of Flight on Boeing Field. Flights are offered on sunny weekends, and, if you have a gift certificate, weekday flights can also be arranged (weather permitting). A 20-minute flight along the Seattle waterfront to the Space Needle costs $99 for two people; other flights range in price from $149 to $395 for two people.

Seattle really isn't known as a hot-air ballooning center, but if you'd like to try floating over the Northwest landscape not far outside the city, contact **Over the Rainbow** (© 206/364-0995; www.letsgoballooning.com), which flies over the vineyards of the Woodinville area. Flights are offered both in the morning and in the afternoon and cost $135 to $165 per person.

A RAILWAY EXCURSION

If you're a fan of riding the rails, consider the **Spirit of Washington Dinner Train,** 625 S. Fourth St., Renton (℃ **800/876-RAIL** or 425/227-RAIL; www.spiritofwashingtondinnertrain.com). Running from Renton, at the south end of Lake Washington, to the Columbia Winery near Woodinville, at the north end of Lake Washington, this train rolls past views of the lake and Mount Rainier. Along the way, you're fed a filling lunch or dinner. At the turnaround point, you get to tour a winery and taste some wines. Dinner tours range from $60 to $70; lunch tours range from $50 to $60. The higher prices are for seatings in the dome car, which definitely offers finer views.

THE BOEING TOUR ☆☆

Until Bill Gates and Microsoft came to town, Boeing was the largest employer (by far) in the Seattle area. Although the company announced in 2001 that it was moving its corporate headquarters out of Seattle, Boeing is still a major presence in the city, and it still has something that Microsoft can never claim: the single largest building, by volume, in the world. This building, the company's Everett assembly plant, could easily hold 911 basketball courts, 74 football fields, 2,142 average-size homes, or all of Disneyland (with room left over for covered parking). Tours of the building let you see just how they put together the huge passenger jets that travelers take for granted.

The tours are quite fascinating and well worth the time it takes to get here from downtown Seattle. Guided 1-hour tours of the facility are held Monday through Friday throughout the year. The schedule varies with the time of year, so be sure to call ahead for details and directions to the plant. Tours cost $5 for adults and $3 for seniors and children under 16 who meet the height requirement (minimum of 50 in. tall). Tickets for same-day use are sold on a first-come, first-served basis beginning at 8am (8:30am Oct–May); in summer, tickets for any given day's tours usually sell out by noon. To check availability of same-day tickets, call ℃ **425/342-8500** between 8:30am and 2:00pm. It is possible to make reservations 24 hours or more in advance. However, when making reservations, you'll pay $10 per person regardless of age.

For more information or to make reservations, contact the **Boeing Tour Center,** Wash. 526, Everett, WA (℃ **800/464-1476** or 206/544-1264; www.boeing.com/companyoffices/aboutus/tours/). Everett is roughly 30 miles north of Seattle (a 30- to 45-min. drive) off I-5.

If you're in town without a car, you can book a tour to the plant through **Customized Tours and Charter Service** (℃ **800/770-8769** or 206/878-3965), which charges $40 and will pick you up at your Seattle hotel.

8 Outdoor Pursuits

See section 5, "Parks & Public Gardens," earlier in this chapter, for a rundown of great places to play.

BEACHES

Alki (rhymes with *sky*) **Beach** ☆, across Elliott Bay from downtown Seattle, is the city's most popular beach and is the nearest approximation you'll find in the Northwest to a Southern California beach scene. The paved path that runs along this 2½-mile-long beach is popular with skaters, walkers, and cyclists; and the road that parallels the beach is lined with shops, restaurants, and beachy houses and apartment buildings. But the views across Puget Sound to the Olympic

Mountains confirm that this is indeed the Northwest. Despite the views, this beach lacks the greenery that makes some of the city's other beaches so much more appealing. In the summer, a water taxi operates between the downtown Seattle waterfront and Alki Beach (see "Getting Around," in chapter 3, "Getting to Know Seattle," for details).

For a more Northwestern beach experience (which usually includes a bit of hiking or walking), head to one of the area's many waterfront parks. **Lincoln Park,** 8011 Fauntleroy Ave. SW, south of Alki Beach in West Seattle, has bluffs and forests backing the beach. Northwest of downtown Seattle in the Magnolia area, you'll find **Discovery Park** ☆☆, 3801 W. Government Way (© **206/ 386-4236**), where miles of beaches are the primary destination of most park visitors. To reach Discovery Park, follow the Elliott Avenue north along the waterfront from downtown Seattle, then take the Magnolia Bridge west toward the Magnolia neighborhood and follow Grayfield Street to Galer Street to Magnolia Boulevard.

Golden Gardens Park ☆☆, 8499 Seaview Place NW, which is located north of Ballard and Shilshole Bay, is our favorite Seattle beach park. Although the park isn't very large and is backed by railroad tracks, the views of the Olympic Mountains are magnificent and on summer evenings people build fires on the beach. There are also lawns and shade trees that make this park ideal for a picnic.

There are also several parks along the shores of Lake Washington that have small stretches of beach, many of which are actually popular with hardy swimmers. **Seward Park** ☆, 5898 Lake Washington Blvd., southeast of downtown Seattle, is a good place to hang out by the water and do a little swimming. To reach this park from downtown, take Madison Street east to Lake Washington Boulevard and turn right. Although this isn't the most direct route to Mount Baker Beach or Seward Park, it's the most scenic. Along the way, you'll pass plenty of other small parks.

BIKING

On the waterfront, bike rentals are available from **Blazing Saddles** ☆, 1230 Western Ave. (© **206/341-9994**). Along with your bike you also get detailed route descriptions for popular and fun rides originating on the waterfront, including a route on Bainbridge Island and mountain bike trails on Vashon Island. Choose to ride one of the island routes and you'll get to have the thoroughly Seattle experience of riding a bike onto a huge ferry. With its lush, green back roads, and variety of eateries at the end of a loop ride, Bainbridge Island is our favorite bike excursion from downtown Seattle. Blazing Saddles also rents bikes at Seattle Center. Rental rates range from $7 to $11 per hour and from $28 to $48 per day.

Gregg's Green Lake Cycle, 7007 Woodlawn Ave. NE (© **206/523-1822**); and the **Bicycle Center,** 4529 Sand Point Way NE (© **206/523-8300**), both rent bikes by the hour, day, or week. Rates range from $3 to $7 per hour and $15 to $30 per day. These shops are both convenient to the **Burke-Gilman/ Sammamish River Trail** ☆☆, a 27-mile paved pathway created mostly from an old railway bed. This path is immensely popular and is a great place for a family bike ride or to get in long, vigorous ride without having to deal with traffic. The Burke-Gilman portion of this trail starts in the Ballard neighborhood of north Seattle, but the most convenient place to start a ride is at **Gasworks Park** on the north shore of Lake Union. From here you can ride north and east, by way of the University of Washington, to **Kenmore Logboom Park** at the north end of Lake Washington. Serious riders can then continue on from Kenmore Logboom Park on the Sammamish River portion of the trail, which leads to the north end of Lake Sammamish and Marymoor Park, which is the site of a velodrome (a bicycle racetrack). This latter half of the trail is actually our favorite portion of a ride along this trail. This section of the path follows the Sammamish River and passes through several pretty parks. Riding the entire trail out and back is a 54-mile round-trip ride popular with riders in training for races. There are lots of great picnicking spots along both trails.

The West Seattle bike path along **Alki Beach** is another good place to ride and offers great views of the sound and the Olympics.

GOLF

While Seattle isn't a name that springs immediately to mind when folks think of golf, the sport is just as much a passion here as it is all across the country these days. Should you wish to get in a round of golf while you're in town, Seattle has three conveniently located municipal golf courses: **Jackson Park Golf Course,** 1000 NE 135th St. (© **206/363-4747**); **Jefferson Park Golf Course,** 4101 Beacon Ave. S. (© **206/762-4513**); and **West Seattle Golf Course,** 4470 35th Ave. SW (© **206/935-5187**). All three charge very reasonable greens fees of $25 to $28. For information on the Web, check out **www.seattlegolf.com**.

HIKING

Within Seattle itself, there are several large natural parks laced with enough trails to allow for a few good long walks. Among these are **Seward Park,** 5898 Lake Washington Blvd., southeast of downtown, and **Lincoln Park,** 8011 Fauntleroy Ave. SW, south of Alki Beach in West Seattle. However, the city's largest natural park and Seattleites' favorite quick dose of nature is **Discovery Park,** 3801 W Government Way (© **206/386-4236**), northwest of downtown at the western tip of the Magnolia neighborhood. This park covers more than 500 acres and has many miles of trails and beaches to hike. There are gorgeous views, forest paths, and meadows for lazing in after a long walk. To reach Discovery Park, follow Elliott Avenue north along the waterfront from downtown Seattle, then take the Magnolia Bridge west toward the Magnolia neighborhood and follow Grayfield Street to Galer Street to Magnolia Boulevard.

For more challenging hiking in the real outdoors, head east of Seattle on I-90. Rising abruptly from the floor of the Snoqualmie Valley outside the town of North Bend is **Mount Si** 🌟🌟, with a tiring trail to its summit, but a payoff of awesome views (take lots of water—it's an 8-mile round-trip hike). From I-90, take the North Bend exit (exit 31), drive into town, turn right at the stoplight onto North Bend Way, continue through town, turn left onto Mount Si Rd. and continue 2.1 miles to the trailhead.

Farther east on I-90, at **Snoqualmie Pass** and just west of the pass, there are several trailheads. Some trails lead to mountain summits, others to glacier-carved lakes, and still others past waterfalls deep in the forest. Due to their proximity to Seattle, these trails can be very crowded, and you will need a Northwest Forest Pass ($5 for a 1-day pass) to leave your car at national forest trailheads (though not at the Mount Si trailhead, which is on state land). For more information and to purchase a Northwest Forest Pass, contact the **Snoqualmie Ranger District** (© **425/888-1421**) in North Bend.

IN-LINE SKATING

Throughout the city, there are dozens of miles of paved paths that are perfect for skating. You can rent in-line skates at **Greg's Green Lake Cycle,** 7007 Wood-lawn Ave. NE (© **206/523-1822**), for $20 per day or $7 per hour. The trail around **Green Lake** in north Seattle and the **Burke-Gilman/Sammamish River Trail** (see the description under "Biking," above) are both good places for skating and are convenient to Gregg's. Other favorite skating spots to try include the paved path in **Myrtle Edwards Park** just north of the Seattle waterfront, the paved path along **Lake Washington Boulevard** north of Seward Park, and the **Alki Beach** pathway in West Seattle.

JOGGING

The waterfront, from **Pioneer Square north to Myrtle Edwards Park,** where a paved path parallels the water, is a favorite downtown jogging route. The residential streets of **Capitol Hill,** when combined with roads and sidewalks through **Volunteer Park,** are another good choice. If you happen to be staying in the University District, you can access the 27-mile-long **Burke-Gilman/Sammamish River Trail** or run the ever-popular trail around **Green Lake.** Out in West Seattle, the **Alki Beach** pathway is also very popular and provides great views of the Olympics.

SEA KAYAKING, CANOEING, ROWING & SAILING

If you'd like to try your hand at **sea kayaking** 🌟🌟, try the **Northwest Outdoor Center** 🌟🌟, 2100 Westlake Ave. N. (© **800/683-0637** or 206/281-9694), which is located on the west side of Lake Union. Here you can rent a sea kayak for between $10 and $15 per hour. You can also opt for guided tours lasting from a few hours to several days, and there are plenty of classes available for those who are interested.

Moss Bay Rowing and Kayak Center, 1001 Fairview Ave. N. (© **206/682-2031;** www.mossbay.net), rents sea kayaks (as well as canoes, bicycle boats, and sailboats) at the south end of Lake Union near Chandler's Cove. Rates range from $10 per hour for a single to $15 per hour for a double. Because this rental center is a little closer to downtown Seattle, it makes a better choice if you are here without a car.

The **University of Washington Waterfront Activities Center,** on the university campus behind Husky Stadium (© **206/543-9433**), is open to the public and rents canoes and rowboats for $6.50 per hour. With the marshes of the Washington Park Arboretum directly across a narrow channel from the boat launch, this is an ideal place for the inexperienced to rent a boat.

For information on renting wooden rowboats and sailboats on Lake Union, see **The Center for Wooden Boats** listing on p. 98.

SKIING

One of the reasons Seattleites put up with long, wet winters is because they can go skiing within an hour of the city—with many slopes set up for night skiing, it's possible to leave work and be on the slopes before dinner, ski for several hours, and be home in time to get a good night's rest. The ski season in the Seattle area generally runs from mid-November to the end of April. Equipment can be rented at the ski area listed below, and at **REI,** 222 Yale Ave. N. (© **206/223-1944**).

CROSS-COUNTRY SKIING   In the Snoqualmie Pass area of the Cascade Range, less than 50 miles east of Seattle on I-90, the **Summit Nordic Center**

(© **425/434-7669,** ext. 4531), offers rentals, instruction, and many miles of groomed trails.

There are also several sno-parks along I-90 at Snoqualmie Pass. Some of these have groomed trails while others have trails that are marked but not groomed. When renting skis, be sure to get a **Sno-Park permit.** These are required if you want to park at a cross-country ski area. Sno-park permits are available at ski shops.

DOWNHILL SKIING Jointly known as **The Summit at Snoqualmie,** Alpental, Summit West, Summit Central, and Summit East ski areas (© **425/ 434-7669** for information, or 206/236-1600 for the snow report; www. summit-at-snoqualmie.com) are all located at Snoqualmie Pass, less than 50 miles east of Seattle off I-90. Together, these four ski areas offer more than 65 ski runs, rentals, and lessons. Adult all-day lift ticket prices range from $29 to $37. Call for hours of operation.

TENNIS

Seattle Parks and Recreation operates dozens of outdoor tennis courts all over the city. The most convenient are at **Volunteer Park,** 1247 15th Ave. E. (at East Prospect Street), and at **Lower Woodland Park,** 5851 W. Green Lake Way N.

If it happens to be raining and you had your heart set on playing tennis, there are indoor public courts at the **Seattle Tennis Center,** 2000 Martin Luther King Jr. Way S. (© **206/684-4764**). Rates here are $15 for singles and $20 for doubles for 1¼ hours. This center also has outdoor courts for $6 for 1½ hours.

9 Spectator Sports

With professional football, baseball, basketball, women's basketball, and ice hockey teams, as well as the various University of Washington Huskies teams, Seattle is definitely a city of sports fans. For those many fans, the sports landscape has been changing dramatically in recent years. In 1999, a stunningly beautiful, state-of-the-art baseball stadium was unveiled in the form of the retractable-roof Safeco Field. In 2000, the venerable and much disparaged Kingdome was demolished to make way for a new football stadium that should be ready for the 2002 season.

TicketMaster (© **206/622-HITS;** www.ticketmaster.com) sells tickets to almost all sporting events in the Seattle area. There are TicketMaster outlets at area Rite-Aid, Wherehouse, and Tower Record and Video stores. If they're sold out, try **Pacific Northwest Ticket Service** (© **206/232-0150**).

BASEBALL

Of all of Seattle's major league sports teams, none are more popular than the American League's **Seattle Mariners** (© **800/MY-MARINERS** or 206/ 346-4000; www.mariners.org). Despite the high-profile departures in recent years of superstars Randy Johnson, Ken Griffey Jr., and A-Rod, the Mariners won at an astounding clip in 2001, tying the 1906 Chicago Cubs for the most regular-season wins in baseball history. The team has a devoted following, which only grew more fanatical in 2001 with the addition of Japanese sensation Ichiro Suzuki.

The Mariners' retrostyle **Safeco Field** ✯✯✯, which hosted the All-Star Game in 2001, is indisputably one of the most gorgeous ballparks in the country. It's also one of only a handful of stadiums with a retractable roof (which can open

Jugglers, dancers and an assortment of acrobats fill the street.

She shoots you a wide-eyed look as a seven-foot cartoon character approaches.

What brought you here was wanting the kids

to see something magical while they still believed in magic.

Travelocity.com
A Sabre Company
Go Virtually Anywhere.

With 700 airlines, 50,000 hotels and over 5,000 cruise and vaca-

tion getaways, you can now go places you've always dreamed of.

WORLD'S LEADING TRAVEL WEB SITE, 5 YEARS IN A ROW" WORLD TRAVEL AWARDS

I HAVE TO CALL THE TRAVEL AGENCY AGAIN. DARN, OUT TO LUNCH. NOW I HAVE TO CALL THE AIRLINE. I HATE CALLING THE AIRLINES. I GOT PUT ON HOLD AGAIN. "INSTRUMENTAL TOP-40" ... LOVELY. I HATE GETTING PUT ON HOLD. TICKET PRICES ARE ALL OVER THE MAP. HOW DO I DIAL INTERNA-TIONALLY? OH SHOOT, FORGOT THE RENTAL CAR. I'M STILL ON HOLD. THIS MUSIC IS GIVING ME A HEADACHE. I WONDER IF SOMEONE ELSE HAS CHEAPER FLIGHTS. FORGET IT, CAN'T TAKE IT ANYMORE ... I'M HANGING UP.

YAHOO! TRAVEL 100% MUZAK-FREE

Booking your trip online at Yahoo! Travel is simple. You compare the best prices. You click. You go have fun. Tickets, hotels, rental cars, cruises & more. Sorry, no muzak.

or close in about 10–20 min.), allowing the Mariners to have a real grass playing field without having to worry about getting rained out.

Ticket prices range from $6 to $36. Though you may be able to get a single
ticket on game day at the Safeco Field box office, that's about all (it would be
tough to get two seats together). Mariners' tickets are a hot commodity, so if you
want to ensure that you get good seats, order in advance at Mariners Team Stores
(see below), or through TicketMaster (© 206/622-HITS; www.ticketmaster.
com), which has outlets at many Rite-Aid pharmacies, as well as Wherehouse
and Tower record stores. Parking is next to impossible in the immediate vicinity
of Safeco Field, so plan to leave your car behind.

If you'd like a behind-the-scenes look at the stadium, you can take a 1-hour
tour ($7 for adults, $5 for seniors, and $3 for kids ages 3–12); tickets can be
purchased at the Mariners Team Store at Safeco Field, other Mariners Team
Stores around the city (there are locations at Fourth and Stewart streets downtown and in Bellevue Square), or through TicketMaster. Tour times vary, and
tours are not offered on days when day games are scheduled.

BASKETBALL

The NBA's **Seattle SuperSonics** (© 206/281-5800; www.supersonics.com)
play in the Key Arena at Seattle Center, and though they always seem to trail
behind Portland's Trailblazers, they generally put in a good showing every season. Tickets are $9 to $110 and are available at the arena box office and through
TicketMaster (© 206/628-0888). Tickets can generally be had even on short
notice, except for games against the Lakers and Blazers, which are always well
attended.

The University of Washington Huskies women's basketball team has been
pretty popular for years, and Seattle also has a pro women's basketball team. The
Women's National Basketball Association's (WNBA) **Seattle Storm** (© 206/
217-WNBA; www.storm.wnba.com) brought professional women's basketball
to Seattle's Key Arena. Ticket prices range from $8 to $45 and are available at
the arena box office and through TicketMaster (© 206/628-0888).

For information on the women's and men's Huskies basketball games, contact
University of Washington Sports (© 206/543-2200).

FOOTBALL

Although the NFL's **Seattle Seahawks** (© 888/NFL-HAWK or 206/682-2800;
www.seahawks.com) aren't the most highly regarded of Seattle's professional
sports teams, the people of Washington state obviously didn't want to see the
Seahawks leave town, or they wouldn't have voted to tax themselves in order to
build a new stadium. Starting with the 2002 season, the Seahawks will begin
playing in their new stadium, which stands on the site of the old Kingdome.
Expect the team's popularity to pick up once they're in the new stadium. Tickets run $15 to $68 and are generally available, depending on how well the team
is doing. Games against Oakland, Denver, and a couple of other teams usually
sell out as soon as tickets first go on sale in August. Traffic and parking in the
vicinity of the new stadium will likely be a nightmare on game days, so take the
bus if you can.

Not surprisingly, the **University of Washington Huskies** (© 206/
543-2200), who play in Husky Stadium on the university campus, have a loyal
following. Big games (Nebraska or Washington State) sell out as soon as tickets
go on sale in the summer. Other games can sell out in advance, but there are

usually obstructed-view tickets available on the day of the game. Ticket prices range from $32 to $36.

HOCKEY

The Western Hockey League's **Seattle Thunderbirds** (© **206/448-PUCK;** www.seattle-thunderbirds.com) play major junior ice hockey at the Key Arena in Seattle Center. While Seattle isn't really a hockey town, the Thunderbirds have quite a following. Tickets, which range in price from $8 to $20 are available by calling the above number or TicketMaster (© **206/628-0888**).

HORSE RACING

The state-of-the-art **Emerald Downs,** 2300 Emerald Downs Dr. (© **888/ 931-8400** or 253/288-7711; www.emeralddowns.com) racetrack is located south of Seattle in the city of Auburn off Wash. 167 (reached from I-405 at the south end of Lake Washington). To reach the track, take the 15th Avenue NW exit. Admission prices range from $4 to $6.50. The season runs from mid-April to mid-September.

MARATHON

The **Seattle Marathon** (© **206/729-3660;** www.seattlemarathon.org) takes place the Sunday after Thanksgiving. The race starts and ends at Seattle Center and crosses the I-90 floating bridge to Mercer Island.

SOCCER

If you're a soccer fan, you can catch the United Soccer League's **Seattle Sounders** play (© **800/796-KICK** or 206/622-3415; www.seattlesounders.net) at Seattle Memorial Stadium in Seattle Center. Tickets are $12 to $15 and are available through TicketMaster (© **206/628-0888**).

10 Day Spas

If you prefer pampering to paddling a kayak, facials to fishing, or massages to mountain climbing, then you'll be glad to know that Seattle has plenty of day spas scattered around the metro area. These facilities offer such treatments as massages, facials, seaweed wraps, mud baths, and the like. Seattle day spas include **Aveda,** in the Alexis Hotel, 1015 First Ave. (© **206/628-9605**); **Gene Juarez Salons,** 607 Pine St. (© **206/326-6000;** wwwgenejuarez.com); **Marketplace Salon and Day Spa,** 2001 First Ave. (© **206/441-5511**); and **Ummelina,** 1525 Fourth Ave. (© **206/624-1370**). A wide variety of treatments are available. Expect to pay $150 to $200 for a half day of pampering and $300 to $400 or more for a full day.

7

Strolling Around Seattle

Downtown Seattle is compact and easily explored on foot (if you don't mind hills). Most visitors end up walking between Pioneer Square and Pike Place Market via the waterfront. Everything along the waterfront is right there to be seen, and Pike Place Market is a fascinating maze best enjoyed by getting lost among its shops and stalls for several hours.

Some people make the mistake of dismissing the Pioneer Square area as just a neighborhood of winos and street people, but it is actually far more than that. To help you get the most out of downtown Seattle's only historic neighborhood, we've outlined a walking tour that takes in interesting shops, art galleries, and historic buildings.

The second walking tour will take you through the Fremont District. Home to hippies and other counter-culture types, Fremont is a quirky area filled with tongue-in-cheek art and unusual shops.

WALKING TOUR 1 **THE PIONEER SQUARE AREA**

Start: Pioneer Place at the corner of Yesler Way and First Avenue.
Finish: Elliott Bay Book Company.
Time: Approximately 5 hours, including shopping, dining, and museum stops.
Best Times: Weekdays, when the neighborhood and the Seattle Underground Tour are not so crowded.
Worst Times: Weekends, when the area is very crowded, and Mondays, when galleries are closed.

In the late 19th century, Pioneer Square was the heart of downtown Seattle, so when a fire raged through these blocks in 1889, the city was devastated. However, residents and merchants quickly began rebuilding and set about to remedy many of the infrastructure problems that had faced Seattle in the years before the fire. Today this small section of the city is all that remains of old Seattle. Since one architect, Elmer Fisher, was responsible for the design of many of the buildings constructed after the fire, the neighborhood has a distinctly uniform architectural style.

While wandering these streets, don't bother looking for a specific site called Pioneer Square; you won't find it. The name actually applies to the whole neighborhood, not a plaza surrounded by four streets, as you would surmise. Do keep your eye out for interesting manhole covers, many of which were cast with maps of Seattle or Northwest Coast Indian designs. Also be aware that this neighborhood, the original Skid Row, still has several missions and homeless shelters—consequently, there are a lot of street people in the area.

Some people make the mistake of dismissing the Pioneer Square area as just a neighborhood of winos and street people, but it is actually far more than that.

To get the most out of downtown Seattle's only historic neighborhood, we have outlined a walking tour that takes in interesting shops, art galleries, and historic buildings. Bear in mind that this area was hard hit by the 6.8 earthquake that rocked Seattle on February 28, 2001. At press time, many historic buildings remained unrepaired.

Start your tour of this historic neighborhood at the corner of Yesler Way and First Avenue on:

❶ Pioneer Place

The triangular park at the heart of Pioneer Square is the site of a totem pole that's a replacement for one that caught fire in 1938. The original pole had, in 1890, been stolen from a Tlingit village far to the north of Seattle. Legend has it that after the pole burned, the city fathers sent a check for $5,000 requesting a new totem pole. The Tlingit response was, "Thanks for paying for the first one. Send another $5,000 for a replacement." A 1905 cast-iron pergola that once stood in the park was damaged by a truck in early 2001 and at press time was being rebuilt.

Facing the square are several historic buildings, including the gabled Lowman Building and three buildings noteworthy for their terra-cotta facades. In one of these buildings, at 608 First Ave., you'll find the ticket counter for Seattle's:

❷ Underground Tour

This tour takes a look at the Pioneer Square area from beneath the sidewalks. The tour (✆ **206/682-4646** for information) is a great introduction to the history of the area (if you don't mind off-color jokes) and actually spends quite a bit of time aboveground (duplicating much of the walking tour outlined here).

In the basement of the Pioneer Building, 602 First Ave., one of the architectural standouts on Pioneer Place, you'll find the:

❸ Pioneer Square Antique Mall

This complex (✆ **206/624-1164**) is home to dozens of antiques and collectibles dealers.

Running along the south side of Pioneer Place is:

❹ Yesler Way

This was the original Skid Row. In Seattle's early years, logs were skidded down this road to a lumber mill on the waterfront, and the road came to be known as Skid Road. These days Yesler Way is trying hard to live down its reputation, but, due to the missions in this neighborhood, there are still a lot of street people in the area (and they'll most certainly be asking you for change as you wander the streets).

TAKE A BREAK
Merchants Cafe, 109 Yesler Way (✆ **206/624-1515**) is the oldest restaurant in Seattle and a good place for an inexpensive lunch or dinner. If you skipped the Underground Tour, then cross Yesler Way to the corner of Yesler and First Avenue, to the **Starbucks,** where you can pick up a latte to help fuel you through this walking tour. Right next door to Starbucks, you'll find **Cow Chips,** 102A First Ave. S., where you can get one of the best (though messiest) chocolate chip cookies you'll ever taste.

With cookie and coffee in hand, glance up Yesler Way, past a triangular parking deck (a monstrosity that prompted the movement to preserve the rest of this neighborhood), to:

❺ Smith Tower

This structure, at 506 Second Ave. (✆ **206/622-4004**), was the tallest building west of the Mississippi when it was completed in 1914. The observation floor near the top of this early skyscraper, is open to the public and provides a very different perspective on Seattle than the Space Needle does.

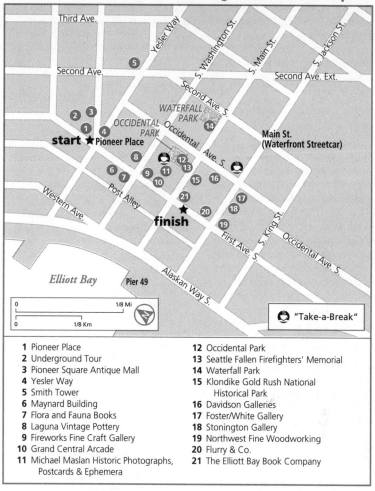

1 Pioneer Place
2 Underground Tour
3 Pioneer Square Antique Mall
4 Yesler Way
5 Smith Tower
6 Maynard Building
7 Flora and Fauna Books
8 Laguna Vintage Pottery
9 Fireworks Fine Craft Gallery
10 Grand Central Arcade
11 Michael Maslan Historic Photographs,
   Postcards & Ephemera

12 Occidental Park
13 Seattle Fallen Firefighters' Memorial
14 Waterfall Park
15 Klondike Gold Rush National
   Historical Park
16 Davidson Galleries
17 Foster/White Gallery
18 Stonington Gallery
19 Northwest Fine Woodworking
20 Flurry & Co.
21 The Elliott Bay Book Company

The ornate lobby and elevator doors are also worth checking out.

Now, walk down back down to First Avenue and turn left, away from Pioneer Place, and at the next corner, Washington Street, look across First Avenue and admire the:

6 Maynard Building

This ornate building, which is named for Seattle founding father David "Doc" Maynard, was the site of Seattle's first bank.

If your fingers aren't too messy from eating your Cow Chip cookie, you might want to stop by:

7 Flora & Fauna Books

Located below street level in the Maynard Building, this specialty bookstore, at 121 First Ave. S. (© **206/623-4727**), is filled with plant and animal field guides, gardening books, and the like.

Heading up Washington Street away from the water for half a block will bring you to:

8 Laguna Vintage Pottery

This shop, at 116 S. Washington St. (© **206/682-6162**), specializes in midcentury pottery, primarily from California. Fiesta, Bauer, and Weller are all well represented.

From here, head back to First Avenue and turn left. On this block, at 210 First Ave. S., you'll find:

⑨ Fireworks Fine Crafts Gallery

This gallery (© 206/682-8707) sells colorful and unusual crafts by Northwest artisans.

Next, at 214 First Ave. S., you'll come to the:

⑩ Grand Central Arcade

Inside this small, European-style shopping arcade, with its brick walls and wine cellar–like basement shops and studios, you'll find:

⑪ Michael Maslan Historic Photographs, Postcards & Ephemera

This store (© 206/587-0187) is crammed full of vintage travel posters, ethnographic photos, and thousands of postcards. Before leaving the Grand Central Arcade, be sure to check out the historic photos in the basement.

TAKE A BREAK
In the arcade you'll also find the **Grand Central Baking Company** (© 206/622-3644), plus some tables and even a fireplace, which together make this a great place to stop for lunch if you didn't already eat. Alternatively, you can grab some food to go and head over to Waterfall Park (see below).

Leaving Grand Central Arcade through the door opposite where you came in will bring you out into:

⑫ Occidental Park

On this shady, cobblestone plaza stand four totem poles carved by Northwest artist Duane Pasco. The tallest is the 35-foot-high *The Sun and Raven,* which tells the story of how Raven brought light into the world. Next to this pole is *Man Riding a Whale.* This type of totem pole was traditionally carved to help villagers during their whale hunts. The other two figures that face each other are symbols of the Bear Clan and the Welcoming Figure.

This shady park serves as a gathering spot for homeless people, so you may not want to linger. However, before leaving the park, be sure to notice the grouping of bronze statues, the:

⑬ Seattle Fallen Firefighters' Memorial

The memorial was designed by students at a local art school.

The statues are adjacent to South Main Street, and if you walk up this street to the corner of Second Avenue, you will come to:

⑭ Waterfall Park

The roaring waterfall here looks as if it had been transported here straight from the Cascade Range. The park is built on the site of the original United Parcel Service (UPS) offices and makes a wonderful place for a rest or a picnic lunch.

Now, walk back the way you came and, across from Occidental Park at 117 S. Main St., you'll find the:

⑮ Klondike Gold Rush National Historical Park

Not really a "park," this small museum (© 206/553-7220) is dedicated to the history of the 1897–98 Klondike gold rush, which helped Seattle grow from an obscure town into a booming metropolis.

Around the corner from this small museum is Occidental Mall, where you'll find a couple of art galleries, including:

⑯ Davidson Galleries

You never know what to expect when you walk through the front door here at 313 Occidental Ave. S. (© 206/624-7684). The gallery sells everything from 16th-century prints to contemporary art by Northwest artists.

TAKE A BREAK
If it's time for another latte, cross the plaza to **Torrefazione,** 320 Occidental Ave. S. (© 206/624-5847), which serves some of the best coffee in Seattle. Be sure to get yours in one of the hand-painted cups.

Diagonally across from Torrefazione, at 123 S. Jackson St., you'll find the:

⑰ Foster/White Gallery

This gallery (② 206/622-2833) is best known for its art glass. It's the Seattle gallery for famed glass artist Dale Chihuly, and always has several of his works on display.

Right next door, at 119 S. Jackson St., you'll find the:

⑱ Stonington Gallery

This gallery (② 206/405-4040) is one of Seattle's top showcases for contemporary Native American arts and crafts. Here you'll find a good selection of Northwest Coast Indian masks, woodcarvings, prints, and jewelry.

Continue to the corner of First Avenue, where you'll find:

⑲ Northwest Fine Woodworking

This large store at 101 S. Jackson St. (② 206/625-0542) sells exquisite, handcrafted wooden furniture, as well as some smaller pieces. It's well worth a visit.

From here, cross South Jackson Street, where you'll find:

⑳ Flury & Co.

This gallery, at 322 First Ave. S. (② 206/587-0260), specializes in prints by photographer Edward S. Curtis, who is known for his portraits of Native Americans. There's also an excellent selection of antique Native American art.

From here, head up First Avenue to the corner of Main Street, where you'll find the:

㉑ Elliott Bay Book Company

One of the city's most popular bookstores, The Elliott Bay Book Company stands at 101 S. Main St. (② 206/624-6600). It boasts an extensive selection of books on Seattle and the Northwest. With so much great browsing to be done here, this bookstore makes a great place to end your walking tour of the Pioneer Square area.

WALKING TOUR 2 FUN, FUNKY FREMONT

Start:	South end of Fremont Bridge near Ponti restaurant.
Finish:	Trolleyman Pub at the corner of Phinney Avenue and 34th Street.
Time:	Approximately 2 hours, not including time spent dining.
Best Times:	Sunday, during the Fremont Sunday Market.
Worst Times:	Early morning or evening, when shops are closed.

Fremont marches to the beat of a different drummer than the rest of the city. Styling itself the Republic of Fremont and the center of the universe, this small, tight-knit community is the most eclectic neighborhood in the city. It has taken as its motto "De Libertas Quirkas," which roughly translated means "free to be peculiar." Fremont residents have focused on art as a way to draw the community together, and in so doing, they've created a corner of the city where silliness reigns. At this crossroads business district, you'll find unusual outdoor art, the Fremont Sunday Market, several vintage clothing and furniture stores, a couple of brewpubs, and many other unexpected and unusual shops, galleries, and cafes. During the summer there are outdoor movies held on Saturday nights, and in June there is the wacky Solstice Parade, a countercultural promenade with giant puppets, wizards, fairies, face paint, and hippies of all ages.

Start your tour by finding a parking spot around the corner from Ponti restaurant at the south end of the:

❶ Fremont Bridge

This is the busiest drawbridge in the United States and spans the Lake

Washington Ship Canal. "Welcome to the center of the Universe" reads the sign at the south end of the bridge.

As you approach the north side of the bridge, glance up and in the window of the bridge-tender's tower on the west side of the bridge, you'll see:

❷ *Rapunzel*

This is a neon sculpture of the famous fairy-tale maiden with the prodigious mane. Her neon tresses cascade down the wall of the tower.

On your immediate right, the big modern building crowding up against the bridge is world headquarters for software giant:

❸ Adobe

This is the Adobe of Illustrator and Photoshop fame. Longtime Fremont residents fear that Adobe's presence in the neighborhood could signal the end of Fremont's funky days, and, indeed, in the past year, this neighborhood has changed considerably, rapidly losing its appealing funkiness.

As you finally land in the Republic of Fremont, you will see, at the end of the bridge on the opposite side of the street from *Rapunzel*, Seattle's most beloved public sculpture:

❹ *Waiting for the Interurban*

This piece features several people waiting for the trolley that no longer runs between Fremont and downtown Seattle. These statues are frequently dressed up by local residents, with costumes changing regularly.

Cross to the far side of 34th Street and walk east along this street past some of Fremont's interesting shops, including:

❺ Portage Bay Goods

This store, at 706 N. 34th St. (© 206/ 547-5221), sells an eclectic array of things that "enrich the soul, support the community, and preserve the environment." Check out the notebooks made from old computer boards.

A few doors down, you'll find:

❻ History House

This neighborhood museum of history (© 206/675-8875) is complete with modern interactive exhibits and a beautiful fence out front.

If it happens to be Sunday, continue 3 blocks east on North 34th Street to the corner of Stone Way North where you'll find the:

❼ Fremont Sunday Market

You never know what you might find at this combination flea market and produce market—perhaps some army surplus Scottish kilts, some organic strawberries, or maybe a rack of vintage Hawaiian shirts.

If it isn't Sunday, turn left at History House and head uphill underneath the Aurora Bridge, which towers high above. If it is Sunday, after visiting the market, return to History House and head up the hill. At the top of the hill, you will see, lurking in the shadows beneath the bridge:

❽ *The Fremont Troll*

This massive monster is in the process of crushing a Volkswagen Beetle. No need to run in fear, though, as a wizard seems to have put a spell on the troll and turned it into cement.

Turn left at the troll and walk a block down North 35th Street to the best little cafe in the neighborhood.

> **TAKE A BREAK**
> **Still Life in Fremont Coffeehouse**, 709 N. 35th St. (© 206/547-9850), is a classic hippie hangout, with a swinging screen door, wood floors, and lots of alternative newspapers on hand at all times. Although oatmeal is a specialty, there are also soups, salads, sandwiches, pastries, and good espresso.

From Still Life in Fremont, it's only a few steps down the hill to the corner of North Fremont Avenue and Fremont Place. Take a left here to reach:

❾ Frank and Dunya

This shop, at 3418 Fremont Ave. N. (© 206/547-6760), sells colorful household decor, including switch plates, cups and saucers, mirrors, jewelry, art, rustic furniture, and little shrines. It's all very playful.

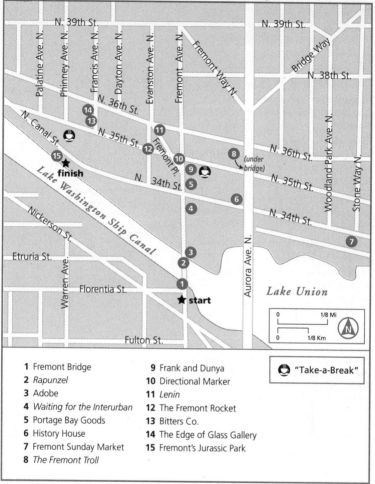

1 Fremont Bridge
2 *Rapunzel*
3 Adobe
4 *Waiting for the Interurban*
5 Portage Bay Goods
6 History House
7 Fremont Sunday Market
8 *The Fremont Troll*
9 Frank and Dunya
10 Directional Marker
11 *Lenin*
12 The Fremont Rocket
13 Bitters Co.
14 The Edge of Glass Gallery
15 Fremont's Jurassic Park

⬤ "Take-a-Break"

Go back up to the corner, cross North Fremont Avenue to the traffic island, where you'll find both the center of the center of the universe and Fremont's:

⑩ Directional marker

This old-fashioned signpost has arrows that point to such important locations as the center of the universe (straight down), the *Fremont Troll, Rapunzel,* Atlantis, and the North Pole.

From the signpost, continue west (away from the intersection) on Fremont Place, and in 1 block (at the corner of N. 36th Street), you will see a larger-than-life statue of:

⑪ *Lenin*

This 20-foot-tall statue in no way reflects the attitudes of the many very capitalistic merchants in the neighborhood.

After communing with Comrade Lenin, cross North 36th Street and walk a block down Evanston Avenue to the:

⑫ The Fremont Rocket

Although there is speculation that this rocket was used by the aliens who founded Fremont, the truth is far stranger. You can read the entire history of the rocket on a map board below the rocket. (If you haven't already figured it out, the locals don't want you getting lost in their neighborhood, so they've put up maps all over to help you find your way from one famous Fremont locale to the next.)

From here, head back up to North 36th Street, and continue west for another couple of blocks to:

⓭ Bitters Co.

This unusual combination import store and wine bar at 513 N. 36th St. (© **206/632-0886**) also has live music on Friday nights. The imports here tend toward the eclectic, rustic, and Asian.

Right next door you'll find:

⓮ The Edge of Glass Gallery

In this showroom at 513 N. 36th St. (© **206/547-6551**), you can often see art-glass artists at work. Even if there's no one blowing glass, there are plenty of beautiful pieces of art glass to see.

From here, continue west on North 36th Street and then turn left on Phinney Avenue North, at the foot of which you'll find:

⓯ Fremont's Jurassic Park

Don't worry, no velociraptors here at the corner of North 34th Street and Phinney Avenue North—just a pair of friendly topiary apotosaurs (sort of like brontosaurs) donated to the neighborhood by the Pacific Science Center. Unfortunately, these dinosaurs weren't yet members of the green party at press time and remained merely a framework ready to have plants added.

And what's that across the street? A brewpub! What a fortuitous end to a most excellent peregrination through the Republic of Fremont.

WINDING DOWN
The Redhook Ale Brewery's little **Trolleyman Pub,** 3400 Phinney Ave. N. (© **206/ 634-4213**), serves pints of draft ESB (Extra Special Bitter), Seattle's favorite craft ale.

8

Seattle Shopping

As the largest city in the state, Seattle has always been where Washingtonians shop. Nordstrom, Eddie Bauer, and REI (all of which were founded in Seattle) have become familiar to shoppers all across the country, and these stores remain some of the busiest in the city. However, in the past few years, as Seattle has developed a national reputation as a great place to put down roots, the retail face of the city has changed considerably.

National chains have taken over many of the storefronts of downtown Seattle, opening up flashy new stores and cashing in on the city's newfound popularity. The names and merchandise at these stores are familiar: Banana Republic, Nike, Levi Strauss, Ann Taylor, FAO Schwartz, Barneys New York. These and many others now have stores in Seattle, so if you forgot to pick up that dress in Chicago or those running shoes in New York, have no fear—you can find them here.

Seattle does, however, have one last bastion of local merchandising, **Pike Place Market.** Whether shopping is your passion or an occasional indulgence, you shouldn't miss this historic market, which is actually one of Seattle's top tourist attractions. Once the city's main produce market (and quite a few produce stalls remain), this sprawling collection of buildings is today filled with hundreds of unusual shops, including **Market Magic** (for magicians and aspiring magicians; © 206/624-4271), **The Spanish Table** (filled with Spanish cooking supplies; © 206/682-2814), **Tenzing Momo** (selling body oils, incense, herbs, and such; © 206/623-9837), **The Rubber Rainbow** (a condom store; © 206/233-9502), **The Women's Hall of Fame** (a feminist bookstore; © 206/622-8427), and **Left Bank Books** (a bookstore for anarchists and their kin; © 206/622-0195). See also the listing for Pike Place Market on p. 95.

After tasting the bounties of the Northwest, it's hard to go back to Safeway, Sanka, and Chicken of the Sea. Sure you can get coffee, wine, and seafood where you live, but do a little food shopping in Seattle and you'll be tapping the source. Washington state wines, coffee from the original Starbucks, and fish that flies—these are a few of the culinary treats that await you here.

1 The Shopping Scene

Although Seattle is a city of neighborhoods, many of which have great little shops, ground zero of the Seattle shopping scene is the corner of **Pine Street and Fifth Avenue.** Within 2 blocks of this intersection are two major department stores (Nordstrom and The Bon Marché) and two upscale urban shopping malls (Westlake Center and Pacific Place). There's even a sky bridge between Nordstrom and Pacific Place to make shopping just that much easier. Fanning out east and south from this intersection are blocks of upscale stores that have begun to take on a very familiar look. Small local shops are rapidly being replaced by national and international boutiques and megastores. Here in this neighborhood you'll now find Ann Taylor, Barneys New York, NIKETOWN, Gap, MaxMara, Banana Republic, and FAO Schwartz. However, you'll still find a few local mom-and-pop stores in the neighborhood.

The city's main tourist shopping district is the **Pike Place Market** neighborhood. Here you'll find dozens of T-shirt and souvenir shops, as well as import shops and stores appealing to teenagers and 20-somethings. Pike Place Market itself is a fascinating warren of cubbyholes that pass for shops. While produce isn't usually something you stock up on while on vacation, there are several market shops that sell ethnic cooking supplies that are less perishable than a dozen oysters or a king salmon. While you may never find anything here you really need, it's still fun to look (at least that's what millions of Seattle visitors each year seem to think).

Just west of Pike Place Market is the Seattle **waterfront,** where you'll find many more gift and souvenir shops.

South of downtown, in the historic **Pioneer Square area,** you'll find the city's greatest concentration of art galleries, some of which specialize in Native American art. This neighborhood also has several antiques stores, but is also home to lots of bars and attracts a lot of homeless people.

As the center of both the gay community and the city's youth culture, **Capitol Hill** has the most eclectic selection of shops in the city. Beads, imports, CDs, vintage clothing, politically correct merchandise, and gay-oriented goods fill the shops along Broadway. Capitol Hill's main shopping plaza is the Broadway Market, which has lots of small shops.

Even funkier than Capitol Hill, the **Fremont** neighborhood just north of Lake Union is filled with retro stores selling vintage clothing, midcentury furniture and collectibles, and curious crafts. However, this neighborhood is undergoing a fairly rapid gentrification that is forcing out many of the smaller and more unusual shops.

A couple of miles east of Fremont there's the **Wallingford** neighborhood, which is anchored by an old schoolhouse that has been converted into a shopping arcade with interesting crafts, fashions, and gifts.

The **University District,** also in north Seattle, has everything necessary to support a student population and also goes upscale at the University Village shopping center.

2 Shopping A to Z
ANTIQUES & COLLECTIBLES

If antiques are your passion, you won't want to miss the opportunity to spend a day browsing the many antiques stores in the historic farm town of **Snohomish.** Located roughly 30 miles north of Seattle off I-5, Snohomish was established in 1859 on the banks of the Snohomish River and was the county seat until 1897. When the county seat was moved to Everett, Snohomish lost its regional importance and development slowed considerably. Today, an abundance of turn-of-the-20th-century buildings are the legacy of the town's early economic growth. By the 1960s, these old homes had begun attracting people interested in restoring them to their original condition, and soon antiques shops began proliferating in the historic downtown area. Today the town has more than 400 antiques dealers and is without a doubt the antiques capital of the Northwest. See also chapter 10, "Side Trips from Seattle."

The Crane Gallery   Chinese, Japanese, and Korean antiquities are the focus of this shop in the Queen Anne neighborhood, which prides itself on selling only the best pieces. Imperial Chinese porcelains, bronze statues of Buddhist deities, rosewood furniture, Japanese ceramics, netsukes, snuff bottles, and Chinese archaeological artifacts are just some of the quality antiques you'll find here. Some Southeast Asian and Indian objects are also available. 104 W. Roy St. (C) 206/298-9425.

Honeychurch Antiques   For high-quality Asian antiques, including Japanese wood-block prints, textiles, furniture, and ivory and woodcarvings, few Seattle antiques stores can approach Honeychurch Antiques. Regular special exhibits give this shop the feel of a tiny museum. The store's annex, called **Glenn Richards,** 964 Denny Way ((C) 206/287-1877), specializes in "entry-level" antiques. 1008 James St. (C) 206/622-1225.

Jean Williams Antiques   If your taste in antiques runs to 18th- and 19th-century French and English formal or country furniture, this Pioneer Square antiques dealer may have something to add to your collection. 115 S. Jackson St. (C) 206/622-1110.

Laguna Vintage Pottery   Twentieth-century art pottery is the specialty of this shop in Pioneer Square. Pieces by such midcentury pottery factories as Fiesta, Roseville, Bauer, Weller, and Franciscan are stacked on the shelves here in this old brick building. This is a great place to look for dinnerware and vintage tiles. 116 S. Washington St. (C) 206/682-6162.

Michael Maslan Vintage Photographs, Postcards & Ephemera Located in the Pioneer Square area's Grand Central Arcade, this store is crammed full of vintage travel posters, ethnographic photos, and thousands of postcards. With a focus on social, industrial, and historical images, Michael Maslan's philosophy is to collect (and sell) just about anything "written, printed, or painted" that's old or interesting. 214 First Ave. S. (C) 206/587-0187.

ANTIQUES MALLS & FLEA MARKETS

Antiques at Pike Place   Located in the Pike Place Market area, this antiques and collectibles mall is one of the finest in Seattle. There are more than 80 dealers, and much of what's available here is fairly small, which means you might be able to fit your find into a suitcase. 92 Stewart St. (C) 206/441-9643. www.antiquesatpikeplace.com.

Fremont Sunday Market   Crafts, imports, antiques, collectibles, and fresh produce all combine to make this Seattle's second favorite public market (after Pike Place Market). The market is open Sunday from 10am to 5pm year-round. N. 34th St. and Stone Way N. (3 blocks east of the Fremont Bridge). (C) 206/781-6776.

Pioneer Square Antique Mall   This underground antiques mall is in the heart of Pioneer Square right beside the ticket booth for the Seattle Underground tour and contains about 60 stalls selling all manner of antiques and collectibles. Look for glass, old jewelry, and small collectibles here. 602 First Ave. (C) 206/624-1164.

ART GALLERIES

The **Pioneer Square area** has for many years been Seattle's main art gallery district, and although there are still quite a few galleries there, many have moved to other parts of the metropolitan area, including the two wealthy east-side suburbs of Bellevue and Kirkland, in the past few years. Still, there are enough galleries left around Pioneer Square that anyone interested in art should be sure to wander around south of Yesler Way. Some galleries are closed on Mondays.

GENERAL ART GALLERIES

Carolyn Staley A wide range of old prints, including a large collection of 19th- and 20th-century Japanese wood-block prints, are on view at this Pioneer Square gallery. Whatever your personal interest, you'll likely find something intriguing in the gallery's large collection. 314 Occidental Ave. S. ℂ 206/621-1888.

Davidson Galleries Located in the heart of the Pioneer Square neighborhood, this gallery is divided into three different areas of focus—contemporary paintings and sculptures (often by Northwest artists); contemporary prints by American and European artists; and antique prints, some of which date from the 1500s. 313 Occidental Ave. S. ℂ 206/624-7684. www.davidsongalleries.com.

Greg Kucera Gallery Established in 1983, this showroom in the Pioneer Square area serves as one of Seattle's most reliably cutting-edge galleries. The shows here tend to have themes that address political or social issues or movements within the art world. Don't miss the outdoor sculpture deck. 212 Third Ave. S. ℂ 206/624-0770. www.gregkucera.com.

Lisa Harris Gallery Landscapes and figurative works, by both expressionist and realist Northwest and West Coast artists, are a specialty of this gallery, which is located on the second floor of a building in Pike Place Market. 1922 Pike Place. ℂ 206/443-3315. www.lisaharrisgallery.com.

ART GLASS

Foster/White Gallery If you are enamored of art glass, as we are, be sure to stop by one or both of the Foster/White galleries, which represent Dale Chihuly in Seattle and always have a few works by this master glass artist for sale. Some of Chihuly's pieces even sell for less than $10,000! Foster/White also represents top-notch Northwest artists in the disciplines of paintings, ceramics, and sculpture. 123 S. Jackson St. ℂ 206/622-2833. www.fosterwhite.com. Also in Kirkland at 126 Central Way (ℂ 425/822-2305).

The Glass Eye Studio The Glass Eye is one of Seattle's oldest art-glass galleries and specializes in colorful hand-blown pieces made from Mount St. Helens ash from the volcano's 1980 eruption. Works by artists from around the country are available, and many pieces are small enough to carry home. 1902 Post Alley, Pike Place Market. ℂ 206/441-3221. www.glasseye.com.

Glasshouse Studio Located in the Pioneer Square area and founded in 1972, Glasshouse claims to be the oldest glass-blowing studio in the Northwest. In the studio, you can watch hand-blown art glass being made, and then, in the gallery, you can check out the works of numerous local glass artists. 311 Occidental Ave. S. ℂ 206/682-9939. www.glasshouse-studio.com.

Phoenix Rising Gallery The art glass here is more high-end than what you'll find at the nearby Glass Eye Gallery. Artists from around the country are represented, and there is always some highly imaginative decorative work on display. This gallery also now sells ceramic pieces and wooden crafts. 2030 Western Ave. ℂ 206/728-2332. www.phoenixrisinggallery.com.

Vetri Vetri, which is affiliated with the prestigious William Traver Gallery, showcases innovative work primarily from emerging glass artists and local area studios, but also works by artists from other countries. It's all high quality and riotously colorful. Prices are relatively affordable. 1404 First Ave. ☎ 206/667-9608. www.vetriglass.com.

William Traver Gallery   In business for more than 25 years, this is one of the nation's top art-glass galleries and showcases the works of 80 glass artists. Works shown here are, so to speak, on the cutting edge of glass art and will give you a good idea of the broad spectrum of work being created by contemporary glass artists. You'll find the gallery on the second floor. 110 Union St. ☎ 206/587-6501. www.travergallery.com.

NATIVE AMERICAN ART

Flury and Company   This Pioneer Square gallery specializes in prints by famed Seattle photographer Edward S. Curtis, who is known for his portraits of Native Americans. The gallery also has an excellent selection of antique Native American art. 322 First Ave. S. ☎ 206/587-0260. www.fluryco.com.

The Legacy Ltd.   The Legacy Ltd. is Seattle's oldest and finest gallery of contemporary and historic Northwest Coast Indian and Alaskan Eskimo art and artifacts. You'll find a large selection of masks, boxes, bowls, baskets, ivory artifacts, jewelry, prints, and books for the serious collector. 1003 First Ave. ☎ 800/729-1562 or 206/624-6350. www.thelegacyltd.com.

Stonington Gallery   This is one of Seattle's top galleries specializing in contemporary Native American arts and crafts. Here you'll find a good selection of Northwest Coast Indian masks, totem poles, mixed-media pieces, prints, carvings, and Northwest Coast–style jewelry. 119 S. Jackson St. ☎ 206/405-4040.

BOOKS

In addition to the stores listed below, you'll find more than a half dozen locations of **Barnes & Nobles** around the metro area, including one downtown at 600 Pine St. (☎ **206/264-0156**). There's also a **Borders** at 1501 Fourth Ave. (☎ **206/622-4599**).

Elliott Bay Book Company   With battered wooden floors, a maze of rooms full of books, and frequent readings and in-store appearances by authors, this Pioneer Square bookstore feels as if it has been around forever. There's an excellent selection of books on Seattle and the Northwest, so if you want to learn more about the region or are planning further excursions, stop by. There is also a good little cafe down in the basement. 101 S. Main St. ☎ 206/624-6600. www.elliott baybook.com.

Flora & Fauna   Gardeners, bird-watchers, and other nature-philes, take note. Down below street level in what passes for the active Seattle underground of the Pioneer Square area, you'll find a store filled with books that'll have you wishing you were in your garden or out in the woods identifying birds and flowers. 121 First Ave. S. ☎ 206/623-4727.

Seattle Mystery Bookshop   If books that keep you wondering whodunit are your passion, don't miss an opportunity to peruse the shelves of this specialty bookstore in the Pioneer Square area. You'll find all your favorite mystery authors, books signings, and lots of signed copies. 117 Cherry St. ☎ 206/587-5737.

COFFEE & TEA

All over the city, on almost every corner, you'll find espresso bars, cafes, and coffeehouses. And while you can get coffee back home, you might want to stock up on whichever local coffee turns out to be your favorite. If you're a latte junkie, you can make a pilgrimage to the shop that started it all, the original Starbucks, listed below.

Starbucks Seattle is well-known as a city of coffeeholics, and Starbucks is the main reason why. This company has coffeehouses all over town (and all over the world), but this is the original. Although you won't find any tables or chairs here, Starbucks fans shouldn't miss an opportunity to get their coffee at the source. 1912 Pike Place, Pike Place Market. © 206/448-8762. www.starbucks.com.

Teahouse Kuan Yin Perhaps you've heard about the health benefits of green tea, or maybe you just want a break from espresso. Whatever your reasons, this Wallingford tea shop serves an amazing variety of teas, from smoky Keemun to flamingo pink Kashmiri chai and frothy, green Japanese tea. All the teas are also available in bulk, and there's plenty of tea paraphernalia as well. 1911 N. 45th St. © 206/632-2055.

Ten Ren Tea Co., Ltd. Ever wondered what $150-a-pound Chinese tea tastes like? At this International District tea shop, you can find out. Not only do they have dozens of different types of teas here, but they also have a little table in back where you can sample various varieties and observe the traditional Chinese tea ceremony. 506 S. King St. © 206/749-9855.

CRAFTS

The Northwest is a leading center for craftspeople, and one place to see what they are creating and meet the artisans themselves is Pike Place Market.

Crackerjack Contemporary Crafts With colorful and imaginative crafts by more than 250 artists from around the country, this shop in the eclectic Wallingford Center shopping arcade (an old schoolhouse) is a great place to check for something interesting and unique to bring home from a trip to Seattle. Lots of interesting jewelry. Wallingford Center, 1815 N. 45th St., Suite 212. © 206/547-4983.

Fireworks Fine Crafts Gallery Playful, outrageous, bizarre, beautiful—these are just some of the terms that can be used to describe the eclectic collection of Northwest crafts on sale at this Pioneer Square gallery. Cosmic clocks, wildly creative jewelry, and artistic picture frames are some of the fine and unusual items you'll find here. 210 First Ave. S. © 206/682-8707. www.fireworks gallery.net. Also at Westlake Center, 400 Pine St. (© 206/682-6462), Bellevue Square, NE Eighth Street and Bellevue Way, Bellevue (© 425/688-0933), and the University Village shopping plaza, 2629 NE University Village Mall (© 206/527-2858).

Frank and Dunya Located in the middle of funky Fremont, this store epitomizes the Fremont aesthetic. The art, jewelry, and crafts here all tend toward the colorful and the humorous, and just about everything is made by Northwest artists and artisans. 3418 Fremont Ave. N. © 206/547-6760.

Northwest Fine Woodworking This store is a showcase for some of the most amazing woodworking you'll ever see. Be sure to stroll through here while in the Pioneer Square area even if you aren't in the market for a one-of-a-kind piece of furniture. The warm hues of the exotic woods are soothing and the designs are beautiful. Furniture, boxes, sculptures, vases, bowls, and much more are created by more than 35 Northwest artisans. 101 S. Jackson St. © 206/625-0542. www.nwfinewoodworking.com. Also in Bellevue at the Bellevue Pedestrian Corridor, 601 108th Ave. NE, Plaza 100 (© 425/462-5382).

Twist This impressively large store is filled with items such as unusual artist-created jewelry, Adirondack chairs made from recycled water skis, twisted glass vases, candlesticks, and ceramics. All are slightly offbeat yet tasteful objets d'art. 1503 Fifth Ave. ⓒ 206/315-8080.

DEPARTMENT STORES

The Bon Marché   Seattle's "other" department store, established in 1890, is every bit as well stocked as the neighboring Nordstrom department store, and with such competition nearby, The Bon, as it's known, tries every bit as hard to keep its customers happy. Third Ave. and Pine St. ⓒ 206/506-6000.

Nordstrom   Known for personal service, Nordstrom stores have gained a reputation for being among the premier department stores in the United States. The company originated here in Seattle (opening its first store in 1901), and its customers are devotedly loyal. This is a state-of-the-art store, with all sorts of little boutiques, cafes, and other features to make your shopping excursion an experience.

Best of all, whether it's your first visit or your 50th, the knowledgeable staff will help you in any way they can. Prices may be a bit higher than those at other department stores, but for your money you get the best service available. The store is packed with shoppers during the half-year sale in June and the anniversary sale in July. You'll also find Nordstrom at area shopping malls. 1601 Fifth Ave. ⓒ 206/628-2111. www.nordstrom.com.

DISCOUNT SHOPPING

Nordstrom Rack *(Value)*   This is the Nordstrom overflow shop where you'll find three floors of discontinued lines as well as overstock, and all at greatly reduced prices. Women's fashions make up the bulk of the merchandise here, but there is also a floor full of men's clothes and shoes, plus plenty of kids' clothes. 1601 Second Ave. ⓒ 206/448-8522.

FASHION

In addition to the stores listed below, you'll find quite a few familiar names in downtown Seattle, including Ann Taylor, Banana Republic, Barneys New York, Eddie Bauer, Gap, and MaxMara.

ACCESSORIES

Byrnie Utz Hats   In the same location since 1934 and boasting the largest selection of hats in the Northwest, this cramped hat-wearer's heaven looks as if it hasn't changed in 50 years. There are Borsalino Panama hats, Kangol caps, and, of course, plenty of Stetsons. 310 Union St. ⓒ 206/623-0233.

CHILDREN'S CLOTHING

Boston St.   Located in the in the renovated old schoolhouse that is now the Wallingford Center shopping arcade, this store stocks fun play clothes, as well as more dressy fashions, for kids. There's lots of locally made 100% cotton clothing, and prices are moderate to expensive. Wallingford Center, 1815 N. 45th Ave. ⓒ 206/634-0580.

MEN'S & WOMEN'S CLOTHING

Eddie Bauer   Eddie Bauer got his start here in Seattle back in 1922, and today the chain is one of the country's foremost purveyors of upscale outdoor fashions—although these days, outdoor fashion is looking quite a bit more urban. 1330 Fifth Ave. ⓒ 206/622-2766. www.eddiebauer.com.

NIKETOWN   Around the country, there are currently more than a dozen NIKETOWNs selling all things Nike and only things Nike. If you don't live near one of these high-tech megastores, and you do wear swooshes, then this store should definitely be on your shopping itinerary. 1500 Sixth Ave. © 206/447-6453.

Northwest Pendleton For Northwesterners, and many other people across the nation, Pendleton is and always will be *the* name in classic wool fashions. This store features tartan plaids and Indian-pattern separates, accessories, shawls, and blankets. 1313 Fourth Ave. © 800/593-6773 or 206/682-4430. www.pendleton blankets.com.

WOMEN'S CLOTHING

Alhambra Alhambra stocks an eclectic collection of women's clothing, jewelry, and home furnishings. Expect to find a fun and quirky selection of dressy hats and accessories as well. 101 Pine St. © 206/621-9571. www.alhambranet.com.

Baby and Co. Claiming stores in Seattle and on Mars, this up-to-the-minute store stocks fashions that can be trendy, outrageous, or out of this world. Whether you're into earth tones or bright colors, you'll likely find something you can't live without. 1936 First Ave. © 206/448-4077.

Coldwater Creek This huge store based out of Sandpoint, Idaho, carries both classic and comfortable casual fashions for women and home furnishings of a rustic nature. And wouldn't you know it—a creek runs through the store. 1511 Fifth Ave. (at Pine St.). © 206/903-0830. www.coldwatercreek.com.

d This little boutique in the Pioneer Square area features hip and sophisticated designs. Displayed here are arty and textural little gossamer sweaters, dresses, and scarves in ephemeral fabrics. everything is in muted colors in the current fashion-conscious Seattle style. 2407 Second Ave. © 206/256-0844.

Passport Clothing Company Soft and easygoing is the current style at this large store near Pike Place Market. Velvet, linen, cotton, rayon, and other natural fibers are the fabrics of choice here. 123 Pine St. © 206/628-9799.

Ragazzi's Flying Shuttle Fashion becomes art and art becomes fashion at this chic boutique-cum-gallery on Pioneer Square. Handwoven fabrics and hand-painted silks are the specialties here, but of course such sophisticated fashions require equally unique body decorations in the form of exquisite jewelry creations. Designers and artists from the Northwest and the rest of the nation find an outlet for their creativity at the Flying Shuttle. 607 First Ave. © 206/343-9762.

GIFTS/SOUVENIRS

Pike Place Market is the Grand Central Station of Seattle souvenirs, with stiff competition from Seattle Center and Pioneer Square.

Made in Washington Whether it's salmon, wine, or Northwest crafts, you'll find a selection of Washington state products in this shop. This is an excellent place to pick up gifts for all those friends and family members who didn't get to come to Seattle with you. Pike Place Market (Post Alley at Pine St.). © 206/467-0788. www.madeinwashington.com. Also in Washington store in downtown's Westlake Center mall (© 206/623-9753).

Portage Bay Goods If you'd like to give a gift with a conscience, drop by this unusual store in the Fremont neighborhood. Almost everything here is made from recycled materials. We like the notebooks with covers made from computer boards, but there are lots of fun decorative home accessories as well. 706 N. 34th St. © 206/547-5221. www.portagebaygoods.com.

Ye Olde Curiosity Shop If you can elbow your way into this waterfront institution, you'll find every inch of space, horizontal and vertical, covered with souvenirs and crafts, both tacky and tasteful (but mostly tacky). Surrounding all this merchandise are the weird artifacts that have made this one of the most visited shops in Seattle. 1001 Alaskan Way, Pier 54. ℰ 206/682-5844. www.yeoldecuriosity shop.com.

HOUSEWARES, HOME FURNISHINGS & GARDEN ACCESSORIES

Kasala Boldly styled contemporary furnishings are this store's main business. While you probably don't want to ship a couch home, they do have lots of easily packed accent pieces (vases, candlesticks, picture frames) that are just as wildly modern as the furniture. 1505 Western Ave. ℰ 206/623-7795. www.kasala.com. Also in Bellevue at 1014 116th Ave. NE (ℰ 425/453-2823).

Kobo Japanophiles won't want to miss this unusual little Capitol Hill shop and gallery, located in one of the most interesting old buildings in the neighborhood. There are all manner of very tasteful decorative items inspired by the Japanese artistic aesthetic, and six times each year, there are exhibits featuring ceramics, textiles, Japanese calligraphy, and other paper arts. 814 E. Roy St. ℰ 206/ 726-0704. www.koboseattle.com.

The Spanish Table If you've decided your life's goal is to prepare the perfect paella, this store will set you on the path to perfection. Paella pans and everything you could ever want for cooking Spanish cuisine fill this Pike Place Market shop. 1427 Western Ave. ℰ 206/682-2827. www.tablespan.com.

Sur La Table Gourmet cooks will not want to miss an opportunity to visit Pike Place Market's Sur La Table, where every imaginable kitchen utensil is available. There are a dozen different kinds of whisks, an equal number of muffin tins, all manner of cake decorating tools, tableware, napkins, cookbooks—simply everything a cook would need. 84 Pine St. ℰ 206/448-2244.

JEWELRY

Unique artist-crafted jewelry can be found at **Ragazzi's Flying Shuttle** (see p. 136) and **Twist** (see p. 134).

Fox's Gem Shop Seattle's premier jeweler, Fox's has been around for 90 years, and always has plenty of a girl's best friends. Colorless or fancy colored diamonds available here are of the finest cut. 1341 Fifth Ave. ℰ 206/623-2528.

MALLS/SHOPPING CENTERS

Bellevue Square Over in Bellevue, on the east side of Lake Washington, you'll find one of the area's largest shopping malls, with more than 200 stores, including Nordstrom, FAO Schwartz, a Disney Store, Banana Republic, Eddie Bauer, and Northwest Pendleton. Bellevue Way and NE 8th Ave., Bellevue. ℰ 425/ 454-2431.

Broadway Market Located in trendy Capitol Hill, the Broadway Market is a stylish little shopping center with a decidedly urban neighborhood feel. The mall houses Urban Outfitters and numerous small shops and restaurants with reasonable prices. There's also a movie theater and a convenient public parking garage. 401 Broadway E. ℰ 206/322-1610.

City Centre This upscale downtown shopping center is the Seattle address of such familiar high-end retailers as Barneys New York, FAO Schwartz, and Ann

Taylor. There are works of art by Dale Chihuly and other Northwest glass artists on display throughout City Centre, and also a very comfortable lounge where you can rest your feet and escape from the Seattle weather. Sixth Ave. and Union St. ✆ 206/624-8800.

Pacific Place   This downtown mall is located adjacent to Nordstrom and contains five levels of upscale shop-o-tainment, including Cartier, Tiffany & Co., J. Crew, MaxMara, five restaurants, and an 11-screen cinema. A huge skylight fills the interior space with much-appreciated natural light, and an adjoining garage ensures that you'll be able to find a place to park (maybe). 600 Pine St. ✆ 206/405-2655. www.pacificplaceseattle.com.

Westlake Center   Before the opening of Pacific Place, this was Seattle's premier downtown, upscale, urban shopping mall. Located in the heart of Seattle's main shopping district, this mall has more than 80 specialty shops, including Godiva Chocolatier, Crabtree & Evelyn, and Made in Washington. There is an extensive food court, and the mall is also the southern terminus for the monorail to Seattle Center. 400 Pine St. ✆ 206/467-3044. www.therousecompany.com.

MARKETS

Pike Place Market   Pike Place Market is one of Seattle's most famous landmarks and tourist attractions. It shelters not only produce vendors, fishmongers, and butchers, but also artists, craftspeople, and performers. There are hundreds of shops and dozens of restaurants (including some of Seattle's best) tucked away in hidden nooks and crannies on the numerous levels of the market. With so much to see and do, a trip to Pike Place Market can easily turn into an all-day affair. See also the sightseeing listing on p. 95. Pike St. and First Ave. ✆ 206/682-7453. www.pikeplacemarket.org.

Uwajimaya   Typically, your local neighborhood supermarket has a section of Chinese cooking ingredients; it's probably about 10 feet long, with half that space taken up by various brands of soy sauce. Now imagine your local supermarket with nothing but Asian foods, housewares, produce, and toys. That's Uwajimaya, Seattle's Asian supermarket in the heart of the International District. There's also a big food court here serving all kinds of Asian food. 600 Fifth Ave. S. ✆ 206/624-6248. www.uwajimaya.com.

MUSICAL INSTRUMENTS

Lark in the Morning Musique Shoppe   At Lark in the Morning, you can find just about any kind of instrument from around the world, from Greek bouzoukis and traditional African drums to didgeridoos and bagpipes. Customers are encouraged to try out the instruments in the store. 1411 First Ave. ✆ 206/623-3440. www.larkinam.com.

RECREATIONAL GEAR

Filson   Ever since the Alaskan gold rush at the end of the 1890s, this Seattle company has been outfitting people headed outdoors. You won't find any high-tech fabrics here, just good old-fashioned wool, and plenty of it. Filson's clothes are meant to last a lifetime (and have the prices to prove it), so if you demand only the best, even when it comes to outdoor gear, be sure to check out this Seattle institution. 1555 Fourth Ave. S. ✆ 206/622-3147. www.filson.com.

The North Face   The North Face is one of the country's best-known names in the field of outdoor gear, and here in their downtown shop you can choose from among their diverse selection. 1023 First Ave. © **206/622-4111.** www.thenorth face.com.

Patagonia Seattle   Patagonia has built up a very loyal clientele based on the durability of its outdoor gear and clothing. Sure the prices are high, but these clothes are built to last. Although there are still plenty of outdoors designs, the clothes sold here these days are just about equally at home on city streets. 2100 First Ave. © **206/622-9700.** www.patagonia.com.

REI   Recreational Equipment, Incorporated (REI), was founded here in Seattle back in 1938 and today is the nation's largest co-op selling outdoor gear. A few years ago, REI opened an impressive flagship store just off I-5 not far from Lake Union. The store, a cross between a high-tech warehouse and a mountain lodge, is massive and sells almost anything you could ever need for pursuing your favorite outdoor sport. The store also has a 65-foot climbing pinnacle, a rain room for testing rain gear, a mountain-bike trail for test-driving bikes, a footwear test trail, even a play area for kids. With all this under one roof, who needs to go outside? Up on the top floor, there's also a World Wraps Cafe with an outstanding view of downtown. 222 Yale Ave. N. © **206/223-1944.**

SALMON

If you think the fish at Pike Place Market looks great, but you could never get it home on the plane, think again. Any of the seafood vendors in Pike Place Market will pack your fresh salmon or Dungeness crab in an airline-approved container that will keep it fresh for up to 48 hours. Alternatively, you can buy vacuum-packed smoked salmon that will keep for years without refrigeration.

Pike Place Fish   Located just behind Rachel, Pike Place Market's life-sized bronze pig, this fishmonger is just about the busiest spot in the market most days. What pulls in the crowds are the antics of the workers here. Order a big silvery salmon and you'll have employees shouting out your order and throwing the fish over the counter. Crowds are always gathered around the stall hoping to see some of the famous "flying fish." 86 Pike Place, Pike Place Market. © **800/542-7732** or 206/682-7181.

Totem Smokehouse   Northwest Coast Indians relied heavily on salmon for sustenance, and to preserve the fish they used alder-wood smoke. This tradition is still carried on today to produce smoked salmon, one of the Northwest's most delicious food products. This store, located at street level in Pike Place Market, sells vacuum-packed smoked salmon that will keep without refrigeration until the package is opened. 1906 Pike Place, Pike Place Market. © **800/972-5666** or 206/443-1710.

TOYS

Archie McPhee   You may already be familiar with this temple of the absurd through its mail-order catalog. Now imagine wandering through aisles full of goofy gags. Give yourself plenty of time and take a friend. You'll find Archie's place in the Ballard neighborhood. 2428 NW Market St. © **206/297-0240.** www. mcphee.com.

Magic Mouse   Adults and children alike have a hard time pulling themselves away from this, the wackiest toy store in downtown Seattle. It is conveniently located in Pioneer Square and has a good selection of European toys. 603 First Ave. © **206/682-8097.**

Wood Shop Toys Despite the name, this toy shop doesn't really have many wooden toys. But if you're a parent and you need to get your kids to go another block, here's a place where you can get something for under $5 to entertain them. This shop is also great for fun and inexpensive stocking stuffers. 320 First Ave. S. ℂ **206/624-1763**.

WINE

Because the relatively dry summers, with warm days and cool nights, provide an ideal climate for growing grapes, the Northwest has become one of the nation's foremost wine-producing regions. After you've sampled Washington or Oregon vintages, you might want to take a few bottles home.

Pike and Western Wine Shop Visit this shop for an excellent selection of Washington and Oregon wines, as well as those from California, Italy, and France. The extremely knowledgeable staff will be happy to send you home (or out on a picnic) with the very best wine available in Seattle. 1934 Pike Place, Pike Place Market. ℂ **206/441-1307**. www.pikeandwestern.com.

Seattle Cellars Wine merchant to the residents of Seattle's Belltown neighborhood, this wine shop sells wines from all over the world, with a substantial selection from Washington and Oregon. If you liked the wine you had last night with dinner, this is a good place to buy a bottle. Prices are quite reasonable, and there are weekly tastings. 2505 Second Ave. ℂ **206/256-0850**.

9

Seattle After Dark

Though Seattleites spend much of their free time enjoying the city's natural surroundings, they do not overlook the more cultured evening pursuits. In fact, the winter weather that keeps people indoors, combined with a long-time desire to be the cultural mecca of the Northwest, have fueled a surprisingly active and diverse nightlife scene. The Seattle Opera is ranked as one of the top operas in the country, and its stagings of Wagner's *Ring* series have achieved near-legendary status. The Seattle Symphony also receives frequent accolades. Likewise, the Seattle Repertory Theatre has won Tony awards for its productions, and a thriving fringe theater scene keeps the city's lovers of avant-garde theater contentedly discoursing in cafes about the latest hysterical or thought-provoking performances. Music lovers will also find a plethora of classical, jazz, and rock offerings.

Much of Seattle's evening entertainment scene is clustered in the Seattle Center Theater District and the Pioneer Square areas. The former hosts theater, opera, and classical music performances; the latter is a nightclub district. Other concentrations of nightclubs can be found in Belltown, Ballard, and on Capitol Hill.

While winters are a time for enjoying the performing arts, summers bring an array of outdoor festivals. While these take place during daylight hours as much as they do after dark, you'll find information on these festivals and performance series in this chapter.

To find out what's going on when you're in town, pick up a free copy of *Seattle Weekly* (www.seattleweekly.com), Seattle's arts-and-entertainment newspaper. You'll find it in bookstores, convenience stores, grocery stores, newsstands, and newspaper boxes around downtown and other neighborhoods. On Friday, the *Seattle Times* includes a section called "Ticket," which is a guide to the week's arts and entertainment offerings.

1 The Performing Arts

While the Seattle Symphony performs in downtown's Benaroya Hall, the main venues for the performing arts in Seattle are primarily clustered in **Seattle Center,** the special events complex that was built for the 1962 Seattle World's Fair. Here, in the shadow of the Space Needle, you'll find the Opera House, Bagley Wright Theater, Intiman Playhouse, Seattle Children's Theatre, Seattle Center Coliseum, Memorial Stadium, and the Experience Music Project's Sky Church performance hall.

OPERA & CLASSICAL MUSIC

The **Seattle Opera** (© 206/389-7676; www.seattleopera.org), which performs at the Seattle Center Opera House, is considered one of the finest opera companies in the country, and *the* Wagnerian opera company. The stagings of Wagner's four-opera *The Ring of the Nibelungen* are breathtaking spectacles that draw crowds from around the country. However, the *Ring* cycle was just staged in 2001, and won't be staged again for several years. In addition to classical operas such as *The Magic Flute* and *The Barber of Seville,* the season usually includes a more contemporary production. Ticket prices range from $31 to $107.

The 90-musician **Seattle Symphony** (© 206/215-4747; www.seattle symphony.org), which performs in the acoustically superb Benaroya Hall, offers an amazingly diverse musical season that runs from September to July. With several different musical series, there is a little something for every type of classical music fan. There are evenings of classical, light classical, and pops, plus afternoon concerts, guest artists, and more. Ticket prices range from $10 to $69.

The **Northwest Chamber Orchestra** (© 206/343-0445; www.nwco.org), a perennial favorite with Seattle classical music fans, is a showcase for Northwest performers. The season runs from September to May, and performances are held primarily in Benaroya Hall in downtown Seattle, although there are also concert series at the Seattle Asian Art Museum. Ticket prices range from $14.50 to $30.

THEATER
MAINSTREAM THEATERS

The **Seattle Repertory Theater** (© 877/900-9285 or 206/443-2222; www.seattlerep.org), which performs at the Bagley Wright and Leo K. theaters, Seattle Center, 155 Mercer St., has been around for more than 30 years. As Seattle's top professional theater, it stages the most consistently entertaining productions in the city. The Rep's season runs from September to June, with five plays performed in the main theater and four more in the more intimate Leo K. Theatre. Productions range from classics to world premieres. Ticket prices range from $15 to $44. When available, rush tickets are available half an hour before shows for $20.

With a season that runs from March to December, the **Intiman Theatre Company** (© 206/269-1900; www.intiman.org), which performs at the Intiman Playhouse, Seattle Center, 201 Mercer St., picks up where the Seattle Rep leaves off, filling in the gap left by those months when the Seattle Rep's lights are dark. Ticket prices range from $27 to $43.

Performing in the historic Eagles Building theater adjacent to the Washington State Convention and Trade Center, **A Contemporary Theater** (**ACT**), 700 Union St. (© 206/292-7676; www.acttheatre.org), offers slightly more adventurous productions than the other major theater companies in Seattle, though it's not nearly as avant-garde as some of the smaller companies. The season runs from the end of May to November (plus *A Christmas Carol* in Dec). Ticket prices usually range from $30 to $42.

FRINGE THEATER

Not only does Seattle have a healthy mainstream performing-arts community, it also has developed the sort of fringe theater life once only associated with such cities as New York, Los Angeles, London, and Edinburgh. The city's more avant-garde performance companies frequently grab their share of the limelight with daring, outrageous, and thought-provoking productions.

Seattle's interest in fringe theater finds its greatest expression each September, when the **Seattle Fringe Theater Festival** (© 206/342-9172; www.seattle fringe.org), a showcase for small, self-producing theater companies, takes over various venues. There are usually performances by more than 70 theater groups from around the country.

Ticket, Please

Full-price advance-purchase tickets to the Seattle Symphony, to many per-forming arts events are handled by TicketMaster (© **206/292-ARTS;** www.ticketmaster.com).

For half-price, day-of-show tickets (and 1-day advance tickets for mati-nees) to a wide variety of performances all over the city, stop by **Ticket/ Ticket** (© **206/324-2744**), which has three sales booths in the Seattle area: one in Pike Place Market, one on Capitol Hill, and one in Bellevue. The Pike Place Market location, in the Pike Place Market information booth, First Avenue and Pike Street, is open Tuesday through Sunday from noon to 6pm. The Capitol Hill booth is in the Broadway Market, 401 Broadway E., and is open Tuesday through Saturday from noon to 7pm and Sunday from noon to 6pm. The Bellevue booth is in the Meydenbauer Center, NE Sixth Street and 112th Avenue, and is open Tuesday through Sunday from noon to 6pm. Ticket/Ticket charges a small service fee, the amount of which depends on the ticket price.

Even if you don't happen to be in town for Seattle's annual fringe binge, check the listings in *Seattle Weekly* or the *Seattle Times'* Friday "Ticket" entertainment guide to see what's going on during your visit. The following venues are some of Seattle's more reliable places for way-off Broadway productions, performance art, and spoken word performances:

- **Book-It Repertory Theater** (© **206/216-0877** for information, or 206/325-6500 for tickets; www.book-it.org). Works by local playwrights, adaptations of literary works. Performances are held at various venues around the city.
- **Empty Space Theatre,** 3509 Fremont Ave. N. (© **206/547-7500;** www.emptyspace.org). One of Seattle's biggest little theaters, Empty Space stages mostly comedies and is popular with a young crowd.
- **Northwest Asian-American Theater,** Theatre Off Jackson, 409 Seventh Ave. S. (© **206/340-1049**). Works by Asian-American writers, actors, and musicians.
- **Theater Schmeater,** 1500 Summit St. (© **206/324-5801;** www. schmeater.org). Lots of weird and sometimes wonderful comedy, including ever-popular live late-night stagings of episodes from *The Twilight Zone.*

DANCE

Although it has a well-regarded ballet company and a theater dedicated to con-temporary dance and performance art, Seattle is not nearly as devoted to dance as it is to theater and classical music. This said, there is hardly a week that goes by without some sort of dance performance being staged somewhere in the city. Touring companies of all types, the University of Washington Dance Depart-ment faculty and student performances, UW World Dance Series (see below for details), and the Northwest New Works Festival (see below) all bring plenty of creative movement to the stages of Seattle. When you're in town, check *Seattle Weekly* or the *Seattle Times* for a calendar of upcoming performances.

The **Pacific Northwest Ballet,** Seattle Center Opera House, 301 Mercer St. (© **206/441-2424;** www.pnb.org), is Seattle's premier dance company. During the season, which runs from September to June, the company presents a wide range of classics, new works, and (the company's specialty) pieces choreographed by George Balanchine (tickets $15–$115). This company's performance of *The Nutcracker,* with outstanding dancing and sets and costumes by children's book author Maurice Sendak, is the highlight of every season.

Much more adventurous choreography is the domain of **On the Boards,** Behnke Center for Contemporary Performance, 100 W. Roy St. (© 206/ 217-9888; www.ontheboards.org), which, although it stages a wide variety of performance art, is best known as Seattle's premier modern-dance venue (tickets $7–$20). In addition to dance performances by Northwest artists, there are a variety of productions each year by internationally known artists.

MAJOR PERFORMANCE HALLS

With ticket prices for shows and concerts so high these days, it pays to be choosy about what you see, but sometimes *where* you see it is just as important. Benaroya Hall, the Seattle Symphony's downtown home, has such excellent acoustics that it's worth attending a performance here just for the sake of hearing how a good symphony hall should sound. Seattle also has two restored historic theaters that are as much a part of a performance as what goes on up on the stage.

Benaroya Hall (© 206/215-4747), on Third Avenue between Union and University streets in downtown Seattle, is the home of the Seattle Symphony. This state-of-the-art performance hall houses two concert halls—the main hall and a smaller recital hall. The concert hall is also home to the Watjen concert organ, a magnificent pipe organ. There's also a Starbucks, a cafe, and a symphony store. But all the amenities aside, it's the main hall's excellent acoustics that are the main attraction here.

The **5th Avenue Theatre,** 1308 Fifth Ave. (© **206/625-1418** for information, or 206/292-ARTS for tickets; www.5thavenuetheatre.org), which first opened its doors in 1926 as a vaudeville house, is a loose re-creation of the imperial throne room in Beijing's Forbidden City. In 1980, the theater underwent a complete renovation that restored this Seattle jewel to its original splendor, and today the astounding interior is as good a reason as any to see a show here. Don't miss an opportunity to attend a performance. Broadway shows are the theater's mainstay (tickets $15–$65).

The **Paramount Theatre,** 911 Pine St. (© **206/682-1414;** www. theparamount.com), one of Seattle's few historic theaters, has been restored to its original beauty and today shines with all the brilliance it did when it first opened. New lighting and sound systems have brought the theater up to contemporary standards. The theater stages everything from rock concerts to Broadway musicals (tickets $11.50–$65). Tickets are available through TicketMaster.

PERFORMING ARTS SERIES

When Seattle's own resident performing arts companies aren't taking to the dozens of stages around the city, various touring companies from around the world are. If you're a fan of Broadway shows, check the calendars at the Paramount Theatre and the 5th Avenue Theatre, both of which regularly serve as Seattle stops for touring shows.

The **UW World Series** (© 206/543-4880), held at Meany Hall on the University of Washington campus, is actually several different series including a chamber music series, a classical piano series, a dance series, and a world music and theater series. Together these four series keep the Meany Hall stage busy between October and May. Special events are also scheduled (tickets $28–$55).

Seattle loves the theater, and each March the city binges on the fringes with the **Seattle Fringe Theater Festival** (see "Fringe Theater," above). Avant-garde performances are also the specialty of the **Northwest New Works Festival** (© 206/217-9888; www.ontheboards.org), while **On the Boards'** annual barrage of contemporary dance and performance art is held each spring.

Another series worth checking out is the **Seattle Art Museum's "After Hours."** Every Thursday from 5 to 9pm, the museum hosts live music, frequently jazz, and sets up a bar in its main lobby. Shows are free with museum admission.

Summer is a time of outdoor festivals and performance series in Seattle, and should you be in town during the sunny months, you'll have a wide variety of alfresco performances from which to choose. The city's biggest summer music festivals are the **Northwest Folklife Festival** over Memorial Day weekend and **Bumbershoot** over Labor Day weekend. See the "Seattle Calendar of Events" in chapter 2, "Planning Your Trip to Seattle," for details.

AT&T Wireless Summer Nights at the Pier (© 206/628-0888; www.summernights.org) presents a summer's worth of big-name acts at Pier 62/63 on the waterfront. Blues, jazz, rock, and folk acts generally pull in a 30-something to 50-something crowd (tickets range from $15–$45).

At **Woodland Park Zoo** (© 206/615-0076; www.zoo.org), the Zoo Tunes concert series brings in more big-name performers from the world of jazz, easy listening, blues, and rock (tickets $12–$18).

In Woodinville, on the east side of Lake Washington, Chateau Ste. Michele, 14111 NE 145th St., stages the area's most enjoyable outdoor summer concert series. The **Summer Festival On The Green** (© 425/415-3300 for information, or 206/628-0888 for tickets) is held at the winery's amphitheater, which is surrounded by beautiful estatelike grounds. Chateau Ste. Michele is Washington's largest winery, and plenty of wine is available. Once again the lineup is calculated to appeal to the 30- to 50-something crowd (A Prairie Home Companion, Diana Krall, Gipsy Kings, Ringo Star, Yes).

2 The Club & Music Scene

If you have the urge to do a bit of clubbing and barhopping, there's no better place to start than in **Pioneer Square.** Good times are guaranteed, whether you want to hear a live band, hang out in a good old-fashioned bar, or dance. However, keep in mind that this neighborhood tends to attract a very rowdy crowd and can be pretty rough late at night.

Belltown, north of Pike Place Market, is another good place to club hop. Clubs here are more trend-conscious, as are the customers.

Seattle's other nightlife district is the former Scandinavian neighborhood of **Ballard,** where you'll find more than half of Seattle's nightlife establishments, including a brewpub, taverns, bars, live-music clubs, and a wine bar.

FOLK, ROCK & REGGAE
PIONEER SQUARE

The Pioneer Square area is Seattle's main live music neighborhood, and the clubs have banded together to make things easy on music fans. The **"Joint Cover"** plan lets you pay one admission to get into nine different clubs. The charge is $5 Sunday through Thursday and $10 on Friday and Saturday ($8 from 8–9pm on Fri–Sat; occasionally $12 for national-act nights). Participating clubs currently include Larry's Greenfront Cafe, Doc Maynard's, the Central Saloon, The Bohemian Café, Old Timer's Cafe, Zasu, and the New Orleans. Most of these clubs are short on style and hit-or-miss when it comes to music (which makes the joint cover a great way to find out where the good music is on any given night).

The Bohemian Café, Lounge & Backstage   This Pioneer Square club is Seattle's main venue for reggae, with live music several nights a week. Caribbean food is also served and there is an after-hours scene here on Friday and Saturday nights. 111 Yesler Way. ℂ 206/447-1514, reggae hot line 206/447-9868. www.bohemian reggaeclub.com. Cover $5–$10 (joint cover).

The Central Saloon   Established in 1892, the Central is the oldest saloon in Seattle. As a Seattle institution, it's a must-stop during a night out in Pioneer Square. You might catch sounds ranging from funk to reggae. 207 First Ave. S. ℂ 206/622-0209. Cover $5–$10 (joint cover).

BELLTOWN & ENVIRONS

Crocodile   With its rambunctious decor, this Belltown establishment is a combination nightclub, bar, and restaurant. There's live rock Tuesday through Saturday nights. The music calendar here is always eclectic with everything from rock to folk to jazz, though alternative rock dominates. 2200 Second Ave. ℂ 206/ 441-5611. www.thecrocodile.com. Cover $5–$20.

EMP   The Experience Music Project, Seattle's humongous lump o' color rock museum, isn't just some morgue for dead rockers. This place is a showcase for real live rockers, too. EMP's main hall, the **Sky Church,** plays host to everything from indie rockers to theater productions with live rock accompaniment. There's also the smaller **Liquid Lounge,** a club with no cover and a wide range of musical sensibilities. One night might be a reggae dance party while another night might feature hip-hop or an acoustic show. 325 Fifth Ave. N. ℂ 206/770-2702. www.emplive.com. Cover: Liquid Lounge free; Sky Church $10–$20.

Showbox   Located across the street from Pike Place Market, this club books a wide variety of local and name rock acts. Definitely *the* downtown rock venue for performers with a national following. 1426 First Ave. ℂ 206/628-3151. Cover $10–$30.

Sit and Spin   It's a club, it's a juice bar, it's a cafe, it's a Laundromat! This Belltown cafe/club is all of these and more. A popular hangout for the city's young scene-makers, Sit and Spin books an eclectic range for music. Decor is 1950s funky. 2219 Fourth Ave. ℂ 206/441-9484. No cover–$7.

CAPITOL HILL

Baltic Room   This swanky Capitol Hill hangout for the beautiful people provides live lounge music from 6 to 9pm nightly. Later in the night there's live or DJ dance music ranging from Britpop to hip-hop and house. 1207 Pine St. ℂ 206/ 625-4444. Cover $3–$6.

Century Ballroom   With a beautiful wooden dance floor and a genuine bandstand, this classic ballroom now plays host to some of the best touring acts to come to town. This is also Seattle's top spot for swing and salsa dancing, each of which tops the bill a couple of nights per week. The crowd here is very diverse, with customers of all ages who come to check out a schedule that might include acts like Hot Tuna or evenings of Hawaiian guitar music. 915 E. Pine St. ℂ 206/324-7263. www.centuryballroom.com. Cover $5–$30.

BALLARD

Ballard Firehouse   An eclectic assortment of musical styles finds its way onto the bandstand of this converted firehouse in Ballard. Now it's just the music that's hot, and that's the way they want to keep it. The crowd is young and the music generally ranges from techno/trance to hip hop to the latest local indie rockers. 5429 Russell Ave. NW ℂ 206/784-3516. No cover–$10.

Tractor Tavern   For an ever-eclectic schedule of music for people whose tastes go beyond the latest rap artist, the Tractor Tavern is the place to be. You can catch almost anything form Hawaiian slack-key guitar to rockabilly to singer-songwriters to banjo music to Celtic to folk to alternative. Sound like your kind of place? 5213 Ballard Ave. NW. ℂ 206/789-3599. www.tractortavern.com. No cover–$20.

JAZZ & BLUES

Dimitriou's Jazz Alley   Cool and sophisticated, this Belltown establishment is reminiscent of a New York jazz club and has been around for more than 20 years. Seattle's premier jazz venue, it books only the best performers, including name acts. 2033 Sixth Ave. ℂ 206/441-9729. www.jazzalley.org. Cover $13.50–$30.

New Orleans   If you like your food and your jazz hot, check out the New Orleans in Pioneer Square. Throughout the week, there's Cajun, Dixieland, R&B, jazz, and blues. 114 First Ave. S. ℂ 206/622-2563. Cover $5–$10 (joint cover).

Tula's   This is the real thing: a jazz club that's a popular jazz musicians' after-hours hangout and a good place to catch up-and-coming musicians. American and Mediterranean food is served. 2214 Second Ave. ℂ 206/443-4221. www.tulas.com. Cover $5–$10.

COMEDY, CABARET & DINNER THEATER

The Cabaret at Crepe de Paris   Throughout the year, this club stages a wide variety of entertaining programs of music, dance, and humor. Updated torch songs and numbers from classic musicals assure that the shows here will appeal to young and old alike. Rainier Sq., 1333 Fifth Ave. ℂ 206/623-4111. $45 for dinner and show; $16 show only. Reservations required.

Comedy Underground   This club is located in Pioneer Square, where the Seattle Underground tour has proven that too much time beneath the city streets can lead even normal people to tell bad jokes. 222 S. Main St. ℂ 206/628-0303. www.comedyunderground.com. Cover $4–$10.

The Pink Door   Better known as Pike Place Market's unmarked restaurant, the Pink Door has a hopping after-work bar scene that tends to attract a 30-something crowd. It also doubles as a cabaret featuring Seattle's most eclectic lineup of performers. Lots of fun and not to be missed. 1919 Post Alley. ℂ 206/443-3241. No cover.

DANCE CLUBS

Downunder   Located in the Belltown neighborhood north of Pike Place Market, the Downunder doesn't necessarily play underground music, but it is down a flight of stairs from street level. Wild decor, light shows, and high-energy music, mostly house mix and techno, attract a young crowd. Open Wednesday through Saturday. 2407 First Ave. ℂ 206/728-4053. No cover (before 10pm) or up to $7.

Polly Esther's/Culture Club   If disco, funk, and '80s new wave music are what get your booty shakin', don't miss this club (part of a national chain) across the street from the Experience Music Project. There are two clubs under one roof. As you can imagine, this place tends to attract a clientele that wasn't even born when disco was all the rage. In other words, this is a 20-something pickup joint. 332 Fifth Ave. ℂ **206/441-1970.** www.pollyesthers.com. Cover $10 (free before 9pm).

3 The Bar Scene

BARS

BELLTOWN & ENVIRONS

Alibi Room   If you've been on your feet all day in Pike Place Market and have had it with the crowds of people, duck down the alley under the market clock and slip through the door of this hideaway. The back-alley setting gives this place an atmospheric speakeasy feel. 85 Pike St. ℂ **206/623-3180.**

Two Bells Tavern   Although this is little more than an old tavern and a local hangout for Belltown residents who can still remember the days before all the condos went up, the walls are usually hung with interesting artwork. And they serve great burgers. 2313 Fourth Ave. ℂ **206/441-3050.**

The Virginia Inn   Although the Virginia Inn is located in oh-so-stylish Belltown, this bar/restaurant has a decidedly old Seattle feel, which is due in large part to the fact that this place has been around since 1903. Best of all, this is a nonsmoking bar and it serves French food! 1937 First Ave. ℂ **206/728-1937.**

DOWNTOWN

The Bookstore—a Bar   Located just off the lobby of the posh Alexis Hotel, this cozy little bar is—surprise—filled with books. There are plenty of interesting magazines on hand as well, so if you want to sip a single malt and smoke a cigar but don't want to deal with crowds and noise, this is a great option. Very classy. In the Alexis Hotel, 1007 First Ave. ℂ **206/382-1506.**

McCormick and Schmick's   The mahogany paneling and sparkling cut glass lend this restaurant bar a touch of class, but otherwise the place could have been the inspiration for *Cheers.* Very popular as an after-work watering hole of Seattle moneymakers, McCormick and Schmick's is best known for its excellent and inexpensive happy-hour snacks. 1103 First Ave. ℂ **206/623-5500.**

Restaurant 67 Bar   If you got any closer to the water, you'd have wet feet. Located inside downtown Seattle's only waterfront hotel, this bar boasts what just might be the best bar view in the city. Watch the ferries coming and going, or see the sun set over Puget Sound and the Olympics. In the Edgewater Hotel, Pier 67, 2411 Alaskan Way. ℂ **206/728-7000.**

Oliver's   Oliver's is martini central for Seattle, and year after year this bar keeps claiming top honors in the annual Martini Classic Challenge (which also happens to be sponsored by the Mayflower Park Hotel). Only you can decide. In the Mayflower Park Hotel, 405 Olive Way. ℂ **206/623-8700.**

PIONEER SQUARE

FX McRory's   Located across the street from Seattle's new football stadium and not far from Safeco Field, this bar attracts upscale sports fans (with the occasional Mariners and Seahawks players thrown in for good measure). You'll find Seattle's largest selection of bourbon. There's also an oyster bar and good food. 419 Occidental Ave. S. ℂ **206/623-4800.** www.mickmchughs.com.

Marcus's   Seattle's only underground martini and cigar bar, Marcus's is hidden beneath a Taco del Mar just off First Avenue in Pioneer Square. You'll be drinking below street level with the ghosts of Seattle's past and the lounge lizards of today. A variety of DJ music Tuesday through Saturday. This is a much mellower

Ballard, A Pioneer Square Alternative

If Pioneer Square nightlife is just too crowded, divey, or touristy for your tastes, you might be a candidate for a foray into Seattle's second liveliest scene. Ballard, formerly a Scandinavian enclave in north Seattle, attracts a primarily white, middle-class, not-too-hip, not-too-old crowd, including a lot of college students and techies. It's not the hipster Belltown scene, it's not the Bud-swilling blues scene of Pioneer Square, and it's not the ultracool gay scene of Capitol Hill. Among its offerings:

Old Town Alehouse, 5233 Ballard Ave. NW (© 206/782-8323), has nightly live music, from folk to rock to jazz to blues.

Tractor Tavern, 5213 Ballard Ave. NW (© 206/789-5265), offers Seattle's most eclectic musical calendar.

Ballard Firehouse, 5429 Russell Ave. NW (© 206/784-3516), is a longtime mainstay of the Seattle club scene, featuring mostly indie rock.

Madame K's, 5327 Ballard Ave. NW (© 206/783-9710), is a wine bar and Italian restaurant with a bordello theme and "kick-ass pizza and pasta."

Hattie's Hat, 5231 Ballard Ave. NW (© 206/784-0175), has a great antique back bar combined with a classic diner feel.

Conor Byrne's, 5140 Ballard Ave. NW (© 206/784-3640), hosts a Sunday-night Irish session music—very Irish.

Mr. Spot's Chai House, 2213 NW Market St. (© 206/297-CHAI), looks like a coffeehouse, but tea's the thing here. There's live folk music on weekends.

Grapes Wine Shop & Bistro, 5424 Ballard Ave. NW (© 206/297-1460), primarily a wine and cheese shop, doubles as a wine bar, with wine tastings.

alternative to Pioneer Square's rowdy street-level bars. 88 Yesler Way. © 206/624-3323.

BREWPUBS

Big Time Brewery and Alehouse   Big Time is located in the University District and is done up to look like a turn-of-the-century tavern, complete with a 100-year-old back bar and a wooden refrigerator. The pub serves as many as 12 of its own brews at any given time, and some of these can be pretty unusual. 4133 University Way NE. © 206/545-4509. www.bigtimebrewing.com.

Elysian Brewing Company   Although the brewery at this Capitol Hill brewpub is one of the smallest in the city, the pub itself is quite large and has an industrial feel that says "local brewpub" all over. The stout and strong ales are especially good, and the brewers' creativity here just can't be beat. Hands-down the best brewpub in Seattle. 1221 E. Pike St. © 206/860-1920.

Hales Ales Brewery and Pub   Located about a mile west of the Fremont Bridge heading toward Ballard, this is a much bigger and livelier brewpub than

Redhook Ales' nearby Trolleyman (see below). 4301 Leary Way NW. ☎ **206/782-0737.** www.halesales.com.

The Pike Pub and Brewery Located in an open, central space inside Pike Place Market, this brewpub makes excellent stout and pale ale. There's live instrumental music a couple of nights a week, and, with its comfortable couches, the Pike makes a great place to get off your feet after a day of exploring the market. 1415 First Ave. ☎ **206/622-6044.**

Pyramid Ale House Located south of Pioneer Square in a big old warehouse, this pub is part of the brewery that makes Thomas Kemper lagers and Pyramid ales and is a favorite spot for dinner and drinks before or after baseball games at Safeco Field. There's good pub food, too. 1201 First Ave. S. ☎ **206/682-3377.**

Trolleyman Pub This is the taproom of the Redhook Ale Brewery, one of the Northwest's most celebrated craft breweries, and is located in a restored trolley barn across the street from the Lake Washington Ship Canal. You can sample the ales brewed here, have a bite to eat, and even tour the brewery if you're interested. Redhook has a second (and much larger) brewery and pub in Woodinville at 14300 NE 145th St. (☎ **425/483-3232**) on the east side of Lake Washington. 3400 Phinney Ave. N. ☎ **206/634-4213.**

IRISH PUBS

Kells At one time the space now occupied by this pub was the embalming room of a mortuary. However, these days the scene is much more lively and has the feel of a casual Dublin pub. They pull a good pint of Guinness and feature live traditional Irish music 7 nights a week. Kells is also serves traditional Irish meals. 1916 Post Alley, Pike Place Market. ☎ **206/728-1916.** www.kellsirish.com. Cover Fri–Sat only, $4.

Fadó This Irish pub is part of a national pub chain but has the feel of an independent. Lots of antiques, old signs, and a dark, cozy feel make it a very comfortable place for a pint. There's live Irish music several nights a week. 801 First Ave. ☎ **206/264-2700.** www.fadoirishpub.com.

T. S. McHugh's Located in the Lower Queen Anne neighborhood adjacent to Seattle Center and many of Seattle's mainstream theaters, T. S. McHugh's has a very authentic feel. It's a good place to relax after an afternoon spent exploring the Seattle Center. 21 Mercer St. ☎ **206/282-1910.**

4 The Gay & Lesbian Scene

Capitol Hill is Seattle's main gay neighborhood, where you'll find the greatest concentration of gay and lesbian bars and dance clubs. Look for the readily available *Seattle Gay News* (☎ **206/324-4297**), where you'll find ads for many of the city's gay bars and nightclubs.

BARS

C. C. Attle's Located across the street from Thumpers, this bar is a Seattle landmark on the gay bar scene. This bar is well known for its cheap, strong cocktails, but it can be something of a regulars' scene. There are a couple of patios and three separate bars. 1501 E. Madison St. ☎ **206/726-0565.**

Thumpers Perched high on Capitol Hill with an excellent view of downtown Seattle, Thumpers is a classy bar/restaurant done up in oak. The seats by the fireplace are perfect on a cold and rainy night, and for sunny days there are two decks with great views. There's live music Thursday through Sunday. 1500 E. Madison St. ☎ 206/328-3800.

Wildrose This friendly restaurant/bar is a long-time favorite with the Capitol Hill lesbian community and claims to be the oldest lesbian bar on the West Coast. During the spring and summer, there is an outdoor seating area. 1021 E. Pike St. ☎ 206/324-9210.

DANCE CLUBS
Neighbours This has been the favorite dance club of Capitol Hill's gay community for years. As at other clubs, different nights of the week feature different styles of music. You'll find this club's entrance down the alley. 1509 Broadway Ave. ☎ 206/324-5358. Cover $1–$5.

Re-Bar Each night there's a different theme, with the DJs spinning everything from world beat to funk and hip-hop. This club isn't exclusively gay, but Thursday nights are currently Queer Disco Night, and Saturday nights are women's night. 1114 Howell St. ☎ 206/233-9873. Cover $3–$6.

Timberline Spirits If the boot-scootin' boogie is your favorite dance, the Timberline is the place to be. There's dancing to C&W music several nights a week. This place is also home to Seattle's largest tea dance, and also plays disco and trance. 2015 Boren Ave. ☎ 206/622-6220. Cover free–$3.

5 More Entertainment
MOVIES
Movies come close behind coffee and reading as a Seattle obsession, and you'll find a surprising number of theaters in Seattle showing foreign and independent films. These include **Grand Illusion,** 1403 NE 50th St. at University Way NE (☎ 206/523-3935); **Harvard Exit,** 807 E. Roy St. at Broadway Avenue East (☎ 206/323-8986); the **Egyptian,** 805 E. Pine St. (☎ 206/32-EGYPT); and the **Varsity,** 4329 University Way NE (☎ 206/632-3131).

There's no better place in town to catch a mainstream movie than **Cinerama,** 2100 Fourth Ave. (☎ 206/441-3080), a space-age 1950s wide-screen theater brought up to 21st-century standards of technology.

The **Seattle International Film Festival** (SIFF; www.seattlefilm.com) takes place each May and early June, with around 150 films shown at various theaters. For information, check the website or, at festival time, the local papers.

At the **Seattle Art Museum,** 100 University St. (☎ 206/625-8900; www. seattleartmuseum.org), there are Thursday-night screenings of classics and foreign films. If you're a movie buff, be sure to check out this series.

The **Paramount Theatre,** 911 Pine St. (☎ 206/682-1414 for information, or 206/628-0888; www.theparamount.com), does Silent Movie Mondays, with classic silent films and musical accompaniment on a Wurlitzer organ. Tickets are $11.50 ($8.50 for seniors and students) and are available through TicketMaster.

In Fremont, there's the **Fremont Saturday Nite Outdoor Movies** series (☎ 206/781-4230; www.outdoorcinema.com), a summer event that shows modern classics, B movies (sometimes with live overdubbing by a local improv comedy company), and indie shorts. Films are screened in the parking lot across from the Trolleyman Pub, N. 35th St and Phinney Avenue N. The parking lot opens at 7:30pm, and there is a $5 suggested donation.

AT&T Outdoor Cinema screens movies at the Seattle Center Mural Stage and in Marymoor Park in Redmond. For information on these movies, contact

Lunar Flicks (© **206/720-1058;** www.lunarflicks.com). Gates open at 6pm, with music at 7pm and movies at dusk.

6 Only in Seattle

While Seattle has plenty to offer in the way of performing arts, some of the city's best after-dark offerings have nothing to do with the music. There's no better way to start the evening (that is, if the day has been sunny or only partly cloudy) than to catch the **sunset from the waterfront.** The Bell Street Pier and Myrtle Edwards Park are two of the best and least commercial vantages for taking in nature's evening light show. Keep in mind that sunset can come as late as 10pm in the middle of summer.

Want the best view of the city lights? Hold off on your elevator ride to the top of the **Space Needle** until after dark. Alternatively, you can hop a ferry and sail off into the night. Now, what could be more romantic?

Well, I suppose a **carriage ride** could be as romantic. Carriages can be found parked and waiting for customers, couples and families alike, on the waterfront.

For a cheap date, nothing beats the **first Thursday art walk.** On the first Thursday of each month, galleries in Pioneer Square stay open until 8 or 9pm. There are usually appetizers and drinks available and sometimes live music. On those same first Thursdays, the Seattle Art Museum, the Seattle Asian Art Museum, the Frye Art Museum, the Henry Art Gallery, the Burke Museum, and the Museum of Flight all stay open late, and most also waive their usual admission charges. All of these museums are open late every Thursday, though you'll have to pay on those other nights (except at the Frye, which never charges an admission).

The **Elliott Bay Book Co.,** 101 S. Main St. (© **206/624-6600**), is not only a great place to hang out after dark (or during the day for that matter), but it also schedules frequent readings by touring authors. Stop by or call to check the schedule. There are also frequent art lectures at the Seattle Art Museum and Seattle Asian Art Museum.

Want to learn to dance? Up on Capitol Hill, there are **brass dance steps** inlaid into the sidewalk along Broadway. Spend an evening strolling the strip, and you and your partner could teach yourselves several classic dance steps in between noshing a piroshki and savoring a chocolate torte.

10

Side Trips from Seattle

After you've explored Seattle for a few days, consider heading out of town on a day trip. Within 1 to 1½ hours of the city you can find yourself hiking in a national park, cruising up a fjordlike arm of Puget Sound, exploring the San Juan Islands, or sampling a taste of the grape at some of Washington's top wineries. With the exception of the San Juan Islands, the excursions listed below are all fairly easy day trips that will give you glimpses of the Northwest outside the Emerald City. Another possible excursion is to Mount St. Helens National Volcanic Monument. I list this excursion as a day trip from Portland, in chapter 20, "Side Trips from Portland," simply because it takes about an hour less to reach the monument from Portland than it does from Seattle.

For more in-depth coverage of the areas surrounding Seattle, pick up a copy of *Frommer's Washington State.*

1 The San Juan Islands

On a late afternoon on a clear summer day, the sun slants low, suffusing the scene with a golden light. The fresh salt breeze and the low rumble of the ferry's engine lulls you into a half-waking state. All around you, rising from a shimmering sea, are emerald-green islands, the tops of glacier-carved mountains flooded at the end of the last Ice Age. A bald eagle swoops from its perch on a twisted madrona tree. Off the port bow, the knifelike fins of two orca whales slice the water. As the engine slows, you glide toward a narrow wooden dock with a simple sign above it that reads "San Juan Island." With a sigh of contentment, you step out onto the San Juan Islands and into a slower pace of life.

There's something magical about traveling to the San Juans. Some people say it's the light, some say it's the sea air, some say it's the weather (temperatures are always moderate, and rainfall is roughly half what it is in Seattle). Whatever it is that so entrances, the San Juans have become the favorite getaway of urban Washingtonians, and if you make time to visit these idyllic islands, we think you too will fall under their spell.

There is, however, one caveat. The San Juans have been discovered. In summer, there can be waits of several hours to get on ferries if you're driving a car. One solution is to leave your car on the mainland and come over either on foot or with a bicycle. If you choose to come over on foot, you can rent a car, moped, or bicycle, take the San Juan or Orcas island shuttle bus, or use taxis to get around. Then again, you can just stay in one place and really relax.

Along with crowded ferries come hotels, inns, and campgrounds that can get booked up months in advance and restaurants that can't seat you unless you have a reservation. If it's summer, don't come out here without a room reservation and expect to find a place to stay.

In other seasons, it's a different story. Spring and fall are often clear, and in spring, the islands' gardens and hedgerows of wild roses burst into bloom, making this one of the best times of year to visit. Perhaps best of all, in spring and fall room rates are much less than they are in the summer.

Depending on whom you listen to there are between 175 and 786 islands in the San Juans. The lower number constitutes those islands large enough to have been named, while the larger number represents all the islands, rocks, and reefs that poke above the water on the lowest possible tide. Of all these islands, only four (San Juan, Orcas, Lopez, and Shaw) are serviced by the Washington State Ferries and of these, only three (San Juan, Orcas, and Lopez) have anything in the way of tourist accommodations.

VISITOR INFORMATION

Contact the **San Juan Island Chamber of Commerce,** P.O. Box 98, Friday Harbor, WA 98250 (© **360/378-5240;** www.sanjuanisland.org); or the **Orcas Island Chamber of Commerce,** P.O. Box 252, Eastsound, WA 98245 (© **360/ 376-2273;** www.sanjuanweb.com/orcasislandchamber).

On the Web, check out www.sanjuanweb.com, www.orcasisle.com, www. guidetosanjuans.com, www.thesanjuans.com, or www.lopezisland.com.

GETTING THERE

If it's summer and you'd like to visit the San Juans without a car, we recommend booking passage through Victoria Clipper (see below), which operates excursion boats from the Seattle waterfront. If you're traveling by car, you'll need to drive north from Seattle to Anacortes and head out to the islands via Washington State Ferries.

Washington State Ferries (© **800/84-FERRY** or 888/808-7977 in Washington, or 206/464-6400; www.wsdot.wa.gov/ferries/) operates ferries between Anacortes and four of the San Juan Islands (Lopez, Shaw, Orcas, and San Juan) and Sidney, British Columbia (on Vancouver Island near Victoria). The fare for a vehicle and driver from Anacortes to Lopez is $17 to $21.25, to Shaw or Orcas $20 to $25, to San Juan $22.50 to $28.25, and to Sidney $29.75 to $41. The higher fares reflect a summer surcharge.

The fare for passengers from Anacortes to any of the islands is $6.80 (though it's $11 to Sidney). The fare for a vehicle and driver on all westbound interisland ferries is $9 to $11.25, and foot passengers ride free. Except for service from Sidney, fares are not collected on eastbound ferries, nor are walk-on passengers charged for interisland ferry service. If you plan to explore the islands by car, you'll save some money by starting your tour on San Juan Island and making your way back east through the islands.

During the summer you may have to wait several hours to get on a ferry, so arrive early.

To cross into Canada and return to the United States, adult U.S. citizens born in the United States need two pieces of identification, such as a passport, driver's license, birth certificate, voter registration card, or credit card. U.S. citizens who were not born in the United States need a passport or certificate of naturalization. If you are a foreign citizen but a permanent resident of the United States, be sure to carry your A.R.R. card. Foreign citizens who are only visiting the United States must carry a passport when traveling to or from Canada. Children traveling to or from Canada with both parents must have a birth certificate; a child traveling with only one parent should have both a birth certificate and a

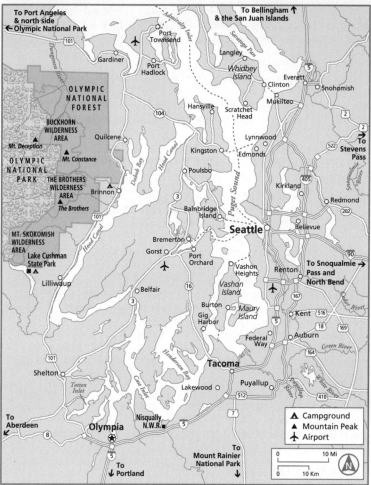

notarized letter from the other parent giving permission for the child to travel out of the country.

There are also passenger-ferry services from several cities around the region. **Victoria Clipper** (© **800/888-2535** or 206/448-5000; www.victoriaclipper. com) operates excursion boats between Seattle and both Friday Harbor on San Juan Island and Rosario Resort on Orcas Island and also stops in Victoria. The round-trip fare to Friday Harbor is $59 round-trip; the fare to Rosario Resort is $69 round-trip. Advance-purchase discounts are available on round-trip tickets.

If you're short on time, it's also possible to fly to the San Juans. **Kenmore Air,** 950 Westlake Ave. N. (© **800/543-9595** or 425/486-1257; www.kenmoreair. com), offers flights in floatplanes that take off from Lake Union (and also from the north end of Lake Washington). Round-trip fares to the San Juans are between $150 and $160 (lower for children). Flights operate to Friday Harbor and Roche Harbor on San Juan Island, Rosario Resort and Westsound on Orcas Island, and the Lopez Islander on Lopez Island.

You can also get from Sea-Tac Airport to the San Juan Islands ferry terminal in Anacortes on the **Airporter Shuttle** (© **866/235-5247** or 360/380-8800; www.airporter.com), which charges $31 one-way and $56 round-trip.

SAN JUAN ISLAND

Although neither the largest nor the prettiest of the islands, San Juan is the most populous and touristy of the San Juan Islands. **Friday Harbor,** where the ferry docks, is the county seat for San Juan County and is the only real town on all of the islands. As such, it is home to numerous shops, restaurants, motels, and bed-and-breakfast inns that cater to tourists, as well as such necessities of island life as grocery and hardware stores. With its large, well-protected marina, it's also one of the most popular places in the islands for boaters to drop anchor.

GETTING AROUND

Car rentals are available on San Juan Island from **Susie's Mopeds** (© **800/ 532-0087** or 360/378-5244; www.susiesmopeds.com), the **Inn at Friday Harbor** (© **800/752-5752** or 360/378-3031; www.theinns.com) and **M&W Auto Sales** (© **360/378-2886**). Expect to pay $45 to $96 per day.

You can also rent scooters and mopeds. They're available in Friday Harbor by the hour or by the day from **Island Scooter Rental,** 85 Front St. (© **360/ 378-8811**) or **Susie's Mopeds** (© **800/532-0087** or 360/378-5244; www. susiesmopeds.com), both of which are located at the top of the ferry lanes. Expect to pay $16 per hour or $48 per day for a moped or scooter.

For a cab, call **San Juan Taxi** (© **360/378-3550**).

San Juan Transit (© **800/887-8387,** or 360/378-8887 on San Juan; www. sanjuantransit.com) operates a shuttle bus during the summer. This shuttle can be boarded at the ferry terminal and operates frequently throughout the day, stopping at all the major attractions on the island, which makes this a great way to get around if you come out without a car. Day passes are $10 for adults, $9 for seniors, and $5 for kids ages 5 to 12, with discounted 2-day rates available. One-way ($4 for everyone over age 13, $2 for kids 12 and under) and round-trip ($7 adults, $3 kids 12 and under) tickets are also available. Children ages 4 and under always ride free.

EXPLORING THE ISLAND

If you arrived by car, you'll first want to find a parking space, which can be difficult in the summer. Once on foot, stroll around town admiring the simple wood-frame shop buildings built in the early 20th century. At that time, Friday Harbor was thought of as the southernmost port in Alaska and was a busy harbor. Schooners and steamships hauled the island's fruit, livestock, and lime (for cement) off to more populous markets. Today these pursuits have all died off, but reminders of the island's rural roots linger on, and these memories have fueled the island's new breadwinner: tourism. Many of the town's old buildings now house art galleries and other interesting shops.

One of your first stops should be the tasting room at **Island Wine Company,** Cannery Landing (© **360/378-3229**), which is the only place you can buy wine from San Juan Cellars (which makes its wine with grapes from eastern Washington). You'll find the wine shop on the immediate left as you leave the ferry.

Whale-watching is one of the most popular summer activities in the San Juans, and before you head out, stop by the **Whale Museum** ✸, 62 First St. N. (© **800/946-7227** or 360/378-4710; www.whale-museum.org). Here you can see whale skeletons and models of whales and learn all about the area's pods of

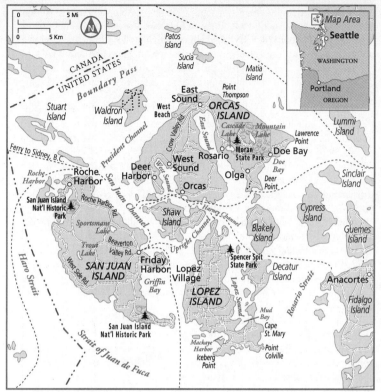

orcas (also known as killer whales). Between Memorial Day and Labor Day, the museum is open daily from 9am to 5pm (10am–5pm other months); admission is $5 for adults, $4 for seniors, and $2 for children 5 to 18 and college students.

Here in Friday Harbor, you'll also find the headquarters of the **San Juan National Historic Park** ✸ (**(C) 360/378-2240**), at the corner of Spring and First streets. It's open daily from 8:30am to 5pm in summer (Mon–Fri 8:30am–4:30pm in winter). This park commemorates the San Juan Island Pig War, one of North America's most unusual and least remembered confrontations. Way back in 1859, San Juan Island nearly became the site of a battle between the British and the Americans. The two countries had not yet agreed upon the border between the United States and Canada when a British pig on San Juan Island decided to have dinner in an American garden. The owner of the garden didn't take too kindly to this and shot the pig. The Brits, rather than welcoming this succulent addition to their evening's repast, threatened redress. In less time than it takes to smoke a ham, both sides were calling in reinforcements. Luckily, this pigheadedness was defused and a more serious confrontation was avoided. While the park's headquarters is here in Friday Harbor, the main historic sites are English Camp, at the north end of the island, and American Camp, at the south end of the island. At both camps, you can visit historic buildings that are much as they might have looked in 1859.

Most of the island's main attractions can be seen on a long loop drive around the perimeter of the island. Start the drive by following Roche Harbor signs north out of Friday Harbor (take Spring Street to Second Street to Tucker Avenue). In about 3 miles, you'll come to **San Juan Vineyards** ⊛, 2000 Roche Harbor Rd. (© **360/378-WINE**), which makes wines both from grapes grown off the island and also from its own estate-grown Siegrebbe and Madeline Angevine grapes. The tasting room is housed in an old schoolhouse that was built in 1896 and is open daily 11am to 6pm in summer and on weekends only mid-October through December and February through May.

Continuing north to the north end of the island, you'll find **Roche Harbor Resort** ⊛⊛, which was once the site of large limestone quarries that supplied lime to much of the West Coast. Today many of the quarries' old structures are still visible, giving this area a decaying industrial look, but amid the abandoned machinery stands the historic Hotel de Haro, a simple whitewashed wooden building with verandahs across its two floors. Stop and admire the old-fashioned marina and colorful gardens. The deck of the hotel's lounge is one of the best places on the island to linger over a drink.

South of Roche Harbor, on West Valley Road, you'll find **English Camp.** Set amid shady trees and spacious lawns, the camp is the picture of British civility. There's even a formal garden surrounded by a white picket fence. You can look inside the reconstructed buildings and imagine the days when this was one of the most far-flung corners of the British Empire. If you're full of energy, hike up to the top of 650-foot **Mount Young** for a panorama of the island. An easier hike is out to the end of **Bel Point.**

South of English Camp, watch for the Bay Road turnoff. This connects to the Westside Road, which leads down the island's west coast. Along this road, you'll find **San Juan County Park,** a great spot for a picnic. A little farther south you'll come to **Lime Kiln State Park** ⊛⊛, the country's first whale-watching park and a great place to spot these gentle giants in summer.

At the far south end of the island is the windswept promontory on which stood the **American Camp** during the Pig War. Here you'll find a visitor center and a few reconstructed buildings. Before the American Camp was built here, this was the site of a Hudson's Bay Company farm. The meadows sweeping down to the sea were once grazed by sheep and cattle, but today you'll see only rabbits browsing amid the high grasses and wildflowers. **Hiking trails** here lead along the bluffs and down to the sea. One trail leads through a dark forest of Douglas firs to **Jackle's Lagoon,** which is a great spot for bird watching. Keep your eyes peeled for bald eagles, which are relatively plentiful around here.

SPORTS & OUTDOOR PURSUITS

BIKING ⊛ Winding country roads are ideal for leisurely trips. If you didn't bring your own wheels, you can rent from **Island Bicycles,** 380 Argyle St., in Friday Harbor (© **360/378-4941**), which charges $6 per hour (2-hr. minimum) and $25 per day.

SEA KAYAKING ⊛⊛ Two- to four-hour **sea-kayak tours** ($39–$49) are offered by **San Juan Safaris** (© **360/378-1323**) at Roche Harbor Resort, **Leisure Kayak Adventures** (© **800/836-1402** or 360/378-5992; www.leisure kayak.com), and **Crystal Seas Kayaking** (© **877/SEAS-877** or 360/378-7899; www.crystalseas.com). Most of these companies also offer full-day and overnight trips.

Three- and four-day trips are offered by **San Juan Kayak Expeditions** (© **360/378-4436;** www.sanjuankayak.com), which charges $325 and $420, respectively, for its outings.

WHALE-WATCHING ★★ When it's time to spot some whales, you have two choices. You can take a whale-watching cruise or head over to **Lime Kiln State Park** ★★, where a short trail leads down to a rocky coastline from which orca whales, minke whales, Dall's porpoises, and sea lions can sometimes be seen. The best months to see orcas are June to September, but it's possible to see them throughout the year.

Whale-watching cruises lasting from 4 to 6 hours are offered in the summer by **San Juan Excursions** (✆ **800/80-WHALE** or 360/378-6636; www.watch whales.com), which operates out of Friday Harbor. Cruises are $49 for adults and $35 for children age 4 to 12. Three-hour whale-watching trips from Roche Harbor Resort, on the north side of the island, are offered by **San Juan Safaris** (✆ **360/378-1323;** www.sanjuansafaris.com), which charges $49 for adults and $39 for children 4 through 12.

WHERE TO STAY

Friday Harbor House ★★ With its contemporary yet distinctly Northwest architecture, this luxurious little boutique hotel brings urban sophistication to Friday Harbor. The hotel's bluff-top location assures excellent views of the ferry landing, the adjacent marina, and, in the distance, Orcas Island. With their fireplaces and double whirlpool tubs, guest rooms are designed for romantic getaways, and as you relax in your tub, you can gaze out at the view and your own crackling fire. Most rooms also have decks or balconies. If you enjoy contemporary styling, these are the best rooms in all the San Juan Islands. The dining room here is one of the best on the island and serves Northwest cuisine.

130 West St. (P.O. Box 1385), Friday Harbor, WA 98250. ✆ **360/378-8455.** Fax 360/378-8453. www.friday harborhouse.com. 20 units. Memorial Day–Sept $200–$300 double; Oct–Memorial Day $130–$185 double, $265 suite. Rates include continental breakfast. AE, MC, V. **Amenities:** Restaurant (Northwest); access to nearby health club; Jacuzzi; concierge; massage. *In room:* TV, fax, dataport, minibar, fridge, coffeemaker, hair dryer, iron, safe.

Olympic Lights Bed and Breakfast ★★ Located at San Juan's dry southwestern tip, the Olympic Lights is a Victorian farmhouse surrounded by windswept meadows, and if it weren't for the sight of Puget Sound out the window, you could easily mistake the setting for the prairies of the Midwest. There are colorful gardens, an old barn, even some hens to lay the eggs for your breakfast. The ocean breezes, nearby beach, and friendliness of innkeepers Christian and Lea Andrade lend a special feel to this American classic. Our favorite room here is the Ra Room, which is named for the Egyptian sun god and features a big bay window. The view out the windows is enough to settle the most stressed-out soul.

146 Starlight Way, Friday Harbor, WA 98250. ✆ **888/211-6195** or 360/378-3186. Fax 360/378-2097. www. olympiclightsbnb.com. 4 units. $120–$140 double. Rates include full breakfast. No credit cards. *In room:* Hair dryer, no phone.

Roche Harbor Village ★★ *(Kids)* Located at the north end of the island, Roche Harbor Village is steeped in island history, with the historic Hotel de Haro, established in 1886, serving as the resort's centerpiece. A brick driveway and manicured gardens provide the foreground for the white two-story hotel, which overlooks the marina and has porches running the length of both floors. Although the rooms in the Hotel de Haro are quite basic (all but four have shared bathrooms) and have not been updated in years, the building has loads of atmosphere. The best accommodations here, however, are the four new luxury McMillin suites in a restored home adjacent to the historic hotel. The modern condominiums are good bets for families. The resort's dining room has a view of the marina, and the deck makes a great spot for a sunset cocktail. In addition to amenities listed below, there are whale-watching cruises, sea-kayak tours, a marina, and a general store.

P.O. Box 4001, Roche Harbor, WA 98250. © 800/451-8910 or 360/378-2155. Fax 360/378-6809. www. rocheharbor.com. Historic hotel: 20 units (16 with shared bathroom). Modern accommodations: 25 condos, 9 cottages, 4 suites. May–Sept $79–$99 double with shared bathroom; $139–$319 suite; $179–$299 condo; $159–$239 cottage. Lower rates Oct–Apr. AE, MC, V. **Amenities:** 3 restaurants (Continental/Northwest, American), lounge; outdoor pool; 2 tennis courts; Jacuzzi; bike and moped rentals; shopping arcade; coin-op laundry. *In room:* hair dryer, iron.

WHERE TO DINE

In addition to the restaurants listed below, there are several other places in Friday Harbor where you can get a quick, simple meal. At the top of the ferry lanes, on A Street, you'll find **Madelyn's Bagel Bakery** (© 360/378-4545), a small bagel and sandwich shop, and not far away is the **Garden Path Café,** 135 Second St. (© 360/378-6255), which usually has a good selection of deli salads, soups, and baked goods.

Duck Soup Inn 🍂🍂 NORTHWEST/INTERNATIONAL   North of Friday Harbor 4½ miles you'll find the Duck Soup Inn, a barnlike restaurant beside a pond frequented by—you guessed it—ducks. Inside this quintessentially Northwestern building you'll find lots of exposed wood and a fieldstone fireplace. The menu changes frequently, depending on the availability of fresh produce, but is always very creative. The chef has a penchant for the flavors of Asia and you might find sesame calamari with Korean dipping sauce or spicy Sri Lankan prawns. Specials always incorporate whatever produce is freshest that week. In spring and fall, you might even find duck soup on the menu!

50 Duck Soup Lane. © 360/378-4878. www.ducksoupinn.com. Reservations highly recommended. Main courses $19.50–$28. DISC, MC, V. Summer Wed–Sun 5:30–9:30pm; spring and fall Fri–Sat 5:30–9:30pm. Closed Nov–early Apr.

The Place Next to the San Juan Ferry 🍂🍂 NORTHWEST/INTERNATIONAL   Located on the waterfront to the right as you get off the ferry and housed in a small wooden building that was once part of a U.S. Coast Guard station, this aptly named establishment is San Juan Island's finest waterfront restaurant. With lots of local art on the wall, this place aims to attract the upscale Seattle market, and it's right on target. The menu changes regularly with an emphasis on seafood preparations such as Asian-style crab cakes and Pacific Rim bouillabaisse.

1 Spring St. © 360/378-8707. Reservations highly recommended. Main courses $17–$32. MC, V. Daily 5:30–9pm (Tues–Sat in winter).

ORCAS ISLAND

Shaped like a horseshoe and named for an 18th-century Mexican viceroy (not for the area's orca whales, as is commonly believed), Orcas Island has long been a popular summer-vacation spot and is the most beautiful of the San Juan Islands. Orcas is a particular favorite of nature lovers, who come to enjoy the views of green rolling pastures, forested mountains, and fjordlike bays. **Eastsound** is the largest town on the island and has several interesting shops and good restaurants. Other, smaller villages include Deer Harbor, West Sound, and Olga.

To rent a car on Orcas Island, contact **Rosario Resort** (© 800/562-8820 or 360/376-2222). Expect to pay $45 to $96 per day. If you need a cab, call **Orcas Island Taxi** (© 360/376-8294).

Around the island you'll find several interesting pottery shops. A few miles west of Eastsound off Enchanted Forest Road is **Orcas Island Pottery** (© 360/376-2813), the oldest pottery studio in the Northwest; and, at the end of this same road, on West Beach across from the West Beach Resort, you'll find **The Right Place Pottery Shop** (© 360/376-4023). Between Eastsound and Orcas on Horseshoe Highway is **Crow Valley Pottery** (© 360/376-4260), in an 1866 log cabin. On the east side of the island in the community of Olga, you'll find **Orcas Island Artworks,** Horseshoe Highway (© 360/376-4408), which is full of beautiful work by island artists.

SPORTS & OUTDOOR PURSUITS

Moran State Park ✶✶ (© 360/376-2326), which covers 5,252 acres of the island, is the largest park in the San Juans and the main destination for most island visitors. If the weather is clear, you'll find great views from the summit of Mount Constitution, which rises 2,409 feet above Puget Sound. There are also five lakes, 32 miles of hiking trails, and an environmental learning center. Fishing, hiking, boating, mountain biking, and camping (campsite reservations through **Reservations Northwest,** © 800/452-5687) are all popular park activities. The park is off Horseshoe Highway, approximately 12½ miles from the ferry landing.

BIKING ✶ Although Orcas is considered the most challenging of the San Juan Islands for biking, plenty of cyclists still pedal the island's roads. One of the best places to rent bikes here is **Dolphin Bay Bicycles** (© 360/376-4157; www.rockisland.com/~dolphin), located just to the right as you get off the ferry. From here you can explore Orcas Island or take a free ferry to Lopez Island or Shaw Island. Bikes rent for $25 per day, $55 for 3 days, and $75 per week. Guided bike rides are also sometimes available. In Eastsound, you can rent bikes from **Wildlife Cycles,** North Beach Road, Eastsound (© 360/376-4708; www.wildlifecycles.com). Bikes rent for about $10 to $12 per hour or $30 to $35 per day.

BOAT CHARTERS If you're interested in heading out on the water in a 33-foot sailboat, contact Capt. Don Palmer at **Amante Sail Tours** (© 360/376-4231), which charges $35 per person (with a two-person minimum and a maximum of six) for a half-day sail.

HIKING With 32 miles of hiking trails, **Moran State Park** ✶✶ offers hikes ranging from short, easy strolls alongside lakes, to strenuous, all-day outings. South of the community of Olga, on the east arm of the island, you'll also find a ½-mile trail through **Obstruction Pass Park** ✶✶. This trail leads to a quiet little cove that has a few walk-in/paddle-in campsites. The park is at the end of Obstruction Pass Road.

SEA KAYAKING ✶✶ The best way to see the Orcas Island coast is by sea kayak. Located right at the Orcas Island ferry landing, **Orcas Outdoors** (© 360/376-4611; www.orcasoutdoors.com) offers guided sea-kayak tours lasting from 1 hour ($25) to overnight ($220). Three-hour guided tours ($44) are also offered by **Shearwater Adventures** (© 360/376-4699; www.shearwaterkayaks.com). Two-hour paddles ($25) are offered by **Spring Bay Inn** (© 360/376-5531; www.springbayinn.com), which is located on the east side of the island near the village of Olga. These trips are in an area where bald eagles nest in the summer.

WHALE-WATCHING 🦌🦌   If you want to see some of the orca whales for which the San Juans are famous, you can take a whale-watching excursion with **Deer Harbor Charters** (© 800/544-5758 or 360/376-5989; www.deerharbor charters.com), which operates out of both Deer Harbor and Rosario Resort and charges $45 for adults and $30 for children, or **Orcas Island Eclipse Charters** (© **800/376-6566** or 360/376-6566), which operates out of the Orcas Island ferry dock and charges $46.50 for adults and $30 for children.

WHERE TO STAY

Orcas Hotel 🦌   Located right at the Orcas ferry landing, this attractive old Victorian hotel has been welcoming guests since 1904 and is a good choice for anyone coming over without a car. The guest rooms, done in a simple country style, vary in size, but all are carpeted and furnished with antiques, and all are non-smoking. On the first floor of the three-story building you'll find a quiet lounge, bakery, cafe, and restaurant.

P.O. Box 155, Orcas, WA 98280. © **888/672-2792** or 360/376-4300. Fax 360/376-4399. www.orcashotel. com. 12 units (4 with shared bathroom, 3 with half bathroom). $79–$109 double with shared bathroom, $129–$159 double with half bathroom, $149–$198 double with private bathroom. Rates include continental breakfast. AE, MC, V. **Amenities:** 2 restaurants, lounge; access to nearby health club; concierge; massage. *In room:* No phone.

The Resort at Deer Harbor 🦌🦌   Set on an open hillside above the spectacular Deer Harbor inlet, this casual resort looks across the water to a forested cliff and offers the best views on the island. Add to this a few small islands at the mouth of the inlet and a marina with sailboats bobbing at anchor, and you have the quintessential island setting. All the cottages here have hot tubs on their porches. However, the 11 large modern cottages, which are the most luxurious accommodations here, also have double whirlpool tubs in the bathrooms, fireplaces, and separate seating areas. The restaurant here, a casual and moderately priced bistro, is under the same management as Christina's, one of the best restaurants in the San Juans.

P.O. Box 200, Deer Harbor, WA 98243. © **888/376-4480** or 360/376-4420. Fax 360/376-5523. www.deer harbor.com. 26 units. May 15–Sept 30 $189–$399 suite or cottage; Oct 1–May 14 $149–$299 suite or cottage. Rates include continental breakfast. AE, DISC, MC, V. **Amenities:** Restaurant (International); outdoor pool. *In room:* TV, coffeemaker.

Rosario Resort & Spa 🦌🦌🦌 *Kids*   Rosario is the most luxurious accommodation on Orcas Island and is the only place in the San Juans that can actually claim to be a resort. Its centerpiece remains the 1904 Moran Mansion, an imposing white stucco building on the shore of Cascade Bay. The mansion houses the resort's main dining room, lounge, spa, and library. The larger and more luxurious rooms (with fireplaces, good views, and French country decor) are across the marina and up a steep hill from this main building, so if you aren't keen on walking, request a room in one of the buildings directly adjacent to the Moran Mansion. Sailing charters are available from the marina here.

1 Rosario Way, Eastsound, WA 98245. © **800/562-8820** or 360/376-2222. Fax 360/376-2289. www.rosario resort.com. 127 units. June–Sept $219–$329 double; $319–$629 suite; Oct–May $89–$249 double; $239–$499 suite. AE, DC, DISC, MC, V. **Amenities:** 3 restaurants (seafood), lounge; 1 indoor and 2 outdoor pools; 2 tennis courts; exercise room; spa; Jacuzzi; sauna; watersports equipment rentals; bike rentals; children's center; concierge; car-rental desk; shopping arcade; room service; massage; babysitting; coin-op laundry; laundry service. *In room:* TV, dataport, fridge, coffeemaker, hair dryer, iron.

Spring Bay Inn ☆☆ Just by virtue of being one of the only waterfront B&Bs in the San Juans, this inn would deserve a recommendation. However, innkeepers Sandy Playa and Carl Burger, both retired park rangers, make a stay here both fun and educational, and the setting and inn itself are great for a romantic getaway. You can soak in the hot tub on the beach and watch the sunset, spot bald eagles from just outside the inn's front door, hike on the nature trails, and best of all, go for a guided sea-kayak tour each morning. Four of the five guest rooms have fireplaces, two have views from their tubs, and two have balconies.

P.O. Box 97, Olga, WA 98279. ℂ 360/376-5531. Fax 360/376-2193. www.springbayinn.com. 5 units. $220–$260 double (2-night minimum). Rates include continental breakfast, brunch, and daily kayak tour. DISC, MC, V. **Amenities:** Access to nearby health club; Jacuzzi; concierge. *In room:* fridge, hair dryer.

Turtleback Farm Inn ☆☆ Nowhere on Orcas will you find a more idyllic setting than this bright-green restored farmhouse overlooking 80 acres of farmland at the foot of Turtleback Mountain. Simply furnished with antiques, the guest rooms range from cozy to spacious, and each has its own special view. Our favorite room in the main house is the Meadow View Room, which has a private deck and claw-foot tub. The four rooms in the orchard house are among the biggest and most luxurious on the island (gas fireplaces, claw-foot tubs, balconies, wood floors, kitchenettes). Days here start with a big farm breakfast served at valley-view tables that are set with bone china, silver, and linen. Finish your day with a nip of sherry by the fire.

1981 Crow Valley Rd., Eastsound, WA 98245. ℂ 800/376-4914 or 360/376-4914. Fax 360/376-5329. www. turtlebackinn.com. 11 units. Main house: May 1–Oct 15 $80–$160 double; Orchard House: June 15–Sept 15 $210 double. Lower rates other months. Rates include full breakfast. 2-night minimum stay June 15–Sept 15, weekends, and holidays. DISC, MC, V. **Amenities:** Access to nearby health club; concierge. *In room:* hair dryer.

WHERE TO DINE

For soups, sandwiches, and lattes, you can't beat the **Comet Café,** Eastsound Square, North Beach Road, Eastsound (ℂ 360/376-4220). For baked goods, imported cheeses, and other gourmet foodstuffs, stop by **Rose's Bread and Specialties** (ℂ 360/376-5805), which is also in Eastsound Square. For great cookies, don't miss **Teezer's Cookies** (ℂ 360/376-2913) at the corner of North Beach Road and A Street.

Café Olga ☆ *Finds* INTERNATIONAL Housed in an old strawberry-packing plant that dates from the days when these islands were known for their fruit, Café Olga is the best place on the island for breakfast or lunch. Everything here is homemade, using fresh local produce whenever possible. The blackberry pie is a special treat, especially when accompanied by Lopez Island Creamery ice cream. This building also houses Orcas Island Artworks, a gallery representing more than 70 Orcas Island artists.

Horseshoe Hwy., Olga. ℂ 360/376-5098. Main courses $7–$15. MC, V. Daily 10am–6pm (until 5pm in Nov–Dec). Closed Jan–Feb.

Christina's ☆☆ NORTHWEST Located on the second floor of an old waterfront building in Eastsound, Christina's has a beautiful view down the sound, just right for sunsets. If the weather is pleasant, the deck is *the* place on the island for sunset dinner. The menu here is short, changes regularly, and features innovative cuisine prepared with an emphasis on local ingredients. For the most part, Christina's showcases its creativity in its appetizers rather than in its entrees, so whether you crave the unusual or the more familiar, you'll likely be satisfied here. The desserts can be heavenly.

Horseshoe Hwy., Eastsound. © 360/376-4904. Reservations highly recommended. Main courses $24–$34. AE, DISC, MC, V. Daily 5:30–9 or 9:30pm. Closed for 3 weeks in Nov and all of Jan.

The Inn at Ship Bay 😗😗 NORTHWEST   About midway between Eastsound and the turnoff for the Rosario Resort, you'll spot the Inn at Ship Bay, an old white house that sits in a field high above the water. (Should you arrive after dark and be tempted to walk over to the water, be aware that the restaurant's front yard ends in a sheer cliff.) Inside, you'll find a traditional maritime decor and plenty of windows to let you gaze out to sea. Oysters are a specialty here; you can opt for pan-fried oysters, oyster shooters, and of course, fresh local oysters on the half shell. You can make a meal on oysters alone, but the entree menu includes plenty of other tempting dishes.

Horseshoe Hwy. © 360/376-5886. Reservations recommended. Main courses $15–$23. AE, DC, DISC, MC, V. Tues–Sun 5:30–8:30pm (closed Sun in fall and spring). Closed Thanksgiving through Feb.

LOPEZ ISLAND

Of the three islands with accommodations, Lopez is the least developed. Although it is less spectacular than Orcas or San Juan, it is flatter, which makes it popular with bicyclists who prefer easy grades over stunning panoramas. Lopez maintains more of its agricultural roots than either of the two previously mentioned islands, and likewise has fewer activities for tourists. If you just want to get away from it all and hole up with a good book for a few days, Lopez may be the place for you. Lopez Islanders are particularly friendly in that they wave to everyone they pass on the road. The custom has come to be known as the Lopez Wave.

For a taxi on Lopez, call **Lopez Cab** (© 360/468-2227).

Lopez Village is the closest this island has to a town, and here you'll find almost all of the island's restaurants and shops, as well as the **Lopez Island Historical Museum** (© 360/468-2049), where you can learn about the island's history and pick up a map of historic buildings. In July and August the museum is open Wednesday through Sunday from noon to 4pm, and in May, June, and September, it's open Friday through Sunday from noon to 4pm.

Lopez Island Vineyards 😗 (© 360/468-3644), which is located on Fisherman Bay Road between the ferry landing and Lopez Village, was until recently the only winery that actually made wine from fruit grown here in the San Juans. Both their Siegerrebe and their Madeleine Angevine are from local grapes, as are their organic fruit wines. They also make wines from grapes grown in the Yakima Valley. The winery tasting room is open between April or May and September Wednesday through Saturday from noon to 5pm.

SPORTS & OUTDOOR ACTIVITIES

Eight county parks and one state park provide plenty of access to the woods and water on Lopez Island. The first park off the ferry is **Odlin County Park** (© 360/468-2496 for information, or 360/378-1842 for reservations, which are taken between noon and 4pm Mon–Fri), which has a long beach, picnic tables, and a campground. Athletic fields make this more of a community sports center than a natural area, so this should be a last resort camping choice.

For a more natural setting for a short easy hike, check out **Upright Channel Park,** which is on Military Road (about a mile north of Lopez Village in the northwest corner of the island).

A little farther south and over on the east side of the island you'll find **Spencer Spit State Park** 😗 (© 360/468-2251), which also has a campground. Here, the forest meets the sea on a rocky beach that looks across a narrow channel to Frost Island. You can hike the trails through the forest or explore the beach.

South of Lopez Village on Bay Shore Road, you'll find the small **Otis Perkins Park,** which is between Fisherman Bay and the open water and has one of the longest beaches on the island.

Down at the south end of the island, you'll find the tiny **Shark Reef Sanctuary** 𝓡𝓡, where a short trail leads through the forest to a rocky stretch of coast that is among the prettiest on all the ferry-accessible islands. Small islands offshore create strong currents that swirl past the rocks here. Seals and occasionally whales can be seen just offshore. This is a great spot for a picnic.

BIKING 𝓡𝓡   Because of its size, lack of traffic, numerous parks, and relatively flat terrain, Lopez is a favorite of cyclists. You can rent bikes for $5 an hour or $25 a day from **Lopez Bicycle Works & Kayaks,** 2847 Fisherman Bay Rd. (𝓒 **360/468-2847**), at the marina on Fisherman Bay Road.

SEA KAYAKING 𝓡𝓡   If you want to explore the island's coastline by kayak, contact **Lopez Island Sea Kayaks** (𝓒 **360/468-2847;** www.lopezkayaks.com), which is located at the marina on Fisherman Bay Road and is open May through October. Tours cost $75 for a full-day trip with lunch included. Single kayaks can also be rented here for $12 to $25 per hour, or $25 to $50 per half-day. Double kayaks rent for $20 to $35 per hour and $40 to $60 per half-day.

WHERE TO STAY

Edenwild Inn 𝓡𝓡   Located right in Lopez Village, this modern Victorian B&B is a good choice if you've come to Lopez to go biking or if you just want to use your car as little as possible. Within a block of the inn are all the island's best restaurants. Most of the guest rooms here are quite large, and most also have views of the water. All the rooms have interesting antique furnishings, and several have fireplaces. In summer, colorful gardens surround the inn, and guests can breakfast on a large brick patio. The front veranda, overlooking Fisherman Bay, is a great place to relax in the afternoon.

132 Lopez Rd. (P.O. Box 271), Lopez Island, WA 98261. 𝓒 **800/606-0662** or 360/468-3238. Fax 360/468-4080. www.edenwildinn.com. 8 units. $110–$170 double. Rates include full breakfast. AE, MC, V. *In room:* No phone.

Lopez Farm Cottages and Tent Camping 𝓡𝓡 *(Value*   Set on 30 acres of pastures, old orchards, and forest between the ferry landing and Lopez Village, these modern cottages are tucked into a grove of cedar trees on the edge of a large lawn (in the middle of which stand three huge boulders). From the outside, the board-and-batten cottages look like old farm buildings, but inside you'll find a combination of Eddie Bauer and Scandinavian design. There are kitchenettes, plush beds with lots of pillows, and, in the bathrooms, showers with double shower heads. If showering together isn't romantic enough for you, there's a hot tub tucked down a garden path. Also on the property is a deluxe tents-only campground.

555 Fisherman Bay Rd., Lopez Island, WA 98261. 𝓒 **800/440-3556.** www.lopezfarmcottages.com. 4 units. $99–$150 double. Tent sites (available May–Oct) $28 double. Cottage rates include continental breakfast. MC, V. **Amenities:** Jacuzzi. *In room:* Kitchenette, coffeemaker.

Lopez Islander 𝓡 *(Kids*   Located about a mile south of Lopez Village, the Lopez Islander may not look too impressive from the outside, but it's a very comfortable lodging. All the rooms have great views of Fisherman Bay, and most rooms have balconies. The more expensive rooms also have coffeemakers, wet bars, microwaves, and refrigerators. In addition to amenities listed below, the Islander also has a full-service marina with kayak rentals.

Fisherman Bay Rd. (P.O. Box 459), Lopez Island, WA 98261. ℂ 800/736-3434 or 360/468-2233. Fax 360/468-3382. www.lopezislander.com. 28 units. July–Sept $79.50–$139.50 double; $199.50–$259.50 suite. Lower rates Oct–June. AE, DISC, MC, V. **Amenities:** Restaurant (American), lounge; outdoor pool; exercise room; Jacuzzi; bike rentals; children's center; coin-op laundry. *In room:* TV, fridge.

WHERE TO DINE

When it's time for coffee, you'll find the island's best in Lopez Village at **Caffé Verdi,** Lopez Plaza (ℂ **360/468-2257**); and right next door, you'll find divinely decadent pastries and other baked goods at **Holly B's Bakery** (ℂ **360/ 468-2133**). Across the street, in Lopez Island Pharmacy, you'll find the old-fashioned **Lopez Island Soda Fountain** (ℂ **360/468-2616**).

Bay Café ⊛⊛ NORTHWEST/INTERNATIONAL   Housed in an eclectically decorated old waterfront commercial building with a deck that overlooks Fisherman Bay, the Bay Café serves some of the best food in the state. This is the sort of place where diners animatedly discuss what that other flavor is in the savory cheesecake with macadamia-cilantro pesto, where the dipping sauces with the pork satay are unlike anything you've ever tasted before, and where people walk through the door and exclaim, "I want whatever it is that smells so good." The menu, though short, spans the globe and changes frequently. Come with a hearty appetite; meals include soup and salad, and the desserts are absolutely to die for (imagine velvety pumpkin crème caramel decorated with a nasturtium flower and candied ginger). Accompany your meal with a bottle of wine from Lopez Island Vineyards for the quintessential Lopez dinner.

Village Center, Lopez Village. ℂ 360/468-3700. Reservations highly recommended. Main courses $8–$15 at lunch, $15–$28 at dinner. AE, DISC, MC, V. Summer daily 3:30–9pm; hours vary other months.

Bucky's ⊛ AMERICAN   With a laid-back island feeling and an outside waterfront deck, this tiny place is where the locals hang out. The food, though simple, is consistently good—nothing fancy, just delicious. The black-and-blue burger with blue cheese and Cajun spices definitely gets our vote for best burger in the islands. If you're feeling more like seafood, there are fish tacos and fish and chips.

Lopez Village Plaza. ℂ 360/468-2595. Reservations taken for parties of 5 or more only. Main courses $5–$15. MC, V. Apr–Sept Sun–Thurs 11:30am–8:30pm, Fri–Sat 11:30am–9pm; usually closed other months.

2 Mount Rainier

Weather forecasting for Seattleites is a simple matter: Either "The Mountain" is out and the weather is good, or it isn't (out or good). "The Mountain" is of course Mount Rainier, the 14,410-foot-tall dormant volcano that looms over Seattle on clear days; and though it looks as if it were on the edge of town, it's actually 90 miles southeast of the city.

The mountain and 235,625 acres surrounding it are part of **Mount Rainier National Park,** which was established in 1899 as the fifth U.S. national park. From downtown Seattle, the easiest route to the mountain is via I-5 south to exit 127. Then take Wash. 7 south, which in some 30 miles becomes Wash. 706. The route is well marked. Allow yourself about 2½ hours to reach the park's Paradise area.

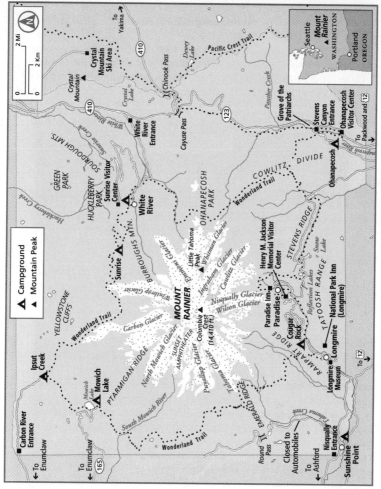

EXPLORING THE PARK

You'd be well advised to leave as early in the day as possible, especially if you're heading to the mountain on a summer weekend. Traffic along the route and crowds at the park can be daunting.

Before leaving, you might contact the park for information: **Mount Rainier National Park,** Tahoma Woods, Star Route, Ashford, WA 98304-9751 (© **360/569-2211,** ext 3314; www.nps.gov/mora). Keep in mind that during the winter only the Henry M. Jackson Memorial Visitor Center at Paradise is open, and then only on weekends and holidays. Park entrances other than the Nisqually entrance are closed by snow throughout the winter.

Mount Rainier National Park admission is $10 per motor vehicle or $5 per person for pedestrians, motorcyclists, and bicyclists.

Just past the **main southwest entrance (Nisqually),** you'll come to Longmire, site of the National Park Inn, the **Longmire Museum** (exhibits on the park's natural and human history), a **hiker information center** that issues back-country permits, and a **ski-touring center** where you can rent cross-country skis and snowshoes in winter.

The road then climbs to **Paradise** (elevation 5,400 ft.), the aptly named mountainside aerie that affords a breathtaking close-up view of the mountain. Paradise is the park's most popular destination, so expect crowds. During July and August the meadows here are ablaze with wildflowers. The circular **Henry M. Jackson Memorial Visitor Center** provides 360° panoramic views, and a short walk away is a spot from which you can look down on Nisqually Glacier. Many miles of other **trails** lead out from Paradise, looping through meadows and up onto snowfields above timberline. It's not unusual to find plenty of snow at Paradise as late as July. In 1972, the area set a world's record for snowfall in one year: 93.5 feet! This record held until the 1998–99 winter season, during which La Niña climatic conditions produced record-breaking conditions on Mount Baker to the north of Mount Rainier. More than 94 feet fell on Mount Baker that season.

In summer, you can continue beyond Paradise to the **Ohanapecosh Visitor Center,** where you can walk through a forest of old-growth trees, some more than 1,000 years old.

Continuing around the mountain, you'll reach the turnoff for **Sunrise.** At 6,400 feet, Sunrise is the highest spot in the park accessible by car, and a beautiful old log lodge serves as the visitor center. From here you can see not only Mount Rainier, seemingly at arm's length, but also Mounts Baker and Adams. Some of the park's most scenic trails begin here at Sunrise. This area is usually less crowded than Paradise.

At both Paradise and Sunrise, hikers can choose from a good variety of outings, from short, flat nature walks to moderately difficult loops to long, steep out-and-back hikes.

If you want to see a bit of dense forest or hike without crowds, head for the park's **Carbon River entrance** in the northwest corner. Carbon River is formed by the lowest-elevation glacier in the contiguous 48 states. A long day hike in this area provides an opportunity not only to come face to face with the Carbon Glacier but also to enjoy some superb alpine scenery. This is the least visited region of the park because it only offers views to those willing to hike several miles uphill. At 3 miles up the main trail, you'll encounter the glacier plowing through the middle of the rain forest, and at about 5 miles you reach meadows and in-your-face views of the northwest flank of Mount Rainier. The road into this area is in very bad shape, however, and a high-clearance vehicle is recommended. Be sure to call the park for a road-condition update before heading this way.

WHERE TO STAY

Besides the two accommodations listed below, there are several **campgrounds** in Mount Rainier National Park. Two of the park's campgrounds—Cougar and Ohanapecosh—take reservations, and these should be made several months in advance for summer weekends. To make reservations, contact the **National Park Reservation Service** (© **800/365-2267;** http://reservations.nps.gov).

National Park Inn ⊛   Located in Longmire, in the southwest corner of the park, this rustic lodge opened in 1920. Because the setting here is not as spectacular as that of the Paradise Inn, this lodge is not nearly as popular, and consequently room reservations are easier to come by. The inn's front veranda does, however, have a view of the mountain, and it is here that guests often gather at sunset on clear days. Because this lodge stays open in the winter, it is popular with cross-country skiers and snowshoers. Guest rooms vary in size and have rustic furnishings. The inn's restaurant manages to have something for everyone. There's also a lounge with a river-rock fireplace that's perfect for winter-night relaxing. A gift shop and cross-country ski/snowshoe rental shop are adjacent to the inn.

Mount Rainier National Park, Ashford, WA 98304. © **360/569-2275**. www.guestservices.com/rainier. 25 units (7 with shared bathroom). $75 double with shared bathroom, $104–$150 double with private bathroom. AE, DC, DISC, MC, V. Free parking. **Amenities:** Restaurant (American), lounge. *In room:* No phone.

Paradise Inn 🌟🌟   Built in 1917 high on the flanks of Mount Rainier in an area aptly known as Paradise, this rustic lodge should be your first choice of accommodations in the park (book early). Cedar-shake siding, huge exposed beams, cathedral ceilings, and a gigantic stone fireplace make this the quintessential mountain retreat. Offering breathtaking views of the mountain, the inn is also the starting point for miles of trails that in summer wander through flower-filled meadows. Guest rooms, which vary in size, all have carpets, drapes, and rustic hickory furniture. The Sunday brunch in the inn's large dining room is legendary. A snack bar and lounge are dining options.

Mount Rainier National Park, Ashford, WA 98304. © **360/569-2275**. www.guestservices.com/rainier. 117 units (33 with shared bathroom). $76 double with shared bathroom, $114–$150 double with private bathroom; $155 suite. AE, DC, DISC, MC, V. Closed early Oct to mid-May. Free parking. **Amenities:** 2 restaurants (American, snack bar), lounge. *In room:* no phone.

3 Ferry Excursions from Seattle

Among Seattle's most popular excursions are ferry trips across Puget Sound to Bainbridge Island (Seattle's quintessential bedroom community) and Bremerton (home of the Naval Shipyards). If your interests run to shopping, small towns, wineries, parks, and gardens, you'll want to head over to Bainbridge Island. If, on the other hand, you're more interested in naval history and antiques and collectibles, you'll want to visit Bremerton. It's also possible to link these two excursions together by taking one ferry out and the other ferry back. It's not a long drive between Bainbridge Island and Bremerton (less than 1 hr.), but if you stop often to enjoy the sights, you can certainly have a long day's journey.

BAINBRIDGE ISLAND & POULSBO

Start the trip by taking the **Bainbridge Island ferry** from the Colman Dock ferry terminal at Pier 52 on the Seattle waterfront. For a current sailing schedule, contact **Washington State Ferries** (© **800/84-FERRY** or 888/808-7977 in Washington, or 206/464-6400; www.wsdot.wa.gov/ferries/). On board, you can see the Seattle skyline, and on a clear day, Mount Rainier to the southeast and the Olympic Mountains to the west. One-way fares from Seattle to Bainbridge Island (a 35-min. crossing) are $8 ($10 from mid-May to mid-Oct) for a car and driver, $4.50 for adult car passengers or walk-ons, $2.20 for seniors, and $3.20 for children ages 5 to 18. Car passengers and walk-ons only pay fares on westbound ferries.

Between mid-June and Labor Day weekend, if you'd like to do a little paddling in a sea kayak or canoe, turn left as you get off the ferry and head to Waterfront Park, where you'll find **Bainbridge Island Boat Rentals** (© **206/ 842-9229**), which rents single sea kayaks ($12 per hr.) and double kayaks ($18 per hr.). This company also rents swan boats, rowboats, and sailboats ($18 per hr.) and a motorboat ($25 per hr.).

With its water views and winding country roads, Bainbridge is a favorite of bicyclists. You can rent from **B. I. Cycle Rentals,** 162 Bjune Ave. (© **206/ 842-6413**), which is located a block off Winslow Way near the corner of Madison Avenue (in downtown Bainbridge Island/Winslow just a few blocks from the ferry) and charges $5 per hour or $25 a day for mountain bikes. They can also give you a map of the island and outline a good ride for you. This shop also rents bikes right at the ferry landing.

Just up the hill from the Bainbridge Island ferry terminal is the island's main shopping district, where you'll find some interesting shops and restaurants. If you'd like to sample some local wines, drop in at the **Bainbridge Island Vineyards and Winery,** 682 Wash. 305 (© **206/842-9463**), which is located half a mile up the hill from the ferry landing and specializes in European-style white wines made from estate-grown grapes. These wines are quite good and are only available here and at a few select restaurants. The winery is open Wednesday through Sunday from noon to 5pm.

Down at the south end of the island, you'll find **Fort Ward State Park** (© **206/842-4041**) on the quiet shore of Rich Passage. The park offers picnicking and good bird watching. Garden enthusiasts will want to call ahead and make a reservation to visit the **Bloedel Reserve** ⊛, 7571 NE Dolphin Dr. (© **206/842-7631**), which is 6 miles north of the ferry terminal off Wash. 305 (turn right on Agate Point Road). Expansive and elegant grounds are the ideal place for a quiet stroll amid plants from around the world. Admission is $6 for adults and $4 for seniors. Nearby, at the northern tip of the island, you'll find **Fay Bainbridge State Park** (© **206/842-3931**), which offers camping and great views across the sound to the Seattle skyline.

After crossing the Agate Pass Bridge to the mainland of the Kitsap Peninsula, take your first right, and in the village of **Suquamish,** you'll see signs for the grave of Chief Sealth, for whom Seattle was named. Nearby (turn at the Texaco station on the edge of town) you'll also find **Old Man House State Park,** which preserves the site of a large Native American longhouse. The Old Man House itself is long gone, but you'll find an informative sign and a small park with picnic tables. From Suquamish, head back to Wash. 305, continue a little farther west and watch for signs to the **Suquamish Museum,** 15838 Sandy Hook Rd. (© **360/394-5275**), on the Port Madison Indian Reservation. The museum houses a compelling history of Puget Sound's native people, with lots of historic photos and quotes from tribal elders about growing up in the area. May through September, the museum is open daily from 10am to 5pm; October through April, it's open Friday through Sunday from 11am to 4pm. Admission is $4 for adults and $3 for seniors, and $2 for children 12 and under.

Continuing north on Wash. 305, you next come to the small town of **Poulsbo,** which overlooks fjordlike Liberty Bay. Settled in the late 1880s by Scandinavians, Poulsbo was primarily a fishing, logging, and farming town until it decided to play up its Scandinavian heritage. Shops in the Scandinavian-inspired downtown sell all manner of Viking and Scandinavian souvenirs, but there are also several good art galleries and other interesting shops. Throughout the year there are numerous Scandinavian-theme celebrations. For more information, contact the **Greater Poulsbo Chamber of Commerce,** 19168 Jensen Way NE (P.O. Box 1063), Poulsbo, WA 98370 (© **877/768-5726** or 360/ 779-4848; www.poulsbo.net).

Between downtown and the waterfront, you'll find Liberty Bay Park, and at the south end of Front Street, you'll find the **Poulsbo Marine Science Center,** 18743 Front St. NE (© **360/779-5549;** www.poulsbomsc.org), which houses interpretive displays on the Puget Sound and is a great place to bring the kids. The center is open daily 11am to 5pm. Admission is $4 for adults, $3 for seniors and teenagers, and $2 for children ages 2 through 12.

If you're interested in seeing Poulsbo from the water, you can rent a sea kayak from **Olympic Outdoor Center,** 18971 Front St. (© **360/697-6095;** www. kayakproshop.com), which charges $12 to $17 per hour or $30 to $50 by the day.

If you have time and enjoy visiting historic towns, continue north from Poulsbo on Wash. 3 to **Port Gamble,** which looks like a New England village dropped down in the middle of the Northwest woods. This community was established in 1853 as a company town for the Pope and Talbot lumber mill. Along the town's shady streets are many Victorian homes that were restored by Pope and Talbot. Stop by the Port Gamble Country Store, which now houses the **Port Gamble Historical Museum** (© **360/297-8074**), a collection of local memorabilia. Admission is $2.50 for adults and $1.50 for seniors and students (children 5 and under are free). From May 1 to October 31, the museum is open daily from 10:30am to 5pm; the rest of the year, it's open by appointment. The same location is home to the **Of Sea and Shore Museum** (© **360/297-2426**), which houses an exhibit of seashells from around the world. This museum is open daily from 9am to 5pm, and admission is free.

BREMERTON & ITS NAVAL HISTORY

If your interests run to big ships and naval history, you'll want to ride the ferry from Seattle to Bremerton (see above for information on Washington State Ferries).

Bremerton is home to the Puget Sound Naval Shipyard, where mothballed U.S. Navy ships have included the aircraft carriers USS *Nimitz* and USS *Midway* and the battleships USS *Missouri* and USS *New Jersey.* If you'd like to see the shipyards and mothballed fleet from the water, take a tour with **Kitsap Harbor Tours,** 110 Harrison Ave. (© **360/876-1260**). From June through August, tours are offered daily between 11am and 4pm. Tours are $8.50 for adults, $7.50 for seniors, and $5.50 for children ages 5 to 12. This company also offers dinner tours to Tillicum Village (a reproduction Native American long house) on Blake Island, which is a state park. These tours, which are offered May through September, include dinner and performances of traditional Native American dances. Dinner tours are $55 for adults, $50 for seniors, $22 for children ages 5 to 12, and free for children 4 and under.

One mothballed destroyer, the USS *Turner Joy,* is now operated by the **Bremerton Historic Ships Association** (© **360/792-2457**) and is open to the public as a memorial to those who have served in the U.S. Navy and who have helped build the navy's ships. The *Turner Joy* is docked about 150 yards east of the Washington State Ferries terminal. From May through September, the ship is open daily from 10am to 5pm; call for hours in other months. Admission is $7 for adults, $6 for seniors and military, and $5 for children ages 5 to 12. Combination *Turner Joy*–Harbor Tour tickets are also available.

Nearby is the **Bremerton Naval Museum,** 130 Washington Ave. (© **360/ 479-7447**), which showcases naval history and the historic contributions of the Puget Sound Naval Shipyard. From Memorial Day to Labor Day, the museum is open Monday through Saturday from 10am to 5pm and Sunday from 1 to 5pm; other months the museum is closed on Monday. Admission is free.

Heading north from Bremerton on Wash. 3, you'll soon see signs for the **Naval Undersea Museum,** Garnett Way (© **360/396-4148**), which is located 3 miles east of Wash. 3 on Wash. 308 near the town of Keyport. The museum examines all aspects of undersea exploration, with interactive exhibits, models, and displays that include a deep-sea exploration and research craft, a Japanese kamikaze torpedo, and a deep-sea rescue vehicle. The museum is open daily from 10am to 4pm (closed on Tues between Oct–May), and admission is free. The reason this museum is here is that the **Bangor Navy Base,** home port for a fleet of Trident nuclear submarines, is nearby. The base is on Hood Canal, a long narrow arm of Puget Sound.

4 East of the City: A Waterfall & Wineries Loop

While Seattle has become a sprawling city of congested highways and high housing prices, there is a reason why so many people put up with the city's drawbacks. Less than an hour east lie mountains so vast and rugged that you can hike for a week without ever crossing a road. Between the city and this wilderness lie the wineries and farmlands of the **Snoqualmie Valley,** the Seattle region's last bit of bucolic countryside. Here you'll find small towns, pastures full of spotted cows, "U-pick" farms, and even a few unexpected attractions, including an impressive (and familiar) waterfall and a medieval village. While driving the back roads of the Snoqualmie Valley, keep an eye out for historic markers that include old photos and details about the valley's past.

Snoqualmie Falls ⊛⊛, the valley's biggest attraction, plummet 270 feet into a pool of deep blue water. The falls are surrounded by a park owned by Puget Power, which operates a hydroelectric plant inside the rock wall behind the falls. The plant, built in 1898, was the world's first underground electric-generating facility. Within the park you'll find two overlooks near the lip of the falls and a half-mile-long trail leading down to the base of the falls. The river below the falls is popular both for fishing and for white-water kayaking. These falls will be familiar to anyone who remembers the opening sequence of David Lynch's *Twin Peaks,* which was filmed in this area. To reach the falls, take I-90 east from Seattle for 35 to 45 minutes and get off at exit 27. If you're hungry for lunch, try the restaurant at Salish Lodge, the hotel at the top of the falls.

Snoqualmie Falls are located just outside the town of **Snoqualmie,** which is where you'll find the restored 1890 railroad depot that houses the **Northwest Railway Museum,** Wash. 202 (© **425/888-3030**). The museum, which is an absolute must for anyone with a child who is familiar with Thomas the Tank Engine, operates the **Snoqualmie Valley Railroad** on weekends May through October. The 40-minute railway excursions, using steam or diesel trains, run between here and the town of **North Bend.** Fares are $7 for adults, $6 for seniors, and $5 for children ages 3 to 12. Be sure to call ahead for a current schedule. The museum, which is free, displays railroad memorabilia and also has a large display of rolling stock. A big hit with kids!

Outside of North Bend rises **Mount Si,** one of the most frequently hiked mountains in the state. This mountain, carved by glaciers long ago, presents a dramatic face to the valley, and if you're the least bit athletic, it is hard to resist the temptation to hike to the top. For more information see "Hiking" in chapter 6, "Exploring Seattle."

Between North Bend and the town of **Carnation,** you'll pass several "U-pick" farms, where you can pick your own berries during the summer or pumpkins in the fall.

The Snoqualmie Valley is also the site of **Camlann Medieval Village,** 10320 Kelly Rd. NE (© **425/788-8624;** www.camlann.com), which is located north of Carnation off Wash. 203. On weekends between mid-July and late August, this reproduction of a medieval village is home to knights and squires, minstrels, and assorted other costumed merrymakers. There are crafts stalls, food booths, and, the highlight each day, jousting matches. Medieval clothing is available for rent if you forgot to pack yours. Throughout the year, there is a wide variety of banquets and seasonal festivals, and the village's Bors Hede restaurant is open Tuesday through Sunday for traditional dinners. Fair admission is $9 for adults, $5 for seniors and children age 12 and under. Admission to both the fair and a banquet is $39.

From Fall City, you can follow Wash. 202 for 22 miles northwest to the Woodinville area where you will find several **wineries.** The first winery you'll come to is the **Columbia Winery,** 14030 NE 145th St., Woodinville (© **800/488-2347** or 425/488-2776; www.columbiawinery.com), which has Washington's largest wine-tasting bar, and produces a wide range of good wines (open daily 10am–7pm).

Across Wash. 202 from the Columbia Winery, you'll find the largest and most famous of the wineries in the area, **Chateau Ste. Michelle** ✨, 14111 NE 145th St., Woodinville (© **425/415-3300;** www.ste-michelle.com). This is by far the most beautiful winery in the Northwest, located in a grand mansion on a historic 1912 estate. It's also the largest winery in the state, and is known for its consistent quality (daily 10am–4:30pm). Tours of the winery are offered available, and an amphitheater on the grounds stages big-name music performances throughout the summer.

Continuing north on Woodinville-Redmond Road (Wash. 202), you'll next come to **Silver Lake Winery,** 15029 Woodinville-Redmond Rd. NE, Woodinville (© **425/486-1900;** www.washingtonwine.com). This winery crafts some good reds but can be hit-and-miss (open Apr–Dec daily noon–5pm; Jan–Mar Wed–Sun noon–5pm). Next up the road heading north is the small **Facelli Winery,** 16120 Woodinville-Redmond NE (© **425/488-1020**), which is open Saturday and Sunday noon to 4pm and produces some of our favorite Washington red wines. Don't miss this hidden gem.

If **beer** is more to your taste, you can stop in at the pub at the large **Redhook Ale Brewery,** 14300 NE 145th St., Woodinville (© **425/483-3232**), right next door to Columbia Winery. Tours are available and there is a pub as well.

Finish your day with a walk around downtown **Kirkland,** along the Moss Bay waterfront on Lake Washington. You can stroll along the waterfront and stop in at interesting shops and any of more than a dozen art galleries. There are also several decent restaurants in the area. For restaurant recommendations, see "The Eastside (Including Bellevue & Kirkland)" section of chapter 5, "Where to Dine in Seattle." To get back to Seattle, take I-405 south to Wash. 520 or I-90.

WHERE TO STAY

Salish Lodge and Spa ✨✨✨   Set at the top of 270-foot Snoqualmie Falls and only 35 minutes east of Seattle on I-90, Salish Lodge is a popular weekend getaway spot for folks from Seattle. With its country lodge atmosphere, the Salish aims for casual comfort and hits the mark, though the emphasis is clearly on luxury. Guest rooms, which are designed for romantic weekend getaways, all have fireplaces and whirlpool baths, feather beds, and down comforters. To make this an even more attractive getaway, there's a full-service spa. The lodge's country breakfast is a legendary feast that will likely keep you full right through to. By the way, if you were a fan of *Twin Peaks*, you'll immediately recognize this hotel.

6501 Railroad Ave. SE (P.O. Box 1109), Snoqualmie, WA 98065. © 800/826-6124, 800/2-SALISH, or 425/888-2556. www.salishlodge.com. 91 units. $199–$389 double; $499–$999 suite (all rates plus $12.50 resort fee). AE, DC, MC, V. Valet parking $5. **Amenities:** Restaurant (Northwest), lounge with view of the falls; exercise room; full-service spa with Jacuzzis and saunas; complimentary mountain bikes; activities desk; room service; massage; laundry service; dry cleaning. *In room:* A/C, TV, dataport, minibar, coffeemaker, hair dryer, iron.

Willows Lodge ★★★ *(Finds)*
Located on the banks of the Sammamish River (which, unfortunately is little more than a shallow canal) about 30 minutes north of Seattle and adjacent to the much-celebrated Herbfarm restaurant, this lodge is a beautiful blending of rustic and contemporary. From the moment you turn in to the lodge's parking lot, you'll recognize that this is someplace special. A huge fire-darkened tree stump is set like a sculpture right outside the front door, and the landscaping has a distinctly Northwest feel.

Inside, the abundance of polished woods (some of which were salvaged from an old building in Portland) gives the lodge something of a Japanese aesthetic. It's all very soothing and tranquil, an ideal retreat from which visit the nearby wineries. In the guest rooms, you'll find beds with lamb's wool mattress pads, European linens, down duvets; slate tables made from salvaged pool tables; and all kinds of high-tech amenities (including digital shower thermostats).

14580 NE 145th St., Woodinville, WA 98072. © 877/424-3930 or 425/424-3900. Fax 425/424-2585. www.willowslodge.com. 88 units. $220–$290 double; $350–$750 suite. Rates include continental breakfast. AE, DC, DISC, MC, V. Pets accepted ($200 refundable deposit). **Amenities:** Restaurant (Northwest), lounge; exercise room; full-service spa; Jacuzzi; sauna; bike rentals; room service; massage; laundry service; dry cleaning. *In room:* A/C, TV, dataport, minibar, fridge, coffeemaker, hair dryer, iron, safe.

WHERE TO DINE

If you aren't out this way specifically to have dinner at The Herbfarm and just want a decent meal while you tour the area, try the **Forecaster's Public House** at the Redhook Ale Brewery, 14300 NE 145th St., Woodinville (© **425/483-3232**). Other good area choices include the dining rooms at the Salish Lodge and Willows Lodge (see above).

The Herbfarm Restaurant ★★★ NORTHWEST
The Herbfarm, the most highly acclaimed restaurant in the Northwest, is known across the nation for its extraordinarily lavish meals. The menu changes throughout the year, with different themes to match the seasons. Wild gathered vegetables, Northwest seafoods and meats, organic vegetables, wild mushrooms, and of course the generous use of fresh herbs from the Herbfarm gardens are the ingredients from which the restaurant's chef, Jerry Traunfeld, creates his culinary extravaganzas. Dinners are paired with complementary Northwest wines (and occasionally something particularly remarkable from Europe).

So what's dinner here like? Well to start with, the restaurant is housed in a reproduction country inn beside a contemporary Northwest-style lodge. Some of the highlights of a recent spring forager's dinner included a paddlefish caviar tart; nettle, green garlic, and lovage soup; fiddlehead ferns and black morel served with an unusual risotto; Douglas fir sorbet; coriander-crusted loin of lamb; cured foie gras; and, for dessert, maple-blossom crème brûlée, sweet cicely–and-currant ice cream. Sure it's expensive, but if you're a foodie, you need to do something like this at least once in your life.

The Herbfarm's dinners are so incredibly popular that reservations are taken only a couple of times each year, so you'll have to plan far in advance if you want to be sure of an Herbfarm experience. However, you can try calling on short notice; cancellations often open up tables.

14590 NE 145th St., Woodinville. © 206/784-2222. www.theherbfarm.com. Reservations required. Fixed-price 9-course dinner $149–$169 per person with 5 or 6 matched wines ($50 per-person deposit required). AE, MC, V. Seatings Thurs–Sat at 7pm, Sun 4:30pm.

11

The Best of Portland

Situated at the confluence of the Willamette and Columbia rivers, Portland, Oregon, with a population of roughly 1.7 million in the metropolitan area, is a city of discreet charms. That the city claims a rose garden as one of its biggest attractions should give you an idea of just how laid-back it is. Sure, Portlanders are just as attached to their cell phones and pagers as residents of other major metropolitan areas, but this is the City of Roses, and people still take time to stop and smell the flowers. Spend much time here, and you, too, will likely feel the city's leisurely pace seeping into your bones.

While Seattle has zoomed into the national consciousness, Portland has, until recently, managed to dodge the limelight and the problems that come with sky-rocketing popularity. For many years now Portland has looked upon itself as a small, accessible city, vaguely European in character. *Clean* and *friendly* are the two terms that crop up most often in descriptions of the city. However, as word has spread about overcrowding in Seattle, people looking for the good life and affordable housing have turned to Portland, which is now experiencing the same sort of rapid growth that Seattle began going through more than a decade ago.

Portland does not have any major sights to pull in tourists—no Space Needle, no waterfront piers, no Experience Music Project. Instead, it is a city of quiet charms that must be searched for and savored—the shade of the stately elms in the South Park Blocks, the tranquility of the Japanese Garden, the view from the grounds of Pittock Mansion, the miles of hiking trails in Forest Park. Sure, there's a good art museum and a world-class science museum, but these are not nearly as important to the city's citizenry as its many parks and public gardens. Not only does Portland claim beautiful rose gardens, the most authentic Japanese Garden in North America, and the largest classical Chinese garden in the country, but it also can lay claim to both the world's smallest city park and the largest forested urban park in the country.

The city's other claim to fame is as the nation's microbrew capital. Espresso may be the beverage that gets this town going in the morning (this *is* the Northwest), but it is microbrewed beer that helps the city maintain its mellow character. There are so many brewpubs here in Portland that the city has been nicknamed Munich on the Willamette. While in other cities craft beer has given way to cocktails and wine, here in Portland microbrews are still the drink of choice. Wine is a close second, though, which shouldn't come as a surprise, considering how close the city is to wine country.

Portland itself may be short on things for visitors to do, but the city's surroundings certainly are not. Within a 1½- to 2-hour drive from Portland, you can be strolling a Pacific Ocean beach, strolling beside a waterfall in the Columbia Gorge, hiking on Mount Hood (a dormant volcano as picture perfect as Mount Fuji), driving through the Mount St. Helens blast zone, or sampling world-class pinot noirs in the Oregon wine country (see chapter 20, "Side Trips from Portland," for details on all these excursions). It is this proximity to the outdoors that makes Portland a great city to use as a base for exploring some of the best of the Northwest.

1 Frommer's Favorite Portland Experiences

- **Strolling the Grounds at the Japanese Garden.** This is the best Japanese Garden in the United States, perhaps the best anywhere outside of Japan. Our favorite time to visit is in June when the Japanese irises are in bloom. There's no better stress-reducer in the city.

- **Beer Sampling at Brewpubs.** They may not have invented beer here in Portland, but they've certainly turned it into an art form. Whether you're looking for a cozy corner pub or an upscale tap room, you'll find a brewpub where you can feel comfortable sampling what local brewmeisters are concocting.

- **Kayaking Around Ross Island.** Seattle may be the sea-kayaking capital of the Northwest, but Portland's not a bad spot for pursuing this sport either. You can paddle on the Columbia or Willamette River, but our favorite easy outing is around Ross Island in the Willamette River. You can even paddle past the submarine at the Oregon Museum of Science and Industry and pull out at Tom McCall Waterfront Park.

- **Mountain-Biking the Leif Erikson Trail.** Forest Park is the largest forested city park in the country, and running its length is the unpaved Leif Erikson Trail. The road is closed to cars and extends for 12 miles. Along the way, there are occasional views of the Columbia River. This is a pretty easy ride, without any strenuous climbs.

- **Driving and Hiking in the Gorge.** No matter what time of year it is, the drive up the Columbia Gorge is spectacular, and there are dozens of easily accessible hiking trails throughout the gorge. If you've got time to spare, take the scenic highway; if not, take I-84. No matter which road you take, be sure to pull off at Multnomah Falls. For an alternative point of view, drive the Washington side of the river and stop to hike to the top of Beacon Rock.

- **Hiking and Skiing on Mount Hood.** Located less than an hour from Portland, Mount Hood offers year-round skiing and hiking. Timberline Lodge, high on this dormant volcano's slopes, was built by the WPA during the Great Depression and is a showcase of craftsmanship. In summer, hiking trails radiate out from the lodge, and in winter there are ski slopes both above and below the lodge.

- **Hanging Out at Powell's.** They don't call Powell's the City of Books for nothing. This bookstore, which sells both new and used books, is so big you have to get a map at the front door. No matter how much time we spend here, it's never enough. A large cafe makes it all that much easier to while away the hours.

- **Free Rides on the Vintage Trolleys.** Tri-Met buses, MAX light-rail trolleys, and Portland Streetcars are all free within a large downtown area known as the Fareless Square. That alone should be enough to get you on some form of public transit while you're in town, but if you're really lucky, you might catch one of the

Site Seeing: The Best Portland Websites

If you're surfing the Web in search of information on Portland, the following websites will provide you with lots of useful information.

- **http://portland.citysearch.com**: Another in CitySearch's excellent line of city sites, CitySearch Portland offers, in a familiar format, much of what a visitor needs to know about the culinary, artistic, theatrical, and musical scenes in town. The site is searchable by time, venue, date, or neighborhood. Also check out the dozens of restaurant reviews, listed by cuisine type.
- **www.pova.com**: The Portland Oregon Visitors Association (POVA) is eager to have you see and do all you can in its city. Click on "Visitor Information" for advice on sightseeing, performing arts, shopping, outdoor activities, and an online hotel reservation service. The site also offers a calendar of events with special activities highlighted, as well as tools to help business travelers plan meetings and conventions.
- **www.oregonlive.com**: A service of the state's largest newspaper, the *Oregonian*, Oregon Live offers news updates, events calendars, local entertainment listings, online classifieds, and chat rooms.
- **www.portlandairportpdx.com**: Check out arrivals and departures online—no need to burrow through an automated phone system to see whether your plane is on time. You can also get a complete rundown on parking options and local ground transportation.
- **www.tri-met.org**: Tri-Met is Portland's public transportation agency and here at its website, there is information on Portland's system of public buses, light-rail trolleys, and stretcars. Get routes, timetables, and fares, or download the Tri-Met trip planner to find the shortest route between two points via light rail and bus systems.

---

vintage trolley cars. There aren't any San Francisco–style hills, but these old trolley cars are still fun to ride.

- **People-Watching at Pioneer Courthouse Square.** This is the heart and soul of downtown Portland, and no matter what time of year or what the weather, people gather here. Grab a latte at the Starbucks and sit by the waterfall fountain. In summer, there are concerts here, both at lunch and in the evenings, and any time of year you might catch a rally, performance, or installation of some kind. Don't miss the *Weather Machine* show at noon.

- **An Afternoon at the Portland Saturday Market.** This large arts-and-crafts market is an outdoor showcase for hundreds of the Northwest's creative artisans. You'll find fascinating one-of-a-kind clothes, jewelry, kitchenware, musical instruments, and much, much more. The food stalls serve up some great fast food, too.
- **Concerts at the Schnitz.** The Arlene Schnitzer Concert Hall, home to the Oregon Symphony, is a restored 1920s movie palace and is the city's most impressive place to attend a performance. Even if the show doesn't meet

your expectations, you can enjoy the classic architectural details.

- **Summertime Concerts at the Washington Park Zoo.** Summertime in Portland means partying with the pachyderms. Two to three evenings a week throughout the summer, you can catch live music at the zoo's amphitheater. Musical styles include blues, rock, bluegrass, folk, Celtic, and jazz. For the price of zoo admission, you can catch the concert and tour the zoo (if you arrive early enough). Picnics are encouraged, but no alcohol is allowed into the zoo (however, beer and wine are on sale during concerts).
- **Summer Festivals at Waterfront Park.** Each summer, Tom McCall Waterfront Park, which stretches along the Willamette River in downtown Portland, becomes the staging ground for everything from Rose Festival events to the Oregon Brewers Festival. Some special events are free and some have small cover charges, but all are lots of fun.
- **First Thursday Art Walk.** On the first Thursday of every month, Portland goes on an art binge. People get dressed up and go gallery hopping from art opening to art opening. There are usually hors d'oeuvres and wine available, and sometimes there's even live music. The galleries stay open until 9pm.

2 Best Hotel Bets

See chapter 14, "Where to Stay in Portland," for complete reviews of all the places mentioned below.

- **Best Historic Hotel:** With its sepia-tone murals of Lewis and Clark on the lobby walls and comfortable overstuffed leather chairs by the fireplace, the **Governor Hotel,** 611 SW 10th Ave. (© **800/554-3456** or 503/224-3400; www.govhotel.com), built in 1909, captures both the spirit of the Northwest and the luxury of a classic hotel in both its public areas and its guest rooms.
- **Best for Business Travelers:** With fax machines and two-line speaker phones with dataports in every room, plenty of room for spreading out your work, a convenient business center, a good restaurant, a day spa, evening wine tastings, and 24-hour room service, the **5th Avenue Suites Hotel,** 506 SW Washington St. (© **800/711-2971** or 503/222-0001; www.5th avenuesuites.com), has everything necessary for a smooth, successful business trip.

- **Best for a Romantic Getaway:** If you're looking for the most romantic room in town, book a starlight room at the **Hotel Vintage Plaza,** 422 SW Broadway (© **800/243-0555** or 503/228-1212; www.vintageplaza.com). Located on one of the hotel's upper floors, these rooms are basically solariums with curving walls of glass that let you lie in bed and gaze up at the stars. Just be sure to come in the summer when there aren't as many clouds in the sky.
- **Best Lobby for Pretending That You're Rich:** With its walnut paneling, Italian marble, and crystal chandeliers, **The Benson,** 309 SW Broadway (© **800/426-0670** or 503/228-2000; www.benson hotel.com), is the pinnacle of 19th-century elegance. Order a snifter of brandy, sink into one of the leather chairs by the fireplace, and you can conjure up your past life as a railroad baron.
- **Best for Families:** Although it is located in Vancouver, Washington, 20 minutes from downtown

Portland, the **Homewood Suites Hotel Vancouver/Portland,** 701 SE Columbia Shores Blvd. (℗ **800/CALL-HOME** or 360/750-1100; www.homewood-suites.com), is a good bet for families. Guest rooms are more like apartments (with full kitchens); rates include breakfast and a big spread of evening appetizers. There's also a 5-mile-long paved riverside trail across the street.

- **Best Moderately Priced Hotel:** Although it is totally unassuming from the outside, the **Four Points Hotel Sheraton,** 50 SW Morrison Ave. (℗ **800/899-0247** or 503/221-0711; www.fourpointsportland.com), with its very contemporary interior decor, is one of Portland's most stylish hotels. Add to this the fact that Waterfront Park and the Willamette River are just across the street, and you've got a great deal (if you can reserve far enough in advance to get a low rate).

- **Best Inexpensive Hotel:** How about a waterfront motel in Portland's most prestigious suburb for under $80? Try the **Lakeshore Inn,** 210 N. State St., Lake Oswego (℗ **800/215-6431** or 503/636-9679; www.thelakeshoreinn.com), a small motel right on the lake, with a swimming pool on a dock. The catch is that it's 7 miles from downtown Portland.

- **Best B&B:** With views, attractive gardens, a secluded feel, and the shops, restaurants, and cafes of NW 23rd Avenue only blocks away, the **Heron Haus,** 2545 NW Westover Rd. (℗ **503/274-1846;** www.heronhaus.com), is Portland's most luxurious and conveniently located B&B.

- **Best Service:** Though quite unpretentious, the historic **Heathman Hotel,** 1001 SW Broadway (℗ **800/551-0011** or 503/241-4100; www.heathmanhotel.com), is one of Portland's finest hotels and is long on personal service.

- **Best Location:** Though it's only a few blocks from downtown businesses, the **RiverPlace Hotel,** 1510 SW Harbor Way (℗ **800/227-1333** or 503/228-3233; www.riverplacehotel.com), a boutique hotel wedged between the Willamette River and Tom McCall Riverfront Park, feels a world away from the city. In summer, the park hosts countless festivals—if you book the right room, you can have a box seat for a concert in the park.

- **Best Health Club:** If you stay at the **Governor Hotel,** 611 SW 10th Ave. (℗ **800/554-3456** or 503/224-3400; www.govhotel.com), you need only head down to the basement for a total workout at the Princeton Athletic Club. For about the same cost as a movie ticket, you can use the lap pool, running track, exercise room, whirlpool spas, saunas, and steam rooms.

- **Best Views:** So, you've seen that photo of the Portland skyline with Mount Hood in the distance and you want that view while you're in town. Sorry, you'll have to sleep in Washington Park for that one. But the next best bet is an east-side room on an upper floor of the **Portland Marriott Downtown,** 1401 SW Naito Pkwy. (℗ **800/228-9290** or 503/226-7600; www.marriott.com/htls/pdxor).

- **Best Westside Hotel:** If you're here on high-tech business in the Beaverton/Hillsboro area or just prefer a little greenery around you, there is no better choice than the **Greenwood Inn,** 10700 SW Allen Blvd. (℗ **800/289-1300** or 503/643-7444; www.greenwoodinn.com). This resortlike hotel has a great restaurant, fun lounge, and very attractive rooms, and all only 15 minutes from downtown Portland.

- **Best for Travelers with Disabilities:** Located right in the heart of downtown, on the bus mall, the **Embassy Suites,** 319 SW Pine St. (© **800/EMBASSY** or 503/279-9000; www.embassyportland.com), is an excellent choice for any traveler restricted to a wheelchair. Most of the rooms here are suites, which means you won't have to deal with a cramped hotel room. The location in the heart of downtown also puts you close to all of Portland's main downtown attractions.

- **Best Uncategorizable Hotel:** What can you say about a hotel that's located in a renovated poor farm and has a brewery, winery, distillery, movie theater, and golf course? Cheers! At **McMenamins Edgefield,** 2126 SW Halsey St., Troutdale (© **800/669-8610** or 503/669-8610; www.mcmenamins. com), on the eastern edge of the Portland Metro area, a local brewpub empire has produced one of the most unusual lodgings in the state. The affiliated **McMenamins Kennedy School,** 5736 NE 33rd Ave. (© **888/249-3983** or 503/ 249-3983), is very similar and closer in.

3 Best Dining Bets

- **Best Spot for a Romantic Dinner:** With dramatic lighting, dark corners, sensuous food, and superb wines, **Assaggio,** 7742 SE 13th Ave. (© **503/232-6151**), a neighborhood trattoria in the Sellwood district, is a sure bet for a romantic dinner.

- **Best Place to Close a Deal:** The **London Grill,** 309 SW Broadway (© **503/228-2000**), at the Benson Hotel, a hotel favored by presidents and other power lunchers, is an unparalleled place for business schmoozing.

- **Best Spot for a Celebration:** With a decor that harkens back to the days of fin de siècle Paris, **Brasserie Montmartre,** 626 SW Park Ave. (© **503/224-5552**), has live jazz and a performing magician several nights a week. Plus, your entire party can color all over the (paper) tablecloths with crayons.

- **Best Decor:** If sleek contemporary decor appeals to you, **Wildwood,** 1221 NW 21st Ave. (© **503/248-WOOD**), one of the anchors of NW 21st Avenue's

Restaurant Row, is the place. The hard-edged interior is straight out of *Architectural Digest*.

- **Best View:** Set high on an east-facing hill south of downtown, the **Chart House,** 5700 SW Terwilliger Blvd. (© **503/246-6963**), has a view that takes in both Mount Hood and Mount St. Helens, plus the Willamette River and most of Portland.

- **Best Wine List:** You can sample some of the best wines around at **Paley's Place,** 1204 NW 21st Ave. (© **503/243-2403**), which has Wednesday-night wine tastings and occasional winemaker dinners. The food here is vibrantly flavorful Northwest and French-inspired cuisine.

- **Best Value:** If you happen to be a frugal gourmet whose palate is more sophisticated than your wallet can afford, you'll appreciate the **Western Culinary Institute International Dining Room,** 1316 SW 13th Ave. (© **800/666-0312** or 503/294-9770), where a five-course lunch will set you back only about $10 (reservations required).

- **Best for Kids:** The **Old Spaghetti Factory,** 0715 SW Bancroft St. (© **503/222-5375**), may not serve the best Italian food in town, but it certainly is some of the cheapest, and the waterfront location and eclectic decor are a hit with kids and parents alike.
- **Best Gourmet Fast Food:** It's just a tiny place, but **Ken's Home Plate,** 1208 NW Glisan St. (© **503/517-8935**), is crammed full of irresistible goodies to stay or to go. If Ken's were in our neighborhood, we'd never cook again.
- **Best French: Couvron,** 1126 SW 18th Ave. (© **503/225-1844**), a tiny cottage French restaurant not far from downtown, serves the most eclectic and creative French and French-influenced meals in the city.
- **Best Italian:** Far removed from the mainstream of high-end restaurants in Portland, **Genoa,** 2832 SE Belmont St. (© **503/ 238-1464**), has for many years now been Portland's premier Italian restaurant. The multicourse dinners are meant to be lingered over for the entire evening, and, although the meals aren't cheap, you get far more for your money than at many of the city's trendier establishments.
- **Best Northwest:** The **Heathman Restaurant,** 1001 SW Broadway (© **503/790-7758**), at the elegant Heathman Hotel, features the very best Northwest meat, seafood, wild game, and produce, all with a French accent. Chef Philippe Boulot won the 2001 James Beard Foundation "Best Chef in the Northwest" award.
- **Best Mexican:** With an outpost on either side of the river, **Chez**

José East, 2200 NE Broadway (© **503/280-9888**), serves the most creative and unusual Mexican food in the city. It's not what you'd expect from a Mexican restaurant, which is exactly what makes it so good.
- **Best Seafood:** Get 'em while they're hot at **Jake's Famous Crawfish,** 401 SW 12th Ave. (© **503/226-1419**). Crawfish are the stars of the menu here, and have been for years, but you can also get lots of other fresh seafood.
- **Best Pizza:** Portland's best pizza (crispy crusts and creative ingredients) can be found at the numerous **Pizzicato Gourmet Pizza** restaurants around the city. The downtown outpost is at 705 SW Alder St. (© **503/226-1007**).
- **Best Desserts: Papa Haydn,** 701 NW 23rd Ave. (© **503/228-7317**), offers a symphony that includes lemon chiffon torte, raspberry gâteau, and Irish coffee Charlotte, to name but a few. There's usually a line at the door, but don't let that deter you. There's another location at 5829 SE Milwaukie Ave. (© **503/232-9440**) in Sellwood.
- **Best Outdoor Dining:** You just can't get any closer to the river than the **Newport Bay Restaurant,** 0425 SW Montgomery St. (© **503/227-3474**), which is in a floating building in the marina at Portland's RiverPlace shopping-and-dining complex. The Newport Bay provides excellent views of the river and the city skyline, especially from the deck.
- **Best Brunch:** The most lavish brunch in Portland is served at The Benson Hotel's **London Grill,** 309 SW Broadway (© **503/ 228-2000**), located downstairs from the marble-floored lobby.

12

Planning Your Trip to Portland

One of your first considerations when planning your trip should be when to visit. Summer is the peak season in the Northwest, the season for sunshine and outdoor festivals and events. During the summer months, hotel and car reservations are almost essential; the rest of the year they're highly advisable but not nearly as imperative. Keep in mind, however, that when booking a plane, hotel, or rental car, you can usually get better rates by reserving weeks in advance.

1 Visitor Information

For information on Portland and the rest of Oregon, contact the **Portland Oregon Visitors Association** (**POVA**), 1000 SW Broadway, Suite 2300, Portland, OR 97205 (© **877/ 678-5263** or 503/275-9750; www. travelportland.com). See also "Visitor Information" in chapter 13, "Getting to Know Portland."

If you're surfing the Net, you can also get additional Portland information at the following websites: *Willamette Week* (**www.wweek.com**), Portland's arts and entertainment weekly, or *The Oregonian* (**www. oregonian.com**), Portland's daily newspaper.

2 Money

ATMs can be found at banks, convenience stores, in many nightclubs, at the Saturday Market, at festivals (portable machines), and other locations around the city. Expect to pay a $1.50 service charge if you use an ATM that is not affiliated with your own bank, in addition to what your home bank charges. The most common ATM networks are Star, Cirrus, PLUS, Accel, and the Exchange.

ATMs have made **traveler's checks** all but obsolete. Although they're generally accepted at most restaurants, hotels, and shops in neighborhoods frequented by tourists, such as downtown and Nob Hill, they're not nearly as widely accepted as credit cards.

See chapter 2, "Planning Your Trip to Seattle," for further details on obtaining traveler's checks and using credit cards, and what to do in case of theft.

3 When to Go

While summer is the sunniest season in Portland, and the obvious time to visit, it's also the most crowded time of year. Although the city is not yet so popular that you can't usually get a

room in town at the last minute, you'll definitely have more choices if you plan ahead. If, on the other hand, you visit in one of the rainier months, between October and May, you'll find lower hotel room rates and almost as much to see and do.

THE WEATHER

This is the section you've all been looking for. You've all heard about the horrible weather in the Northwest. It rains all year, right? Wrong! The Portland area has some of the most beautiful summer weather in the country—warm, sunny days with clear blue skies and cool nights perfect for sleeping. During July, August, and September, it almost never rains.

And the rest of the year? Well, yes, it rains in those months and it rains regularly. But the rain is generally a fine mist—not the torrential downpours most people associate with the word rain. The average annual rainfall in Portland is less than it is in New York, Boston, Washington, D.C., or Atlanta (but Portland has more days of rain and more cloudy days). A raincoat and a sweater or jacket are all a

way of life in this part of the country, with Gore-Tex the preferred material. Portlanders seldom use umbrellas since the rain is rarely more than a steady drizzle.

Winters here aren't too bad, either. They're warmer than in the Northeast, although there is snow in nearby mountains. In fact, there's so much snow on Mount Hood—only 90 minutes from downtown Portland—that you can ski right through the summer.

All in all, the best months to visit are August and September, and if you're headed to the coast, September is definitely the best month. Octobers can be very pleasant if the rainy season starts slowly. Even in the spring there are often weeks, here and there, when the sun shines, and even when it doesn't, the spring flower displays around Portland are so colorful that you hardly notice that the skies are gray.

Of course you're skeptical, so here are the statistics.

Portland's Average Temperature & Days of Rain

	Jan	Feb	Mar	Apr	May	June	July	Aug	Sept	Oct	Nov	Dec
Temp. (°F)	40	43	46	50	57	63	68	67	63	54	46	41
Temp. (°C)	4	6	8	10	14	17	20	19	17	12	8	5
Rain (Days)	18	16	17	14	12	10	4	5	8	13	18	19

PORTLAND CALENDAR OF EVENTS

For a calendar of special events in and around Portland, contact the **Portland Oregon Visitors Association** (see section 1 of this chapter, above), which lists special events in a couple of its publications and also on its website (**www.travelportland. com**). *The Oregonian* newspaper also lists special events at **www.oregonlive.com**. To find out what's going on during your visit, pick up a free copy of *Willamette Week* (online at **www.wweek.com**) or buy the Friday or Sunday *Oregonian*. Some of the larger and more popular special and free events are listed there.

Every summer, **Portland Parks and Recreation** (✆ 503/823-2223) also sponsors a variety of concerts in several parks throughout the city.

February

Portland International Film Festival (✆ **503/221-1156;** www.nw film.org). Though it's not one of the country's top film festivals, it does book plenty of interesting films. Screenings are held at various theaters around the city. Tickets go on sale 2 weeks before the festival starts, and weekend shows usually sell out. Last 3 weeks of February.

May

Cinco de Mayo Fiesta (✆ **503/ 222-9807;** www.cincodemayo.org), in downtown Portland at Tom McCall Waterfront Park. This Hispanic celebration with food and entertainment is the largest Cinco de Mayo Fiesta in the country. It's staged in conjunction with Portland's sister city, Guadalajara, Mexico. Early May.

Mother's Day Rhododendron Show (☎ 503/771-8386 or 503/777-1734; www.arsportland.org), Crystal Springs Rhododendron Gardens. This show comes when the rhododendron blooms are just about at their peak. Mother's Day.

Memorial Day Wine Tastings (☎ 503/646-2985; www.yamhill wine.com), throughout the wine country surrounding Portland. Memorial Day weekend is one of 2 weekends celebrated by Yamhill County and other area wineries with special tastings and events. Many wineries not usually open to the public open on this weekend.

June

Rhythm and Zoo Concerts, Oregon Zoo (☎ 503/226-1561; www. oregonzoo.org). Wednesday and Thursday nights from June to August, the zoo's amphitheater hosts performances of folk, jazz, blues, country, and ethnic music with both local and national acts. The ticket price of $8 includes zoo admission.

Zoo Beat Concerts, Oregon Zoo (☎ 503/226-1561; www.oregon zoo.org). On selected weekend nights from June to August name performers appear at the zoo. Tickets are $16 to $22.

Portland Rose Festival. From its beginnings back in 1888, when the first rose show was held, the Rose Festival has blossomed into Portland's biggest celebration. The festivities now span nearly a month and include a rose show, parade, rose queen contest, music festival, art show, car races, footrace, boat races, and even an air show. For more details, contact the Portland

Rose Festival Association, 5603 SW Hood Ave., Portland, OR 97201 (☎ 503/227-2681; www.rose festival.org), or TicketMaster (☎ 503/224-4400) for tickets to specific events. Tickets are also available through the Rose Festival website. Most of the events (some of which are free) take place during the middle 2 weeks of June, and hotel rooms can be hard to come by, so plan ahead.

Portland Arts Festival (☎ 503/227-2681; www.rosefestival.org), South Park Blocks at Portland State University. More than 100 regional artists are juried into this fine art and crafts show ensuring good-quality art-buying opportunities. Music, theater, local wines and microbrews too. Mid-June.

July

Fourth of July Fireworks, Fort Vancouver, Washington (☎ 360/693-5481). This is the largest fireworks display west of the Mississippi. They're set off from Vancouver, just across the river, and you can see them from many spots in Portland. For a close-up view, head up to Jantzen Beach, or for an elevated perspective, drive up into the West Hills.

Waterfront Blues Festival, Waterfront Park (☎ 503/973-3378; www. waterfrontbluesfest.com). Attracting both national and regional acts, this festival in downtown Portland's Tom McCall Waterfront Park on the bank of the Willamette River is one of the biggest blues festivals in the country. The festival is a benefit for the Oregon Food Bank, and the suggested daily admission is $5 plus two cans of food. Early July.

High Noon Tunes (☎ 503/223-1613), Pioneer Courthouse Square. This is a series of free lunchtime concerts featuring everything from classical music to bluegrass to jazz to Japanese taiko drumming. They're held every Wednesday from July through August.

Oregon Brewers Festival (© 503/ 778-5917; www.oregonbrewfest. com), Tom McCall Waterfront Park. America's largest festival of independent craft brewers features lots of local and international microbrews and music. Last weekend in July.

August

Mount Hood Jazz Festival (© 503/219-9833; www.mthood jazz.com), Mount Hood Community College, Gresham (less than 30 min. from Portland). For the serious jazz fan, this is *the* festival of the summer, featuring the greatest names in jazz. Tickets are $28.50 to $50 per day or $70 to $175 for a 3-day pass. Tickets are available through the Web address or Fastixx (© 800/992-8499 or 503/224-8499). First weekend in August.

The Bite—A Taste of Portland (© 503/248-0600), Tom McCall Waterfront Park. Portland's finest restaurants serve up sample portions of their specialties at this food and music festival. It's a true gustatory extravaganza, and also includes wine tasting. This is a benefit for the Special Olympics. Mid-August.

September

Reptile and Amphibian Show, Oregon Museum of Science & Industry (© 503/797-4588). Hundreds of reptiles and amphibians are brought in for a holiday weekend show that's the biggest of its kind in the Northwest. Kids love this venomous event! Labor Day weekend.

Portland Creative Conference, Downtown Portland (© 503/234-1641; www.cre8con.org). Directors, actors, designers and other creative sorts gather to celebrate and explore the human creative spirit. Past presenters have included local celebs

Gus Van Sant and Matt Groening. Mid-September.

Rheinlander Oktoberfest, Oaks Park Amusement Center (© 503/ 233-5777). A large and crowded Oktoberfest with lots of polka in the beer hall. Late September.

North by Northwest (NXNW), in clubs around the Portland area (© 503/243-2122, ext. 380, or 512/ 467-7979; www.nxnw.com). This contemporary music binge features 300 of the hottest regional bands. In addition to the music showcases, there are panels, workshops, and a trade show. Late September.

Portland Marathon, Downtown Portland (© 503/226-1111). Includes a variety of competitions including a 26.2-mile walk, a 5-mile run, and a kid's run. End of September.

October

Howloween, Oregon Zoo (© 503/ 226-1561; www.oregonzoo.org). Sort of a trick-or-treat scavenger hunt, with lots of activities for kids. Last weekend in October.

November

Wine Country Thanksgiving, Yamhill County (© 503/646-2985; www.yamhillwine.com). About 30 miles outside of Portland, more than two dozen wineries open their doors for tastings of new releases, usually with food and live music. Thanksgiving weekend.

Christmas at Pittock Mansion, Pittock Mansion (© 503/823-3623). Each year, this grand French Renaissance–style château is decorated according to an annual theme. Thanksgiving to end of December.

December

Holiday Parade of Ships, Willamette and Columbia rivers (www.christmasships.org). Boats decked out in fanciful holiday lights parade and circle on the rivers after nightfall. Mid-December.

Zoo Lights, Oregon Zoo (© **503/ 226-1561;** www.oregonzoo.org). One of Portland's most impressive holiday light shows is at the Oregon Zoo. No, they don't put lights on the animals, but just about everything else seems to get covered. Month of December (closed Dec 24–25).

4 Tips for Travelers with Special Needs

FOR TRAVELERS WITH DISABILITIES

All major hotels listed in this book feature handicapped-accessible rooms, but when making a hotel reservation, be sure to ask. B&Bs, on the other hand, are often in old homes with stairs, and rarely have handicapped-accessible rooms.

All MAX light-rail system stations have wheelchair lifts, and there are two wheelchair spaces available on each train. Be sure to wait on the platform lift. Many of the Tri-Met buses are also equipped with wheelchair lifts and wheelchair spaces. Look for the wheelchair symbol on buses, schedules, and bus stops. There is also a special door-to-door service provided for people who are not able to use the regular Tri-Met service, but as a visitor you must have an eligibility card from another public transportation system. For more information, contact Tri-Met at © **503/962-2455** or 503/ 802-8200.

Broadway Cab (© **503/227- 1234**) and **Radio Cab** (© **503/ 227-1212**) both have vehicles for transporting persons with disabilities.

See also "Tips for Travelers with Special Needs" on p. 17 of chapter 2,

"Planning Your Trip to Seattle." There you'll find a list of useful websites, publications, and advocacy groups.

FOR GAY & LESBIAN TRAVELERS

Gay and lesbian travelers visiting Portland should be sure to pick up a free copy of *Just Out* (© **503/236-1252;** www.justout.com), a bimonthly newspaper for the gay community covering local and national news. You can usually find copies at **Powell's Books,** 1005 W. Burnside St. *Just Out* also publishes the *Just Out Pocketbook,* a statewide gay and lesbian business directory.

Another publication to look for once you're in Portland is *Portland's Gay & Lesbian Community Yellow Pages* (© **503/230-7701;** www.pdx gayyellowpages.com), which is also usually available at Powell's.

See also "Tips for Travelers with Special Needs" on pp. 18–19 of chapter 2, "Planning Your Trip to Seattle." There you'll find a list of useful websites, publications, and advocacy groups.

FOR SENIORS

Most Portland attractions, many theaters and performance venues, many

---

Health & Insurance

For tips on staying healthy while you travel, handling medical emergencies while you're on the road, and purchasing travel insurance, see section 4, "Health & Insurance," in chapter 2, "Planning Your Trip to Seattle." Also see "Fast Facts: Portland" at the end of chapter 13, "Getting to Know Portland"; entries there will help you track down a doctor, dentist, pharmacy, clinic, or hospital if you need one.

budget hotels and motels, and Portland's public transportation system all offer senior discounts.

See also "Tips for Travelers with Special Needs" on p. 19 of chapter 2, "Planning Your Trip to Seattle." There you'll find a list of useful websites and publications, plus tips on travel discounts.

FOR FAMILIES

For information on traveling with your kids, see "Tips for Travelers with Special Needs" on p. 20 of chapter 2, "Planning Your Trip to Seattle." Also see the "Family-Friendly Hotels" box in chapter 14, "Where to Stay in Portland"; the "Family-Friendly Restaurants" box in chapter 15, "Where to Dine in Portland"; and section 7, "Especially for Kids," in chapter 16, "Exploring Portland," which gives a rundown of fun family attractions and activities.

5 Getting There

BY PLANE

Almost 20 carriers serve **Portland Airport** (www.portlandairportpdx.com) from some 100 cities worldwide. The major airlines include **Alaska Airlines** (© 800/426-0333; www.alaskaair.com), **America West** (© 800/235-9292; www.americawest.com), **American Airlines** (© 800/433-7300; www.im.aa.com), **Continental** (© 800/525-0280; www.continental.com), **Delta** (© 800/221-1212; www.delta.com), **Frontier Airlines** (© 800/432-1359; www.frontierairlines.com), **Hawaiian** (© 800/367-5320; www.hawaiianair.com), **Horizon Air** (© 800/547-9308; www.horizonair.com), **Northwest/KLM** (© 800/225-2525; www.nwa.com), **Skywest** (© 800/241-6522; www.skywest.com), **Southwest** (© 800/435-9792; www.southwest.com), **TWA** (© 800/221-2000; www.twa.com), and **United Airlines** (© 800/241-6522; www.united.com).

Important note: For valuable advice on getting the best airfare, see p. 22 in the "Getting There" section of chapter 2, "Planning Your Trip to Seattle."

For information on flights to the United States from other countries, see "Getting to the United States" in Appendix B, "For International Visitors."

BY CAR

Portland is linked to the rest of the United States by a number of interstate highways and smaller roads. I-5 runs north to Seattle and south as far as San Diego. I-84 runs east as far as Salt Lake City. I-405 arcs around the west and south of downtown Portland. I-205 bypasses the city to the east. U.S. 26 runs west to the coast.

Portland is 640 miles from San Francisco, 175 miles from Seattle, 350 miles from Spokane, and 285 miles from Vancouver, B.C.

AAA (© **800/222-4357;** www.aaa.com) will supply members with emergency road service if you have car trouble during your trip. You also get maps and detailed Trip-Tiks that give precise directions, including up-to-date information about areas of construction.

See "Getting Around" in chapter 13, "Getting to Know Portland," for details on driving, parking, and car rentals in Portland.

BY TRAIN

Amtrak's (© **800/872-7245;** www.amtrak.com) *Coast Starlight* train connects Portland with Seattle, San Francisco, Los Angeles, and San Diego and stops at historic **Union Station,** 800 NW Sixth Ave. (© **503/273-4866**), about 10 blocks from the heart of downtown Portland. Between

Portland and Seattle there are both regular trains and modern European-style Talgo trains, which make the trip in 3½ to 4 hours versus 4½ hours for the regular train. One-way fares on either type of train run $23 to $36. Talgo trains run between Eugene, Oregon, and Vancouver, British Columbia.

Like the airlines, Amtrak offers several discounted fares; although they're not all based on advance purchase, you have more discount options by reserving early. Amtrak's website features a bargain fares service, Rail SALE.

BY BUS

Portland is served by **Greyhound Bus Lines.** The bus station is at 550 NW Sixth Ave. (© **800/231-2222** or 503/243-2357;   www.greyhound.com). From Seattle to Portland it's $24 one-way or $42 round-trip, and takes about 3½ to 4½ hours. From San Francisco to Portland it's $29 to $55 one-way or $55 to $105 round-trip (lower prices available with 7-day advance purchase), and takes anywhere from 15 to 21 hours.

13

Getting to Know Portland

Portland's compactness makes it an easy city to get to know. However, a little bit of information on city layout and getting around always proves helpful, and that's exactly what you'll find in this chapter. At the end of the chapter is a list of handy "Fast Facts" that'll tell you everything from where to find a pharmacy to where to check your e-mail.

1 Orientation

ARRIVING

BY PLANE

Portland International Airport (PDX) (℗ 877/739-4636; www.portland airportpdx.com) is located 10 miles northeast of downtown Portland, adjacent to the Columbia River. For the past several years, the airport has been undergoing a massive expansion and remodeling to handle the increasing traffic, but by the time you arrive, all construction should be completed. When it's done, the airport should once again be a well-designed, compact, and efficiently laid-out facility.

There's an information booth by the baggage-claim area where you can pick up maps and brochures and find out about transportation into the city. Many hotels near the airport provide courtesy shuttle service to and from the airport; be sure to ask when you make a reservation.

GETTING INTO THE CITY BY CAR   If you've rented a car at the airport and want to reach central Portland, follow signs for downtown. These signs will take you first to I-205 and then I-84 west, which brings you to the Willamette River. Take the Morrison Bridge exit to cross the river. The trip into town takes about 20 minutes and is entirely on interstate highways. For more information on renting a car, see section 2 of this chapter, "Getting Around," below.

GETTING INTO THE CITY BY TAXI, SHUTTLE, BUS, OR LIGHT RAIL   If you haven't rented a car at the airport, the best way to get into town is to take the new **Airport MAX (Red Line)** light-rail system, which at press time, which began operating in September 2001. This light-rail line will operate daily every 15 minutes between 5am and 11:30pm and will take approximately 40 minutes to make the trip from the airport to Pioneer Courthouse Square in downtown Portland. (All but one or two of the downtown hotels lie within 4 or 5 blocks of the square; plan on walking this distance, since there are not usually any taxis waiting at the square. Folks arriving with a lot of luggage will be better of taking a cab or shuttle van from the airport.) The fare is $1.55. For information on this new service, contact **Tri-Met** (℗ 503/238-7433; www. tri-met.org).

Alternatively, you can take the **Gray Line Airport Shuttle** (℗ 800/422-7042 or 503/285-9845), which picks you up outside the baggage-claim area. Gray Line

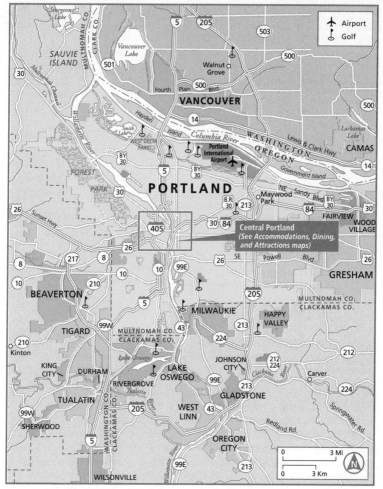

drops off at more than a dozen downtown hotels. It takes almost 45 minutes to stop at all the downtown hotels, so keep this additional time in mind when doing your scheduling. One-way fares are $15 for adults, $12 seniors, $8 for children ages 4 to 12, and under age 4 free. It operates every 45 minutes from 5:15am to midnight.

Tri-Met public bus no. 12 leaves the airport approximately every 15 minutes from 5:30am to 11:45pm for the trip to downtown Portland. The trip takes about 40 minutes and costs $1.25. The bus between downtown and the airport operates between 5:15am and 12:30am and leaves from SW Sixth Avenue and Main Street.

A taxi to downtown generally costs between $20 and $25, which ends up being cheaper and faster than the Gray Line Airport Shuttle if there are two or more of you traveling together.

BY TRAIN/BUS

Amtrak trains stop at the historic **Union Station,** 800 NW Sixth Ave. (© **503/ 273-4866**), about 10 blocks from the heart of downtown Portland. Taxis are usually waiting to meet trains and can take you to your hotel. Alternatively, you might be able to get your hotel to send a van to pick you up, or, if you are renting a car from a downtown car-rental office, you can usually get the agency to pick you up at the station. Public buses stop within a block of the station and are free within the downtown area if you catch the bus south of Hoyt Street (2 blocks away).

The **Greyhound Bus Lines** station is at 550 NW Sixth Ave. (© **800/ 231-2222** or 503/243-2357) on the north side of downtown near Union Station. As with getting into downtown from the train station, if you walk south 2 blocks to Hoyt Street, you reach the edge of downtown Portland's Fareless Square area, within which all buses and light-rail trolleys are free.

Although you could easily walk from the station into the heart of downtown, you have to pass through a somewhat rough neighborhood for a few blocks. This area is currently undergoing a renaissance and is not nearly as bad as it once was.

VISITOR INFORMATION

The **Portland Oregon Visitors Association (POVA) Information Center,** 701 SW Sixth Ave, Suite 1 (© **877/678-5263** or 503/275-9750; www.travel portland.com), is in Pioneer Courthouse Square in downtown Portland. There's also an information booth by the baggage-claim area at the Portland Airport.

If you happen to see a person walking down a Portland street wearing a very bright green jacket, he or she is probably a member of the **Portland Guides** service run by the Association for Portland Progress (© **503/224-7383**). The guides will be happy to answer any question you have about the city.

CITY LAYOUT

Portland is located in northwestern Oregon at the confluence of the Columbia and Willamette rivers. To the west are the West Hills, which rise to more than 1,000 feet. Some 90 miles west of the West Hills are the spectacular Oregon coast and the Pacific Ocean. To the east are rolling hills that extend to the Cascade Range, about 50 miles away. The most prominent peak in this section of the Cascades is Mount Hood (11,235 ft.), a dormant volcanic peak that looms over the city on clear days. From many parts of Portland it's also possible to see Mount St. Helens, the volcano that famously erupted in 1980.

With about 1.8 million people in the entire metropolitan area, Portland remains a relatively small city, a fact that's especially evident when you begin to explore the compact downtown area. Nearly everything is accessible on foot, and the city authorities do everything they can to encourage walking.

MAIN ARTERIES & STREETS   I-84 (**Banfield Freeway or Expressway**) enters Portland from the east. East of the city is **I-205,** which bypasses downtown Portland and runs past the airport. **I-5 (East Bank Freeway)** runs

---

Impressions

We want you to visit our State of Excitement often. Come again and again. But for heaven's sake, don't move here to live. Or if you do have to move in to live, don't tell any of your neighbors where you are going.
—Gov. Tom McCall, 1971

> ## ⓘ Did You Know?
>
> - The flasher in the famous "Expose Yourself to Art" poster is none other than Bud Clark, the former mayor of Portland.
> - Portland is the only city in the United States with an extinct volcano—Mount Tabor—within the city limits.
> - Matt Groening, creator of *The Simpsons,* got his start in Portland.
> - More Asian elephants have been born in Portland (at the Metro Washington Park Zoo) than in any other city in the United States or Canada.
> - Twenty downtown water fountains were a gift to the city from teetotaling, turn-of-the-century timber baron Simon Benson, who wanted his mill workers to have something other than alcohol to drink during the day.

through on a north-south axis, passing along the east bank of the Willamette River directly across from downtown. **I-405 (Stadium Freeway and Foothills Freeway)** circles around the west and south sides of downtown. **U.S. 26 (Sunset Highway)** leaves downtown heading west toward Beaverton and the coast. **Oregon Hwy. 217 (Beaverton-Tigard Highway)** runs south from U.S. 26 in Beaverton.

The most important artery within Portland is **Burnside Street.** This is the dividing line between north and south Portland. Dividing the city from east to west is the **Willamette River,** which is crossed by eight bridges in the downtown area. From north to south these bridges are the Fremont, Broadway, Steel, Burnside, Morrison, Hawthorne, Marquam, and Ross Island. There are also additional bridges beyond the downtown area, including the Sellwood Bridge between downtown and Lake Oswego and the St. John's Bridge from northwest Portland to north Portland.

For the sake of convenience, we have defined downtown Portland as the 300-block area within the **Fareless Square.** This is the area (shaded on our map at the beginning of this chapter) in which you can ride for free on the city's public buses and the MAX light-rail system. In downtown, the Fareless Square is bounded by I-405 on the west and south, by Hoyt Street on the north, and by the Willamette River on the east. A Fareless Square extension now allows transit riders to travel between downtown Portland and both the Oregon Convention Center and Lloyd Center Mall for free. There is no charge to ride either the MAX light-rail trolleys or any of the 10 buses that connect downtown with the Rose Quarter and Lloyd District across the Willamette River in northeast Portland.

FINDING AN ADDRESS   Finding an address in Portland can be easy. Almost all addresses in Portland, and even extending for miles beyond the city, include a map quadrant—NE (Northeast), SW (Southwest), and so forth. The dividing line between east and west is the Willamette River; between north and south it's Burnside Street. Any downtown address will be labeled either SW (Southwest) or NW (northwest). An exception to this rule is the area known as North Portland, which is the area across the Willamette River from downtown going toward Jantzen Beach. Streets here have a plain "North" designation. Also, Burnside Street is designated either "East" or "West."

Avenues run north-south and streets run east-west. Street names are the same on both sides of the Willamette River. Consequently, there is a Southwest Yamhill Street and a Southeast Yamhill Street. In northwest Portland, street names are alphabetical going north from Burnside to Wilson. Naito Parkway is the street nearest the Willamette River on the west side, and Water Avenue is the nearest on the east side. Beyond these are numbered avenues. On the west side you'll also find Broadway and Park Avenue between Sixth Avenue and Ninth Avenue. With each block, the addresses increase by 100, beginning at the Willamette River for avenues and at Burnside Street for streets. Odd numbers are generally on the west and north sides of the street, and even numbers on the east and south sides.

Here's an example: You want to go to 1327 SW Ninth Ave. Because it's in the 1300 block, you'll find it 13 blocks south of Burnside and, because it's an odd number, on the west side of the street.

STREET MAPS   Stop by the **Portland Oregon Visitors Association Information Center,** 701 SW Sixth Ave, Suite 1 (© 877/678-5263 or 503/275-9750; www.travelportland.com), in Pioneer Courthouse Square in downtown Portland for a free map of the city; they also have a more detailed one for sale.

Powell's City of Books, 1005 W. Burnside St. (© 800/878-7323 or 503/228-4651), has an excellent free map of downtown that includes a walking-tour route and information on many of the sights you'll pass along the way.

Members of the **American Automobile Association** can obtain a free map of the city at the AAA offices at 600 SW Market St. (© 503/222-6734; www.aaa.com).

THE NEIGHBORHOODS IN BRIEF

Portland's neighborhoods are, in large part, dictated by its geography. The Willamette River forms a natural dividing line between the eastern and western portions of the city, while the Columbia River forms a boundary with the state of Washington on the north. The West Hills, comprising Portland's prime residential neighborhoods, are a beautiful backdrop for this attractive city. Covered in evergreens, the hills rise to a height of 1,000 feet at the edge of downtown. Within these hills are the Oregon Zoo, the International Rose Test Garden, the Japanese Garden, and several other attractions.

For a map of Portland neighborhoods, turn to the "Portland Attractions" map on p. 246.

DOWNTOWN This term usually refers to the business and shopping district south of Burnside and north of Jackson Street between the Willamette River and 13th Avenue. Within this area, you'll find a dozen or more high-end hotels, dozens of restaurants of all types, and loads of shopping (including the major department stores). Within downtown's **Cultural District** (along Broadway and the South Park Blocks), you'll also find most of the city's performing arts venues and a couple of museums.

For the sake of convenience, we have defined downtown Portland as the 300-block area within the **Fareless Square.** This is the area (shaded in on our map) in which you can ride for free on the city's public buses and the MAX light-rail system. In downtown, the Fareless Square is bounded by I-405 on the west and south, by Hoyt Street on the north, and by the Willamette River on the east.

SKIDMORE HISTORIC DISTRICT Also known as Old Town, this is Portland's original commercial core, and centers around Southwest Ankeny Street and Southwest First Avenue. Many of the restored buildings have become retail stores, but despite the presence of the **Saturday Market,** the neighborhood has never become a popular shopping district, mostly because of its welfare hotels, missions, street people, and drug dealing. However, with its many clubs and bars, it has become the city's main nightlife district.

CHINATOWN Portland has had a Chinatown almost since its earliest days. Today, this small area, with its numerous Chinese groceries and restaurants, is wedged between the Pearl District and the Skidmore Historic District and is entered through the colorful Chinatown Gate at West Burnside Street and Fourth Avenue. The neighborhood's main attraction is the impressive **Portland Classical Chinese Garden.** As you would expect, there are also some good Chinese restaurants in the area. Because of its proximity to bars on West Burnside Street and the homeless missions and welfare hotels in Old Town, this is not a good neighborhood explore late at night.

THE PEARL DISTRICT This neighborhood of galleries, residential and business lofts, cafes, breweries, and shops is bounded by the North Park Blocks, Lovejoy Street, I-405, and Burnside Street. Crowds of people come here on **First Thursday** (the first Thurs of every month) when the galleries and other businesses are open late. This is currently Portland's bid for a hip urban loft scene and is one of the city's main upscale restaurant neighborhoods.

NORTHWEST/NOB HILL Located along Northwest 23rd and Northwest 21st avenues, this is Portland's most fashionable neighborhood. Here you'll find

many of the city's most talked-about restaurants (mostly along NW 21st Avenue), as well as lots of cafes, boutiques, and ever more national chain stores such as the Gap and Pottery Barn. Surrounding the two main business streets of the neighborhood are blocks of restored Victorian homes on shady tree-lined streets. This is where you'll find the city's liveliest street scene.

IRVINGTON Though neither as attractive nor as large as the Northwest/Nob Hill neighborhood, Irvington, centered around Broadway in northeast Portland, is almost as hip. For several blocks along Broadway (around NE 15th Avenue) you'll find interesting boutiques and numerous excellent but inexpensive restaurants.

HAWTHORNE/BELMONT DISTRICT This enclave of southeast Portland is full of eclectic boutiques, moderately priced restaurants, and hip college students from nearby **Reed College.** Just south of Hawthorne Boulevard, beginning at SE 12th Avenue, you'll find the interesting **Ladd's Addition** neighborhood, which has five rose gardens, a great pastry shop, and a brewpub that features live music several nights a week. Along Belmont Street, just north of Hawthorne Boulevard, you'll find one of the city's up-and-coming hip neighborhoods that still has a funky streak.

SELLWOOD/WESTMORE-LAND Situated in Southeast Portland, this is the city's antiques district and contains many restored Victorian houses. Just north of the Sellwood antiques district, surrounding the intersection of SE Milwaukie Avenue and SE Bybee Boulevard, you'll find the heart of the Eastmoreland neighborhood, which is home to numerous good restaurants.

2 Getting Around

BY PUBLIC TRANSPORTATION

FREE RIDES   Portland is committed to keeping its downtown uncongested, and to this end it has invested heavily in its public transportation system. The single greatest innovation and best reason to ride the Tri-Met public buses and the MAX light-rail system is that they're free within an area known as the **Fareless Square.** That's right, free!

There are 300 blocks of downtown included in the Fareless Square, and as long as you stay within the boundaries, you don't pay a cent. The Fareless Square covers the area between I-405 on the south and west, Hoyt Street on the north, and the Willamette River on the east. A Fareless Square extension now also makes it possible to take public transit (either the bus or the MAX light-rail trolley) between downtown Portland and both the Rose Quarter (site of the Oregon Convention Center) and the Lloyd District (site of the Lloyd Center Mall), which are both across the Willamette River in northeast Portland.

BY BUS   Tri-Met buses operate daily over an extensive network. You can pick up the **Tri-Met Guide,** which lists all the bus routes with times, or individual route maps and time schedules, at the **Tri-Met Customer Assistance Office,** behind and beneath the waterfall fountain at Pioneer Courthouse Square (© **503/238-7433;** www.tri-met.org). The office is open Monday through Friday from 7:30am to 5:30pm. Bus and MAX passes and transit information are also available at area Fred Meyer, Safeway, and most Albertson grocery stores. Nearly all Tri-Met buses pass through the Transit Mall on SW Fifth Avenue and SW Sixth Avenue.

Outside the Fareless Square, adult fares on both Tri-Met buses and MAX are $1.25 or $1.55, depending on how far you travel. Seniors 65 years and older pay 60¢ with valid proof of age; children ages 7 through 18 pay 95¢. You can also make free transfers between the bus and the MAX light-rail system. A day ticket costing $4 is good for travel to all zones and is valid on both buses and MAX. Day tickets can be purchased from any bus driver. The **Adventure Pass,** good for 3 days of unlimited rides on both buses and MAX, costs $10 and is available at the Tri-Met Customer Assistance Office and at any of the other outlets mentioned above.

BY LIGHT RAIL   The **Metropolitan Area Express (MAX)** is Portland's aboveground light-rail system that connects downtown Portland with the airport (as of Sept 2001), the eastern suburb of Gresham, and the western suburbs of Beaverton and Hillsboro. MAX is basically a modern trolley, but there are also reproductions of vintage trolley cars (© **503/323-7363**) operating between downtown Portland and the Lloyd Center on Sundays between noon and 6pm. One of the most convenient places to catch the MAX is at Pioneer Courthouse Square. The MAX light-rail system crosses the Transit Mall on SW Morrison Street and SW Yamhill Street. Transfers to the bus are free.

As with the bus, MAX is free within the Fareless Square, which includes all the downtown area. A Fareless Square extension now also makes it possible to ride the MAX between downtown Portland and both the Rose Quarter (site of the Oregon Convention Center) and the Lloyd District (site of the Lloyd Center Mall), which are both across the Willamette River in northeast Portland. If you are traveling outside of the Fareless Square, be sure to buy your ticket and stamp it in the time-punch machine on the platform before you board MAX. There are ticket-vending machines at all MAX stops that tell you how much to pay for your destination; these machines also give change. The MAX driver cannot sell tickets. Fares are the same as on buses. There are ticket inspectors who randomly check tickets, so be sure you get one, and also stamp it before boarding.

In July 2001, the new **Portland Streetcar** (© **503/238-RIDE;** www.portland streetcar.org) began operating between the Portland State University neighborhood of downtown through the Pearl District to the Nob Hill neighborhood. This streetcar route takes in not only the attractions of the Cultural District, but also all the restaurants and great shopping in the Pearl District and along Northwest 21st and 23rd avenues, which makes this streetcar a great way for visitors to get from the downtown (where most of the hotels are located) and the neighborhoods with the greatest concentrations of restaurants. On Saturdays and Sundays, vintage streetcars operate free of charge (though donations are encouraged to help maintain these old streetcars). Streetcar fares for trips outside the Fareless Square are $1.25 for adults, 95¢ for youths, and 60¢ for seniors.

BY CAR

CAR RENTALS   Portland is a compact city, and public transit will get you to most attractions within its limits. However, if you are planning to explore outside the city—and Portland's greatest attractions, such as Mount Hood and the Columbia River Gorge, lie not in the city itself but in the countryside within an hour of the city—you'll definitely need a car.

The major car-rental companies are all represented in Portland and have desks at Portland International Airport, which is the most convenient place to pick up a car. There are also many independent and smaller car-rental agencies listed in the Portland Yellow Pages. Currently, weekly rates for an economy car in July (high-season rates) are about $188 with no discounts. Expect lower rates in the rainy months.

On the ground floor of the airport parking deck, across the street from the baggage-claim area, you'll find the following companies: **Avis** (© 800/831-2847 or 503/249-4950; www.avis.com), **Budget** (© 800/527-0700 or 503/ 249-6500; www.budget.com), **Dollar** (© 800/800-4000 or 503/249-4792; www.dollar.com), **Hertz** (© 800/654-3131 or 503/249-8216; www.hertz.com), and **National** (© 800/227-7368 or 503/249-4900; www.nationalcar.com). Outside the airport, but with desks adjacent to the other car-rental desks, are **Alamo** (© 800/327-9633 or 503/252-7039; www.alamo.com), **Enterprise** (© 800/736-8222 or 503/252-1500; www. enterprise.com), and **Thrifty,** at 10800 NE Holman St. (© 800/367-2277 or 503/254-6563; www.thrifty.com).

PARKING   Parking downtown can be a problem, especially if you show up after workers have gotten to their offices on weekdays. There are a couple of very important things to remember when parking downtown:

When parking on the street, be sure to notice the meter's time limit. These vary from as little as 15 minutes (these are always located right in front of the restaurant or museum where you plan to spend 2 hr.) to long term (read: long walk). Most common are 30- and 60-minute meters. You don't have to feed the meters after 6pm or on Sunday.

The best parking deal in town is at the **Smart Park** garages, where the cost is 95¢ per hour for the first 4 hours (but after that the hourly rate jumps

> **/Value** **Driving a Bargain in Portland**
>
> If there's any way you can arrange to pick up your car somewhere other than the airport, you can save the 11% airport concession fee. If you can pick up your car in Beaverton or Hillsboro (western suburbs of Portland), you can also avoid the 12.5% Multnomah county tax that applies at the airport and at downtown Portland car-rental offices.
>
> For more tips on how to save money on a car rental, see the box titled "Driving a Bargain in Seattle" on p. 34.

considerably and you'd be well advised to move your car to another lot), $2 for the entire evening after 6pm, or $5 all day on the weekends. Look for the red, white, and black signs featuring Les Park, the friendly parking attendant. You'll find Smart Park garages at First Avenue and Jefferson Street, Fourth Avenue and Yamhill Street, Tenth Avenue and Yamhill Street, Third Avenue and Alder Street, O'Bryant Square, and Naito Parkway and Davis Street. More than 200 downtown merchants also validate Smart Park tickets if you spend at least $25, so don't forget to take your ticket along with you.

Rates in other public lots range from about $1.50 up to about $4 per hour.

SPECIAL DRIVING RULES   You may turn right on a red light after a full stop, and if you are in the far left lane of a one-way street, you may turn left into the adjacent left lane of a one-way street at a red light after a full stop. Everyone in a moving vehicle is required to wear a seat belt.

You don't have to feed parking meters after 6pm or on Sunday.

BY TAXI

Because most everything in Portland is fairly close, getting around by taxi can be economical. Although there are almost always taxis waiting in line at major hotels, you won't find them cruising the streets—you'll have to phone for one. **Broadway Cab** (© **503/227-1234**) and **Radio Cab** (© **503/227-1212**) both offer 24-hour radio-dispatched service and accept American Express, Discover, MasterCard, and Visa. Fares are $2.50 for the first mile, $1.50 for each additional mile, and $1 for additional passengers. Up to four passengers can share a taxi.

ON FOOT

City blocks in Portland are about half the size of most city blocks elsewhere, and the entire downtown area covers only about 13 blocks by 26 blocks. These two facts make Portland a very easy place to explore on foot. The city has been very active in encouraging people to get out of their cars and onto the sidewalks downtown. The sidewalks are wide, and there are many small parks with benches for resting, fountains for cooling off, and works of art for soothing the soul.

As mentioned above, if you happen to spot a person walking around downtown wearing a bright green jacket, he or she is probably a **Portland Guide.** These informative souls are there to answer any questions you might have about Portland—like "Where's the nearest latte stand?" Their job is simply to walk the streets and answer questions.

FAST FACTS: Portland

AAA The **American Automobile Association** (© **800/222-4357**; www. aaa.com) has a local Portland office at 600 SW Market St. (© **503/ 222-6734**), which offers free city maps to members.

Airport See "Getting There" in chapter 12, "Planning Your Trip to Portland," and "Arriving," in section 1, earlier in this chapter.

American Express The **American Express Travel Service Office,** 1100 SW Sixth Ave. (© **503/226-2961**), at the corner of Sixth and Main, is open Monday through Friday from 8:30am to 5:30pm. You can cash American Express traveler's checks and exchange the major foreign currencies here. For card member services, phone © **800/528-4800.** Call © **800/AXP-TRIP** or go online to **www.americanexpress.com** for other city locations or general information.

Area Codes The Portland metro area has two area codes—503 and 971— and consequently it is necessary to dial all 10 digits of a telephone number, even when making local calls.

Babysitters If your hotel doesn't offer babysitting services, call **Northwest Nannies** (© **503/245-5288**).

Business Hours Banks are generally open weekdays from 9am to 5pm, with later hours on Friday; some have Saturday morning hours. Offices are generally open weekdays from 9am to 5 or 6pm. Stores typically open Monday through Friday between 9 and 10am and close between 5 and 6pm. Department stores tend to stay open later (until between 7–9pm), as do stores in malls. Bars stay open until 1 or 2am; dance clubs often stay open much later.

Car Rentals See section 2, "Getting Around," earlier in this chapter.

Climate See section 3, "When to Go," in chapter 12, "Planning Your Trip to Portland."

Dentist If you need a dentist while you're in Portland, contact **Oregon Dental Referral** (© **800/800-1705**) or the **Multnomah Dental Society** (© **503/223-4731**) for a referral.

Doctor If you need a physician referral while in Portland, contact the **Medical Society of Metropolitan Portland** (© **503/222-0156**). The **Oregon Health Sciences University Hospital,** 3181 SW Sam Jackson Park Rd. (© **503/494-8311**), has a drop-in clinic.

Emergencies For police, fire, or medical emergencies, phone © **911.**

Eyeglass Repair Check out **Binyon's Eyeworld Downtown,** 803 SW Morrison St. (© **503/226-6688**).

Hospitals Three conveniently located area hospitals include **Legacy Good Samaritan,** 1015 NW 22nd Ave. (© **503/413-7711**); **Providence Portland Medical Center,** 4805 NE Glisan St. (© **503/215-1111**); and the **Oregon Health Sciences University Hospital,** 3181 SW Sam Jackson Park Rd. (© **503/494-8311**), which is just southwest of the city center and has a drop-in clinic.

Hot Lines The **Portland Center for the Performing Arts Event Information Line** is © **503/796-9293.** The **Oregonian's Inside Line** (© **503/225-5555**), operated by Portland's daily newspaper, provides information on every-thing from concerts and festivals to sports and the weather.

Information See "Visitor Information" in section 1, earlier in this chapter.

Internet Access If you need to check e-mail while you're in Portland, first check with your hotel. Otherwise, visit a **Kinko's.** There's one downtown at 221 SW Alder St. (© 503/224-6550) and in Northwest at 950 NW 23rd Ave. © 503/222-4133). You can also try the **Multnomah County Library,** 801 SW 10th Ave. (© 503/988-5123), which is Portland's main library and offers online services.

Liquor Laws The legal minimum drinking age in Oregon is 21. Aside from on-premise sales of cocktails in bars and restaurants, hard liquor can only be purchased in liquor stores. Beer and wine are available in convenience stores and grocery stores. Brewpubs tend to sell only beer and wine, but some also have licenses to sell hard liquor.

Maps See "City Layout," in section 1, earlier in this chapter.

Newspapers & Magazines Portland's morning daily newspaper is *The Oregonian.* For arts and entertainment information and listings, consult the "A&E" section of the Friday *Oregonian* or pick up a free copy of *Willamette Week* at Powell's Books and other bookstores, convenience stores, or cafes.

Pharmacies Convenient to most downtown hotels, **Central Drug,** 538 SW Fourth Ave. (© 503/226-2222), is open Monday to Friday from 9am to 6pm, on Saturday from 10am to 4pm.

Photographic Needs **Wolfcamera,** 900 SW Fourth Ave. (© **503/224-6776**) and 733 SW Alder (© **503/224-6775**), offers 1-hour film processing. **Camera World,** 400 SW Sixth Ave. (© 503/205-5900), is the largest camera and video store in the city.

Police To reach the police, call © **911.**

Restrooms There are public restrooms underneath Starbucks coffee shop in Pioneer Courthouse Square, in downtown shopping malls, and in hotel lobbies.

Safety Because of its small size and progressive emphasis on keeping the downtown alive and growing, Portland is still a relatively safe city; in fact, strolling the downtown streets at night is a popular pastime. Take extra precautions, however, if you venture into the entertainment district along West Burnside Street or Chinatown at night. Certain neighborhoods in north and northeast Portland are the centers for much of the city's gang activity, so before visiting any place in this area, be sure to get very detailed directions so you don't get lost. If you plan to go hiking in Forest Park, don't leave anything valuable in your car. This holds true in the Skidmore Historic District (Old Town) as well.

Smoking Although many of the restaurants listed in this book are smoke-free, there are also many Portland restaurants that allow smoking. At most high-end restaurants, the smoking area is usually in the bar/lounge, and although many restaurants have separate bar menus, most will serve you off the regular menu even if you are eating in the bar. There are very few non-smoking bars in Portland.

Taxes Portland is a shopper's paradise—there's no sales tax. However, there is an 11.5% tax on hotel rooms within the city and a 12.5% tax on car rentals (plus an additional airport use fee if you pick up your rental car at the airport; this fee is usually an additional 11%). Outside the city, the room tax varies.

Taxis See section 2, "Getting Around," earlier in this chapter.

Time Zone Portland is on Pacific time, 3 hours behind the East Coast. In the summer, daylight saving time is observed and clocks are set forward 1 hour.

Transit Info For bus and MAX information, call the **Tri-Met Customer Assistance Office** (© **503/238-7433**).

Weather If it's summer, it's sunny; otherwise, there's a chance of rain. This almost always suffices, but for specifics, call **Weatherline Forecast Service** (© **503/243-7575**) or the Portland Oregon Visitor Association's **weather information hot line** (© **503/275-9792**). If you want to know how to pack before you arrive, check **www.cnn.com/weather** or **www.weather.com**.

14

Where to Stay in Portland

Portland has been undergoing a downtown hotel renaissance for the past decade. Several historic hotels have been renovated, and other historic buildings have been retrofitted to serve as hotels. The Benson, the Governor Hotel, The Heathman Hotel, the Hotel Vintage Plaza, the 5th Avenue Suites, and the Embassy Suites (formerly the Multnomah Hotel) are all part of this trend. Today these hotels offer some of Portland's most comfortable and memorable accommodations. Several other new hotels have also opened in the past two years.

The city's largest concentrations of hotels are in downtown and near the airport. If you don't mind the high prices, downtown hotels are the most convenient for visitors.

However, if your budget won't allow for a first-class business hotel, try near the airport or elsewhere on the outskirts of the city (Troutdale and Gresham on the east side; Beaverton and Hillsboro on the west; Wilsonville and Lake Oswego in the south; and Vancouver, Washington in the north), where you're more likely to find inexpensive to moderately priced motels.

You'll find the greatest concentration of bed-and-breakfast inns in the Irvington neighborhood of northeast Portland. This area is close to downtown and is generally quite convenient even if you are here on business.

In the following listings, price categories are based on the rate for a double room in high season (most hotels charge the same for a single or double room). Keep in mind that the rates listed do not include local room taxes, which vary between 7% and 11.5%.

For comparison purposes, we list what hotels call "rack rates," or walk-in rates—but you should never have to pay these highly inflated prices. Various discounts (AAA, senior citizen, corporate, Entertainment Book) often reduce these rates, so be sure to ask (and check each hotel's website for Internet specials). In fact, you can often get a discounted corporate rate simply by flashing a business card (your own, that is). At inexpensive chain motels, there are almost always discounted rates for AAA members and senior citizens.

You'll also find that room rates are almost always considerably lower October through April (the rainy season), and large downtown hotels often offer weekend discounts of up to 50% throughout the year. Some of the large, upscale hotel chains have now gone to an airline-type rate system based on occupancy, so if you call early enough before a hotel books up you might get a really good rate. On the other hand, call at the last minute and you might catch a cancellation and still be offered a low rate. Also be sure to ask about special packages (romance, golf, theater), which most of the more expensive hotels usually offer.

A few hotels include breakfast in their rates; others offer complimentary breakfast only on certain deluxe floors. Parking rates are per day.

Although Portland is not nearly as popular with tourists as Seattle, it's still advisable to make reservations as far in advance as possible if you're planning to visit during the busy summer months.

Most all hotels in the Portland area now offer no-smoking rooms, and most bed-and-breakfast inns are exclusively nonsmoking. Most hotels also offer wheelchair-accessible rooms.

HELPING HANDS

If you're having trouble booking a room for your visit, try contacting the **Portland Oregon Visitors Association** (**POVA**), 1000 SW Broadway, Suite 2300, Portland, OR 97205 (© **877/678-5263** or 503/275-9750; www.pova.com), which offers a reservation service for the Portland metro area.

For information on **bed-and-breakfast inns** in the Portland area, call the **Portland Oregon Visitors Association** (© **877/678-5263** or 503/275-9750; www.pova.com). Also try contacting the **Oregon Bed and Breakfast Guild,** P.O. Box 3187, Ashland, OR 97520 (© **800/944-6196;** www.obbg.org). You can also try the **Northwest Bed and Breakfast Reservation Service** (© **877/243-7782** or 503/243-7616; www.nwbedandbreakfast.com).

1 Downtown

VERY EXPENSIVE

RiverPlace Hotel ★★★   With the Willamette River at its back doorstep and the sloping lawns of Waterfront Park to one side, the RiverPlace is Portland's only downtown waterfront hotel. This fact alone would be enough to recommend this hotel, but its quiet boutique-hotel atmosphere would make the River-Place an excellent choice even if it weren't right on the water. During the summer, the hotel is particularly popular when there are music festivals in the adjacent park. (If you're planning a weekend visit, be sure to find out if there's a festival scheduled; depending on your interest in the event, you'll either find this to be a great location, or you might not want to deal with the crowds.)

The river-view standard king rooms here are the hotel's best deal, but the junior suites are only slightly more expensive and provide a bit more space. In general, furnishings here are neither as elegant nor as luxurious as at The Heathman or The Benson, but what you're paying for is, of course, the waterfront locale. More than half the rooms here are suites, and some come with wood-burning fireplaces and whirlpool baths. There are also condominiums available for long stays.

The hotel's restaurant overlooks the river, and just off the lobby there's a comfortable bar with live piano music and a casual menu. The bar also has a patio dining area overlooking the river.

1510 SW Harbor Way, Portland, OR 97201. © **800/227-1333** or 503/228-3233. Fax 503/295-6161. www. riverplacehotel.com. 84 units. $219–$379 double; $249–$389 junior suite; $279–$979 suite. Rates include continental breakfast. AE, DC, DISC, MC, V. Valet parking $18. Pets accepted with $45 nonrefundable cleaning fee. **Amenities:** Restaurant (Northwest/continental), lounge; indoor pool; access to nearby health club; day spa; Jacuzzi; sauna; concierge; babysitting; 24-hour room service; massage; laundry/dry cleaning. *In room:* A/C, TV, fax, dataport, minibar, hair dryer, iron.

EXPENSIVE

The Benson ★★★   Built in 1912, The Benson exudes old-world sophistication and elegance. In the French baroque lobby, walnut paneling frames a marble fireplace, Austrian crystal chandeliers hang from the ornate plasterwork ceiling, and a marble staircase provides the perfect setting for grand entrances. The fact that presidents stay here whenever they're in town is a good clue that

Portland Accommodations

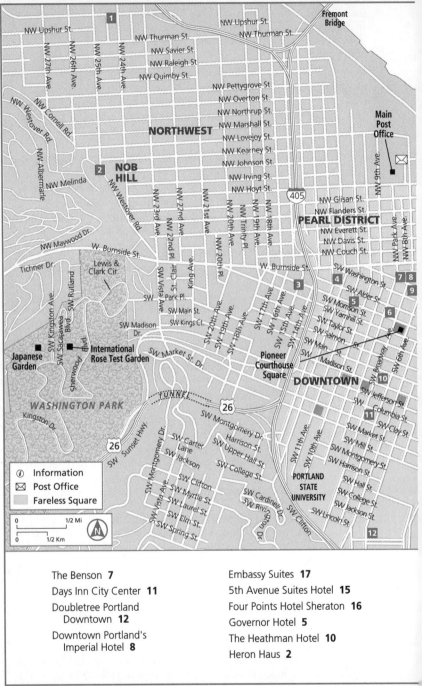

The Benson **7**

Days Inn City Center **11**

Doubletree Portland
Downtown **12**

Downtown Portland's
Imperial Hotel **8**

Embassy Suites **17**

5th Avenue Suites Hotel **15**

Four Points Hotel Sheraton **16**

Governor Hotel **5**

The Heathman Hotel **10**

Heron Haus **2**

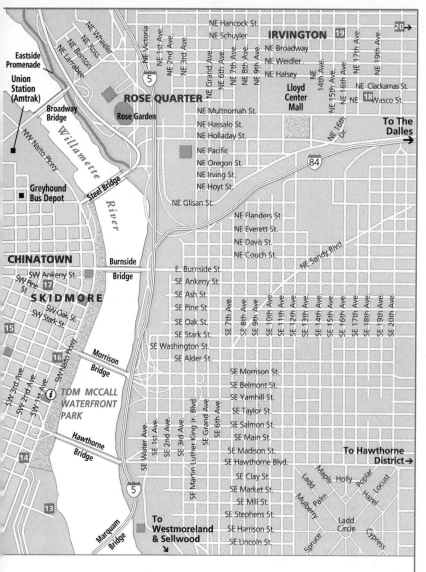

Hotel Vintage Plaza **9**

The Lion and the Rose **19**

Mallory Hotel **3**

The Mark Spencer Hotel **4**

Portland Marriott
Downtown **14**

Portland's White House **20**

RiverPlace Hotel **13**

Silver Cloud Inn Portland
Downtown **1**

Sullivan's Gulch B&B **18**

The Westin Portland **6**

these are the poshest digs in Portland. The guest rooms, housed in two towers (only one of which is part of the original hotel), vary considerably in size, but all are luxuriously furnished in a plush Euro-luxe styling. The deluxe kings are particularly roomy, but the corner junior suites are the hotel's best deal. Not only are these quite large, but the abundance of windows makes them much cheerier than other rooms. Bathrooms, unfortunately, include little shelf space for spreading out your toiletries.

In the vaults below the lobby you'll find **The London Grill** (see the full review in chapter 15, "Where to Dine in Portland"), which is well known for its Sunday brunch. Just off the lobby, there's El Gaucho steak house, and in the Lobby Bar, there's live jazz in the evenings.

309 SW Broadway, Portland, OR 97205. (C) **800/426-0670** or 503/228-2000. Fax 503/226-4603. www. bensonhotel.com. 287 units. $150–$170 double; $285 junior suite; $500–$900 suite. AE, DC, DISC, MC, V. Valet parking $21. Pets accepted ($100 fee). **Amenities:** Restaurant (Northwest/continental), lounge; exercise room and access to nearby health club; concierge; business center; 24-hour room service; massage; dry cleaning. *In room:* A/C, TV, dataport, minibar, coffeemaker, hair dryer, iron.

Embassy Suites ★★ *Kids Value*   Located in the restored Multnomah Hotel, which originally opened in 1912, the Embassy Suites has a beautiful large lobby that is a masterpiece of gilded plasterwork, successfully conjuring up the hotel's heyday. The accommodations here are primarily two-room suites, with the exception of a handful of studio suites. In keeping with the historic nature of the hotel, the suites have classically styled furnishings. However, what's much more important is that they give you lots of room to spread out, a rarity in downtown hotels, which tend to have fairly small units. The hotel's Portland Steak and Chophouse is just what its name implies, with a classic dark and woody steakhouse decor and a large bar. There's also a nightly complimentary evening manager's reception.

319 SW Pine St., Portland, OR 97204-2726. (C) **800/EMBASSY** or 503/279-9000. Fax 503/497-9051. www. embassyportland.com. 276 units. $129–$209 double. Rates include full breakfast. AE, DC, DISC, MC, V. Valet parking $15; self-parking $15. **Amenities:** Restaurant (steaks), lounge; indoor pool; exercise room and access to nearby health club; day spa; Jacuzzi; sauna; concierge; car-rental desk; business center; room service; massage; laundry/dry cleaning. *In room:* A/C, TV, dataport, fridge, coffeemaker, hair dryer, iron.

5th Avenue Suites Hotel ★★   Located a block from Pioneer Courthouse Square and within a few blocks of the best downtown shopping, this unpretentious yet sophisticated hotel is housed in what was originally a department store. Artwork by Northwest artists fills the lobby, and in the afternoon there are complimentary tastings of Oregon and Washington wines.

Guest rooms, most of which are suites, are furnished in a turn-of-the-century country style but also have fax machines and two-line speakerphones for 21st-century convenience. Plush chairs and beds with padded headboards and luxurious comforters assure that business travelers (and others) will be comfortable in their home away from office. Bathrooms have lots of counter space. In the suites, sliding French doors with curtains divide the living room from the bedrooms, but don't provide much privacy.

The **Red Star Tavern and Roast House** is a popular and traditionally styled restaurant specializing in upscale American comfort food (see chapter 15 for a full review).

506 SW Washington St., Portland, OR 97204. (C) **800/711-2971** or 503/222-0001. Fax 503/222-0004. www.5thavenuesuites.com. 221 units. $139–$169 double; $169–$300 suite. AE, DC, DISC, MC, V. Valet parking $21. **Amenities:** Restaurant (American), lounge; pool; exercise room; Aveda day spa; concierge; business center; 24-hour room service; laundry/dry cleaning. *In room:* A/C, TV, fax, dataport, minibar, coffeemaker, hair dryer, iron.

Governor Hotel ★★★   This historic hotel pays homage to the Lewis and Clark Expedition, and you'll spot references to the famous explorers throughout. However, the historical references are just the icing on the cake at this plush hotel.

Guest rooms vary considerably in size but are all attractively decorated, with perks like two-line phones and voice mail. The least expensive rooms are rather small but are nevertheless very comfortable. Still, we'd opt for one of the deluxe guest rooms. Unfortunately, bathrooms are, in general, quite cramped by today's standards and lack counter space, although their tile work does give them a classic feel. Suites, on the other hand, are spacious, and some even have huge patios overlooking the city.

Be sure to take a peek at the Dome Room, which is just off the lobby and has a stunning stained-glass skylight. Jake's Grill, a large, old-fashioned restaurant located just off the lobby, serves grilled steak and seafood. There's also a complimentary evening wine tasting Monday through Thursday.

611 SW 10th Ave., Portland, OR 97205. ℂ **800/554-3456** or 503/224-3400. Fax 503/241-2122. www.gov hotel.com. 100 units. $165–$195 double; $200 junior suite; $210–$500 suite. AE, DC, DISC, MC, V. Valet parking $16. **Amenities:** Restaurant (American), lounge; pool; access to adjacent health club with indoor pool, Jacuzzi, saunas, indoor running track; concierge; business center; 24-hour room service; laundry service; dry cleaning. *In room:* A/C, TV, dataport, minibar, coffeemaker, hair dryer, iron.

The Heathman Hotel ★★★   With its understated luxury and superb service, The Heathman, which abuts the Portland Center for the Performing Arts, is one of the finest hotels in the city. Although this is primarily a top-end business hotel, it's also the address of choice for visiting culture hounds, with its proximity to the theater and an outstanding collection of art ranging from 18th-century oil paintings to Andy Warhol prints. Don't look for a bowl-you-over lobby here; although there is plenty of marble and teak, the lobby itself is tiny. However, just off the lobby is the Tea Court, where the original eucalyptus paneling creates a warm, old-world atmosphere.

The basic rooms here tend to be quite small, but are nonetheless attractively furnished and set up for business travelers. There are no real views to speak of, but rooms on the west side of the hotel look out to a mural done just for the hotel. Basically what you get here is luxury in a small space. Ask for a corner room, which gets more light and feels more spacious.

The **Heathman Restaurant and Bar** is one of Portland's finest, with a menu that emphasizes creatively prepared fresh local produce, seafood, and game (see the complete review in chapter 15, "Where to Dine in Portland"). Afternoon tea is served in the Lobby Lounge, and there's usually live jazz nightly. There are also complimentary wine tastings several nights a week.

1001 SW Broadway at Salmon St., Portland, OR 97205. ℂ **800/551-0011** or 503/241-4100. Fax 503/790-7110. www.heathmanhotel.com. 150 units. $169–$209 double; $305–$775 suite. AE, DC, DISC, MC, V. Parking $19. Pets accepted for $25. **Amenities:** Restaurant (Northwest), lounge; exercise room and access to nearby health club; concierge; room service; laundry service; dry cleaning. *In room:* A/C, TV, dataport, high-speed Internet access, minibar, coffeemaker, hair dryer, iron.

Hotel Vintage Plaza ★★   This hotel, which was built in 1894 and is on the National Register of Historic Buildings, is *the* place to stay in Portland if you are a wine lover. A wine theme predominates in the hotel's decor and there are complimentary evening tastings of Northwest wines. There are a wide variety of room types here, and though the standard rooms are certainly recommendable, the starlight rooms and bilevel suites are the real scene-stealers. The starlight rooms in particular are truly extraordinary. Though small, they have greenhouse-style wall-into-ceiling windows that provide very romantic views at night and let in floods of light during the day. The bilevel suites, some with Japanese soaking tubs and one with a spiral staircase, are equally attractive spaces.

Pazzo Ristorante, one of Portland's best Italian restaurants, is a dark and intimate trattoria.

422 SW Broadway, Portland, OR 97205. (C) **800/243-0555** or 503/228-1212. Fax 503/228-3598. www. vintageplaza.com. 107 units. $150–$225 double; $325–$400 suite. AE, DC, DISC, MC, V. Valet parking $21. Pets accepted. **Amenities:** Restaurant (Italian), lounge; exercise room and access to nearby health club; concierge; business center; 24-hour room service; massage; laundry service; same-day dry cleaning. *In room:* A/C, TV, fax, dataport, minibar, hair dryer, iron.

Portland Marriott Downtown *ₐₐ*   Located just across Waterfront Park and Naito Parkway from the Willamette River, the high-rise Portland Marriott offers great views of Mount Hood from its upper east-side rooms, and this alone would be reason enough to stay here. That the park across the street serves as the site of virtually all of Portland's main festivals also makes it a good choice if you're in town for one of these festivals. (If you're planning a weekend visit, be sure to find out if there's a festival scheduled; depending on your interest in the event, you'll either find this to be a great location, or you might not want to deal with the crowds.) Otherwise, this standard corporate high-rise doesn't have a whole lot of character, though there is a nice Japanese-style garden outside the front door. Most of the guest rooms have small balconies, and if you ask for a room overlooking the river, throw back the glass door to the balcony and think about the fact that the view used to be of a noisy freeway (it was torn out to build the park). All the rooms have been recently redone.

1401 SW Naito Pkwy., Portland, OR 97201. (C) **800/228-9290** or 503/226-7600. Fax 503/221-1789. www. marriott.com/htls/pdxor. 503 units. $114–$199 double; $450–$600 suite. AE, DC, DISC, MC, V. Valet parking $19. Pets accepted with $50 nonrefundable fee. **Amenities:** 2 restaurants (American), 2 lounges (1 sports bar, 1 more sedate lobby lounge); indoor pool; exercise room; Jacuzzi; sauna; concierge; business center; room service; coin-op laundry; laundry service; dry cleaning; concierge level. *In room:* A/C, TV, dataport, coffeemaker, hair dryer, iron.

The Westin Portland *ₐₐ*   This is one of the newest business hotels in downtown Portland and is by far the most stylish, combining contemporary styling with original works by regional artists. Guest rooms are set up primarily for business travelers and are among the most attractive and luxurious standard guest rooms in the city. Bathrooms are large and have separate tubs and showers. There are even CD players in all the rooms (plus a few CDs for your listening pleasure). If you'd prefer a room with a little more light, ask for a corner room; if you need extra work space, opt for one of the "guest office" rooms. The hotel's restaurant is plush and stylish (complete with curtained booths), but the food can be inconsistent.

750 SW Alder St., Portland, OR 97205. (C) **800/WESTIN-1** or 503/294-9000. Fax 503/241-9565. www.westin portland.com. 205 units. $99–$215 double; $179–$960 suite. AE, DC, DISC, MC, V. Valet parking $19. Pets accepted ($25 fee). **Amenities:** Restaurant (Asian/Mediterranean), lounge; exercise room; children's programs; concierge; business center; 24-hour room service; dry cleaning. *In room:* A/C, TV, dataport, minibar, coffeemaker, hair dryer, iron, safe.

MODERATE

Days Inn City Center *ₐ*   Although this 1960s vintage hotel lacks much in the way of character or charm, it's one of the few economical choices for anyone wishing to stay in downtown Portland. A renovation a few years back has

kept the hotel looking decent, and in the guest rooms, you'll find modern furnishings.

1414 SW Sixth Ave., Portland, OR 97201. © **800/DAYS-INN** or 503/221-1611. Fax 503/226-0447. www.days inn.com. 173 units. $89–$139 double. AE, DC, DISC, MC, V. Free parking. **Amenities:** Restaurant (American), lounge; small outdoor pool; access to nearby health club; room service; dry cleaning. *In room:* A/C, TV, dataport.

Doubletree Portland Downtown ★★

Situated on a shady tree-lined street about a mile south of Pioneer Courthouse Square and on the southern edge of downtown Portland, this low-rise hotel offers the convenience of a downtown location and the casual appeal of a suburban business hotel. The design and landscaping reflect the Northwest, and in the courtyard surrounding the swimming pool are lush plantings of evergreens and other shrubs. Keep in mind that in summer, this hotel only qualifies for the inexpensive category on weekends. The best rooms are those on the third floor overlooking the pool courtyard. Although slightly more expensive, these rooms are quiet and have pleasant views. They also get plenty of that precious Northwest sunlight (when the sun shines), although all the rooms have large windows.

310 SW Lincoln St., Portland, OR 97201. © **800/222-TREE** or 503/221-0450. Fax 503/226-6260. www. doubletreehotels.com. 235 units. $79–$149 double; $200–$400 suite. AE, DC, DISC, MC, V. Parking $10. Pets accepted with $25 deposit. **Amenities:** Restaurant (American), lounge; outdoor pool; exercise room; concierge; room service; laundry/dry cleaning. *In room:* A/C, TV, coffeemaker, hair dryer.

Downtown Portland's Imperial Hotel ★ *(Value)*

Although it doesn't quite live up to its regal name, this remodeled older hotel across the street from the Benson is a good bet for moderately priced accommodations downtown. While the staff may be young and not as polished as those at more expensive hotels, they usually are good about seeing to guests' needs. Rooms are quite up-to-date, and the location can't be beat. The corner king rooms, with large windows, should be your first choice; barring this, at least ask for an exterior room. These might get a little street noise, but they're bigger than the interior rooms and get more sunlight (when the sun shines at all, that is). Free local calls are a nice perk.

400 SW Broadway, Portland, OR 97205. © **800/452-2323** or 503/228-7221. Fax 503/223-4551. www. hotel-imperial.com. 128 units. $90–$130 double. Rates include continental breakfast. AE, DC, DISC, MC, V. Valet parking $15. Pets accepted ($10 fee). **Amenities:** Highly regarded restaurant (Thai), lounge with live jazz; access to nearby health club; dry cleaning. *In room:* A/C, TV, dataport, fridge, hair dryer, iron, safe.

Four Points Hotel Sheraton ★★ *(Value)*

Overlooking Waterfront Park and located on the MAX light-rail line, this 1960s vintage hotel looks nondescript from the outside, but the inside has been renovated and given a contemporary look that makes it one of the most stylish hotels in town. You are only steps from the Willamette River (although not actually on the water), and are also close to businesses, fine restaurants, and shopping. Guest rooms are as boldly contemporary in design as the lobby and restaurant, which are sort of downscale *Architectural Digest.* If this is your style, make this your Portland choice.

50 SW Morrison St., Portland, OR 97204-3390. © **800/899-0247** or 503/221-0711. Fax 503/274-0312. www.fourpointsportland.com. 140 units. $99–$140 double. AE, DC, DISC, MC, V. Parking $10. Pets accepted. **Amenities:** Restaurant (American/international), lounge; access to nearby health club; room service; massage; dry cleaning. *In room:* A/C, TV, dataport, coffeemaker, hair dryer, iron.

Mallory Hotel ★ *(Finds)*

The Mallory, which is right on the west-side Max line and thus convenient for exploring the city by light rail, has long been a favorite of Portland visitors who want the convenience of staying downtown but aren't on a bottomless expense account. This is an older hotel, and the lobby, with its ornate gilt plasterwork trim and crystal chandeliers, has a certain classic (and faded) grandeur. Time seems to have stood still here (there's a lounge straight out of the 1950s).

The standard rooms are not as luxurious as the lobby might suggest and are smaller than comparable rooms at the Imperial or Days Inn, but are comfortable and clean. With rates this low, you might even want to go for one of the king-size suites, which are as big as they come, with walk-in closets, refrigerators, and sofa beds. Free local calls are a nice perk.

The dining room at the Mallory continues the grand design of the lobby. Heavy drapes hang from the windows, and faux-marble pillars lend just the right air of imperial grandeur.

729 SW 15th Ave., Portland, OR 97205-1994. ℂ **800/228-8657** or 503/223-6311. Fax 503/223-0522. www. malloryhotel.com. 130 units. $95–$160 double; $160 suite. AE, DC, DISC, MC, V. Free parking. Pets accepted ($10 fee). **Amenities:** Restaurant (American), lounge; access to nearby health club; concierge; room service. *In room:* A/C, TV, dataport, fridge, iron, safe.

The Mark Spencer Hotel ℛ   If you're planning an extended stay in Portland and need to be right downtown, this is the place for you. Although the hotel is not in the best neighborhood (there are lots of nightclubs and bars in the vicinity), it's just around the corner from both Powell's City of Books and Jake's Famous Crawfish, one of Portland's oldest and best seafood restaurants. The rooms and suites here have rather dated decor but all have kitchenettes, which is the main draw here for people planning on spending a week or more in town. The hotel offers afternoon tea, and there's also a great rooftop garden deck. The Mark Spencer is a favorite with the casts of touring Broadway shows, and is also a good choice for any gay travelers interested in checking out the nearby bars.

409 SW 11th Ave., Portland, OR 97205. ℂ **800/548-3934** or 503/224-3293. Fax 503/223-7848. www.mark spencer.com. 101 units. $89–$109 double; $109–$129 suite. Rates include continental breakfast. AE, DC, MC, V. Free parking. Pets accepted with $25 nonrefundable deposit. **Amenities:** Access to nearby health club; coin-op laundry; laundry service; dry cleaning. *In room:* A/C, TV, dataport, kitchen, fridge, coffeemaker.

2 Nob Hill & Northwest Portland

EXPENSIVE

Heron Haus ℛℛ   A short walk from the bustling Nob Hill shopping and dining district of northwest Portland, the Heron Haus B&B offers outstanding accommodations, spectacular views, and tranquil surroundings. Surprisingly, the house still features some of the original plumbing. In most places, this would be a liability, but not here, since the plumbing was done by the same man who plumbed Portland's famous Pittock Mansion. Many of that building's unusual bathroom features are to be found at the Heron Haus as well. One shower has two shower heads; another has *seven*. In another room, there's a modern whirlpool spa that affords excellent views of the city. All the rooms have fireplaces.

2545 NW Westover Rd., Portland, OR 97210. ℂ **503/274-1846.** Fax 503/248-4055. www.heronhaus.com. 6 units. $135–$350 double. Rates include continental breakfast. MC, V. Free parking. *In room:* A/C, TV, dataport, hair dryer, iron.

MODERATE

Silver Cloud Inn Portland Downtown ℛ   This hotel is located on the edge of Portland's trendy Nob Hill neighborhood, and though it faces the beginning of the city's industrial area, it is still a very attractive and comfortable place (ask for a room away from Vaughn Street). Reasonable rates are the main draw here,

Kids Family-Friendly Hotels

The Lakeshore Inn *(see p. 215)*   Located 7 miles south of downtown in the affluent suburb of Lake Oswego, this small motel directly on the lake has a pool on its back deck. Rates are economical, and from here you can take a vintage trolley to downtown.

Embassy Suites *(see p. 206)*   Located in the center of the city, this renovated historic hotel offers spacious rooms (mostly two-room suites). You and the kids will have room to spread out, and can hang out by the indoor pool when you tire of exploring Portland.

Homewood Suites by Hilton Vancouver/Portland *(see p. 212)* Although this hotel is across the Columbia River in Vancouver, Washington, its location right across the street from the river, a paved riverside trail, a fun family restaurant, and a brewpub all add up to convenience for families. That you'll get a one- or two-bedroom apartment with a full kitchen just makes life on vacation that much easier.

but the rooms are also well designed and filled with plenty of conveniences, like free local calls. Although the minisuites have wet bars, microwave ovens, and separate seating areas, the king rooms with whirlpool tubs, which happen to be the most expensive rooms, are our favorites. However, the best thing about the hotel is its location within a 5-minute drive (or 15-min. walk) of half a dozen of the city's best restaurants. To find the hotel, take I-405 to Ore. 30 west and get off at the Vaughn Street exit.

2426 NW Vaughn St., Portland, OR 97210. © **800/205-6939** or 503/242-2400. Fax 503/242-1770. www.silvercloud.com. 83 units. $89–$139 double. Rates include continental breakfast. AE, DC, DISC, MC, V. Free parking. **Amenities:** Exercise room; Jacuzzi; business center; coin-op laundry; laundry service; dry cleaning. *In room:* A/C, TV, dataport, coffeemaker, hair dryer, iron.

3 Jantzen Beach (North Portland) & Vancouver, Washington

Located on Hayden Island in the middle of the Columbia River, Jantzen Beach, named for the famous swimwear company that got its start here, is a beach in name only. Today this area is a huge shopping mall complex aimed primarily at Washingtonians, who come to Oregon to avoid Washington's sales tax. Jantzen Beach is also home to a pair of large convention hotels that are among the city's only waterfront hotels. Both hotels are, however, in the flight path for the airport, and although the rooms themselves are adequately insulated against noise, the swimming pools and sundecks can be pretty noisy.

MODERATE

Doubletree Hotel Portland Columbia River 🌟🌟   Attractive landscaping and an interesting low-rise design that's slightly reminiscent of a Northwest Coast Indian longhouse give this convention hotel a very resortlike feel and have kept it popular for many years. Although rush-hour traffic problems can make this a bad choice if you're here to explore Portland, it's a good location if you plan to visit Mount St. Helens. You're also within walking distance of a large shopping mall. Guest rooms are large, though rather nondescript, but many of them have views of the Columbia River. Be sure to ask for one of these.

1401 N. Hayden Island Dr., Portland, OR 97217. ℂ **800/222-TREE** or 503/283-2111. Fax 503/283-4718. www.doubletreehotels.com. 351 units. $100–$125 double; $200–$250 suite. AE, DC, DISC, MC, V. Free parking. Pets accepted with $30 nonrefundable deposit. **Amenities:** 2 restaurants (Northwest, American), 2 lounges; outdoor pool; access to exercise room at adjacent hotel; Jacuzzi; concierge; courtesy airport shuttle; room service; laundry/dry cleaning. *In room:* A/C, TV, dataport, coffeemaker, hair dryer, iron.

The Heathman Lodge ★★ *(Value)*   Mountain lodge meets urban chic at this suburban Vancouver hotel adjacent to the Vancouver Mall, and though it's a 20-minute drive to downtown Portland, the hotel is well placed for exploring both the Columbia Gorge and Mount St. Helens. With its log, stone, and cedar-shingle construction, this hotel conjures up the Northwest's historic mountain lodges. As at Timberline Lodge, this hotel is filled with artwork and embellished with rugged Northwest-inspired craftwork, including totem poles, Eskimo kayak frames, and Pendleton blankets. Guest rooms feature a mix of rustic pine and peeled-hickory furniture as well as rawhide lampshades and Pendleton-inspired bedspreads.

7801 NE Greenwood Dr., Vancouver, WA 98662. ℂ **888/475-3100** or 360/254-3100. Fax 360/254-6100. www.heathmanlodge.com. 143 units. $89–$139 double; $159–$550 suite. AE, DC, DISC, MC, V. Free parking. **Amenities:** Restaurant (Northwest), lounge; indoor pool; exercise room; Jacuzzi; sauna; concierge; business center; room service; laundry service; dry cleaning. *In room:* A/C, TV, dataport, fridge, microwave, coffeemaker, hair dryer, iron.

Homewood Suites by Hilton Vancouver/Portland ★★ *(Kids)*   Located across the street from the Columbia River, this modern suburban all-suite hotel is a great choice for families. The hotel charges surprisingly reasonable rates for large apartment-like accommodations that include full kitchens. Rates also include not only a large breakfast but afternoon snacks as well (Mon–Thurs). These snacks are substantial enough to pass for dinner if you aren't too hungry. The hotel is right across the street from both a beach-theme restaurant and a brewpub. Across the street, you'll also find a paved riverside path that's great for walking or jogging. The only drawback is that it's a 15- to 20-minute drive to downtown Portland.

701 SE Columbia Shores Blvd., Vancouver, WA 98661. ℂ **800/CALL-HOME** or 360/750-1100. Fax 360/750-4899. www.homewood-suites.com. 104 units. $99–$119 double. Rates include full breakfast. AE, DC, DISC, MC, V. Free parking. Pets accepted with $25 nonrefundable deposit plus $10 per night. **Amenities:** Outdoor pool; exercise room; Jacuzzi; sports court; business center; coin-op laundry. *In room:* A/C, TV, dataport, kitchen, fridge, coffeemaker, hair dryer, iron.

4 The Rose Quarter & Irvington
EXPENSIVE
The Lion and the Rose ★★   This imposing Queen Anne–style Victorian inn is located in the Irvington District; it's 1 block off Northeast Broadway and within walking distance of several good restaurants, which makes it an appropriate choice if you want to keep your driving to a minimum. Within 4 blocks are not only restaurants and cafes, but also a number of eclectic boutiques and a huge shopping mall. Yet, the Lion and Rose itself is in a fairly quiet residential neighborhood. Even if this inn were not so splendidly located, it would still be a gem. Guest rooms each have a distinctively different decor. In the Lavonna room, there are bright colors and a turret sitting area, while in the deep green Starina room you'll find an imposing Edwardian bed and armoire. Both the Garden room and the Lavonna Room's shared bathroom have claw-foot tubs, while some rooms have rather cramped, though attractive, bathrooms. If you have

problems climbing stairs, ask for the ground floor's Rose room, which has a whirlpool tub. Breakfasts are sumptuous affairs that are meant to be lingered over.

1810 NE 15th Ave., Portland, OR 97212. (C) **800/955-1647** or 503/287-9245. Fax 503/287-9247. www.lion rose.com. 6 units (1 with shared bathroom). $95–$140 double. AE, DISC, MC, V. **Amenities:** Concierge. *In room:* A/C, TV, hair dryer, iron.

MODERATE

McMenamins Kennedy School ★★ *Finds*   The Kennedy School is from the same folks who turned Portland's old poor farm into the most entertaining and unusual B&B in the state (see the listing for McMenamins Edgefield, below, in section 5 of this chapter). This inn, located well north of stylish Irvington in an up-and-coming neighborhood that dates from the early years of the 20th century, was an elementary school from 1915 to 1975. In the guest rooms you'll still find the original blackboards and great big school clocks (you know, like the one you used to watch so expectantly). However, the classroom/guest rooms here now have their own bathrooms, so you won't have to raise your hand or walk down the hall. On the premises you'll also find a restaurant, a beer garden, a movie theater pub, a cigar bar, and a big hot soaking pool.

5736 NE 33rd Ave., Portland, OR 97211. (C) **888/249-3983** or 503/249-3983. www.mcmenamins.com. 35 units. $99–$109 double. Rates include full breakfast. AE, DISC, MC, V. **Amenities:** Restaurant (American), 5 lounges; soaking pool; massage. *In room:* dataport.

Portland's White House ★★   With massive columns framing the entrance, semicircular driveway, and in the front garden, a bubbling fountain, this imposing Greek-revival mansion bears a more than passing resemblance to its namesake in Washington, D.C. Behind the mahogany front doors, a huge entrance hall with original hand-painted wall murals is flanked by a parlor, with French windows and a piano, and the formal dining room, where the large breakfast is served beneath sparkling crystal chandeliers. A double staircase leads past a large stained-glass window to the second-floor accommodations. Canopy and brass queen beds, antique furnishings, and bathrooms with claw-foot tubs further the feeling of classic luxury here. Request the balcony room and you can gaze out past the Greek columns and imagine you're in the Oval Office. There are also three rooms in the restored carriage house.

1914 NE 22nd Ave., Portland, OR 97212. (C) **800/272-7131** or 503/287-7131. Fax 503/249-1641. www. portlandswhitehouse.com. 9 units. $98–$169 double. Rates include full breakfast. AE, DISC, MC, V. *In room:* A/C, dataport, fridge, hair dryer, iron.

INEXPENSIVE

Hollywood Express Inn   Located in the Hollywood District of Northeast Portland about halfway between the airport and downtown, this economical choice is in a rather unusual spot (tucked away several blocks from the interstate, but worth finding if you need a budget accommodation). Rooms on the third floor are the largest and are worth requesting. The neighborhood takes its name from the Mission-Revival buildings and Craftsman bungalows that are reminiscent of old Hollywood.

3939 NE Hancock St., Portland OR 97212. (C) **503/288-6891.** Fax 503/288-1995. 48 units. $53–$80 double. AE, DC, DISC, MC, V. Free parking. *In room:* A/C, TV.

Sullivan's Gulch B&B ★   Set on a quiet, tree-shaded street just a couple of blocks off busy Northeast Broadway, this inn is a 1907 home filled with an eclectic mix of Mission-style furniture, Asian artifacts, and contemporary art.

Our favorite room here is the Northwest Room, which is decorated with Northwest Coast Native American masks and has an old Hudson's Bay Company blanket on the bed. There's also a room that draws on Montana and Western art for its decor. A pretty little deck out back is a pleasant place to hang out in summer. The inn is popular with gay and lesbian travelers, and with the MAX stop just a few blocks away it's convenient to get downtown.

1744 NE Clackamas St., Portland, OR 97232. Ⓒ **503/331-1104.** Fax 503/331-1575. www.sullivansgulch. com. 4 units (2 with shared bathroom). $70–$85 double. AE, MC, V. Pets accepted. *In room:* TV, fridge; no phone.

5 The Airport Area & Troutdale

Moderately priced hotels have been proliferating in the airport area in the past few years, which makes this a good place to look for a room if you arrive with no reservation.

EXPENSIVE

Shilo Inn Suites Hotel Portland Airport ★★   If you want to stay near the airport and want a spacious room and the facilities of a deluxe hotel, this is one of your best bets. All the rooms here are called suites, and although they don't actually have separate seating and sleeping rooms, they do have plenty of room and lots of other amenities. There are large closets with mirrored doors, lots of bathroom counter space, double sinks, and three TVs in the rooms (including one in the bathroom). The main drawback here is that this is a convention hotel and is often very crowded. To find the Shilo, head straight out of the airport, drive under the I-205 overpass, and watch for the hotel ahead on the left.

11707 NE Airport Way, Portland, OR 97220-1075. Ⓒ **800/222-2244** or 503/252-7500. Fax 503/254-0794. www.shiloinns.com. 200 units. $79–$169 double. Rates include full breakfast. AE, DC, DISC, MC, V. Free parking. **Amenities:** Restaurant (American), lounge; indoor pool; exercise room; Jacuzzi; sauna; tour desk; courtesy airport shuttle; business center; room service; coin-op laundry; dry cleaning. *In room:* A/C, TV, dataport, fridge, coffeemaker, hair dryer, iron, safe.

MODERATE

McMenamins Edgefield ★ *(Finds*   B&Bs don't usually have more than 100 rooms, but this is no ordinary inn. Located 30 minutes east of downtown Portland and ideally situated for exploring the Columbia Gorge and Mount Hood, this flagship of the McMenamin microbrewery empire is the former Multnomah County poor farm. Today the property includes not only tastefully decorated guest rooms with antique furnishings, but a brewery, a pub, a beer garden, a restaurant, a movie theater, a winery, a wine-tasting room, a distillery, a golf course, a cigar bar in an old shed, and extensive gardens. With so much in one spot, this makes a great base for exploring the area. The beautiful grounds give this inn the feel of a remote retreat, though you're still within a short drive of everything Portland has to offer.

2126 SW Halsey St., Troutdale, OR 97060. Ⓒ **800/669-8610** or 503/669-8610. Fax 5-3/492-7750. www.mcmenamins.com. 114 units (101 with shared bathroom), 24 hostel beds. $85–$105 double with shared bathroom, $115–$130 double with private bathroom; $20 hostel bed per person. Rates include full breakfast (not included with hostel). AE, DISC, MC, V. **Amenities:** 3 restaurants (Northwest, American), 6 lounges; 18-hole par-3 golf course; exercise room and access to nearby health club; Jacuzzi; sauna; business center; massage. *In room:* no phone.

Silver Cloud Inn Portland Airport ★ *(Value*   Conveniently located right outside the airport, this hotel has one of the best backyards of any hotel in the Portland area. A lake, lawns, and trees all add up to a tranquil setting despite the proximity of both the airport and a busy nearby road. Rooms are designed primarily for business travelers, but even if you aren't here on an expense account, the rooms are a good value, especially those with whirlpool tubs (and you even get free local calls). Some suites have gas fireplaces. Best of all, with the exception of two suites, every room has a view of the lake. An indoor pool is another big plus here. To find this hotel, take the complimentary airport shuttle or head straight out of the airport, drive under the I-205 overpass, and watch for the hotel sign ahead on the left.

11518 NE Glenn Widing Dr., Portland, OR 97220. © 800/205-7892 or 503/252-2222. Fax 503/257-7008. www.silvercloud.com. 102 units. $89–$105 double; $129–$139 suite. Rates include continental breakfast. AE, DC, DISC, MC, V. Free parking. **Amenities:** Indoor pool; exercise room; Jacuzzi; courtesy airport shuttle; business center; coin-op laundry; dry cleaning. *In room:* A/C, TV, dataport, fridge, coffeemaker, microwave, hair dryer, iron.

INEXPENSIVE

The **Super 8 Motel,** 11011 NE Holman St. (© **503/257-8988**), just off Airport Way after you go under the I-205 overpass, is conveniently located but charges a surprisingly high $66 to $81 a night for a double in summer. Also not far away, in Troutdale, at the mouth of the Columbia Gorge, you'll find a **Motel 6,** 1610 NW Frontage Rd., Troutdale (© **503/665-2254**), charging $43 to $52 per night for a double.

6 The Southwest Suburbs (Lake Oswego & Beaverton)

MODERATE

Greenwood Inn ★★   The Greenwood Inn is a resortlike, low-rise hotel with beautifully landscaped grounds that reflect the garden style of the Pacific Northwest. This is Beaverton's best hotel and is located only 15 to 20 minutes from downtown Portland. A good restaurant and an atmospheric lounge make this an all-around good choice. If you're in the area to do business in the "Silicon Forest," the Greenwood is a good location. Guest rooms are large and comfortable and most are designed with business travelers in mind, and in the bathrooms, you'll find plenty of counter space for toiletries. Executive rooms, which cost a little extra, are exceptional, with original artwork on the walls, three phones, and a well-lighted desk/work area.

10700 SW Allen Blvd., Beaverton, OR 97005. © 800/289-1300 or 503/643-7444. Fax 503/626-4553. www.greenwoodinn.com. 251 units. $79–$118 double; $150–$375 suite. AE, DC, DISC, MC, V. Free parking. Pets accepted ($25 fee). **Amenities:** Restaurant (Italian), lounge; 2 outdoor pools; exercise room and access to nearby health club; Jacuzzi; sauna; business center; room service; coin-op laundry; laundry service; dry cleaning. *In room:* A/C, TV, dataport, fridge, coffeemaker, hair dryer, iron.

INEXPENSIVE

The Lakeshore Inn ★ *(finds) (kids)*   Considering that the town of Lake Oswego is Portland's most affluent bedroom community, this motel is quite reasonably priced. It's located right on the shore of the lake, and there's a pool on a deck built right on the water's edge, making this a great place to stay during a summer visit. Rooms have standard motel furnishings but are large and have kitchenettes. There are also one- and two-bedroom suites. The 7-mile drive into downtown Portland is quite pleasant, passing along the Willamette River. There are several restaurants and cafes within walking distance of the motel.

210 N. State St., Lake Oswego, OR 97034. © 800/215-6431 or 503/636-9679. Fax 503/636-6959. www.the lakeshoreinn.com. 33 units. $69–$99 double; $89–$129 suite. AE, DC, DISC, MC, V. **Amenities:** Outdoor pool; access to nearby health club; coin-op laundry. *In room:* A/C, TV, dataport, kitchenette, coffeemaker, hair dryer, iron.

15

Where to Dine in Portland

In the past few years the Portland restaurant scene has gotten so fired up that the city has developed almost as much of a reputation as Seattle. Excellent new restaurants keep popping up around the city. Several distinct dining districts are full of upscale restaurants, and though you aren't likely to choose to eat at one of these places on the spur of the moment (reservations are usually imperative), the close proximity of establishments makes it easy to check out a few places before making a decision for later.

The Pearl District's renovated warehouses currently claim the trendiest restaurants, while Nob Hill's

Northwest 21st Avenue boasts half a dozen terrific restaurants within a few blocks. The Sellwood and Westmoreland neighborhoods of Southeast Portland make up another of the city's hot restaurant districts, and for good inexpensive food, it's hard to beat the many offerings along NE Broadway in the Irvington neighborhood.

With Oregon wines, especially pinot noir and pinot gris, continuing to receive widespread acclaim, a dinner out in Portland isn't complete without a local wine. However, expect to pay a bit more for an Oregon wine than you would for one from California.

1 Restaurants by Cuisine

AMERICAN

Huber's ✸ (Downtown, $$, p. 224)

Red Star Tavern and Roast House ✸✸ (Downtown, $$, p. 225)

Western Culinary Institute International Dining Room ✸ (Downtown, $, p. 227)

Zell's, An American Café ✸ (Hawthorne, Belmont & Inner Southeast Portland, $, p. 239)

BAKERIES/DESSERT PLACES

Palio Dessert House ✸ (Hawthorne, Belmont & Inner Southeast Portland, $, p. 241)

Papa Haydn West ✸✸ (Northwest Portland, $$, p. 241)

Pearl Bakery ✸✸ (Northwest Portland, $$, p. 241)

Rimsky-Korsakoffee House ✸ (Hawthorne, Belmont & Inner Southeast Portland, $, p. 241)

Rosie's Boulangerie ✸ (Hawthorne, Belmont & Inner Southeast Portland, $, p. 241)

BREAKFAST/BRUNCH

Bijou Café ✸ (Downtown, $, p. 226)

Bread and Ink Cafe ✸✸ (Hawthorne, Belmont & Inner Southeast Portland, $$, p. 237)

Hands on Café ✸ (Northwest Portland, $, p. 233)

The London Grill ✸✸✸ (Downtown, $$$, p. 223)

Red Star Tavern and Roast House ✸✸ (Downtown, $$, p. 225)

Southpark Seafood Grill & Wine Bar ✸✸ (Downtown, $$, p. 226)

Key to Abbreviations: $$$$ = Very Expensive $$$ = Expensive $$ = Moderate $ = Inexpensive

Salty's on the Columbia ✵
    (Northeast Portland, $$$,
    p. 234)
Wildwood ✵✵ (Northwest
    Portland, $$$, p. 230)
Zell's, An American Café ✵
    (Hawthorne, Belmont & Inner
    Southeast Portland, $, p. 239)

CAFES

Café Lena (Hawthorne, Belmont
    & Inner Southeast Portland, $,
    p. 240)
Coffee Time (Northwest Portland,
    $, p. 240)
Common Grounds (Hawthorne,
    Belmont & Inner Southeast
    Portland, $, p. 240)
Palio Dessert House ✵
    (Hawthorne, Belmont & Inner
    Southeast Portland, $, p. 241)
Peet's Coffee ✵ (Downtown, $,
    p. 241)
Pied Cow (Hawthorne, Belmont
    & Inner Southeast Portland, $,
    p. 241)
Rimsky-Korsakoffee House ✵
    (Hawthorne, Belmont & Inner
    Southeast Portland, $, p. 241)
Torrefazione Italia ✵✵ (Northwest
    Portland, $, p. 241)
World Cup Coffee & Tea ✵
    (Northwest Portland, $, p. 241)

CAJUN

Le Bistro Montage ✵ (Hawthorne,
    Belmont & Inner Southeast
    Portland, $, p. 239)

CHINESE

Fong Chong ✵ (Downtown, $,
    p. 226)

CONTINENTAL

The London Grill ✵✵✵
    (Downtown, $$$, p. 223)
Western Culinary Institute
    International Dining Room ✵
    (Downtown, $, p. 227)

DELICATESSEN

Elephant's Delicatessen (Northwest
    Portland, $, p. 242)

Kornblatts (Northwest Portland, $,
    p. 233)

FRENCH

bluehour ✵ (Northwest Portland,
    $$$, p. 227)
Brasserie Montmartre ✵
    (Downtown, $$, p. 224)
Café des Amis ✵✵ (Northwest
    Portland, $$, p. 231)
Castagna ✵✵ (Hawthorne,
    Belmont & Inner Southeast
    Portland, $$$, p. 237)
Couvron ✵✵✵ (Downtown,
    $$$$, p. 222)
The Heathman Restaurant and Bar
    ✵✵✵ (Downtown, $$$, p. 222)
L'Auberge ✵✵ (Northwest
    Portland, $$$, p. 228)
Paley's Place ✵✵ (Northwest
    Portland, $$$, p. 229)

GREEK

Alexis Restaurant ✵ (Downtown,
    $$, p. 223)

INDIAN

Plainfield's Mayur Restaurant and
    Art Gallery ✵✵ (Northwest
    Portland, $$$, p. 229)
Swagat ✵ (Northwest Portland,
    Southwest Portland & the West
    Side, $, p. 233)

INTERNATIONAL

Briggs and Crampton Caterers
    Table for Two ✵✵ (Northwest
    Portland, $$$, p. 228)
Hands on Café ✵ (Northwest
    Portland, $, p. 233)
Ken's Home Plate ✵ (Northwest
    Portland, $, p. 233)
Old Wives' Tales ✵ (Hawthorne,
    Belmont & Inner Southeast
    Portland, $, p. 239)

ITALIAN

Assaggio ✵✵ (Hawthorne,
    Belmont & Inner Southeast
    Portland, $$, p. 237)
bluehour ✵ (Northwest Portland,
    $$$, p. 227)

Caffé Mingo ★★ (Northwest
  Portland, $$, p. 231)
Castagna ★★ (Hawthorne,
  Belmont & Inner Southeast
  Portland, $$$, p. 237)
Fratelli ★★ (Northwest Portland,
  $$, p. 231)
Genoa ★★★ (Hawthorne,
  Belmont & Inner Southeast
  Portland, $$$$, p. 236)
Il Piatto ★★ (Hawthorne,
  Belmont & Inner Southeast
  Portland, $$, p. 237)
The Old Spaghetti Factory ★
  (Southwest Portland, $, p. 234)
Pasta Veloce ★ (Downtown, $,
  p. 227)
Rustica Italian Caffe ★ (Northeast
  Portland, $$, p. 235)
Serratto ★ (Northwest Portland,
  $$$, p. 230)

JAPANESE

Saburo's Sushi House ★★
  (Westmoreland & Sellwood, $$,
  p. 240)

LAOTIAN

Tara Thai ★ (Northwest Portland,
  $$, p. 232)

LATE-NIGHT DINING

Brasserie Montmartre ★
  (Downtown, $$, p. 224)
Garbonzo's (Northwest Portland
  and other locations, $, p. 232)
Le Bistro Montage ★ (Hawthorne,
  Belmont & Inner Southeast
  Portland, $, p. 239)
L'Auberge ★★ (Northwest
  Portland, $$$, p. 228)
Southpark Seafood Grill & Wine
  Bar ★★ (Downtown, $$,
  p. 226)

MEDITERRANEAN

Bread and Ink Cafe ★★
  (Hawthorne, Belmont & Inner
  Southeast Portland, $$, p. 237)
Higgins ★★★ (Downtown, $$$,
  p. 222)

Southpark Seafood Grill & Wine
  Bar ★★ (Downtown, $$,
  p. 226)

MEXICAN

Aztec Willie & Joey Rose
  Tacqueria (Northeast Portland,
  $, p. 235)
Café Azul ★★ (Northwest
  Portland, $$$, p. 228)
Chez José East ★ (Northeast
  Portland, $, p. 236)
El Palenque (Westmoreland &
  Sellwood, $, p. 240)
Mayas Tacqueria (Downtown, $,
  p. 227)

MIDDLE EASTERN

Garbonzo's (Northwest Portland
  and other locations, $, p. 232)
Nicholas's (Hawthorne, Belmont
  & Inner Southeast Portland, $,
  p. 239)

NATURAL FOODS

Bijou Café ★ (Downtown, $,
  p. 226)
Daydream Café ★ (Hawthorne,
  Belmont & Inner Southeast
  Portland, $, p. 238)

NEW AMERICAN

Veritable Quandary ★★
  (Downtown, $$$, p. 223)
Wildwood ★★ (Northwest
  Portland, p. 230)

NORTHWEST

Brasserie Montmartre ★
  (Downtown, $$, p. 224)
Bread and Ink Cafe ★★
  (Hawthorne, Belmont & Inner
  Southeast Portland, $$, p. 237)
Caprial's Bistro and Wine ★★
  (Westmoreland & Sellwood,
  $$$, p. 239)
The Heathman Restaurant and Bar
  ★★★ (Downtown, $$$, p. 222)
Higgins ★★★ (Downtown, $$$,
  p. 222)
L'Auberge ★★ (Northwest
  Portland, $$$, p. 228)

The London Grill ✹✹✹
(Downtown, $$$, p. 223)
Paley's Place ✹✹ (Northwest
Portland, $$$, p. 229)

NUEVO LATINO
¡Oba! ✹ (Northwest Portland,
$$$, p. 229)

PIZZA
Pizza Schmizza ✹ (Northeast
Portland, $, p. 236)

QUICK BITES
Chez Machin (Hawthorne,
Belmont & Inner Southeast
Portland, $, p. 242)
Elephant's Delicatessen (Northwest
Portland, $, p. 242)
Good Dog/Bad Dog (Downtown,
$, p. 242)
In Good Taste ✹ (Northwest
Portland, $, p. 242)
Kitchen Table Café (Hawthorne,
Belmont & Inner Southeast
Portland, $, p. 242)
Pizzicato Gourmet Pizza ✹
(Several locations, $, p. 242)

SALVADORAN
El Palenque (Westmoreland &
Sellwood, $, p. 240)

SEAFOOD
Chart House ✹✹ (Southwest
Portland, $$$, p. 234)
Dan and Louis Oyster Bar ✹
(Downtown, $, p. 226)
Jake's Famous Crawfish ✹✹
(Downtown, $$, p. 224)
McCormick and Schmick's ✹✹
(Downtown, $$, p. 225)
McCormick and Schmick's
Harborside Restaurant ✹✹
(Downtown, $$, p. 225)
Newport Bay Restaurant ✹
(Downtown, $$, p. 225)

Salty's on the Columbia ✹
(Northeast Portland, $$$,
p. 234)
Southpark Seafood Grill & Wine
Bar ✹✹ (Downtown, $$,
p. 226)

SOUTHWEST
Chez Grill ✹ (Hawthorne,
Belmont & Inner Southeast
Portland, $, p. 238)

SPANISH
Tapeo ✹✹ (Northwest Portland,
$$, p. 231)
Colosso ✹ (Northeast Portland, $,
p. 236)

STEAK
RingSide West ✹ (Northwest
Portland, $$$, p. 230)
Ruth's Chris Steak House
(Downtown, $$$, p. 222)

TEA
The Heathman Hotel (Downtown,
$, p. 241)
Tao of Tea ✹✹ (Hawthorne,
Belmont & Inner Southeast
Portland, $, p. 242)

TEX-MEX
Esparza's Tex-Mex Café ✹
(Hawthorne, Belmont & Inner
Southeast Portland, $, p. 238)

THAI
Tara Thai ✹ (Northwest Portland,
$$, p. 232)
Thai Orchid Restaurant ✹
(Northwest Portland, $$,
p. 232)
Typhoon! ✹ (Northwest Portland,
Downtown, $$, p. 232)

VEGETARIAN
Old Wives' Tales ✹ (Hawthorne,
Belmont & Inner Southeast
Portland, $, p. 239)

Portland Dining

Alexis Restaurant **54**
Assaggio **82**
Aztec Willie & Joey Rose
   Taqueria **58**
Bijou Café **53**
bluehour **28**
Brasserie Montmartre **36**
Bread and Ink Cafe **73**
Briggs & Crampton
   Caterers Table for Two **3**
Café Azul **30**
Café des Amis **15**

Café Lena **76**
Caffe Mingo **10**
Caprial's Bistro & Wine **83**
Castagna **79**
Chart House **43**
Chez Grill **75**
Chez José East **61**
Chez Machin **77**
Coffee Time **11**
Colosso **60**
Common Grounds **74**
Couvron **23**

Dan & Louis Oyster Bar **55**
Daydream Café **78**
El Palenque **84**
Elephants Delicatessen **18**
Esparza's Tex-Mex Café **63**
Fong Chong **56**
Fratelli **24**
Garbonzo's **7**
Genoa **72**
Good Dog/Bad Dog **37**
Hands On Café **19**

The Heathman Restaurant **40**
Higgins **41**
Huber's **49**
Il Piatto **64**
In Good Taste **29**
Jake's Famous Crawfish **32**
Ken's Home Plate **26**
Kitchen Table Café **66**
Kornblatts **14**
L'Auberge **2**
Le Bistro Montage **81**
The London Grill **52**

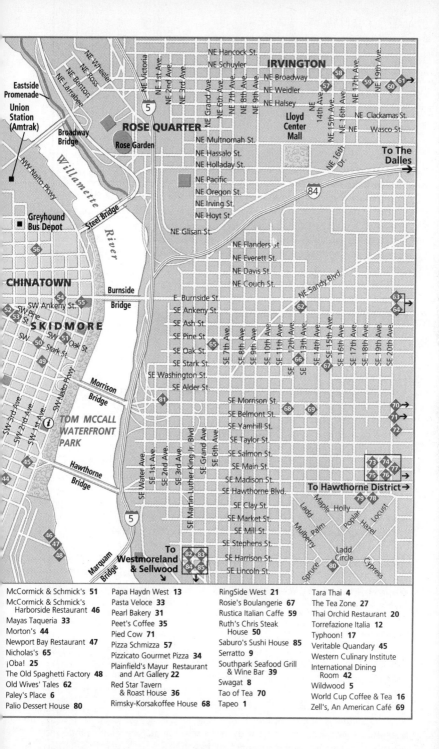

McCormick & Schmick's **51**
McCormick & Schmick's Harborside Restaurant **46**
Mayas Taqueria **33**
Morton's **44**
Newport Bay Restaurant **47**
Nicholas's **65**
¡Oba! **25**
The Old Spaghetti Factory **48**
Old Wives' Tales **62**
Paley's Place **6**
Palio Dessert House **80**

Papa Haydn West **13**
Pasta Veloce **33**
Pearl Bakery **31**
Peet's Coffee **35**
Pied Cow **71**
Pizza Schmizza **57**
Pizzicato Gourmet Pizza **34**
Plainfield's Mayur Restaurant and Art Gallery **22**
Red Star Tavern & Roast House **36**
Rimsky-Korsakoffee House **68**

RingSide West **21**
Rosie's Boulangerie **67**
Rustica Italian Caffe **59**
Ruth's Chris Steak House **50**
Saburo's Sushi House **85**
Serratto **9**
Southpark Seafood Grill & Wine Bar **39**
Swagat **8**
Tao of Tea **70**
Tapeo **1**

Tara Thai **4**
The Tea Zone **27**
Thai Orchid Restaurant **20**
Torrefazione Italia **12**
Typhoon! **17**
Veritable Quandary **45**
Western Culinary Institute International Dining Room **42**
Wildwood **5**
World Cup Coffee & Tea **16**
Zell's, An American Café **69**

2 Downtown (Including the Skidmore Historic District & Chinatown)

VERY EXPENSIVE

Couvron ✷✷✷ CONTEMPORARY FRENCH   Located in the Goose Hollow neighborhood at the foot of the West Hills and only a few blocks from the PGE Park baseball stadium, this diminutive French restaurant has an utterly unremarkable façade yet a thoroughly French and unpretentiously sophisticated interior. However, the menu is one of the most extraordinary in the city, featuring the finest of ingredients in unusual flavor combinations that almost always hit the mark. Dinners here are multicourse affairs that change with the seasons. Expect such interesting creations as an ahi salad with avocado, fresh wasabi, and citrus vinaigrette; chilled tomato soup; smoked quail with organic fingerling potatoes, truffles, truffle oil, and wine sauce; saddle of rabbit with lentils and sautéed foie gras; and lobster with polenta, corn, chanterelles, and port-wine sauce. If you're in town for a very special occasion and are looking for the most memorable restaurant in town, Couvron will fill the bill.

1126 SW 18th Ave. © **503/225-1844.** www.couvron.com. Reservations required. Prix fixe menus only: $65 vegetarian, $75, or $95 grand menu. AE, MC, V. Tues–Sat 5:30–9pm.

EXPENSIVE

In addition to the restaurants listed below, the nation's two big, high-end steakhouse chains—**Ruth's Chris Steak House,** 309 SW Third Ave. (© **503/ 221-4518**), and **Morton's,** 213 SW Clay St. (© **503/248-2005**)—both have restaurants in downtown Portland.

The Heathman Restaurant and Bar ✷✷✷ NORTHWEST/FRENCH This grand dame of Northwest-style restaurants serves Northwest cuisine with a French accent, and in 2001, executive chef Philippe Boulot received the James Beard Foundation's "Best Chef in the Northwest" award. Boulot's menu changes seasonally, but one thing remains constant: The ingredients used are the very freshest of Oregon and Northwest seafood, meat, wild game, and produce. With a simple Art Deco–inspired interior, the restaurant exudes a bistro atmosphere. The menu changes daily and is always quite long. We advise picking appetizers and entrees from the "Northwest Specialties" lists, but the dishes from the grill are also good choices. The bar offers Northwest microbrewery beers on tap, while an extensive wine list spotlights Oregon wines.

The Heathman Hotel has an extensive collection of classic and contemporary art, and on the walls here in the restaurant, you'll find Andy Warhol's *Endangered Species* series of portraits—a rhino, zebra, lion, panda, and others.

In the Heathman Hotel, 1001 SW Broadway. © **503/790—7758.** Reservations highly recommended. Main courses $7.25–$15 at lunch, $16–$30 at dinner. AE, DC, MC, V. Mon–Fri 6:30–11am and 11:30am–2pm, Sat–Sun 7am–2pm; Mon–Thurs 5–10pm, Fri–Sat 5–11pm.

Higgins ✷✷✷ NORTHWEST/MEDITERRANEAN   Higgins, located just up Broadway from the Heathman Hotel, where chef Greg Higgins first made a name for himself in Portland, strikes a balance between contemporary and classic in both decor and cuisine. The menu, which changes frequently, explores contemporary culinary horizons, while the decor in the trilevel dining room opts for wood paneling and elegant place settings. Yet despite all this, the restaurant remains unpretentious. Portions here can be surprisingly generous for a high-end restaurant. Flavors change with the season, but are often both subtle and earthy. A recent entree of roast pork loin with grilled sweet Walla Walla onions, cherry glacé, and Swiss rösti-style potatoes highlighted the restaurant's ability to balance creativity with familiarity. Be sure to leave room for dessert, and if you happen to be a beer lover, you'll be glad to know that Higgins has one of the most interesting beer selections in town (plenty of good wine, too).

1239 SW Broadway. ℰ 503/222-9070. Reservations recommended. Main courses $7.75–$13.75 at lunch, $16.50–$26.50 at dinner. AE, DC, MC, V. Mon–Fri 11:30am–2pm and 5–10:30pm; Sat–Sun 5–10:30pm; bistro menu served in the bar daily until midnight.

The London Grill ★★★ NORTHWEST/CONTINENTAL/BREAKFAST/ BRUNCH   When you really want to feel like a major player, there's only one place in Portland that will do. The London Grill, located below the lobby of the luxurious Benson Hotel, has long been one of Portland's top restaurants. The restaurant is modeled after the original London Grill, which was a favorite with Queen Elizabeth I. Vaulted ceilings give the restaurant a wine-cellar feel, while mahogany paneling reflects the glowing chandeliers. Service is impeccable, and both breakfast and lunch are popular with business executives.

The chef uses many of the Northwest's finest fresh fruits and vegetables in dishes such as salmon glazed with sake and ginger, veal medallions with brandy-paprika cream sauce, and chicken Wellington (stuffed with foie gras, roasted tomatoes, and mushrooms). The Sunday champagne brunch is the most elegant in the city (be sure to make reservations). There is also a wine cellar available for a private dining.

In the Benson Hotel, 309 SW Broadway. ℰ 503/228-2000. Reservations highly recommended. Main courses $25–$40; Sun brunch $25.50. AE, DC, DISC, MC, V. Mon–Tues 6:30am–2pm and 5–9pm; Wed–Sat 6:30am–2pm and 5–10pm; Sun 9:30am–2pm (brunch) and 5–9pm.

Veritable Quandary ★★ NEW AMERICAN   Located in an old brick building just a block off Tom McCall Waterfront Park, this restaurant is a must for summer meals. The restaurant's garden patio faces a small park and has the prettiest restaurant patio in the city. Although the prices here are fairly high for Portland, you can enjoy the food and the garden by coming at lunch. At dinner, the osso bucco is not to be missed. The menu changes daily, but keep your eyes out for the grilled prawns, which might be served with strawberries and green peppercorn sauce. The chef here pulls in all kinds of influences, so don't be surprised if you find grilled beef skewers with a Peruvian marinade or prosciutto with fig molasses, fresh figs, and warm bruschetta, or springs rolls filled with duck confit, shiitakes, and Chinese cabbage (served with a side of wasabi-ginger sauce).

1220 SW First Ave. ℰ 503/227-7342. Reservations recommended. Main courses $16–$25. AE, DC, DISC, MC, V. Mon–Fri 11:30am–3pm, Sat–Sun 9:30am–3:30pm; Sun–Thurs 5–10pm, Fri–Sat 5–11pm.

MODERATE

There's an outpost of **Typhoon!** at 400 SW Broadway (ℰ **503/224-8285**), in the Imperial Hotel. See the complete review on p. 232.

Alexis Restaurant ★ GREEK   Alexis is a classic Greek taverna, and the crowds keep it packed as much for the great food as for the fun atmosphere. On weekends there's belly dancing, and if you happen to be in town on March 25, you can help Alexis celebrate Greek Independence Day with a rousing big party. The menu has all your Greek favorites, and although the main dishes are good, the appetizers are even better. The not-to-be-missed list includes *saganaki* (pan-fried cheese flamed with ouzo), *kalamarakia* (perfectly fried squid), octopus, and the tart and creamy avgolemono soup. Accompany these with Alexis's own fresh bread, and wash it all down with a bottle of Demestica wine for a meal beyond compare. Although you're likely to be panhandled in front of the door (this is Portland's main mission district), don't let this put you off.

215 W. Burnside St. ℂ **503/224-8577.** Reservations recommended. Appetizers $3.50–$9; main courses $11–$14. AE, DC, DISC, MC, V. Mon–Fri 11:30am–2pm; Mon–Thurs 5–10pm, Fri–Sat 5–11pm.

Brasserie Montmartre ✦ NORTHWEST/FRENCH/LATE-NIGHT DINING Though the menu lacks the creativity of other Northwest and French restaurants in Portland, and dishes are sometimes disappointing, The Bra (as it's known) is popular for its fun atmosphere. There's live jazz nightly, and several nights each week, a magician performs amazing feats of digital dexterity. On every table you'll find a paper tablecloth and a container of crayons, so you let your artistic ambitions run wild. This hip playfulness is balanced out by dark, formal dining rooms, with massive faux marble pillars, black-and-white tile floors, velvet banquettes, and silk lamp shades that lend an air of fin de siècle Paris. You might start your meal with a *ménage à trois* of pâtés, then have a cup of onion soup with three cheeses, move on to Oregon snapper with crabmeat and *beurre blanc,* and finish off with one of the divinely decadent pastries. The wine list is extensive and includes many reasonably priced choices.

626 SW Park Ave. ℂ **503/224-5552.** www.brasseriemontmartre.com. Reservations recommended. Main courses $6–$12 at lunch, $12–$20 at dinner. AE, DC, MC, V. Daily 11am–2pm and 5–10pm; bistro menu available Sun–Thurs 2pm–1am and Fri–Sat 2pm–3am.

Huber's ✦ *Finds* AMERICAN Huber's, Portland's oldest restaurant, first opened its doors to the public in 1879 and is tucked inside the Oregon Pioneer Building down a quiet hallway. The main room here has a vaulted stained-glass ceiling, Philippine mahogany paneling, and the original brass cash register.

Turkey dinner with all the trimmings is the house specialty, so there really isn't any question of what to order. However, you can also now gobble turkey enchiladas, turkey Parmesan, and even Moroccan turkey. The other house specialty here is Spanish coffee, which is made with rum, Kahlúa, Triple Sec, coffee, and cream. Preparation of Spanish coffee, which includes flaming the rum in a wine glass, is a very impressive tableside production. Because Huber's has become a popular bar recently, you'll likely enjoy your meal more if you come for lunch instead of dinner. Be sure to ask for a table in the old vaulted room.

411 SW Third Ave. ℂ **503/228-5686.** www.hubers.com. Reservations recommended. Main courses $6–$20 at lunch, $8–$20 at dinner. AE, DC, DISC, MC, V. Mon–Thurs 11:30am–midnight, Fri 11:30am–1am, Sat noon–1am.

Jake's Famous Crawfish ✦✦ SEAFOOD Jake's is a Portland institution and has been serving up crawfish and other seafood dishes since 1909 in a space that holds a back bar that came all the way around Cape Horn in 1880. Much of the rest of the decor looks just as old and well worn as the back bar, but therein lies this restaurant's charm. However, it is the great seafood at reasonable prices that really makes this place a winner.

There's a daily fresh sheet listing a dozen or more specials, but there's really no question about what to eat at Jake's: crawfish, which are always on the menu and are served several different ways. Monday through Friday from 3 to 6pm, bar appetizers are only $1.95. The noise level after work, when local businesspeople pack the bar, can be high, and the wait for a table can be long if you don't make a reservation. However, don't let these obstacles put you off.

401 SW 12th Ave. ℂ **503/226-1419.** Reservations recommended. Main courses $5–$13 at lunch, $10–$43 at dinner. AE, DC, DISC, MC, V. Mon–Fri 11:30am–11pm, Sat 4–11pm, Sun 4–10pm.

McCormick and Schmick's ★★ SEAFOOD   A classic seafood restaurant, McCormick and Schmick's is noted for the freshness of its ingredients. The daily fresh sheet begins with a listing of what's available that day and might list as many as 25 different types of seafood. Whether it's king salmon or Dungeness crab, seafood is king here. The oysters go by their first names: Quilcene, Willapa Bay, Hammersley—you get the picture. If you aren't interested in oysters on the half shell as an appetizer, there are plenty of other seafood dishes to get you started. Main courses draw on a wide range of culinary influences, so you're sure to find something that grabs you. The extensive wine list features lots of good Oregon wines. Both the "up-and-coming" and the "already-there" crowds keep this place bustling. Free parking is available most nights after 5pm at Oak Street and Front Avenue.

235 SW First Ave. © **503/224-7522.** Reservations highly recommended. Main courses $7.50–$13 at lunch, $12–$25 at dinner; bar meals $1.95. AE, DC, DISC, MC, V. Mon–Thurs 11:30am–10:30pm, Fri 11:30am–11pm, Sat 5–11pm, Sun 5–10pm; bar meals Mon–Fri 1:30–6:30pm and 9:30pm–closing, Sat 5–6:30pm, Sun 4:30pm–closing.

McCormick and Schmick's Harborside Restaurant ★★ SEAFOOD Anchoring the opposite end of RiverPlace Esplanade from the RiverPlace Hotel, this large and glitzy seafood restaurant offers a view of the Willamette to go with its excellent seafood. Four dining levels assure everyone a view of the river and marina below, and in summer, customers head out to tables on the Esplanade. Because it's so popular, the place tends to be noisy and the help can sometimes be a bit harried; however, this doesn't detract from the fine food. Although seafood (such as blackened cod with cilantro-lime butter or macadamia-encrusted mahimahi with tropical fruit salsa) is the main attraction here, the menu is quite extensive. The clientele is mostly upscale, especially at lunch and during the after-work hours.

0309 SW Montgomery St. © **503/220-1865.** Reservations recommended. Main courses $9.75–$24. AE, DC, DISC, MC, V. Mon–Thurs 11am–10pm, Fri–Sat 11am–11pm, Sun 10am–3pm and 4–10pm.

Newport Bay Restaurant ★ Kids SEAFOOD   Though there are Newport Bay restaurants all over the Portland area, this one has by far the best location— floating on the Willamette River. Located in the marina at Portland's beautiful RiverPlace shopping-and-dining complex, the Newport Bay provides excellent views of the river and the city skyline, especially from the deck. Popular with young couples, families, and boaters, this place exudes a cheery atmosphere and service is efficient. Nearly everything on the menu has some sort of seafood in it, even the quiche, salads, and pastas. Entrees are mostly straightforward and well prepared—nothing too fancy. Sunday brunch is a very good deal.

0425 SW Montgomery St. © **503/227-3474.** www.newportbay.com. Reservations recommended. Main courses $10–$23; lunches and light main courses $6–$12. AE, DC, DISC, MC, V. Summer hours Mon–Thurs 11am–11pm, Fri–Sat 11am–midnight, Sun 10am–3pm (brunch) and 3–10pm. Closes 1 hour earlier in winter.

Red Star Tavern and Roast House ★★ AMERICAN/BREAKFAST/ BRUNCH   Big and always busy, the Roast House is an American bistro serving up just what many Portlanders crave: big portions of well-prepared and upscale down-home comfort food. With a wood oven, rotisseries, and a smoker, roasted meats are the specialty here, with the spit-roasted pork loin a particular favorite. However, you can also get such things as seared scallops with forest-mushroom risotto cakes. Decor in the large, open restaurant is a comfortable mix of plush and rustic, with interesting murals on the walls.

503 SW Alder St. ⓒ **503/222-0005.** Reservations recommended. Main courses $10.50–$25. AE, DC, DISC, MC, V. Mon–Fri 6:30–10am and 11:30am–2:30pm, Sat–Sun 8am–3pm (brunch); Sun–Thurs 5–10pm, Fri–Sat 5–11pm.

Southpark Seafood Grill & Wine Bar ★★ *(Value)* MEDITERRANEAN/ SEAFOOD/LATE-NIGHT DINING/BREAKFAST/BRUNCH Can it be true? An upscale restaurant/wine bar with downscale prices? Yes, that's exactly what you'll find here at Southpark (no relation to the TV show). So what's the catch? Wine prices are not as reasonable as the food prices, so what you save on your food bill, you'll likely spend on your wine. With its high ceiling, long heavy drapes, halogen lights, and interesting wall mural, the wine bar is a contemporary interpretation of a late-19th-century Parisian, and the main dining room is both comfortable and classy. For a starter, don't pass up the fried calamari served with salt-preserved lemons bursting with flavor. Equally delicious is the butternut squash and ricotta-filled ravioli with toasted hazelnuts, which comes in a rich marsala wine sauce that begs to be sopped up with the crusty bread. An extensive wine list presents some compelling choices, and the desserts are consistently fine.

901 SW Salmon St. ⓒ **503/326-1300.** www.southpark.citysearch.com. Reservations recommended. Main courses $8–$20. AE, DC, DISC, MC, V. Mon–Thurs 11:30am–midnight, Fri 11:30am–1am, Sat 11am–1am, Sun 10am–midnight.

INEXPENSIVE

Bijou Café ★ NATURAL FOODS/BREAKFAST/BRUNCH The folks who run the Bijou take both food and health seriously. They'll serve you a bowl of steamed brown rice and raisins for breakfast, but you can also get delicious fresh oyster hash or brioche French toast. However, the real hits here are the sautéed potatoes and the muffins, which come with full breakfasts. Don't leave without trying these two. Local and organic products are used as often as possible at this comfortably old-fashioned cafe.

132 SW Third Ave. ⓒ **503/222-3187.** Reservations not necessary. Breakfast and lunch $4–$9. MC, V. Mon–Fri 7am–2pm, Sat–Sun 8am–2pm.

Dan and Louis Oyster Bar ★ *(Value)* *(Kids)* SEAFOOD Dan and Louis has been serving up succulent oysters since 1907, and half the fun of eating here is enjoying the old-fashioned surroundings. The front counter is stacked high with candies much as it would have been in the 1920s. The walls are covered with founder Louis Wachsmuth's own collection of old and unusual plates. Beer steins line the shelves, and nautical odds and ends are everywhere. Louis began his restaurant business serving only two items: oyster stew and oyster cocktails. These two are still on the menu, and are as good today as they were 85 years ago. Main courses are simple, no-nonsense seafood dishes, mostly fried. The quality can be uneven, but the prices are great.

208 SW Ankeny St. ⓒ **503/227-5906.** www.danandlouis.citysearch.com. Reservations recommended. Main courses $7–$19. AE, DC, DISC, MC, V. Sun–Thurs 11am–10pm, Fri–Sat 11am–11pm.

Fong Chong ★ CHINESE This popular Chinese restaurant is in a grocery store, but don't worry, you won't be eating in the aisles; the restaurant occupies its own room. Although most of the food here is above average, the dim sum is the best in the city. Flag down a passing cart and point to the most appetizing looking little dishes. We really like the shrimp dumplings wrapped in crispy taro. Be careful, though, or you might end up with a plate of chicken feet. At the end of the meal, your bill is calculated by the number of plates you've ordered.

301 NW Fourth Ave. ✆ **503/220-0235.** Reservations not accepted. Main courses $6–$12; dim sum items $2.50–$5. MC, V. Daily 10:30am–10pm; dim sum 10:30am–3pm daily.

Mayas Tacqueria MEXICAN   Nothing fancy here, just good home-cooked Mexican food. You can watch the cooks prepare your meal just as in any tacqueria in Mexico. The menu above the counter lists the different meals available, and on a separate list you'll find the choice of meats, which include chicken mole, pork or chicken chile verde, chicken chile Colorado, and carne asada. To find this place, just watch for the Mayan-style murals on the walls out front.

   Sante Fe Tacqueria, 831 NW 23rd Ave. (✆ **503/220-0406**), and **Aztec Willie & Joey Rose Tacqueria,** 1501 NE Broadway (✆ **503/280-8900**), are run by the same folks and serve equally delicious food.

1000 SW Morrison St. ✆ **503/226-1946.** $3–$9. AE, DISC, MC, V. Daily 10am–10pm.

Pasta Veloce ✰ ITALIAN   Pasta Veloce, which translates roughly as "noodles in a hurry," really lives up to its name—it's a quick, cheap place to get a tasty Italian meal downtown. And there are two convenient locations. Portions are not huge, but they are satisfying, and come with rustic grilled bread. We really like the gnocchi with chicken, broccoli, and walnuts in a Gorgonzola sauce. Wine and beer are available at prices that match those of the pastas.

933 SW Third Ave. (✆ **503/223-8200**) and 1022 SW Morrison St. (✆ **503/916-4388**). Main courses $5.25–$7.50. AE, DISC, MV, V. Third Ave. location Mon–Thurs 11am–8pm, Fri 11am–8:30pm, Sat noon–8:30pm; Morrison St. location Mon–Thurs 11:30am–9pm, Fri 11:30am–9:30pm, Sat noon–9:30pm.

Western Culinary Institute International Dining Room ✰ (Value) CONTI-NENTAL/AMERICAN   If you happen to be a frugal gourmet whose palate is more sophisticated than your wallet can afford, you'll want to schedule a meal here. The dining room serves five- to six-course gourmet meals prepared by advanced students at prices even a budget traveler can afford. The dining room decor is modern and unassuming, and the students who wait on you are eager to please. For each course you have a choice among two to half a dozen offerings. A sample dinner menu might begin with velouté Andalouse followed by sautéed vegetables in a puff pastry, a pear sorbet, grilled ahi tuna with black bean salsa, Chinese salad with smoked salmon, and mocha cheesecake. Remember, that's all for under $20! The five-course lunch for only $9.95 is an even better deal.

1316 SW 13th Ave. ✆ **800/666-0312** or 503/294-9770. Reservations required. 5-course lunch $9.95; 6-course dinner $19.95; Thurs buffet $19.95. AE, MC, V. Tues–Fri 11:30am–1pm and 6–8pm.

3 Northwest Portland (Including the Pearl District & Nob Hill)

EXPENSIVE

bluehour ✰ (Overrated) FRENCH/ITALIAN   Restaurateur Bruce Carey has long dominated the Portland restaurant scene, and here at is latest high-style restaurant, he continues to woo and wow the local trendsetters. Despite the location in a recently converted warehouse that serves as headquarters for Portland advertising giant Wieden+Kennedy, bluehour has a very theatrical atmosphere. With the likes of pan-seared foie gras and smoked goose prosciutto on the menu, it's obvious that this restaurant wants to raise the sophistication level among Portland's high-end restaurants. However, despite the cultured cuisine, the cacophonous noise level and close proximity of tables to one another severely detracts from the experience here. If you value conversation with your meal, steer clear of bluehour. This is definitely the sort of place where being seen by the right people is more important than the food.

250 NW 13th. © **503/226-3394.** www.bluehour.com. Reservations highly recommended. Main dishes $17.50–$30. AE, MC, V. Mon–Thurs 11:30am–2:30pm and 6–10pm, Fri 11:30am–2:30pm and 6–10:30pm, Sat 5:30–10:30pm.

Briggs and Crampton Caterers Table for Two ★★ INTERNATIONAL
Dubbing their dining room "The World's Smallest Restaurant," Briggs and Crampton Caterers puts on a special lunch for two people only (make reservations well in advance) at a house in Northwest Portland. This pampering experience, which occurs in a screened-off area of the front parlor, begins with an appetizer, followed by a sorbet, breads, the main course with side dishes, dessert, and coffee. Dishes are influenced by whatever is in season, be it a certain type of fish, morel mushrooms, or fresh berries, or by the preferences of those dining (with special attention to dietary restrictions). The chef doubles as the waiter, so attention is concentrated on your special needs and desires. The wine list has some fine selections. Reservations are taken quarterly, in January, April, July, and October.

1902 NW 24th Ave. © **503/223-8690.** Reservations several months in advance. 4-course lunch for 2 people $75. MC, V. Tues–Fri 12:30pm.

Café Azul ★★ GOURMET MEXICAN
Located in the Pearl District in what was clearly once an old warehouse, Café Azul is a long and narrow space softened by expanses of warm yellow and terra-cotta walls. The food here includes some of the best regional Mexican dishes you're likely to find this side of the border. Tasty margaritas are generous, and can be made with a number of different tequilas; sangrita, a spicy nonalcoholic ancho chile and orange drink, also gets two thumbs up. Start by spreading some dangerously tasty chile butter on a crusty roll, then follow this with a taco sampler platter that includes handmade corn tortillas served with Yucatecan-style pork roasted in banana leaves. From Oaxaca, Mexico, comes the inspiration for Café Azul's mole, a rich and spicy sauce that is made with more than two dozen ingredients, including toasted nuts, chocolate, and chile, and which might be served over chicken or duck. The house-made ice creams and sorbets, often made with unusual tropical fruits are always a fitting finale. This may be expensive for Mexican food, but it's well worth it.

112 NW Ninth Ave. © **503/525-4422.** Reservations recommended. Main courses $16.50–$25. DISC, MC, V. Tues–Thurs 5–9pm, Fri–Sat 5–9:30pm.

L'Auberge ★★ (Value) FRENCH/NORTHWEST/LATE-NIGHT DINING
Located at the edge of an industrial district in a building that in France could pass very nicely as a country inn, L'Auberge has stood the test of time—while other restaurants have come and gone, it's been around for more than 30 years. As such, it's a favorite of the old guard and a popular special-occasion restaurant. There are two settings for dining here: the casual lounge area and the more formal dining room, although both serve the same menu. In summer, the large, gardenlike deck is especially popular. Simply prepared classic French dishes with a handful of more creative Northwest and Pacific Rim offerings provide just enough variety to make things interesting. Some of the same dishes from the dinner menu appear at lunch for about half price, making this a good choice if you appreciate good French cooking but usually can't afford it.

Great Brunch Choices

If you're looking for someplace to do brunch on a leisurely Sunday, try the **London Grill** (you'll want to dress up for this one, and reservations are imperative), **Wildwood** (for the trendiest brunch in town), **Newport Bay** (for a seafood brunch at a floating restaurant on the Willamette River), **Salty's on the Columbia** (seafood brunch with a view of the Columbia River), **Bread and Ink Cafe** (a three-course Yiddish repast; don't feel guilty if you can't finish your meal), or **Hands on Café** (for a casual brunch on an art school campus). Complete listings for these restaurants are found under the appropriate neighborhood headings throughout this chapter.

2601 NW Vaughn St. ✆ **503/223-3302.** Reservations recommended for dinner. Main courses $10–$14 at lunch, $18–$26 at dinner. AE, DC, MC, V. Tues–Fri 11:30am–2:30pm; Tues–Sun 5–10pm.

¡Oba! ✿ NUEVO LATINO   Lively, with a very Latin American feeling both in color and design, ¡Oba! (Portuguese for "oh yeah!") is one of the Portland's currently trendy Pearl District watering holes. And oh, what a rumbling buzz of conversation fills the air. The big bar is guaranteed to be filled with people wearing the requisite black and sipping fresh fruit margaritas or Roberto Roys. Service is polished and personable, something you wouldn't expect from the latest hip restaurant. Get away from some of the noise by asking for one of the cozy and romantic booths. Memorable appetizers include crispy coconut prawns with jalapeño-citrus marmalade and perfectly seared rare ahi tuna. The sauces, such as the passion fruit sauce that spices up the Chilean sea bass, are standouts. Desserts are most unusual. Some hit, some miss, but they're all pretty extravagant.

555 NW 12th Ave. ✆ **503/228-6161.** Reservations recommended. Main courses $14–$22. AE, DISC, MC, V. Sun–Mon 5:30–9pm, Tues–Thurs 5:30–10pm, Fri–Sat 5:30–10:30pm. Bar opens at 4:30pm and stays open later than restaurant.

Paley's Place ✿✿ NORTHWEST/FRENCH   Located in a turn-of-the-20th-century Victorian house, Paley's is a favorite of Portland foodies. The menu ranges from traditional bistro fare to dishes with a hint of Northwest inspiration and relies extensively on the freshest local organic ingredients. Chef Vitaly Paley and his wife, Kimberly, run the show here and continue to receive accolades year after year. Whether you're in the mood for steamed mussels or something more unusual (pasta with chickpeas, preserved tuna, dried tuna roe, and mint), you'll certainly find something that appeals. If you've never tried sweetbreads, this is the place to do so, and the signature *frites,* with a mustard aioli, are not to be missed. Big on wines, Paley's offers wine tasting on Wednesdays and an occasional winemaker dinner. For dessert, we can't pass up the warm chocolate soufflé with ice cream. In good weather, the front porch is the preferred place to dine, while inside, the restaurant is small and stylishly comfortable but can be quite noisy.

1204 NW 21st Ave. ✆ **503/243-2403.** www.paleysplace.citysearch.com. Reservations highly recommended. Main courses $15–$26. AE, MC, V. Mon–Thurs 5:30–10pm, Fri–Sat 5:30–11pm, Sun 5–10pm.

Plainfield's Mayur Restaurant and Art Gallery ✿✿ INDIAN   In the words of a friend, "With an Indian restaurant like Mayur's, who needs anything else?" Located in an elegant old Portland home, this is the city's premier Indian restaurant. The prices are high, the atmosphere is refined, and the service is informative and gracious (definitely not the sort of downscale Indian restaurant most people are familiar with). The food here is almost always perfectly spiced so that the complex flavors and aromas of Indian cuisine shine through. Instead of the usual plethora or chicken and lamb dishes you find on most Indian menus, this restaurant serves such unusual dishes as lobster, tandoori rack of lamb, and halibut filets. The dessert list is also an unexpected and pleasant surprise, and the wine list is one of the finest in the city. In addition to the two floors of dining rooms inside, there's also a patio out back. Be sure to take a peek at the cooks preparing bread and tandoori chicken in the tandoori show kitchen.

852 SW 21st Ave. ✆ 503/223-2995. www.plainfields.com. Reservations recommended. Main courses $15–$28. AE, DC, DISC, MC, V. Daily 5:30–10pm.

RingSide West ✦ STEAK   Despite the location on a rather unattractive stretch of West Burnside Street, RingSide has long been a favorite Portland steakhouse. Boxing may be the main theme of the restaurant, but the name is a two-fisted pun as well, referring to the incomparable onion rings that should be an integral part of any meal here. Have your rings with a side order of one of their perfectly cooked steaks for a real knockout meal.

There's also a **RingSide East** at 14021 NE Glisan St. (✆ **503/255-0750**), on Portland's east side, with basically the same menu but not as much atmosphere; this one is open for lunch during the week.

2165 W. Burnside St. ✆ **503/223-1513.** www.ringsidesteakhouse.com. Reservations highly recommended. Steaks $14–$27; other main courses $15–$38. AE, DC, DISC, MC, V. Mon–Sat 5pm–midnight, Sun 4–11:30pm.

Serratto ✦ ITALIAN   Italian restaurants continue to be all the rage in Portland, as evidenced by the row of three good ones on one block of Northwest 21st Avenue. Because of all the competition, the quality and creativity tends to be high at all of these restaurants. Serratto is the largest of the three and features a modern "rustic" look and a wine cafe (La Vineria), where you can have a glass of wine and also order food if the main restaurant is too crowded and you're stuck without a reservation. If you have your heart set on pasta with a thick tomato sauce, you might want to try elsewhere. Here you're more likely to encounter a salad of arugula, fresh trout, diced potatoes, and pine nuts with a blood-orange vinaigrette or perhaps grilled halibut with black-olive risotto cakes and fresh roma tomato puree.

2112 NW Kearney St. ✆ 503/221-1195. Reservations recommended. Main courses $14–$20. AE, DISC, MC, V. Sun–Thurs 5–10pm, Fri–Sat 5–10:30pm.

Wildwood ✦✦ NEW AMERICAN/BREAKFAST/BRUNCH   With a menu that changes daily and an elegant and spare interior decor straight out of *Architectural Digest,* Wildwood has for many years now been considered one of the best restaurants in Portland. However, lately dishes have been a bit hit-and-miss, with the appetizers, salads, and desserts often outshining the entrees. However, if you love creative cuisine, you'll want to give this place a try. Fresh seasonal ingredients combined into simple-yet-imaginative dishes are the hallmark of chef Cory Schreiber's cooking, and often there are no more than four ingredients in a dish so as to let each of the flavors shine through. Results are usually artful, not pretentious. On a recent evening, there were skillet-roasted Washington mussels with garlic, tomato, and saffron and an excellent oyster-topped salad with pancetta and aioli. This is the only non-Indian restaurant we know of that has a tandoor oven, and you can usually count on the meat dishes that are roasted in this oven. Salads and sorbets are exceptionally good. If you can't get a reservation, you can still usually get served at the bar.

1221 NW 21st Ave. © **503/248-WOOD.** www.wildwoodrestaurant.citysearch.com. Reservations highly recommended. Main courses $9–$13 at lunch, $16–$25 at dinner. AE, MC, V. Mon–Sat 11:30am–2:30pm and 5:30–10pm; Sun 10am–2pm (brunch).

MODERATE

Café des Amis ★★ FRENCH   This neighborhood French restaurant is tucked into an out-of-the-way corner of Northwest Portland, and its walls are so covered with ivy that it's easy to miss. With a menu split between economical bistro dishes and more expensive entrees, Café des Amis serves some reliable French fare in an unpretentious atmosphere. In business for many years, the cafe has developed a loyal following for such well-prepared dishes as tender duck with blackberry sauce and excellent beef filet with Port wine and garlic sauce. The dining room is small, quiet, and sedate (no hustle-bustle here) and frequented by an older, conservative crowd that has come for the dining experience, not to be part of a scene.

1987 NW Kearney St. © **503/295-6487.** Reservations recommended. Main courses $10–$27. AE, MC, V. Mon–Sat 5:30–9:30 or 10pm.

Caffé Mingo ★★ *(Finds)* ITALIAN   If there's any problem with this intimate little neighborhood restaurant, which is immensely popular and doesn't take reservations, it's that you almost always have to wait for a table. The solution? Get here as close to opening as possible. The interior is as attractive as that of any other upscale restaurant here on Restaurant Row, but the prices are less expensive, which is why Caffé Mingo is so popular. The quality of the food also has a lot to do with the popularity. The menu is short, and focuses on painstakingly prepared Italian comfort food. Just about all of the items on the menu are winners, from the antipasti platter, which might include roasted fennel, fresh mozzarella, and roasted red pepper, to an unusual penne pasta dish with tender beef braised in Chianti and espresso. The *panna cotta* dessert ("cooked cream" with fruit) is reason enough to come back here again and again, even if you have to wait in the rain to get a seat.

807 NW 21st Ave. © **503/226-4646.** Reservations accepted only for parties of 6 or more. Main courses $8.50–$18. AE, DISC, MC, V. Sun–Thurs 5–10pm, Fri–Sat 5–11pm.

Fratelli ★★ REGIONAL ITALIAN   In this rustic-yet-chic restaurant, cement walls provide a striking contrast to dramatic draperies and candles that drip casually onto the tabletops. Dishes are consistently good, with surprisingly moderate prices for the Pearl District. There's excellent olive oil to go with your bread and an antipasti plate that's far more creative than your usual platter of meat, cheese, and pickled vegetables. On a recent visit, everything we tasted, from spring beans with arugula and octopus to chicken wrapped in prosciutto to rabbit *crepinette* (a sort of sausage) to a luscious *panna cotta* (cooked cream) dessert, was thoroughly satisfying. This restaurant has a similar aesthetic and menu to Caffé Mingo (see above), but at Fratelli you can make reservations.

1230 NW Hoyt St. © **503/241-8800.** Reservations recommended. Main courses $11–$16.50. AE, DC, MC, V. Sun–Thurs 5:30–9pm, Fri–Sat 5:30–10pm.

Tapeo ★★ *(Finds)* SPANISH   With the feeling of an old European restaurant, this small yet plush neighborhood spot located deep in Northwest Portland seems intimate, but the noise level rises considerably when the place is full—which is often. People wait around for the tables, which are placed so close together that you might as well be sitting with your neighbor. But it's worth the wait for authentic Spanish tapas such as an excellent grilled eggplant that is thinly sliced and stuffed with goat cheese or deliciously crispy fried calamari served with aioli. The flan is the richest you'll ever taste. Prices on wines, both by the glass and bottle, are decent. All in all, this a great place for a light meal or a romantic evening out.

2764 NW Thurman St. ⓒ **503/226-0409**. Reservations not accepted. Tapas $1.75–$9. DISC, MC, V. Tues–Thurs 5:30–10pm, Fri–Sat 5–10:30pm.

Tara Thai ✱ NORTHERN THAI/LAOTIAN   Tara Thai is recommendable both for its location on one of the prettiest blocks of Northwest Portland and its attractive outdoor deck. However, the real attraction here is the chance to try a bit of Laotian food. (Despite the term *Thai* in this restaurant's name, Laotian food is the real specialty.) Although it's a bit odd by Western standards, the combination platter of *som tum* (green papaya salad), beef jerky, and sticky rice is delicious. Other tasty standouts include the curries and *ban seo*, an Asian-style crepe filled with chicken and bean sprouts, garnished with cilantro and mint, and served with a sweet chile sauce. In season, Tara Thai serves mango and sticky rice, one of our all-time favorite desserts.

1310 NW 23rd Ave. ⓒ **503/222-7840**. Reservations not necessary. Main courses $7.50–$15.50. AE, DISC, MC, V. Mon–Thurs 11am–9pm and 4–9pm, Fri 11am–10pm, Sat noon–10pm, Sun noon–9pm.

Thai Orchid Restaurant ✱ THAI   Although this place is on an unattractive stretch of West Burnside Street and has almost nothing in the way of atmosphere, it serves some of the best and most consistent Thai food in Portland. So popular is this place that it has spun off no fewer than six other restaurants located around the Portland metro area. The pad Thai is excellent, as are most of the curries. To start your meal, be sure to order the *miang kum*, a traditional Thai bar food (for a description, see the review of Typhoon!, immediately below). For another unusual taste treat, try the *som tum*, a spicy salad made from green papaya.

2231 W. Burnside St. ⓒ **503/226-4542**. www.thaiorchidrestaurant.com. Reservations taken only for parties of 6 or more. Main courses $8–$14. AE, DISC, MC, V. Mon–Fri 11:30am–2:30pm; Mon–Thurs 4:30–9:30pm, Fri 4:30–10:30pm, Sat noon–10:30pm, Sun noon–9:30pm.

Typhoon! ✱ THAI   Located just off NW 23rd Avenue, this trendy spot is a bit pricey for a Thai restaurant, but the unusual menu offerings generally aren't available at other Portland Thai restaurants. Be sure to start a meal with the *miang kum*, which consists of dried shrimp, tiny chiles, ginger, lime, peanuts, shallots, and toasted coconut drizzled with a sweet-and-sour sauce and wrapped up in a spinach leaf. The eruption of flavors that takes place on your taste buds is absolutely astounding (we first had this in Thailand and waited years to get it here in the United States). The whole front wall of the restaurant slides away for Thai-style open-air dining in the summer. There is an extensive tea list.

There's another **Typhoon!** at 400 SW Broadway (ⓒ **503/224-8285**), in the Imperial Hotel.

2310 NW Everett St. ⓒ **503/243-7557**. Reservations recommended. Main courses $7–$20. AE, DC, DISC, MC, V. Mon–Fri 11:30am–2:30pm; Sat noon–3pm; Mon–Thurs 5–9:30pm, Fri–Sat 5–10:30pm, Sun 4:30–9:30pm.

INEXPENSIVE

Garbonzo's MIDDLE EASTERN/LATE-NIGHT DINING   This casual little place calls itself a falafel bar and is a popular spot for a late-night meal (but it's also good for lunch or dinner). The menu includes all the usual Middle Eastern offerings, most of which also happen to be American Heart Association approved. You can eat at one of the tiny cafe tables or get your order to go. They even serve beer and wine.

Other Garbonzo's are at 3433 SE Hawthorne Blvd. (© **503/239-6087**) and 6341 SW Capitol Hwy. (© **503/293-7335**).

922 NW 21st Ave. © **503/227-4196.** Sandwiches $4–$5; dinners $7–$9. AE, DISC, MC, V. Sun–Thurs 11:30am–12:30am, Fri–Sat 11:30am–2am (closed 1 hour earlier Oct–June).

Hands on Café ⋆ *(Finds)* INTERNATIONAL/BREAKFAST/BRUNCH This cafe is located at the Oregon College of Arts and Crafts, a 10-minute drive west of downtown Portland (take West Burnside Street) and convenient if you are spending the morning or afternoon at any of the attractions at Washington Park. Here at this student cafe, you can enjoy healthful and light foods such as Indonesian chicken-noodle curry, homemade soups, salads, breads, and muffins, and soak up the ambience of an art school, which is housed in cedar-shingled buildings on a tree-shaded campus. There are artworks by students on the walls, and you can visit the craft shop and gallery if they're open. An outside patio is enjoyable in the warm weather.

8245 SW Barnes Rd. © **503/297-1480.** Reservations not accepted. $3.50–$7. No credit cards. Mon–Fri 11:30am–2pm; Mon–Thurs 5:30–7:30pm; Sun 9:30am–1:30pm (brunch).

Ken's Home Plate ⋆ *(Finds)* INTERNATIONAL This little hole-in-the-wall in the trendy Pearl District could easily be overlooked, but once you step inside and see the beautiful prepared foods in the display cases, you'll likely be as hooked as we are. One meal here is enough to have you dreaming about living in the neighborhood so you could get all your meals here. Chef/owner Ken Gordon turns out dishes that would do justice to the best restaurants in town, and on any give day, there are 15 to 20 different entrees such as salmon strudel, Tuscan meatloaf, chicken marsala, and Louisiana gumbo, available. However, you might have trouble getting past the delicious sandwiches, which come with a side of any of more than half a dozen different salads. Desserts are prominently displayed on the countertop, making them very difficult to ignore. Although this is primarily a take-out place, there are a few tables in case you can't wait to dig in.

1208 NW Glisan St. © **503/517-8935.** Plates and sandwiches $5–$8.50. MC, V. Tues–Sat 11am–8pm, until 9pm on first Thurs of each month.

Kornblatts DELICATESSEN In the heart of NW 23rd Avenue, a dozen tables and a take-out corner are the setting for some very satisfying (and kosher) Jewish soul food. The corned beef and pastrami come directly from New York, and the bagels are made on the premises. If Nova lox, whitefish salad, knishes, potato latkes, or blintzes don't tempt you, how about a selection of five different kinds of cheesecake?

628 NW 23rd Ave. © **503/242-0055.** Reservations not accepted. Sandwiches $5–$10. AE, MC, V. Mon–Fri 7am–8pm, Sat–Sun 7:30am–9pm.

Swagat ⋆ INDIAN Located on the same corner as Garbonzo's (see above) is an exceptionally good Indian restaurant specializing in south Indian dishes. The *dosas,* crepes made of lentil flour stuffed with vegetable curry and served with a variety of sauces, are deliciously savory, and the tandoori chicken is deliciously smoky. Be sure to start your meal with the sambar, a thin but flavorful soup. We also like the vegetable samosas, crisp turnovers stuffed with potatoes and peas, and the *keema mattar* (ground lamb with peas). Don't forget to order some of the puffy nan. At lunch, there is an extensive buffet, that's a very good deal.

Another Swagat is located in the west-side suburb of Beaverton at 4325 SW 109th Ave. (© **503/626-3000**).

2074 NW Lovejoy St. © **503/227-4300.** Reservations not accepted. Main courses $7–$14. AE, DISC, MC, V. Daily 11:30am–2:30pm and 5–10pm.

4 Southwest Portland

EXPENSIVE

Chart House ✹✹ SEAFOOD   Although this place is a part of a national restaurant chain with lots of outposts all over California and the rest of the West, it also happens to boast the best view of any restaurant in Portland. On top of that, it serves the best New England clam chowder in the state (the recipe repeatedly won awards in a Boston chowder competition). While you savor your chowder, you can marvel at the views of the Willamette River, Mount Hood, Mount St. Helens, and nearly all of Portland's east side. Fresh fish, either grilled, baked, or blackened is the house specialty, and on any given day, there'll be a short selection of the day's fresh fish. You'll also find a selection of excellent steaks for the problem child in your group who just won't eat seafood. No dinner here is complete without the hot chocolate lava cake, which has to be ordered at the start of your meal if you want it to be ready when you are.

The Chart House is in an out-of-the-way spot about a 10-minute drive from downtown Portland; be sure to call ahead and get driving directions.

5700 SW Terwilliger Blvd. © **503/246-6963.** Reservations recommended. Main courses $10–$16 at lunch, $15–$40 at dinner. AE, DC, DISC, MC, V. Mon–Fri 11:30am–2pm; Mon–Sat 5–10pm, Sun 5–9pm.

INEXPENSIVE

For Middle Eastern fare, there's a branch of Garbonzo's at 6341 SW Capitol Hwy. (& 503/293-7335). See the complete review on p. 232.

The Old Spaghetti Factory ✹ *Kids* ITALIAN   Sure, this is a chain restaurant, but incredibly low prices, great decor, a waterfront location on the bank of the Willamette River, and the fact that the chain was born right here in Portland are reason enough to give this place a chance. This is the best waterfront restaurant in town for kids, and it's a lot of fun for grown-ups, too. Sort of a cross between a church, a trolley depot, and a Victorian brothel, this restaurant will keep you entertained and won't cost much more than McDonald's. Although this place is less than a mile from downtown, you should call for directions, then, as you're driving, watch for the big building with the blue tile roof.

0715 SW Bancroft St. © **503/222-5375.** www.osf.com. Reservations accepted only for large parties. Main courses $5.75–$9.25. AE, DISC, MC, V. Mon–Thurs 11:30am–2pm and 5–10pm, Fri 11:30am–2pm and 5–11pm, Sat 11:30am–11pm, Sun 11:30am–10pm (Memorial Day to Labor Day: Mon–Fri 11:30am–10pm, Sat 11:30am–11pm, Sun 11:30am–10pm).

5 Northeast Portland (Including Irvington)

EXPENSIVE

Salty's on the Columbia ✹ SEAFOOD/BREAKFAST/BRUNCH   Located out on the Columbia River near the airport, Salty's is one of Portland's best waterfront restaurants, with views that take in the river, mountains, and forests. Preparations here are creative, the portions are large, and the salmon dishes are

Kids Family-Friendly Restaurants

Aztec Willie & Joey Rose Tacqueria (see p. 235)   Cheap Mexican and a glassed-in children's play area make this a good choice for families on a budget.

Dan and Louis Oyster Bar (see p. 226)   You'll feel like you're eating in the hold of an old sailing ship, and all the fascinating stuff on the walls will keep the kids entertained.

Old Wives' Tales (see p. 239)   This is just about the best place in Portland to eat if you've got small children. There are children's menus at all meals, and in the back of the restaurant there's a playroom that will keep your kids entertained while you enjoy your meal.

The Old Spaghetti Factory (see p. 234)   This chain of inexpensive Italian restaurants got its start here in Portland, and the restaurant here just might have the best location of any in the chain—right on the bank of the Willamette River. Kids love the food and parents enjoy the atmosphere and low prices.

particularly good. Try some seared salmon with chanterelle-zinfandel reduction or blackened salmon on a Caesar salad. A few choice offerings of steak and chicken dishes offer options to those who don't care for seafood. *A warning:* Though the decks look appealing, the noise from the airport can make conversation difficult.

3839 NE Marine Dr. (C) **503/288-4444.** www.saltys.com. Reservations highly recommended. Main courses $8–$17 at lunch, $20–$33 at dinner. AE, DC, DISC, MC, V. Mon–Thurs 11:15am–3pm and 5–10pm, Sat 11:15am–3pm and 5–10:30pm, Sun 9:30am–2pm (brunch) and 4:30–9pm.

MODERATE

Rustica Italian Caffe (Kids) ITALIAN   If you're looking for good, moderately priced Italian food in Northeast Portland, look no further than Rustica. The menu is long, portions are large, and they have a nice selection of Chiantis and great bread. What more could you ask for? In addition, the atmosphere is unpretentious, the space light and airy, and it's a popular spot for families. There is also a small pizzeria adjacent to the main restaurant. Among our favorite dishes here are the smoked-salmon cannelloni and the prawns sautéed in olive oil with grapefruit, rosemary, chile flakes, and cream.

1700 NE Broadway. (C) **503/288-0990.** Reservations recommended. Main courses $11–$17. AE, DISC, MC, V. Mon–Fri 11:30am–2:30pm; Mon–Thurs 5–9:30pm, Fri–Sat 5–10:30pm, Sun 5–9pm.

INEXPENSIVE

Aztec Willie & Joey Rose Tacqueria (Kids) MEXICAN   With a copper pyramid over the front door and Mayan glyphs decorating the facade, it's hard to miss this hip-yet-casual Mexican place on NE Broadway. Associated with the ever-popular Mayas Tacqueria in downtown Portland, Aztec Willie is a big place where you order cafeteria-style. For adults, there's a bar, and for kids, there's a glassed-in play area.

1501 NE Broadway. (C) **503/280-8900.** Reservations not accepted. Main courses $3–$9. AE, DISC, MC, V. Daily 11am–11pm.

Chez José East ⭐ *Kids* MEXICAN   It's immediately obvious both from the hip decor and the menu that this isn't Taco Bell. While a squash enchilada with peanut sauce (spicy and sweet with mushrooms, apples, jicama, and sunflower seeds) sounds weird, it actually tastes great. Don't worry, though, there's plenty of traditional fare on the menu, too (and at traditional cheap prices). Because the restaurant doesn't take reservations, it's a good idea to get here early, before the line starts snaking out the door. This is a family-friendly place, so don't hesitate to bring the kids, and if the kids are under 6, they'll eat for free between 5 and 7pm.

2200 NE Broadway. ✆ **503/280-9888.** Reservations accepted only for parties of 7 or more. Main courses $5.75–$11.50. AE, MC, V. Mon–Thurs 11:30am–11pm, Fri–Sat 11:30am–midnight, Sun 5–10pm.

Colosso ⭐ SPANISH   For cheap chic and tasty tapas, you can't beat Colosso. Inside, this little neighborhood hangout has gold-painted stucco walls and the music (usually rock) is loud. In summer, if the music is too much for you, you can sit at a table out on the sidewalk. There are several excellent Spanish Rioja wines available by the glass, and cocktails made with fresh-squeezed juice. The varied selection of tapas includes baked Spanish omelets, seared eggplant with tomatoes and goat cheese in a pomegranate glaze, grilled calamari in garlic and red-wine vinegar, and grilled prawns in salsa verde. As far as we can tell, this is a dud-free menu. Hip waiters provide surprisingly attentive service.

1932 NE Broadway. ✆ **503/288-3333.** Reservations not accepted. Tapas and plates $2.50–$12. DISC, MC, V. Daily 5pm–midnight or later.

Pizza Schmizza ⭐ PIZZA   With creative pizzas and wacky decor, Pizza Schmizza is a great place to grab a slice or an entire pie. Of course there are old favorites such as cheese and pepperoni, but there are also such pizzas as spicy Thai and Yucatán-style, and several that have spaghetti as well as other ingredients on them. You can go Northwest and get a smoked salmon pizza, or try a Cajun pizza with alligator meat.

1422 NE Broadway ✆ **503/517-9981.** www.schmizza.com. Pizzas $12–$28. AE, DISC, MC, V. Mon–Thurs 11am–10pm, Fri–Sat 11am–11pm, Sun noon–9pm.

6 Hawthorne, Belmont & Inner Southeast Portland

VERY EXPENSIVE

Genoa ⭐⭐⭐ REGIONAL ITALIAN   This has long been the best Italian restaurant in Portland, and with fewer than a dozen tables, it's also one of the smallest. Everything, from the breads to the luscious desserts, is made fresh in the kitchen with the best of locally available seasonal ingredients. This is an ideal setting for a romantic dinner, and service is attentive—the waiter explains dishes in detail as they are served, and dishes are magically whisked away as they're finished. The fixed-price menu changes every couple of weeks, but a typical dinner might start with *bagna cauda,* a creamy garlic and anchovy fondue, followed by spicy mussel soup. The pasta course could be a lasagna, with braised fresh artichokes layered with a béchamel sauce and Parmigiano-Reggiano cheese. There's always a choice of main courses, such as trout stuffed with chanterelle mushrooms, prosciutto, and tomatoes; or pan-roasted rabbit with fennel and white wine. It takes Herculean restraint to choose from a selection that includes chocolate and nut tortes, fresh berry tarts, or liqueur-infused desserts.

2832 SE Belmont St. ✆ **503/238-1464.** www.genoarestaurant.com. Reservations required. Fixed-price 4-course dinner $56, 7-course dinner $68. AE, DC, DISC, MC, V. Mon–Sat 5:30–9:30pm (4-course dinner limited to 5:30 and 6pm seatings only).

EXPENSIVE

Castagna ✦✦ FRENCH/ITALIAN   Located on a rather nondescript stretch of Hawthorne Boulevard and much removed from the hustle and bustle of this boulevard's central commercial area, Castagna is a magnet for Portland foodies. Considering the less than stylish setting and minimalist (though thoroughly designed) interior, it's obvious that the food's the thing here. Dishes tend toward simple preparations that allow the freshness of the ingredients to express themselves. A friend swears the New York steak, served with a heaping mound of shoestring potatoes, is the best he's ever had; no wonder it's a house favorite here. However, less familiar entrees—such as salmon with fingerling potatoes and preserved Meyer lemon salsa or grilled rack of lamb with mint salsa verde and fava bean salad—flesh out the menu. In addition to the main dining room, there is a more casual and inexpensive cafe dining room serving much simpler fare.

1752 SE Hawthorne Blvd. ℂ **503/231-7373.** Reservations highly recommended. Main dishes $20–$28; cafe main courses $9–$18. AE, DC, DISC, MC, V. Tues–Thurs 6–10pm, Fri 6–10:30pm, Sat 5:30–10:30pm.

MODERATE

Assaggio ✦✦ RUSTIC ITALIAN   This trattoria in the Sellwood neighborhood focuses its attention on pastas and wines, and to that end, the menu lists 15 pastas and the wine list includes more than 100 wines, almost all of which are from Italy. The atmosphere of this tiny place is theatrical, with indirect lighting, dark walls, and the likes of Mario Lanza playing in the background. While pastas are the main attraction, this doesn't mean the flavors are not robust. Don't be surprised if after taking your first bite, you suddenly hear a Verdi aria. *Assaggio* means a sampling or a taste, and that is exactly what you get if you order salad, bruschetta, or pasta Assaggio style—a sampling of several dishes, all served family style. This is especially fun if you're here with a group.

7742 SE 13th Ave. ℂ **503/232-6151.** www.assaggiorestaurant.com. Reservations accepted (and recommended) only Tues–Thurs or for parties of 6 or more. Main courses $10–$16. MC, V. Tues–Thurs 5–9:30pm, Fri–Sat 5–10pm.

Bread and Ink Cafe ✦✦ NORTHWEST/MEDITERRANEAN/BREAKFAST/BRUNCH   This place has been around for years, and nothing about it suggests the year 2002. It's simple and stark, with linoleum floors, old chairs, pen-and-ink drawings on the walls, and large storefront windows that look out onto Hawthorne Boulevard. This very timelessness (plus friendly service and consistently good food prepared using fresh Northwest ingredients) has kept this place popular with the locals throughout the years. A recent spring menu included such interesting dishes as balsamic-roasted chicken with garlic, rosemary, and olive oil served with basil mashed potatoes and pork tenderloin in filo pastry with fennel, lavender, mustard, and roasted onions. Desserts are a mainstay for Bread and Ink's loyal patrons, and should not be missed. The Yiddish Sunday brunch is one of the most filling in the city.

3610 SE Hawthorne Blvd. ℂ **503/239-4756.** Reservations recommended. Main courses $7–$9.25 at lunch, $11.50–$18.50 at dinner. AE, DISC, MC, V. Mon–Fri 7am–3pm, Sat 8am–3pm, Sun 9am–2pm (brunch); Sun–Thurs 5–9pm, Fri–Sat 5–10pm.

Il Piatto ✦✦ ITALIAN   Il Piatto is a small neighborhood restaurant with a romantic atmosphere, and the antiqued walls, dried flowers, and overstuffed chairs in the lounge area provide a comfortable place for sipping a glass of good Italian wine while waiting for your table. Start your meal with oven-dried tomato pesto spread on crusty bread. The pastas, such as lasagna layered with

Late-Night Bites

If you're ravenous at midnight or later in Portland, you can try **Garbonzo's** or **Le Bistro Montage**, or, for something more upscale, **Southpark Seafood Grill** or **Brasserie Montmartre**. See the listings in the appropriate neighborhood sections throughout this chapter.

roasted eggplant and yams with a pine nut crust, are wonderful, as is the *risotto al pollo,* which is made with arborio rice cooked in red wine with grilled chicken, grilled pears, Gorgonzola cheese, and fresh basil. The marinated rabbit also gets rave reviews. Italian desserts such as tiramisu made with cornmeal cake are all made here in the kitchen by the pastry chef.

2348 SE Ankeny St. ✆ **503/236-4997.** www.ilpiatto.citysearch.com. Reservations highly recommended Thurs–Sat. Main courses $7–$13 at lunch, $11.50–$18.50 at dinner. DISC, MC, V. Tues–Fri 11:30am–2pm; Tues–Thurs and Sun 5:30–9:30pm, Fri–Sat 5:30–10:30pm (in summer, open 30 minutes later for dinner).

INEXPENSIVE

For Middle Eastern fare, there's a branch of Garbonzo's at 3433 SE Hawthorne Blvd. (✆ **503/239-6087**). See the complete review on p. 232.

Chez Grill ✯ SOUTHWEST   Brought to you by the owners of Portland's popular Chez José restaurants, Chez Grill leans a bit more toward nuevo Mexican or Southwestern flavors. Although the restaurant is at the western end of the Hawthorne district, it looks as if it could have been transported straight from Tucson or Santa Fe. Whatever you do, don't miss the grilled fish tacos; they're the best in town! Also, the grilled prawn enchilada is exquisite, although you only get one enchilada (with rice and beans). Be sure to start a meal with the rough-cut guacamole, and for a strangely sweet appetizer, try the unusual stuffed avocado.

2229 SE Hawthorne Blvd. ✆ 503/239-4002. www.chezgrill.citysearch.com. Main courses $6.25–$14. DISC, MC, V. Mon–Thurs 4–10pm, Fri–Sat 4–11pm, Sun 5–10pm (bar open later nightly).

Daydream Café ✯ *Finds* NATURAL FOODS   The Daydream Café is a casual little neighborhood joint frequented by locals for its superb baked polenta, a hearty and creamy affair loaded with vegetables and Asiago cheese. Other items on the menu are also a vegetarian's delight, such as the gnocchi with hazelnuts and Gorgonzola cream sauce (although nonveggie choices such as the salmon burger are pretty good, too). Everything here is as organic as possible, including the desserts, most of which are baked in-house.

1740 SE Hawthorne Blvd. ✆ 503/233-4244. Main courses $6–$9. DISC, MC, V. Mon–Sat 7am–5pm, Sun 8am–5pm.

Esparza's Tex-Mex Café ✯ *Finds* TEX-MEX   With red-eyed cow skulls on the walls and marionettes, model planes, and stuffed iguanas and armadillos hanging from the ceiling, the decor here can only be described as Tex-eclectic, an epithet that is equally appropriate when applied to the menu. Sure there are enchiladas and tamales and tacos, but they might be filled with ostrich, buffalo meat, or smoked salmon. Rest assured Esparza's also serves standard ingredients such as chicken and beef. Main courses come with some pretty good rice and beans, and if you want your meal hotter, they'll toss you a couple of jalapeño peppers. The *nopalitos* (fried cactus) are worth a try, and the margaritas just might be the best in Portland. While you're waiting for a seat (there's almost always a wait), check out the vintage tunes on the jukebox.

2725 SE Ankeny St. ✆ **503/234-7909.** Reservations not accepted. Main courses $7.25–$14.50. AE, DC, DISC, MC, V. Tues–Sat 11:30am–10pm (in summer Fri–Sat until 10:30pm).

Le Bistro Montage ✸ CAJUN/LATE-NIGHT DINING   A cacophony of voices and throbbing music punctuated by waiters bellowing out orders for oyster shooters slams you in the face as you step through the door of this "in" spot *under* the Morrison Bridge. They've definitely got the right idea here—Cajun dishes such as blackened catfish, jambalaya, frogs' legs, and alligator salad (and at beguilingly moderate prices). A lengthy wine menu and cocktail list promises you'll find something to your liking. If you hate noisy places, don't even think of eating here—otherwise, it's great fun.

301 SE Morrison St. ✆ **503/234-1324.** www.montage.citysearch.com. Reservations not accepted. Main courses $4.50–$16. No credit cards. Mon–Fri 11am–2pm; Sun–Thurs 6pm–2am, Fri–Sat 6pm–4am.

Nicholas's *Finds* MIDDLE EASTERN   This little hole-in-the-wall on an unattractive stretch of Grand Avenue is usually packed at mealtimes, and it's not the decor or ambience that pulls people in. The big draw is the great food and cheap prices. In spite of the heat from the pizza oven and the crowded conditions, the customers and wait staff still manage to be friendly. Our favorite dish is the *Manakish,* Mediterranean pizza with thyme, oregano, sesame seeds, olive oil, and lemony-flavored sumac. Also available are a creamy hummus, baba ghanoush, kabobs, and falafel and gyros sandwiches.

318 SE Grand Ave. (between Pine and Oak sts.). ✆ **503/235-5123.** Reservations not accepted. Main courses $4.25–$10.75. No credit cards. Mon–Sat 11am–9pm, Sun noon–9pm.

Old Wives' Tales ✸ *Kids* INTERNATIONAL/VEGETARIAN   Old Wives' Tales is a Portland countercultural institution. The menu is mostly vegetarian, with multiethnic dishes such as spanakopita and burritos and a smattering of chicken and seafood dishes. Breakfasts here are excellent and are served until 2pm daily. Old Wives' Tales's other claim to fame these days is as the city's best place to eat out with kids if you aren't into the fast-food scene. The restaurant has plenty of meal choices for children, and there's a big playroom where the kids can stay busy while you enjoy your meal.

1300 E Burnside St. ✆ **503/238-0470.** Reservations recommended for parties of 5 or more. Breakfasts $5–$7; lunch and dinner main courses $6–$13. AE, DC, DISC, MC, V. Sun–Thurs 8am–9pm, Fri–Sat 8am–10pm.

Zell's, An American Café ✸ *Finds* AMERICAN/BREAKFAST/BRUNCH   Once a pharmacy and now famed for delicious breakfasts such as German apple pancakes, real corned beef hash, and baked salmon benedict, Zell's has for years been one of Portland's best breakfast spots. There are also unusual breakfast specials such as paella and eggs and frittatas with prosciutto. Although breakfast is served until closing, you can also get sandwiches, soups, and salads at lunchtime. Service is friendly, and children are welcome.

1300 SE Morrison St. ✆ **503/239-0196.** Reservations not accepted. Breakfast and lunch $4.25–$9. AE, DISC, MC, V. Mon–Fri 7am–2pm, Sat 8am–2pm, Sun 8am–3pm.

7 Westmoreland & Sellwood

EXPENSIVE

Caprial's Bistro and Wine ✸✸ NORTHWEST   If you're a foodie, you're probably already familiar with celebrity chef Caprial Pence, who helped put the Northwest on the national restaurant map and has since gone on to write several cookbooks and host TV and radio food shows. That her eponymously named restaurant is a fairly casual place tucked away in a quiet residential neighborhood in Southeast Portland may come as a surprise. The menu changes monthly and is limited to four or five main dishes and about twice as many appetizers. Entrees combine perfectly cooked meats and seafood with vibrant sauces such as cherry barbecue sauce. Pork loin is always a good bet here, as are the seasonal seafood dishes. Desserts are usually rich without being overly sweet. There is also a wine bar offering a superb selection of wines at reasonable prices.

7015 SE Milwaukie Ave. ⓒ **503/236-6457.** Dinner reservations highly recommended. Main courses $7–$12 at lunch, $20–$26 at dinner. MC, V. Tues–Fri 11am–3pm, Sat 11:30am–3pm; Tues–Thurs 5–9pm, Fri–Sat 5–9:30pm.

MODERATE

Saburo's Sushi House ⭐⭐ JAPANESE   This tiny sushi restaurant is so enormously popular that there is almost always a line out the door, and as people linger over their sushi, frequently ordering "just one more," the line doesn't always move very fast. But when you finally do get a seat and your sushi arrives, you'll know it was worth the wait. The big slabs of fresh fish drape over the sides of the little cubes of rice, leaving no question about whether you get your money's worth here. Our favorite is the *sabu* roll with lots of fish, and the maguro tuna sushi, with generous slabs of tuna. Most Westerners don't care for the sea urchin, but you can try it if you're brave.

1667 SE Bybee Blvd. ⓒ **503/236-4237.** Reservations not accepted. Main courses $8–$16; sushi $2.50–$7. DISC, MC, V. Mon–Thurs 5–9:30pm, Fri 5–10:30pm, Sat 4:30–10pm, Sun 4:30–9pm.

INEXPENSIVE

El Palenque *Finds* SALVADORAN/MEXICAN   Though El Palenque also bills itself as a Mexican restaurant, the Salvadoran dishes are the real reason to come. If you've never had a *pupusa*, this is your chance; it's basically an extra thick corn tortilla with a meat or cheese filling, accompanied by spicy shredded cabbage. Instead of adding the filling after the tortilla is cooked, the filling goes in beforehand, so you end up with a sort of griddle-cooked turnover. Accompany your pupusa with some fried plantains and a glass of *horchata* (sweet and spicy rice drink) for a typical Salvadoran meal.

8324 SE 17th Ave. ⓒ **503/231-5140.** Main courses $5–$13. AE, MC, V. Daily 11:30am–9:30pm.

8 Coffee, Tea, Bakeries & Pastry Shops

CAFES

If you'd like to sample some cafes around Portland that serve not only the full range of coffee drinks, but also have atmosphere, we recommend the following:

Café Lena, 2239 SE Hawthorne Blvd. (ⓒ **503/238-7087**), located in the funky Hawthorne District, has occasional live music and tasty food but is best known for its poetry nights.

Coffee Time, 712 NW 21st Ave. (ⓒ **503/497-1090**), is a favorite Northwest neighborhood hangout with tables outside, and a variety of atmospheres inside—a cafe with big wooden booths, a lounge with cracked leather chairs and a fake fireplace, and a dark Victorian drawing room. Take your pick. Popular with the young retrohippie crowd.

Located out beyond Hawthorne Boulevard's main shopping district, **Common Grounds,** 4321 SE Hawthorne Blvd. (ⓒ **503/236-4835**), is a countercultural hangout where the magazine rack is filled with literary reviews, small press journals, and other lefty literature. The crowd of coffee drinkers tends to be tattooed and pierced.

Peet's Coffee ⭐, 508 SW Broadway (© **503/973-5540**), is a relative newcomer in Portland, and is notable not only for its great (and strong) coffee, but also for the fact that the space here is much larger than at any Peet's you'd find in Berkeley, California, where the chain originated.

Pied Cow, 3244 SE Belmont St. (© **503/230-4866**), in a Victorian house decorated in Bohemian chic, has a couch on which to lounge and an outdoor garden. Soups and snack-type foods are served, too.

Torrefazione Italia ⭐⭐, 838 NW 23rd Ave. (© **503/228-1255**), serves its classic brew in hand-painted Italian crockery, and has a good selection of pastries to go with your drink. Order a latte just to see what a wonderful job they do with the foam. Other locations are at 1403 NE Weidler (© **503/288-1608**) and 1140 NW Everett (© **503/224-9896**).

World Cup Coffee & Tea ⭐, 1740 NW Glisan St. (© **503/228-4152**), is a sophisticated little place on a tree-lined street in northwest Portland. Located away from any major shopping districts, this place has the feel of an undiscovered neighborhood gem.

BAKERIES & PASTRY SHOPS

Pearl Bakery ⭐⭐, 102 NW Ninth Ave. (© **503/827-0910**), in the heart of the Soho-like Pearl district, is famous for its breads and European-style pastries. The gleaming bakery cafe is a also good place for such sandwiches as roasted eggplant and tomato pesto on crusty bread.

The **Rimsky-Korsakoffee House** ⭐, 707 SE 12th Ave. (© **503/232-2640**), a classic old-style coffeehouse (complete with mismatched chairs), has been Portland's favorite dessert hangout for more than a decade. Live classical music and great desserts keep patrons loyal (the mocha fudge cake is small but deadly). There's no sign on the old house, but you'll know this is the place as soon as you open the door. Open after 7pm.

If you're in southeast earlier in the day and find yourself craving a pastry, search out **Rosie's Boulangerie** ⭐, 1406 SE Stark St. (© **503/232-4775**), which is tucked away in a residential neighborhood. This little bakery produces excellent French-style pastries and breads. Don't miss the ravioli dolce or the lavender cookies.

Say the words *Papa Haydn* to a Portlander and you'll see a blissful smile appear. What is it about this little bistro that sends locals into accolades of superlatives? Just desserts. **Papa Haydn West** ⭐⭐, 701 NW 23rd Ave. (© **503/ 228-7317**), is legendary for such desserts as lemon chiffon torte, raspberry gâteau, black velvet, and tiramisu. There's another location at 5829 SE Milwaukie Ave. (© **503/232-9440**) in Sellwood.

Located in Ladd's Addition, an old neighborhood full of big trees and Craftsman-style bungalows, **Palio Dessert House** ⭐, 1996 SE Ladd Ave. (© **503/232-9412**), is a very relaxed place with a timeless European quality. Hang out, play chess, or listen to music while you enjoy a slice of Key lime pie or banana bread. To get there, take Hawthorne Boulevard east to the corner of 12th and Hawthorne, then go diagonally down Ladd Avenue.

TEA

In the Heathman Hotel's lobby lounge, tea hostesses in lace aprons serve finger sandwiches, scones, pastries, and of course excellent tea. On chilly afternoons, a fire crackles in the fireplace. Tea at **The Heathman Hotel,** 1001 SW Broadway at Salmon Street (© **503/241-4100**), is a welcome respite from shopping or business meetings. Since it's mainly a winter holiday tradition here, tea isn't served during the summer season.

For a very different sort of tea experience, drop by the **Tao of Tea** ⋇⋇, 3430 SE Belmont St. (© **503/736-0198**), an exotic-looking place filled with bamboo and old tea-shipping crates that have been turned into tables. All kinds of exotic teas are available here by the cup, pot, or pound.

Tea gets a contemporary spin at the Pearl District's **The Tea Zone,** 510 NW 11th Ave. (© **503/221-2130**). Here you can get rare teas by the cup or by the ounce in the form of bulk, dry tea. One of the oddest offerings here is known as bubble tea, a milky iced tea with tapioca or coconut balls at the bottom of the glass. Sounds strange, but it's actually pretty good. Cookies, pastries, and smoothies are also available.

9 Quick Bites & Cheap Eats

If you're just looking for something quick, cheap, and good to eat, there are lots of great options around the city. Downtown, at **Good Dog/Bad Dog,** 708 SW Alder St. (© **503/222-3410**), you'll find handmade sausages. The bratwurst with kraut and onions is a good deal.

Designer pizzas topped with anything from roasted eggplant to wild mushrooms to Thai peanut sauce can be had at **Pizzicato Gourmet Pizza** ⋇. Find them downtown at 705 SW Alder St. (© **503/226-1007**); in Northwest at 505 NW 23rd Ave. (© **503/242-0023**); and in Southeast at 2811 E. Burnside (© **503/236-6045**).

In the Pearl District, there's **In Good Taste** ⋇ at 231 NW 11th Ave. (© **503/ 241-7960**), a cooking school and store that also serves a bistro lunch. Order such items as caramelized tomato tart and maple-spice pork loin sandwich at the counter, and take a seat anywhere you like.

Over in Southeast Portland, you can't miss the **Kitchen Table Café,** 400 SE 12th Ave. (© **503/230-6977**), in the yellow and purple building on the corner of SE Oak and SE 12th streets. This is a great place for homemade soups, salads, and sandwiches.

If you're in the mood for a picnic, **Elephant's Delicatessen,** 13 NW 23rd Place (© **503/224-3955**), is a good place to go for your supplies, including cheeses, sandwiches, wines, and yummy desserts. Head up to nearby Washington Park to enjoy it all.

If you find your energy flagging while shopping in the funky Hawthorne district, do as the French do and a grab a filling little crepe. **Chez Machin,** 3553 SE Hawthorne Blvd. (© **503/736-9381**), can whip up any of more than two dozen sweet or savory crepes for you. If you've got a sweet tooth, be sure to try the Nutella custard crepe. This place also operates a crepe cart on NW 23rd Avenue.

16

Exploring Portland

Most American cities boast about their museums and historic buildings, shopping, and restaurants; Portland, as always, is different. Ask a Portlander about the city's must-see attractions and you'll likely be directed not to the Portland Art Museum or any historic district, but to the Japanese Garden, the International Rose Test Garden, and the Portland Saturday Market.

This isn't to say that the art museum, which specializes in blockbuster exhibits, isn't worth visiting or that there are no historic buildings around (there's plenty of pioneer history on view in nearby Oregon City and Vancouver, Washington). It's just that Portland's gardens, thanks to the weather here, are some of the finest in the country. What's more, all the rainy weather seems to keep artists indoors creating beautiful art and crafts for much of the year, work that many artists sell at the Portland Saturday Market.

Gardening is a Portland obsession, and there are numerous world-class public gardens and parks within the city. Visiting all the city's gardens alone can take up 2 or 3 days of touring, so leave plenty of time in your schedule if you have a green thumb.

Once you've seen the big attractions, it's time to start learning why everyone loves living here so much. Portlanders for the most part are active types, who enjoy snow skiing on Mount Hood and hiking in the Columbia Gorge just as much as going to art museums. So no visit to Portland would be complete without venturing out into the Oregon countryside. Within 1½ hours you can be skiing on Mount Hood, walking beside the chilly waters of the Pacific, sampling pinot noir in wine country, or hiking beside a waterfall in the Columbia Gorge. However, for those who prefer urban activities, the museums and parks listed below should satisfy.

SUGGESTED ITINERARIES

If You Have 1 Day

Start your day in Washington Park at the **Rose Garden** (the roses are in bloom from June to September) and the **Japanese Garden** (lovely any time of year). After touring these two gardens, head downhill into downtown Portland. If you can make it to **Pioneer Courthouse Square** by noon, you can catch the day's weather prediction on the *Weather Machine* sculpture. From here, head over to the South Parks Blocks and visit the **Portland Art Museum,** which usually has some big show going on. Across the park from this museum is the **Oregon History Center,** where you can finish your day. If it's the weekend, be sure to squeeze in time to visit the **Saturday Market** (open both Sat–Sun; closed Jan–Feb), in the Skidmore Historic District.

If You Have 2 Days

Follow the outline above for your first day in town. On your second day, head up the **Columbia Gorge** to see its many beautiful waterfalls. If you get an early start, you can loop all the way around **Mount Hood** and maybe get in a little hiking from historic Timberline Lodge.

If You Have 3 Days

Follow the 2-day strategy as outlined above. On your third day, explore some of the historic blocks in the **Old Town** neighborhood (take in the Saturday Market if you haven't already), and perhaps visit the **Oregon Maritime Center and Museum.** Then walk through **Tom McCall Waterfront Park,** at the south end of which you can catch a historic trolley that runs to the posh suburb of **Lake Oswego.** Alternatively, you could take a scenic **cruise** on the river or do some paddling on a guided **sea kayak tour** on the Willamette.

If You Have 4 Days or More

Follow the 3-day strategy as outlined above. On Day 4, head over to the beach; it's only about 1½ hours away. You can stroll around artsy **Cannon Beach** and explore nearby **Ecola State Park.** Then make your way down the coast, stopping at other small state parks along the way. You can head back to Portland from **Tillamook.** If you have time, do part or all of the **Three Capes Scenic Loop** outside of Tillamook before returning to Portland.

On Day 5, venture north to **Mount St. Helens** for the day to see the devastation that was caused when this volcano erupted back in 1980. Along the way, you could stop and visit historic Fort Vancouver in **Vancouver, Washington.** If you're a wine fancier, skip Mount St. Helens and instead head west from Portland for some **wine tasting.**

1 Downtown Portland's Cultural District

Any visit to Portland should start at the corner of Southwest Broadway and Yamhill Street on **Pioneer Courthouse Square,** which is Portland's outdoor living room. The brick-paved square is an outdoor stage for everything from flower displays to concerts to protest rallies, but not too many years ago this beautiful square was nothing but a parking lot. The parking lot had been created by the controversial razing in 1951 of the Portland Hotel, an architectural gem of a Queen Anne–style château.

Today the square, with its tumbling waterfall fountain, and free-standing columns, is Portland's favorite gathering spot, especially at noon, when the **Weather Machine** *☆*, a mechanical sculpture, forecasts the weather for the 24 hours to come. Amid a fanfare of music and flashing lights, the Weather Machine sends up clouds of mist and then raises either a sun (clear weather), a dragon (stormy weather), or a blue heron (clouds and drizzle).

Keep your eyes on the square's brick pavement, too. Every brick contains a name (or names) or statement, and some are rather curious (see "Walking Tour 2" in chapter 17, "Strolling Around Portland"). Also on the square, you'll find the **Portland Oregon Visitor Association Information Center,** a Starbucks espresso bar, and Powell's Travel Store. Unfortunately, you'll also find plenty of street kids hanging out here all hours of the day and night, so don't be surprised if kids ask you for spare change.

Also not to be missed in this neighborhood are **Portlandia** *☆☆* and the **Portland Building,** 1120 SW Fifth Ave. Symbol of the city, *Portlandia* is the second-largest hammered bronze statue in the country, second only to the Statue of Liberty. The massive kneeling figure holds a trident in one hand and reaches toward the street with the other. This classically designed figure perches incongruously above the entrance to the controversial Portland Building, considered to be the first postmodern structure in the country. Today anyone familiar with the bizarre constructions of Los Angeles architect Frank Gehry would find it difficult to understand how such an innocuous and attractive building could have ever raised such a fuss, but it did just that in the early '80s.

Oregon History Center ✯   In the middle of the 19th century, the Oregon Territory was a land of promise and plenty. Thousands of hardy individuals set out along the Oregon Trail, crossing a vast and rugged country to reach the fertile valleys of this region. Others came by ship around the Horn. Today the state of Oregon is still luring immigrants, and those who wish to learn about the people who discovered Oregon before them should visit this well-designed museum.

Oregon history from before the arrival of the first Europeans to well into the 20th century is chronicled in fascinating educational exhibits. The displays incorporate Native American artifacts, a covered wagon, nautical and surveying instruments, and contemporary objects such as snow skis, dolls, and bicycles. Museum docents, with roots stretching back to the days of the Oregon Trail, are often on hand to answer questions. There's also a research library that includes many journals from early pioneers. You can't miss this complex—look for the eight-story-high trompe l'oeil mural stretching across the front.

1200 SW Park Ave. ✆ 503/222-1741. www.ohs.org. Admission $6 adults and seniors, $3 students, $1.50 children 6–12, children under 6 free, seniors free on Thurs. Tues–Sat 10am–5pm (Thurs until 8pm), Sun noon–5pm. Bus: 6. MAX: Library Station. Portland Streetcar: Art Museum (northbound); 11th Ave. & Jefferson St. (southbound).

Portland Art Museum ✯✯   While this relatively small art museum has a respectable collection of European, Asian, and American art, the museum has in recent years been positioning itself as the Northwest stop for touring blockbuster exhibits. Scheduled June 1 to September 22, 2002, is "Splendors of Imperial Japan (Arts of the Meiji Period from the Khalili Collection);" and, from August 17 to December 1, 2002, the museum will be showing "Grandma Moses in the 21st Century." An expansion a couple of years ago added several new galleries and a small sculpture court to the museum. The galleries of Native American art and Northwest art are now the museum's most impressive displays. October through May, on Wednesday nights, the Museum After Hours program presents live music. The adjacent **Northwest Film Center** is affiliated with the Art Museum and shows an eclectic mix of films.

1219 SW Park Ave. ✆ 503/226-2811. www.portlandartmuseum.org. Admission $7.50 adults, $6 seniors and students, $4 ages 5–18, children under 5 free. Tues–Sat 10am–5pm (Oct–May Wed 10am–8pm), Sun noon–5pm; first Thurs of each month until 8pm. Bus: 6. MAX: Library Station. Portland Streetcar: Art Museum (northbound); 11th Ave. & Jefferson St. (southbound).

2 Skidmore Historic District & the Willamette River Waterfront

If Pioneer Courthouse Square is the city's living room, **Tom McCall Waterfront Park** ✯, along the Willamette River, is the city's party room and backyard play area. There are acres of lawns, shade trees, sculptures, and fountains, and the paved path through the park is popular with in-line skaters and joggers. This park also serves as the site of numerous festivals each summer. Also in the park

Portland Attractions

American Advertising Museum **14**

CM2—Children's Museum
Second Generation **6**

International Rose Test Garden **1**

Japanese Garden **2**

Mill Ends Park **18**

The Old Church **7**

Oregon History Center **9**

Oregon Maritime Center
and Museum **17**

Oregon Museum of Science
& Industry (OMSI) **19**

Oregon Zoo **4**

Pioneer Courthouse Square **11**

Portland Art Museum **8**

Portland Classical Chinese Garden **15**

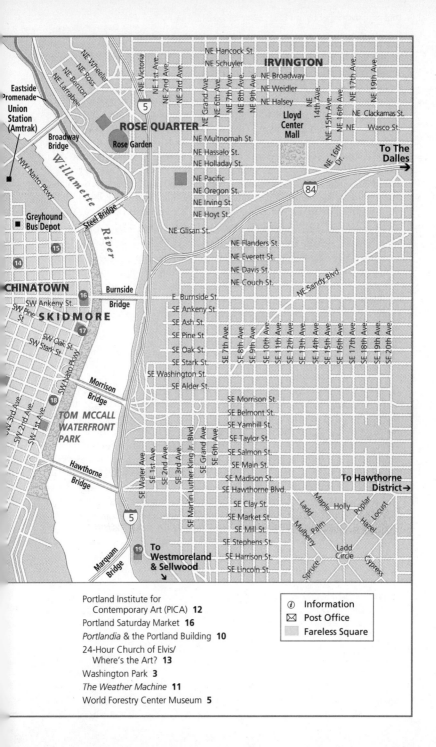

Portland Institute for
Contemporary Art (PICA) **12**
Portland Saturday Market **16**
Portlandia & the Portland Building **10**
24-Hour Church of Elvis/
Where's the Art? **13**
Washington Park **3**
The Weather Machine **11**
World Forestry Center Museum **5**

ⓘ Information
⊠ Post Office
Fareless Square

are the Waterfront Story Garden, dedicated to storytellers, and the Japanese-American Historical Plaza, dedicated to Japanese Americans who were sent to internment camps during World War II.

Just north of this plaza, a pedestrian walkway crosses the Steel Bridge to the east side of the Willamette River and the new **Eastside Promenade,** which stretches for about 1.5 miles along the east bank of the river. Although this paved multiuse path gets a lot of traffic noise from the adjacent freeway, it offers great views of the Portland skyline. Along the route there are small parks and gardens, interesting sculptures, and benches for sitting and soaking up the view. The highlight of this path is a section that floats right on the river and is attached to pilings in much the same way that a floating dock is constructed. You can access the Eastside Promenade by way of the pedestrian pathway on the Steel Bridge. This bridge is at the north end of Waterfront Park.

Oregon Maritime Center and Museum   Inside this museum you'll find models of ships that once plied the Columbia and Willamette. Also on display are early navigation instruments, artifacts from the battleship *Oregon,* old ship hardware, and other maritime memorabilia. The historic steam-powered stern-wheeler *Portland,* moored across Waterfront Park from the museum, is also open to the public. Inside this old steam-powered paddle-wheel tugboat there are more displays about maritime history, and docents are on hand to answer questions about the boat itself.

113 SW Naito Pkwy. ✆ **503/224-7724.** Admission $4 adults, $3 senior citizens, $2 youths 8 and older, free under 8. Fri–Sun 11am–4pm (sometimes also open Wed–Thurs in summer). Bus: 12, 19, 20. MAX: Skidmore Fountain Station.

Oregon Museum of Science and Industry (OMSI) ✮ *Kids*   Located on the east bank of the Willamette River across from the south end of Waterfront Park, this modern science museum has six huge halls, and both kids and adults find the exhibits fun and fascinating. This is a hands-on museum, and everyone is urged to get involved with displays, from a discovery space for toddlers to physics and chemistry labs for older children. Simulated earthquakes and tornadoes are perennial favorites. There's plenty of pure entertainment at an **OMNI-MAX theater** and the **Murdock Sky Theater,** which features laser-light shows and astronomy presentations. The USS *Blueback* submarine (used in the film *The Hunt for Red October*) is docked here, and tours are given daily.

Between mid-June and late September, **Samtrak** (✆ **503/653-2380**), a small open-air train, runs between OMSI and Oaks Park Amusement Center. OMSI is also the departure point for several different boat cruises up and down the Willamette River.

1945 SE Water Ave. ✆ **800/955-6674** or 503/797-4000. www.omsi.edu. Museum or OMNIMAX $7 adults, $5 seniors and children 4–13; $4 submarine tours, $4 planetarium shows, laser-light shows $4 matinee, $7 evening; discounted combination tickets available. Thurs 2pm until closing all tickets are 2-for-1. Mid-June to Labor Day daily 9:30am–7pm; Labor Day to Mid-June Tues–Sun 9:30am–5:30pm. Closed Dec 25. Bus: 63.

Portland Saturday Market ✮✮   The Portland Saturday Market (actually held on both Sat–Sun) is arguably the city's single most important and best-loved event. For years the Northwest has attracted artists and craftspeople, and every Saturday and Sunday nearly 300 of them can be found selling their creations here. In addition to the dozens of crafts stalls, you'll find ethnic and unusual foods and lots of free entertainment. This is one of the best places in

Portland to shop for one-of-a-kind gifts. The atmosphere is always cheerful and the crowds colorful. Located at the heart of the Skidmore District, Portland Saturday Market makes an excellent starting or finishing point for a walk around Portland's downtown historic neighborhood. Don't miss this unique market. On Sunday, on-street parking is free.

Underneath the west end of the Burnside Bridge between SW First Ave. and SW Naito Pkwy. (✆) **503/ 222-6072.** www.portlandsaturdaymarket.com. Free admission. First weekend in Mar to Christmas Eve, Sat 10am–5pm and Sun 11am–4:30pm. Bus: 12, 19, 20. MAX: Skidmore Fountain Station.

3 Washington Park & Portland's West Hills

Portland is justly proud of its green spaces, and foremost among them are **Washington Park** and **Forest Park.**

Within Washington Park, you'll find the Japanese Garden and International Rose Test Garden, which are adjacent to one another on the more developed east side of the park (see the listings below). On the west side of the park (farther from the city center), you'll find not only the Hoyt Arboretum but also the Oregon Zoo, World Forestry Center, and CM2—Children's Museum 2nd Generation.

The 175-acre **Hoyt Arboretum** ✿ (✆ **503/228-8733**), which is planted with 800 species of trees and shrubs from temperate regions around the world. The arboretum has 10 miles of hiking trails and is a great place for a quick hike. Between April and October, there are free 1-hour guided tours of the arboretum on Saturdays and Sundays at 2pm. At the south end of the arboretum, adjacent to the World Forestry Center and the Oregon Zoo, is the **Vietnam Veterans Living Memorial.** At the Visitor Center, 4000 SW Fairview Blvd. (open daily 9am–3pm), you can pick up maps and guides to the arboretum. The arboretum can be reached either from the Oregon Zoo/World Forestry Center/CM2— Children's Museum 2nd Generation area or by following the arboretum signs from West Burnside Street.

To the north of Hoyt Arboretum is **Forest Park** ✿✿ (✆ **503/823-PLAY**), which, with nearly 5,000 acres of forest, is the largest forested city park in the United States. Within the park, there are more than 65 miles of trails and old fire roads for hiking, jogging, and mountain biking. More than 100 species of birds call this forest home, making the park a great spot for some urban bird watching. Along the forest trails, you can see huge old trees and find quiet picnic spots tucked away in the woods. One of the most convenient park access points is at the top of NW Thurman Street (just keep heading uphill until the road dead-ends). However, if you park at the Hoyt Arboretum Visitor Center (see above) or the Audubon Society (see below), can pick up a map of Forest Park and head out from either of these locations.

Adjacent to Forest Park, you'll also find the **Portland Audubon Society,** 5151 NW Cornell Rd. (✆ **503/292-9453**), which has a couple of miles of hiking trails on its forested property. In keeping with its mission to promote enjoyment, understanding, and protection of the natural world, these nature trails are open to the public. You can also visit the Nature Center or Wildlife Care Center here. To find this facility from downtown Portland, first drive to NW 23rd Avenue, and then head uphill on NW Lovejoy Street, which becomes NW Cornell Road. (*Warning:* Car break-ins are commonplace at the parking area just down the road from the Audubon Society, so don't leave anything of value in your car.)

✐ Great Photo Ops

If you've seen a photo of Portland with conical snow-covered Mount Hood looming in the background and you want to snap a similar photo while you're in town, there are several places to try. Most popular are probably the terraces of the International Rose Test Garden and from behind the pavilion at the Japanese Garden. Another great view can be had from the grounds of the Pittock Mansion. All three of these places are described in detail elsewhere in this chapter.

One other view is located atop Council Crest, a hilltop park in Portland's West Hills. To reach this park, take the Sylvan exit off U.S. 26 west of downtown Portland, turn south and then east (left) on Humphrey Boulevard, and then follow the signs. Alternatively, you can follow SW Broadway south out of downtown Portland and follow the signs. This road winds through attractive hillside neighborhoods for a ways before reaching Council Crest.

By car, the easiest route to the Washington Park attractions from downtown Portland is to take SW Jefferson Street west, turn right onto SW 18th Avenue, left on SW Salmon Street, right on SW King Street, and then left onto SW Park Place. Although this sounds confusing, you'll find most of the route well marked with SCENIC DRIVE signs. Alternatively, you can drive west on West Burnside Street and watch for signs to the arboretum, or take the zoo exit off U.S. 26. All of these attractions can also be reached via Bus 63. You can also take the MAX line to the Washington Park Station, which is adjacent to the Oregon Zoo, World Forestry Center, CM2—Children's Museum 2nd Generation, and Hoyt Arboretum. From here, it is possible (in the summer months) to take a bus shuttle to the Japanese Garden and International Rose Test Garden. There's also a miniature train that runs from the zoo to a station near the two public gardens. However, to ride this train, you must first pay zoo admission.

International Rose Test Garden 🌟🌟   Covering 4½ acres of hillside in the West Hills above downtown Portland, these are among the largest and oldest rose test gardens in the United States and are the only city-maintained test gardens to bestow awards on each year's best roses. The gardens were established in 1917 by the American Rose Society and are used as a testing ground for new varieties of roses. Though you will likely see some familiar roses in the Gold Medal Garden, most of the 400 varieties on display here are new hybrids being tested before marketing. Among the roses in bloom from late spring to early winter, you'll find a separate garden of miniature roses. There's also a Shakespeare Garden that includes flowers mentioned in the Bard's works. After seeing these acres of roses, you'll understand why Portland is known as the City of Roses and why the Rose Festival in June is the city's biggest annual celebration. The small Rose Garden Store (✆ **503/227-7033**), is packed with rose-inspired products.

400 SW Kingston Ave., Washington Park. ✆ **503/823-3636**. Free admission (donations accepted). Daily dawn–dusk. Bus: 63.

Japanese Garden 🌟🌟🌟   Considered the finest example of a Japanese garden in North America, Portland's Japanese Garden is one of the city's most popular attractions. Don't miss it. Not only are there five different styles of Japanese gardens scattered over 5½ acres, but there's also a view of volcanic Mount Hood, which has a strong resemblance to Mount Fuji.

While Japanese gardens are traditionally not designed with colorful floral displays in mind, this garden definitely has its seasonal highlights. In early spring there are the cherry trees, in midspring there are the azaleas, in late spring a huge wisteria bursts into bloom, and in early summer, huge Japanese irises color the banks of a pond. Among the gardens, there's a beautiful and very realistic waterfall.

This is a very tranquil spot and is even more peaceful on rainy days when the crowds stay away, so don't pass up a visit just because it's raining. Also, on the third Saturday of each of the summer months, there's a demonstration of the Japanese tea ceremony in the garden's tea house. There are also many special events held here throughout the year (ikebana, bonsai, Japanese-inspired art).

611 Kingston Ave. (in Washington Park). (𝄢 503/223-1321. www.japanesegarden.com. Admission $6 adults, $4 seniors, $3.50 students, children under 6 free. Apr 1–Sept 30 Tues–Sun 10am–7pm, Mon noon–7pm; Oct 1–Mar 31 Tues–Sun 10am–4pm, Mon noon–4pm. Closed Thanksgiving, Christmas, and New Year's Day. Bus: 63. MAX: Washington Park Station (then, in summer months, take the shuttle bus or the Zoo Train).

Oregon Zoo 𝄢 *(Kids)*   Perhaps best known for its elephants, the Oregon Zoo has the largest breeding herd of elephants in captivity. However, in recent years, the zoo has been continually adding new exhibits and has been branching out beyond the world of pachyderms. The Africa exhibit, which includes a very life-like rain forest and a savanna populated by zebras, rhinos, giraffes, hippos, and other animals, is one of the most true-to-life habitats you'll ever see at a zoo. Equally impressive is the Alaskan tundra exhibit, with grizzly bears, wolves, and musk oxen. The Cascade Crest exhibit includes mountain goat habitat, and in the Steller Cove exhibit, you can watch the antics of Steller sea lions and sea otters. Also, don't miss the bat house. At press time, there were plans to open a new Amazon Flooded Forest exhibit in late 2001.

In the summer, there are **outdoor concerts** in the zoo's amphitheater; admission prices vary.

4001 SW Canyon Rd., Washington Park. (𝄢 503/226-1561. www.oregonzoo.org. Admission $7.50 adults, $6 seniors, $4.50 children ages 3–11, free under 2; free second Tues of each month from 1pm to closing. Apr 1–Sept 30 daily 9am–6pm; Oct 1–Mar 31 daily 9am–4pm. Bus: 63. MAX: Washington Park Station.

Pittock Mansion 𝄢   At nearly the highest point in the West Hills, 1,000 feet above sea level, stands the most impressive mansion in Portland. Once slated to be torn down to make way for new housing, this grand château, built by the founder of Portland's *Oregonian* newspaper, is fully restored and open to the public. Built in 1914 in a French Renaissance style, the mansion featured many innovations, including a built-in vacuum system and amazing multiple shower heads in the baths. Today it's furnished with 18th- and 19th-century antiques, much as it might have been at the time the Pittocks occupied the building. With an expansive view over the city to the Cascade Range, the lawns surrounding the

---

All Aboard!

The **Washington Park and Zoo Railway** travels between the zoo and the International Rose Test and Japanese gardens. Tickets for the miniature railway are $2.75 for adults, $2 for seniors and children 3 to 11.

mansion are a great spot for a picnic. You can also access Forest Park's Wildwood Trail from here.

3229 NW Pittock Dr. ⓒ **503/823-3624**. Admission $5.50 adults, $5 seniors, $3 ages 6–18. Daily noon–4pm. Closed 3 days in late Nov, most major holidays, and the month of Jan.

World Forestry Center Museum ⭐   Although Oregon depends less and less on the timber industry with each passing year, the World Forestry Center Museum is still busy educating visitors about the importance of our forest resources. Step inside the huge wooden main hall and you come face to bark with a very large and very lifelike tree. Press a button at its base and it tells you the story of how trees live and grow. In other rooms you can see exhibits on forests of the world, old-growth trees, a petrified wood exhibit, and a rain forest exhibit developed by the Smithsonian Institution. There are also interesting temporary exhibits staged here throughout the year, from photographic exhibits to displays of the woodworker's art.

4033 SW Canyon Rd. ⓒ **503/228-1367**. www.worldforestry.org. Admission $4.50 adults, $3.50 seniors and children under 6. Daily 10am–5pm (9am–5pm from Memorial Day to Labor Day). Closed Christmas Day. Bus: 63. MAX: Washington Park Station.

4 Other In-Town Attractions

American Advertising Museum ⭐   Like it or not, advertising is here to stay. In this small museum, you'll learn about its history, from the 1700s to the present, through displays on historic advertisements, celebrities, and jingles. Tapes of old TV commercials provide a popular trip down memory lane. Lots of 20th-century advertising icons are on display, and the most influential ads of the past century are chronicled in detail. Definitely a fun and unusual little museum.

211 NW Fifth Ave. ⓒ **503/226-0000**. www.admuseum.org. Admission $5 adults, $4 seniors and children ages 4–12. Wed–Sun noon–5pm.

Portland Institute for Contemporary Art (PICA)   The Portland Institute for Contemporary Art (PICA) was created as a resource for exploring and supporting experimental art and new music in Portland. Here, at the Institute's gallery facility, PICA presents visual art exhibitions focusing on contemporary trends in the regional, national, and international art scene. These exhibitions are always innovative and thought-provoking. At various venues around the city, PICA hosts performances by both well-known and less-established performance artists and musicians.

219 NW 12th Ave. ⓒ **503/242-1419**. www.pica.org. Admission $3 (free on first Thurs noon–9pm. Wed–Sun noon–6pm. Bus: 17 or 20. Portland Streetcar: 10th Ave. and Couch St. (northbound); 11th Ave. and Couch St. (southbound).

24-Hour Church of Elvis/Where's the Art? *Finds*   This is Portland's longtime temple of kitsch, the city's most bizarre attraction. Coin-operated art, a video psychic, cheap (though not legal) weddings, and other absurd assemblages, interactive displays, and kitschy contraptions (such as the Vend-O-Matic Mystery Machine with whirling dolls' heads) cram this second-floor oddity. As celebrity-spokes-model/minister S. G. Pierce says, "the tour *is* the art form." If you pass the customer test, you can even buy a Church of Elvis T-shirt. Great fun if you're a fan of Elvis, tabloids, or the unusual; and if you've seen Elvis anytime in the past decade, a visit is absolutely mandatory.

720 SW Ankeny St. ⓒ **503/226-3671**. www.churchofelvis.com. Free admission (with $1 purchase at gift shop). Flexible hours; almost always open on weekends. Any downtown bus

5 Portland's Other Public Gardens

For Portland's two best-loved public gardens, the **International Rose Test Garden** and the **Japanese Garden,** see section 3, "Washington Park & Portland's West Hills," earlier in this chapter.

If roses are your passion, you'll also want to check out the **Peninsula Park Rose Garden** at the corner of N. Portland Boulevard and N. Albina Avenue (take the Portland Boulevard exit off I-5 and go 2 blocks east), which has even more rose bushes than the International Rose Test Garden.

The Berry Botanic Garden   Originally founded as a private garden, the Berry Botanic Garden is now one of Portland's favorite public gardens. Among the highlights is a large, forestlike collection of mature rhododendron shrubs. There's also a native plant trail, a fern garden, and rock gardens with unusual plants. The garden is open by reservation only.

11505 SW Summerville Ave. © **503/636-4112.** www.berrybot.org. Adults $5. Open daylight hours by appointment. Bus: 35 or 36.

Crystal Springs Rhododendron Garden ⚐   Nowhere do rhododendrons do better than in the cool, rainy Northwest, and nowhere in Portland is there a more impressive planting of rhodies than at Crystal Springs. Eight months out of the year this is a tranquil garden, with a waterfall, a lake, and ducks to feed. But when the rhododendrons and azaleas bloom from March to June, it becomes a spectacular mass of blazing color. The Rhododendron Show and Plant Sale is held here on Mother's Day weekend.

SE 28th Ave. (1 block north of SE Woodstock Blvd.). © **503/771-8386** or 503/777-1734. Admission $3 from Mar 1 to Labor Day Thurs–Mon 10am–6pm; free at other times. Open year-round daily dawn–dusk. Bus: 19.

Elk Rock Garden of the Bishop's Close ⚐   Set on a steep hillside above the Willamette River between Portland and Lake Oswego, this was once a private garden but was donated to the local Episcopal bishop of Oregon on the condition that it be opened to the public. The mature gardens are at their best through the spring and early summer. There's also an excellent view of Mount Hood from the grounds.

11800 SW Military Lane. © **503/636-5613.** Free admission. Daily 8am–5pm. Bus: 35 or 36.

The Grotto—National Sanctuary of Our Sorrowful Mother   Although this forested 62-acre sanctuary is first and foremost a Catholic religious shrine (with a marble replica of Michelangelo's Pietà set in a shallow rock cave at the foot of a cliff), the gardens are quite beautiful. The gardens are at their best in the early summer and during the Christmas season when the grounds are decorated with thousands of lights and a choral festival is held. An elevator ride to the top of the bluff offers panoramic views of the Cascade Range, the Columbia River, and Mount St. Helens. There are also a couple of chapels on the grounds, a gift shop, and a coffee shop. The Grotto is open to visitors of all faiths.

NE 85th Ave. and Sandy Blvd. © **503/254-7371.** www.thegrotto.org. Free admission (except during Christmas Festival of Lights: $6 adults, $3 ages 3–12, free for children 2 and under); elevator $2. Open daily summer 9am–7:30pm, winter 9am–4pm, spring 9am–5:30pm. Closed Christmas and Thanksgiving. Bus: 12.

Portland Classical Chinese Garden ⚐⚐   This classically styled Chinese garden takes up an entire city block and is the largest of its type outside of China. The gardens, located in Portland's Chinatown, are surrounded by walls that serve to separate the urban 21st century from the timeless Chinese

The World's Smallest Park

Don't blink as you cross the median strip on Naito Parkway at the corner of Southwest Taylor Street, or you might just walk right past **Mill Ends Park,** the smallest public park in the world.

Covering a whopping 452.16 square inches of land, this park was the whimsical creation of local journalist Dick Fagen. After a telephone pole was removed from the middle of Naito Parkway (then known as Front Avenue), Fagen dubbed the phone pole hole Mill Ends Park (Mill Ends, a lumber mill term, was the name of Fagen's newspaper column). The columnist, whose office looked down on the hole in the middle of Front Avenue, peopled the imaginary park with leprechauns and would often write of the park's goings-on in his column. On St. Patrick's Day 1976, it was officially designated a Portland city park. Rumor has it that despite its diminutive size, the park has been the site of several weddings (although the parks department has never issued a wedding permit for it).

landscape that lies within. That landscape is designed to evoke the wild mountains of China and to create a tranquil oasis within an urban setting. The gardens are centered around a small pond, at one end of which stands a rock wall meant to conjure up the sort of images often seen in Chinese scroll paintings. Numerous pavilions, a small bridge, and a winding pathway provide ever-changing views of the gardens. With its many paved paths and small viewing pavilions, this garden has a completely different feel than the Japanese Garden. Try to visit as soon as the gardens open in the morning; when the crowds descend and the guided tours start circulating—well, so much for tranquility. Be sure to stop and have a cup of tea and maybe a snack in the garden's tea room.

NW Everett St. and NW Third Ave. ✆ 503/228-8131. Admission $6 adults, $5 seniors, $5 college students and ages 6–18, children 5 and under free. Apr 1–Oct 31 daily 9am–6pm; Nov 1–Mar 31 daily 10am–5pm.

6 Outlying Historical Attractions

VANCOUVER, WASHINGTON

The city of Vancouver, Washington, which is located directly across the Columbia River from Portland (a 20-min. drive north on I-5 from downtown), was one of the first settlements in the Northwest and consequently has a long pioneer and military history. After the British, in the guise of the Hudson's Bay Company, gave up Fort Vancouver, it became the site of the Vancouver Barracks U.S. military post. Stately homes were built for the officers of the post, and these buildings and their attractive surroundings are now preserved as part of the **Vancouver National Historic Reserve** ⊛. You'll find the tree-shaded row of 21 homes, as well as Fort Vancouver, in the 1-square-mile Central Park, which is located just east of I-5 (take the East Mill Plain Boulevard exit just after you cross the bridge into Washington).

Start a visit to Officer's Row at the **O. O. Howard House,** 750 Anderson St. (✆ **360/992-1849**), a restored Victorian mansion that was once an NCO club for the military post and now serves as the information center for the national historic reserve.

After learning a bit about the history of this area, you can stroll the grounds admiring the well-kept homes. Two of the old homes here are open to the public. The **Grant House,** 1101 Officers' Row, was the first commanding officer's quarters and is named for President Ulysses S. Grant, who was stationed here as quartermaster in the 1850s. Today this building houses the **Grant House Folk Art Center** (© **360/694-5252**), which is open Monday through Saturday from 11am to 3pm, and Sunday from 10am to 2pm (admission is free). Here in the Grant House, you'll also find the **Grant House Restaurant** (© **360/696-1727**), which serves fresh Northwest cuisine and is a good place to stop for lunch.

Further along Officers' Row, you'll find the **George C. Marshall House,** 1301 Officers' Row (© **360/693-3103**), a Victorian-style building that replaced the Grant House as the commanding officer's quarters. This home is furnished much the way it might have looked in the late 1800s when it was built (admission is free; open Mon–Fri 9am–5pm and sometimes, if no wedding party has rented the building, Sat–Sun 11am–6pm).

Fort Vancouver National Historic Site ⋆   It was here in Vancouver, at the Hudson's Bay Company (HBC) Fort Vancouver, that much of the Northwest's important early pioneer history unfolded. The HBC, a British company, came to the Northwest in search of furs, and for most of the first half of the 19th century it was the only authority in this remote region. Fur trappers, mountain men, missionaries, explorers, and settlers all made Fort Vancouver their first stop in Oregon country. Today Fort Vancouver houses several reconstructed buildings that are furnished as they might have been in the middle of the 19th century. In summer, there are costumed interpreters on hand giving demonstrations of activities that once took place here at the fort. Outside the fort is a large formal garden.

1501 E. Evergreen Blvd. © **360/696-7655**. www.nps.gov/fova. Admission $2. Daily 9am–5pm (until 4pm in winter).

Pearson Air Museum   A very different piece of history is preserved at this small air museum on the far side of Fort Vancouver from Officers' Row. This airfield was established in 1905, making it the oldest operating airfield in the United States. Dozens of vintage aircraft, including several World War I–era biplanes are on display. In August, the museum has a biplane fly-in.

1115 E. Fifth St. © **360/694-7026**. www.pearsonairmuseum.org. Admission $5 adults, $4 seniors, $3 ages 13–18, $2 ages 6–12, children under 6 free. Tues–Sun 10am–5pm.

OREGON CITY

When the first white settlers began crossing the Oregon Trail in the early 1840s, their destination was Oregon City and the fertile Willamette Valley. At the time Portland had yet to be founded, and Oregon City, set beside powerful Willamette Falls, was the largest town in Oregon. However, with the development of Portland and the shifting of the capital to Salem, Oregon City began to lose its importance. Today this is primarily an industrial town, though one steeped in Oregon history and well worth a visit. To get here from downtown Portland, drive south on SW First Avenue and continue on SW Macadam Avenue, which is Ore. 43. Follow this road for roughly 12 miles to reach Oregon City (it should take 30–45 min.).

To get to Oregon City from Portland, you can take I-5 south to I-205 east or you can head south from downtown Portland on SW Riverside Drive and drive through the wealthy suburbs of Lake Oswego and West Linn. Once in Oregon City, your first stop should be just south of town at the **Willamette Falls**

overlook ⑂ on Ore. 99E. Though the falls have been much changed by industry over the years, they are still an impressive sight.

Oregon City is divided into upper and lower sections by a steep bluff, with a free municipal elevator connecting the two halves of the city and providing a great view from its observation area at the top of the bluff. You'll find the 100-foot-tall elevator at the corner of Seventh Street and Railroad Avenue. It's in the upper section of town that you will find the town's many historic homes, including the McLoughlin House (listed below) and the **Ermatinger House,** Sixth and John Adams streets (⑆ **503/650-1851** or 503/557-9199), which is Oregon City's oldest house and is open to the public Friday through Sunday from 1pm to 4pm. Admission is $3 for adults.

End of the Oregon Trail Interpretive Center ⑂   With its three Paul Bunyan–size wagons parked in the middle of Abernethy Green (the official end of the Oregon Trail), this interpretive center is impossible to miss. Inside the first of the giant wagons, you'll find an exhibit hall, hands-on area, and gift shop. After looking around this first wagon, you'll then be led through the next one by costumed interpreters who explain the difficulties of provisioning for the overland trek. The third wagon houses a multimedia presentation based on three Oregon Trail diaries.

1726 Washington St. ⑆ **503/657-9336.** www.endoftheoregontrail.org. Admission $6.50 adults, $5.50 seniors, $4 ages 5–12, children under 5 free. Mon–Sat 9am–5pm, Sun 10am–5pm. Tour hours vary with day and season.

McLoughlin House   Oregon City's most famous citizen, retired Hudson's Bay Company chief factor, John McLoughlin, helped found this mill town on the banks of the Willamette River in 1829. By the 1840s, immigrants were pouring into Oregon, and McLoughlin provided food, seeds, and tools to many. Upon retirement in 1846, McLoughlin moved to Oregon City, where he built what was at that time the most luxurious home in Oregon. Today McLoughlin's house is a National Historic Site and is furnished as it would have been in McLoughlin's days. Many of the pieces on display are original to the house.

713 Center St. ⑆ **503/656-5146.** www.mcloughlinhouse.org. Admission $4 adults, $3 seniors, and $2 children ages 6–17, free under 6. Tues–Sat 10am–4pm, Sun 1–4pm. Closed Jan and major holidays.

Museum of the Oregon Territory   This small museum houses collections of historic memorabilia and old photos from this area. There's the obligatory covered wagon, as well as a display of Native American petroglyphs. Your admission ticket to this museum will also get you into the **Stevens Crawford House,** 603 Sixth St., a foursquare-style home that is furnished with late-19th-century antiques and looks as if the family just stepped out.

211 Tumwater Dr. ⑆ **503/655-5574.** Admission $4 adults, $3 seniors, $2 ages 6–18. Mon–Fri 10am–5pm, Sat–Sun 1–5pm. Closed Thanksgiving, Christmas, New Years Day.

AURORA

Another interesting chapter in Oregon pioneer history is preserved in the town of Aurora, which was founded in 1855 as a Christian communal society. Similar in many ways to other more famous communal experiments as the Amana Colony and the Shaker communities, the Aurora Colony lasted slightly more than 20 years.

Today Aurora is a National Historic District, and the large old homes of the community's founders have been restored. Many of the old commercial buildings now house antiques stores, which are the main reason most people visit the town. You can learn about Aurora's history at the **Old Aurora Colony Museum,** Second and Liberty streets (© **503/678-5754**). Between April and October, the museum is open Tuesday through Saturday from 10am to 4pm and on Sunday from noon to 4pm; other months the schedule varies. Admission is $3.50 for adults, $3 for seniors, and $1.50 for ages 6 to 18.

Aurora is located 13 miles south of Oregon City on Ore. 99E. You can also get to Aurora by driving south from Portland on I-5 and taking the signed Aurora exit.

7 Especially for Kids

In addition to the attractions listed below, the kids will likely enjoy the **Oregon Museum of Science and Industry,** which has lots of hands-on exhibits (see the listing on p. 248 for details), and the **Oregon Zoo** (see p. 251). From inside the zoo, it's possible to take a small train through Washington Park to the International Rose Test Garden, below which there is the **Rose Garden Children's Park,** a colorful play area for younger children. The **Salmon Street Springs fountain,** in downtown's Tom McCall Waterfront Park (at SW Naito Parkway and SW Salmon Street), is another fun place to take the kids. During hot summer months, there are always lots of happy kids playing in the jets of water that erupt from the pavement here. There are also big lawns here in **Waterfront Park,** so the kids can run off plenty of excess energy.

CM2—Children's Museum 2nd Generation ★ *Kids*   Located across the parking lot form the Oregon Zoo, this new children's museum opened in mid-2001. With much more space than the old museum, this "second generation" museum includes exhibits for children from age six months to 13 years. Kids can experiment with gravity, act out fairy tales, or explore a magical forest. However, it is the Water Works exhibit that is likely to make the biggest splash with your kids. There area also six studios that will have changing exhibits and opportunities for exploring the visual, literary, and performing arts. Together with the nearby zoo, this museum now makes for an easy all-day kid-oriented outing.

4015 SW Canyon Rd. © **503/223-6500**. www.portlandcm2.org. Admission $5 adults and children, under 1 year free. Tues–Thurs 9am–5pm, Fri 9am–8pm, Sun 11am–5pm (open some school holiday Mondays). Closed some national holidays. Bus: 63. MAX: Washington Park Station

Oaks Park Amusement Center *Kids*   What would summer be without the screams of happy thrill-seekers risking their lives on a roller coaster? Pretty boring, right? Just ask the kids. They'll tell you that the real Portland excitement is at Oaks Park. Covering more than 44 acres, this amusement park first opened in 1905 to coincide with the Lewis and Clark Exposition. Beneath the shady oaks for which the park is named, you'll find waterfront picnic sites, miniature golf, music, and plenty of thrilling rides. The largest wood-floored roller-skating rink in the west and an organist still plays the Wurlitzer for the skaters.

East end of the Sellwood Bridge. © **503/233-5777**. www.oakspark.com. Free admission; individual-ride tickets $1.50, limited-ride bracelet $9.75, deluxe-ride bracelet $12.25. Mid-June to Labor Day Tues–Thurs noon–9pm, Fri–Sat noon–10pm, Sun noon–7pm (separate hours for skating rink); May to mid-June and Sept (after Labor Day) Sat–Sun noon–7pm (weather allowing). Bus: 40.

CHILDREN'S THEATER

The **Oregon Children's Theatre Company** (© **503/228-9571**) performs stage adaptations of classic children's stories and every December does a special holiday production. The season is limited to only three productions. Shows are held at various venues, and ticket prices range from $10 to $14 for children and seniors and from $13 to $19 for adults.

More children's theater productions are staged by the **Northwest Children's Theater and School,** 1819 NW Everett St. (© **503/222-2190**), which holds its performances in the Northwest Neighborhood Cultural Center in northwest Portland. The schedule includes as many as seven productions per year, which means you're more likely to luck into a performance here than at the Oregon Children's Theatre Company. Tickets are $5 to $16 for adults and $5 to $11 for children.

Tears of Joy Theater (© **503/248-0557** or 360/695-0477) performs exciting puppet theater for both children and adults. Productions range from the familiar to the foreign with the occasional new work. Lots of fun. Performances are held in the Winningstad Theatre at the Portland Center for the Performing Arts. Tickets are $14 for adults and $9 for children.

8 Organized Tours

CRUISES

With two rivers, the Columbia and the Willamette, Portland has a lot of water running through it, and if you'd like to see the city from the water, you've got plenty of options.

Traditionalists will want to book a tour on the **Sternwheeler** *Columbia Gorge* ⚔ (© **503/223-3928**), which offers sternwheeler cruises through Portland on the Willamette River between October and late June. During the summer months, this boat operates out of Cascade Locks on the Columbia River and does trips in the scenic Columbia Gorge. While it's fun to see the city from the water, the summer trips beneath the towering cliffs of the Columbia Gorge are far more impressive—a definite must on a summertime visit to Portland. Two-hour cruises are $14.95 for adults and $8.95 for children. Call for information on brunch, dinner, and dance cruises.

Alternatively, you can do a cruise on the **Sternwheeler** *Rose* (© **503/286-7673**), a small sternwheeler offering Portland harbor tours, as well as brunch and dinner cruises. Prices range from $12 for a 1-hour harbor cruise to $35 for a 2-hour dinner cruise.

If a modern yacht is more your speed, try the *Portland Spirit* (© **800/224-3901** or 503/224-3900; www.portlandspirit.com). This 75-foot yacht specializes in dinner cruises and seats 350 people on two decks. Lunch, brunch, and dinner cruises feature Northwest cuisine with views of the city skyline out the cabin windows. Saturday nights the *Portland Spirit* becomes a floating nightclub with live bands or a DJ, and there are also Friday afternoon cocktail cruises in the summer. Call for reservations and schedule. Prices range from $15 to $52 for adults and $9 to $47 for children.

For high-speed tours up the Willamette River, there are the **Willamette Jetboat Excursions** ⚔ (© **888/JETBOAT** or 503/231-1532; www.jetboatpdx.com). The high-powered open-air boats blast their way from downtown Portland to the impressive Willamette Falls at Oregon City. The 2-hour tours, which start at OMSI, are $25 for adults and $15 for children ages 4 to 11, free for 3 and under. Tours are offered May through mid-October.

BUS TOURS

If you want to get a general overview of Portland, **Gray Line** (© **800/422-7042** or 503/285-9845) offers several half-day and full-day tours. One itinerary takes in the International Rose Test Garden and the grounds of Pittock Mansion; another stops at the Japanese Garden and the World Forestry Center. There are also tours up to see the waterfalls in the Columbia Gorge, to Mount Hood, and to the Oregon coast. Tour prices range from $27 to $47 for adults, and from $13.50 to $23.50 for children.

ECOTOURS
Ecotours of Oregon (© **503/245-1428;** www.ecotours-of-oregon.com) offers a variety of tours and hikes. They travel to the Columbia River Gorge, Mount Hood, Mount St. Helens, the Oregon coast, ancient forests, and places to whale-watch or experience Native American culture. Visits to wineries, microbreweries, and custom tours can all be arranged. Tours to Mount St. Helens are $47.50 (plus $6 national monument admission) while a whale-watching excursion to the Oregon coast is $59.50.

RAIL EXCURSIONS
While Portland is busy reviving trolleys as a viable mass transit option, the **Willamette Shore Trolley** ✯ (© **503/222-2226**) is offering scenic excursions along the Willamette River in historic trolley cars from the early part of the 20th century (including a double-decker). The old wooden trolleys rumble over tres-tles and through a tunnel as they cover the 7 miles between Portland and the prestigious suburb of Lake Oswego (a 45-min. trip). Along the way, you pass through shady corridors with lots of views of the river and glimpses into the yards of posh riverfront homes. The trip takes about 45 minutes each way. In Lake Oswego, the trolley station is on State Street, between "A" Avenue and Foothills Road. In downtown Portland, the station is just south of the River-Place Athletic Club on Harbor Way (off Naito Parkway at the south end of Tom McCall Waterfront Park). The round-trip fare is $8 for adults, $7 for seniors, and $4 for children age 3 to 12. Call for a schedule. They also do an annual Fourth of July fireworks run from Oaks Park on the east bank of the Willamette River, and a Christmas run to see the Holiday Parade of Ships.

SCENIC FLIGHTS
For an air tour straight out of *The English Patient,* contact **Jim's Biplane Rides** (© **800/FLY-1929** or 503/515-1929), which offers biplane rides in a restored 1929 Travel Air. From May to October, flights depart from the Troutdale Air-port near the mouth of the Columbia Gorge and from Hillsboro Airport west of Portland, where rides take flyers over Sauvie Island and the rolling farmland of the area. Rates for two people range from $129 to $299.

WALKING TOURS
Peter's Walking Tours of Portland (© **503/665-2558** or 503/680-4296; famchausse@aol.com), led by university instructor Peter Chausse, are a great way to learn more about Portland. The walking tours of downtown take 2½ hours, cover about 1½ miles, and take in the fountains, parks, historic places, art, and architecture that make Portland the energetic city that it is. Tours are by reservation and cost $10 for adults (children 12 and under are free with a paying adult).

Two to three times a year, Sharon Wood Wortman, author of *The Portland Bridge Book,* offers a **Bridge Tour and Urban Adventure** that explores several Portland bridges. These tours are offered through the Outdoor Recreation Program of **Portland Parks and Recreation** (© **503/823-5132**). Many other walking tours are also available through Portland Parks and Recreation.

The seamy underbelly of history is laid bare on **Portland Underground Tours** ⋆ (© 503/622-4798), which head down below street level in the historic Old Town neighborhood. On these unusual tours, which aren't for anyone who isn't steady on his feet and able to duck under pipes and joists and such, you'll hear tales of the days when Portland was known as one of the most dangerous ports on the Pacific Rim. Sailors were regularly shanghaied from bars and brothels in this area and a vast network of tunnels and underground rooms developed to support the shanghaiing business. Although these tours are similar to the much more famous Seattle Underground tours, the Portland Underground Tours are still pretty casual outings. Tours cost $10 and are offered on an irregular basis. Reservations are required

WINERY TOURS

If you're interested in learning more about Oregon wines and want to tour the nearby wine country with a guide, contact **Grape Escape** (© 503/283-3380; www.grapeescapetours.com), which offers an in-depth winery tour of the Willamette Valley. All-day tours include stops at several wineries, appetizers, lunch, and dessert, and pickup and drop-off at your hotel ($85 per person). For people with less time, there are half-day afternoon trips that take in two or three wineries ($60 per person). A number of other tours are also available.

For information on touring wine country on your own, see "A Winery Tour" in chapter 20, "Side Trips from Portland."

9 Outdoor Pursuits

If you're planning ahead for a visit to Portland, contact **Metro Regional Parks and Greenspaces,** 600 NE Grand Ave., Portland, OR 97232-2736 (© 503/797-1850; www.metro-region.org), for its *Metro GreenScene* publication that lists tours, hikes, classes, and other outdoor activities and events being held in the Portland metro area.

BEACHES

The nearest ocean beaches are **Cannon Beach** (a charming village) and **Seaside** (an old-fashioned family beach town), about 90 miles to the west. See "The Northern Oregon Coast" in chapter 20, "Side Trips from Portland," for more information.

There are a couple of freshwater beaches on the Columbia River within 45 minutes of Portland. **Rooster Rock State Park,** just off I-84 east of Portland, includes several miles of sandy beach as does **Sauvie Island,** off Oregon Hwy. 30 northwest of Portland. You'll need to obtain a parking permit for Sauvie Island; it's available at the convenience store located just after you cross the bridge onto the island. Both beaches include clothing-optional sections, though these are well separated from the more popular clothing-required beaches.

BIKING

Portland is a very bicycle-friendly city, and you'll notice plenty of bicyclists on Portland streets. There are also lots of miles of paved bike paths around the city, and a some good mountain biking areas as well. However, if you want to get rolling with everyone else, you don't have too many choices for rentals, but at **Fat Tire Farm,** 2714 NW Thurman St. (© 503/222-3276), you can rent a mountain bike for $40 a day. Straight up Thurman Street from the bike shop, you'll find the trailhead for the **Leif Erikson Trail,** and old gravel road that is

Impressions

While the people of Portland are not mercurial or excitable—and by Cal-
ifornians or people "east of the mountains" are even accused of being
lymphatic, if not somnolent—they are much given . . . to recreation and
public amusements.

—Harvey Scott, editor of the *Oregonian,* 1890

Forest Park's favorite route for cyclists and runners (the road is closed to motor vehicles); the trail is 12 miles long.

BOARDSAILING

Serious enthusiasts already know about the boardsailing Mecca of **Hood River,** an hour east of Portland on the Columbia River. The winds come howling down the gorge with enough force to send sailboards airborne. Several shops in Hood River rent boardsailing equipment.

Right in Portland you can take a lesson at **Gorge Performance Windsurfing,** 7400 SW Macadam Blvd. (© **503/246-6646**), which happens to be conveniently close to **Willamette Park,** the city's best boardsailing spot. You'll find this park at the corner of SW Macadam Boulevard and SW Nebraska Street, on the Willamette River.

The many miles of sandy beaches on **Sauvie Island** are another good spot for experienced sailors to try.

The easiest spot for beginners is across the Columbia River in Vancouver, Washington, at **Vancouver Lake State Park,** which is reached by taking the Fourth Plain exit of I-5 and driving west on NW New Lower River Road.

GOLF

If you're a golfer, don't forget to bring your clubs along on a trip to Portland. There are plenty of public courses around the area, and greens fees at municipal courses are as low as $21 for 18 holes on a weekday and $35 on weekends and holidays. Municipal golf courses operated by the Portland Bureau of Parks and Recreation include **Redtail Golf Course,** 8200 SW Scholls Ferry Rd. (© **503/646-5166**); **Eastmoreland Golf Course,** 2425 SE Bybee Blvd. (© **503/775-2900**), which is the second oldest golf course in the state (this one gets our vote for best municipal course); **Heron Lakes Golf Course,** 3500 N. Victory Blvd. (© **503/ 289-1818**), a Robert Trent Jones design; and **Rose City Golf Course,** 2200 NE 71st Ave. (© **503/253-4744**), on the site of a former country club.

If you want to tee off where the pros play, head west from Portland 20 miles to **Pumpkin Ridge Golf Club** ⚘⚘, 12930 NW Old Pumpkin Ridge Rd. (© **503/647-4747**), which has hosted the U.S. Women's Open. Greens fees are $120 ($135 with cart) and $65 after 3pm Monday to Thursday.

Also west of the city, on the south side of Hillsboro, you'll find the **Reserve Vineyards & Golf Club** ⚘⚘, 4805 SW 229th Ave., Aloha (© **503/649-8191;** www.reservegolf.com). Greens fees are $65 Monday through Thursday and $79 Friday through Sunday.

HIKING

Hiking opportunities in the Portland area are almost unlimited. For shorter hikes, you need not leave the city. Bordered by West Burnside Street on the south, Newberry Road on the north, St. Helens Road on the east, and Skyline Road on the west, **Forest Park** is the largest forested city park in the country.

You'll find more than 50 miles of trails through this urban wilderness. One of our favorite access points is at the top of NW Thurman Street in northwest Portland (after a hike, you can stop by one of the neighborhood brewpubs, an espresso bar, or bakery along NW 23rd or NW 21st Avenue for a postexercise payoff). The Wildwood Trail is the longest trail in the park and offers the most options for loop hikes along its length. For a roughly 2.5-mile hike, head up Leif Erikson Drive to a left onto the Wild Cherry Trail to a right onto the Wildwood Trail to a right onto the Dogwood Trail, and then a right on Leif Erikson Drive to get you back to the trailhead. There are also good sections of trail to hike in the vicinity of the Hoyt Arboretum. To reach the arboretum's visitor center, 4000 SW Fairview Boulevard (open daily 9am–3pm), drive west on West Burnside Street from downtown Portland and follow signs to the arboretum. You can get a trail map here at the visitor center.

About 5 miles south of downtown, you'll find **Tryon Creek State Park** on Terwilliger Road. This park is similar to Forest Park and is best known for its displays of trillium flowers in the spring. There are several miles of walking trails within the park, and a bike path to downtown Portland starts here.

If you head over to **Mount Hood National Forest** (less than an hour away), you can get on the **Pacific Crest Trail** and hike all the way to Mexico. Of course, there are also plenty of shorter hikes. Among our favorites are the sections of the Timberline Trail heading out from Timberline Lodge, which is Mount Hood's main man-made attraction. From the lodge you can to an out-and-back hike of whatever length you're up for. Another good choice is the Mirror Lake Trail, which has its trailhead right on U.S. 26 just before you reach the community of Government Camp (if you're coming up from Portland). It's a 4-mile round-trip hike to Mirror Lake and a 6.4-mile round-trip hike to the top of nearby Tom, Dick, and Harry Mountain. However, if you want to avoid the crowds, head around the mountain (take U.S. 26 to Ore. 35 north toward Hood River, and then take Cooper Spur Road for 12.5 miles to the Cloud Cap Campground). From Cloud Cap, you can hike up above treeline on the treeless east slopes of the mountain or head through the trees and meadows on the mountains north side. For information on hiking trails on Mount Hood, contact the **Mount Hood Information Center,** 65000 E. U.S. 26, Welches (© **503/622-7674**).

If you're interested in a more strenuous mountain experience, the Mount Hood area offers plenty of mountain- and rock-climbing opportunities. **Timberline Mountain Guides** (© **541/312-9242;** www.timberlinemtguides.com) leads summit climbs on Mount Hood. They also offer snow, ice, and rock-climbing courses. A 2-day Mount Hood mountaineering course with summit climb costs $375.

You can buy or rent camping equipment from **REI Co-op,** 1798 Jantzen Beach Center (© **503/283-1300**), or 7410 SW Bridgeport Rd., Tualatin (© **503/624-8600**). This huge outdoor recreation supply store also sells books on hiking in the area.

If you have been keeping up with the controversy over saving the remaining old-growth forests of the Northwest, you might want to go see an ancient forest for yourself. Though there isn't much publicly accessible ancient forest right in Portland, you can find plenty within 1½ hours' drive. Along the coast, Ecola State Park, Oswald West State Park, Cape Meares State Park, and Cape Lookout State Park all have trails through stands of old-growth trees. See "The Northern Oregon Coast," in chapter 20, for details.

SEA KAYAKING

If you want to check out the Portland skyline from water level, arrange for a sea kayak tour through the **Portland River Company** 𝒜𝒜, 0315 SW Montgomery St. (℃ **888/238-2059** or 503/229-0551; www.portlandrivercompany.com), which operates out of the RiverPlace Marina at the south end of Tom McCall Waterfront Park. A 2½-hour tour that circles nearby Ross Island costs $35 per person. All-day trips on the lower Columbia River are also offered ($75 per person) and will get you off an urban river and into a wildlife refuge. This company also rents sea kayaks (to experienced paddlers) for $15 to $20 for the first hour and $10 to $15 per hour after that.

SKIING

There are several ski resorts within about an hour's drive of Portland, on the slopes of Mount Hood. Timberline Ski Area even boasts summer skiing. There are also many miles of marked cross-country ski trails. The best cross-country skiing on Mount Hood is at the Nordic center at Mount Hood Meadows, and at Teacup Lake, which is along Ore. 35 near the turnoff for Mount Hood Meadows. You'll find numerous ski and snowboard rental shops in the town of Sandy, which is on the way from Portland to Mount Hood, and ski areas also rent equipment.

Timberline Ski Area 𝒜 (℃ **503/272-3311** for information, or 503/222-2211 for snow report; www.timberlinelodge.com) is the highest ski area on Mount Hood and has one slope that is open all the way through summer. This is the site of the historic Timberline Lodge, which was built during the Depression by the WPA. Adult lift ticket prices range from $18 for night skiing to $37 for an all-day pass. Call for hours of operation.

Mount Hood Meadows 𝒜𝒜 (℃ **503/337-2222,** or 503/227-7669 for snow report; www.skihood.com) is the largest ski resort on Mount Hood, with more than 2,000 skiable acres, 2,777 vertical feet, and a wide variety of terrain. Lift ticket prices range from $18 for night skiing to $41 for a weekend all-day pass. Call for hours of operation.

Mt. Hood SkiBowl (℃ **503/272-3206,** or 503/222-2695 for snow report; www.skibowl.com), the closest ski area to Portland, offers 1,500 vertical feet of skiing and has more expert slopes than any other ski area on the mountain. Ski-Bowl is also one of the largest lighted ski areas in the country. Adult lift ticket prices range from $18 for midweek night skiing to $31 for a weekend all-day pass. Call for hours of operation.

All of the ski areas mentioned above allow snowboarding. Mount Hood Meadows and Mt. Hood SkiBowl both have cross-country skiing (though only Mount Hood Meadows has a Nordic Center and groomed fee-access trails).

TENNIS

Portland Parks and Recreation operates more than 120 tennis courts, both indoors and out, all over the city. Outdoor courts are generally free and available on a first-come, first-served basis. Our personal favorites are those in Washington Park just behind the International Rose Test Garden. If you want to be certain of getting a particular court time, some of these courts can be reserved by contacting Portland Parks and Recreation at ℃ **503/823-2525,** ext. 6.

If the weather isn't cooperating, head for the **Portland Tennis Center,** 324 NE 12th Ave. (℃ **503/823-3189**). They have indoor courts and charge about $5.75 to $7.75 per hour per person for singles matches and $3.75 to $5 per hour per person for doubles.

WHITE-WATER RAFTING

The Cascade Range produces some of the best white-water rafting in the country, and the Deschutes, White Salmon, Sandy, and Clackamas rivers all offer plenty of opportunities to shoot within an hour or two of Portland. The Sandy and the Clackamas are the two closest rivers.

Portland River Company, 0315 SW Montgomery St. (© **888/238-2059** or 503/229-0551; www.portlandrivercompany.com), offers day trips on the Deschutes and North Umpqua rivers ($75 per person) and 2- to 3-day trips on the Deschutes River ($260–$360 per person). Trips on the Sandy, Clackamas, North Santiam, and Hood rivers are offered by **Blue Sky Whitewater Rafting** (© **800/898-6398;** www.blueskyrafting.com), which charges $30 to $35 for a half-day trip and $55 to $60 for a full-day trip. **River Drifters** (© **800/972-0430** or 800/226-1001; www.riverdrifters.net) offers trips on the Deschutes, White Salmon, Clackamas, Wind River, North Santiam, and Klickitat rivers for between $65 and $75 for a full day. **Zoller's Outdoor Odysseys, Inc.,** 1248 Hwy. 141, White Salmon, WA (© **800/366-2004** or 509/493-2641; www.zooraft.com), offers trips on the White Salmon for $60.

If you already have some rafting experience and just want to rent a raft for the easy Class 1-plus rapids on the lower Sandy River (between Oxbow Park and Dabney Park), contact **River Trails,** 336 E Columbia River Hwy., Troutdale (© **503/667-1964**), which charges $50 per day for a four-person raft.

10 Spectator Sports

Tickets to most games, including those of the Trail Blazers, the Portland Winter Hawks, and the Portland Beavers, are sold through **TicketMaster** (© **503/224-4400;** www.ticketmaster.com).

Tickets to events at the Rose Garden arena and Memorial Coliseum are also sold through the **Rose Quarter** box office (© **503/797-9617** for tickets, or 503/321-3211 event information hot line; www.rosequarter.com). The Rose Garden arena is home to the Portland Trail Blazers and the Portland Winter Hawks and is the main focal point of Portland's **Rose Quarter.** This sports and entertainment neighborhood is still more an idea than a reality, but it does include the Rose Garden, Memorial Coliseum, and several restaurants and bars. To reach the Rose Garden or adjacent Memorial Coliseum, take the Rose Quarter exit off I-5. Parking is expensive, so you might want to consider taking the MAX light-rail line from downtown Portland.

AUTO RACING   Portland International Raceway, West Delta Park, 1940 N. Victory Blvd. (© **503/823-RACE**), hosts road races, drag races, motocross and other motorcycle races, go-kart races, and even vintage-car races. February to October are the busiest months here.

BASEBALL   The Portland Beavers Baseball Club (© **503/553-5555;** www.pgepark.com), the AAA affiliate of the San Diego Padres, plays minor-league ball at the recently renovated PGE Park, SW 20th Avenue and Morrison Street. Tickets are $3.25 to $8.75.

BASKETBALL   The NBA's Portland Trail Blazers (© **503/231-8000** or 503/234-9291; www.nba.com/blazers) do well enough each year to have earned them a very loyal following. Unfortunately, they have a habit of not quite making it all the way to the top. The Blazers pound the boards at the Rose Garden arena. Call for current schedule and ticket information. Tickets are $10 to $127. If the Blazers are doing well, you can bet that tickets will be hard to come by.

ICE HOCKEY   The **Portland Winter Hawks** (© **503/238-6366;** www. winterhawks.com), a junior-league hockey team, carve up the ice at Memorial Coliseum and the Rose Garden from October to March. Call for schedule and ticket information. Tickets are $14 to $21.50.

MARATHON   The **Portland Marathon** (© **503/226-1111;** www. portlandmarathon.org) is held in late September or early October each year. The 26.2-mile run is also supplemented by shorter runs.

11 Day Spas

If you'd rather opt for a massage than a hike in the woods, consider spending a few hours at a day spa. These facilities typically offer massages, facials, seaweed wraps, and the like. Portland day spas include **Aveda Lifestyle Store and Spa,** 5th Avenue Suites Hotel, 500 Washington St. (© **503/248-0615**); **Urbaca,** 120 NW Ninth Ave., Suite 101 (© **503/241-5030**); and **Salon Nyla—The Day Spa,** adjacent to the Embassy Suites hotel at 327 SW Pine St. (© **503/228-0389**). Expect to pay about $65 to $75 for a 1-hour massage and $150 to $435 for a multitreatment spa package.

17

Strolling Around Portland

Portland's compactness makes it an ideal city to explore on foot. There's no better way to gain a feel for this city than to stroll through the Skidmore Historic District, down along Tom McCall Waterfront Park, and through Pioneer Courthouse Square. If you're here on the weekend, you'll also be able to visit the Portland Saturday Market.

You're never far from an outdoor sculpture or fountain in downtown Portland, and these public works of art are as much a part of the local art scene as anything in a gallery or museum. Our second walking tour outlines a route that will take you past some of the best outdoor art the city has to offer. Keep your eyes peeled for other works of art not mentioned in this walking tour.

If you're up for a long walk, these two tours can be linked together into one extended walk around downtown. For additional information on several stops in these two strolls, see chapter 16, "Exploring Portland."

WALKING TOUR 1	OLD TOWN & DOWNTOWN

Start:	Skidmore Fountain.
Finish:	Skidmore Fountain.
Time:	Allow approximately 3 to 4 hours, including breaks, museum visits, and shopping stops.
Best Times:	Saturday and Sunday between March and December, when the Portland Saturday Market is open.
Worst Times:	After dark, when the Skidmore neighborhood is not as safe as in daylight.

Although Portland was founded in 1843, most of the buildings in Old Town date only from the 1880s. A fire in 1872 razed much of the town, which afterward was rebuilt with new vigor. Ornate pilasters, pediments, and cornices grace these brick buildings. However, the most notable features of Old Town's buildings are the cast-iron facades.

Begin your exploration of this 20-block historic neighborhood in the heart of Old Town. At the corner of SW First Avenue and Ankeny Street is:

❶ Skidmore Fountain
Erected in 1888, the fountain was intended to provide refreshment for "horses, men, and dogs," and it did that for many years. Today, however, the bronze and granite fountain is primarily decorative.

Across SW First Avenue is the:

❷ New Market Block
Constructed in 1872 to house the unlikely combination of a produce market and a theater, the New Market Block contains some unusual shops and budget restaurants, as do many of

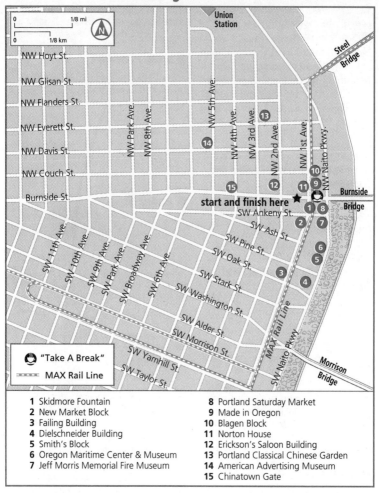

0   1/8 mi
0   1/8 km

Union Station

Steel Bridge

NW Hoyt St.
NW Glisan St.
NW Flanders St.
NW Everett St.
NW Davis St.
NW Couch St.
Burnside St.

NW Park Ave.
NW 8th Ave.
NW 5th Ave.
NW 4th Ave.
NW 3rd Ave.
NW 2nd Ave.
NW 1st Ave.
NW Naito Pkwy.

start and finish here ★

SW Ankeny St.
SW Ash St.
SW Pine St.
SW Oak St.
SW Stark St.
SW Washington St.
SW Alder St.
SW Morrison St.
SW Yamhill St.
SW Taylor St.

SW 11th Ave.
SW 10th Ave.
SW 9th Ave.
SW Park Ave.
SW Broadway Ave.
SW 6th Ave.

MAX Rail Line
SW Naito Pkwy.

Burnside Bridge

Morrison Bridge

🍵 "Take A Break"
MAX Rail Line

1 Skidmore Fountain
2 New Market Block
3 Failing Building
4 Dielschneider Building
5 Smith's Block
6 Oregon Maritime Center & Museum
7 Jeff Morris Memorial Fire Museum
8 Portland Saturday Market
9 Made in Oregon
10 Blagen Block
11 Norton House
12 Erickson's Saloon Building
13 Portland Classical Chinese Garden
14 American Advertising Museum
15 Chinatown Gate

the restored historic buildings in this area. The free-standing wall of archways extending out from the New Market Building was salvaged from an Old Town structure that didn't survive the urban renewal craze of the 1960s.

Two blocks south, at 235 SW First Ave., is the:

❸ Failing Building

Built in 1886, this attractive structure integrates French and Italian influences. (This building houses McCormick and Schmick's seafood restaurant, a good place for lunch if the Saturday Market is closed.)

Turn left on SW Oak Street and you'll pass by the:

❹ Dielschneider Building

This structure at 71 SW Oak St. was originally a foundry. Built in 1859, it's the third oldest commercial building in Portland. The casting initials of one of the first tenants, Oregon Ironworks, can be seen on the building's threshold plates.

Take a left on SW Naito Parkway (Front Avenue) where you'll find:

⑤ Smith's Block

Located from 111–117 SW Naito Parkway, it contains some of the most beautifully restored buildings in Old Town. At one time this whole district was filled with elegant structures such as these. The cast-iron filigree appears both solid and airy at the same time.

Here, at 113 SW Naito Pkwy., you'll find the:

⑥ Oregon Maritime Center and Museum

This museum is dedicated to Oregon's shipping history. See the complete listing in chapter 16 for details.

Continue along SW Naito Parkway to SW Ankeny, where you'll see the:

⑦ Jeff Morris Memorial Fire Museum

It houses several pieces of old firefighting equipment, including historic horse-drawn steamers from the early part of the 20th century. Because this museum is part of an active fire station and because the equipment is packed so tightly together, you can't actually go inside the museum. You'll have to be satisfied with looking through the glass doors that face the street.

If it's a Saturday or Sunday between March and December, you will no doubt have noticed the crowds under the Burnside bridge ahead of you. This is the:

⑧ Portland Saturday Market

Here you'll find the best of Northwest crafts being sold by their makers. There typically are more than 250 booths plus entertainers and food vendors. See the complete listing in chapter 16, "Exploring Portland," for more details.

> **TAKE A BREAK**
> **Portland Saturday Market** makes an excellent refueling stop in this neighborhood. In the market's food court you can get all manner of delicious, healthful, and fun foods.

After you've visited the market, walk north on the east side of NW First Avenue. Just out from under the shadow of the Burnside Bridge, at 10 NW First Ave., you'll find:

⑨ Made in Oregon

This shop sells all things Oregon, from Pendleton blankets to local wines. This is a great place to pick up more gifts if you haven't already spent more than you should have at the Saturday Market.

From here, continue up NW First Avenue to the corner of NW Couch (pronounced *Kooch*) Street, where you'll find the:

⑩ Blagen Block

This is another excellent example of the ornate cast-iron facades that appeared on nearly all the buildings in this area at one time. Note the cast-iron figures of women wearing spiked crowns. They are reminiscent of the Statue of Liberty, which was erected 2 years before this building opened in 1888.

Across First Avenue, you'll see the covered sidewalk of the:

⑪ Norton House

Though this is not the original covered sidewalk, it is characteristic of Portland buildings from 100 years ago.

Walk west to Second Avenue, where at the southwest corner you'll see:

⑫ Erickson's Saloon Building

Back in the late 1800s this building at 9 NW Second Ave. housed the very popular Erickson's Saloon, with a 684-foot-long bar, card rooms, and a brothel.

From here, walk north on Second Avenue to the corner of Everett Street and turn left. At the corner of Everett Street and Third Avenue, you'll find the:

⑬ Portland Classical Chinese Garden

This is the largest classical Suzhou-style Chinese garden outside of China. With its tiled roofs, pond, bridges, and landscaping that conjures up images from Chinese scroll paintings, the garden is an urban oasis. See the listing in chapter 16 for more information.

From here, walk back south on NW Third Avenue to the corner of Davis Street, turn right, and in 2 blocks, you'll see, on the northwest corner, the :

14 American Advertising Museum

Located at 211 NW Fifth Ave., this museum houses fun displays on the history of advertising. Inside, you can watch videos of some of the most unforgettable TV commercials of the past 50 years, follow the history of advertising in the United States, and get face to face with the likes of Aunt Jemima, Mr. Peanut, and Big Boy. See the complete listing in chapter 16, "Exploring Portland."

From here, walk back to Fourth Avenue, turn right, and ahead of you, at the corner of Fourth Avenue and Burnside Street, you'll see the:

15 Chinatown Gate

Since you're already in Chinatown, you'll have to cross to the opposite side of the brightly painted three-tiered gateway to appreciate its ornate design, including two huge flanking bronze Chinese lions.

From here, cross West Burnside Street, turn left on Ankeny, and walk 3 blocks back to the Skidmore Fountain to end the tour.

WALKING TOUR 2   FOUNTAINS & PUBLIC ART

Start:	Pioneer Courthouse Square.
Finish:	Pioneer Courthouse Square.
Time:	Allow approximately 2 hours, not including museum visits, breaks, and shopping stops.
Best Times:	Saturday and Sunday between March and December, when the Portland Saturday Market is open. The best starting time is noon, when you can see the *Weather Machine* in action.
Worst Times:	After dark, when the Skidmore neighborhood is not as safe as in daylight and the artworks aren't as easy to see.

Portland is proud of its public art, and the **Regional Arts & Culture Council** (**RACC**), 620 SW Main St., Suite 420 (© **503/823-5111**), has put together a booklet outlining several walking tours in the Portland downtown area. These walking tours will help you find many of the city's most interesting pieces of art and architecture. You can get a free copy by stopping by the Portland Oregon Visitors Association information center, which is located right on Pioneer Courthouse Square.; the RACC office; or the Portland Art Museum, 1219 SW Park Ave.

Start your art and fountain tour at the stroke of noon, if at all possible, by grabbing a latte and parking yourself on a terrace at:

1 Pioneer Courthouse Square

The square is bordered by Yamhill and Morrison streets, Sixth Avenue, and Broadway. Known as Portland's living room, this brick plaza has several sculptures, a waterfall fountain, a Starbucks, Powell's Travel Store, and the Portland Oregon Visitors Association information center.

The reason to get here at noon is to witness the day's weather forecast by the fascinating *Weather Machine*, a sculpture that displays creatures to represent the current weather—a sun (sunny), a dragon (stormy), or a blue heron (drizzle). A weathervane, thermometer, and puffs of smoke are all part of this unusual weather-oriented sculpture. Other works of art on the square include *Allow Me* (a bronze sculpture of a man carrying an umbrella), and *Running Horses*.

From the square, walk east on SW Yamhill Street, past Pioneer Courthouse. Along the sidewalk here, you'll see:

❷ *Animals in Pools*
These are among the best-loved statues in the city. Included among these bronze statues are a mother bear with two cubs, a doe and fawn, and two curious river otters.

Turn right on SW Fifth Avenue, and you'll see:

❸ *Soaring Stones*
This unusual sculpture consists of granite boulders on steel columns. Because the five boulders are staggered above the sidewalk, they appear to be flying.

Continue up SW Fifth Avenue to the intersection with SW Salmon Street. Here you'll find one of the:

❹ Simon Benson Fountains
These drinking fountains and many just like them were donated to the city in 1917 by local timber magnate Simon Benson after he tried to get a glass of water in a saloon and was told he had to first buy a glass of beer or whiskey.

Continue another block south, and you'll come to:

❺ *Portlandia* and the Portland Building
These landmarks are located between SW Main and SW Madison streets. The building, designed by Michael Graves, is considered the first postmodern building in the world. Out front is Raymond Kaskey's hammered-copper statue *Portlandia*, the second-tallest beaten-copper statue in the world (second only to the Statue of Liberty).

From here, walk east on SW Main Street 1½ blocks to the:

❻ Elk Fountain
This life-size bronze elk and water fountain were installed here in this park in 1900 and once served as a watering stop for horses.

Continue south on SW Fourth Avenue for 4 blocks to the:

❼ Ira Keller Memorial Fountain
Consisting of a complex waterfall, this fountain, surrounded by a tree-filled park, is meant to conjure up images of waterfalls in the nearby Cascade Range.

After lounging around the falls, head back 7 blocks on SW Fourth Avenue to SW Yamhill Street, and turn left to find:

❽ *Street Wise*
This is an installation of granite paving blocks that are engraved with sayings and quotations. "You blocks, you stones, you worse than senseless things" (William Shakespeare) and "I've been on a calendar but never on time" (Marilyn Monroe) are just two of our favorites.

From here, head back east to SW Naito Parkway, turn right, and go 1 block to the corner of SW Taylor Street. Cross Naito Parkway, stopping in the middle of the street to visit:

❾ Mill Ends Park
This is the smallest public park in the world. Once merely a hole left over when a telephone pole was removed, this little circle of flowers became a park after a popular local newspaper columnist began writing of the exploits of the park's leprechauns.

Continuing across the street, you come to the much larger:

❿ Tom McCall Waterfront Park
The park is the site of many of Portland's outdoor festivals. Here you'll find Portlanders biking, skating, or simply enjoying the outdoors.

One block south is the:

⓫ Salmon Street Springs fountain
This amounts to a public sprinkler system for kids (and the occasional adult) to play in on hot summer days. It's also fun to just sit and watch these ever-changing fountains.

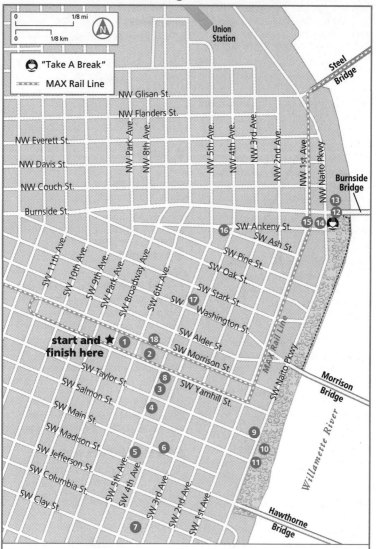

0   1/8 mi
0   1/8 km

Union Station

Steel Bridge

🐚 "Take A Break"

⋯⋯ MAX Rail Line

NW Glisan St.

NW Flanders St.

NW Everett St.

NW Davis St.

NW Couch St.

Burnside St.

NW Park Ave.
NW 8th Ave.
NW 5th Ave.
NW 4th Ave.
NW 3rd Ave.
NW 2nd Ave.
NW 1st Ave.
NW Naito Pkwy

Burnside Bridge

13

12

15 14 🐚

16 SW Ankeny St.

SW Ash St.

SW Pine St.

SW Oak St.

SW Stark St.

SW 17 Washington St.

SW 11th Ave.
SW 10th Ave.
SW 9th Ave.
SW Park Ave.
SW Broadway Ave.
SW 6th Ave.

start and ★ 1
finish here

18

2

SW Alder St.

SW Morrison St.

SW Taylor St.

8

3

SW Yamhill St.

SW Salmon St.

4

SW Main St.

9

SW Madison St.

SW Jefferson St.

5

6

10

11

SW Columbia St.

SW 5th Ave.
SW 4th Ave.
SW 3rd Ave.
SW 2nd Ave.
SW 1st Ave.

SW Clay St.

7

MAX Rail Line

SW Naito Pkwy

Morrison Bridge

Willamette River

Hawthorne Bridge

1 Pioneer Courthouse Square
2 *Animals in Pools*
3 *Soaring Stones*
4 Simon Benson Fountain
5 *Portlandia* and the Portland Building
6 Elk Fountain
7 Ira Keller Memorial Fountain
8 *Street Wise*
9 Mill Ends Park

10 Tom McCall Waterfront Park
11 Salmon Street Springs Fountain
12 Waterfront Park Story Garden
13 Japanese American Historical Plaza/ Bill of Rights Memorial
14 Portland Saturday Market
15 Skidmore Fountain
16 *Untitled*
17 *Kvinneakt*
18 *Animals in Pools*

From here walk north through the park on the paved riverside path and in 10 blocks you'll come to the:

⑫ Waterfront Park Story Garden

This fascinating installation is a cross between a maze and a board game, made up of carved granite paving stones scattered along a cobblestone pathway maze. Carved on the paving stones are images of everything from 1950s board game characters to Northwest Coast Indian images. Other stones ask questions (What is your joy? What is your failure? What is your secret?). You could easily spend half an hour or more just wandering through this mazelike installation.

A few steps away is the:

⑬ Japanese American Historical Plaza/Bill of Rights Memorial

Standing boulders inscribed with poetry are scattered throughout the plaza. In spring, the cherry trees are covered with blossoms.

From here, cross NW Naito Parkway, turn left on NW First Avenue, and under the Burnside Bridge you'll find the:

⑭ Portland Saturday Market

The market, held on Saturdays and Sundays, is filled with artists from all over the region and has a fascinating assortment of one-of-a-kind art and interesting crafts. This is perhaps Portland's greatest public art treasure.

TAKE A BREAK
If it is Saturday or Sunday and the market is set up, this is a great place to grab some good, cheap eats. There are all kinds of inexpensive meals available at market stalls. Other days of the week, you'll find budget eateries in the New Market Block building across SW First Avenue from the market.

Across the market is the:

⑮ Skidmore Fountain

Erected in 1888 and intended to provide refreshment for "horses, men, and dogs," it did just that for many years. Today, however, the bronze and granite fountain is primarily decorative.

From here, walk up SW Ash Street 4 blocks to:

⑯ *Untitled*

This is a large sculpture fountain vaguely reminiscent of a giant brass musical instrument.

From here, turn left and head south 4 blocks on SW Fifth Avenue to the corner of SW Washington Street. Here you'll find:

⑰ *Kvinneakt*

You're looking at the most notorious piece of public art in Portland. This bronze sculpture of a nude woman was made famous in a poster titled "Expose Yourself to Art," which featured a man in a trench coat flashing the statue. The man in the photo was Bud Clark, local tavern owner and Portland's most colorful former mayor.

Continue another 2 blocks on Fifth Avenue, turn right on SW Morrison Street, and you will see more of the bronze:

⑱ *Animals in Pools* sculptures

On this side of the Pioneer Courthouse you'll see a pair of beavers and a family of seals. Pioneer Courthouse Square, the end point of this stroll, is just across SW Sixth Avenue.

18

Portland Shopping

Portland may not be as much of a shopping mecca as Seattle, but it has one thing going for it that Seattle can't claim: There's no sales tax here. This fact alone makes Portland a popular shopping destination with Washingtonians, who cross the Columbia River to avoid paying their state's substantial sales tax.

1 The Shopping Scene

The **blocks around Pioneer Courthouse Square** are the heartland of upscale shopping in Portland. It's here that you'll find Nordstrom, NIKETOWN, Saks Fifth Avenue, Tiffany, Pioneer Place shopping mall, and numerous upscale boutiques and shops.

However, Portland's hippest shopping district is the **Nob Hill/Northwest neighborhood** along NW 23rd Avenue beginning at West Burnside Street. Here you'll find block after block of unusual boutiques as well as such chains as Gap, Urban Outfitters, and Pottery Barn.

For shops with a more down-to-earth, funky flavor, head out to the **Hawthorne District,** which is the city's counterculture shopping area (lots of tie-dye and imports).

In the **Pearl District,** of which NW Glisan Street and NW 10th Avenue are the center, you'll find the city's greatest concentration of art galleries.

Most small stores in Portland are open Monday through Saturday from 9 or 10am to 5 or 6pm. Shopping malls are usually open Monday through Friday from 9 or 10am to 9pm, on Saturday from 9 or 10am to between 6pm and 9pm, and on Sunday from 11am until 6pm. Many department stores stay open past 6pm. Most art galleries and antiques stores are closed on Monday.

2 Shopping A to Z
ANTIQUES

The **Sellwood** neighborhood (south of downtown at the east end of the Sell-wood Bridge) is Portland's main antiques-shopping district, with about 30 antiques shops and antiques malls along 12 blocks of SE 13th Avenue. Spend the day browsing these many shops and you're certain to find something to add to your collection of whatever it is you collect. With its old Victorian homes and turn-of-the-century architecture, Sellwood is an ideal setting for these shops. There are plenty of good restaurants in the area in case it turns into an all-day outing.

You'll also find three more large antiques malls (all under the same ownership) nearby on Milwaukie Boulevard: **Stars,** at 6717 SE Milwaukie Blvd. (© **503/235-9142**), and at 7027 SE Milwaukie Blvd. (© **503/239-0346**); and **Star & Splendid,** 7030 SE Milwaukie Blvd. (© **503/235-5990**).

ART GALLERIES

If you're in the market for art, try to arrange your visit to coincide with the **first Thursday of the month.** On these days galleries in downtown Portland schedule coordinated openings in the evening. Stroll from one gallery to the next, meeting artists and perhaps buying an original work of art.

A guide listing dozens of Portland galleries is available at galleries around Portland.

GENERAL ART GALLERIES

Augen Gallery   When it opened 17 years ago, the Augen Gallery focused on internationally recognized artists such as Jim Dine, Andy Warhol, and David Hockney. Today, the gallery has expanded its repertoire to regional contemporary painters and printmakers as well. 817 SW Second Ave. ℂ **503/224-8182.** www.augengallery.com.

Blackfish Gallery   Artist-owned since 1979, the Blackfish is a large and relaxing space in which to contemplate contemporary images. Since this gallery is a cooperative run by artists, it doesn't have the same constraints as a commercial art gallery and thus can present more cutting-edge and thought-provoking work. 420 NW Ninth Ave. ℂ **503/224-2634.**

Butters Gallery Ltd.   The Butters Gallery has a beautiful and airy loft space on the second floor, where the works of regional and national painters and high-quality artworks in metal, natural fibers, and glass are featured. 520 NW Davis St. ℂ **503/248-9378.** www.buttersgallery.com.

The Laura Russo Gallery   The focus here is on Northwest contemporary artists, showcasing talented emerging artists as well as the estates of well-known artists. Laura Russo has been on the Portland art scene for a long time and is highly respected. 805 NW 21st Ave. ℂ **503/226-2754.**

Margo Jacobsen Gallery   In the heart of the Pearl District, this gallery is where you'll find most of the crowds milling about on First Thursdays. Margo Jacobsen promotes contemporary painters, printmakers, and photographers, with a focus on ceramics and glass. 1039 NW Glisan St. ℂ **503/224-7287.**

Pulliam Deffenbaugh Gallery   This gallery represents a long list of both talented newcomers and masters from the Northwest. Solo shows and salon-style group shows are held here at the Pearl District location, and also at the Pulliam Deffenbaugh Broadway Gallery downtown at 507 SW Broadway (ℂ **503/ 228-8208**). 522 NW 12th Ave. ℂ **503/228-6665.**

Quintana Galleries   This large, bright space is virtually a small museum of Native American art, selling everything from Northwest Indian masks to contemporary paintings and sculptures by various Northwest coast Indian and Inuit artists. They also carry a smattering of Northwest and Southwest Indian antiquities. The jewelry selection is outstanding. Prices, however, are not cheap. 501 SW Broadway. ℂ **503/223-1729.**

ART GLASS

The Bullseye Connection   Located in the Pearl District, the Bullseye Connection is a large open exhibition and sales space for glass artists. Pieces sold here include sculptures, delightful glass jewelry, paperweights, and even marbles. There's even a Dale Chihuly chandelier of pink fruitlike objects on display. Workshops and lectures related to glassmaking are also offered. The **Bullseye**

Connection Gallery, which is across the street at 300 NW 13th St. (℃ **503/ 227-0222**), shows work of internationally acclaimed glass artists. 1308 NW Everett St. ℃ **503/227-2797.**

Fireborne . . . Creations in Glass   Located at Morgan's Alley, this shop carries a wide variety of glass creations by Northwest artists. Ranging from whimsical to elegant, the pieces here include hand-blown, fused, and cast glass incarnated as paperweights, vases, and things that are just plain pretty to look at. Many pieces are small enough to pack conveniently into a carry-on bag. 515 SW Broadway. ℃ **503/227-6585.**

BOOKS

Major chain bookstores in Portland include **Barnes & Noble** at 1231 NE Broadway (℃ **503/335-0201**) and 1720 Jantzen Beach Center (℃ **503/ 283-2800**), and **Borders** at 708 SW Third Ave. (℃ **503/220-5911**).

If you have a special child in mind, try **A Children's Place,** 4807 NE Fremont St. (℃ **503/284-8294**), a this small independent children's bookstore, which has a wide selection of books, tapes, and CDs. Besides author signings, there is a Saturday-morning story time.

CRAFTS

For the largest selection of local crafts, visit the **Portland Saturday Market** (see "Markets," below), which is a showcase for local crafts.

Contemporary Crafts Gallery   In business since 1937 and located in a residential area between downtown and the John's Landing neighborhood, this is the nation's oldest nonprofit art gallery showing exclusively artwork in clay, glass, fiber, metal, and wood. The bulk of the large gallery is taken up by glass and ceramic pieces in ongoing thematic exhibitions. There are also several cabinets of jewelry. 3934 SW Corbett Ave. ℃ **503/223-2654.**

Graystone Gallery   This gallery in the Hawthorne district is full of fun and whimsical artwork and home furnishings, including paintings, jewelry, ceramics, and greeting cards. 3279 SE Hawthorne Blvd. ℃ **503/238-0651.**

Hoffman Gallery   The Hoffman Gallery is located on the campus of the Oregon College of Art and Craft, which has been one of the nation's foremost crafts education centers since 1906. The gallery hosts installations and group shows by local, national, and international artists. The adjacent gift shop has a good selection of handcrafted items. The grounds are serene and relaxing, and there is also a cafe open to the public. 8245 SW Barnes Rd. ℃ **503/297-5544.**

The Real Mother Goose   This is Portland's premier fine crafts shop, and one of the top such shops in the United States. It showcases only the very best contemporary American crafts, including imaginative ceramics, colorful art glass, intricate jewelry, exquisite wooden furniture, and sculptural works. Hundreds of craftspeople and artists from all over the United States are represented here. Even if you're not buying, stop by to see the best of American craftsmanship. 901 SW Yamhill St. ℃ **503/223-9510.** www.therealmothergoose.com. Also at Washington Square; Tigard (℃ **503/620-2243**); and Portland International Airport, Main Terminal (℃ **503/284-9929**).

Twist   This large store has quite a massive selection of wildly colorful and imaginative furniture, crockery, glassware, and lamps, and also a limited but intense selection of handmade jewelry from artists around the United States. Pioneer Place, 700 SW Fifth Ave. ℃ **503/222-3137.** Also at 30 NW 23rd Place (℃ **503/224-0334**).

The City of Books

Portland's own **Powell's City of Books,** 1005 W. Burnside St. (© **800/ 878-7323** or 503/228-4651; www.powells.com), is the bookstore to end all bookstores. Powell's, which covers an entire city block three floors deep, claims to be the world's largest bookstore. Those books, roughly three-quarters of a million at any given time, are shelved side by side— well-thumbed old paperbacks next to the latest hardcover books— which is why browsing is what Powell's is all about.

Once inside the store, be sure to pick up a store map, which will direct you to the color-coded rooms. In the Gold Room, you'll find science fiction and mysteries. The Rose Room has books on ornithology, the outdoors, and sports, among other subjects, as well as children's books. In the Orange Room, there are books on cooking, gardening, business, and crafts. Serious book collectors won't want to miss a visit to the Rare Book Room.

One warning: If you haven't got at least an hour of free time, enter at your own risk. It's so easy to lose track of time at Powell's that many customers miss meals and end up in the store's in-house cafe.

Believe it or not, City of Books is even bigger than what you see here; it has several satellite stores. There's **Powell's Technical Bookstore,** 33 NW Park St. (© **503/228-3906**); **Powell's Books for Cooks and Gardeners,** 3747 SE Hawthorne Blvd. (© **503/235-3802**); **Powell's Books on Hawthorne,** 3723 SE Hawthorne Blvd. (© **503/238-1668**); **Powell's Travel Store,** Pioneer Courthouse Square, SW Sixth Avenue and Yamhill Street (© **503/228-1108**); **Powell's Books in Beaverton,** at the Progress exit off Ore. 217 in Beaverton (© **503/643-3131**); and **Powell's Books at PDX,** Portland International Airport (© **503/ 249-1950**).

DEPARTMENT STORES

Meier and Frank   Meier and Frank is a Portland institution and has been doing business here for more than 100 years. The flagship store on Pioneer Courthouse Square was built in 1898 and, with 10 stories, was at one time the tallest store in the Northwest. Today those 10 floors of consumer goods and great sales still attract crowds of shoppers. The store is open daily, with Friday usually the latest night. 621 SW Fifth Ave. © 503/223-0512. Also at 1100 Lloyd Center (© 503/281-4797) and 9300 SW Washington Square Rd. in Tigard (© 503/620-3311).

Nordstrom   Directly across the street from Pioneer Courthouse Square and a block away from Meier and Frank, Nordstrom is a top-of-the-line department store that originated in the Northwest and takes great pride in its personal service and friendliness. This pride is well founded—the store has devoutly loyal customers who would never dream of shopping anywhere else. 701 SW Broadway. © 503/224-6666. Also at 1001 Lloyd Center (© 503/287-2444) and 9700 SW Washington Square Rd. in Tigard (© 503/620-0555).

FASHION

SPORTSWEAR

Columbia Sportswear Company   This flagship store is surprisingly low-key, given that the nearby Nike flagship store and the new REI in Seattle are designed to knock your socks off. Displays showing the Columbia line of outdoor clothing are rustic, with lots of natural wood. The most dramatic architectural feature of the store is the entryway, in which a very wide tree trunk seems to supports the roof. 911 SW Broadway. *C* **503/226-6800.**

Columbia Sportswear Company Outlet Store *Value*   This outlet store in the Sellwood neighborhood south of downtown and across the river sells well-made outdoor clothing and sportswear from one of the Northwest's premiere outdoor clothing manufacturers. You'll pay 30% to 50% less here than you will at the downtown flagship store (though the clothes will likely be last year's). 1323 SE Tacoma St. *C* **503/238-0118.**

The Jantzen Store   Jantzen is another of Portland's famous sportswear manufacturers. The company got its start when a local rowing team requested wool outfits to keep out the chill, but nowadays Jantzen is supplying outfits for warmer weather. The full line of attractive and innovative swimsuit styles are sold right here, and there are even occasional sales. 921 SW Morrison St. (in the Galleria). *C* **503/221-1443.** www.jantzen.com.

NIKETOWN   Sure, you may have a NIKETOWN back home, but this one is the closest to Nike's headquarters in nearby Beaverton, which somehow makes it just a little bit special. Matte black decor, kinetic displays, and edgy music give NIKETOWN the feel of a sports museum or disco. A true shopping experience. 930 SW Sixth Ave. *C* **503/221-6453.**

Nike Portland Factory Store *Value*   The Nike outlet is one season behind the current season at NIKETOWN, selling swoosh brand running, aerobic, tennis, golf, basketball, kids, and you-name-it sports clothing and accessories at discounted prices. 2650 NE Martin Luther King Jr. Blvd. *C* **503/281-5901.**

MEN'S & WOMEN'S

Langlitz Leathers   This family run shop produces the Rolls Royce of leather jackets. Even though there may be a wait (the shop turns out only six handmade jackets a day), motorcyclists ride their Harleys all the way from the East Coast to be fitted. It's rumored that Jay Leno bought a jacket here before he became famous. 2443 SE Division St. *C* **503/235-0959.**

Norm Thompson   Known throughout the country for its mail-order catalogs, Norm Thompson is a mainstay of the well-to-do in Portland. Classic styling for men and women is the name of the game here. 1805 NW Thurman St. *C* **503/221-0764.** Also at Portland International Airport (*C* **503/249-0170**).

The Portland Pendleton Shop   Pendleton wool is as much a part of life in the Northwest as forests and salmon. This company's fine wool fashions for men and women define the country-club look in the Northwest and in many other parts of the country. Pleated skirts and tweed jackets are de rigueur here, as are the colorful blankets that have warmed generations of Northwesterners through long chilly winters. 900 SW Fifth Ave. (entrance is actually on Fourth Ave. between Salmon and Taylor). *C* **503/242-0037.**

For Serious Pendleton Fans

If you'd like to see how Pendleton's famous wool blankets and classic wool fashions are made, drive 16 miles east of Vancouver, Washington, on Wash. 14 to the town of **Washougal,** where you can visit the **Pendleton Woolen Mills and Outlet Shop,** 217th Street (📞 **800/568-2480** or 360/835-1118). The store is open Monday through Friday from 8am to 5pm, Saturday from 9am to 5pm, and Sunday from 1 to 5pm, with free mill tours offered Monday to Friday at 9, 10, and 11am, and 1:30pm.

CHILDREN'S CLOTHING

Hanna Andersson   Based on Swedish designs and made with comfort and warmth in mind, Hanna's carries 100% cotton clothing for babies, kids, and women. Striped Swedish long johns, snuggly baby suits, and girl's dresses are some of the items you'll find here. 327 NW Tenth Ave. 📞 800/222-0544 or 503/321-5275.

MEN'S CLOTHING

John Helmer   This is a classic, old-fashioned men's haberdasher and has been dressing Portland men since 1921. The hat selection is the best in the city. 969 SW Broadway. 📞 **503/223-4976.**

Mario's   Located inside the Galleria, Mario's sells self-consciously stylish European men's fashions straight off the pages of *GQ.* Prices are as high as you would expect. If you long to be European, but if your birth certificate says otherwise, here you can at least adopt the look. 921 SW Morrison St. 📞 **503/227-3477.**

WOMEN'S CLOTHING

Byrkit   Byrkit specializes in natural fabric clothing of cotton, silk, rayon, and linen for women. The contemporary designs, including dresses, jumpers, and separates, are built for comfort but include a lot of style. 2200 NE Broadway. 📞 503/282-3773.

Changes   Located next door to The Real Mother Goose gallery, this shop specializes in handmade clothing, including hand-woven scarves, jackets, shawls, hand-painted silks, and other wearable art. 927 SW Yamhill St. 📞 **503/223-3737.**

Elizabeth Street   You'll find a small and basic selection of casual but up-to-the-minute women's fashions, accessories, and jewelry. This store also stocks trendy fashions for men and shares space with Zelda's Shoe Bar (see below). 635 NW 23rd Ave. 📞 **503/243-2456.**

The Eye of Ra   Women with sophisticated tastes in ethnic fashions will want to visit this shop in The Water Tower at John's Landing shopping center. Silk and rayon predominate, and there's ethnic jewelry by creative designers to accompany any ensemble you might put together here. Ethnic furniture and home decor are also for sale. 5331 SW Macadam Ave. 📞 **503/224-4292.**

M. Sellin Ltd.   Located in the relaxed and low-key Hawthorne district, this shop carries women's "soft dressing" clothing made of natural fabrics with comfortable styling along the lines of designers such as Mishi and Amanda Gray. There's also a good selection of jewelry at reasonable prices. 3556 SE Hawthorne Blvd. 📞 **503/239-4605.**

Mario's   Flip through the pages of a European edition of *Vogue* magazine and you'll get an idea of the fashions you can find at the women's version of fashionable Mario's (located across the street from Mario's for men, above). Up-to-the-minute and back-to-the-future European fashions fill the racks. 811 SW Morrison St. ☎ 503/241-8111.

Mercantile   This specialty store carries modern classic clothing from blue jeans to black tie. Designers represented are both European and American, from Zannela Italian separates to the whimsical fashions of Nicole Miller. You'll find stylish purses, exquisite formal wear, and cashmere sweaters. The occasional sale yields some good selections at discount prices. 735 SW Park St. (across the street from Nordstrom). ☎ 503/223-6649.

Zelda's Shoe Bar   Nothing's cheap here, but if you're looking for a fake calf-skin-covered ballerina flat or the latest in a velvet-flocked cowboy boot, they've got it. 633 NW 23rd Ave. ☎ 503/226-0363.

FOOD
The **Made in Oregon** shops offer the best selection of local food products such as hazelnuts, marion-berry and raspberry jam, and smoked salmon. See "Gifts & Souvenirs," below, for details.

GIFTS & SOUVENIRS
For unique locally made souvenirs, your best bet is the **Portland Saturday Market** (see "Markets," below, for details). See also the listing for **Urbino** under "Home Furnishings," below.

Made in Oregon   This is your one-stop shop for all manner of made-in-Oregon gifts, food products, and clothing. Every product sold is either grown, caught, or made in Oregon. You'll find smoked salmon, filberts, jams and jellies, Pendleton woolens, and Oregon wines. All branches are open daily, but hours vary from store to store. 921 SW Morrison St. (in the Galleria). ☎ 800/828-9673 or 503/241-3630. www.madeinoregon.com. Also at Portland International Airport (☎ 503/282-7827); in Lloyd Center mall, SE Multnomah Street and SE Broadway (☎ 503/282-7636); and in Old Town at 10 NW First Ave. (☎ 503/273-8354).

HOME FURNISHINGS
Urbino   This store is artistic and lush, selling special things for the home and body. You'll find, among other items, handmade candles, hand-milled soaps, napkins, scarves, ceramics, jewelry, pillows, and picture frames. 521 NW 23rd Ave. ☎ 503/220-0053.

JEWELRY
For some of the most creative jewelry in Portland, visit **Twist,** the **Graystone Gallery,** the **Hoffman Gallery,** the **Contemporary Craft Gallery,** and the **Real Mother Goose.** See "Crafts," above.

MALLS & SHOPPING CENTERS
Lloyd Center   This large shopping mall in inner northeast Portland has five anchor stores and more than 200 specialty shops, including a Nordstrom and a Meier and Frank. A food court, ice-skating rink, and eight-screen cinema complete the mall's facilities. Bounded by SE Multnomah St., NE Broadway, NE 16th Ave., and NE Ninth Ave. ☎ 503/282-2511.

Pioneer Place   Located only a block from Pioneer Courthouse Square, this is Portland's most upscale downtown shopping center. Anchored by a Saks Fifth Avenue, Pioneer Place is filled with stores selling designer fashions and expensive gifts. You'll find the city's only Godiva chocolatier here and Todai, a Japanese restaurant with a 160-foot sushi bar. 700 SW Fifth Ave. (between Third and Fifth aves.). © 503/228-5800.

The Water Tower at Johns Landing   As you're driving south from downtown on Macadam Avenue, you can't miss the old wooden water tower for which this unusual mall is named. Standing high above the roof, it was once used as a storage tank for fire-fighting water. Hardwood floors, huge overhead beams, and a tree-shaded courtyard paved with Belgian cobblestones from Portland's first paved streets give this place plenty of character. There are about 40 specialty shops and restaurants here. 5331 SW Macadam Ave. © 503/242-0022. www.watertoweratjohnslanding.com.

MARKETS

Portland Saturday Market   The Portland Saturday Market (held on both Sat and Sun, despite its name) is arguably the city's single most important and best-loved event. For years, the Northwest has attracted artists and craftspeople, and every weekend, nearly 300 of them can be found selling their creations here. In addition to the dozens of crafts stalls, you'll find ethnic and unusual foods, and lots of free entertainment. This is one of the best places in Portland to shop for one-of-a-kind gifts. The atmosphere is always cheerful and the crowds are always colorful. Don't miss it. On Sunday, on-street parking is free. Open the first weekend in March through Christmas Eve, Saturday 10am to 5pm, Sunday 11am to 4:30pm; closed January and February. Under the west end of the Burnside Bridge (between SW First Ave. and SW Naito Pkwy.). © 503/222-6072. www.portlandsaturday market.com.

TOYS

Finnegan's Toys and Gifts   This is the largest toy store in downtown Portland. It'll have your inner child kicking and screaming if you don't buy that silly little toy you never got when you were young. 922 SW Yamhill St. © 503/221-0306. www.finneganstoys.com.

Paint the Sky Kites   Forget the little jockey or pink flamingos on the front lawn. What you need is one of the colorful wind-driven nylon whirligigs or pennants they sell here. You can't miss this store on trendy NW 23rd Avenue. Just look for the spinning and flapping rainbow of colors in front of an old Victorian building. There are all kinds of kites and plenty of fun toys, too. 828 NW 23rd Ave. © 503/222-5096. www.paintthesky.com.

WINE

Great Wine Buys   Oenophiles who have developed a taste for Oregon wines may want to stock up here before heading home. This is one of the best little wine shops in Portland and has a tasting bar where you can sample the wines. The staff is always very helpful. 1515 NE Broadway. © 503/287-2897. www.greatwine buys.citysearch.com.

Oregon Wines on Broadway   This cozy wine bar/shop is located diagonally across from the Hotel Vintage Plaza in downtown Portland. Here you can taste some of Oregon's fine wines, including 30 different pinot noirs, as well as chardonnays, and gewürztraminers and Washington state cabernet sauvignons and merlots. 515 SW Broadway. © 503/228-4655.

19

Portland After Dark

Portland is the Northwest's number two cultural center (after Seattle, of course). The city's symphony orchestra, ballet, and opera are all well regarded, and the many theater companies offer classic and contemporary plays. If you're a jazz fan, you'll feel right at home—there's always a lot of live jazz being played around town. In summer, festivals move the city's cultural activities outdoors.

To find out what's going on during your visit, pick up a copy of *Willamette Week,* Portland's free weekly arts-and-entertainment newspaper. The *Oregonian,* the city's daily newspaper, also publishes lots of entertainment-related information in its Friday "A&E" section and also in the Sunday edition of the paper.

1 The Performing Arts

For the most part, the Portland performing arts scene revolves around the **Portland Center for the Performing Arts** (**PCPA**), 1111 SW Broadway (© **503/248-4335**), which is comprised of five performances spaces in three different buildings. The **Arlene Schnitzer Concert Hall,** Southwest Broadway and Southwest Main Street, known locally as the Schnitz, is an immaculately restored 1920s movie palace that still displays the original Portland theater sign and marquee out front and is home to the Oregon Symphony. This hall also hosts popular music performers, lecturers, and many other special performances. Directly across Main Street from the Schnitz, at 1111 SW Broadway, is the sparkling glass jewel box known as the **New Theater Building.** This building houses both the **Newmark** and **Dolores Winningstad** theaters and **Brunish Hall.** The **Newmark** Theatre is home to Portland Center Stage, while the two theaters together host stage productions by local and visiting companies. Free tours of all three of these theaters are held Wednesdays at 11am, Saturdays every half hour between 11am and 1pm, and the first Thursday of every month at 6pm. A few blocks away from this concentration of venues is the 3,000-seat **Keller Auditorium,** SW Third Avenue and SW Clay Street, the largest of the four halls and the home of the Portland Opera and the Oregon Ballet Theatre. The auditorium was constructed shortly after World War I and completely remodeled in the 1960s. In addition to resident companies mentioned above, these halls together host numerous visiting companies each year, including touring Broadway shows.

Note that tickets to PCPA performances are sold through either **Ticket Master** (© **503/224-4400**) or **Fastixx** (© **503/224-8499**), depending on the show. PCPA's box office is open for ticket sales only for 2 hours before a show. All other times, you can purchase tickets at **Ticket Central** (© **503/275-8358**), which is located at the **Portland Oregon Visitors Association** (**POVA**) **Information Center,** 701 SW Sixth Ave, Suite 1, in Pioneer Courthouse Square. This ticket office also sells day-of-show, half-price tickets to many area performances.

Ticket, Please

Tickets for many of the venues listed below can be purchased through either **TicketMaster** (© **503/224-4400**; www.ticketmaster.com), which has outlets at area G. I. Joe's and Meier and Frank stores, or **Fastixx** (© **800/ 992-TIXX** or 503/224-8499; www.fastixx.com), which has outlets at area Safeway stores. More convenient for many visitors will be **Ticket Central** (© **503/275-8358**), which is located at the Portland Oregon Visitors Association (POVA) Information Center, 701 SW Sixth Ave, Suite 1, in Pioneer Courthouse Square. This one-stop walk-up ticket-shopping desk sells tickets to events and performances at almost all Portland venues. Half-price, day-of-show tickets are available.

Many theaters and performance halls in Portland offer discounts to students and senior citizens, who can often save money by buying tickets on the day of a performance or within a half hour of curtain time.

For much more daring and cutting-edge performances, check out the calendar of the **Portland Institute for Contemporary Art** (**PICA**), 219 NW 12th Ave. (© **503/242-1419;** www.pica.org), which was created as a resource for exploring and supporting experimental art and new music in this city. PICA presents innovative performances by both well-known and less-established performance artists and musicians, as well as visual exhibitions focusing on contemporary trends in the regional, national, and international art scene. Call for a current schedule of performance events, which are held at various venues around town (tickets $16–$23).

One other performing arts venue worth checking out is **The Old Church,** 1422 SW 11th Ave. (© **503/222-2031;** www.oldchurch.org). Built in 1883, this wooden Carpenter Gothic church is a Portland landmark. It incorporates a grand traditional design, but was constructed with spare ornamentation. Today the building serves as a community facility, and every Wednesday at noon it hosts free lunchtime classical music concerts. There are also many other performances held here throughout the year.

OPERA & CLASSICAL MUSIC

Founded in 1896, the **Oregon Symphony** (© **800/228-7343** or 503/228-1353; www.orsymphony.org), which performs at the Arlene Schnitzer Concert Hall, 1111 SW Broadway (see above), is the oldest symphony orchestra on the West Coast. Under the expert baton of conductor James de Preist, the symphony has achieved national recognition and each year between September and June stages several series, including classical, pops, Sunday matinees, and children's concerts. Ticket prices range from $15 to $55 (seniors and students may purchase half-price tickets 1 hr. before a classical or pops concert; Monday nights there are $5 student tickets).

Each season, the **Portland Opera** (© **503/241-1802;** www.portlandopera. org), which performs at Keller Auditorium, SW Third Avenue and SW Clay Street (see above), offers five different productions that include both grand opera and light opera. The season runs from September to May. Ticket prices range from $25 to $155.

Summer is the time for Portland's annual chamber music binge. **Chamber Music Northwest** (© **503/294-6400;** www.cmnw.org) is a 5-week-long series that starts in late June and attracts the world's finest chamber musicians. Performances are held at Reed College and Catlin Gable School (tickets $17–$33).

THEATER

Portland Center Stage (℡ **503/274-6588;** www.pcs.org), which stages performances at the Portland Center for the Performing Arts, 1111 SW Broadway (see above), is Portland's largest professional theater company. They stage a combination of six classic and contemporary plays during their September-to-April season (tickets $16–$44).

The play's the thing at **Tygres Heart Shakespeare Co.** (℡ **503/288-8400;** www.tygresheart.org), which performs at the Dolores Winningstad Theatre, 1111 SW Broadway (see above), and old Will would be proud. Tygres Heart remains true to its name and stages only works by the bard himself. The three-play season runs from September to May (tickets $11–$32).

If it's musicals you want, you've got a couple of options in Portland. At the Keller Auditorium, you can catch the **Portland Opera Presents the Best of Broadway** series (℡ **503/241-1802;** www.broadwayseries.com). Tickets range from around $15 to $69. For other classics from Broadway's past, check the schedule of the **Musical Theatre Company** (℡ **503/916-6592** or 503/224-5411; www.themusicaltheatrecompany.com), a semiprofessional company that performs at the Eastside Performance Center, SE 14th Avenue and SE Stark Street. The season runs September to May (tickets are $26–$30 for adults, $24–$28 for seniors, and $16 for students).

For more daring theater productions, see what's on tap at the **Artists Repertory Theater,** 1516 SW Alder St. (℡ **503/241-1278;** www.artistsrep.org); **IMAGO Theatre,** 17 SE Eighth Ave. (℡ **503/231-9581;** www.imagotheatre. com), which is best known for its fun *Frogz* performance piece; or **Miracle Theater/Teatro Milagro,** 425 SE Sixth Ave. (℡ **503/236-7253;** www. milagro.org), which specializes in Latino-inspired theater. Also, at 3430 SE Belmont St., you'll find Theater! Theatre!, which is home to three of Portland's more adventurous theater companies: **Stark Raving Theater** (℡ **503/ 232-7072;** www.starkravingtheatre.org), which, among other performances, stages an annual "New Plays Festival" featuring works-in-progress by Northwest playwrights; **Triangle Productions** (℡ **503/239-5919;** www.tripro.org), which stages numerous plays with gay themes; and **Profile Theatre Project** (℡ **503/ 242-0080**), which each season stages the plays of a single playwright (Harold Pinter in the 2001–02 season).

DANCE

Although the **Oregon Ballet Theatre** (℡ **888/922-5538** or 503/222-5538; www.obt.org), which performs at the Keller Auditorium and the Newmark Theatre (see above), is best loved for its sold-out performances each December of *The Nutcracker,* this company also stages the annual American Choreographers Showcase. This latter performance often features world premiers. Rounding out the season are performances of classic and contemporary ballets (tickets $5–$80).

More unusual dance performances are staged by **White Bird** (℡ **503/ 245-1600;** www.whitebird.com), which brings a wide range of touring companies to town. Among the companies being brought to town for the 2001-02 season are Les Ballets Trockadero de Monte Carlo (Jan 23, 2002), Pilobolus (Mar 13, 2002), and the Lyon Opera Ballet (May 8, 2002). Tickets generally cost between $18 and $39.

PERFORMING ARTS SERIES

The **Museum After Hours** series at the **Portland Art Museum's North Wing**, 1119 SW Park Ave. (☏ **503/226-2811**), is a great place to catch some of the best local jazz, blues, rock, and folk bands. Performances are held October through April on Wednesday nights from 5:30 to 7:30pm, and admission is $6.

When summer hits, Portlanders like to head outdoors to hear music. The city's top outdoor music series is held at **Washington Park Zoo,** 4001 SW Canyon Rd. (☏ **503/226-1561;** www.oregonzoo.org), which brings in the likes of Bonnie Raitt, John Prine, and Leo Kottke.

Summer also brings the annual **Portland International Performance Festival** (**PIPFest;** ☏ **800/547-8887,** ext. 3307, or 503/725-3307; www.extended. pdx.edu/pipf/), a month-long binge of theater, film/video, dance, performance art, music, and photography. The festival, which takes place between late June and late July, is sponsored by Portland State University and brings lots of great cutting edge performances to town. Main stage tickets are $18 ($14 for seniors and students).

2 The Club & Music Scene

ROCK, BLUES & FOLK

Aladdin Theater   This former movie theater now serves as one of Portland's main venues for touring performers such as Richard Thompson, the Buena Vista Social Club, and Brian Wilson. The very diverse musical spectrum represented here includes blues, rock, ethnic, country, folk, and jazz. There are also regular singer-songwriter programs. 3017 SE Milwaukie Ave. ☏ **503/233-1994.** www.show man.com. Tickets $10–$25.

Berbati's Pan   Located in Old Town, this is currently one of Portland's most popular rock clubs. A wide variety of acts, primarily the best of the local rock scene and bands on the verge of breaking into the national limelight, play here. 231 SW Ankeny St. ☏ **503/248-4579.** www.berbati.citysearch.com. Cover $5–$15.

Crystal Ballroom   The Crystal Ballroom first opened before 1920, and since then has seen performers ranging from early jazz musicians to James Brown, Marvin Gaye, and The Grateful Dead. The McMenamin Brothers (of local brewing fame) renovated the Crystal Ballroom several years back and refurbished its dance floor, which, due to its mechanics, feels as if it's floating. The ballroom now hosts a variety of performances and special events nearly every night of the week. Lola's Room, a smaller version of the Ballroom, is located downstairs on the second floor and also has a floating dance floor. You'll find Ringlers Pub (a colorful brewpub) on the ground floor. 1332 W. Burnside St. ☏ **503/225-0047,** ext. 239 for box office, or 503/225-5555, ext. 8811 for concert information. www.danceonair.com. Cover free–$28.

Roseland Theater & Grill   The Roseland Theater, though it isn't all that large, is currently Portland's premier live music club for touring national name acts. You might encounter the likes of the Neville Brothers, Tower of Power, or Steel Pulse. There's also a restaurant affiliated with the club. 8 NW Sixth Ave. ☏ **503/219-9929.** Cover $5–$35.

JAZZ

Brasserie Montmartre   Located just a block off Broadway and a block away from Pioneer Courthouse Square, this is downtown Portland's most popular spot for live jazz. The Bra, as its known by regulars, is also a favorite French restaurant, and customers tend to dress up. There's live jazz nightly. 626 SW Park Ave. ⒸＴ **503/224-5552.** No cover.

Heathman Hotel Lobby Lounge   Jazz is big with downtown hotels, and along SW Broadway, there are no less than three hotel lounges featuring live jazz. Although it isn't quite as swank a place as the Lobby Court at The Benson, this place is plenty upscale. There's live music Tuesday through Saturday nights. In the Heathman Hotel, 1001 SW Broadway. Ⓒ **503/790-7752.**

Jazz De Opus   Located in the Old Town nightlife district, this restaurant/bar has long been one of Portland's bastions of jazz, with a cozy room and smooth sounds on the stereo. You can also catch live performances nightly by jazz musicians. 33 NW Second Ave. Ⓒ **503/222-6077.** Cover $5 on weekends.

The Lobby Court   Hands down the most elegant and old-world bar in Portland, the Lobby Court is in the lobby of the city's most luxurious hotel. The Circassian walnut paneling and crystal chandeliers will definitely put you in the mood for a martini or single malt. Tuesday through Saturday, there's live jazz in the evening. In the Benson Hotel, 309 SW Broadway. Ⓒ **503/228-2000.**

Typhoon! Imperial Lounge   Located off the lobby of downtown Portland's Imperial Hotel, this bar has live jazz Thursday through Saturday nights. Big windows fronting on the sidewalk let you check out the scene before venturing in. An eclectic array of musicians makes this place a bit different from other area jazz clubs. In the Imperial Hotel, 400 SW Broadway. Ⓒ **503/224-8285.** No cover.

COMEDY, CABARET & DINNER THEATER

ComedySportz Arena   This is the home of the ever-popular ComedySportz improv comedy troupe. Shows are Friday at 9pm and Saturday at 7:30 and 9:30pm. Reservations are highly recommended, especially between September and April. The nature of the beast is that you never know what to expect. Have fun. 1963 NW Kearney St. Ⓒ **503/236-8888.** www.cpmedysportz.com. Cover $12 ($10 with a can of food for the Food Bank).

Darcelle's XV   In business since 1967 and run by Portland's best-loved cross-dresser, this cabaret is a campy Portland institution with a female-impersonator show that has been a huge hit for years. There are shows Wednesday through Saturday. Reservations are recommended. 208 NW Third Ave. Ⓒ **503/222-5338.** www.darcellexv.citysearch.com. Cover $10.

DANCE CLUBS

See also the listing for Saucebox, below, under "The Bar Scene"; this restaurant and bar becomes a dance club after 10pm, when a DJ begins spinning tunes.

Andrea's Cha-Cha Club   Located in the Grand Cafe and open on Wednesday through Saturday nights, this is Portland's premier dance spot for fans of Latin dancing. Whether it's cha-cha, salsa, macarena, or the latest dance craze from south of the border, they'll be doing it here. Lessons are available between 8:30 and 9:30pm. 832 SE Grand Ave. Ⓒ **503/230-1166.** Cover $1–$3.

Bar 71   Located in the Old Town nightlife district, Bar 71 is a mixed-use sort of place. It offers DJ dancing Thursday through Saturday on the back patio, pool tables in front, and good bar food. It's the classiest of the Old Town bars. In summer, you can dance under the stars. 71 SW Second Ave. Ⓒ **503/241-0938.** No cover before 9:30pm, $5 9:30–10pm, $10 after 10pm.

Fernando's Hideaway   Located upstairs from a popular Spanish tapas restaurant and bar, this is the hottest Latin dance club in Portland. The dance floor is tiny and the place gets packed, but that's just fine with the cruising singles who hang out here. Open Thursday through Saturday nights. 824 SW First Ave. ℭ 503/248-4709. Cover $5.

3 The Bar Scene

BARS

The Brazen Bean   What started out as a late-night coffeehouse is now a very hip cocktail and cigar bar with a fin-de-siècle European elegance in Northwest Portland. This is mainly a man's domain, but cigar-puffing women will appreciate it as well. 2075 NW Glisan St. ℭ 503/294-0636.

Jake's Famous Crawfish   In business since 1892, Jake's is a Portland institution and should not be missed (see the full dining review in chapter 15, "Where to Dine in Portland"). Although this historic fish house is best known for its crawfish, the bar here also happens to be one of the busiest in town when the downtown offices let out. 401 SW 12th Ave. ℭ 503/226-1419.

McCormick and Schmick's Harborside Pilsner Room   Located at the south end of Tom McCall Waterfront Park overlooking the Willamette River and RiverPlace Marina, this restaurant/bar is affiliated with Hood River's Full Sail brewery and keeps 10 Full Sail brews on tap (plus 15 other area beers). However, the bar also does a brisk cocktail business. The crowd is upscale, and the view is one of the best in town. See chapter 15 for a full review of the restaurant here. 0309 SW Montgomery St. ℭ 503/220-1865. www.mccormickandschmicks.com.

¡Oba!   Currently one of the trendiest bars in Portland, this big Pearl District bar/nuevo Latino restaurant has a very tropical feel despite the warehouse district locale (see chapter 15 for a full dining review). After work, the bar is always packed with the stylish and the upwardly mobile. Don't miss the tropical-fruit margaritas! 555 NW 12th Ave. ℭ 503/228-6161.

Paragon   Dark and cavernous, this Pearl District warehouse makeover is among the hippest hangouts in town, and regulars like to dress to impress. Not so overdone that you can't recognize the space's industrial heritage, this place has a sort of Edward-Hopper-meets-the-21st-century feel. There's live music on Wednesday and Thursday nights and a DJ on Fridays and Saturdays. 1309 NW Hoyt St. ℭ 503/833-5060. www.paragonrestaurant.com.

Saucebox   Popular with the city's scene-makers, this downtown hybrid restaurant-bar is a large, dramatically lit dark box that can be very noisy. If you want to talk, you'd better do it before 10pm, when the DJ arrives to transform this place from restaurant into dance club. Great cocktails. 214 SW Broadway. ℭ 503/241-3393.

Veritable Quandary   This tiny old brick building sits alone in the shadow of the Hawthorne Bridge and looks like a relic from the past. Inside you'll find not only an excellent restaurant (see chapter 15 for a full review) but also a lively bar scene that pulls in a young professional crowd. There's also a long list of wines by the glass. 1220 SW First Ave. ℭ 503/227-7342.

Who-Song and Larry's   Sure it's a bar in a Mexican restaurant chain, but the location right on the Willamette River is hard to beat. Grab a table out on the deck and watch the boats drift by. Happy hour specials from 4 to 7pm on weekdays (except for Wed) pull in the after-work crowd. 4850 SW Macadam Ave. ℭ 503/223-8845.

WINE BARS

In addition to the wine bars listed here, you'll also find a winery of sorts in Portland. **Urban Wineworks,** 407 NW 16th Ave. (✆ **503/226-WRXS**), doesn't actually make its wines here on the premises, but it does operate a tasting room. You can try not only the wines from this winery but also those from guest wineries.

The Empire Room Wine Bar   Located at the eastern end of the Hawthorne neighborhood, this little wine bar has a casual and Bohemian feel; it's the sort of place where poets would feel comfortable. The wine list focuses on European wines, and there's live music several nights a week. 4260 SE Hawthorne Blvd. ✆ 503/231-9225. www.jazzwineblues.com.

Oregon Wines on Broadway   As the name implies, this tiny place, with just a handful of stools at the bar and a couple of cozy tables, is devoted almost exclusively to Oregon wines, and on any given night, there will be 30 Oregon pinot noirs available by the glass. Plenty of white wines, too. This is the best place in Portland to learn about Oregon wines. 515 SW Broadway. ✆ 503/228-4655.

Southpark Seafood Grill & Wine Bar   With its high ceiling, long heavy drapes, halogen lights, and lively wall mural, the wine bar at Southpark (see the full dining review in chapter 15, "Where to Dine in Portland") is a contemporary interpretation of a Parisian cafe from the turn of the last century. Very romantic. 901 SW Salmon St. ✆ 503/326-1300.

BREWPUBS

They're brewing beers in Portland the likes of which you won't taste in too many other places on this side of the Atlantic. If you're a beer connoisseur, you'll probably find yourself with little time out from your brew tasting to see any of Portland's other attractions. This is the heart of the Northwest craft-brewing explosion, and although many of Portland's craft beers are available in restaurants, you owe it to yourself to go directly to the source.

Brewpubs have become big business in Portland, and there are now glitzy upscale pubs as well as funky warehouse-district locals. What this means is that no matter what vision you have of the ideal brewpub, you're likely to find your dream come true here in Portland. Whether you're wearing bike shorts or a three-piece suit, there's a pub in Portland where you can get a handcrafted beer, a light meal, and a vantage for enjoying the convivial atmosphere that only a pub can provide.

With almost three dozen brewpubs in the Portland metropolitan area, the McMenamins chain is Portland's biggest brewpub empire, and the owners of this empire think of themselves as its court jesters. McMenamins pubs tend to mix brewing fanaticism with a Deadhead aesthetic. Throw in a bit of historic preservation and a strong belief in family friendly neighborhood pubs and you'll understand why these joints are so popular.

DOWNTOWN

McMenamins Ringlers Pub   With mosaic pillars framing the bar, Indonesian antiques, and big old signs all around, this cavernous place is about as eclectic a brewpub as you'll ever find. A block away are two associated pubs in a flat-iron building; one is below street level with a beer cellar feel and the other has walls of multipaned glass. These three pubs are the most atmospheric alehouses in town. 1332 W. Burnside St. ✆ 503/225-0627. www.mcmenamins.com.

Tugboat Brewpub   This tiny brewpub on an alleylike street just off Broadway near The Benson hotel is just what a good local pub should be. With its picnic-table decor, it's decidedly casual, but the shelves of books lend the place a literary bent. Good brews, too. 711 SW Ankeny St. ✆ 503/226-2508.

NORTHWEST PORTLAND

BridgePort Brewery and BrewPub   Located in the trendy Pearl District, Portland's oldest microbrewery was founded in 1984 and is housed in the city's oldest industrial building (where workers once produced rope for sailing ships). The ivy-draped old brick building has loads of character, just right for enjoying craft ales, of which there are usually four to seven on tap on any given night (including several cask-conditioned ales). The pub also makes great pizza. 1313 NW Marshall St. ✆ **888/834-7546** or 503/241-7179. www.bridgeportbrew.com.

New Old Lompoc   Boasting the best beer garden in the city, this comfortable neighborhood pub at the north end of trendy NW 23rd Avenue is also one of Portland's outposts of strong ales and other unusual brews. If you've had it with hefeweizen and berry beers, check this place out. 1616 NW 23rd Ave. ✆ **503/225-1855.**

Portland Brewing Company's Brewhouse Tap Room and Grill   With huge copper fermenting vats proudly displayed and polished to a high sheen, this is by far the city's most ostentatious, though certainly not its largest, brewpub. We aren't particularly fond of the brews here, but Portland Brewing's MacTarnahan's Scottish-style amber ale does have some very loyal fans. 2730 NW 31st Ave. ✆ 503/228-5269.

Rogue Ales Public House   This Pearl District pub is an outpost of a popular microbrewery headquartered in the Oregon coast community of Newport. Rogue produces just about the widest variety of beers in the state, and, best of all, keeps lots of them on tap at this pub. If you're a fan of barley-wine ale, don't miss their Old Crustacean. 1339 NW Flanders St. ✆ 503/241-3800.

SOUTHEAST

BridgePort Ale House   This neighborhood pub is a satellite of the ever-popular BridgePort Brew Pub in the Pearl District and serves the same great beers. It has a very California feel, with lots of wood and an upscale bar. Lots of firkins (cask-conditioned ales) as well as standard taps. Good menu. 3632 SE Hawthorne Blvd. ✆ **503/233-6540.** www.bridgeportbrew.com.

The Lucky Labrador Brew Pub   With a warehouse-size room, industrial feel, and picnic tables on the loading dock out back, this brewpub is a classic southeast Portland local. The crowd is young, and dogs are welcome (they don't even have to be Labs). 915 SE Hawthorne Blvd. ✆ 503/236-3555. www.luckylab.com.

NORTHEAST & NORTH PORTLAND PUBS

Alameda Brewhouse   With its industrial chic interior, this high-ceilinged neighborhood pub brews up some of the most unusual beers in Portland. How about a rose-petal bock, a juniper berry porter, or heather-flower ales made without hops? Some work, some don't, but fans of craft beers have to appreciate the willingness to experiment. 4765 NE Fremont St. ✆ 503/460-9025.

McMenamins Kennedy School   Never thought they'd ever start serving beer in elementary school, did you? However, in the hands of the local McMenamins brewpub empire, an old northeast Portland school has been transformed into a sprawling complex complete with brewpub, beer garden, movie theater pub, a cigar-and-cocktails room, even a bed-and-breakfast inn. Order up a pint and wander the halls checking out all the cool artwork. 5736 NE 33rd Ave. ✆ **503/ 288-2192.** www.mcmenamins.com.

Portland's Brewing Up a Microstorm

Though espresso is the drink that drives Portland, relaxing over a flavorful pint of ale is what draws educated beer drinkers to the city's dozens of brewpubs. No other city in America has such a great concentration of brewpubs, and it was here that the craft brewing business got its start in the mid-1980s. Today, brewpubs continue to proliferate, with cozy neighborhood pubs vying for business with big, polished establishments.

To fully appreciate what the city's craft brewers are concocting, it helps to have a little beer background. There are four basic ingredients in beer: malt, hops, yeast, and water. The first of these, malt, is made from grains, primarily barley and wheat, which are roasted to convert their carbohydrates into the sugar needed to grow yeast. The amount of roasting the grains receive during the malting process will determine the color and flavor of the final product. The darker the malt, the darker and more flavorful the beer or ale. There is a wide variety of malts, each providing its own characteristic flavor. Yeast in turn converts the malt's sugar into alcohol; there are many different strains of yeast that all lend different characters to beers. The hops are added to give beer its characteristic bitterness. The more "hoppy" the beer or ale, the more bitter it becomes. The Northwest is the nation's only commercial hop-growing region, with 75% grown in Washington and 25% grown in Oregon and Idaho.

Lagers, which are cold-fermented, are the most common beers in America and are made from pale malt with a lot of hops added to give them their characteristic bitter flavor. **Pilsner,** a style of beer that originated in the mid–19th century in Czechoslovakia, is a type of lager. **Ales,** which are the most common brews served at microbreweries, are made using a warm fermentation process and usually with more and darker malt than is used in lagers and pilsners. **Porters** and **stouts** get their characteristic dark coloring and flavor from the use of dark, even charred, malt.

To these basics, you can then add a few variables. Fruit-flavored beers, which some disparage as soda pop beer, are actually an old European tradition and, when considering the abundance of fresh fruits in the Northwest, are a natural here. If you see a sign for nitro beer in a pub, it isn't referring to their explosive brews—it means they've got a keg charged with nitrogen instead of carbon dioxide. The nitrogen gives the beer an extra creamy head. (A nitro charge is what makes Guinness Stout so distinctive.) Cask-conditioned ales, served almost room temperature and with only their own carbon dioxide to create the head, are also gaining in popularity. While some people find these brews flat, others appreciate them for their unadulterated character.

It all adds up to is a lot of variety in Portland pubs. Cheers!

McMenamins St. Johns Pub   Housed in a pavilion built for the 1905 Lewis & Clark Exposition, this building was another great score for the McMenamins, who have snapped up historic buildings left and right over the years. Unusual chandeliers and tapestries give this place a unique atmosphere. 8203 N. Ivanhoe St. ✆ 503/283-8520. www.mcmenamins.com.

Widmer Brewing and Gasthaus   Located in an industrial area just north of the Rose Garden arena, this place has the feel of a classic blue-collar pub. This is the brewery for Portland's largest craft brewing company, which is best known for its hefeweizen. German and American food is served. 955 N. Russell St. ✆ 503/281-3333. www.widmer.com.

OUTLYING BREWPUBS

Cornelius Pass Roadhouse   Housed in an old farmhouse, a hexagonal barn, a new barn made from salvaged wood, and a couple of other restored farm buildings, this pub is surrounded by shade trees, lawns, and picnic tables. This McMenamin brothers pub has a quintessentially Oregonian atmosphere and is a favorite summertime after-work watering hole for Intel employees and others from the area's many high-tech companies. On sunny weekends the picnic tables stay packed all day long. 4045 NW Cornelius Pass Rd., Hillsboro. ✆ 503/640-6174. www.mcmenamins.com. Take U.S. 26 (Sunset Hwy.) west to Cornelius Pass Rd. exit.

McMenamins on the Columbia   Located right on the Columbia River just over the bridge into Washington from north Portland, this is one of the only waterfront brewpubs in the area. Sip your ale and watch the mighty Columbia roll on (and see the jets coming and going from the airport across the river). 1801 SE Columbia River Dr., Vancouver, Washington. ✆ 360/699-1521 or 503/255-9879. www.mcmenamins.com.

Power Station Pub   Located on the grounds of the former Multnomah County poor farm, this McMenamins brewpub has both a pub and a theater pub. Also on the grounds here are an upscale restaurant, a winery and wine-tasting room, a beer garden, The Little Red Shed (a tiny cigar bar), a lodge (the McMenamins Edgefield; see chapter 14, "Where to Stay in Portland"), a nine-hole golf course, and a distillery and bar. An ideal stop on the way back from the Columbia Gorge. 2126 SW Halsey St., Troutdale. ✆ 503/492-4686. www.mcmenamins.com.

IRISH & ENGLISH PUBS

Fadó   This pub may be located in a building that also houses a Gap store, but it's about as authentic as you can get in a stateside Irish pub. Lots of traditional Irish food to go with your pint of Guinness. 2307 NW Westover Rd. (at the corner of W. Burnside St. and NW 23rd Ave.). ✆ 503/221-6621. www.fadoirishpub.com.

Horse Brass Pub   If not for this east-side pub, the local microbrew scene may never have developed. It was here that many of Portland's big-name brewers used to hang out way back in the days when people could only dream of beers as good as those in Europe. There are nearly 50 beer taps here, and you'll find some obscure and delicious brews. There's an adjacent store selling all things beer related, including lots of imported bottled beers. 4534 SE Belmont St. ✆ 503/232-2202. www.horsebrass.com.

Kells   Located in Old Town, Kells is a traditional Irish pub and restaurant. In addition to pulling a good pint of Guinness, it boasts one of the most extensive Scotch whiskey lists on the West Coast. You can listen to live music here every night. 112 SW Second Ave. ✆ 503/227-4057.

4 The Gay & Lesbian Scene

A DANCE CLUB

Embers Avenue   Though this is still primarily a gay disco, it's also popular with straights. There are always lots of flashing lights and sweaty bodies until the early morning. Look for drag shows 6 nights a week; on Mondays, movies are shown on a giant-screen TV. 110 NW Broadway. ℂ 503/222-3082. Cover Fri–Sat $5, Sun–Thurs free.

BARS

The area around the intersection of **SW Stark Street and West Burnside Street** has the largest concentration of gay bars in Portland.

Eagle PDX   If leather and Levi's are your uniform, then you'll feel right at home in this dive bar. Loud rock music plays in the background, and it's popular with a young crowd. Long happy hours with good prices. 1300 W. Burnside St. ℂ 503/241-0105.

The Egyptian Club   Billing itself as a "girl's bar," this solidly lesbian establishment provides an eclectic range of entertainment: live bands, karaoke, "chick flicks," belly dancing, butch strip nights, and even a nude revue. 3701 SE Division St. ℂ 503/236-8689.

Scandal's & The Otherside Lounge   In business for more than 20 years, this bar/restaurant is at ground zero of the gay bar scene. There always seems to be some special event going on here. 1038 SW Stark St. ℂ 503/227-5887. www. scandals.citysearch.com.

5 At the Movies

Portland brewpub magnates the McMenamin brothers have a novel way to sell their craft ales—in movie pubs. Although it's often hard to concentrate on the screen, it's always a lot of fun to attend a show. The movies are usually recent releases that have played the main theaters but have not yet made it onto video. Theaters include the **Bagdad Theater,** 3702 SE Hawthorne Blvd. (ℂ 503/236-9234), a restored classic Arabian Nights movie palace; the **Mission Theater,** 1624 NW Glisan St. (ℂ 503/223-4527), which was the first McMenamins theater pub; the **Kennedy School Theater,** 5736 NE 33rd Ave. (ℂ 503/288-2192), in a former elementary school; and the **Edgefield Theater,** 2126 SW Halsey St., Troutdale (ℂ 503/492-4686).

Located in the heart of downtown, the **Fox Tower 10,** SW Park Avenue and Taylor Street (ℂ 503/225-5555, ext. 4604), is Portland's main theater for first-run foreign and independent films. Buy tickets early—most of the screening rooms here are small and often sell out.

Cinema 21, 616 NW 21st Ave. (ℂ 503/223-4515), is a reliable art-film house screening more daring films than make it to the Fox Tower 10. This is also where you can catch animation festivals and the occasional revival of an obscure classic.

The **Northwest Film Center,** 1219 SW Park Ave. (ℂ 503/221-1156; www.nwfilm.org), affiliated with the Portland Art Museum, is a repertory cinema that schedules an eclectic blend of classics, foreign films, daring avant-garde films, documentaries, visiting artist programs, and thematic series. There's no telling what might turn up on a given night. Some films are shown at the nearby **Guild Theatre,** SW Ninth Avenue and SW Taylor Street.

Side Trips from Portland

Portland likes to boast about how close it is to both mountains and ocean, and no visit would be complete without a trip or two to saltwater or snow. In 1½ hours you can be walking on a Pacific Ocean beach or skiing in the Cascade Range—even in the middle of summer, when there is lift-accessed snow skiing on Mount Hood.

A drive through the Columbia River Gorge, a National Scenic Area, is an absolute must; and if wine is your interest, you can spend a day visiting wineries and driving through the rolling farmland that enticed pioneers to travel the Oregon Trail beginning in the 1840s.

1 The Columbia Gorge & Mount Hood Loop

If you have time for only one excursion from Portland, I strongly urge you to do the Mount Hood Loop. This is a long trip, so start your day as early as possible.

To begin your trip, take I-84 east out of Portland. At Troutdale, take the exit marked **Historic Columbia River Highway** (U.S. 30) ☆☆, which was built between 1913 and 1922. The highway was an engineering marvel in its day, but it is dwarfed by the spectacular vistas that present themselves whenever the scenic road emerges from the dark forest. To learn more about the road and how it was built, stop at **Vista House** ☆☆, 733 feet above the river on **Crown Point.** There are informative displays with old photos and a spectacular view of the gorge, including **Beacon Rock** ☆☆, an 800-foot-tall monolith on the far side of the river.

Between Troutdale and Ainsworth State Park, 22 miles east, you'll pass numerous waterfalls, including Latourelle, Shepherds Dell, Bridal Veil, Wahkeena, Horsetail, Oneonta, and **Multnomah Falls** ☆☆☆. At 620 feet from lip to pool, Multnomah Falls is the tallest waterfall in Oregon and is one of the state's top tourist attractions. Expect crowds. A paved trail leads from the base of the falls to the top and connects with other unpaved trails that are usually not at all crowded.

Not far beyond Multnomah Falls, you'll come to the narrow **Oneonta Gorge** ☆☆. This narrow cleft in the rock has long been a popular summertime walk for the sure of foot. The gorge can usually be explored for about half a mile upstream to a waterfall that pours into a small pool of very cold water. There is no trail here; you just hike up the creek itself, so wear shoes that can get wet. Due to an unstable logjam at the mouth of Oneonta Gorge, the Forest Service has been discouraging people from hiking into this little gorge. Enter at your own risk.

The next stop on your tour should be **Bonneville Lock and Dam** ☆. One of the dam's most important features, attracting thousands of visitors each year, is its fish ladder, which allows the upriver migration of salmon and other *anadromous* fish (fish that are spawned in freshwater, mature in saltwater, and return to

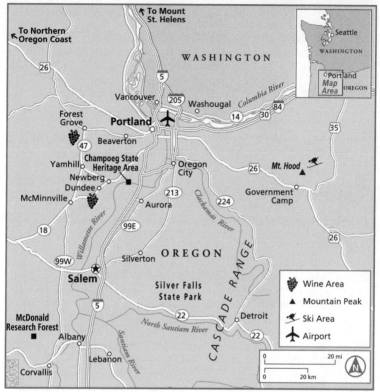

freshwater to spawn). Underwater windows permit visitors to see fish as they pass through the ladder. Visit the adjacent fish hatchery to see how trout, salmon, and sturgeon are raised before they are released into the river. June and September are the best months to observe salmon at the fish ladder.

This is the first of many dams on the Columbia River and, along with the other dams, is currently the focus of a heated environmental debate over saving the region's dwindling native wild salmon populations. Despite fish ladders and fish hatcheries, wild salmon have been fighting an upstream battle for survival. Adult salmon heading upstream to spawn have to contend with fish ladders, fishermen (both commercial and sport), and spawning beds that are sometimes destroyed or silted up, often by the common practice of clear-cutting timber from steep mountainsides. Among the perils faced by young salmon heading downstream are slow, warm waters that delay the journey to the Pacific Ocean, electrical turbines in dams (these kill countless numbers of fish), and irrigation culverts that often lead salmon out into farm fields. With many populations now listed as threatened species (one step below endangered species), a plan for salmon survival is being hammered out. It is hoped that the dams that once brought prosperity and cheap electricity to the Northwest won't bring about the demise of the salmon.

Not far past the dam is the **Bridge of the Gods,** a two-lane toll bridge that connects Oregon to Washington at the site where an Indian legend says a natural bridge once stood. Geologists are now convinced that this legend has its basis in a relatively recent geological event—a massive landslide that may have occurred as recently as 250 years ago. The slide completely blocked the river, and when the Columbia finally poured over the top of this natural dam, the water unleashed a 100-foot flood downstream and rapidly eroded the natural earthen dam leaving only huge slabs of rocks in the riverbed. These rocks created the Cascades for which both the Cascade Range and Cascade Locks were named.

On the Washington side of the Columbia River, east of the Bridge of the Gods, is the **Columbia Gorge Interpretive Center** ✿✿, 990 SW Rock Creek Dr., Stevenson (© **800/991-2338;** www.columbiagorge.org). This modern museum is the single best introduction to the natural and human history of the Columbia Gorge and has an awesome view (when it's not cloudy). Exhibits focus on the Gorge's early Native American inhabitants and the development of the area by white settlers. A relic here that you can't miss is a 37-foot-high replica of a 19th-century fish wheel, which helps show how salmon runs were decimated in the past. Admission is $6 for adults, $5 for seniors and students, $4 for children 6 to 12, and free for children under 6. The center is open daily from 10am to 5pm.

Just beyond Bridge of the Gods on the Oregon side are the **Cascade Locks.** These navigational locks were built to enable river traffic to avoid the treacherous passage through the cascades that once existed at this spot. In earlier years, many boats were portaged around the cascades instead of attempting the dangerous trip. When the locks were opened in 1896, they made traveling between The Dalles and Portland much easier. But the completion of the Historic Columbia River Highway in 1922 made the trip even easier by land. With the construction of the Bonneville Dam, the cascades were flooded, and the locks became superfluous.

There are two small museums here at the locks, one of which also holds the ticket office for the **Sternwheeler** *Columbia Gorge* ✿ (© **800/643-1354,** 503/223-3928 in Portland, or 541/374-8427 in Cascade Locks), which makes regular trips on the river between mid-June and late September. These boat tours provide a fascinating glimpse of the Columbia Gorge and are highly recommended. Tours, which last 2 hours, cost $14.95 for adults and $8.95 for children.

Anyone who boardsails has likely heard of the town of **Hood River** ✿✿. This section of the Columbia River is one of the most popular boardsailing spots in the world because of the strong winds that blow through the gorge in summer. Almost every other car in this once-sleepy little town seems to have a sailboard on the roof. If you want to try this sport yourself, stop by one of the many sailboard shops downtown for information on rentals and lessons.

If you are staying overnight on the loop, you might want to consider getting out of your car and riding the rails. The **Mount Hood Railroad** ✿, 110 Railroad Ave., Hood River (© **800/872-4661**), operates an excursion train from late March to late December carrying passengers up the Hood River Valley from the town of Hood River to Parkdale and back. The railroad cars are vintage Pullman coaches, and the Mount Hood Railroad Depot is a National Historic Site. The excursions last 4 hours, and fares are $22.95 for adults, $20.95 for seniors, and $14.95 for children 2 to 12. The schedule varies with the season, so call ahead to make a reservation. There are also regularly scheduled dinner, brunch, and other specialty excursions. Mid-April's Fruit Blossom Express runs when the fruit orchards are in bloom, and in mid-October, there are Harvest Festival excursions.

The Columbia Gorge & Mount Hood Loop

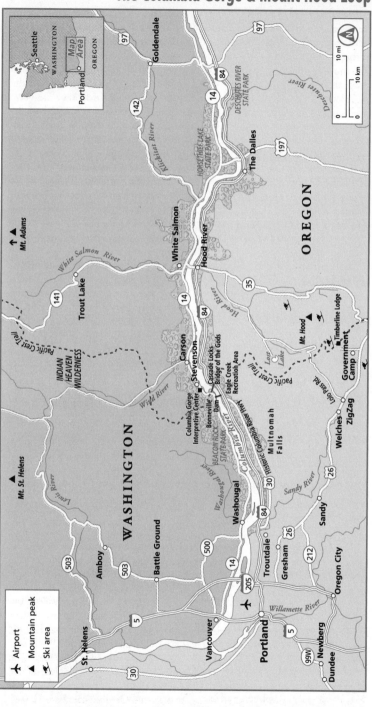

From Hood River, turn south on Oregon Hwy. 35, passing through thousands of acres of apple and pear orchards. Every fall, roadside stands in this area sell fresh fruit and fruit products. The orchards are especially beautiful in the spring, when the trees are in bloom. No matter what time of year, you will have the snow-covered peak of Mount Hood in view as you drive through the orchards, making them all the more spectacular.

Just after Hwy. 35 merges into U.S. 26, turn right onto the road to **Timberline Lodge** 👍👍. As the name implies, this lodge is at the timberline, and a July or August walk on one of the trails in the vicinity will lead you through wildflower-filled meadows. Surprisingly, because of the glacier and snowfields above the lodge, you can also ski and snowboard here all summer long.

Between Government Camp and the community of Zig Zag, watch for the roadside marker that marks the western end of the **Barlow Trail** toll road, a section of the Oregon Trail that circled around Mount Hood in order to avoid the dangerous downriver journey through the cascades of the Columbia River. There is a reproduction of the gate that once stood on this spot, and you can still see the trail itself, which is now open only to hikers, mountain bikers, and horseback riders.

To return to Portland just stay on Oregon Hwy. 26 all the way back to town or follow the signs for I-84.

WHERE TO STAY

Columbia Gorge Hotel 👍👍   Located just west of the town of Hood River off I-84 and opened shortly after the Columbia River Scenic Highway was completed in 1915, this little oasis of luxury offers the same genteel atmosphere that was once enjoyed by the likes of Rudolph Valentino and Clark Gable. With its yellow-stucco walls and red-tile roofs, this hotel would be right at home in Beverly Hills, and the hotel gardens could hold their own in Victoria, British Columbia. Despite the attractive furnishings and gardens, it is almost impossible to notice anything but the view from the windows. The hotel is perched more than 200 feet above the river on a steep cliff.

Guest rooms are all a little different, with a mixture of antique and classic furnishings. There are canopy beds, brass beds, and even some hand-carved wooden beds. Unfortunately, many of the rooms are rather cramped, as are the bathrooms, most of which have older fixtures. However, some rooms have soaking tubs and fireplaces.

4000 Westcliff Dr., Hood River, OR 97031. ☎ **800/345-1921** or 541/386-5566. Fax 541/387-5414. www.columbiagorgehotel.com. 39 units. $169–$279 double. Rates include multicourse breakfast. AE, DC, DISC, MC, V. Pets accepted with $25 fee. **Amenities:** Restaurant (Northwest/Continental), lounge; concierge; room service; massage. *In room:* A/C, TV, dataport, hair dryer, iron, safe.

Dolce Skamania Lodge 👍👍👍   Boasting the most spectacular vistas of any hotel in the Gorge, Skamania Lodge is also the only golf resort in the area. Although golf is the preferred sport here, the hotel is well situated whether you brought your sailboard, hiking boots, or mountain bike. The interior decor is classically rustic, with lots of rock and natural wood, and throughout the hotel there are Northwest Indian artworks and artifacts on display. Huge windows in the lobby take in a superb view of the Gorge. Of course, the river-view guest rooms are more expensive than the forest-view rooms (which overlook more parking lot than forest), but these rooms are well worth the extra cost. There are also rooms with fireplaces available. The lodge was planning to add 59 new rooms in late 2001, so you might want to request one of these new units.

P.O. Box 189, Stevenson, WA 98648. © 800/221-7117 or 509/427-7700. www.dolce.com/skamania. 253 units. $169–$199 double; $239–$385 suite. Lower rates in winter. AE, DC, DISC, MC, V. **Amenities:** Restaurant (Northwest), lounge; indoor pool; 18-hole golf course; 2 tennis courts; exercise room; Jacuzzi; sauna; bike rentals; children's programs; activities desk; business center; babysitting; room service; massage; laundry service. In room: A/C, TV, dataport, minibar, coffeemaker, hair dryer, iron.

Timberline Lodge ✰✰ Constructed during the Great Depression of the 1930s as a WPA project, this classic alpine ski lodge overflows with craftsmanship. The grand stone fireplace, huge exposed beams, and wide plank floors of the lobby impress every first-time visitor. Details are not overlooked either. Woodcarvings, imaginative wrought-iron fixtures, hand-hooked rugs, and handmade furniture complete the rustic picture. Rooms vary in size considerably, with the smallest rooms lacking private bathrooms. However, no matter which unit you stay in, you'll be surrounded by the same rustic furnishings. Unfortunately, room windows are not very large, but you can always retire to the Ram's Head lounge for a better view of Mount Hood.

Timberline, OR 97028. © 800/547-1406 or 503/622-7979. Fax 503/622-0710. www.timberlinelodge.com. 70 units (10 without private bathroom). $75 double with shared bathroom, $115–$225 double with private bathroom. AE, DISC, MC, V. Sno-park permit required in winter, but hotel will provide guests with one. **Amenities:** 2 restaurants (Northwest/American), 2 lounges; small outdoor pool; Jacuzzi; sauna; children's ski programs; coin-op laundry. In room: TV, dataport, hair dryer, iron, safe.

2 The Northern Oregon Coast

One of the most beautiful coastlines in the United States, the spectacular Oregon coast is this state's main tourist destination and is offers countless summer vacation spots along its length. The beach is less than 2 hours away from Portland and offers everything from rugged coves to long sandy beaches, artists' communities to classic family beach towns.

The quickest route from Portland to the Oregon coast (80 miles) is via U.S. 26, also called the **Sunset Highway.** Outlined here is a driving tour that takes in the very best of the northern Oregon coast. It's a long day's drive, so be sure to get an early start.

Just before reaching the coast and the junction with U.S. 101, watch for a sign for the **world's largest Sitka spruce tree.** This giant, more than 750 years old, is located in a small park just off the highway. Trees of this size were once common throughout the Coast Range, but almost all have now been cut down. The fight to preserve the remaining big trees is a bitter one that has divided the citizens of Oregon.

If you've got kids with you, turn north at the junction with U.S. 101 and head into **Seaside,** the coast's most traditional beach town (beachside promenade, saltwater taffy, arcade games, the works).

Otherwise, head south and watch for the turnoff to **Cannon Beach** ✰✰✰, the artsiest little town on the Oregon coast. Cannon Beach, though quite touristy, still has so much charm, you'll likely start scheming a way to retire here yourself.

Located just north of the town of Cannon Beach is **Ecola Beach State Park** ✰✰ (© 800/551-6949 or 503/436-2844), which provides some of the most spectacular views on the coast. Here in the park, there are stands of old-growth spruce, hemlock, and Douglas fir, and several trails offer a chance to walk through this lush forest. The park's Indian Beach is popular with surfers. For great views to the south, head to the Ecola Point picnic area, which is to your left just after you enter the park. A relatively easy 3-mile round-trip hiking trail connects this picnic area with Indian Beach.

Cannon Beach was named for a cannon off the USS *Shark,* which washed ashore here after that ship sank in 1849. Just offshore from the south end of town is **Haystack Rock** ☆☆, a massive 235-foot-tall island that is the most photographed rock on the coast. Only a few feet out from the beach, it's a popular destination of beachcombers and tide-pool explorers. In town, there are many art galleries and interesting shops.

Every summer, in early June, Cannon Beach celebrates **Sandcastle Day,** a festival that attracts numerous sand sculptors and thousands of appreciative viewers. Any time of year you'll find the winds here ideal for kite flying. However, forget about doing any swimming; the waters here, and all along the Oregon coast are too cold and rough for swimming.

Heading south out of Cannon Beach on U.S. 101, watch for the **Arcadia Beach State Recreation Site** ☆☆. This is one of the prettiest little beaches in the area, with haystack rocks and a headland that blocks the northwest winds in the summer months.

A little farther south, you'll come to **Hug Point State Recreation Site** ☆☆, with more headland-framed beach. Here you can also see an old stretch of the original coast highway. Although the old highway was mostly just the beach, here at Hug Point, the road was blasted into a headland, thus hugging the point.

A little farther south you'll come to the rugged **Oswald West State Park** ☆☆ (© **800/551-6949** or 503/436-2844), named for the governor who promoted legislation to preserve all Oregon beaches as public property. The beach is in a cove that can only be reached by walking a few hundred yards through dense forest; once you're there, all you'll hear is the crashing of the surf. The beach is strewn with huge driftwood logs that give it a wild look. High bluffs rise up at both ends of the cove and it is possible to hike to the top of them. There are plenty of picnic tables and a walk-in campground. This is another popular surfing spot.

U.S. 101 continues south from Oswald West State Park and climbs up over **Neahkahnie Mountain** ☆. Legend has it that at the base of this ocean-side mountain, the survivors of a wrecked Spanish galleon buried a fortune in gold. Keep your eyes open for elk, which frequently graze in the meadows here.

Just below this windswept mountain is the quiet beach town of **Manzanita** ☆☆. Tucked under the fir, spruce, and hemlock trees are attractive summer homes. With Neahkahnie Mountain rising to the north, a long stretch of sandy beach fronting the town, and a **Nehalem Bay State Park** ☆ (© **800/551-6949** or 503/368-5154) to the south of town, Manzanita is one of our favorite Oregon beach towns.

Tillamook Bay is one of the largest bays on the Oregon coast and at its north end is the small town of **Garibaldi,** which is a popular sportfishing spot. If you aren't an angler, you can still go for a cruise either around the bay or to look for whales.

Two miles north of the busy farm town of **Tillamook** on U.S. 101, you will come to the **Tillamook Cheese Factory** ☆ (© **503/815-1300;** www.tilla mookcheese.com). This region is one of Oregon's main dairy-farming areas, and much of the milk is turned into cheddar cheese and butter. Today this is one of the most popular attractions on the Oregon coast, and you can watch the cheese-making process through large windows. The cheese-factory store is a busy

Campground ▲

Mountain peak ▲

S.R.S.–State Recreation Site
S.N.A.–State Natural Area
S.P.–State Park
S.S.V.–State Scenic Viewpoint

WASHINGTON

Columbia River

Fort Canby S.P. ■
Fort Stevens S.P. ■ ▲
Lewis and Clark N.W.R. ■
Astoria
Warrenton ○
To Portland ➘
30

Gearhart ○
Youngs River
Lewis and Clark River
Seaside ○
Tillamook Head
Saddle Mtn. S.N.A.
▲ Saddle Mtn.
Ecola S.P. ■ ■ World's largest Sitka spruce
Cannon Beach ○
Haystack Rock ■
26
Elsie ○
Arcadia S.R.S. ■
Hug Point S.R.S. ■
Arch Cape ○
53
Oswald West S.P. ■ ▲
Nehalem River
To Portland ➘

PACIFIC
OCEAN

Manzanita ○ **Nehalem** ○
Nehalem Bay S.P. ■ ▲
Wheeler ○
Nehalem Bay

Rockaway Beach ○
Wilson River
To Portland ➘
Garibaldi ○
Tillamook Bay
Bay City ○
Cape Meares ■ Cape Meares S.S.V. ■
6
Oceanside ○ **Tillamook** ○
Trask River
Netarts Bay
101
Cape Lookout S.P. ▲
Cape Lookout

C O A S T   R A N G E S

Beaver ○

Tierra Del Mar ■
Cape Kiwanda S.N.A. ■
Cape Kiwanda ○ **Woods** ○
SIUSLAW NATIONAL FOREST
Nestucca Bay
Pacific City

Seattle
WASHINGTON
Map Area
Portland
OREGON

0   10 mi
0   10 km

N

place (especially the ice cream counter), but the lines move quickly and you can be on your way to the next picnic area with an assortment of tasty cheeses.

From Tillamook the **Three Capes Scenic Route** 🎭🎭 leads to Cape Meares, Cape Lookout, and Cape Kiwanda, all of which provide stunning vistas of rocky cliffs, misty mountains, and booming surf. As the name implies, this is a very scenic stretch of road, and there are plenty of places to stop and enjoy the views and the beaches.

Cape Meares State Scenic Viewpoint 🎭 perches high atop the cape, with the Cape Meares lighthouse just a short walk from the parking lot. This lighthouse, 200 feet above the water, was built in 1890. Today it has been replaced by an automated light a few feet away. Be sure to visit the **octopus tree** here in the park. This Sitka spruce has been twisted and sculpted by harsh weather.

As you come down from the cape, you'll reach the village of **Oceanside** 🎭, which clings to the steep mountainsides of a small cove. One tavern, one restaurant, and one cafe are the only commercial establishments, and that's the way folks here like it. If you walk north along the beach, you'll find a pedestrian tunnel through the headland that protects this hillside community. Through the tunnel is another beautiful stretch of beach.

South of Oceanside, the road runs along a flat stretch of beach before reaching **Cape Lookout State Park** ✯✯ (© **800/551-6949** or 503/842-4981). Cape Lookout, a steep forested ridge jutting out into the Pacific, is an excellent place for whale watching in the spring. A trail leads out to the end of the point from either the main (lower) parking area or the parking area at the top of the ridge. From the upper parking lot it is a 5-mile round-trip to the point.

South of Cape Lookout, you come to **Pacific City** and **Cape Kiwanda** ✯✯, the last of the three capes on this scenic loop. Cape Kiwanda, a state natural area, is a sandstone headland backed by a huge sand dune that is popular with hang gliders. It's also fun to climb to the top and then run down. From the top of this giant dune, it is sometimes possible to spot spouting whales. Just offshore is another **Haystack Rock** ✯✯ every bit as picturesque as the one in Cannon Beach. Because this huge rock breaks the waves, the beach here is used by beach-launched dories, as well as surfers. The Pelican Pub & Brewery right on the beach here makes a good spot for dinner before heading back to Portland.

From Pacific City, follow signs to U.S. 101 and head north to **Tillamook,** where Ore. 6 heads east toward Portland. Ore. 6 joins U.S. 26 about 25 miles west of Portland. Allow about 2½ hours to get back from Tillamook.

3 A Winery Tour

For many years now, Oregon wines, particularly pinot noirs, have been winning awards. This isn't surprising when you consider that Oregon is on the same latitude as the wine-growing regions of France. The climate is also very similar—cool, wet winters and springs and long, dry summers with warm days and cool nights. These are ideal conditions for growing wine grapes, and local vineyards are making the most of a good situation.

An Oregon winery guide describing more than 70 Oregon wineries is available from the **Oregon Wine Advisory Board,** 1200 NW Naito Pkwy., Suite 400, Portland, OR 97209 (© **503/228-8336;** www.oregonwine.org), or at the **Portland Oregon Visitors Association Information Center,** 1000 SW Broadway, Suite 2300, Portland, OR 97205 (© **877/678-5263** or 503/275-9750; www.travelportland.com).

There are more than two dozen wineries within an hour's drive of Portland. You could easily spend a week getting to know the area's many wineries. However, for an afternoon of wine tasting, we suggest visiting only three or four wineries. A trip through wine country is a chance not only to sample a wide range of wines but also to see the fertile valleys that lured pioneers across the Oregon Trail. We recommend taking along a picnic lunch, which you can of course supplement with a wine purchase. Most wineries have picnic tables, and many of them have lovely views. During the summer, many wineries stage weekend festivals that include live music.

The easiest way to visit the Oregon wine country is to head southwest out of Portland on Ore. 99W. Between the towns of Newberg and Dundee, you'll find about half a dozen wineries right alongside the highway and an equal number tucked into the hills within a few miles of the highway. Along the Ore. 99W, wineries are well marked by official highway department signs. The first winery you'll come to on this route is **Rex Hill Vineyards,** 30835 N. Hwy. 99W, Newberg (☎ **503/538-0666**); followed by **Duck Pond Cellars,** 23145 Hwy. 99W, Dundee (☎ **800/437-3213**); **Dundee Springs,** Hwy. 99W and Fox Farm Rd., Dundee (☎ **503/554-8000**); **Ponzi Wine Bar,** Hwy. 99W and SW Seventh St., Dundee (☎ **503/554-1500**); **Argyle,** 691 Hwy. 99w, Dundee (☎ **503/538-8520**); and **Sokol Blosser,** 5000 Sokol Blosser Lane, Dundee (☎ **800/582-6668**).

If you opt for this easy, straight-line wine tour, consider stopping for dinner in the town of Dundee, which has several excellent restaurants. **Tina's,** 760 Hwy. 99W (☎ **503/538-8880**), is a small place with a menu limited to about half a dozen well-prepared dishes. **Red Hills Provincial Dining,** 276 Hwy. 99W (☎ **503/538-8224**), in an old house beside the highway, serves a combination of Northwest and Mediterranean cuisine. Reservations are highly recommended at both of these restaurants. The **Dundee Bistro,** 100-A SW Seventh St. (☎ **503/554-1650**), operated by nearby Ponzi Vineyards, serves a wide variety of meals from simple to complex and is affiliated with the adjacent Ponzi Wine Bar.

Alternatively, if you'd like to avoid the crowds and the traffic congestion along busy Ore. 99W, try the wine tour outlined below, which takes in some of the region's best wineries and also some of the most beautiful countryside. To begin this alternative winery tour, head west out of Portland on U.S. 26 (Sunset Highway) and then take Ore. 47 south toward Forest Grove.

After a few miles on this two-lane highway, watch for a sign to **David Hill Winery,** 46350 NW David Hill Rd. (☎ **503/992-8545**). Although the original winery here went out of business during Prohibition, the first grapes were planted on this site in the late 1800s. Today David Hill produces excellent pinot noir and sparkling wines by the *méthode champenoise.* The winery is open March through December Tuesday through Sunday from noon to 5pm.

Continue through Forest Grove on Ore. 47 and just south of town, you'll see a sign for **Montinore Vineyards,** 3663 SW Dilley Rd. (☎ **503/359-5012**), which has its tasting room in an old Victorian mansion at the top of a tree-lined driveway. This is one of the largest wine producers in the state and enjoys an enviable location with sweeping views across the Tualatin Valley to the Cascade Range. Landscaped grounds invite a stroll or picnic after tasting a few wines. Pinot Noir, Pinot Gris, Chardonnay, and Riesling are among the more popular wines produced here. Between April and December, the winery is open daily from 11am to 5pm; other months, it's open on weekends from 11am to 4pm.

Back on Ore. 47, continue south to the small town of Gaston, where you'll find **24° Brix,** 108 Mill St. (☎ **503/985-3434**), a combination sandwich shop and wine-tasting room representing several small wineries that are not usually open to the public. About 14 miles south of Gaston on Ore. 47, you'll come to the town of Carlton, which is home to **The Tasting Room,** Main and Pine streets (☎ **503/852-6733**), another wine-tasting room specializing in wines from wineries that aren't regularly open to the public.

From Carlton, head back north to Gaston, and turn right on East Main Street. In slightly more than a mile turn left at a T-intersection and then turn right on Dixon Mill Road, which turns to gravel. At the end of this road, turn right on Unger Road, which will bring you to **Lion Valley Vineyards,** 35040 SW Unger Rd. (☎ **503/628-5458**), which produces very drinkable, fruit-forward pinot noirs. Open on Saturday and Sunday from noon to 5pm.

From Lion Valley, continue downhill (east) on Unger Road to Ore. 219, turn left, and then turn right onto Burkhalter Road to reach **Oak Knoll Winery,** 29700 SW Burkhalter Rd., Hillsboro (✆ **503/648-8198**). This winery produces a wide range of wines, including a delicious raspberry dessert wine. From here, continue east on Burkhalter Road, turn right on Rood Bridge Road and then left (east) on Ore. 10 (Farmington Road), which will take you to Beaverton, where you can get on Ore. 217 north to U.S. 26 east to Portland.

4 Mount St. Helens National Volcanic Monument

Once it was regarded as the most perfect of the Cascade peaks, a snow-covered cone rising above lush forests, but on May 18, 1980, all that changed. On that day, a massive volcanic eruption blew out the entire north side of Mount St. Helens, laying waste to a vast area and darkening the skies of the Northwest with billowing clouds of ash. Although today the volcano is quiet and life has returned to the once devastated landscape, this volcano and much of the land surrounding it has been designated the Mount St. Helens National Volcanic Monument.

The monument is located roughly 90 miles north of Portland off I-5 (take the Castle Rock exit). Admission to one monument visitor center (or Ape Cave) is $3 ($1 for children 5–15) and to two or more visitor centers (and Ape Cave), is $6 ($2 for children 5–15). If you just want to park at one of the monument's trailheads and go for a hike, all you need is a valid Northwest Forest Pass, which costs $5 per day. If it's winter, you'll need a sno-park Permit ($8 per day).

For more information, contact **Mount St. Helens National Volcanic Monument** (✆ **360/247-3900;** www.fs.fed.us/gpnf/mshnvm).

The best place to start an exploration of the monument is at the **Mount St. Helens Visitor Center** (✆ **360/274-2100**), which is located at Silver Lake, 5 miles east of Castle Rock on Wash. 504. The visitor center houses extensive exhibits on the eruption and its effects on the region. This center is open daily from 9am to 5pm. Before even reaching this center, you can stop and watch a 25-minute, 70mm film about the eruption at the **Mount St. Helens Cinedome Theater** (✆ **877/ERUPTION** or 360/274-9844), which is located at exit 49 off I-5 (tickets $6 adults, $5 seniors and children).

Continuing east from the visitor center, you'll come to the **Hoffstadt Bluffs Visitor Center** (✆ **360/274-7750**) at milepost 27 (open daily 9am–7pm in summer; shorter hours in winter), which has a snack bar and is the takeoff site for 20-minute helicopter flights over Mount St. Helens ($99 with a three-person minimum).

A few miles farther, just past milepost 33, you'll arrive at the **Forest Learning Center** (✆ **360/414-3439**), which is open mid-May through September daily 10am to 6pm and in October daily 10am to 5pm. This is primarily a promotional center for the timber industry, but, in a theater designed to resemble an ash-covered landscape, you can watch a short, fascinating video about the eruption. There are also displays on how forests destroyed by the blast have been replanted. Outside either of these centers you can usually see numerous elk on the floor of the Toutle River valley far below.

The **Coldwater Ridge Visitor Center** (✆ **360/274-2131**), which is at milepost 47 on Wash. 504, only 8 miles from the crater, is the second of the national monument's official visitor centers. This center features interpretive displays on the events leading up to the eruption and the subsequent slow regeneration of

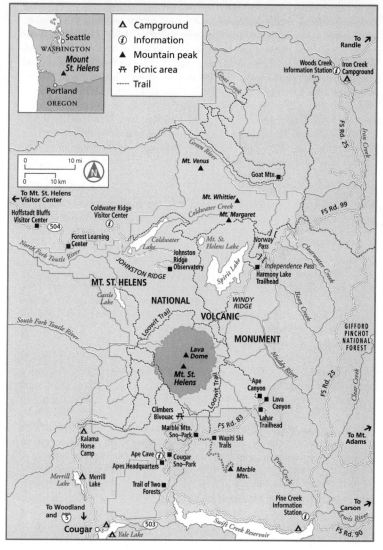

life around the volcano. You'll also find a picnic area, interpretive trail, restaurant, and boat launch at Coldwater Lake. Hours are late April through late September daily 10am to 6pm, and late September through late April daily 10am to 5pm.

Of all the many visitor centers, none offers a more awe-inspiring view than that from the **Johnston Ridge Observatory** (© **360/274-2140**), which is located 10 miles past the Coldwater Ridge Visitor Center. Built into the mountainside and designed to blend into the landscape, this observatory houses the equipment that is still used to monitor activity within Mount St. Helens. The observatory is open May through October daily from 10am to 6pm. If you're up for a bit of hiking, the single best trail on this side of the monument is the **Boundary Ridge Trail,** which heads east from the Johnston Ridge Observatory, with a jaw-dropping view of the blast zone the entire way. This trail leads for many miles across the monument, so you can hike as much or as little as you want. There is a good turnaround point about 1 mile out from the observatory.

For a different perspective on the devastation wrought by Mount St. Helens' eruption, drive around to the mountain's east side and the road up to **Windy Ridge.** Although it takes a couple of hours longer to get to this side of the mountain, you'll be rewarded by equaling amazing views, better hiking opportunities, and smaller crowds. To reach the east side of the mountain, take U.S. 12 east from exit 68 off I-5. In Randle, head south on Local Route 25. The **Woods Creek Information Station,** on Route 25 just before the junction with Route 26, has information on this part of the monument.

South of Woods Creek, watch for Route 99, the road to the **Windy Ridge Viewpoint.** This road crosses many miles of blown-down trees, and though the sight of the thousands of trees that were felled by a single blast is quite bleak, it reminds one of the awesome power of nature. More than two decades after the eruption, life is slowly returning to this devastated forest. At the Windy Ridge Viewpoint, visitors get one of the best close-up views of the crater. A staircase of 439 stairs climbs 220 feet up the hill above the parking area for even better views. Below Windy Ridge lies Spirit Lake, which was once one of the most popular summer vacation spots in the Washington Cascades. Today the lake is desolate and lifeless. The 1-mile-long Harmony Trail leads down to the shore of Spirit Lake and is a very worthwhile hike. Just keep in mind that it is a 600-foot climb back up to the trailhead parking lot

If you are an experienced hiker in good physical condition, you may want to consider **climbing to the top of Mount St. Helens.** From the trailhead on the south side of the mountain, it is an 8- to 10-hour, 10-mile hike, and can require an ice ax. Permits ($15) are required April through October, and because this is a very popular climb, it is advisable to make a reservation (© **360/247-3961**). Reservations are taken beginning on February 1, and summer weekends book up fast. However, if you don't have a reservation, you can try your luck by stopping by **Jack's Restaurant and Store** on Wash. 503, 5 miles west of the town of Cougar. Each evening at 6pm this store has a lottery of climbing permits for the next day. Between November 1 and March 31, permits are free and no reservation is necessary, but expect lots of snow.

On the south side of the monument, you can explore the **Ape Cave,** a lava tube that was formed 1,900 years ago when lava poured from the volcano. When the lava finally stopped flowing, it left a 2-mile-long cave that is the longest continuous lava tube in the Western Hemisphere. At the Apes Headquarters (open late May–early Sept), you can join a regular ranger-led exploration of the cave or rent a lantern for exploring the cave on your own.

Hikers who aren't doing the climb to the summit will find many other hiking trails within the monument, some in blast zones and some in forests that were left undamaged by the eruption. Ask at any visitor center for trail information.

Appendix A:
Seattle & Portland in Depth

Want to learn a little more about Seattle and Portland? Spend a little time thumbing through this appendix and you'll get to know these two Northwest cities quite a bit better. Although neither city is very old even by American standards, both cities have had interesting histories that have led them to be among the nation's most livable (and visitable) cities.

1 Seattle Past & Present

A LOOK AT SEATTLE'S PAST

Seattle got a late start in U.S. history. Although explorers had visited the region as early as the late 1700s, the first settlers didn't arrive until 1851. Capt. George Vancouver of the British Royal Navy—who lent his name to both Vancouver, British Columbia, and Vancouver, Washington—had explored Puget Sound as early as 1792. However, there was little to attract anyone permanently to this remote region. Unlike Oregon to the south, Washington had little rich farmland, only acres and acres of forest. It was this seemingly endless supply of wood that finally enticed the first settlers.

The region's first settlement was on Alki Point, in the area now known as West Seattle. Because this location was exposed to storms, within a few years the settlers moved across Elliott Bay to a more protected spot, the present downtown Seattle. The new location for the village was a tiny island surrounded by mud flats. Although some early settlers wanted to name the town New York—even then Seattle had grand aspirations—the name Seattle was chosen as a tribute to Chief Sealth, a local Native American who had befriended the newcomers.

In the middle of town, on the waterfront, Henry Yesler built the first steam-powered lumber mill on Puget

Dateline

- **1792** Capt. George Vancouver of the British Royal Navy explores Puget Sound.
- **1841** Lt. Charles Wilkes surveys Puget Sound and names it Elliott Bay.
- **1851** The first white settlers arrive in what will become West Seattle's Alki Point.
- **1852** These same settlers move to the east side of Elliott Bay from Alki Point, which is subject to storms.
- **1853** Washington Territory is formed.
- **1864** The transcontinental telegraph reaches Seattle, connecting it with the rest of the country.
- **1866** Chief Sealth, for whom Seattle is named, dies and is buried across Puget Sound at Suquamish.
- **1875** Regular steamship service begins between Seattle and San Francisco.
- **1889** The Great Seattle Fire levels most of downtown.
- **1893** The railroad reaches Seattle.
- **1897** The steamer *Portland* arrives from Alaska carrying more than a ton of gold, thus starting the Yukon gold rush.
- **1907** Pike Place Market is founded.
- **1916** William Boeing launches his first airplane from Lake Union, beginning an industry that will become Seattle's lifeblood.
- **1940** The Mercer Island Floating Bridge opens.
- **1962** The Century 21 exposition is held in Seattle, and the Space Needle is erected.

continues

Sound. It stood at the foot of what is now Yesler Way, which for many years was simply referred to as Skid Road, a reference to the way logs were skidded down to the sawmill from the slopes behind town. Over the years Skid Road developed a reputation for its bars and brothels. Some say that after an East Coast journalist incorrectly referred to it as Skid Row in his newspaper, the name stuck and was subsequently applied to derelict neighborhoods all over the country. To this day, despite attempts to revamp the neighborhood, Yesler Way continues to attract the sort of visitors

- **1971** Starbucks Coffee is founded in Seattle.
- **1999** Safeco Field, the Seattle Mariners' retractable-roof baseball stadium, opens for business. Riots erupt during meeting of World Trade Organization (WTO).
- **2000** The Kingdome is demolished to make way for a new football stadium. Experience Music Project opens at Seattle Center.
- **2001** Riots break out during annual Fat Tuesday celebration. An earthquake damages numerous historic buildings in Pioneer Square area. The Mariners enjoy a record-setting season.

one would expect (due in part to the presence in the neighborhood of missions and homeless shelters), but it is also in the center of the Pioneer Square Historic District, one of Seattle's main tourist destinations.

By 1889 the city had more than 25,000 inhabitants and was well on its way to becoming the most important city in the Northwest. On June 6 of that year, however, 25 blocks in the center of town burned to the ground. By that time the city, which had spread out to low-lying land reclaimed from the mud flats, had begun experiencing problems with mud and sewage disposal. The fire gave citizens the opportunity they needed to rebuild their town. The solution to the drainage and sewage problems was to regrade the steep slopes to the east of the town and raise the streets above their previous levels. Because the regrading lagged behind the rebuilding, the ground floors of many new buildings eventually wound up below street level. When the new roads and sidewalks were constructed at the level of what had previously been the second floor of most buildings, the old ground-floor stores and businesses moved up into the light of day and the spaces below the sidewalk were left to businesses of shady character. Today sections of this Seattle underground can be toured (see the box titled "Good Times in Bad Taste" in chapter 6, "Exploring Seattle," for details).

Among the most amazing engineering feats that took place after the fire were the regradings of Jackson Street Hill and Denny Hill. Although Seattle once had eight hills, there are now only six—nothing is left of either Denny Hill or Jackson Street Hill. Hydraulic mining techniques, which used high-powered water jets to dig into the hillsides, were used to level both of these hills. Today the Jackson Street Hill is the flat area to the west of the International District, and Denny Hill, now known as the Denny Regrade, is a flat neighborhood just south of Seattle Center.

The new buildings went up quickly after the fire, and 8 years later another event occurred that changed the city almost as much as the fire. On July 17, 1897, the steamship *Portland* arrived in Seattle from Alaska carrying a ton of gold from the recently discovered Klondike goldfields. Within the year Seattle's population swelled with prospectors heading north. Few of them ever struck it rich, but they all stopped in Seattle to purchase supplies and equipment, thus lining the pockets of Seattle merchants and spreading far and wide the name of this obscure Northwest city. When the prospectors came south again with their hard-earned gold, much of it never left Seattle, sidetracked by beer halls and brothels.

In 1916, not many years after the Wright brothers made their first flight, Seattle residents William Boeing and Clyde Esterveld launched their first airplane, a floatplane, from the waters of Lake Union. Their intention was to operate an airmail service to Canada. Their enterprise eventually became the Boeing Company, which has since grown to become one of the two largest employers in the area. Unfortunately, until recently Seattle's fortunes were so inextricably bound to those of Boeing that hard times for the aircraft manufacturer meant hard times for the whole city. In recent years, however, industry in the Seattle region has become much more diversified, and the 2001 announcement by Boeing that they would move their headquarters away from Seattle barely even caused a stir. Leading the region in its new role as high-tech development center is software giant Microsoft, the presence of which has attracted many other computer-related companies. Also located here in the Seattle area are high-tech companies Adobe and Amazon.

The single most recognizable structure on the Seattle skyline is, of course, the Space Needle. Built in 1962 for Century 21, the Seattle World's Fair, the Space Needle was at the time a very futuristic observation tower. Situated just north of downtown in the Seattle Center complex that was the site of the World's Fair, the Space Needle provides stupendous views of the city and all its surrounding natural beauty. Today, the design looks far less 21st century than it once did, and over the 40 years since the Space Needle was erected, the skyline it overlooks has changed radically. At the beginning of the 21st century, the Seattle skyline has become more and more dominated by towering skyscrapers, symbols of Seattle's ever-growing importance as a gateway to the Pacific Rim.

The 1962 World's Fair was far more than a fanciful vision of the future—it was truly prophetic for Seattle. The emergence of this city as an important Pacific Rim trading center is a step toward a bright 21st century. The Seattle area has witnessed extraordinary growth in recent years, with the migration of thousands of people in search of jobs, a higher quality of life, and a mild climate. To keep pace with its sudden prominence on the Pacific Rim, Seattle has also been rushing to transform itself from a sleepy Northwest city into a cosmopolitan metropolis. New restaurants, theaters, and museums have been cropping up around the city as new residents demand more cultural attractions. Visitors to Seattle will immediately sense the quickening pulse of this vibrant city.

However, with the bursting of the dot.com bubble, Seattle has been fairly hard hit, with a lot less disposable income changing hands than just a year or two earlier. Fewer people seem to be eating out, which is hurting all the new high-end restaurants around town. By the time you visit, don't be too surprised if you find that some of the restaurants listed in this book have gone out of business. The flip side is that right now it's easy to get last-minute dinner reservations and many downtown hotels are offering discounted rates even in summer.

SEATTLE TODAY

Seattle is a city in the midst of profound change. This rapid urbanization and upscaling can be seen on the bags that downtown shoppers carry. Where once the names were Pendleton, Eddie Bauer, and REI (all Northwest companies), today they are just as likely to be Banana Republic, Pottery Barn, Williams-Sonoma, even Cartier and Tiffany. Where a decade ago, the downtown area was left to the winos and barflies at night, today people are working and living downtown. All along First Avenue and Alaskan Way, high-rise water-view condominiums are changing the city's skyline. No longer is the city just a conglomeration of quaint neighborhoods. Today the downtown is as alive and active as any major Atlantic seaboard city.

The Sixth Avenue and Pine Street shopping district and the Belltown neighborhood are where the change is most evident, but it isn't limited to these areas. North Seattle's Fremont neighborhood, long a bastion of artistic and hippie aesthetics, is now home to software giant Adobe. Amazon.com claims a hilltop location in South Seattle. The Ballard neighborhood, long a middle-class Scandinavian neighborhood, has taken on a much more contemporary feel and has become one of the city's main nightlife districts.

Positioning itself as a major metropolis has meant thinking big, and to this end, Seattle has been busy adding (and subtracting) large, sometimes controversial structures to its ever-changing cityscape. In 2000, Microsoft cofounder Paul Allen opened his Experience Music Project, a museum of rock and roll that started out as a simple memorial to hometown rocker Jimi Hendrix. The museum building, designed by visionary architect Frank Gehry, is meant to conjure up images of a melted electric guitar and is one of the most bizarre-looking buildings on the planet.

Also in 2000, and also by the hand of Paul Allen, Seattle's venerable and much-disparaged Kingdome came crashing down in a cloud of dust as demolition experts imploded the massive cement structure in order to make way for a new football stadium for the Seattle Seahawks football team, which happens to be owned by Paul Allen. That new stadium, which now stands side by side with the Seattle Mariners' gorgeous Safeco Field, is scheduled for completion in time for the 2002 football season. Paul Allen has also been behind the redevelopment of much of the land that once surrounded the Kingdome, including a renovation of the old Union Station.

Not all of the changes around the city are big ones. Upscale restaurants continue to proliferate in downtown Seattle, especially in Belltown. Walk along First and Second avenues just north of Pike Place Market and you'll find interesting and pricey restaurants on every block. The average price for an entree in one of these places is around $20, a reflection of the affluent tastes of the neighborhood's condo residents.

However, recent years have not been all sunshine and grande espressos here in Latte Land. The World Trade Organization riots in 1999 focused the world's attention on Seattle, casting the city in a less-than-flattering light. In 2001, riots broke out again, this time during the city's annual Fat Tuesday celebrations (similar to Mardi Gras). The city was then rocked by a powerful earthquake that left many historic Pioneer Square buildings severely damaged. With the crash of the dot.com economy, Seattle has been particularly hard hit, but so far Microsoft and most of Seattle's largest tech companies have managed to weather the storm.

By all rights, Seattle residents should have taken on a gloomy outlook on life in 2001, but one thing helped keep them cheerful through one dot.com closure after another: The Mariners, against all odds, had a stellar year. Despite trading away or failing to sign superstars Randy Johnson, Ken Griffey Jr., and A-Rod over the past few years, the team, which plays at gorgeous Safeco Field under a retractable roof (or under clear skies, as the case may be), reeled off an incredible winning season before being eliminated by the Yankees in the ALCS.

2 Portland Past & Present

HISTORY 101

Portland was once a very inexpensive piece of property. In 1844 it sold for $50, double the original price of Manhattan Island. Before that, however, it had been purchased for just 25¢, although the original purchaser had to borrow the quarter. This was a wilderness, and anyone who thought it would ever be anything more was either foolish or extremely farsighted.

Asa Lovejoy and William Overton, the two men who staked the original claim to Portland, were the latter: farsighted. From this spot on the Willamette River they could see snow-capped Mount Hood 50 miles away; they liked the view and figured other people might also. These two were as disparate as a pair of founding fathers could be. Overton was a penniless drifter. No one is sure where he came from, or where he went when he left less than a year later. Lovejoy had attended Harvard College and graduated from Amherst. He was also one of the earliest settlers to venture by wagon train to the Oregon country.

These two men were traveling by canoe from Fort Vancouver, the Hudson's Bay Company fur-trading center on the Columbia River, to the town of Oregon City on the Willamette River. Midway through their journey they stopped to rest at a clearing on the west bank of the Willamette. Overton suggested they stake a claim to the spot. It was commonly believed that Oregon would soon become a U.S. territory and that the federal government would pass out free 640-acre land claims. Overton wanted to be sure that he got his due. Unfortunately, he didn't have the 25¢ required to file a claim. In exchange for half the claim, Lovejoy loaned him the money. Not a bad return on a 25¢ investment!

Wanderlust struck Overton before he could do anything with his claim, and he bartered his half to one Francis Pettygrove for $50 worth of supplies and headed off for parts unknown. Overton must have thought he had turned a pretty deal—from a borrowed quarter to $50 in under a year is a respectable return. Pettygrove, a steadfast Yankee like Lovejoy, was a merchant with ideas on

Dateline

- **1805** Lewis and Clark expedition travels down the Columbia River on its journey to the Pacific Ocean.
- **1834** Methodist missionaries settle at the confluence of the Columbia and Willamette rivers.
- **1843** Asa Lovejoy and William Overton file a claim for 640 acres on the site of present-day Portland. Filing fee: 25¢.
- **1844** Francis Pettygrove enters into partnership with Lovejoy, buying Overton's share for $50.
- **1845** The name Portland wins over Boston in a coin toss between Pettygrove and Lovejoy.
- **1851** Portland is incorporated.
- **1872** Fire levels most of city.
- **1873** A second fire devastates Portland.
- **1888** First Portland rose show.
- **1905** Lewis and Clark Exposition celebrates centennial of explorers' trip.
- **1907** Annual rose show becomes Portland Rose Festival.
- **1927** Downtown wharves are demolished, and a seawall is built.
- **1974** Expressway removed from the west bank of Willamette River to create Waterfront Park.
- **1996** February floodwaters come within inches of spilling out of the Willamette River and into downtown Portland.
- **1998** Westside MAX Light Rail begins operating.
- **2000** Portland Art Museum expands. Classical Chinese Garden opens. Oregon Zoo adds Steller Cove exhibit.
- **2001** Airport MAX light-rail line opens. Portland Streetcar line opens.

how to make a fortune. Today, aside from a single street name, Overton has pretty much been forgotten as a founding father.

Pettygrove lost no time in setting up a store on the waterfront, and now with a single building on the site, it was time to name the town. Pettygrove was from Maine and wanted to name the new town for his beloved Portland; Lovejoy was from Boston and wanted that name for the new settlement. A coin was flipped, Pettygrove called it correctly, and a new Portland was born.

Portland was a relative latecomer to the region. Oregon City, Fort Vancouver, Milwaukie, and St. Helens were all doing business in the area when Portland was still just a glimmer in the eyes of Lovejoy and Overton. However, in 1846 things changed quickly. Another New Englander, Capt. John Couch, sailed up the Willamette, dropped anchor in Portland, and decided to make this the headquarters for his shipping company.

Another enterprising gentleman, a southerner named Daniel Lownsdale, opened a tannery outside town and helped build a road through the West Hills to the wheat farms of the Tualatin Valley. With a road from the farm country and a small port to ship the wheat to market, Portland became the most important town in the region.

With the 1848 discovery of gold in California, and the subsequent demand for such Oregon products as grain and timber, Portland became a booming little town of 800 residents.

By the late 1880s Portland was connected to the rest of the country by several railroad lines, and by 1900 the population had grown to 90,000. In 1905 the city hosted the Lewis and Clark Exposition, that year's World's Fair, which celebrated the centennial of the explorers' journey to the Northwest. The fairgrounds, landscaped by John Olmsted, son and successor to New York City's Central Park designer Frederick Law Olmsted, were a great hit. The city of Portland also proved popular with visitors; by 1910 its population had exploded to 250,000.

By this time, however, the city boasted even more roses than people. Since 1888 Portland had been holding an annual rose show, but in 1907 it had blossomed into a full-fledged Rose Festival. Today the festival, held each June, is still Portland's favorite celebration. More than 400 varieties bloom in the International Rose Test Gardens in Washington Park, lending Portland the sobriquet "City of Roses."

The 20th century was a roller-coaster ride of boom and bust for Portland, but by the turn of 21st century, the city was in a new boom period. While timber and agriculture are still the mainstays of the Oregon economy, the Portland area has developed a high-tech industrial base that has allowed its economy to diversify and continue to prosper. Driven by the many high-tech manufacturing plants in the area, the city's population has been booming for the past few years.

Portlanders, however, tend to have a different idea of prosperity than residents of most other cities. Nature and the city's relationship to it have been an integral part of life here. As early as the beginning of the 20th century, the Willamette River was a favored recreation site, with canoe clubs racing on its clean waters. However, over the course of the 20th century, various industries filled the river with so much pollution that the river ceased to be a recreational attraction. Downtown Portland eventually lost its preeminence as a shipping port, and the wharves were torn down and replaced by a freeway, an act that was akin to cutting out Portland's very heart and soul. The freeway, however, didn't last long.

Of Shanghaied Sailors & Floating Brothels

While polite, clean, and livable are the sort of adjectives that are used to describe Portland these days, there was a time when wild and wicked were far more appropriate.

Back in the late 1800s, Joseph "Bunco" Kelly and "Sweet Mary" summed up the sort of Wild West enterprising spirit that characterized the young Portland. At the time, the city was one of the West Coast's main port towns, and as is the case with such waterfront communities, it attracted a few unsavory characters. Kelly, a local hotelier, was well known by ship's captains, who would rely on him to shanghai crew members when a ship was ready to sail and didn't yet have a full complement of sailors. Kelly would get men drunk and then haul them off to a ship about to set sail. As unscrupulous an occupation as shanghaiing was, Kelly outdid himself when he happened upon a group of men who had mistakenly been drinking embalming fluid in a basement mortuary they had stumbled into. With men both dead and dying, Kelly saw a chance to turn a tidy profit and foisted them off on a desperate ship's captain as merely dead drunk. On another occasion he wrapped a cigar store wooden Indian in blankets and convinced a captain that it was a soon-to-be able-bodied seamen.

As one of the city's most notorious madams, "Sweet Mary" saw to the needs of ship's captains and sailors alike. However, even in the late 19th century, Portland had laws against prostitution. Sweet Mary took full advantage of a loophole in the law by setting up shop on a barge that she floated up and down the Willamette River. On the river, she was outside the jurisdiction of the city, and also managed to avoid paying taxes.

With the heightened environmental awareness of the 1960s and 1970s, Portland's basic character and love of nature began to resurface. A massive cleanup of the Willamette River was undertaken, which helped the river's salmon runs and also restored the river's importance as a magnet for boaters and anglers. The freeway was torn up and replaced with Tom McCall Waterfront Park, a large expanse of lawns, trees, fountains, and promenades. But this is only one in a grand network of parks, a so-called "Emerald Necklace" that was first envisioned by the Olmsteds back in the early 1900s. Today the city is ringed with parks, including Forest Park (the largest wooded city park in the United States) and Washington Park (home to the International Rose Test Gardens, Japanese Garden, Oregon Zoo, and Hoyt Arboretum). It is this deep-rooted love of nature and the outdoors that seems to have molded this city for more than a century now and will hopefully continue to guide the city in its future growth.

PORTLAND TODAY

Today the Portland metropolitan area is facing a battle over how best to grow and develop while still maintaining its distinctive character. As a "big little city," Portland has tried to emphasize quality of life over economic progress, and for now seems to be succeeding. In late 2001, the city's ever-growing light-rail system opened to Portland International Airport, making Portland the only city on the West Coast with a light-rail-serviced airport. The summer of 2001 also saw the opening the new Portland Streetcar line, which is the nation's first new streetcar line in 50 years. The new streetcar links downtown, the stylish Pearl District, and northwest Portland's Nob Hill neighborhood. Together, these two systems (along with the extensive system of bus routes) offer Portlanders an alternative to automobile commuting and visitors a way of getting around the city without a car.

To keep the city beautiful, Portland also has a Percent for Art program that requires every new public building to spend slightly more than 1% of building costs on public art.

To anyone who lives in Portland, however, the city's greatest attributes are its ease of accessibility to the mountains and the coast and the close proximity of idyllic rural settings. Within a 30 minutes' drive from downtown, you can be out in the country, and within an hour and a half, you can be walking on the beach, skiing on Mount Hood, fishing in the Sandy River, hiking the Timberline Trail, or sampling a pinot noir at a winery.

The city's distinct boundary between urban and rural is no accident. Portland's Urban Growth Boundary (UGB) was a demarcation line drawn in the 1970s to prevent the city from experiencing the sort of suburban sprawl characteristic of California cities. The UGB has worked well, and while it was recently extended, the expansion is still far less than the sprawl that might have taken place if Portland had no UGB. To help prevent further sprawl, new light rail–oriented suburban developments are changing the face of the Portland metropolitan area and are being held up as models for compact development.

With growth has also come the renovation and gentrification of long-neglected neighborhoods throughout Portland. The greatest change in recent years has been in the Pearl District, a neighborhood of modern condominiums and old warehouses converted into upscale lofts. This has been the center of the city's art gallery scene for several years now, but now it has also become one of the city's main upscale restaurant neighborhoods, joining nearby Northwest 21st Avenue as the best neighborhoods in the city for dining out.

Northwest Portland's Nob Hill has become the city's most upscale and fashion-conscious neighborhood, with national chains such as the Gap, Pottery Barn, and Urban Outfitters all taking up residence here. Fans of funky shops, budget eateries, and eclectic boutiques find their fill of such places in the Irvington, Hawthorne, Southeast Belmont Street, Sellwood, Alberta, and Multnomah Village neighborhoods.

The Skidmore Historic District (also known as Old Town), a neighborhood that should be the busiest in the city, has never managed to slough off its negative image. Home to both the city's finest restored historic buildings and several missions and soup kitchens for the homeless, the area attracts street people and drug dealers, which together keep most other people from venturing into this area, except on weekends when the Portland Saturday Market is in full swing. This market is a major point of pride for Portlanders, who like to show off the creativity of the region's many craftspeople. By night, Old Town is the city's main nightlife district, with a dozen or more clubs and bars featuring everything from live jazz and alternative rock to salsa dancing.

Although Portland's Chinatown, adjacent to Old Town, is quite small, in 2000 it became the site of the largest urban Suzhou-style Chinese garden outside of China. The walled garden, with its tile-roofed pavilions, ponds, and evocative plantings and miniature landscapes, takes up an entire city block and serves as an oasis in this very urban neighborhood.

Another positive aspect of Portland's current growth is its restaurant renaissance. Where once good restaurants were confined to a few neighborhoods, today you are as likely to find a great French restaurant in an obscure residential neighborhood as you are to find one downtown. Although, with the slowing of the economy, fewer new high-end restaurants have been opening, there are still plenty around, and most seem to be weathering the economic downturn.

Portland today is growing quickly, though so far with a deliberation that has not compromised the city's values and unique character. Whether this controlled and intelligent growth can continue remains to be seen. However, for now Portland remains a city both cosmopolitan and accessible.

Appendix B:
For International Visitors

Although American trends have spread across Europe and other parts of the world to the extent that America may seem like familiar territory before your arrival, there are still many peculiarities and uniquely American situations that any foreign visitor will encounter.

1 Preparing for Your Trip

ENTRY REQUIREMENTS

Check at any U.S. embassy or consulate for current information and requirements. You can also obtain a visa application and other information online at the **U.S. State Department**'s website, at **www.travel.state.gov**.

VISAS The U.S. State Department has a **Visa Waiver Program** that allows citizens of certain countries to enter the United States without a visa for stays of up to 90 days. At press time, this visa waiver program applied to citizens of Andorra, Argentina, Australia, Austria, Belgium, Brunei, Denmark, Finland, France, Germany, Iceland, Ireland, Italy, Japan, Liechtenstein, Luxembourg, Monaco, the Netherlands, New Zealand, Norway, Portugal, San Marino, Singapore, Slovenia, Spain, Sweden, Switzerland, the United Kingdom, and Uruguay. Citizens of these countries need only a valid passport and a round-trip air or cruise ticket in their possession upon arrival. Further information is available from any U.S. embassy or consulate.

Canadian citizens may enter the United States without visas; they need only proof of residence.

Citizens of all other countries must have: (1) a valid passport that expires at least 6 months later than the scheduled end of their visit to the United States, and (2) a tourist visa, which may be obtained from any U.S. consulate.

To obtain a visa, you must submit a completed application form (either in person or by mail) with two 1½-inch-square photos and a US$45 fee, and must demonstrate binding ties to a residence abroad. Usually you can obtain a visa at once or within 24 hours, but it may take longer during the summer rush from June through August. If you cannot go in person, contact the nearest U.S. embassy or consulate for directions on applying by mail. Your travel agent or airline office may also be able to provide you with visa applications and instructions. The U.S. consulate or embassy that issues your visa will determine if you will be issued a multiple- or single-entry visa and any restrictions regarding the length of your stay.

British subjects can obtain up-to-date passport and visa information by calling the **U.S. Embassy Visa Information Line** (© 09061/500-590) or the **London Passport Office** (© 0870/521-0410 for recorded information), or by checking the website www.usembassy.org.uk.

Inquiries about visa cases and the application process can be made by calling © 202/663-1225.

MEDICAL REQUIREMENTS   Unless you're arriving from an area known to be suffering from an epidemic (particularly cholera or yellow fever), inoculations or vaccinations are not required for entry into the United States. If you have a disease that requires treatment with narcotics or syringe-administered medications, carry a valid, signed prescription from your physician to allay any suspicions that you may be smuggling narcotics.

Upon entering the United States, foreign nationals are required to declare any dangerous contagious diseases they carry, which includes infection with HIV, the AIDS virus. Anyone who has such a disease is excluded from entry as a tourist. However, you may be able to apply for a waiver if you are attending a conference or have another compelling nontourism reason for your visit (call the **Immigration and Naturalization Service [INS]** at © **800/375-5283** to inquire). Doubtless many HIV-positive visitors come in without declaring their condition, their way of dealing with an archaic law that was originally intended to halt the spread of tuberculosis and the like. The U.S. Immigration and Naturalization Service receives so many questions about the confusing and frequently changing policy regarding HIV-positive visitors that the public affairs office has issued a fact sheet on the subject: **"HIV Infection: Inadmissibility and Waiver Policies."** (Call the number above and ask for it.) Or for even more up-to-the-minute information, contact the Centers for Disease Control's **National Center for HIV** (© **800/HIV-0440;** www.hivatis.org) or the **Gay Men's Health Crisis** (© **800/AIDS-NYC;** www.gmhc.org).

DRIVER'S LICENSES   Foreign driver's licenses are mostly recognized in the United States, although you may want to get an international driver's license if your home license is not written in English.

CUSTOMS

WHAT YOU CAN BRING IN   Every visitor over 21 years of age may bring in, free of duty, the following: (1) 1 liter of wine or hard liquor; (2) 200 cigarettes, 150 cigars (but not from Cuba), or 3 pounds of smoking tobacco; and (3) $100 worth of gifts. These exemptions are offered to travelers who spend at least 72 hours in the United States and who have not claimed them within the preceding 6 months.

Foreign tourists may bring in or take out up to $10,000 in U.S. or foreign currency with no formalities; larger sums must be declared to U.S. Customs upon entering or leaving, which includes filing form CM 4790.

Declare any medicines you are carrying and be prepared to present a letter or prescription from your doctor demonstrating you need the drugs; you may bring in no more than you would normally use in the duration of your visit.

For many more details on what you can and cannot bring, check the informative U.S. Customs website at **www.customs.ustreas.gov** and click "Traveler Information." You can also call the **U.S. Customs** office at © **202/354-1000.** Ask for a copy of "Visiting the United States," which offers travelers more information about what U.S. Customs allows you to bring in. You can also call the **U.S. Department of Agriculture's Animal and Plant Health Inspection Service** (© **301/734-8645**) and ask for a copy of "Traveler's Tips," which provides detailed information on bringing food, plant, and animal products into the United States. You can also find this information on the USDA's website at **www.aphis.usda.gov/travel.html**.

WHAT YOU CAN BRING HOME   Rules governing what you can bring back duty-free vary from country to country, and are subject to change, but they're generally posted on the Web. **Canadians** should check the booklet *I Declare,* which you can download or order from Revenue Canada (℡ **800/ 461-9999** in Canada, or 613/993-0534;). An even clearer explanation is found in the publication *Bon Voyage, But . . .* , found at **www.dfait-maeci.gc.ca** (click on "Travel" and then click on "Bon Voyage"), or by ordering the publication from the 800-number listed above. Both booklets are free. **British** citizens should contact HM Customs & Excise (℡ **020/7202-4227;** www.hmce. gov.uk). **Australians** can contact the Australian Customs Service (℡ **1-300/ 363-263** within Australia, or 61-2/6275-6666 from outside Australia; www. customs.gov.au). **New Zealand** citizens should contact New Zealand Customs (℡ **09/359-6655;** www.customs.govt.nz/).

INSURANCE

Although it's not required of travelers, health insurance is highly recommended. Unlike many European countries, the United States does not usually offer free or low-cost medical care to its citizens or visitors. Doctors and hospitals are expensive, and in most cases will require advance payment or proof of coverage before they render their services. Travel insurance policies can cover everything from the loss or theft of your baggage and trip cancellation to the costs of an accident, repatriation, or death. See "Health & Insurance" on p. 16 (in chapter 2, "Planning Your Trip to Seattle") for more information. Packages such as **Europ Assistance** in Europe are sold by automobile clubs and travel agencies at attractive rates. **Worldwide Assistance Services, Inc.** (℡ **800/821-2828** or 703/ 204-1897; www.worldwideassistance.com) is the agent for Europ Assistance in the United States. **Specialty Risk International** (℡ **800/335-0611;** www. specialtyrisk.com) is another insurance company that offers packages to travelers from countries around the world.

Though lack of health insurance may prevent you from being admitted to a hospital in nonemergencies, don't worry about being left on a street corner to die: The American way is to fix you now and bill the living daylights out of you later.

MONEY

CURRENCY   The U.S. monetary system has a decimal base: one American **dollar** ($1) = 100 **cents** (100¢).

The most common **bills** (all ugly, all green) are the $1 (colloquially, a "buck"), $5, $10, and $20 denominations. There are also $2 bills (seldom encountered), $50 bills, and $100 bills (the last two are usually not welcome as payment for small purchases). Note that redesigned bills were introduced in the last few years, but the old-style bills are still legal tender.

There are six denominations of **coins:** 1¢ (1 cent, or a penny); 5¢ (5 cents, or a nickel); 10¢ (10 cents, or a dime); 25¢ (25 cents, or a quarter); 50¢ (50 cents, or a half dollar); and the rare $1 piece (the older, large silver dollar and the newer, small Susan B. Anthony coin). In 2000, a new gold-toned $1 piece was introduced.

Note that U.S. coins are not stamped with their numeric value.

CURRENCY EXCHANGE   You'll find currency exchange services in major airports with international service. Seattle-Tacoma International Airport provides Thomas Cook services (℡ **206/248-0401**), and at Portland International Airport there is Travelex America (℡ **503/281-3045**), on the main floor across from the Southwest Airlines desk. Elsewhere, they may be quite difficult to come by.

To exchange money in Seattle, go to **American Express,** 600 Stewart St. (*C* **206/441-8622**), or **Thomas Cook,** at Westlake Center (*C* **206/682-4525**). In Portland, go to **American Express,** 1100 SW Sixth Ave. in the Standard Plaza Building (*C* **503/226-2961**), or **Thomas Cook** at Powell's Travel Store at Pioneer Courthouse Square, 701 SW Sixth Ave. (*C* **503/222-2665**).

TRAVELER'S CHECKS   Though traveler's checks are widely accepted, *make sure that they're denominated in U.S. dollars,* as foreign-currency checks are often difficult to exchange. The three traveler's checks that are most widely recognized—and least likely to be denied—are **Visa, American Express,** and **Thomas Cook/MasterCard.** Be sure to record the numbers of the checks, and keep that information separately in case they get lost or stolen. Most businesses are pretty good about taking traveler's checks, but you're better off cashing them in at a bank (in small amounts, of course) and paying in cash. *Remember:* You'll need identification, such as a driver's license or passport, to change a traveler's check.

CREDIT CARDS   Credit cards are the most widely used form of payment in the United States: **Visa** (BarclayCard in Britain), **MasterCard** (Eurocard in Europe, Access in Britain, and Chargex in Canada), **American Express, Diners Club, Discover,** and **Carte Blanche;** you'll also find that some vendors may accept international cards like **enRoute, Eurocard,** and **JCB,** but not as universally as Amex, MasterCard, or Visa. There are, however, a handful of stores and restaurants that do not take credit cards, so be sure to ask in advance. And be aware that often businesses require a minimum purchase price, usually around $10 or $15, to use a credit card.

ATMs   You'll find automated-teller machines (ATMs) all over both cities. Most ATMs will allow you to draw U.S. currency against your bank account back home. Check with your bank before leaving home, and ask if you'll need to reprogram your PIN number in the United States. Expect to be charged up to $3 per transaction, however, if you're not using your own bank's ATM.

SAFETY
GENERAL SAFETY SUGGESTIONS   While tourist areas are generally safe, U.S. urban areas tend to be less safe than those in Europe or Japan. You should always stay alert. This is particularly true of large U.S. cities. Ask your hotel front desk staff or the city's or area's tourist office if you're in doubt about which neighborhoods are safe.

Avoid deserted areas, especially at night, and don't go into public parks at night unless there's a concert or similar occasion that will attract a crowd.

Avoid carrying valuables with you on the street, and don't display expensive cameras or electronic equipment. If you are using a map, consult it inconspicuously—or better yet, try to study it before you leave your room. Hold onto your pocketbook, and place your billfold in an inside pocket. In theaters, restaurants, and other public places, keep your possessions in sight.

Remember also that hotels are open to the public, and in a large hotel, security may not be able to screen everyone entering. Always lock your room door—don't assume that once inside your hotel you are automatically safe and no longer need to be aware of your surroundings.

DRIVING   Ask your rental agency about personal safety or request a brochure of traveler safety tips when you pick up your car. Get written directions or a map with the route marked in red from the agency to show you how to get to your destination. If possible, arrive and depart during daylight hours.

Recently more and more crime has involved cars and drivers. If you drive off a highway into a doubtful-looking neighborhood, leave the area as quickly as possible. If you have an accident, even on the highway, stay in your car with the doors locked until you assess the situation or until the police arrive. If you are bumped from behind on the street or are involved in a minor accident with no injuries, and the situation appears to be suspicious, motion to the other driver to follow you to the nearest police precinct, gas station, or open store. *Never* get out of your car in such situations.

Park in well-lit, well-traveled areas if possible. Always keep your car doors locked, whether the vehicle is attended or unattended. Look around you before you get out of your car and never leave any packages or valuables in sight.

If someone attempts to rob you or steal your car, do *not* try to resist the thief/carjacker—report the incident to the police department immediately by calling © **911.**

Also, make sure that you have enough gasoline in your tank to reach your intended destination, so that you're not forced to look for a service station in an unfamiliar and possibly unsafe neighborhood, especially at night.

2 Getting to the United States

BY PLANE

For an extensive listing of airlines that fly into Seattle and Portland, see "Getting There" in chapter 2 and chapter 12, "Planning Your Trip to Portland."

A number of U.S. airlines offer service from Europe to the United States. If they do not have direct flights from Europe to Seattle or Portland, they can book you straight through on a connecting flight. You can make reservations by calling the following numbers in Great Britain: **American Airlines** (© 0345/789-789; www.im.aa.com), **Continental** (© 0800/776-464; www.continental.com), **Delta** (© 0800/414-767; www.delta.com), **Northwest/KLM** (© 08705/074-074; www.nwa.com), or **United** (© 0800/888-555; www.united.com).

International carriers that fly from Europe to Los Angeles and San Francisco include **Aer Lingus** (© 01/886-8888 in Ireland; www.aerlingus.com) and **British Airways** (© 0845/773-3377; www.britishairways.com), which also flies direct to Seattle from London.

From New Zealand and Australia, there are flights to Los Angeles on **Qantas** (© 13 13 13; www.qantas.com.au) and **Air New Zealand** (© 0800/737-000 in Auckland; www.airnewzealand.co.nz). From there, you can continue on to Seattle or Portland on a regional airline such as **Alaska Airlines** (© 800/426-0333; www.alaskaair.com) or **Southwest** (© 800/435-9792; www.iflyswa.com).

From Toronto, there are flights to Seattle and Portland on **Air Canada** (© 888/247-2262; www.aircanada.ca), **American Airlines** (© 800/433-7300; www.aa.com), **Northwest** (© 800/225-2525; www.nwa.com), and **United** (© 800/241-6522; www.united.com).

From Vancouver, B.C., there are flights to Seattle and Portland on **Air Canada, United,** and **Alaska Airlines** (© 800/426-0333; www.alaskaair.com).

Operated by the European Travel Network, **www.discount-tickets.com** is a great online source for regular and discounted airfares. ETN operates another useful site at **www.etn.nl**. Students should also try **Campus Travel** (© **0870/ 240-1010** in England, or 0131/668-3303 in Scotland; www.usitcampus.co.uk).

For more money-saving airline advice, see the "Getting There" section of chapter 2.

BY TRAIN

There is **Amtrak** (© **800/872-7245;** www.amtrak.com) service from Vancouver, B.C., to Seattle, a trip that takes about 4 hours (from there, it's another 3½–4 hr. to continue on to Portland). One-way fares from Vancouver to Seattle are usually between $23 and $34, and fares between Seattle and Portland are usually between $23 and $36. Booking earlier will get you a less expensive ticket. Amtrak also operates service between Vancouver and Eugene, Oregon, and runs bus service between Vancouver and Seattle.

Like the airlines, Amtrak offers several discounted fares; although they're not all based on advance purchase, you have more discount options by reserving early.

BY FERRY

If you are traveling between Victoria, British Columbia, and Seattle, there are several options available from **Victoria Clipper,** Pier 69, 2701 Alaskan Way (© **800/888-2535** from outside Seattle and Victoria, 206/448-5000, or 250/382-8100 in Victoria; www.victoriaclipper.com). Throughout the year, a ferry taking either 2 or 3 hours makes the trip ($79–$125 round-trip for adults).

3 Getting Around the United States

For specific information on traveling to and around Seattle and Portland, see "Getting There" in chapters 2 and 12 and "Getting Around" in chapter 3, "Getting to Know Seattle," and chapter 13, "Getting to Know Portland."

BY PLANE

Some large U.S. airlines (including American, Continental, Northwest, United, and Delta) offer travelers on their transatlantic or transpacific flights special discount tickets allowing travel between U.S. destinations at minimum rates. (Two such programs are American's **Visit USA** and Delta's **Discover America.**) These tickets are not on sale in the United States and must be purchased before you leave home. This is the best, easiest, and fastest way to see the United States at low cost. Obtain information well in advance from your travel agent or airline, since the conditions attached to these discount tickets can be changed without advance notice.

If you are arriving by air, allow lots of time to make connections between international and domestic flights—an average of 2 to 3 hours at least.

BY TRAIN

International visitors, except Canadians, can buy a **USA Railpass,** good for 15 or 30 days of unlimited travel on **Amtrak** (© **800/USA-RAIL;** www.amtrak.com). The pass is available through many foreign travel agents. Prices in 2001 for a nationwide 15-day pass were $295 off-peak, $440 peak; a nationwide 30-day pass cost $385 off-peak, $550 peak. (With a foreign passport, you can also buy passes at some Amtrak offices in the United States, including locations in San Francisco, Los Angeles, Chicago, New York, Boston, and Washington, D.C.) Reservations should be made for each part of your trip as early as possible.

If your travel plans include visiting both the United States and Canada, you need to purchase a **North American Railpass.** Also available through Amtrak is an **Airail** pass, a joint venture of United Airlines and Amtrak that's available as part of **Amtrak Vacations packages** (© **800/321-8684**).

BY BUS

Although bus travel is often the most economical form of public transit for short hops between U.S. cities, it can also be slow and uncomfortable—certainly not an option for everyone (particularly when Amtrak, which is far more luxurious, offers similar rates). **Greyhound/Trailways** (© **800/231-2222**), the sole nationwide bus line, offers an **International Ameripass** for unlimited travel for specified amounts of time, from 4 days for $135, to 60 days at $449. You can buy International Ameripasses online, at **www.greyhound.com,** or at participating international travel agents in your country. In this country, you can purchase the domestic versions, simply the **Ameripass,** but they cost a little more; for example, the 60-day pass is $509 (prices good in 2001). You can buy the regular Ameripass online or at Greyhound terminals.

ℰ FAST FACTS: **For the International Traveler**

Automobile Organizations Auto clubs will supply maps, suggested routes, guidebooks, accident and bail-bond insurance, and emergency road service. The **American Automobile Association (AAA)** is the major auto club in the United States. If you belong to an auto club in your home country, inquire about AAA reciprocity before you leave. You may be able to join AAA even if you're not a member of a reciprocal club; to inquire, call AAA (© **800/222-4357;** www.aaa.com). AAA has a nationwide emergency road service telephone number (© **800/AAA-HELP**).

Business Hours The following are general open hours; specific establishments may vary. **Banks:** Monday through Friday from 9am to 5pm (some are also open on Sat mornings); there's usually 24-hour access to ATMs at most banks and other outlets. **Offices:** generally open weekdays from 9am to 5pm. **Stores:** typically open Monday through Saturday between 9 and 10am and close between 5 and 6pm. Some department stores have later hours and are open on Sunday from 11am to 5 or 6pm, and stores in malls are usually open until 9pm. **Bars:** stay open until 1 or 2am; dance clubs often stay open much later.

Climate See "When to Go" in chapters 2 and 12.

Currency & Currency Exchange See section 1 of this chapter.

Drinking Laws The legal age for purchase and consumption of alcoholic beverages is 21; proof of age is required and often requested at bars, nightclubs, and restaurants, so it's always a good idea to bring ID when you go out.

Do not carry open containers of alcohol in your car or any public area that isn't zoned for alcohol consumption. The police can fine you on the spot. And nothing will ruin your trip faster than getting a citation for DUI ("driving under the influence"), so don't even think about driving while intoxicated.

See also the "Liquor Laws" entry in the "Fast Facts" at the end of chapters 3 and 13.

Electricity Like Canada, the United States uses 110 to 120 volts AC (60 cycles), compared to 220 to 240 volts AC (50 cycles) in most of Europe, Australia, and New Zealand. If your small appliances use 220 to 240 volts, you'll need a 110-volt transformer and a plug adapter with two flat parallel pins to operate them here. Downward converters that change 220 to 240 volts to 110 to 120 volts are difficult to find in the United States, so bring one with you.

Embassies & Consulates All embassies are located in Washington, D.C. If your country isn't listed below, call for directory information in Washington, D.C. (✆ **202/555-1212**), for the number of your embassy.

The embassy of **Australia** is at 1601 Massachusetts Ave. NW, Washington, D.C. 20036 (✆ **202/797-3000;** www.austemb.org). The nearest consulate is in **San Francisco** at 625 Market St, Suite 200, San Francisco, CA 94105-3304 (✆ **415/536-1970**). There are also consulates in Atlanta, New York, Honolulu, and Los Angeles.

The embassy of **Canada** is at 501 Pennsylvania Ave. NW, Washington, D.C. 20001 (✆ **202/682-1740;** www.canadianembassy.org). The regional consulate is at Plaza 600 Building, Sixth Avenue and Stewart Street, Seattle, WA 98101-1286 (✆ **206/443-1777**). Other Canadian consulates are in Buffalo (New York), Detroit, New York, and Los Angeles.

The embassy of **Ireland** is at 2234 Massachusetts Ave. NW, Washington, D.C. 20008 (✆ **202/462-3939;** www.irelandemb.org). The nearest consulate is at 44 Montgomery St., Suite 3830, San Francisco, CA 94104 (✆ **415/392-4214**). Other Irish consulates are in Boston, Chicago, and New York.

The embassy of **New Zealand** is at 37 Observatory Circle NW, Washington, D.C. 20008 (✆ **202/328-4800;** www.nzemb.org). There is a consulate in Los Angeles at 12400 Wilshire Blvd., Suite 1150, Los Angeles, CA 90025 (✆ **310/207-1605**). Other New Zealand consulates are in Atlanta, Boston, Chicago, Hawaii, Houston, New York, Salt Lake City, San Diego, and San Francisco. There is also an honorary consulate in Seattle.

The embassy of the **United Kingdom** is at 3100 Massachusetts Ave. NW, Washington, D.C. 20008 (✆ **202/462-1340;** www.britain-info.org). There is a consulate in Seattle at 900 Fourth Ave., Suite 3001, Seattle, WA 98164 (✆ **206/622-9255**). Other British consulates are in Atlanta, Boston, Chicago, Dallas, Denver, Houston, Los Angeles, Miami, New York, and San Francisco.

Emergencies Call ✆ **911** to report a fire, call the police, or get an ambulance. This is a toll-free call (no coins are required at a public telephone).

Gasoline (Petrol) Petrol is known as gasoline (or simply "gas") in the United States, and petrol stations are known as both gas stations and service stations. Gasoline costs much less here than it does in Europe (about $1.65 per gallon at press time); and taxes are already included in the printed price. One U.S. gallon equals 3.8 liters or .85 Imperial gallons.

Holidays Banks, government offices, post offices, and many stores, restaurants, and museums are closed on the following legal national holidays: January 1 (New Year's Day), the third Monday in January (Martin Luther King Day), the third Monday in February (Presidents' Day, Washington's Birthday), the last Monday in May (Memorial Day), July 4

(Independence Day), the first Monday in September (Labor Day), the second Monday in October (Columbus Day), November 11 (Veterans' Day/Armistice Day), the fourth Thursday in November (Thanksgiving Day), and December 25 (Christmas).

Legal Aid If you are pulled over for a minor infraction (for example, of the highway code, such as speeding), never attempt to pay the fine directly to a police officer; this could be construed as attempted bribery, a much more serious crime. Pay fines by mail, or directly into the hands of the clerk of the court. If accused of a more serious offense, say and do nothing before consulting a lawyer. Here the burden is on the state to prove a person's guilt beyond a reasonable doubt, and everyone has the right to remain silent, whether he or she is suspected of a crime or actually arrested. Once arrested, a person can make one telephone call to a party of his or her choice. Call your embassy or consulate.

Mail Generally found at intersections, mailboxes are blue with a white eagle logo and carry the inscription U.S. MAIL. If your mail is addressed to a U.S. destination, don't forget to add the five-digit postal code (or ZIP code) after the two-letter abbreviation of the state to which the mail is addressed.

At press time, domestic postage rates were 22¢ for a postcard and 34¢ for a letter. For international mail, a first-class letter of up to 1 ounce costs 80¢ (60¢ to Canada and Mexico); a first-class postcard costs 70¢ (50¢ to Canada and Mexico); and a preprinted postal aerogramme costs 70¢.

Safety See section 1 of this chapter.

Taxes The United States does not have a value-added tax (VAT) or other indirect tax at a national level. Every state, and each county and city in it, is allowed to levy its own local tax on purchases and services (including hotel and restaurant bills, airline tickets, and so on). Taxes are already included in the price of certain services, such as public transportation, cab fares, telephone calls, and gasoline.

In Seattle, the sales tax rate is 8.8%. In Portland and the rest of Oregon, there is no sales tax. Also, you'll pay 28.5% in taxes and concession fees when you rent a car at Seattle-Tacoma Airport. At Portland International Airport, you'll pay 23% when you rent a car. You'll save 11% to 23% by renting somewhere other than the airport. Hotel room taxes range from around 11.5% to 15.8%. Travelers on a budget should keep both car-rental and hotel-room taxes in mind when planning a trip.

Telephone & Fax The telephone system in the United States is run by private corporations, so rates can vary widely. Generally, hotel surcharges on long-distance and local calls are astronomical, so you're usually better off using a **public pay telephone,** which you'll find clearly marked in most public buildings and private establishments as well as on the street. Convenience grocery stores and gas stations always have them. Many convenience groceries and packaging services sell **prepaid calling cards** in denominations up to $50, though these aren't always the least expensive way to call home. Many public phones at airports now accept American Express, MasterCard, and Visa credit cards. **Local calls** made from public pay phones in most locales cost either 25¢ or 35¢. Pay phones do not accept pennies, and few will take anything larger than a quarter.

Most long-distance and international calls can be dialed directly from any phone. **For calls within the United States and to Canada,** dial 1 followed by the area code and the seven-digit number. **For other international calls,** dial 011 followed by the country code, city code, and the telephone number of the person you are calling. Some country and city codes are as follows: **Australia** 61, Melbourne 3, Sydney 2; **Ireland** 353, Dublin 1; **New Zealand** 64, Auckland 9, Wellington 4; **United Kingdom** 44, Belfast 232, Birmingham 21, Glasgow 41, London 71 or 81.

If you're **calling the United States from another country,** the country code is 01.

Calls to area codes **800, 888,** and **877** are toll-free. However, calls to numbers in area codes **700** and **900** (chat lines, bulletin boards, "dating" services, and so on) can be very expensive—usually 95¢ to $3 or more per minute, and they sometimes have minimum charges that can run as high as $15 or more.

For **reversed-charge or collect calls,** and for person-to-person calls, dial 0 (zero, not the letter O) followed by the area code and number you want; an operator will then come on the line, and you should specify that you are calling collect, or person-to-person, or both. If your operator-assisted call is international, ask for the overseas operator.

For **local directory assistance** (information), dial ℂ **411;** for **long-distance information,** dial 1, then the appropriate area code and ℂ **555-1212.**

Most hotels have **fax machines** available for guest use (be sure to ask about the charge to use it). A less expensive way to send and receive faxes may be at stores such as **Kinkos** (see "Internet Access," in "Fast Facts" sections of chapters 3 and 13) or **Mail Boxes Etc.,** a national chain of packing service shops (look in the Yellow Pages directory under "Packing Services").

There are two kinds of telephone directories in the United States. The so-called **White Pages** list private households and business subscribers in alphabetical order. The inside front cover lists emergency numbers. The first few pages will tell you how to make long-distance and international calls, complete with country codes and area codes. Government numbers are usually printed on blue paper within the White Pages. Printed on yellow paper, the so-called **Yellow Pages** list all local services, businesses, industries, and houses of worship according to activity with an index at the front or back.

Time The United States is divided into six time zones. From east to west, they are eastern standard time (EST), central standard time (CST), mountain standard time (MST), Pacific standard time (PST), Alaska standard time (AST), and Hawaii standard time (HST). Seattle and Portland run on Pacific standard time.

Tipping Tipping is so ingrained in the American way of life that the annual income tax of tip-earning service personnel is based on how much they *should* have received in light of their employers' gross revenues.

In hotels, tip **bellhops** about $1 per bag, and tip the **maid** at least $1 to $2 per day (more if you've left a disaster area to clean up, or if you're traveling with kids and/or pets). Tip the **doorman** or **concierge** only if he or she has provided you with some specific service (for example, calling a cab for you or obtaining difficult-to-get theater tickets). Tip the **valet parking attendant** $1 every time you get your car.

In restaurants, bars, and nightclubs, tip your waiter or waitress at least 15% of the check (up to 20% if service was very good), tip **bartenders** about $1 per drink ordered, tip **checkroom attendants** $1 per garment, and tip **valet-parking attendants** $1 per vehicle. Tipping is not expected in cafeterias and fast-food restaurants.

Tip **cab drivers** 15% of the fare.

Tip **skycaps** at airports at least $1 per bag ($2–$3 if you have a lot of luggage) and tip **hairdressers** and **barbers** 15% to 20%. Tipping gas-station attendants and ushers at movies and theaters is not expected.

Toilets You won't find public toilets or "restrooms" on the streets in most U.S. cities, but they can be found in hotel lobbies, bars, coffee bars, restaurants, museums, department stores, and gas stations. Note, however, that restaurants and bars may reserve their restrooms for the use of their patrons. You can ignore this sign or, better yet, avoid arguments by paying for a cup of coffee or a soft drink, which will qualify you as a patron. Large hotels and fast-food restaurants are probably your best bet for good, clean facilities.

Index

See also Accommodations and Restaurant indexes, below.

GENERAL INDEX

A AA (American
Automobile Association),
36, 199, 320
Accommodations
for gays and lesbians, 19
Portland, 202–215
bed & breakfasts,
203, 210, 213, 214
best bets, 179–181
family-friendly, 211
reservations and book-
ing services, 203
Seattle, 38–60
bed & breakfasts,
39, 49, 50, 55
best bets, 8
family-friendly, 56
reservations and book-
ing services, 39
what's new, 1
senior discounts, 19–20
**A Contemporary Theater
(ACT) (Seattle), 142**
Addresses, finding
Portland, 193–194
Seattle, 27–28
Adobe (Seattle), 126
Airfares, Seattle, 22
Airlines, 319
Portland, 188
San Juan Islands, 155–156
Seattle, 21
to the United States, 318
**Airport MAX (Portland),
2, 190**
Airports
Portland, 190
Seattle, 7, 25–26
**Alki Beach (Seattle), 114,
116, 117**
All Day Pass (Seattle), 32
Allen, Paul, 4, 91, 98, 308
**American Advertising
Museum (Portland), 3,
252, 269**

**American Camp (San Juan
Island), 158**
American Express
Portland, 199
Seattle, 36
Amtrak
for disabled passengers, 18
Seattle, 24, 26
senior discounts, 19
***Animals in Pools* sculptures
(Portland), 270, 272**
Antiques and collectibles
Portland, 273
Seattle, 130–131
Ape Cave, 304
Aquarium, Seattle, 95, 107
Arboretum (Seattle), 7–8
**Arcadia Beach State Recre-
ation Site, 298**
Area codes
Portland, 199
Seattle, 36
**Arlene Schnitzer Concert
Hall (Portland), 178–179,
281**
Art galleries
Portland, 179, 274–275
Seattle, 131–133
first Thursday art walk,
152
Art glass
Portland, 274–275
Seattle, 103, 125, 128,
132–133
**Art Museum, Bellevue,
2, 105–106**
Fair, 15
**Art Museum, Frye (Seattle),
102**
Art Museum, Portland, 245
**Art Museum, Seattle, 97,
151**
**Art Museum, Seattle Asian,
102**
Ashford, 167, 169
**ATMs (automated-teller
machines), 317**
Seattle, 12

**AT&T Family Fourth at Lake
Union (Seattle), 15**
**AT&T New Year's at the
Needle (Seattle), 16**
**AT&T Wireless Summer
Nights at the Pier
(Seattle), 145**
**Augen Gallery (Portland),
274**
Aurora, 256–257
Auto racing, Portland, 264

B ainbridge Island,
31, 169–170
Bakeries and pastry shops
Lopez Island, 166
Orcas Island, 163
Portland, 241
Seattle, 89–90, 122, 124
Ballard (Seattle), 31
nightlife, 147, 149
Ballet, Seattle, 143–144
Bangor Navy Base, 172
**Bank of America Tower
(Seattle), 100**
Barlow Trail, 296
Bars
Portland, 286–290
gay and lesbian, 291
Seattle, 148–150
gay and lesbian,
150–151
Baseball
Portland, 264
Seattle, 118–119
Basketball
Portland, 264
Seattle, 119
**Bauhaus Coffee & Books
(Seattle), 89**
Beaches
near Portland, 260
Northern Oregon coast,
297–300
Seattle, 114–115
Beacon Rock, 292

Beaverton, accommodations, 215

Bed & breakfasts
Portland, 203, 210, 213, 214
Seattle, 39, 49, 50, 55

Beer
ingredients and types of, 289
Rheinlander Oktoberfest (Portland), 186

Bellevue. See also Eastside
accommodations, 58–60

Bellevue Art Museum, 2, 105–106

Bellevue Art Museum Fair, 15

Bellevue Botanical Gardens, 108

Bellevue Square, 137

Belltown (Seattle), 30
accommodations, 48–50
bakeries and pastry shops, 89
coffeehouses and tea shops, 88
nightlife, 145, 146, 148
restaurants, 72–78

Belmont district (Portland). See Hawthorne/Belmont district

Benaroya Hall (Seattle), 103, 144

Berry Botanic Garden (Portland), 253

Biking and mountain biking
Bainbridge Island, 170
Lopez Island, 165
Orcas Island, 161
Portland, 177, 260
San Juan Island, 158
Seattle, 8, 115–116

Bill of Rights Memorial (Portland), 272

Bird-watching, in San Juan Island, 158

Bite, The—A Taste of Portland, 186

Bite of Seattle, 15

Bitters Co (Seattle), 128

Blackfish Gallery (Portland), 274

Blagen Block (Portland), 268

Bloedel Reserve (Bainbridge Island), 170

Blues
Portland, 284
Seattle, 147

Boardsailing, Hood River, 261, 294

Boating. See also Canoeing; Sea kayaking
Bainbridge Island, 169–170
Bremerton, 171
Seattle, Opening Day of Boating Season, 14

Boats and ships
Bremerton, 171–172
Portland, Holiday Parade of Ships, 186
Seattle
Center for Wooden Boats, 98
Seafair, 15
Seattle Christmas Ships, 16
Seattle International Boat Show, 14
Wooden Boat Festival, 15

Boat Show, Seattle International, 14

Boat trips and tours. See also Ferries
Bremerton, 171
Orcas Island, 161
Portland, 258
Seattle, 92, 94, 111–113

Boeing tour (Seattle), 114

Bon Marché (Seattle), 135

Bonneville Lock and Dam, 292–293

Bookstores
Portland, 177, 275, 276
Seattle, 133

Bothell. See Eastside

Boulangerie (Seattle), 90

Bremerton, 171–172

Bremerton Naval Museum, 171

Brewpubs and breweries
Portland, 176, 177, 287–290
Oregon Brewers Festival, 186
Redhook Ale Brewery (Woodinville), 173
Seattle, 149–150

Bridge of the Gods, 293–294

Broadway Market (Seattle), 137

Bucket shops (consolidators), 22

Bullseye Connection (Portland), 274

Bullseye Connection Gallery (Portland), 274–275

Bumbershoot, the Seattle Arts Festival, 6, 15–16, 145

Burke-Gilman/Sammamish River Trail (Seattle), 115, 117

Burke Museum (Seattle), 104

Burnside Street (Portland), 193

Business hours, 320
Portland, 199

Bus tours
Portland, 258–259
Seattle, 110–111

Bus travel, 320
for disabled travelers, 18
Portland, 189, 191, 196
Seattle, 24, 26, 32

Butters Gallery Ltd. (Portland), 274

Cabaret, Seattle, 147

Cabs
Lopez Island, 164
Portland, 191, 198
San Juan Island, 156
Seattle, 25, 35

Café Allegro (Seattle), 89

Café Lena (Portland), 240

Cafes
Portland, 240–241
Seattle, 88–89

Caffe Appassionato (Seattle), 88

Caffe Ladro Espresso Bar & Bakery (Seattle), 88–89

Calendar of events
Portland, 184–187
Seattle, 14–16

Camlann Medieval Village (near Carnation), 173

Campgrounds, Mount Rainier National Park, 168

Canada, crossing into, 154–155

Cannon Beach, 260, 297–298

Canoeing
Bainbridge Island, 169
Seattle, 117

Cape Kiwanda, 300

Cape Lookout State Park, 300

Cape Meares State Scenic Viewpoint, 299

Capitol Hill (Seattle), 30
accommodations, 55–57
brass dance steps, 152
chocolate shop, 90
coffeehouse, 89
nightlife, 146
restaurants, 84–85
shopping, 130
sights and attractions, 102–103

Carl S. English, Jr. Ornamental Gardens, 108
Carlton, 301
Carnation, 173
Carolyn Staley (Seattle), 132
Car rentals
    for disabled travelers, 17
    Orcas Island, 161
    Portland, 197, 198
    San Juan Island, 156
    Seattle, 33–34
Carriage rides, Seattle, 152
Car travel
    Portland, 188, 190
    safety suggestions, 318
    Seattle, 23, 33
Cascade Locks, 294
Center for Wooden Boats (Seattle), 98
Chateau Ste. Michelle (Woodinville), 173
Cherry Blossom and Japanese Cultural Festival (Seattle), 14
Chief Seattle Days, 15
Chihuly, Dale, 103
Children, families with
    Portland, 188
        accommodations, 179–180
        restaurants, 182
        sights and attractions, 257–258
    Seattle
        accommodations, 8, 56
        information and resources, 20–21
        restaurants, 69
        Seattle International Children's Festival, 15
        sights and attractions, 109–110
Children's Museum (Seattle), 109
Chinatown (Portland), 195
    restaurants, 222–227
Chinatown (Seattle), walking tours, 110
Chinatown Gate (Portland), 269
Chinatown/International District Summer Festival (Seattle), 15
Chinese New Year (Seattle), 14
Chittenden Locks (Seattle), 107
Christmas at Pittock Mansion (Portland), 186

Cinco de Mayo Fiesta (Portland), 184–185
City Centre (Seattle), 137–138
City Centre shopping arcade (Seattle), 103
Classical Chinese Garden, Portland (Portland), 253
Classical music
    Portland, 282–283
    Seattle, 141–142
Club and music scene
    Portland, 284–286
    Seattle, 145–148
CM2—Children's Museum 2nd Generation (Portland), 3, 257
Coffeehouses and coffee bars
    Portland, 240–241
    Seattle, 5, 6, 88–89, 127
Coffee Time (Portland), 240
Columbia Gorge, 177, 292–297
Columbia Sportswear Company (Portland), 277
Columbia Winery (Woodinville), 173
Comedy clubs
    Portland, 285
    Seattle, 147
Common Grounds (Portland), 240
Concerts. See also Classical music
    Portland, 185, 251
    Seattle, 15
Consolidators (bucket shops), 22
Contemporary Crafts Gallery (Portland), 275
Council Crest (Portland), 250
Cow Chips (Seattle), 122
Crackerjack Contemporary Crafts (Seattle), 134
Crafts
    Portland, 275
    Seattle, 134
Credit cards, 13, 317
Cross-country skiing, near Seattle, 117–118
Crumpet Shop (Seattle), 88
Crystal Springs Rhododendron Garden (Portland), 253
Currency and currency exchange, 316–317
Customs regulations, 315–316

D ance
    Portland, 283
    Seattle, 143–144
Dance clubs
    Portland, 285–286
        gay, 291
    Seattle, 147–148
        gay and lesbian, 151
David Hill Winery, 301
Davidson Galleries (Seattle), 124, 132
Day spas
    Portland, 265
    Seattle, 120
DeLaurenti, 90
Dentists
    Portland, 199
    Seattle, 36
Department stores
    Portland, 276
    Seattle, 135
Dielschneider Building (Portland), 267
Dilettante Chocolates (Seattle), 90
Dinner cruises, Seattle, 112
Dinner train, Seattle, 114
Directional marker (Seattle), 127
Disabilities, travelers with
    Portland, 187
        accommodations, 181
    Seattle, 17–18
Discovery Park (Seattle), 106, 115, 116
Doctors
    Portland, 199
    Seattle, 36
Downtown Portland, 194
    accommodations, 203–210
    brewpubs, 287–288
    restaurants, 222–227
    sights and attractions, 244–245
    walking tour, 266–269
Downtown Seattle, 28
    accommodations, 39–47
    bars, 148
    restaurants, 65–70
Driver's licenses, foreign, 315
Driving rules
    Portland, 198
    Seattle, 35
Drugstores
    Portland, 200
    Seattle, 36
Dundee, 300, 301

East Seattle
accommodations, 55–57
chocolate shop, 90
coffeehouse, 89
restaurants, 84–85
Eastside (Kirkland, Bellevue, Redmond, Bothell), 31
accommodations, 58–60
restaurants, 87–88
sights and attractions, 105–106
Eastside Promenade (Portland), 248
Eastsound (Orcas Island), 160
Ecola Beach State Park, 297–298
Ecotours, Portland, 259
Edge of Glass Gallery (Seattle), 128
Electricity, 321
Elephant's Delicatessen (Portland), 242
Elk Fountain (Portland), 270
Elk Rock Garden of the Bishop's Close (Portland), 253
Elliott Bay Book Company (Seattle), 125, 133, 152
Elliott's Oyster New Year (Seattle), 16
Embassies and consulates, 321
Emerald Downs (Seattle), 120
Emergencies, 321
Seattle, 36
End of the Oregon Trail Interpretive Center (Oregon City), 256
English Camp (San Juan Island), 158
Entry requirements, 314–315
Erickson's Saloon Building (Portland), 268
Ermatinger House (Oregon City), 256
Experience Music Project (EMP) (Seattle), 98, 109, 146

Facelli Winery (Woodinville), 173
Failing Building (Portland), 267
Fallen Firefighters' Memorial, Seattle, 124

Famous Pacific Dessert Company (Seattle), 89
Fareless Square (Portland), 2–3, 177–178, 193, 194, 196
Fashions (clothing)
Portland, 277–279
Seattle, 135–136
Fax machines, 323
Fay Bainbridge State Park, 170
Ferries, 1. See also Boat trips and tours
San Juan Islands, 154
Seattle, 6, 23–24, 33
excursions from Seattle, 169–172
from Victoria (British Columbia), 319
Festivals and special events
Portland, 184–187
Seattle, 14–16
5th Avenue Theatre (Seattle), 6, 144
Film Festival, Portland International, 184
Film Festival, Seattle International (SIFF), 14, 151
Fireborne . . . Creations in Glass (Portland), 275
Fireworks Fine Crafts Gallery (Seattle), 124, 134
First Hill (Pill Hill) (Seattle), 28
accommodations, 39–47
restaurants, 65–70
sights and attractions, 102–103
Flea market, Seattle, 131
Flight, Museum of (Seattle), 105, 109, 152
Flora & Fauna Books (Seattle), 123, 133
Flury and Company (Seattle), 125, 133
Folk music
Portland, 284
Seattle, 145–147
Food stores, Orcas Island, 163
Football, Seattle, 119
Forest Park (Portland), 249, 261–262
Fort Vancouver National Historic Site (Vancouver, WA), 255
Fort Ward State Park (Bainbridge Island), 170
Foster/White Gallery (Seattle), 103, 125, 132

Fourth of Jul-Ivar's fireworks (Seattle), 15
Fourth of July Fireworks (Portland), 185
Frank and Dunya (Seattle), 126, 134
Freeway Park (Seattle), 106
Fremont (Seattle), 6, 31
restaurants, 85–86
shopping, 130
sights and attractions, 104
walking tour, 125–128
Fremont Bridge (Seattle), 125–126
Fremont Fair (Seattle), 15
Fremont Rocket (Seattle), 127–128
Fremont Sunday Market (Seattle), 126, 131
Fremont Troll (Seattle), 126
Friday Harbor (San Juan Island), 156
Frye Art Museum (Seattle), 102
Fun Forest (Seattle), 109

Gardens
Portland, 243
Berry Botanic Garden, 253
Crystal Springs Rhododendron Garden, 253
Elk Rock Garden of the Bishop's Close, 253
The Grotto—National Sanctuary of Our Sorrowful Mother, 253
International Rose Test Garden, 250
Japanese Garden, 250–251
Peninsula Park Rose Garden, 253
Portland Classical Chinese Garden, 253–254
Seattle, 108–109
Carl S. English, Jr. Ornamental Gardens, 108
Japanese Garden, 108
Northwest Flower & Garden Show, 14
Garibaldi, 298
Gasoline (petrol), 321
Gaston, 301

Gasworks Park (Seattle), 107, 115
Gay and Lesbian Travelers
    information and resources, 18–19
    Portland, 187
        nightlife, 291
    Seattle, 30
        accommodations, 19, 55, 56
        nightlife, 150–151
George C. Marshall House (Vancouver, WA), 255
Gifts and souvenirs
    Portland, 279
    Seattle, 136–137
Glass, art
    Portland, 274–275
    Seattle, 103, 125, 128, 132–133
Glass Eye Studio (Seattle), 132
Glasshouse Studio (Seattle), 132
Golden Access Passport, 18
Golden Age Passport, 20
Golden Gardens (Seattle), 108
Golden Gardens Park (Seattle), 115
Golf
    Portland, 261
    Seattle, 116
Grand Central Arcade (Seattle), 124
Grand Central Baking Company (Seattle), 89, 124
Grant House (Vancouver, WA), 255
Grant House Folk Art Center (Vancouver, WA), 255
Graystone Gallery (Portland), 275
Green Lake (Seattle), 8, 117
Green Lake Park (Seattle), 107
Greg Kucera Gallery (Seattle), 132
Grotto, The—National Sanctuary of Our Sorrowful Mother (Portland), 253

H awthorne/Belmont district (Portland), 195, 273
    restaurants, 236–239
Haystack Rock, 298, 300
Health, 16
Henry Art Gallery (Seattle), 104

High Noon Tunes (Portland), 185–186
Hiking
    Columbia Gorge, 177
    Lopez Island, 164, 165
    Mount Hood, 177
    Mount Rainier National Park, 168
    Mount St. Helens National Volcanic Monument, 304
    Orcas Island, 161
    Portland, 249, 261–262
    San Juan Island, 158
    Seattle, 116
Hing Hay Park (Seattle), 101
Hiram M. Chittenden Locks (Seattle), 107
History
    Portland, 309–313
    Seattle, 305–308
History House (Seattle), 126
Hockey, Seattle, 120
Hoffman Gallery (Portland), 275
Holiday Parade of Ships (Portland), 186
Holidays, 321–322
Hood, Mount, 262
Hood River, 261, 294, 296
Horse racing, Seattle, 120
Hospitals
    Portland, 199
    Seattle, 36
Housewares and home furnishings
    Portland, 279
    Seattle, 137
Howloween (Portland), 186
Hoyt Arboretum (Portland), 249
Hug Point State Recreation Site, 298

I ce hockey, Portland, 265
IMAXDome Theater (Seattle), 95
Information sources
    Portland, 183
    Seattle, 12, 26–27
In-line skating, Seattle, 117
Insurance, 316
    travel, 17
International District (Seattle), 30
    accommodations, 48
    bakery, 89
    restaurants, 70–72
    sights and attractions, 101–102

International Fountain (Seattle), 109
International Rose Test Garden (Portland), 250
International visitors, 314–324
Internet access
    Portland, 200
    Seattle, 36
Intiman Theatre Company (Seattle), 142
Ira Keller Memorial Fountain (Portland), 270
Irish pubs
    Portland, 290
    Seattle, 150
Irvington (Portland), 195
    accommodations, 212–214
    restaurants, 234–236
Island Wine Company (San Juan Island), 156
Issaquah, 107
    Salmon Days Festival, 16

J ackle's Lagoon (San Juan Island), 158
Jackson Park Golf Course (Seattle), 116
Jantzen Beach (North Portland), accommodations, 211–212
Jantzen Store (Portland), 277
Japanese American Historical Plaza (Portland), 272
Japanese Garden (Portland), 176, 177, 250–251
Japanese Garden (Seattle), 108
Jazz
    Portland, 284–285
    Seattle, 147
Jefferson Park Golf Course (Seattle), 116
Jeff Morris Memorial Fire Museum (Portland), 268
Jogging, Seattle, 8, 117
Johnston Ridge Observatory, 303–304
Jurassic Park (Seattle), 128

K ayaking
    Bainbridge Island, 169–170
    Lopez Island, 165
    Orcas Island, 161–162
    Portland, 177, 263
    Poulsbo, 171
    San Juan Island, 158
    Seattle, 8, 117
Keller Auditorium (Portland), 281

Kenmore Logboom Park
  (Seattle), 116
Kerry Viewpoint (Seattle),
  100
Kirkland, 173. *See also*
  Eastside
Klondike Gold Rush National
  Historical Park (Seattle),
  97, 124
Kvinneakt (Portland), 272

L add's Addition (Port-
  land), 195
Laguna Vintage Pottery
  (Seattle), 123
Lake Oswego, accommoda-
  tions, 215
Lake Union (Seattle)
  accommodations, 54–55
  restaurants, 82–84
  sea kayaking, 8
  sights and attractions,
    98–101
Laura Russo Gallery
  (Portland), 274
Legacy Ltd., The (Seattle),
  133
Legal aid, 322
Leif Erikson Trail (Portland),
  177, 260
Lenin (Seattle), 128
Le Panier (Seattle), 89
Lime Kiln State Park (San
  Juan Island), 158, 159
Lincoln Park (Seattle),
  115, 116
Lion Valley Vineyards, 301
Liquor laws, 320
  Portland, 200
  Washington state, 36
Lisa Harris Gallery (Seattle),
  132
Live-music clubs, 145
Lloyd Center (Portland), 279
Longmire, 167–169
Longmire Museum (Mount
  Rainier National Park),
  167–168
Lopez Island, 164–166
Lopez Island Historical
  Museum, 164
Lopez Island Vineyards, 164
Lower Woodland Park
  (Seattle), 118

M cLoughlin House
  (Oregon City), 256
Macrina (Seattle), 89

Made in Oregon (Portland),
  268, 279
Madison Park (Seattle), 30
Magnolia (Seattle), 31
Mail and post offices, 322
Manzanita, 298
Marathon
  Portland, 186
  Seattle, 16, 120
Margo Jacobsen Gallery
  (Portland), 274
Markets
  Portland, 280
  Seattle, 138
Marshall, George C., House
  (Vancouver, WA), 255
Maynard Building (Seattle),
  123
Medical requirements for
  entry, 315
Meier and Frank (Portland),
  276
Memorial Day Wine Tastings
  (Portland), 185
Metropolitan Area Express
  (MAX) (Portland), 196–197
Michael Maslan Historic
  Photographs, Postcards &
  Ephemera (Seattle), 124
Mill Ends Park (Portland),
  254, 270
MOHAI (Museum of History
  and Industry), 104–105
Money, 316–317
  Portland, 183
  Seattle, 12–13
Monorail, Seattle, 6, 33
Montinore Vineyards, 301
Moran State Park, 161
Mother's Day Rhododendron
  Show (Portland), 185
Mountain biking. *See* Biking
  and mountain biking
Mount Hood Jazz Festival
  (Gresham), 186
Mount Hood Loop, 292–297
Mount Hood Meadows, 263
Mount Hood National
  Forest, 262
Mount Hood Railroad
  (Hood River), 294
Mount Rainier National
  Park, 166–169
Mount St. Helens National
  Volcanic Monument,
  302–304
Movies
  Portland, 291
  Seattle, 151–152
Mt. Hood SkiBowl, 263

Multnomah Falls, 292
Murdock Sky Theater
  (Portland), 248
Museum of Flight (Seattle),
  105, 109, 152
Museum of History and
  Industry (MOHAI),
  104–105
Museum of the Oregon
  Territory (Oregon City),
  256
Music. *See also* Classical
  music; Concerts; Jazz;
  Live-music clubs
  Experience Music Project
    (Seattle), 98
Music festivals
  Portland, 185, 186
  Seattle
    Bumbershoot, the
      Seattle Arts Festival,
      6, 15–16, 145
    Northwest Folklife
      Festival, 14–15
    Summer Festival On
      The Green (Wood-
      inville), 145
Myrtle Edwards Park
  (Seattle), 94, 106, 117

N ative Americans, 15,
  133, 170
Naval Undersea Museum
  (Bremerton), 172
Neahkahnie Mountain, 298
Nehalem Bay State Park, 298
Neighborhoods
  Portland, 194–195
  Seattle, 28, 30–31
    sights and attractions,
    101–106
New Market Block
  (Portland), 266–267
Newspapers and magazines
  Portland, 200
  Seattle, 36
New Theater Building
  (Portland), 281
Nightlife and entertainment
  Portland, 281–291
    bars, 286–290
    club and music scene,
    284–286
    performing arts,
    281–284
  Seattle, 141–152
    advance-purchase
    tickets, 143
    club and music scene,
    145–148

current listings, 141
major performance
halls, 144
performing arts,
141–145
Nob Hill (Portland). *See*
Northwest/Nob Hill
Nordstrom (Portland), 276
Nordstrom (Seattle), 135
North by Northwest
(NXNW), 186
Northeast Portland. *See also*
Irvington
accommodations, 213
brewpubs, 288, 290
restaurants, 234–236
Northern Oregon coast,
297–300
North Face (Seattle),
138–139
North Seattle (Fremont,
Montlake, Wallingford,
University District). *See
also* Fremont; University
District; Wallingford
accommodations, 57–58
coffeehouses and tea
shops, 89
pastry shop, 90
restaurants, 85–86
Northwest Chamber Orches-
tra (Seattle), 142
Northwest Children's The-
ater and School (Portland),
258
Northwest Film Center
(Portland), 245
Northwest Fine Woodwork-
ing (Seattle), 125, 134
Northwest Flower & Garden
Show (Seattle), 14
Northwest Folklife Festival
(Seattle), 14–15, 145
Northwest/Nob Hill (Port-
land), 194, 195. *See also*
Pearl District
accommodations, 210–211
brewpubs, 288
restaurants, 227–234
shopping, 273
Northwest Puppet Center
(Seattle), 109
Northwest Railway Museum
(Snoqualmie), 172
Northwest Seaport/Maritime
Heritage Center (Seattle),
98, 100
Norton House (Portland),
268

O. O. Howard House
(Vancouver, WA), 254–255
Oak Knoll Winery, 302
Oaks Park Amusement
Center (Portland), 257
Occidental Park (Seattle),
124
Oceanside, 299–300
Odlin County Park, 164
Odyssey—The Maritime Dis-
covery Center (Seattle), 95
Of Sea and Shore Museum
(Port Gamble), 171
Old Aurora Colony Museum,
257
Old Church (Portland), 282
Old Man House State Park,
170
Old Town (Portland). *See*
Skidmore Historic District
Olympic National Park, 18,
20
OMNIMAX theater (Port-
land), 248
Oneonta Gorge, 292
Opera
Portland, 282
Seattle, 141–142
Orcas Island, 160–164
Orcas Island Pottery, 161
Oregon Brewers Festival
(Portland), 186
Oregon Children's Theatre
Company (Portland),
257–258
Oregon City, 255–256
Oregon History Center
(Portland), 245
Oregon Maritime Center and
Museum (Portland), 248,
268
Oregon Museum of Science
and Industry (OMSI) (Port-
land), 248, 257
Oregon Symphony
(Portland), 282
Oregon Zoo, 187
Oregon Zoo (Portland), 251,
257
Oswald West State Park, 298
Otis Perkins Park, 165
Outdoor activities. *See also
specific activities*
Portland, 260–264
Seattle, 8, 114–118
Out to Lunch (Seattle), 15

P acific City, 300
Pacific Crest Trail, 262

Pacific Place (Seattle), 138
Pacific Science Center
(Seattle), 100–101
Paradise (Mount Rainier
National Park), 168
Paramount Theatre (Seattle),
144
Parking
Portland, 197–198
Seattle, 35
Parks
Portland, 243, 270
Seattle, 8, 106–108
Pastry shops
Portland, 241
Seattle, 89–90
Patagonia Seattle, 139
Pearl Bakery (Portland), 241
Pearl District (Portland), 195,
273
restaurants, 227–234
Pearson Air Museum (Van-
couver, WA), 255
Peet's Coffee (Portland), 241
Pendleton Woolen Mills and
Outlet Shop (Washougal),
278
Peninsula Park Rose Garden
(Portland), 253
Performing arts
Portland, 281–284
Seattle, 141–145
Petrol (gasoline), 321
Pharmacies
Portland, 200
Seattle, 36
Phoenix Rising Gallery
(Seattle), 132
PICA (Portland Institute for
Contemporary Art), 252,
282
Picnics (picnic fare)
Portland, 242
Seattle, 90
Pied Cow (Portland), 241
Pike Place Fish (Seattle), 139
Pike Place Market and
neighborhood (Seattle),
6, 91
accommodations, 48–50
bakeries and pastry shops,
89
coffeehouses and tea
shops, 88
restaurants, 72–78
shopping, 129–132, 134,
136, 138, 139
sights and attractions,
95–97
tours, 96–97

Pike Place Market Festival (Seattle), 15
Pilchuck School for art glass (near Seattle), 103
Pill Hill (Seattle). See First Hill
Pioneer Courthouse Square (Portland), 178, 244, 269–270, 273
Pioneer Place (Portland), 279–280
Pioneer Place (Seattle), 122
Pioneer Square (Seattle), 28, 30, 130
    accommodations, 48
    art galleries, 131–132
    bakery, 89
    bars, 148–149
    cafes and coffee bars, 88
    nightlife, 145–146
    restaurants, 70–72
    sights and attractions, 95–97
    walking tour, 121–125
Pioneer Square Antique Mall (Seattle), 122, 131
Piroshky, Piroshky (Seattle), 90
Pittock Mansion (Portland), 250, 251–252
Police, 37, 200
Portage Bay Goods (Seattle), 126, 136
Portfolio Glass (Seattle), 103
Port Gamble, 171
Port Gamble Historical Museum, 171
Portland Art Museum, 245
Portland Arts Festival, 185
Portland Audubon Society, 249
Portland Building, 244, 245, 270
Portland Center for the Performing Arts (PCPA), 281
Portland Classical Chinese Garden, 195, 253–254, 268
Portland Creative Conference, 186
Portlandia (Portland), 244–245, 270
Portland Institute for Contemporary Art (PICA), 252, 282
Portland International Airport (PDX), 190
    accommodations near, 214–215
Portland International Film Festival, 184

Portland International Performance Festival (PIPFest), 284
Portland Marathon, 186, 265
Portland Opera, 282
Portland Oregon Visitors Association (POVA), 2
Portland Rose Festival, 185
Portland Saturday Market, 248–249, 268, 272, 275, 280
Portland Streetcar, 2
Portland Trail Blazers, 264
Post offices, 322
Poulsbo, 170–171
Poulsbo Marine Science Center, 171
Powell's City of Books (Portland), 177, 194, 276
Private Eye on Seattle tours, 113
Puget Sound, ferries, 6
Pulliam Deffenbaugh Gallery (Portland), 274

Queen Anne (Seattle)
    accommodations, 50–54
    coffeehouses and tea shops, 88–89
    pastry shop, 89
    restaurants, 78–82
Queen Anne Hill (Seattle), 30
Quintana Galleries (Portland), 274

Rail travel. See Train travel and rail excursions
Rain
    Portland, 184
    Seattle, 13–14
Rainier, Mount, 5, 166–169
    for disabled travelers, 18
    senior discounts, 20
Rapunzel (Seattle), 126
Real Mother Goose (Portland), 275
Recreational gear, Seattle, 138–139
Redhook Ale Brewery (Woodinville), 173
Redmond. See Eastside
Reed College (Portland), 195, 283
Reggae, Seattle, 146
Regional Arts & Culture Council (RACC) (Portland), 269

REI (Seattle), 139
Reptile and Amphibian Show (Portland), 186
Restaurants
    Bite of Seattle, 15
    Portland, 216–242
        best bets, 181–182
        for brunch, 229
        by cuisine, 216–217, 220–221
        family-friendly, 235
        late-night, 238
        quick bites and cheap eats, 242
        what's new, 3
    Seattle, 61–90
        best bets, 10
        for brunch, 74
        cafes, coffee bars and tea shops, 88–89
        by cuisine, 62–65
        family-friendly, 69
        quick bites, 90
        what's new, 1–2
Restrooms, 37, 324
Rheinlander Oktoberfest (Portland), 186
Rhythm and Zoo Concerts (Portland), 185
Rimsky-Korsakoffee House (Portland), 241
Roche Harbor Resort (San Juan Island), 158
Rock music
    Portland, 284
    Seattle, 145–147
Rooster Rock State Park, 260
Rose Garden Children's Park (Portland), 257
Rose Quarter (Portland), 196, 264
    accommodations, 212–214
Rosie's Boulangerie (Portland), 241
Ross Island, kayaking, 177
Rowing, in Seattle, 117
Running. See Jogging; Marathon

Safeco Field (Seattle), 118–119
Safety
    general suggestions, 317–318
    Portland, 200
    Seattle, 37
Sailing, in Seattle, 117
St. Helens, Mount, 302–304

Salmon
Bonneville Lock and Dam, 292–293
Issaquah Salmon Hatchery, 107
Seattle
Hiram M. Chittenden Locks (Seattle), 107
Seattle Aquarium, 107
shopping, 139
Salmon Days Festival (Issaquah), 16
Salmon Street Springs fountain (Portland), 257, 270
Samtrak (Portland), 248
Sandcastle Day (Cannon Beach), 298
San Juan County Park (San Juan Island), 158
San Juan Island, 156–160
San Juan Islands, 153–166
traveling to, 154–156
visitor information, 154
San Juan National Historic Park, 157
San Juan Vineyards (San Juan Island), 158
Saturday Market, Portland, 178, 195, 248–249, 268, 272, 275, 280
Sauvie Island, 260, 261
SBC (Seattle's Best Coffee), 88
Scenic flights and hot-air balloon rides
Portland, 259
Seattle, 113
Seafair (Seattle), 15
Sea kayaking. *See* Kayaking
Seaplane rides, Seattle, 113
Seaside, 260, 297
Seasons, Portland, 183–184
Sea-Tac Airport, 7, 25–26
accommodations near, 58
Seattle Aquarium, 95, 107
Seattle Art Museum, 97, 151
Seattle Asian Art Museum, 102
Seattle Center, 109, 141
accommodations, 50–54
coffeehouses and tea shops, 88–89
pastry shop, 89
restaurants, 78–82
sights and attractions, 98–101
Seattle Children's Theatre, 109
Seattle Christmas Ships, 16

Seattle Duck Tours, 111
Seattle Fallen Firefighters' Memorial, 124
Seattle Fringe Theatre Festival, 16, 142–143
Seattle International Boat Show, 14
Seattle International Children's Festival, 15
Seattle International Film Festival (SIFF), 14, 151
Seattle Marathon, 16, 120
Seattle Mariners, 118–119
Seattle Monorail, 33
Seattle Opera, 141–142
Seattle Repertory Theater, 142
Seattle Seahawks, 119
Seattle Sounders, 120
Seattle Storm, 119
Seattle SuperSonics, 119
Seattle Symphony, 142
Seattle-Tacoma (Sea-Tac) International Airport, 7, 25–26
accommodations near, 58
Seattle Thunderbirds, 120
Seattle Times, 7
Seattle Weekly, 7
Sellwood/Westmoreland (Portland), 195
restaurants, 239–240
Seniors
Portland, 187–188
Seattle, 19
Seward Park (Seattle), 107, 115, 116
Shark Reef Sanctuary (Lopez Island), 165
Shopping
Portland, 273–280
Seattle, 129–140
Shopping centers and malls
Portland, 279–280
Seattle, 137–138
antiques and collectibles, 131
Si, Mount, 116, 172
Sights and attractions
Portland, 243–260
Frommer's favorite experiences, 177–179
for kids, 257–258
organized tours, 258–260
suggested itineraries, 243–244
what's new, 3

Seattle, 91–114
Frommer's favorite experiences, 6–8
gardens, 108–109
for kids, 109–110
neighborhoods, 101–106
organized tours, 110–114
parks, 106–108, 115
saving money on, 94
suggested itineraries, 91–92
what's new, 2
Silver Lake Winery (Woodinville), 173
Simon Benson Fountains (Portland), 270
Skidmore Fountain (Portland), 266, 272
Skidmore Historic District (Old Town), 194–195
restaurants, 222–227
sights and attractions, 245–249
walking tour, 266–269
Skiing
near Portland, 263
near Seattle, 117, 118
Smith's Block (Portland), 268
Smith Tower (Seattle), 100, 122, 123
Smoking
Portland, 200
Seattle, 37
Snoqualmie, 172
Snoqualmie, Summit at, 118
Snoqualmie Falls, 172
Snoqualmie Pass (near Seattle), 116
Snoqualmie Valley, 172
Soaring Stones (Portland), 270
Soccer, Seattle, 120
Southeast Portland. *See also* Hawthorne/Belmont district
brewpubs, 288
restaurants, 236–239
South Seattle, sights and attractions, 105
Southwest Portland, restaurants, 234
Space Needle (Seattle), 101, 109, 152
Spas, day
Portland, 265
Seattle, 120

Special events and festivals
　Portland, 184–187
　Seattle, 14–16
Spectator sports
　Portland, 264–265
　Seattle, 118–120
Spencer Spit State Park,
　164–165
Spring Flower and Garden
　Show (Seattle), 6
Starbucks, in Seattle, 88,
　122, 134, 144
Stevens Crawford House
　(Oregon City), 256
Still Life in Fremont Coffee-
　house (Seattle), 89
Stonington Gallery (Seattle),
　125, 133
Story Garden (Portland), 272
Streetcars, Seattle, 32
Streetcars (trolleys), Port-
　land, 177–178, 197, 259
Street maps
　Portland, 194
　Seattle, 28
Street Wise (Portland), 270
Summer Festival On The
　Green (Woodinville), 145
Summit at Snoqualmie, 118
Sunday Market, Fremont
　(Seattle), 126, 131
Sunrise (Mount Rainier
　National Park), 168
Suquamish, 170
Suquamish Museum, 170

Tacoma Art Museum, 103
Tao of Tea (Portland), 242
Taxes, 322
　Portland, 201
　Seattle, 37
Taxis
　Lopez Island, 164
　Portland, 191, 198
　San Juan Island, 156
　Seattle, 25, 35
Teahouse Kuan Yin (Seattle),
　89, 134
Tears of Joy Theater
　(Portland), 258
Tea shops
　Portland, 241–242
　Seattle, 88–89, 134
Tea Zone (Portland), 242
Telephone, 322–323
Temperature, average
　Portland, 184
　Seattle, 14
Tennis
　Portland, 263
　Seattle, 118

Ten Ren Tea Co., Ltd
　(Seattle), 134
Theater
　Portland, 283
　　children's theater,
　　　257–258
　Seattle, 142–143
　　Seattle Fringe Theatre
　　　Festival, 16,
　　　142–143
Three Capes Scenic Route,
　299
Three Girls Bakery (Seattle),
　89, 90
Ticket Central (Portland), 2
Tillamook, 298, 300
Tillamook Bay, 298
Tillamook Cheese Factory,
　298, 299
Tillicum Village, 92, 94,
　111–112, 171
Timberline Lodge, 296
Timberline Ski Area, 263
Time zones, 37, 201, 323
Tipping, 323–324
Toilets, 324
Tom McCall Waterfront Park
　(Portland), 179, 245, 248,
　257
　　special events, 184–186
　　Story Garden (Portland),
　　　272
Torrefazione Italia (Port-
　land), 241
Torrefazione Italia (Seattle),
　88, 125
Totem Smokehouse
　(Seattle), 139
Tourist information
　Portland, 183
　Seattle, 12, 26–27
Tours, 122
　for disabled travelers, 18
　Seattle, 110
　　boat tours, 111–113
　　Boeing tour, 114
　　bus tours, 110–111
　　Pike Place Market,
　　　96–97
　　Safeco Field, 119
　　scenic flights and hot-
　　　air balloon rides,
　　　113
　　Spirit of Washington
　　　Dinner Train, 114
　　Underground Tour, 96,
　　　109, 122
　　Victoria excursions,
　　　113
　　walking tours, 110
　for seniors, 20

Toys
　Portland, 280
　Seattle, 139–140
Train travel and rail excur-
　sions, 319–320
　for disabled travelers, 18
　Mount Hood Railroad
　　(Hood River), 294
　Portland, 188–189, 192,
　　196, 259
　　Airport Max, 2, 190
　Seattle, 24
　Snoqualmie Valley
　　Railroad, 172
　Spirit of Washington Dinner
　　Train (Seattle), 114
Transportation
　Portland, 2–3, 177,
　　196–198
　Seattle, 32–35
　　information, 37
Traveler's checks, 12–13,
　183, 317
Travel insurance, 17
Trip-cancellation insurance,
　17
Trolleyman Pub (Seattle),
　128
Troutdale (Portland), accom-
　modations, 214–215
Tryon Creek State Park, 262
Tully's (Seattle), 88
Turner Joy, USS (Bremerton),
　171
24-Hour Church of
　Elvis/Where's the Art?
　(Portland), 252
Twist (Portland), 275
Twist (Seattle), 134–135

Underground Tour,
　Seattle, 96, 109, 122
Underground Tours, Portland,
　260
Union, Lake (Seattle)
　accommodations, 54–55
　restaurants, 82–84
　sights and attractions,
　　98–101
University District (Seattle),
　30, 130
　accommodations, 57–58
　restaurants, 85–86
　sights and attractions, 104
University of Washington,
　sports teams, 119–120
Upright Channel Park, 164
Uptown Espresso (Seattle),
　89
Uwajimaya (Seattle), 138
UW World Series, 144–145

Vancouver, Washington
accommodations, 211–212
sights and attractions,
254–255
Vancouver Lake State Park,
261
Vancouver National Historic
Reserve, 254
Vetri (Seattle), 132–133
Victoria (Canada), 155
Victor Steinbrueck Park
(Seattle), 96
Vietnam Veterans Living
Memorial (Portland), 249
Visas, 314
Visitor information
Portland, 183, 192
Seattle, 12, 26–27
Volunteer Park (Seattle),
6–7, 100, 102, 106–107,
117, 118
Volunteer Park Conservatory
(Seattle), 103

Waiting for the
Interurban (Seattle), 126
Walking
in Portland, 198
in Seattle, 35
Walking tours
Portland
guided tours, 259–260
self-guided tours,
266–272
Seattle
guided, 110
self-guided, 121–128
Wallingford (Seattle), 31, 130
restaurants, 85–86
Washington, Lake (Seattle),
5, 27, 31
accommodations, 8, 59
cruises, 112
parks and beaches, 107,
115
restaurants, 87
Washington Park (Portland),
249
Washington Park and Zoo
Railway (Portland), 251
Washington Park Arboretum
(Seattle), 108–109
Washington Park Zoo
(Portland), 179
Washington State
Convention and Trade
Center (Seattle), 103
Washington State Ferries,
1, 33, 111
website, 7

Washougal, 278
Waterfall Park (Seattle), 124
Waterfalls
Multnomah Falls (near
Portland), 292
Snoqualmie Falls (near
Seattle), 172
Waterfront, Seattle, 28, 130
accommodations, 47–48
catching the sunset from,
152
harbor tours, 92
parks, 94, 106, 108, 115
restaurants, 70
sights and attractions,
94–95
Waterfront Blues Festival
(Portland), 185
Waterfront Park (Portland),
179, 245, 248, 257
special events, 184–186
Story Garden (Portland),
272
Water taxis, Seattle, 33
Water Tower at Johns
Landing (Portland), 280
Weather
Portland, 184, 201
Seattle, 13–14, 37
Weather Machine (Portland),
244
Websites
Portland, 178, 183
Seattle, best, 7
travel-planning and book-
ing, 22–23
Westlake Center (Seattle),
138
Westmoreland (Portland). *See*
Sellwood/Westmoreland
West Seattle, 31
restaurants, 86–87
West Seattle Golf Course,
116
Whale Museum (San Juan
Island), 156–157
Whale-watching
Orcas Island, 162
San Juan Island, 159
White-water rafting, near
Portland, 264
Willamette Falls, 255–256
Willamette Park (Portland),
261
Willamette River. *See* Tom
McCall Waterfront Park
William Traver Gallery
(Seattle), 133
Wine bars, Portland, 287
Wine Country Thanksgiving
(near Portland), 186

Wines and vineyards, 173
Bainbridge Island, 170
Lopez Island, 164
Portland and environs,
300–302
shopping, 280
tours, 260
Wine Country Thanks-
giving, 186
San Juan Island, 156, 158
Seattle and environs, 140,
173
Wing Luke Asian Museum
(Seattle), 101–102
Wooden Boat Festival
(Seattle), 15
Woodinville, 145, 173
Woodland Park Zoo
(Seattle), 2, 105, 145
World Class Chili (Seattle),
90
World Cup Coffee & Tea
(Portland), 241
World Forestry Center
Museum (Portland), 252

Ye Olde Curiosity Shop
(Seattle), 96, 109, 137
Yesler Way (Seattle), 122
Young, Mount, 158
Youth hostels, Seattle, 47

Zeitgeist Art/Coffee
(Seattle), 88
Zoo
Oregon Zoo (Portland),
187, 251, 257
Woodland Park (Seattle),
7, 105, 145
Zoo Beat Concerts
(Portland), 185
Zoo Lights (Portland), 187

**SEATTLE AND
ENVIRONS
ACCOMMODATIONS**

Ace Hotel, 50
Alexis Hotel, 9, 10, 39, 42
The Bacon Mansion Bed &
Breakfast, 19, 55
Bellevue Club Hotel, 9, 59
Best Western Bellevue Inn,
59
Best Western Pioneer Square
Hotel, 48
Best Western University
Tower Hotel, 9, 57

Chambered Nautilus Bed and Breakfast Inn, 57

Comfort Suites Downtown/Seattle Center, 51

Days Inn Town Center, 51

Edenwild Inn (Lopez Island), 165

The Edgewater, 9, 47–48

Elliott Grand Hyatt Seattle, 1, 8, 42

Executive Pacific Plaza Hotel, 46

Extended StayAmerica–Bellevue, 60

Four Seasons Olympic Hotel, 8, 42

Friday Harbor House (San Juan Island), 159

The Gaslight Inn, 9, 19, 56

The Georgian, 42–43

Hostelling International–Seattle, 47

Hotel Monaco, 43

Hotel Vintage Park, 43

Howard Johnson Express Inn, 9, 54

Inn at Harbor Steps, 44–45

Inn at Queen Anne, 51

Inn at the Market, 8, 48–49

The Inn at Virginia Mason, 46

Lopez Farm Cottages and Tent Camping (Lopez Island), 165

Lopez Islander (Lopez Island), 165–166

MarQueen Hotel, 51, 56

Mayflower Park Hotel, 45

Moore Hotel, 50

Motel 6, 58

The MV Challenger, 54–55

National Park Inn (Ashford), 168–169

Olympic Lights Bed and Breakfast (San Juan Island), 159

Orcas Hotel (Orcas Island), 162

Paradise Inn (Ashford), 169

Pensione Nichols, 49

Renaissance Madison Hotel, 43–44

The Resort at Deer Harbor (Orcas Island), 162

Roche Harbor Village (San Juan Island), 159–160

The Roosevelt, A WestCoast Hotel, 46–47

Rosario Resort & Spa (Orcas Island), 162

Salisbury House, 56–57

Salish Lodge and Spa (Snoqualmie), 173–174

Seattle Downtown-Lake Union Marriott Residence Inn, 55

Seattle Marriott Sea-Tac Airport, 56, 58

Sheraton Seattle Hotel and Towers, 9, 45

Silver Cloud Inns Seattle–Lake Union, 8, 54, 56

Sorrento Hotel, 44

Spring Bay Inn (Orcas Island), 163

Summerfield Suites by Wyndham, 47

Super 8 Motel, 58

Travelodge Seattle Airport, 58

Travelodge—Seattle City Center, 54

Turtleback Farm Inn (Orcas Island), 163

University Inn, 57–58

The Wall Street Inn, 49

WestCoast Sea-Tac Hotel, 58

WestCoast Vance Hotel, 49–50

The Westin Seattle, 45–46

Willows Lodge (Woodinville), 1, 174

The Woodmark Hotel on Lake Washington, 8, 59

W Seattle, 8, 44

PORTLAND AND ENVIRONS ACCOMMODATIONS

The Benson, 179, 203, 206

Columbia Gorge Hotel (Hood River), 296

Days Inn City Center, 208–209

Dolce Skamania Lodge (Stevenson, WA), 296–297

Doubletree Hotel Portland Columbia River, 211–212

Doubletree Portland Downtown, 209

Downtown Portland's Imperial Hotel, 209

Embassy Suites, 181, 206, 211

5th Avenue Suites Hotel, 179, 206

Four Points Hotel Sheraton, 180, 209

Governor Hotel, 179, 180, 207

Greenwood Inn (Beaverton), 180, 215

The Heathman Hotel, 180, 207

The Heathman Lodge (Vancouver, WA), 212

Heron Haus, 180, 210

Hollywood Express Inn, 213

Homewood Suites by Hilton Vancouver/Portland, 180, 211, 212

Hotel Vintage Plaza, 179, 207–208

Lakeshore Inn, 180

The Lakeshore Inn (Lake Oswego), 211, 215

The Lion and the Rose, 212–213

McMenamins Edgefield, 181, 214

McMenamins Kennedy School, 181, 213

Mallory Hotel, 209–210

The Mark Spencer Hotel, 210

Motel 6, 215

Portland Marriott Downtown, 180, 208

Portland's White House, 213

RiverPlace Hotel, 180, 203

Shilo Inn Suites Hotel Portland Airport, 214

Silver Cloud Inn Portland Airport, 214–215

Silver Cloud Inn Portland Downtown, 210–211

Sullivan's Gulch B&B, 213–214

Super 8 Motel, 215

Timberline Lodge, 297

The Westin Portland, 208

SEATTLE AND ENVIRONS RESTAURANTS

Afrikando, 2, 73–74

Andaluca, 68

Anthony's Pier 66 & Bell Street Diner, 10, 70

Assaggio, 74

Bay Café (Lopez Island), 166

Beach Café, 2, 87–88

Belltown Pub and Cafe, 11, 78

Bluwater Bistro, 82

The Brooklyn Seafood, Steak, and Oyster House, 65

Bucky's (Lopez Island), 166

Cafe Campagne, 74

Cafe Flora, 84–85

Café Olga (Orcas Island), 163
Caffé Verdi, 166
Campagne, 10, 73
Canlis, 10, 79
Chez Shea, 10, 73
Chinook's at Salmon Bay, 2, 85
Christina's (Orcas Island), 163–164
Comet Café (Orcas Island), 163
Cucina!Cucina!, 10, 69, 83–84
Dahlia Lounge, 74–75
Duck Soup Inn (San Juan Island), 160
El Gaucho, 72–73
Elliott's, 70
Etta's Seafood, 11, 75
The Famous Pacific Dessert Company, 11
Fandango, 75
The 5 Spot, 82
Flying Fish, 75
Forecaster's Public House (Woodinville), 174
Fuller's, 65, 68
Garden Path Café (San Juan Island), 160
The Georgian, 65
Gravity Bar, 85
The Herbfarm Restaurant (Woodinville), 1, 87, 174–175
Himalayan Sherpa Restaurant, 86
Hing Loon, 71
Icon Grill, 75–76
Il Bistro, 73
Il Terrazzo Carmine, 11, 71
The Inn at Ship Bay (Orcas Island), 164
Ivar's Salmon House, 69, 83
Kaspar's Restaurant & Wine Bar, 79
Koraku, 2, 71–72
Le Pichet, 2, 76
McCormick and Schmick's, 69
McCormick and Schmick's Harborside, 83
Madelyn's Bagel Bakery (San Juan Island), 160
Maggie Bluffs Marina Grill, 69, 82
Marco's Supperclub, 76
Matt's in the Market, 76
Merchants Cafe, 72, 122
Metropolitan Grill, 11, 68
Noodle Ranch, 10, 78
The Painted Table, 68
Palace Kitchen, 11, 77

Palisade, 10, 79
Palomino, 69
Pecos Pit BBQ, 72
The Pink Door, 77
Pizzeria Pagliacci, 82, 84
The Place Next to the San Juan Ferry (San Juan Island), 160
Ponti Seafood Grill, 85
Ray's Boathouse and Cafe, 86
Red Mill Burgers, 86
Rover's, 11, 84
Salty's on Alki Beach, 86–87
Salumi, 72
Serafina, 83
Shea's Lounge, 77
Shiro's, 1, 77–78
Siam on Broadway, 84
Siam on Lake Union, 84
SkyCity at the Needle, 10, 78–79
Still Life in Fremont Coffeehouse, 127
Third Floor Fish Cafe, 87
Torrefazione, 11, 124
Trattoria Mitchelli, 71
Uwajimaya food court, 70–71
Virginia Inn, 78
Wild Ginger Asian Restaurant and Satay Bar, 69–70
Yarrow Bay Grill, 87

PORTLAND AND ENVIRONS RESTAURANTS

Alexis Restaurant, 223–224
Assaggio, 181, 237
Aztec Willie & Joey Rose Tacqueria, 227, 235
Bijou Café, 226
bluehour, 227–228
Brasserie Montmartre, 181, 224
Bread and Ink Cafe, 229, 237
Briggs and Crampton Caterers Table for Two, 228
Café Azul, 228
Café des Amis, 231
Caffé Mingo, 231
Caprial's Bistro and Wine, 239–240
Castagna, 237
Chart House, 3, 181, 234
Chez Grill, 238
Chez José East, 182, 236
Chez Machin, 242
Colosso, 236

Couvron, 182, 222
Dan and Louis Oyster Bar, 226, 235
Daydream Café, 238
Dundee Bistro, 301
El Palenque, 240
Esparza's Tex-Mex Café, 238–239
Fong Chong, 226–227
Fratelli, 231
Garbonzo's, 232–234, 238
Genoa, 182, 236
Good Dog/Bad Dog, 242
In Good Taste, 242
Grant House Restaurant (Vancouver, WA), 255
Hands on Café, 229, 233
The Heathman Restaurant and Bar, 182, 222, 241–242
Higgins, 222–223
Huber's, 224
Il Piatto, 237
Jake's Famous Crawfish, 182, 224
Ken's Home Plate, 182, 233
Kitchen Table Café, 242
Kornblatts, 233
L'Auberge, 228
Le Bistro Montage, 239
London Grill, 181, 182, 229
The London Grill, 223
McCormick and Schmick's, 225
McCormick and Schmick's Harborside Restaurant, 225
Mayas Tacqueria, 227
Morton's, 222
Newport Bay, 229
Newport Bay Restaurant, 182, 225
Nicholas's, 239
¡Oba!, 229
The Old Spaghetti Factory, 182, 234, 235
Old Wives' Tales, 235, 239
Paley's Place, 181, 229
Palio Dessert House, 241
Papa Haydn, 182
Papa Haydn West, 241
Pasta Veloce, 227
Pizza Schmizza, 236
Pizzicato Gourmet Pizza, 182, 242
Plainfield's Mayur Restaurant and Art Gallery, 229–230
Red Hills Provincial Dining (Dundee), 301
Red Star Tavern and Roast House, 225

RingSide East, 230
RingSide West, 230
Rustica Italian Caffe, 235
Ruth's Chris Steak House, 222
Saburo's Sushi House, 240
Salty's on the Columbia, 229, 234–235
Sante Fe Tacqueria, 227

Serratto, 230
Southpark Seafood Grill & Wine Bar, 226
Swagat, 233
Tapeo, 231–232
Tara Thai, 232
Thai Orchid Restaurant, 232
Tina's (Dundee), 301
24° Brix (Gaston), 301

Typhoon!, 223, 232
Veritable Quandary, 3, 223
Western Culinary Institute International Dining Room, 181–182, 227
Wildwood, 181, 229, 230–231
Zell's, An American Café, 239

FROMMER'S® COMPLETE TRAVEL GUIDES

Alaska
Amsterdam
Argentina & Chile
Arizona
Atlanta
Australia
Austria
Bahamas
Barcelona, Madrid & Seville
Beijing
Belgium, Holland & Luxembourg
Bermuda
Boston
British Columbia & the Canadian
  Rockies
Budapest & the Best of Hungary
California
Canada
Cancún, Cozumel & the Yucatán
Cape Cod, Nantucket &
  Martha's Vineyard
Caribbean
Caribbean Cruises & Ports of Call
Caribbean Ports of Call
Carolinas & Georgia
Chicago
China
Colorado
Costa Rica
Denmark
Denver, Boulder & Colorado Springs
England
Europe
European Cruises & Ports of Call
Florida
France

Germany
Great Britain
Greece
Greek Islands
Hawaii
Hong Kong
Honolulu, Waikiki & Oahu
Ireland
Israel
Italy
Jamaica
Japan
Las Vegas
London
Los Angeles
Maryland & Delaware
Maui
Mexico
Montana & Wyoming
Montréal & Québec City
Munich & the Bavarian Alps
Nashville & Memphis
Nepal
New England
New Mexico
New Orleans
New York City
New Zealand
Nova Scotia, New Brunswick &
  Prince Edward Island
Oregon
Paris
Philadelphia & the Amish Country
Portugal
Prague & the Best of the Czech
  Republic

Provence & the Riviera
Puerto Rico
Rome
San Antonio & Austin
San Diego
San Francisco
Santa Fe, Taos & Albuquerque
Scandinavia
Scotland
Seattle & Portland
Shanghai
Singapore & Malaysia
South Africa
South America
Southeast Asia
South Florida
South Pacific
Spain
Sweden
Switzerland
Texas
Thailand
Tokyo
Toronto
Tuscany & Umbria
USA
Utah
Vancouver & Victoria
Vermont, New Hampshire
  & Maine
Vienna & the Danube Valley
Virgin Islands
Virginia
Walt Disney World & Orlando
Washington, D.C.
Washington State

FROMMER'S® DOLLAR-A-DAY GUIDES

Australia from $50 a Day
California from $70 a Day
Caribbean from $70 a Day
England from $75 a Day
Europe from $70 a Day

Florida from $70 a Day
Hawaii from $80 a Day
Ireland from $60 a Day
Italy from $70 a Day
London from $85 a Day

New York from $90 a Day
Paris from $80 a Day
San Francisco from $70 a Day
Washington, D.C., from $80
  a Day

FROMMER'S® PORTABLE GUIDES

Acapulco, Ixtapa & Zihuatanejo
Alaska Cruises & Ports of Call
Amsterdam
Aruba
Australia's Great Barrier Reef
Bahamas
Baja & Los Cabos
Berlin
Big Island of Hawaii
Boston
California Wine Country
Cancún
Charleston & Savannah
Chicago
Disneyland

Dublin
Florence
Frankfurt
Hong Kong
Houston
Las Vegas
London
Los Angeles
Maine Coast
Maui
Miami
New Orleans
New York City
Paris

Phoenix & Scottsdale
Portland
Puerto Rico
Puerto Vallarta, Manzanillo &
  Guadalajara
San Diego
San Francisco
Seattle
Sydney
Tampa & St. Petersburg
Vancouver
Venice
Virgin Islands
Washington, D.C.

FROMMER'S® NATIONAL PARK GUIDES

Family Vacations in the National
  Parks
Grand Canyon

National Parks of the American
  West
Rocky Mountain
Yellowstone & Grand Teton

Yosemite & Sequoia/
  Kings Canyon
Zion & Bryce Canyon

FROMMER'S® MEMORABLE WALKS

Chicago
London

New York
Paris

San Francisco

FROMMER'S® GREAT OUTDOOR GUIDES

Arizona & New Mexico
New England

Northern California
Southern New England

Vermont & New Hampshire

SUZY GERSHMAN'S BORN TO SHOP GUIDES

Born to Shop: France
Born to Shop: Hong Kong,
  Shanghai & Beijing

Born to Shop: Italy
Born to Shop: London

Born to Shop: New York
Born to Shop: Paris

FROMMER'S® IRREVERENT GUIDES

Amsterdam
Boston
Chicago
Las Vegas
London

Los Angeles
Manhattan
New Orleans
Paris
Rome

San Francisco
Seattle & Portland
Vancouver
Walt Disney World
Washington, D.C.

FROMMER'S® BEST-LOVED DRIVING TOURS

Britain
California
Florida
France

Germany
Ireland
Italy

New England
Scotland
Spain

HANGING OUT™ GUIDES

Hanging Out in England
Hanging Out in Europe

Hanging Out in France
Hanging Out in Ireland

Hanging Out in Italy
Hanging Out in Spain

THE UNOFFICIAL GUIDES®

Bed & Breakfasts and Country
  Inns in:
    California
    New England
    Northwest
    Rockies
    Southeast
Beyond Disney
Branson, Missouri
California with Kids
Chicago
Cruises
Disneyland

Florida with Kids
Golf Vacations in the
  Eastern U.S.
The Great Smokey &
  Blue Ridge Mountains
Inside Disney
Hawaii
Las Vegas
London
Mid-Atlantic with Kids
Mini Las Vegas
Mini-Mickey
New England & New York
  with Kids

New Orleans
New York City
Paris
San Francisco
Skiing in the West
Southeast with Kids
Walt Disney World
Walt Disney World for
  Grown-ups
Walt Disney World for Kids
Washington, D.C.
World's Best Diving Vacations

SPECIAL-INTEREST TITLES

Frommer's Adventure Guide to Australia & New
  Zealand
Frommer's Adventure Guide to Central America
Frommer's Adventure Guide to India & Pakistan
Frommer's Adventure Guide to South America
Frommer's Adventure Guide to Southeast Asia
Frommer's Adventure Guide to Southern Africa
Frommer's Britain's Best Bed & Breakfasts and
  Country Inns
Frommer's France's Best Bed & Breakfasts and
  Country Inns
Frommer's Italy's Best Bed & Breakfasts and Country
  Inns
Frommer's Caribbean Hideaways

Frommer's Exploring America by RV
Frommer's Gay & Lesbian Europe
Frommer's The Moon
Frommer's New York City with Kids
Frommer's Road Atlas Britain
Frommer's Road Atlas Europe
Frommer's Washington, D.C., with Kids
Frommer's What the Airlines Never Tell You
Israel Past & Present
The New York Times' Guide to Unforgettable
  Weekends
Places Rated Almanac
Retirement Places Rated

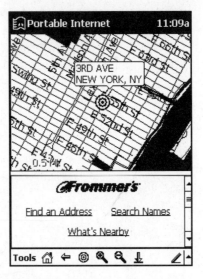